Canadian Fifth Edition

Volume III

Horngren | Harrison | Bamber | Lemon | Norwood

Accounting

Charles T. Horngren
Stanford University

Walter T. Harrison, Jr.
Baylor University

Linda Smith Bamber
University of Georgia

W. Morley Lemon
University of Waterloo

Peter R. Norwood
Langara College

Prentice
Hall

Toronto

Canadian Cataloguing in Publication Data

Main entry under title:

Accounting

Canadian 5th ed.
Canadian ed. published under title: Accounting/Charles T. Horngren,
Walter T. Harrison, W. Morley Lemon; with Carol E. Dilworth.
Contents: v. 1. Chapters 1–11—v. 2. Chapters 12–18—v. 3. Chapters 19–26.
ISBN 0-13-089693-4 (v. 1) ISBN 0-13-089694-2 (v. 2) ISBN 0-13-089695-0 (v. 3)

1. Accounting. 2. Managerial accounting. I. Horngren, Charles T., 1926-   .

HF5635.H8125 2002   657'.044   C00.933091-7

0-13-089695-0

Vice President, Editorial Director: Michael Young
Senior Acquisitions Editor: Samantha Scully
Executive Marketing Manager: Cas Shields
Developmental Editor/Copy Editor: Anita Smale, CA
Production Editor: Mary Ann McCutcheon
Production Coordinator: Deborah Starks
Page Layout: Bill Renaud
Permissions/Photo Research: Susan Wallace-Cox
Art Director: Mary Opper
Interior Design: Alex Li
Cover Design: Alex Li
Cover Image: Mel Curtis/Photonica

2 3 4 5   06 05 04 03 02

Printed and bound in U.S.A.

BRIEF
Contents

Contents

Tejal Govande

---

*In each chapter, Assignment Material includes Questions, Exercises, Beyond the Numbers, an Ethical Issue, and Problems (Group A and B, and Challenge Problems).

About the Authors

Charles T. Horngren is the Edmund W. Littlefield Professor of Accounting, Emeritus, at Stanford University. A graduate of Marquette University, he received his MBA from Harvard University and his Ph.D. from the University of Chicago. He is also the recipient of honourary doctorates from Marquette University and DePaul University.

A Certified Public Accountant, Horngren served on the Accounting Principles Board for six years, the Financial Accounting Standards Board Advisory Council for five years, and the Council of the American Institute of Certified Public Accountants for three years. For six years, he served as a trustee of the Financial Accounting Foundation, which oversees the Financial Accounting Standards Board and the Government Accounting Standards Board.

Horngren is a member of the Accounting Hall of Fame.

A member of the American Accounting Association, Horngren has been its President and its Director of Research. He received its first annual Outstanding Accounting Educator Award.

The California Certified Public Accountants Foundation gave Horngren its Faculty Excellence Award and its Distinguished Professor Award. He is the first person to have received both awards.

The American Institute of Certified Public Accountants presented its first Outstanding Educator Award to Horngren.

Horngren was named Accountant of the Year, Education, by the national professional accounting fraternity, Beta Alpha Psi.

Professor Horngren is also a member of the Institute of Management Accountants, where he has received its Distinguished Service Award. He was a member of the Institute's Board of Regents, which administers the Certified Management Accountant examinations.

Horngren is the author of other accounting books published by Prentice-Hall and Pearson Education: *Cost Accounting: A Managerial Emphasis*, Second Canadian Edition, 2000 (with George Foster, Srikant Datar and Howard D. Teall); *Introduction to Financial Accounting*, Third Canadian Edition, 2001 (with Gary L. Sundem, John A. Elliot, and Howard D. Teall); *Management Accounting*, Fourth Canadian Edition, 2002 (with Gary L. Sundem, William O. Stratton, and Howard D. Teall); and *Financial Accounting*, Fourth Edition, 2001 (with Walter T. Harrison, Jr.).

Horngren is the Consulting Editor for the Charles T. Horngren Series in Accounting.

Walter T. Harrison, Jr. is Professor of Accounting at the Hankamer School of Business, Baylor University. He received his B.B.A. degree from Baylor University, his M.S. from Oklahoma State University, and his Ph.D. from Michigan State University.

Professor Harrison, recipient of numerous teaching awards from student groups as well as from university administrators, has also taught at Cleveland State Community College, Michigan State University, the University of Texas, and Stanford University.

A member of the American Accounting Association and the American Institute of Certified Public Accountants, Professor Harrison has served as Chairman of the Financial Accounting Standards Committee of the American Accounting Association, on the Teaching/Curriculum Development Award Committee, on the Program Advisory Committee for Accounting Education and Teaching, and on the Notable Contributions to Accounting Literature Committee.

Professor Harrison has lectured in several foreign countries and published articles in numerous journals, including *The Accounting Review, Journal of Accounting*

Research, Journal of Accountancy, Journal of Accounting and Public Policy, Economic Consequences of Financial Accounting Standards, Accounting Horizons, Issues in Accounting Education, and *Journal of Law and Commerce.* He is coauthor of *Financial Accounting, Fourth Edition,* 2001 (with Charles T. Horngren) and *Accounting, Fifth Edition* (with Charles T. Horngren and Linda S. Bamber) published by Prentice Hall. Professor Harrison has received scholarships, fellowships, research grants, or awards from Price Waterhouse & Co., Deloitte & Touche, the Ernst & Young Foundation, and the KMPG Peat Marwick Foundation.

Linda Smith Bamber is Professor of Accounting at the J.M. Tull School of Accounting at the University of Georgia. She graduated summa cum laude from Wake Forest University, where she was a member of Phi Beta Kappa. She is a certified public accountant. For her performance on the CPA examination, Professor Bamber received the Elijah Watt Sells Award in addition to the North Carolina Bronze Medal. Before returning to graduate school, she worked in cost accounting at RJR Foods. She then earned an MBA from Arizona State University, and a Ph.D. from The Ohio State University.

Professor Bamber has received numerous teaching awards from The Ohio State University, the University of Florida, and the University of Georgia, including selection as Teacher of the Year at the University of Florida's Fisher School of Accounting.

She has lectured in Canada and Australia in addition to the U.S., and her research has appeared in numerous journals, including *The Accounting Review, Journal of Accounting Research, Journal of Accounting and Economics, Journal of Finance, Contemporary Accounting Research, Auditing: A Journal of Practice and Theory, Accounting Horizons, Issues in Accounting Education,* and *CPA Journal.* She provided the annotations for the *Annotated Instructor's Edition* of Horngren, Foster, and Datar's *Cost Accounting: A Managerial Emphasis,* Seventh, Eighth, and Ninth Editions.

A member of the Institute of Management Accounting, the American Accounting Association (AAA), and the AAA's Management Accounting Section and Financial Accounting and Reporting Section, Professor Bamber has chaired the AAA New Faculty Consortium Committee, served on the AAA Council, the AAA Research Advisory Committee, the AAA Corporate Accounting Policy Seminar Committee, the AAA Wildman Medal Award Committee, the AAA Nominations Committee, and has chaired the Management Accounting Section's Membership Outreach Committee. She served as Associate Editor of *Accounting Horizons,* and is serving as editor of *The Accounting Review* from 1999 to 2002.

W. Morley Lemon is the PricewaterhouseCoopers Professor of Auditing and the Director of the School of Accountancy at the University of Waterloo. He obtained his BA from the University of Western Ontario, his MBA from the University of Toronto, and his PhD from the University of Texas at Austin. Professor Lemon obtained his CA in Ontario. In 1985 he was honoured by that Institute, which elected him a Fellow. He received his CPA in Texas.

Professor Lemon was awarded the University of Waterloo Distinguished Teacher Award at the 1998 convocation at the University.

Professor Lemon is coauthor, with Arens, Loebbecke, and Splettstoesser, of *Auditing and Other Assurance Services,* Canadian Eighth Edition, published by Prentice Hall Canada, and coauthored four previous Canadian editions of that text. He is also coauthor, with Horngren, Harrison, Bamber, and Norwood, of *Accounting,* Canadian Fifth Edition, published by Pearson Education Canada. He coathored the four previous Canadian editions of that text.

He was a member of the Canadian Institute of Chartered Accountants' Assurance Standards Board. He has also served on the Institute of Chartered Accountants of Ontario Council, as well as a number of committees for both bodies. He has chaired and served on a number of committees of the Canadian Academic Accounting Association. Professor Lemon has served on Council and chaired and served on a number of committees of the American Accounting Association.

Professor Lemon has presented lectures and papers at a number of universities and academic and professional conferences and symposia in Canada and the United States. He has chaired and organized six audit symposia held at the University of Waterloo. He has served on the editorial board of and reviewed papers for a number of academic journals including *The Accounting Review*, *Contemporary Accounting Research*, *Issues in Accounting Education*, *Auditing: A Journal of Practice and Theory*, *Advances in Accounting*, *Journal of Accounting and Public Policy*, and *CA Magazine*. Professor Lemon has coauthored two monographs and has had papers published in *Contemporary Accounting Research*, *Research on Accounting Ethics*, *Journal of Accounting, Auditing and Finance*, *The Chartered Accountant in Australia*, *The Journal of Business Ethics*, and *CA Magazine*. He has had papers published in the following collections: *Educating the Profession of Accountancy in the Twenty-First Century*, *Comparative International Accounting Education Standards*, *Comparative International Auditing Standards*, and *The Impact of Inflation on Accounting: A Global View*. Professor Lemon served as a judge for *CA Magazine's* Walter J. Macdonald Award.

Professor Lemon has received a number of research grants and has served as the Director of the Centre for Accounting Ethics, School of Accountancy, University of Waterloo. He has written a number of ethics cases published by the Centre.

Peter R. Norwood is an instructor in accounting and the Chair of the Financial Management Department in the School of Business at Langara College. A graduate of the University of Alberta, he received his MBA from the University of Western Ontario. He is a Chartered Accountant and a Certified Management Accountant.

Before entering the academic community, Mr. Norwood worked in public practice and industry for over fifteen years. He is a member of the Board of Examiners of the Canadian Institute of Chartered Accountants and is the Chair of the Professional Development Management Committee of the Institute of Chartered Accountants of British Columbia. In addition, he has been involved in program development for the Certified Management Accountants of British Columbia and the Chartered Accountants' School of Business. Mr. Norwood has lectured at the University of British Columbia and is the Chair of the Langara Foundation.

Photo Credits

1134 Courtesy Dell Computer Corporation; **1176** Courtesy Big Rock Brewery Ltd.; **1223** Douglas Leighton, © Rocky Mountaineer Railtours (www.rkymtnrail.com), courtesy The Great Canadian Railtour Ltd.; **1269** The Image Works/R. Crandall; **1324** Stock Boston/Bill Horsman; **1376** Courtesy Exxon/Mobil Corporation; **1429** Courtesy Sandestin® Golf & Beach Resort.

To the Student

On behalf of the authors, we would like to welcome you to introductory accounting. Whether you plan to major in accounting or are taking this course for interest, rest assured that a basic understanding of accounting is fundamental to the world of business. Many of the principles you will learn in this course will be useful in whatever career you choose to pursue.

As you will discover in this course, accounting is more than bookkeeeeping. Accounting requires that you understand issues conceptually in addition to developing the technical ability to record, summarize, report, and interpret financial data. If you devote your efforts to understanding both of these aspects of accounting, you will be taking a large step towards developing a greater understanding of business fundamentals.

To maximize the benefit of this course and this text, there are certain responsibilities that you need to accept. As instructors, we know the volume of material covered in introductory accounting can be overwhelming. On a daily basis, you will learn new principles and techniques. In order to fully comprehend the new material, you should consider the following suggestions:

Read the textbook material in advance.   If you have had a chance to review the chapter before it is covered in class, you will find it much easier to grasp the material when it is presented in class.

Use the end-of-chapter material.   We have provided a multitude of exercises and problems at the end of each chapter. They range from single-objective, basic questions to comprehensive, multi-objective problems. These exercises and problems are designed to help provide a good understanding of the accounting issues you have covered in class. Check Figures have been provided at the end of the text to help you check your progress.

Use the resources available.   To help you understand accounting, the most important resource, of course, is your instructor. And don't forget this text! Please look at the next few pages for all the features in the text that will help you succeed in accounting.

Features in *Accounting*

LEARNING accounting can be a bit overwhelming, especially if you have little business or accounting experience. But with a good text and instructor, you will succeed. To help you, we provide features in every chapter of this text to make accounting as easy to understand as possible. Please read through the next few pages to learn more about *Accounting* and the many ways it will help you understand, learn, and apply accounting concepts.

Chapter Objectives are listed on the first page of each chapter. This "roadmap" shows you what will be covered and what is especially important. Each objective is repeated in the margin where the material is first covered. The objectives are summarized at the end of the chapter.

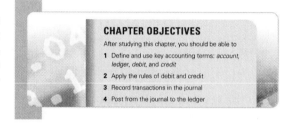

CHAPTER OBJECTIVES

After studying this chapter, you should be able to

1 Define and use key accounting terms: *account, ledger, debit,* and *credit*

2 Apply the rules of debit and credit

3 Record transactions in the journal

4 Post from the journal to the ledger

Chapter openers present a story about a real company or a real business situation, and show why the topics in the chapter are important to real companies. Some of the companies you'll read about include Dell Computer Corporation, Big Rock Brewery, Rocky Mountaineer Railtours, and Intrawest. Students tell us that using real companies makes it easier for them to learn and remember accounting concepts.

Weblinks in the margin give you the internet address for the companies mentioned in the text. If you want to learn more about a company, use these handy references.

Objectives in the margin signal the beginning of the section that covers the objective topic. Look for this feature when you are studying and want to review a particular objective.

Learning Tips in the margin are suggestions for learning or remembering concepts that you might find difficult.

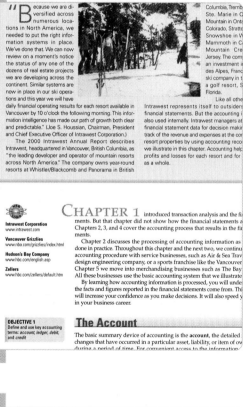

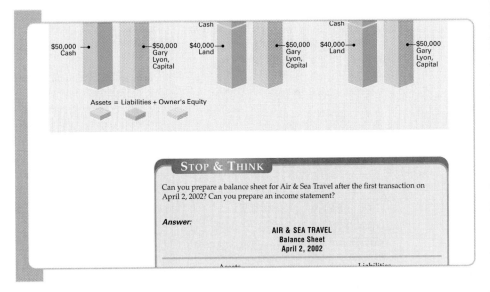

Exhibits are provided in full colour to make the concepts easier to understand and easier to remember.

Stop and Think boxes are "speed bumps" that allow you to slow down for a moment, review and apply to a decision situation material just covered in the text. These serve as an excellent way to check your progress because the answers are provided in the same box.

STOP & THINK

Can you prepare a balance sheet for Air & Sea Travel after the first transaction on April 2, 2002? Can you prepare an income statement?

Answer:

AIR & SEA TRAVEL
Balance Sheet
April 2, 2002

DON'T FORGET the material in the margins! Some

of these items allow you to pause and make sure you understand the material covered in the text. Others are excellent study aids because they help you find material you are looking for quickly. We already mentioned the Objectives, the Weblinks, and the Learning Tips in the margins. Here are some other margin items.

Working It Out are short calculation questions that appear throughout the chapter. Answers are provided to give you immediate feedback. You can use these questions to check your progress and to prepare for exams.

Thinking It Over are short questions about concepts just covered in the text. Answers are provided to give you immediate feedback. Like the Working It Out questions, you can use Thinking It Over questions to check your progress and to prepare for exams.

THINKING IT OVER

Suppose you bought a Pontiac Grand Am for $24,000 and had to borrow $18,000 to pay for the car. Write your personal accounting equation for this transaction.

A:
Assets = Liabilities + Owner's Equity
$24,000 = $18,000 + $6,000

WORKING IT OUT

Compute the missing amounts:

(1) Cash

Bal.	10,000	
	20,000	13,000
Bal.	X	

(2) Accounts Payable

	X	Bal.	12,800
			45,600
		Bal.	23,500

(3) S. Scully, Capital

		Bal.	X
	22,000		56,000
			15,000
		Bal.	73,000

A: (1) The ending balance (X) for Cash is
X = $10,000 + $20,000 − $13,000
X = $17,000
(2) We are given the beginning and ending balances. We can compute the debit entry as follows:
$12,800 + $45,600 − X
= $23,500
$12,800 + $45,600
− $23,500 = X
X = $34,900
(3) The Capital account has an ending credit balance of $73,000. We can calculate the beginning credit balance as follows:
X + $56,000 + $15,000
− $22,000 = $73,000
X = $73,000 − $56,000
− $15,000 + $22,000
X = $24,000

Key Points in the margin highlight important details from the text. These are good review tools for when you prepare for tests or exams.

ᴜꜱʜ

(Right side)
Credit

ᴛe **debit** side, and the right side is called the ᴄan be confusing because they are new. To y remember this:

left side
right side

Mid-Chapter Summary Problem for Your Review gives you another chance to review your understanding of the material covered in the first half of the chapter. A full solution is provided so you can judge whether you should look at the material again or proceed to the last half of the chapter.

Mid-Chapter Summary Problem
for Your Review

On August 1, 2003, Mary Woo opens Woo Computer Consulting. During the business's first ten days of operations, it completes the following transactions:

a. To begin operations, Mary Woo deposits $40,000 of personal funds in a bank account entitled Woo Computer Consulting. The business receives the cash and gives Woo capital (owner's equity).
b. Woo Computer Consulting pays $20,000 cash for a small house to be used as an office and $10,000 for the land on which the house is located.
c. The business purchases office supplies for $500 on account.
d. The business pays $6,000 cash for office furniture.
e. The business pays $150 on the account payable created in Transaction (c).
f. Woo withdraws $1,000 cash for personal use.

Required

1. Prepare the journal entries to record these transactions. Key the journal entries by letter.
2. Post the entries to T-accounts and calculate the ending balance.
3. Prepare the trial balance of Woo Computer Consulting at August 10, 2003.

Solution to Review Problem

Requirement 1

Accounts and Explanation	Ref.	Debit	Credit
a. Cash		40,000	
Mary Woo, Capital			40,000
Record initial investment from owner.			
b. Building		20,000	
Land		10,000	
Cash			30,000
Purchased building for an office and land.			
c. Office Supplies		500	
Accounts Payable			500
Purchased office supplies on account.			

Management Accounting in the Real World or **Accounting and the E-World** appears in most chapters. These boxes illustrate either how management accounting concepts and tools are used by a smaller British Columbia manufacturer or how the world of e-commerce is influencing accounting. These boxes offer interesting views of accounting that might make you think about accounting in different ways.

Management Accounting in the Real World 🌐

From Process Costing to Job Costing?

Canadians will soon be able to pick out a fully custom-built car and drive it away in the same time it takes to tailor a three-piece suit—15 days from order to delivery.

Ford Motor Co. of Canada Ltd. expects to have the technology to make this option available within five years. And these are true custom cars: a mix-and-match design to suit your needs and tastes from about 70,000 permutations and combinations of options. The cost will be based on a list price plus options.

The driver that will make this possible is technology. Car makers are among the first to recognize that technology can turn mass production into true custom crafting on a huge scale.

This is how it would work. Computers capture the specifics of an individual order. Glass-fibre networks relay the order to an assembly plant, where other computers translate it into instructions for building the vehicle on the assembly line. These instructions are programmed into wireless transponders or bar codes that instruct robots and humans on what to add, and when and where.

At each stage, computers track progress, and inventory is counted and ordered, with parts arriving as they are needed, often trucked from factories 1,000 kilometres away.

The wonder is not so much the use of new technology, but the ability to use many different technologies so seamlessly and in concert. "A decade ago, we didn't have things like transponders and radio-scanning systems," says assembly plant manager Rich Wagner. "But now that we have them, they are giving us the ability to do custom production on a mass-production scale."

Source: Terrence Belford, "Dream Car on Fast Track," *Globe and Mail*, February 23, 2001, p. T3.

Process Costing for a Second Department—FIFO Method

Most products require a series of processing steps. In this section, we introduce a second department—the Finishing Department of Recreational Divers Ltd.—to complete the pic-

Decision Guidelines show how the accounting concepts covered in the chapter are used by business people to make business decisions. This feature shows why accounting principles and concepts are important in a broader business context, not just to accountants. The Decision Guidelines also serve as an excellent summary of the chapter topics.

Summary Problem for Your Review pulls together the chapter concepts with an extensive and challenging review problem. Full solutions are given so that you can check your progress.

Summary Problem
for Your Review

The trial balance of Tomassini Computer Service Centre on March 1, 2003, lists the company's assets, liabilities, and owner's equity on that date.

Account Titles	Balance	
	Debit	**Credit**
Cash	$26,000	
Accounts receivable	4,500	
Accounts payable		$ 2,000
John Tomassini, Capital		28,500
Total	$30,500	$30,500

During March the business engaged in the following transactions:

a. Borrowed $45,000 from the bank and signed a note payable in the name of the business.
b. Paid cash of $40,000 to a real estate company to acquire land.
c. Performed service for a customer and received cash of $5,000.
d. Purchased supplies on account, $300.

Summary appears at the end of each chapter. It gives a concise description of the material covered in the chapter and is organized by objective. Use this summary as a starting point for organizing your review when studying for a test or exam.

Summary

1. **Define and use key accounting terms:** *account, ledger, debit,* **and** *credit. Accounts* can be viewed in the form of the letter "T." The left side of each T-account is its *debit* side. The right side is its *credit* side. The *ledger,* which contains a record for each account groups and numbers accounts by category in the following order: assets, liabilities, and owner's equity (and its subparts, revenues and expenses).

2. **Apply the rules of debit and credit.** *Assets* and *expenses* are increased by debits and decreased by credits. *Liabilities, owner's equity,* and *revenues* are increased by credits and decreased by debits. An account's *normal balance* is the side of the account—debit or credit—in which increases are recorded. Thus the normal balance of assets and expenses is a debit, and the normal balance of liabilities, owner's equity, and revenues is a credit. The Withdrawals account, which decreases owner's equity, normally has a debit balance. *Revenues,* which are increases in owner's equity, have a normal credit balance. *Expenses,* which are decreases in owner's equity, have a normal debit balance.

3. **Record transactions in the journal.** The accountant begins the recording process by entering the transaction's information in the *journal,* a chronological list of all the entity's transactions.

4. **Post from the journal to the ledger.** Posting means transferring to the *ledger* accounts. Posting references are used to trace amounts back and forth between the journal and the ledger.

5. **Prepare and use a trial balance.** The *trial balance* is a summary of all the account balances in the ledger. When *double-entry accounting* has been done correctly, the total debits and the total credits in the trial balance are equal.

6. **Set up a chart of accounts for a business.** A *chart of accounts* lists all the accounts in the ledger and their account numbers.

7. **Analyze transactions without a journal.** Decision makers must often make decisions without a complete accounting system. They can analyze the transactions without a journal.

We can now trace the flow of accounting information through these steps:

Business Transaction ⟶ Source Documents

⟶ Journal Entry ⟶ Posting to Ledger

⟶ Trial Balance

Self-Study Questions allow you to test your understanding of the chapter on your own. Page references are given for each of these multiple-choice questions so that you can review a section quickly if you miss an answer. The answers are provided after the Similar Accounting Terms (see below) so you can check your progress.

Accounting Vocabulary lists all the terms that were defined and appeared in bold type in the chapter. The page references are given so you can review the meanings of the terms. These terms are also collected and defined in the Glossary at the end of the text.

Similar Accounting Terms links the accounting terms used in the chapter to similar terms you might have heard outside your accounting class, in the media, in other courses, or in day-to-day business dealings. Knowing similar terms should make it easier to remember the accounting terms.

These are the Answers to the Self-Study Questions, mentioned above.

Self-Study Questions

Test your understanding of the chapter by marking the correct answer for each of the following questions:

1. An account has two sides called the (p. 55)
   a. Debit and credit   c. Revenue and expense
   b. Asset and liability   d. Journal and ledger
2. Increases in liabilities are recorded by (p. 56)
   a. Debits   b. Credits
3. Why do accountants record transactions in the journal? (p. 58)
   a. To ensure that all transactions are posted to the ledger
   b. To ensure that total debits equal total credits
   c. To have a chronological record of all transactions
   d. To help prepare the financial statements
4. Posting is the process of transferring information from the (p. 60)
   a. Journal to the trial balance
   b. Ledger to the trial balance
   c. Ledger to the financial statements
   d. Journal to the ledger
5. The purchase of land for cash is recorded by a (p. 61)
   a. Debit to Cash and a credit to Land
   b. Debit to Cash and a debit to Land
   c. Debit to Land and a credit to Cash
   d. Credit to Cash and a credit to Land
6. The purpose of the trial balance is to (p. 64)
   a. List all accounts with their balances
   b. Ensure that all transactions have been recorded

c. Speed the collection of cash receipts from customers
d. Increase assets and owner's equity

7. What is the normal balance of the Accounts Receivable, Office Supplies, and Rent Expense accounts? (p. 71)
   a. Debit   b. Credit
8. A business has Cash of $3,000, Notes Payable of $2,500, Accounts Payable of $4,300, Service Revenue of $7,000 and Rent Expense of $800. Based on these data, how much are its total liabilities? (p. 74)
   a. $5,500   c. $9,800
   b. $6,800   d. $13,800
9. Smale Transport earned revenue on account. The earning of revenue on account is recorded by (pp. 74–78)
   a. Debit to Cash and a credit to Revenue
   b. Debit to Accounts Receivable and a credit to Revenue
   c. Debit to Accounts Payable and a credit to Revenue
   d. Debit to Revenue and a credit to Accounts Receivable
10. The account credited for a receipt of cash on account is (p. 77)
   a. Cash   c. Service Revenue
   b. Accounts Payable   d. Accounts Receivable

Answers to the Self-Study Questions follow the Similar Accounting Terms.

Accounting Vocabulary

Account (p. 52)	Journal (p. 58)
Chart of accounts (p. 70)	Ledger (p. 52)
Credit (p. 55)	Posting (p. 60)
Debit (p. 55)	Trial balance (p. 64)

Similar Accounting Terms

Cr	Credit; right
Dr	Debit; left
The Ledger	The Books; the General Ledger
Entering the transaction in a journal	Making the journal entry; journalizing the transaction
Withdrawals by owner(s)	In a *proprietorship* or *partnership*, distributions from a company to its owner(s).

Answers to Self-Study Questions
1. a	3. c	5. c	7. a	9. b
2. b	4. d	6. a	8. b ($6,800 = $2,500 + $4,300)	10. d

THE END-OF-CHAPTER
Assignment Material is extensive because often the best way to make sure you grasp new accounting concepts is to practice, practice, practice! The number and variety of questions, exercises, and problems give you every opportunity to test your understanding of the chapter's concepts.

Questions require short, written answers or short calculations, often on a single topic.

Exercises on a single or a small number of topics require you to "do the accounting" and, often, to consider the implications of the result in the same way that real companies would. The objectives covered by each exercise are listed after the brief description of the concepts covered.

Challenge Exercises provide a challenge for those students who have mastered the Exercises.

Beyond the Numbers exercises require analytical thinking and written responses about the topics presented in the chapter.

Ethical Issues are thought-provoking situations that help you recognize when ethics should affect an accounting decision.

Problems are presented in two groups that mirror each other, "A" and "B." Many instructors work through problems from Group A in class to demonstrate accounting concepts, then assign problems from Group B for homework or extra practice. The objectives covered by each problem are listed after the brief description of the concepts covered.

Challenge Problems encourage you to consider the effect of accounting information and apply it to decision situations.

THE EXTENDING Your Knowledge section contains

Decision Problems, which allow you to prepare and interpret accounting information and then make recommendations to a business based on this information.

In addition to the features above that appear in each chapter, an additional feature appears at the end of each part of Volume III.

Comprehensive Problem covers the content addressed in the book so far. This is a relatively long problem that provides an excellent review of all of the topics covered in the chapters in that part. See your instructor for the solution to this problem.

To the Instructor

Welcome to *Accounting*! *Accounting*, Canadian Fifth Edition, provides full introductory coverage of financial and management accounting in a three-volume, full-colour format. Volumes I and II cover financial accounting topics, and Volume III covers management accounting topics. The three-volume format gives *Accounting* the flexibility to be used in a one-, two-, or three-semester introductory accounting course.

Instructors have told us their greatest challenges are effectively teaching students with very different business and accounting backgrounds, and motivating students to give accounting the study time and attention it deserves. *Accounting*'s approach and features were designed to help you address and overcome these challenges. The keys are a supportive text and supplements package, and motivated students.

Accounting continues its tradition of complete and comprehensive coverage of the most widely used accounting theory and practices. We have always believed that it is better to provide instructors with comprehensive coverage that could be trimmed if necessary rather than reduced coverage that might require instructor supplementation. This gives instructors the flexibility to tailor their presentations and coverage to their students' experience level.

Accounting continues to use the easy-to-understand writing style that sets it apart from other accounting texts. Instuctors have told us time and again that if students miss an accounting class, the instructor knows that students can keep up by reading the text. This should help students feel less overwhelmed by the thought of missing a class and having to catch up.

Accounting principles and procedures are illustrated using examples from real Canadian companies. This real-world business context runs throughout the chapters and assignment material, motivating students to think about companies and situations they know, which can help make difficult concepts easier to grasp. Familiar companies enliven the material and illustrate the role of accounting in business. In those situations where "live" data drawn from real companies would complicate the material for introductory students, we illustrate the accounting with realistic examples from generic companies to give students the clearest examples possible.

Changes in the Canadian Fifth Edition of *Accounting*

The most obvious change in this new edition is the attractive, inviting full-colour presentation of the material. Students have said they find concepts easier to understand when key material and exhibits are presented in colour. However, colour is only the beginning—colour cannot make weak features stronger. The features have to stand on their own.

A number of well-received features were introduced in the previous edition of *Accounting*, and most of these features remain in this edition, including Decision Guidelines, Similar Accounting Terms, Working It Out, and Thinking It Over items. A number of new features have been added to this edition—they are described below. For detailed descriptions of all of the features in this text, please refer to the To the Student section earlier in this Preface.

The most significant change in this edition of *Accounting* is the focus on proprietorships in Volume I, especially in Chapters 1 to 5. This change was made after considerable discussion with many instructors from across the country. While most instructors agreed that corporations, large and small, are increasing in number in Canada, the majority of instructors felt that students grasp owner's equity concepts more easily by learning about proprietorships before learning about corporations. However, for those instructors who prefer a corporate focus in Chapters 1 to 5, we will offer a website containing a parallel presentation of Chapters 1 to 5 with a corporate focus in the same full-colour layout as the text.

New **Student-to-Student** boxes appear in Chapters 1 to 18. We asked students to tell us which concepts or ideas they found particularly challenging and which feature or item in *Accounting* helped them overcome the challenge. One student said, "I think that the Student-to-Student boxes are great...they help students realize that other students have read and maybe even struggled with the same concepts that they are struggling with and they give them encouragement to continue."

A new **Accounting and the E-World** or **Accounting Around the Globe** box appears in each chapter. These boxes illustrate how the world of e-commerce is influencing accounting or how accounting differs around the world. These boxes offer interesting views of accounting that motivate students to think about accounting in different ways.

A new **Cyber Coach** box appears after both the Mid-Chapter Summary Problem for Your Review and the Summary Problem for Your Review in Volumes I and II. It is a reminder to students to visit the *Accounting* Companion Website's Online Study Guide and other student resources for extra practice with the new material introduced in the chapter.

A new **Management Accounting in the Real World** box appears in most chapters in Volume III. It shows how the management accounting concepts covered in the chapter, which are typically illustrated using large manufacturers, are used by a real, small business located in British Columbia.

Cash flow statements are introduced in Chapter 1 and covered fully in Chapter 17. To reduce possible student confusion, chapter-by-chapter introductions to portions of the cash flow statement have been eliminated in this edition.

The "generic" Financial Statement Problems in Chapters 1 to 18 have been moved from the text to the Companion Website and the *Instructor's Resource Manual and Video Guide*. However, the Intrawest Corporation Financial Statement Problems are still presented in the text.

What has *not* changed is the quantity, quality, and variety of exercises, questions, and problems presented in the text. All problems have been updated and revised, but the flexibility provided to instructors by the extensive assignment material remains.

Supplements

Accounting is supported by a variety of online course management solutions designed to meet the full range of instructor and student needs, including a Companion Website, a WebCT course, a BlackBoard course, and Pearson Education Canada's proprietary Course Compass course. For more information about any of these solutions, please contact your Pearson Education Canada Sales and Editorial Representative, or visit **www.pearsoned.com/dl**.

Also ask about the other supplements that accompany *Accounting*:

Instructor's Solutions Manual, Vol I: 013-093176-4; Vol II: 013-093177-2;
    Vol III: 013-093178-0
Instructor's Manual and Media Guide, Vol I: 013-093190-X; Vol II: 013-093201-9;
    Vol III: 013-093202-7
Test Item File, Vol I: 013-093193-4; Vol II: 013-093194-2;
    Vol III: 013-093195-0
Test Manager (Computerized Test Item File) for Volume I, II: 013-093276-0; for
    Volume III: 013-044476-6.
CBC/Pearson Education Canada Video Library, 013-093270-1
Solutions Acetates, Vol I: 013-093275-2; Vol II: 013-093277-9;
    Vol III: 013-093279-5
Electronic Transparencies in PowerPoint, 013-093273-6
Adapting Your Lecture Notes if Using Larson et al., *Fundamental Accounting Principles*,
    9/C/E, 013-064588-5
Adapting Your Lecture Notes if Using Weygandt et al., *Accounting Principles*,
    Canadian Edition, 013-064589-3

Acknowledgements for the Canadian Fifth Edition

We would like to thank Chuck Horngren, Tom Harrison, and Linda Bamber for their encouragement and support.

Particular thanks are due to the following people for reviewing the manuscript for Volume I, Volume II, and/or Volume III of this new edition, writing the supplements, or performing technical checks, and for offering many useful suggestions:

Cécile Ashman, Algonquin College
Dave Bopara, Toronto School of Business
Nada Borden, College of the North Atlantic
Michael Bozzo, Mohawk College
Wayne Bridgeman, formerly with CGA-Canada
Chris Burnley, Malaspina University College
Maisie Caines, College of the North Atlantic
K. Suzanne Coombs, Kwantlen University College
Robert Dearden, Red River Community College
Vincent Durant, St. Lawrence College
David Ferries, Algonquin College
Dave Fleming, George Brown College
Augusta Ford, College of the North Atlantic
Donna Grace, Sheridan College
Laurence P. Hanchard, Edmonton
Elizabeth Hicks, Douglas College
Larry Howe, University College of the Fraser Valley
Stephanie Ibach, Northern Alberta Institute of Technology
Laurette Korman, Kwantlen University College
Peter Lubka, University of Waterloo
Rick Martin, College of the North Atlantic
Stella Penner, University of Alberta
Clifton Philpott, Kwantlen University College
Carson Rappell, Dawson College
David Sale, Kwantlen University College
Scott Sinclair, British Columbia Institute of Technology
Bob Sproule, University of Waterloo
Gregg Tranter, Southern Alberta Institute of Technology
H. Barrie Yackness, British Columbia Institute of Technology
Elizabeth Zaleschuk, Douglas College

We are also grateful to the instructors across the country who took the time to respond to surveys conducted during the planning stages of this edition. The thoughts and opinions of these instructors were a valuable guide as we mapped out a strategy for improving this new edition:

Cécile Ashman, Algonquin College
James E. Chambers, St. Clair College
K. Suzanne Coombs, Kwantlen University College
Richard Farrar, Conestoga College
Albert M. Ferris, University of Prince Edward Island
Reiner Frisch, Georgian College
Donna Grace, Sheridan College
Elizabeth Hicks, Douglas College
Wayne Irvine, Mount Royal College
Connie Johl, Douglas College
Allen McQueen, Grant MacEwan Community College

Ann MacGillivary, Mount Saint Vincent University
Tariq Nizami, Champlain Regional College CEGEP
Penny Parker, Fanshawe College
Gabriela Schneider, Grant MacEwan Community College
Scott Sinclair, British Columbia Institute of Technology
Bob Sproule, University of Waterloo
Elizabeth Zaleschuk, Douglas College

We especially want to thank those students who have generously and eloquently contributed Student to Student comments to the text and companion website for Volumes I and II. Our thanks go to those at the following schools who participated in this project. The students' and instructors' enthusiasm was greatly appreciated.

Assiniboine Community College
College of New Caledonia
College of the North Atlantic
Conestoga College
Douglas College
Humber College
Langara College
Malaspina University College
McGill University
St. Lawrence College
University College of the Fraser Valley
University of Waterloo

Thanks are extended to Intrawest Corporation for permission to use its annual report in Volumes I and II of the text. Thanks are extended to JVC Canada Inc. for permission to use its invoice in Chapter 5. Thanks are extended to the Canadian Institute of Chartered Accountants for permission to use materials published by the Institute. We acknowledge the support provided by *The Globe and Mail's Report on Business*, the *Financial Post*, and by the annual reports of a large number of public companies.

We would like to acknowledge the people of Pearson Education Canada, in particular Vice President, Editorial Director Michael Young and Senior Acquisitions Editor Samantha Scully. We would also like to acknowledge especially the editorial and technical support of Anita Smale, CA.

I would like to thank my wife Sandra for her support and encouragement.

W. Morley Lemon

I would like to thank my wife, Helen, and my family very much for their support, assistance, and encouragement.

Peter R. Norwood

19

Introduction to Management Accounting

CHAPTER OBJECTIVES

After studying this chapter, you should be able to

1 Distinguish between financial accounting and management accounting

2 Describe the value chain and classify costs by value-chain function

3 Distinguish direct costs from indirect costs

4 Distinguish among full product costs, inventoriable product costs, and period costs

5 Prepare the financial statements of a manufacturing company

6 Identify major trends in the business environment, and use cost-benefit analysis to make business decisions

7 Use reasonable standards to make ethical judgments

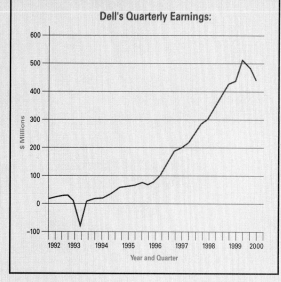

Dell Computer Corporation—the direct-order computer-assembly firm—saw its net income for the year ending in January 2000 leap to nearly $1.9 billion, double its earnings only two years earlier. This phenomenal growth helped Dell pass IBM and become the second-largest U.S. seller of personal computers. But Dell's outlook wasn't always so rosy. Just a few years earlier, the company posted its first-ever net loss—$36 million—after a major product recall and a shareholder lawsuit.

How did Michael Dell turn his company around? What information helped him make wise choices? Michael Dell knew that cost control should drive his business, because most customers prefer a good price over a specific brand name. Dell executives also had to decide how to market and distribute the computers. Should the company sell via the Internet or telephone, and eliminate the intermediaries? Or should it sell computers through discount chains? Should Dell continue to focus on the North American market, or should the company expand into Latin America, Europe, or the Pacific? Decisions! Decisions!

Accounting information helps executives like Michael Dell make these and other decisions. For example, the accounting system provides managers with cost and profit information broken down by

1. Type of product, such as desktop and laptop models
2. Marketing strategy, such as Internet sales versus direct-telephone sales versus sales to retailers
3. Geographic units, such as North American, Latin American, European, or Pacific operations

This kind of information helped Michael Dell steer Dell Computer Corporation in the right direction. The result? Soaring income and stock price. A $1,000 investment in Dell at the end of 1993 would have been worth $143,000 by January 2000.

Source: Based on Gary McWilliams, "Dell's New Push: Cheaper Laptops Built to Order," *Wall Street Journal*, June 19, 1999, p. B1; Louise Lee, "Dell Computer Profit Soars, Tops Forecasts," *Wall Street Journal*, May 21, 1997, p.A3; Toni Mack, "Michael Dell's New Religion," *Forbes*, June 6, 1994, pp. 45-46.

O̲UR STUDY of accounting has focused on reporting information for decision makers *outside* the organization: investors, creditors, and government authorities. Accounting that reports to parties outside the business is called *financial accounting*. In Chapters 1 through 18, we analyzed financial accounting reports—the income statement, the balance sheet, and the cash flow statement. These statements report the *past* performance and position of a business.

We now shift our focus to how accounting information helps shape the business's *future*. We examine accounting through the eyes of the people who run the business. Decision makers *inside* a company are called *managers*, and accounting designed to meet their information needs is called *management accounting*.

The Functions of Management

Business managers perform two broad functions: planning and controlling (Exhibit 19-1). **Planning** means choosing goals and deciding how to achieve them. For example, one goal of Dell Computers is to increase operating income. The company's managers may decide to:

1. Raise sale prices
2. Increase advertising costs to stimulate sales, or
3. Redesign the computers for faster production and servicing

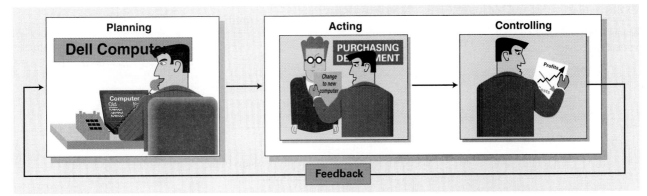

Planning

Dell Computer

Computer
Old

Acting

PURCHASING
DEPARTMENT

Change
to new
computer

Controlling

Profits

Feedback

Suppose Dell's managers decide to adopt alternative 3. Dell's engineers, purchasing officer, and production, marketing, and service managers work together to redesign the laptop computer to speed assembly and servicing while still meeting customer needs. Managers use the new design to budget the cost of the laptops, considering both the cost per laptop and the number of laptops they expect to sell. The **budget** is a quantitative expression of a plan that helps managers coordinate and implement the plan.

Dell's purchasing officer uses the new design and the number of laptops they expect to sell to order component parts, and the production manager alerts the plant workers to the design changes before they begin assembling the laptops. After they implement the plan, controlling begins. **Controlling** means evaluating the results of the business operations by comparing the actual results to the plan. Dell's accounting system records the number of laptops produced. The system also records the purchase prices and number of components used to assemble the laptops.

After completing the day's production, managers can compare the actual costs with the budgeted costs to evaluate the performance of the laptop operation and its employees. If actual costs fall below budgeted costs, that is good news. But if actual costs exceed budgeted amounts, managers may need to take corrective action. The operating costs provide feedback that helps managers decide whether their decision to redesign the laptop was a good decision that increased profits or a bad decision that decreased profits.

The chapter-opening story illustrates both the long-term and the short-term aspects of planning and controlling. In the short term, Dell Computer Corporation executives must decide whether Internet sales will increase market share and reduce marketing costs and thus increase profits. Dell's executives must also plan far into the future when they decide whether to expand in Latin America. Building a new plant in Brazil, for example, will require cash for years to come.

Dell Canada Online
www.dell.ca

Management Accounting and Financial Accounting

Exhibit 19-2 summarizes the differences between management accounting and financial accounting. Consider points 1 and 2 of the exhibit. The decision whether to build a new production plant in Brazil is related to Dell Computer Corporation's future and the decision makers are Dell managers. Dell will budget (predict) the future income and cash flows generated by the plant. Managers will then compare the benefits and costs of operating the plant with the benefits and costs of alternative investments. For example, the money required for the Brazilian plant could be used to develop a new laptop model instead. Dell executives will choose the investment with the greatest expected net benefit to the company.

EXHIBIT 19-2

Management Accounting versus Financial Accounting

	Management Accounting	Financial Accounting
1. Primary users	Internal—company's managers	External—investors, creditors, and government authorities
2. Purpose of information	Help managers plan and control business operations	Helps investors, creditors, and others make investment, credit, and other decisions
3. Focus and time dimension	Relevance and focus on the future—example: 2004 budget prepared in 2003	Reliability, objectivity, and focus on the past—example: 2001 actual performance reported in 2002
4. Type of report	Internal reports not restricted by GAAP—determined by cost-benefit analysis	Financial statements restricted by GAAP
5. Verification	No independent audit	Annual independent audit
6. Scope of information	Detailed reports on parts of the company (products, departments, territories) often on a daily, weekly, or monthly basis	Summary reports primarily on the company as a whole, usually on a quarterly or annual basis
7. Behavioural implications	Concern about how reports will affect employee behaviour	Concern about adequacy of disclosure; behavioural implications are secondary

Now consider point 4 of Exhibit 19-2—accounting reports used by decision makers. There are no GAAP-type standards for preparing the information managers use to plan and control a company's operations. Managers are free to tailor the company's management accounting system to provide information that will help them make better decisions. Managers weigh

- The *benefits* of the system—helping managers make better decisions that increase profit, against
- The *cost* of the system—including costs of training managers, as well as the cost to develop and run the system.

Weighing costs against benefits to aid decision making is called **cost-benefit analysis**. The costs and benefits of any particular management accounting system differ from one company to the next. Different companies create different systems. For example, companies differ in the way they calculate the manufacturing cost of a product, as we shall see in Chapters 20 and 21. For external reporting, though, all businesses must follow GAAP and use the accrual basis of accounting.

Point 6 of Exhibit 19-2 highlights another difference between management accounting and financial accounting—the scope of the information provided. Management accounting generates detailed reports on parts of the company (products, departments, or territories), often on a daily, weekly, or monthly basis. Managers need this more detailed and timely information to help them run the company efficiently and effectively. For example, detailed, timely information can help managers: (a) identify ways to cut costs, (b) set prices that will be competitive yet yield a profit, (c) identify the most profitable products and customers so the company can focus on key strategic profitmakers, and (d) evaluate managers' job performance.

Information technology, from Web-based company Intranet systems to hand-held computers, lets managers access this information with the touch of a button or the click of a mouse.

Point 7 of Exhibit 19-2 highlights the behavioural implications of management accounting reports. Managers' actions are influenced by how their performance is measured, and the accounting system measures performance. For example, the manager of a Laura Secord store will care about cleanliness and cheerful service if her performance evaluation is based on the store's profit. Excellent customer service leads to higher sales, which add to profit. The manager will be less concerned about customer service if she is evaluated only on her ability to control costs. In that case, she may save money by cleaning the store less often. Top executives create incentive plans very carefully due to their effects on employee behaviour.

Service, Merchandising, and Manufacturing Firms

Previous chapters focused on service and merchandising firms. **Service companies** do not sell tangible products. Rather, they provide intangible services such as house painting, hair styling, and legal advice. Labour is typically their most significant cost—often as high as 70 percent of total costs. Well-known service businesses include H & R Block (tax return preparation), Accountemps (temporary personnel services), and e-trade, an on-line brokerage service.

In contrast, merchandisers and manufacturers sell tangible products. **Merchandising companies** resell products previously purchased from suppliers. Footlocker is a merchandising company, which sells athletic shoes. Like other merchandisers, Footlocker buys ready-made inventory for resale to customers. Determining Footlocker's cost of the shoes is relatively easy. Cost is the price that the merchandiser pays for the shoes plus the freight-in costs and any applicable customs duties.

Because merchandise inventory consists only of goods ready for sale, a merchandiser's balance sheet typically reports a single category of inventory.

Companies like those that supply athletic shoes to stores such as Footlocker—New Balance, Nike, Adidas, and others—are **manufacturing companies,** which use their labour forces and factory assets to shape raw materials into finished products. Their manufacturing processes begin with materials (cloth, rubber, plastics, and so on). These materials are cut, glued, stitched, and formed into athletic shoes. The process of converting materials into finished products makes it more difficult to measure the inventory cost of a manufacturer than to measure the inventory cost of a merchandiser.

Manufacturers have three kinds of inventory:

1. **Materials inventory:** *raw materials for use in manufacturing.* For example, a shoe manufacturer's materials include leather, glue, plastic, cloth, and thread. Raw materials for Dofasco include iron ore, coal, and chemicals.

2. **Work in process inventory:** *goods that are partway through the manufacturing process, but not yet complete.* At Dell Computer Corporation, partially completed computers make up work in process inventory. At Petro-Canada, work in process inventory is half-processed crude oil that is being refined into gasoline. Work in process is also called *work in progress* or *goods in process.*

3. **Finished goods inventory:** *completed goods that have not yet been sold.* Finished goods are what the manufacturer sells to a merchandising business. For example, Procter & Gamble (P&G) manufactures Tide laundry soap and Crest toothpaste, which are finished goods that P&G sells to Costco and Shoppers Drug Mart. P&G's finished goods inventory then becomes the inventory of Costco and Shoppers Drug Mart.

H&R Block
www.hrblock.ca

Adidas
www.adidas.com

Nike
www.nike.com

Procter & Gamble
www.pg.com

Shoppers Drug Mart
www.shoppersdrugmart.ca

KEY POINT

A merchandising company *buys* the goods it sells; a manufacturing company *makes* the goods it sells.

KEY POINT

Materials Inventory includes any material that goes into manufactured goods.

KEY POINT

Work in Process Inventory includes all costs associated with units started but not yet completed. Only part of their cost has been added.

KEY POINT

Finished Goods Inventory includes the costs of products that have been completed but not yet sold.

The Value Chain

Consider Dell Computer Corporation. Many people describe Dell (or IBM or Hewlett-Packard) as a manufacturing company. Dell may be described more accurately as a company that does manufacturing. Why? Because manufacturing is only one of its major business functions.

Companies that do manufacturing also do many other things. For example, a company such as Reebok also conducts research and development to determine what new products to introduce into the market. It uses that information to design new products, which then are manufactured, marketed, and distributed. All these business functions collectively are called a **value chain**—the sequence of all business functions in which value is added to a firm's products or services (Exhibit 19-3).

- **Research and development (R&D)**—the process of researching and developing new or improved products or services, or the processes for producing them. For example, market research may identify a need for a lighter laptop computer.

- **Design**—detailed engineering of products and services, or processes for producing them. Example: redesigning the laptop's case and reengineering the manufacturing process to accommodate the new case.

- **Production or purchases**—Resources used to produce a product or service, or the purchase of finished merchandise. Examples: (1) For a manufacturer such as Dell, the actual production of products—for example, the materials, labour, and equipment used to assemble the new laptop. (2) For a merchandiser such as Future Shop, the purchase of merchandise inventory (such as laptop computers) to resell to customers.

- **Marketing**—promotion of products or services. Example: an ad campaign for the new laptop.

- **Distribution**—delivery of products or services to customers. Example: delivery of a new laptop via truck to Future Shop.

- **Customer service**—support provided for customers after the sale. Example: a hotline for owners of Dell's new laptop.

Managers are concerned about the value chain as a whole. They must control the total costs of the entire chain. For example, companies may willingly spend more in product design to enhance product quality and thereby reduce manufacturing costs and the customer service costs of honouring product warranties. Even though product design costs are then higher, the total cost of the product—as measured by the entire value chain—may be lower.

Future Shop
www.futureshop.com

Cost Objects, Direct Costs, and Indirect Costs

Managers need cost data on all aspects of the business to make wise decisions. A **cost object** is anything for which a separate measurement of costs is desired. For example, Dell Computer Corporation's cost objects may include

EXHIBIT 19-3

The Value Chain

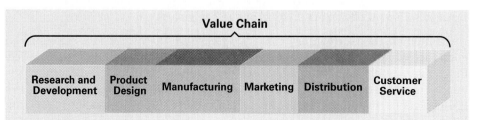

- Individual products (laptop computers or desktop models)

- Alternative marketing strategies (direct telephone sales versus Internet sales)

- Geographical segments of the business (North American, European, or Pacific)

- Departments (personnel, accounting, or information systems)

Costs that can be specifically traced to the cost object are **direct costs**. Costs that cannot be specifically traced to the cost object are **indirect costs**.

A Dell Computer Corporation plant manager wants to know the cost of producing a specific laptop. The cost of the chip in the laptop is a *direct* cost of that computer because the chip can be specifically traced to a particular laptop. In contrast, the plant manager's salary cannot be specifically traced to any one computer, so the plant manager's salary is an *indirect* cost of the laptop.

Consider another example. Suppose Dell headquarters asks for the costs incurred by a production plant. The plant now becomes the cost object. The plant manager's salary becomes a direct cost because it can be traced specifically to the plant.

Now let's focus on the most common cost object: products.

Product Costs

OBJECTIVE 4
Distinguish among full product costs, inventoriable product costs, and period costs

Accountants use the term *product costs* to denote the costs that they assign to products (Exhibit 19-4). The costs assigned depend on the purpose. For external reporting, accountants assign only *inventoriable product costs* to products.

Inventoriable product costs include all costs of a product that are regarded as an asset for external financial reporting. These costs must conform with GAAP. Typically, these costs are reported on the income statement as cost of goods sold and on the balance sheet as the cost of product inventories.

For planning, controlling, and decision making, managers must know full product costs. **Full product costs** are the costs of all resources that are used throughout the value chain for a product. The profit that New Balance earns on a particular shoe model is the difference between its sales revenue and the total cost that New Balance incurs to research, design, manufacture, market, and distribute the model as well as to service the customers who buy it. Before launching a new model, managers must predict all these costs. Also, the company's managers must decide which of their many products to emphasize. If they determine that the profit (revenue minus full product costs) of a children's shoe is less than the profit of another product, they may drop the shoe and use the freed-up production capacity to produce additional units of the more profitable product. The more accurate the assignment of costs to individual products, the more likely managers will make profitable decisions.

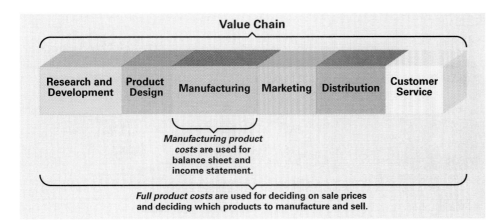

EXHIBIT 19-4

Different Meanings of the Term *Product Costs* and Their Relations to the Value Chain

Definitions of Key Inventoriable Product Costs

Exhibit 19-5 illustrates the major categories of inventoriable product costs for a manufacturer such as New Balance:

Direct Materials   To be considered **direct materials**, materials must meet two requirements: (1) They must become a physical part of the finished product, and (2) their costs must be separately and conveniently traceable through the manufacturing process to finished goods. For New Balance, the leather uppers, the rubber and plastic soles, and the laces of the company's athletic shoes are among its direct materials. They become part of the finished shoe. Also, we can trace their costs directly from materials inventory through work in process to finished goods.

Direct Labour   **Direct labour** is the compensation of employees who physically convert materials into the company's products. For New Balance, direct labour includes the wages of the machine operators and the persons who assemble the shoes. For Dell, direct labour is the pay of employees who work on the computer assembly lines. The effort of these persons can be traced *directly* to finished goods.

Manufacturing Overhead   **Manufacturing overhead** includes all manufacturing costs besides direct materials and direct labour. Examples include indirect materials, indirect labour, factory utilities, repairs, maintenance, rent, insurance, property taxes, and amortization on factory buildings and equipment. Manufacturing overhead also is called **factory overhead** or **indirect manufacturing cost.**

Indirect Materials   The glue and thread used in athletic shoes are materials that become physical parts of the finished product. But, compared with the cost of the leather uppers and rubber soles, the costs of glue and thread are minor. Measuring

New Balance
www.newbalance.com

KEY POINT

Manufacturing overhead includes *only* indirect *manufacturing* costs—that is, indirect costs related to the manufacturing plant.

LEARNING TIP

For a manufacturing company,
  Direct materials
+ Direct labour
+ Manufacturing Overhead
= Inventoriable product costs

EXHIBIT 19-5

Inventoriable Product Costs for a Manufacturer

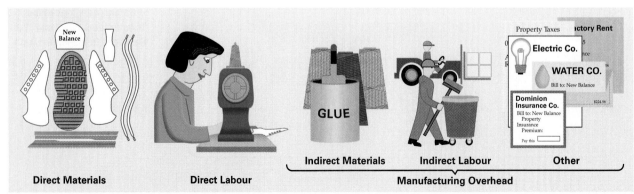

Direct Materials	Direct Labour	Indirect Materials	Indirect Labour	Other
			Manufacturing Overhead	

the costs of those low-priced materials is difficult for a single pair of shoes. How would a supervisor calculate the cost of a brushful of glue? Or the cost of the thread used in a shoe? How useful would such detailed information be? We call materials whose costs cannot conveniently be traced directly to particular finished products **indirect materials**. Indirect materials are accounted for as part of manufacturing overhead cost.

Indirect Labour Some manufacturing labour costs are classified as **indirect labour**. These costs are difficult to trace to specific products. Examples include the pay of forklift operators, janitors, and plant managers. Indirect labour, like indirect materials, is a part of manufacturing overhead.

The balance sheet of New Balance, a manufacturing company, will report the inventoriable product cost of the finished shoes on hand at the end of the period (direct materials, direct labour, and manufacturing overhead) as an asset—Finished Goods Inventory. New Balance's income statement will report as Cost of Goods Sold the inventoriable costs of the shoes the company sells.

Note that New Balance's inventoriable product costs include *only* the manufacturing costs. Remember that *the inventoriable costs are incurred only in the third element of the value chain in Exhibit 19-3*. Costs incurred in other elements of the value chain—such as New Balance's cost to research and develop a new style of shoe, and to advertise and deliver shoes to customers—are *not* inventoriable product costs for external reporting. Instead, these are **period costs** that are expensed in the income statement in the period incurred. Period costs are never part of the inventory asset account.

Exhibit 19-6 summarizes the differences between inventoriable costs and period costs for service, merchandising, and manufacturing companies. Study this exhibit carefully. When are costs like amortization, insurance, utilities, and property taxes treated as inventoriable product costs? Only when those costs are related to the manufacturing plant. A manufacturer treats amortization, insurance, utilities, and property taxes as inventoriable product costs only when these costs are related to manufacturing. When those costs are related to nonmanufacturing activities like R&D or marketing, they are treated as period costs. Service companies and merchandisers do no manufacturing, so they always treat amortization, insurance, utilities, and property taxes as period costs. The difference between inventoriable product costs and period costs is important because these two kinds of cost are treated differently in the financial statements. The next section takes a closer look at how the financial statements of service companies, merchandisers, and manufacturers differ.

EXHIBIT 19-6

Inventoriable Product Costs and Period Costs for Service, Merchandising, and Manufacturing Companies

	Inventoriable Product Costs Initially an asset (inventory), and not expensed (Cost of Goods Sold) until inventory is sold	**Period Costs** Expensed in period incurred; never considered an asset
Service Companies	None	Salaries, amortization expense, utilities, insurance, property taxes, advertising
Merchandising Companies	Purchases plus freight-in	Salaries, amortization expense, utilities, insurance, property taxes, advertising, freight-out
Manufacturing Companies	Direct materials, plus direct labour, plus manufacturing overhead (including indirect materials; indirect labour; amortization on plant and equipment; insurance, utilities and property taxes on plant)	R&D; freight-out; and amortization expense, utilities, insurance, and property taxes on executive headquarters (separate from plant); advertising; CEO's salary

Inventoriable Product Costs and Period Costs in Financial Statements

How do inventoriable product costs and period costs affect companies' financial statements? We begin with a short review to help you see how a manufacturer's financial statements differ from those of service and merchandising companies.

Service Companies

Service companies have the simplest accounting. Exhibit 19-7 shows the income statement of Bailey, Banks, & Hancock Inc. (BBH), a firm of landscape architects. As you would imagine, the firm carries no inventory and thus has no inventoriable product costs. Consequently, BBH's income statement in Exhibit 19-7 includes no Cost of Goods Sold. The income statement groups all expenses (period costs) together. As for most service companies, BBH's largest expense is for the salaries of employees who perform the services.

Merchandising Companies

Exhibit 19-8, Panel A, presents a bird's-eye view of how inventoriable product costs and period costs affect the financial statements of merchandising companies. Apex Showrooms Inc., a merchandiser of lighting fixtures, buys chandeliers and track lights ready for resale. Apex's *only* inventoriable product costs are for the purchase of these goods, plus freight-in.

Panel B of Exhibit 19-8 shows Apex's income statement.[1] In contrast to the service company (Exhibit 19-7), the merchandiser's income statement features the cost of goods sold as the major expense. Merchandisers like Apex can compute cost of goods sold as follows:

Beginning inventory	$9,500	What Apex had at the beginning of the period
+ Purchases and freight-in	110,000	What Apex bought during the period
= Cost of goods available for sale	119,500	Total available for sale during the period
– Ending inventory	13,000	What Apex had at the end of the period
= Cost of goods sold	$106,500	What Apex sold

On the income statement, cost of goods sold is deducted from sales revenue to obtain gross margin. Apex's operating expenses (period costs) are deducted from gross margin to measure operating income.

EXHIBIT 19-7

Service Company Income Statement

BAILEY, BANKS, & HANCOCK INC.
Income Statement
For the Month Ended December 31, 2002

Revenues		$160,000
Expenses:		
Salary expense	$104,000	
Office rent expense	18,000	
Amortization expense—furniture and equipment	3,500	
Marketing expense	2,500	
Other expenses	2,000	(130,000)
Operating income		$30,000

[1]To highlight the roles of beginning inventory, purchases, freight-in, and ending inventory, we assume that Apex uses a periodic inventory system. However, the concepts in this chapter apply equally to companies that use perpetual inventory systems.

PANEL A—Inventoriable Product Costs and Period Costs in Merchandising Companies

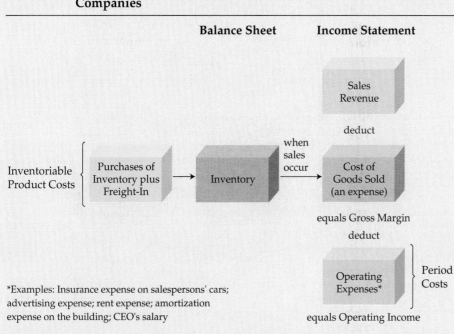

*Examples: Insurance expense on salespersons' cars; advertising expense; rent expense; amortization expense on the building; CEO's salary

PANEL B—Merchandising Company Income Statement

APEX SHOWROOMS INC.
Income Statement
For the Month Ended December 31, 2002

Sales revenue..		$150,000
Cost of goods sold:		
Beginning inventory	$ 9,500	
Purchases and freight-in...	110,000	
Cost of goods available for sale...............................	119,500	
Ending inventory	(13,000)	106,500
Gross margin...		43,500
Operating expenses:		
Showroom rent expense	5,000	
Sales salary expense...	2,500	
Administrative expense...	1,500	9,000
Operating income..		$ 34,500

Manufacturing Companies

Exhibit 19-9, Panel A, shows that manufacturing firms have the most complicated accounting with three kinds of inventory: materials, work in process, and finished goods. Direct labour and manufacturing overhead convert raw materials into finished goods. As shown in Panel A, these are all inventoriable costs.

Consider Top-Flight Inc., a manufacturer of golf equipment and athletic shoes. Compare its income statement in Panel B of Exhibit 19-9 with the merchandiser's income statement in Panel B of Exhibit 19-8. Both Apex and Top-Flight subtract cost of goods sold from sales revenue to obtain gross margin. Both companies subtract operating expenses from gross margin to get operating income. The only difference between the two statements is that the *merchandiser* (Apex) uses *purchases* in

PANEL A—Inventoriable Product Costs and Period Costs in Manufacturing Companies

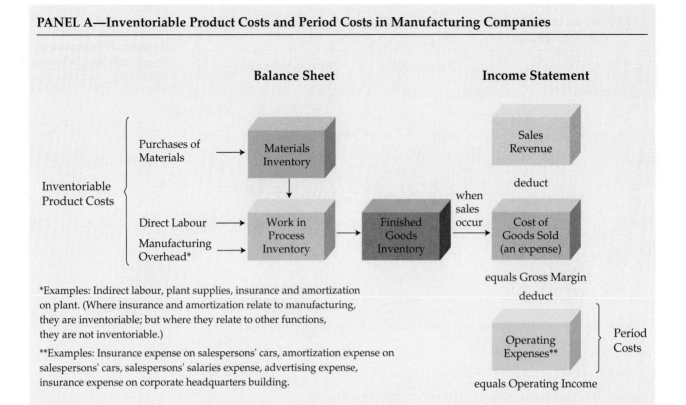

*Examples: Indirect labour, plant supplies, insurance and amortization on plant. (Where insurance and amortization relate to manufacturing, they are inventoriable; but where they relate to other functions, they are not inventoriable.)

**Examples: Insurance expense on salespersons' cars, amortization expense on salespersons' cars, salespersons' salaries expense, advertising expense, insurance expense on corporate headquarters building.

PANEL B—Manufacturing Company Income Statement

TOP-FLIGHT INC.
Income Statement
For the Year Ended December 31, 2002

Sales revenue...		$65,000
Cost of goods sold:		
Beginning finished goods inventory	$ 6,000	
Cost of goods manufactured*.................................	42,000	
Cost of goods available for sale...............................	48,000	
Ending finished goods inventory	(8,000)	
Cost of goods sold..		40,000
Gross margin..		25,000
Operating expenses:		
Sales salary expense...	3,000	
Delivery expense...	5,000	
Administrative expense...	2,000	10,000
Operating income...		$15,000

*From schedule of Cost of Goods Manufactured in Exhibit 19-10.

EXHIBIT 19-9

Manufacturing Company: Inventoriable Product Costs, Period Costs, and the Income Statement

computing cost of goods sold, while the *manufacturer* (Top-Flight) uses the *cost of goods manufactured* in computing cost of goods sold. Otherwise, the format of a manufacturer's income statement is identical to the format of a merchandiser's income statement.

Now let's see how to compute cost of goods manufactured.

Calculating Cost of Goods Manufactured The **cost of goods manufactured** is the manufacturer's counterpart to the merchandiser's purchases—that is, the cost of new completed goods ready for sale that is added to beginning inventory of finished goods during the period.

The cost of goods manufactured computation is more complex than the merchandiser's tabulation of purchases. Panel A of Exhibit 19-10 shows how Top-Flight

EXHIBIT 19-10

Schedule of Cost of Goods Manufactured

Panel A—Manufacturing Company Schedule of Cost of Goods Manufactured

TOP-FLIGHT INC.
Schedule of Cost of Goods Manufactured
December 31, 2002

Beginning work in process inventory.........			$2,000
Add: Direct materials used:			
Beginning materials inventory..................	$ 9,000		
Purchases of direct materials plus freight-in	27,000		
Available for use..	36,000		
Ending materials inventory........................	(22,000)		
Direct materials used		$14,000	
Direct labour..		19,000	
Manufacturing overhead:			
Indirect materials	$ 1,500		
Indirect labour...	3,500		
Amortization—factory building...............	2,000		
Amortization—factory equipment...........	1,000		
Factory utilities and insurance..................	3,500		
Property tax on factory	500	12,000	
Total manufacturing costs			
incurred during the year...........................			45,000
Total manufacturing costs to account for ...			47,000
Less: Ending work in process inventory			(5,000)
Cost of goods manufactured........................			$42,000

Panel B—Flow of Costs Through a Manufacturer's Inventory Accounts

computes cost of goods manufactured—the manufacturing cost of the goods completed during a production period (the year 2002 in Exhibit 19-10). The computation begins with the Work in Process Inventory balance at the beginning of the year ($2,000). To this amount, we add the three components of total manufacturing cost incurred during the year: direct materials used ($14,000), direct labour ($19,000), and manufacturing overhead ($12,000). Adding the sum of these costs ($45,000) to the beginning Work in Process Inventory balance of $2,000 gives the total cost assigned to goods worked on during the year—$47,000. Some of these goods were completed and sent into Finished Goods Inventory during the year; the others are still in process at the end of the year. Thus we subtract the cost of goods in process at the end of the year on December 31 ($5,000) to arrive at the cost of the completed goods—that is, the cost of goods manufactured total of $42,000.

Panel B of Exhibit 19-10 diagrams the flow of costs through a manufacturer's inventory accounts, using a T-account approach. It reveals a similar computational format at all three stages—direct materials, work in process, and finished goods. For example, the cost of direct materials used is the beginning inventory plus purchases minus the ending inventory. The credit amount of each account flows into the next account. This flow of costs through the inventory accounts can be seen in the income statement in Panel B of Exhibit 19-9 and the schedule of cost of goods manufactured in Exhibit 19-10.

STOP & THINK

Goods worked on during a production period may be classified according to when they are begun and when they are completed. For example, some of the goods worked on in 2002 were begun in 2001 and completed in 2002. Other goods worked on 2002 were both begun and completed during 2002. Still others were begun late in 2002 but not completed until 2003. Refer to Exhibit 19-10, Panel A. Suppose that $3,000 of the total manufacturing cost incurred during the year was incurred to complete the beginning work in process inventory (which was begun in 2001). What is the total cost of the goods that were both begun and completed in 2002?

Answer: The total manufacturing costs incurred during the year was $45,000. If $3,000 of that total was incurred to complete the beginning work in process inventory, then $42,000 was incurred to produce goods both begun and completed during 2002 and goods begun in 2002 but not completed as of December 31, 2002. The cost of the incomplete goods is the ending work in process inventory cost of $5,000. Therefore $37,000 ($42,000 − $5,000) is the total cost of the goods both begun and completed during the year.

Perpetual and Periodic Inventory Systems

Chapter 9 compared accounting for inventories under the perpetual system and the periodic system. Most manufacturers use the perpetual system because they need a continuous record of materials, work in process, and finished goods on hand. The perpetual records help managers control operations. During periods of high customer demand, a manufacturer focuses on meeting production schedules. Important accounting controls may be relaxed. As a peak production season winds down, managers may find it difficult to bring accounting information up to date. A

BAILEY, BANKS, & HANCOCK INC. (Service Company)		APEX SHOWROOMS INC. (Merchandising Company)		TOP-FLIGHT INC. (Manufacturing Company)	
Cash...............................	$4,000	Cash	$4,000	Cash	$4,000
Accounts receivable	5,000	Accounts receivable.....	5,000	Accounts receivable.....	5,000
		Inventory (from............		Materials inventory	
		Exhibit 19-8)..............	13,000	(from Exhibit 19-10).	22,000
				Work in process inventory (from Exhibit 19-10)............	5,000
				Finished goods inventory (from Exhibit 19-9)..............	8,000
				Total inventories...........	35,000
Prepaid expenses	1,000	Prepaid expenses..........	1,000	Prepaid expenses..........	1,000
Total current assets	$10,000	Total current assets	$23,000	Total current assets	$45,000

EXHIBIT 19-11

Current Asset Sections of Balance Sheets on December 31, 2002

computerized perpetual system is easier to keep current throughout the year than a manual system. But even companies that use a perpetual system take physical counts of inventories at least annually to check the accuracy of their records.

Manufacturers that use a periodic inventory system follow the general accounting procedures that merchandisers use, as discussed in Chapter 9. Here we concentrate on the perpetual system because it is more commonly used by manufacturers than the periodic system.

Effects on the Balance Sheet

The only difference in the balance sheets of service, merchandising, and manufacturing companies is related to inventories. Exhibit 19-11 shows how the current asset sections of Bailey, Banks, & Hancock Inc. (service company), Apex Showrooms Inc. (merchandising company), and Top-Flight Inc. (manufacturing company) might differ at the end of 2002. Notice that Bailey, Banks, & Hancock Inc. has no inventory at all, Apex Showrooms Inc. has a single category of inventory, and Top-Flight Inc. has three categories of inventory (materials, work in process, and finished goods).

You have now

1. Learned the differences between financial and management accounting

2. Considered the six business functions that comprise the value chain

3. Distinguished direct costs from indirect costs

4. Distinguished among full product costs, inventoriable product costs, and period costs

5. Seen the differences among service, merchandising, and manufacturing companies' financial statements

We will use these concepts many times throughout our discussion of management accounting. It is important that you take time now to review the following Decision Guidelines. Make sure you have a solid understanding of all of these concepts before you read any further.

Decision	Guidelines
What information should management accountants provide? What is the primary focus of management accounting?	Management accounting provides information that helps managers make better decisions. It has a: • *Future* orientation • Focus on *relevance* to business decisions
How do you decide on a company's management accounting system, which is not restricted by GAAP?	Cost-benefit analysis: Design management accounting system so that benefits (from helping managers make wiser decisions) outweigh the costs of the system (including costs of management time and education).
How do you distinguish among service, merchandising, and manufacturing companies? How do their balance sheets differ?	*Service companies:* • Provide customers with intangible services • Have no inventories on the balance sheet *Merchandising companies:* • Resell tangible products they purchased ready-made from suppliers • Have only one category of inventory on the balance sheet *Manufacturing companies:* • Apply labour, plant, and equipment to transform raw materials into new finished products • Have three categories of inventory on the balance sheet: Materials inventory Work in process inventory Finished goods inventory

How do you compute cost of goods sold?	• *Service companies:* No cost of goods sold, because they don't sell tangible goods
	
	• *Merchandising companies:*
	    Beginning inventory
	    + Purchases and freight-in
	    <u>− Ending inventory</u>
	    = Cost of goods sold
	
	• *Manufacturing companies:*
	    Beginning finished goods inventory
	    + Cost of goods manufactured
	    <u>− Ending finished goods inventory</u>
	    = Cost of goods sold

How do you compute the cost of goods manufactured for a manufacturer?	Beginning work in process inventory + Current period manufacturing costs (Direct materials + direct labour + manufacturing overhead) <u>− Ending work in process inventory</u> = Cost of goods manufactured
What costs are initially treated as assets for external reporting? When are these costs expensed?	For external reporting, *inventoriable product costs* are initially treated as assets (Inventory). These costs are expensed (as Cost of goods sold) when the products are sold.
What costs are inventoriable under GAAP?	• *Service companies:* No inventoriable product costs because they do not sell tangible products • *Merchandising companies:* Purchases and freight-in • *Manufacturing companies:* Direct materials used, direct labour, and manufacturing overhead

1. Show how to compute cost of goods manufactured. Use the following amounts: direct materials used ($24,000), direct labour ($9,000), manufacturing overhead ($17,000), and work in process, beginning ($5,000) and ending ($4,000).

2. For a manufacturing company identify the following as either an inventoriable product cost or a period cost:

   a. Amortization on factory equipment

   b. Amortization on salespersons' automobiles

   c. Insurance on factory building

   d. Marketing manager's salary

Solution to Review Problem

1. Cost of goods manufactured:

Beginning work in process inventory		$ 5,000
Add: Direct materials used	$24,000	
Direct labour	9,000	
Manufacturing overhead	17,000	
Total manufacturing costs incurred during the period		50,000
Total manufacturing costs to account for		55,000
Less: Ending work in process inventory		(4,000)
Cost of goods manufactured		$51,000

2. a. Inventoriable product cost; b. Period cost; c. Inventoriable product cost; d. Period cost.

The Modern Business Environment

OBJECTIVE 6
Identify major trends in the business environment, and use cost-benefit analysis to make business decisions

The rest of this textbook describes management accounting tools and techniques designed to help managers make wise business decisions that will maximize shareholder wealth. Before we turn to these specific accounting tools, let's first consider recent trends in business that affect managers' decisions and the management accounting systems that support these decisions. These trends include: the shift toward a service economy, the rise of the global marketplace, time-based competition (including electronic commerce and the just-in-time management philosophy), and total quality management.

Shift Toward a Service Economy

Service companies provide health care, communication, transportation, banking, and other important benefits to society. The last century has seen our economy shift from manufacturing to service. Service companies now make up the largest sector of the Canadian economy and employ 67 percent of the work force. Even companies that do manufacturing, such as General Electric (GE), are shifting their focus toward selling services. It's easy to see why. In GE's jet engine business, services contribute only 30 percent of the revenues, but generate two-thirds of the profit.

General Electric
www.ge.ca

Managers of service companies need information to make decisions. For example, banks must include the cost of servicing chequing and savings accounts in the fees they charge customers. Our discussions will consider how service companies, as well as merchandising and manufacturing firms, use management accounting information.

Competing in the Global Marketplace

The costs of international trade have plummeted over the last decade, largely due to

- Improved telecommunications, including video conferencing, the Internet, and e-mail.
- Improved worldwide transportation, such as UPS's worldwide overnight delivery services
- Reduced barriers to free trade, including the European Union free-trade zone (which includes more than a dozen European countries) and the North American Free Trade Agreement trading bloc (composed of the United States, Canada, and Mexico)

UPS
www.ups.com/canada/
engindex.html

These changes enable foreign companies to compete with local firms, and firms that are not world-class competitors will not survive in the global marketplace. For example, RCA stereos have largely been replaced by Panasonic, Sony, and JVC models. However, global markets do provide competitive companies with tremendous potential. For instance, GE's revenue is growing faster in foreign countries than in North America, and foreign operations account for over 30 percent of GE's revenues. McDonald's is expanding in Russia and China, two countries with billions of consumers.

Manufacturers often move production operations to other countries where labour is less expensive. Suppose that Top-Flight Inc., a golf equipment and athletic shoe company, is considering whether to build a new manufacturing plant in Mexico. Top-Flight's managers will compare the costs with the benefits of building the plant in Mexico. They will decide to build the plant if the benefits (less expensive labour) outweigh the costs of building the new plant.

Globalization has several implications for management accounting:

1. Stiffer competition means that managers need more accurate information to make wise decisions. For example, if Nokia overestimates the cost of its new cell phone model, it may set prices too high and lose business to competitors.
2. Companies must decide whether to expand sales and/or production into foreign countries. To make these decisions, managers need estimates of the costs and benefits of international expansion.
3. Globalization fosters the transfer of management philosophy across international borders. For example, many North American companies now follow the just-in-time philosophy that was developed in Japan.

Time-Based Competition

The Internet, electronic commerce (e-commerce), e-mail, and express delivery services speed the pace of business in the new millenium. Customers who surf the Web and use e-mail to correspond in real time with people all over the world will not wait four weeks to receive their purchases. Companies that do not quickly satisfy customers' demands will not survive. Time is the latest competitive turf for world-class business.

Dell Computer Corporation commits to delivering your desktop computer within a week of receiving your order. Even automakers are getting in on the act: Toyota says that it can now make a car within five days of receiving a custom order. Tom Meredith, Dell's chief financial officer, recently addressed an automakers' conference on the "Dell way" (high-quality custom-built products delivered shortly after the customer places an order). U.S. automakers, who have often kept customers waiting 30 to 60 days for custom orders, were all ears. To compete with Toyota, General Motors plans to cut its order-to-delivery time from 8 weeks in 1999 to no more than 11 days by 2003. How can GM do it? E-commerce and the just-in-time management philosophy are two ways managers speed up responses to customers.

E-commerce How does Dell assemble and deliver your computer within a week after you order it? E-commerce helps. E-commerce is a shorthand for conducting everyday business practices such as budgeting, planning, purchasing, and selling using the Internet. E-commerce is fundamentally changing the way companies do business. Companies realize they must embrace e-commerce to survive in an increasingly competitive globally wired economy. Imagine a sales clerk who can sell to thousands of customers at once. This sales clerk instantly provides every product, option, and price the company offers. It works 24 hours a day, 365 days a year, without ever taking a break or vacation. This sales clerk is an e-commerce Web site.

Business-to-business e-commerce takes this speed and efficiency a big step further. Imagine that you are sitting in your office, anywhere in the world. You enter Dell's Web site and customize your own computer. The site shows computer systems and prices your employer has prenegotiated with Dell. After you fill your virtual shopping cart, the entire process of ordering, approval, and delivery is automated through your employer's business-to-business software. At any time, your employer can obtain a real-time view of recent computer purchases and outstanding orders.

Suppose your employer requires specific approval for computer purchases over $1,000. If falling computer prices mean that the typical purchase, which used to cost about $1,500, now costs less than $1,000, your employer might now require specific approval for purchases over $800. Or your employer may decide to keep the $1,000 cutoff to eliminate a level of approval and further speed computer purchases. Electronic purchases below specified dollar limits are often untouched by human hands, generate little if any paper, and avoid the time and cost of processing this paperwork. General Motors indicates that moving such purchases online will slash the roughly $100 it now costs to process each of the hundreds of thousands of purchase orders it issues each year.

Firms also use the Internet to tap into other companies' business processes. Companies that supply component computer parts to Dell can use the Internet to look into Dell's production process through the virtual window Dell provides each supplier. From this customized window, the supplier can see the current demand for and inventory levels of the parts it supplies to Dell. In addition to automating the size of the next day's order, the virtual window provides current information that can help the supplier forecast trends in demand. Dell's suppliers use this information to plan, or budget, Dell's demand for their products. Access to this real-time information that lets suppliers forecast Dell's demand for their products is a key to Dell's ability to cut order-to-delivery times and to control costs.

In addition to reducing their own processing costs, firms that purchase online can often cut the prices they pay for goods and services. Competition is stiff because buyers can ask vendors throughout the world for price quotes. Firms in some industries, such as the auto industry, are cooperating to establish virtual marketplaces that link manufacturers and suppliers. A small low-cost supplier in Asia that never before had timely information to make competitive bids needs only a password and an Internet browser to enter the online market and bid against every other potential supplier. By joining Ford and General Motors in establishing virtual markets for their purchases, DaimlerChrysler's chairman estimates a cost saving of nearly $1,000 per vehicle. How? The big automakers expect price concessions from their suppliers not only on their own purchases, but on purchases their suppliers make from each other. By reducing costs throughout the value chain, the automakers expect to reap substantial cost reductions.

We have seen how e-commerce is providing suppliers with virtual windows into their customers' business operations, and how Internet marketplaces can cut the prices businesses must pay for purchased goods and services. E-commerce is thus an important means of **supply chain management**, where companies exchange information with their suppliers and their customers to reduce costs, improve quality, and speed delivery of goods and services from suppliers, through the company itself, and on to the end customers.

E-commerce increases firms' ability (and need) to move toward a just-in-time management philosophy.

The Just-in-time Management Philosophy Traditionally, companies held a lot of inventory to ensure they would have enough raw materials for production and enough finished goods to fill customer orders. However, it is expensive to hold these inventories. Money invested cannot be used for other purposes. Inventory held too long becomes obsolete. Storing the inventory requires space. The costs of holding inventory can easily add up to 25 percent of the inventory's value. The just-in-time philosophy helps managers cut these costs and speed the transformation of raw materials into new finished products by reducing the need to hold inventory.

Toyota is generally credited with pioneering the **just-in-time (JIT)** management philosophy. As the name suggests, the JIT philosophy means producing *just in time* to satisfy needs. Materials are purchased and finished goods are completed only as needed to satisfy customer orders. Ideally, materials necessary for today's production are delivered in (small) batches of exactly the right quantities *just in time* to begin production, and finished units are completed just in time for delivery to customers.

Firms adopting JIT report sharp reductions in inventory, often averaging about 50 percent. The reduction in inventory and speeding up of the production process reduces **throughput time**, the time between buying raw materials and selling the finished products. For example, Dell Computer Corporation recently cut its throughput time from 31 days to 7 days. Why is this important? The *Wall Street Journal* estimates that the onrush of technology reduces the value of a completed PC by 1 percent a week.[2] Moving inventory quickly gives Dell pricing and manufacturing advantages over its competitors. For example, Dell can quickly cut sale prices on its computers when the cost of components declines. Less inventory also means that Dell can quickly incorporate new technology.

Manfacturers adopting just-in-time depend on their suppliers to make on-time deliveries of perfect-quality raw materials. Thus JIT requires close communications with suppliers. As we noted earlier, Dell has even designed special Web pages for its major suppliers, giving them a "virtual window" into Dell operations they supply. Suppliers use these windows to decide when and how much raw material to deliver to Dell.

Companies that adopt JIT must strive for perfect quality. Defects stop the production line. To avoid disrupting production, defects must be rare.

Managers considering JIT want to know its costs and benefits. Suppose New-Tell, a computer chip manufacturer, is considering JIT. If New-Tell adopts JIT, the company will incur costs, including employee training, searching for the most reliable suppliers, and lost sales due to initial slowing of production as it makes the transition to JIT. New-Tell estimates that these costs will total $2,000,000. The benefits of adopting JIT include savings on inventory and storage space. JIT also reduces inventory obsolescence and yields higher sales because of better-quality products. New-Tell estimates that these benefits will save an average of $650,000 a year for ten years.

To make a decision, New-Tell must compare the future benefits of adopting JIT with the $2,000,000 cost. The cost of adopting JIT comes immediately, but the

---

[2]"Compaq Stumbles as PCs Weather New Blow," *Wall Street Journal*, March 9, 1998, p. B1.

benefits occur later. New-Tell must determine the present value today of the future benefits of adopting JIT. In business, we refer to this as *discounting* the future amounts to their *present values*. Let's assume that New-Tell's benefits of adopting JIT have a present value of $3,141,450.[3]

The costs of adopting JIT are incurred now, so the cost data are already stated at their present values. With all amounts stated at present values, we can compare New-Tell's costs and benefits of adopting a JIT system. New-Tell's decision follows this rule:

- Present value of JIT's benefits exceed the cost of adopting JIT —> Adopt JIT
- Cost of adopting JIT exceeds the present value of JIT's benefits —> Do not adopt JIT

The analysis is as follows:

Present value of benefits	$3,141,450
Present value of costs	(2,000,000)
Excess of benefits over costs	$1,141,450
Decision: Invest in JIT system	

Total Quality Management

Today, companies must deliver quality goods and services to remain competitive. Hewlett-Packard, Ford, British Telecom, and Toyota view **total quality management (TQM)** as one of the keys to success in a global economy. The goal of total quality management is to attract customers by providing them with superior products and services. Companies achieve this goal by improving quality and by eliminating defects and waste throughout the value chain. Each business function examines its own activities and works to improve by setting higher and higher goals.

TQM emphasizes educating, training, and cross-training employees to do multiple tasks. Motorola's purchasing department is an example. Motorola wanted to reduce the time taken to issue a purchase order. Before starting the project, a departmental team took a two-day company course called High-Commitment, High-Performance Team Training. Team members then reduced the number of steps in handling a purchase order from 17 to 6, slashing average processing time from 30 minutes to 3. The department now processes 45 percent more purchase orders with no added employees.

Like JIT, quality improvement programs cost money today. The benefits usually do not occur until later. Because no one can foresee the future, the amount of the future benefits is not known exactly. Accountants often adjust for this uncertainty.

Consider GE. The company recently started nearly 3,000 quality-related projects at a cost of more than $200 million. The first-year cost savings from these projects totalled only $170 million. Does this mean that GE made a bad decision? Not necessarily. GE expects these projects to continue yielding benefits in the future.

Suppose GE managers predict these projects will be either moderately successful or extremely successful. Assume that if the projects are moderately successful, they will yield additional benefits (cost savings) with a present value of $20 million. If the projects are extremely successful, they will yield extra benefits with a present value of $100 million. GE managers think the projects are more likely to be extremely successful, but they do not know for sure. Suppose they estimate a 60 percent chance that the projects will be extremely successful, and a 40 percent chance that they will be moderately successful.

Ford
www.ford.ca

Hewlett-Packard
www.hewlettpackard.com

Toyota
www.toyota.ca

---

[3]JIT will reduce New-Tell's costs by $650,000 per year for ten years. Using a 16 percent discount rate, the present value of $650,000 per year for ten years is $3,141,450 ($650,000 × 4.833 from the present value table in Appendix A in this text).

In an uncertain environment such as GE's, managers make decisions based on **expected values**. We compute expected values by multiplying the dollar value of each possible outcome by the probability of that outcome, and then add the results:

Outcome (Benefit)	× Probability	=	Expected Value (of Additional Benefit)
Extremely successful:	$100 million × 60% chance	=	$60 million
Moderately successful:	20 million × 40% chance	=	$ 8 million
Total expected value of benefits			$68 million

What does this $68 million mean? If GE faced this exact situation ten times, it would expect to get $100 million in extra benefits six times, and only $20 million of additional benefits four times. The *average* extra benefits across the ten situations is $68 million, calculated as [(6 × $100) + (4 × $20)]/10 = $68. In effect, GE's best guess of the additional benefit is the expected value of $68 million.

The following summary shows that the total benefits expected from GE's quality projects ($238 million) exceeds the $200 million cost of the projects, suggesting that GE's quality project was worthwhile:

	Total Benefits	Total Costs
Initial benefits and costs	$170 million	$200 million
Additional expected benefits	$ 68 million	
Total	$238 million	$200 million

Even after adopting quality programs, companies cannot rest on their laurels. TQM requires that companies (and individual employees) continually look for ways to improve performance. This is the **continuous improvement** philosophy.

How do companies improve? Many businesses find that investments in higher quality earlier in the value chain (R&D and design) generate savings in later stages (production, marketing, and customer service). Successful companies design and build quality into the product or service rather than doubling back to inspect quality and make repairs later. Carefully designed products and better employee training reduce costs of inspections, rework, and warranty claims, all of which decrease profits.

Management Accounting in the Real World 🌐

Management Accounting for Small- and Medium-Sized Businesses

Many of the techniques that we study in management accounting tend to reflect the operations of large manufacturers or large service corporations. Do small- and medium-sized manufacturers and service corporations use these techniques too? Are the techniques modified by smaller companies? Are the techniques used by smaller companies? We will explore these questions in the coming chapters by visiting West Coast Alloys Limited, a medium-sized manufacturer of pipe products used primarily in the forest industry. The company is located in Richmond, British Columbia.

Are modern trends in manufacturing changing the techniques of management accounting? We will also explore this question in the coming chapters, for small and large businesses.

Professional Ethics for Management Accountants

OBJECTIVE 7
Use reasonable standards to make ethical judgments

A key indicator of quality is ethical behaviour. As we've seen throughout this text, ethical behaviour is necessary for the orderly functioning of society and business. How would you feel if parents, teachers, employers, friends, and co-workers constantly lied to you? Relationships necessary for everyday life would break down. Business would become much more difficult to conduct, and the range and quality of goods and services would decline. Because ethical behaviour is so important, society enacts laws that require social responsibility. For example, it is illegal for companies to sell products that are clearly defective, such as automobiles that do not meet government safety standards.

Unfortunately, the ethical path is not always clear. You may want to act ethically and do the right thing, but the consequences involved can make it difficult to decide what to do. Consider the following examples:

- Sarah Baker is examining the expense reports of her staff accountants, who counted inventory at Canadian Tire's warehouses in Ontario. She discovers that Mike Flinders has claimed, but not included, hotel receipts for over $1,000 of accommodation expenses. Each of the other staff members who also claimed $1,000 did attach hotel receipts. When asked about the receipt, Mike admits that he had stayed with an old friend, not in the hotel. His wife is expecting their first child, and he believes that he deserves the money he saved. After all, the company would have paid his hotel bill.

- As the accountant of Entreé Computer Co., you are aware of your company's weak financial condition. Entreé is close to signing a lucrative contract that should ensure its future. To do so, the controller states that the company *must* report a profit this year (ending December 31). He makes the following suggestion. "Two customers have placed orders that are really not supposed to be shipped until early January. Ask production to fill and ship those orders on December 31, so we can record them in this year's sales."

Canadian Tire
www.canadiantire.ca

Certified Management Accountants of Canada (CMA)
www.cma-canada.org

The Society of Management Accountants of Canada (CMA Canada) through its provincial societies, has developed standards to help management accountants deal with these kinds of situations. A summary of the *Rules of Professional Conduct* issued by the Certified Management Accountants of British Columbia appears in Exhibit 19-12. These standards require management accountants to

- Maintain their professional competence
- Preserve the confidentiality of the information they handle
- Act with integrity and objectivity

Let's return to the two preceding ethical dilemmas. By asking to be reimbursed for hotel expenses he did not incur, Mike Flinders clearly violated the CMA's integrity standards (conflict of interest in which he tried to enrich himself at company expense). Because Sarah Baker discovered the inflated expense report, she would not be fulfilling her ethical responsibilities (integrity and objectivity) if she allowed the reimbursement and did not take disciplinary action.

The second dilemma, in which the controller asked you to accelerate the shipments, is less clear-cut. You should discuss the available alternatives and their consequences with others. Many people believe that following the controller's suggestion to manipulate the company's income would violate the standards of competence, integrity, and objectivity. Others would argue that because Entreé Computer Co. already had the customer order, Entreé could behave ethically by shipping the goods and recording the sale in December. If you refused to ship the goods in December and you simply resigned without attempting to find an alternative solution, you might only hurt yourself.

There are fairly clear-cut solutions to many situations, but not to true ethical dilemmas. The CMA's *Rules of Professional Conduct* serve as a reminder that society expects professional accountants to uphold the highest level of ethical behaviour.

You have now seen cost-benefit analysis applied to several different business decisions. The general approach of weighing costs versus benefits to make the best decision comes up again and again in management accounting. Study the "Cost-Benefit Analysis" Decision Guidelines to make sure you understand this important concept.

EXHIBIT 19-12

CMA's Rules of Professional Conduct for Management Accountants (excerpt)

Management accountants have an obligation to the organizations they serve, their profession, the public, and themselves to maintain the highest standards of ethical conduct including:

Competence
- Maintain an appropriate level of professional competence by ongoing development of their knowledge and skills.
- Perform their professional duties in accordance with relevant laws, regulations, and technical standards.

Confidentiality
- Refrain from disclosing confidential information acquired in the course of their work except when authorized, unless legally obligated to do so.

Integrity
- Avoid actual or apparent conflicts of interest and advise all appropriate parties of any potential conflict.
- Refuse any gift, favour, or hospitality that would influence or would appear to influence their actions.
- Communicate unfavourable as well as favourable information and professional judgments or opinions.

Objectivity
- Communicate information fairly and objectively.

Source: Adapted from the Certified Management Accountants Society of British Columbia *Rules of Professional Conduct* (Vancouver, B.C.).

DECISION GUIDELINES *Cost-Benefit Analysis*

Decision	Guidelines
How to compete in a globally wired economy?	Embrace e-commerce and use cooperation to compete more effectively.
How to decide whether to undertake new projects like JIT and TQM?	Cost-benefit analysis: Compute the benefits of the project, and compare with the costs. Undertake the project if benefits exceed costs. Abandon the project if costs exceed benefits.
How to adjust the cost-benefit analysis if the exact amount of the benefit (or cost) is not known?	Compute the expected value of the benefits (or costs) as follows: $$\text{Estimated amount} \times \text{Probability of occurrence} = \text{Expected Value}$$ Then add up the expected values across all possible outcomes.
How to resolve an ethical dilemma?	Weigh the costs and benefits of alternative courses of action. Consult the CMA's *Rules of Professional Conduct* (Exhibit 19-12). Also consult the Framework for Ethical Judgments in Chapter 7.

Summary Problem
for Your Review

Cost-benefit analysis applies to many decisions. This chapter showed how managers can use cost-benefit analysis to decide whether to adopt JIT or TQM. Managers can also use cost-benefit analysis for more specific decisions. This summary review problem shows how you can apply cost-benefit analysis to a more specific decision about international expansion.

EZ-Rider Motorcycles is considering whether to expand into Germany. Public concern over air pollution may cause the government to raise gasoline taxes. If gas prices increase, EZ-Rider expects more interest in fuel-efficient transportation such as motorcycles. Thus EZ-Rider is considering setting up a motorcycle-assembly plant in a Berlin suburb.

EZ-Rider estimates that it will cost $850,000 to convert an existing building to motorcycle production. The workers will need training for specific jobs, at a total cost to the company of $65,000. The CEO of EZ-Rider, Dennis Popper, would have to spend a month in Berlin to organize the business and to establish relationships. He estimates the cost of this travel at $43,000. All these costs would be incurred in the next six months.

Popper sees a 60 percent chance that the price of gasoline in Germany will increase significantly. If this increase occurs, he believes EZ-Rider can sell enough motorcycles over the next eight years to earn profits with a present value of $1,624,000. However, if gas prices remain stable, Popper would expect to earn profits of only about $812,000. He believes that there is a 40 percent chance that gas prices will remain stable.

Required

1. What are the total costs of EZ-Rider's proposed expansion into Germany?
2. Compute the *expected value* of the benefits, or profits, Dennis Popper expects EZ-Rider to receive if EZ-Rider expands into Germany.
3. Do the benefits outweigh the costs of expanding into Germany?

Solution to Review Problem

Requirement 1

The total costs are as follows:

Conversion of manufacturing plant..................	$850,000
Work force training..	65,000
Popper's trip to Berlin...	43,000
Total	$958,000

Requirement 2

Benefit	×	Probability	=	Expected Value
$1,624,000	×	0.60	=	$ 974,400
812,000	×	0.40	=	324,800
				$1,299,200

The expected value of the benefits, or profits, is $1,299,200. This means that if EZ-Rider were to be in this exact situation many times, its average benefits in the form of profits across all the situations would be $1,299,200.

Requirement 3

Yes, the total expected benefits outweigh the costs of the expansion:

Total expected benefits of expansion (from requirement 2)	$1,299,200
Total costs of expansion (from requirement 1)	958,000
Net benefits of expansion	$ 341,200

Summary

1. Distinguish between financial accounting and management accounting. Financial accounting information is used primarily by external groups such as investors, creditors, and government authorities; it focuses on past performance of the company as a whole; and it is restricted by GAAP. Management accounting information is used primarily by internal managers to help plan and control business operations. It focuses on the future, is restricted only by the cost of generating the information versus the benefits of that information, often reports on parts of the company, and is often produced on a daily, weekly, or monthly basis.

2. Describe the value chain and classify costs by value-chain function. The value chain is the sequence of activities that adds value to a firm's products or services. Value-chain functions are research and development, design, production or purchases, marketing, distribution, and customer service. Managers want to control total costs throughout the value chain as a whole.

3. Distinguish direct costs from indirect costs. Managers need cost data on many aspects of a business to make wise decisions. A *cost object* is anything for which management wants a separate measurement of costs. Costs that can be specifically traced to the cost object are *direct costs*. Costs that cannot be specifically traced to the cost object are *indirect costs*.

4. Distinguish among full product costs, inventoriable product costs, and period costs. *Product costs* are costs of producing (or purchasing) tangible products intended for sale. *Full product costs* include the costs of all resources used throughout the value chain. These costs are used for internal decisions. *Inventoriable product costs* include only costs of the *production or purchases* element of the value chain, and must conform to GAAP because they are used for external financial reporting. *Period costs* are operating costs that are always expensed in the period in which they are incurred, and are never part of the Inventory asset account.

5. Prepare the financial statements of a manufacturing company. Manufacturers use three inventory accounts. *Materials Inventory* is the cost of materials on hand for use in production. *Work in Process Inventory* is the cost of goods that are in the manufacturing process but are not yet complete. *Finished Goods Inventory* is the cost of completed goods that have not yet been sold. Manufacturers compute cost of goods sold by adding the *cost of goods manufactured* to beginning finished goods inventory, and subtracting ending finished goods inventory.

6. Identify major trends in the business environment, and use cost-benefit analysis to make business decisions. Major trends in the business environment influencing management accounting are the shift toward a service economy, the rise of the global marketplace, time-based competition, including e-commerce and the just-in-time management philosophy, and total quality management. In making business decisions, managers compare the present value of expected future costs and benefits of alternative courses of action.

7. Use reasonable standards to make ethical judgments. Ethical behaviour is necessary for the orderly functioning of society and business. The Certified Management Accountants of Canada (CMA) standards require management accountants to maintain their professional competence, preserve the confidentiality of the information they handle, and act with integrity and objectivity.

Self-Study Questions

Test your understanding of the chapter by marking the best answer for each of the following questions.

1. The primary user(s) of management accounting information is (are) (p. 1089)
   a. Canada Customs and Revenue Agency
   b. Company management
   c. Financial analysts
   d. Company shareholders

2. Which of the following is an inventory account of a manufacturer but not of a merchandiser? (pp. 1096–1100)
   a. Cost of Goods Manufactured
   b. Merchandise Inventory

c. Work in Process Inventory
d. Direct Labour

3. Cost of goods manufactured is used to compute (p. 1100)
   a. Cost of goods sold
   b. Manufacturing overhead applied
   c. Direct materials used
   d. Finished goods inventory

4. Beginning Work in Process Inventory is $35,000, manufacturing costs for the period total $140,000, and ending Work in Process Inventory is $20,000. What is the cost of goods manufactured? (pp. 1099–1100)
   a. $125,000   c. $175,000
   b. $155,000   d. $195,000

5. Which of the following is a period cost? (p. 1095)
   a. Materials inventory
   b. Direct labour
   c. Manufacturing overhead
   d. Selling expense

6. Firms adopting a just-in-time management philosophy have found sharp reductions in their level of (p. 1106)
   a. Accounts Receivable   c. Inventory
   b. Sales   d. Operating expenses

7. Before implementing a just-in-time program, managers should (p. 1106)
   a. Perform a cost-benefit analysis
   b. Reconfigure production facilities
   c. Identify appropriate suppliers
   d. Reduce inventory levels

8. The goal of total quality management is to (p. 1107)
   a. Reduce inventory levels
   b. Provide customers with superior products or services
   c. Decrease throughput time
   d. Reduce accounts receivable

9. Total quality management focuses on (p. 1107)
   a. Manufacturing functions
   b. Marketing and distribution
   c. The entire value chain
   d. Research and design

10. Standards of ethical conduct require managers to (pp. 1109–1110)
    a. Act with integrity and objectivity
    b. Join professional associations
    c. Maximize profitability
    d. Overstate sales

Answers to the Self-Study Questions follow the Similar Accounting Terms.

Accounting Vocabulary

Budget (p. 1089)
Continuous improvement (p. 1108)
Controlling (p. 1089)
Cost-benefit analysis (p. 1090)
Cost object (p. 1092)
Cost of goods manufactured (p. 1099)
Customer service (p. 1092)
Design (p. 1092)
Direct cost (p. 1093)
Direct labour (p. 1094)
Direct materials (p. 1094)
Distribution (p. 1092)
Expected values (p. 1108)
Factory overhead (p. 1094)

Finished goods inventory (p. 1091)
Full product costs (p. 1093)
Indirect cost (p. 1093)
Indirect labour (p. 1095)
Indirect manufacturing cost (p. 1094)
Indirect materials (p. 1095)
Inventoriable product costs (p. 1093)
Just-in-time (JIT) (p. 1106)
Manufacturing company (p. 1091)
Manufacturing overhead (p. 1094)
Marketing (p. 1092)
Materials inventory (p. 1091)

Merchandising company (p. 1091)
Period costs (p. 1095)
Planning (p. 1088)
Production or purchases (p. 1092)
Research and development (R&D) (p. 1092)
Service company (p. 1091)
Supply chain management (p. 1106)
Throughput time (p. 1106)
Total quality management (TQM) (p. 1107)
Value chain (p. 1092)
Work in process inventory (p. 1091)

Similar Accounting Terms

Work in process   Work in progress; Goods in process
Manufacturing overhead   Factory overhead; Indirect manufacturing costs

Assignment Material

Questions

1. Name three differences between management accounting and financial accounting.

2. How do manufacturing companies differ from service companies and merchandisers? What inventory accounts does each type of company use?

3. Identify the various business functions in the value chain of a manufacturing company. To which functions is management accounting relevant?

4. What is the manufacturer's counterpart to the merchandiser's purchases?

5. Distinguish direct materials from indirect materials and direct labour from indirect labour. Direct materials and direct labour are debited directly to what inventory account when placed in production? What account do indirect materials and indirect labour pass through en route to this inventory account?

6. Give examples of direct materials and indirect materials for a home builder.

7. Identify at least six components of manufacturing overhead. Is Manufacturing Overhead an asset or an expense account?

8. Outline the flow of inventory costs through a manufacturing company's accounting system.

9. Distinguish between inventoriable product costs and period costs. Which represents an asset, and which is used to account for expenses?

10. What costs should managers consider in deciding on the sale price of a product: manufacturing product costs or full product costs? Give your reason.

11. Summarize the computation of cost of goods manufactured. Use any dollar amounts.

12. What is the principal difference between a service company's income statement and the income statements of merchandising and manufacturing companies?

13. What is the primary difference between a merchandiser's and a manufacturer's income statement?

14. List and briefly explain four recent changes in the business environment.

15. Describe two ways managers respond to time-based competition.

16. Explain two ways globalization affects management accounting.

17. Once a company decides to adopt a just-in-time philosophy, what kinds of costs and benefits should it expect?

18. The Certified Management Accountants' *Rules of Professional Conduct* lists four broad requirements. In your own words, list and briefly explain three.

Exercises

Exercise 19-1   *Distinguish between financial and management accounting*   *(Obj. 1)*

Your roommate, who plans to specialize in international business, is considering whether to enroll in the second principles of accounting course. She says, "I don't want to be an accountant, so why do I need a second accounting course? I just spent a whole term on financial accounting. Most of this second course focuses on management accounting, but how can that be so different from what I already learned in financial accounting?" Respond.

Exercise 19-2 *Classifying cost by value chain function* **(Obj. 2)**

List the six business functions in the value chain (Exhibit 19-3, page 1092). Give an example of costs that Coca-Cola might incur in each function.

Exercise 19-3 *Classifying costs by value chain function* **(Obj. 2)**

Classify each of Hewlett-Packard's costs into one of the six business functions in the value chain.

a. Amortization on factory building.

b. Costs of a customer support centre Web site.

c. Transportation costs to deliver printers to retailers.

d. Amortization on research lab.

e. Cost of a prime-time television ad featuring the new Hewlett-Packard logo.

f. Salary of scientists at Hewlett-Packard Laboratories who are developing new printer technologies.

g. Purchase of plastic used in printer casings.

h. Salary of engineers who are redesigning the printer's on-off switch.

i. Amortization on delivery vehicles.

j. Factory manager's salary.

Exercise 19-4 *Direct versus indirect, full versus inventoriable costs* **(Obj. 3, 4)**

Listed below are several terms relating to various cost definitions. Complete the following statements with one of these terms. You may use a term more than once, and some terms may not be used at all.

Cost object	Direct labour	Inventoriable product cost
Direct cost	Full product cost	Manufacturing overhead
Direct materials	Indirect cost	Period cost

a. _____ is expensed in the period incurred.

b. The product cost used for external reporting is called _____.

c. _____ includes all elements of the value chain and is used for internal decisions such as setting long-run average selling prices.

d. _____ is initially considered an asset, and is not expensed until the related products are sold.

e. The sum of direct materials, direct labour, and manufacturing overhead is _____ for a manufacturing company.

f. _____ is all costs incurred in the plant other than direct materials and direct labour.

Exercise 19-5 *Reporting current assets of a manufacturer* **(Obj. 5)**

Consider the following selected amounts and account balances of Brandon Holdings Inc.:

Cost of goods sold	$202,000	Prepaid expenses	$ 12,000
Direct labour	94,000	Marketing expense	78,000
Direct materials	50,000	Work in process inventory	84,000
Accounts receivable	150,000	Manufacturing overhead	52,000
Cash	38,000	Finished goods inventory	144,000
Cost of goods manufactured	188,000	Materials inventory	34,000

Show how Brandon Holdings Inc. would report current assets on the balance sheet. Not all data are used. Is Brandon Holdings Inc. a service company, a merchandiser, or a manufacturer?

Exercise 19-6 *Computing cost of goods manufactured and cost of goods sold* **(Obj. 5)**

Compute cost of goods manufactured and cost of goods sold from the following amounts for Scantext Inc. (the year end is December 31, 2003):

	Beginning of Year	End of Year
Materials inventory	$33,000	$42,000
Work in process inventory	57,000	45,000
Finished goods inventory	27,000	37,500
Purchases of raw materials		117,000
Direct labour		123,000
Indirect labour		22,500
Factory insurance		13,500
Amortization—factory building and equipment		24,000
Repairs and maintenance—factory		6,000
Marketing expenses		115,500
General and administrative expenses		43,500
Income tax expense		45,000

Exercise 19-7 *Preparing a manufacturer's income statement* **(Obj. 5)**

Prepare an income statement for the company in Exercise 19-6. Assume that it sold 30,000 units of its product at a price of $19 during 2003.

Exercise 19-8 *Computing gross margin for a manufacturer* **(Obj. 5)**

Supply the missing amounts from the following computation of gross margin:

Sales revenue				$874,000
Cost of goods sold:				
Beginning finished goods inventory			$182,000	
Cost of goods manufactured:				
Beginning work in process inventory		$104,000		
Direct materials used	$128,000			
Direct labour	?			
Manufacturing overhead	102,000			
Total manufacturing costs incurred during the period		452,000		
Total manufacturing costs to account for		?		
Ending work in process inventory		(80,000)		
Cost of goods manufactured			?	
Goods available for sale			?	
Ending finished goods inventory			(214,000)	
Cost of goods sold				?
Gross margin				$?

Exercise 19-9 *Inventoriable costs; balance sheets of service, merchandising, and manufacturing companies* **(Obj. 4, 5)**

Consider Toyota, Fedex, and Costco. For each company, answer the following questions.

1. Is this a service company, a merchandiser, or a manufacturer?
2. What is the primary output the company sells to customers?
3. What inventory accounts would this company have on its balance sheet?

4. Does this company have any inventoriable product costs? If so, how would you compute these costs?

Exercise 19-10 *Prepare the cost of goods sold section of a merchandiser's income statement (Obj. 5)*

Link Back to Chapter 5. Given the following information for Gemz, a fashion jewellry e-tailer, compute the cost of goods sold.

Web site maintenance.......	$2,000	Delivery expenses...............	$1,000
Freight-in............................	5,000	Purchases............................	60,000
Ending inventory..............	10,000	Revenues	120,000
Marketing expenses..........	12,000	Beginning inventory...........	6,000

Exercise 19-11 *Computing direct materials used (Obj. 5)*

You are a new accounting intern at Que Pasa, Inc. Your boss gives you the following information and asks you to compute direct materials used.

Purchases of direct materials	$69,000
Freight-in...	600
Freight-out	3,000
Ending inventory of direct materials.................	4,500
Beginning inventory of direct materials............	12,000

Exercise 19-12 *Understanding supplier relations under JIT (Obj. 6)*

Pasco Technologies Inc. supplies motherboards to TPC Computers Inc., a manufacturer of computers. Pasco uses the Internet to look into TPC's production process. What potential advantages does this provide for Pasco and TPC?

Exercise 19-13 *Cost and benefits of adopting JIT (Obj. 6)*

Araxis Inc. manufactures casual menswear. Kevin Peters, the CEO, is trying to decide whether he should ask the plant to adopt a just-in-time (JIT) philosophy. He expects that in present-value terms, adopting JIT would save $225,000 in warehousing expenses, and $80,000 in spoilage costs.

Kevin also expects that adopting JIT will require several one-time up-front expenditures: (1) $60,000 for an employee training program, (2) $95,000 to streamline the plant's production process, and (3) $18,000 to identify suppliers that will guarantee zero defects and on-time delivery.

Required

1. What are the total costs of adopting the JIT approach?
2. What are the total benefits of adopting JIT?
3. Should Araxis Inc. adopt JIT? Why or why not?

Exercise 19-14 *Ethics in management accounting (Obj. 7)*

For a little over a year, April Smith has been the assistant controller for Caltronics Ltd., a manufacturer of high-end stereo equipment. Sam Pechet, the senior bookkeeper, called in sick this week. April temporarily took over Sam's duties, which include maintaining the petty cash fund. She found a shortage and confronted Sam when he returned to work. Sam admitted that he occasionally took advantage of his access to petty cash in order to pay for his lunch and other small expenses. April estimated that the amounts have added up to over $2,000. April had earlier wondered about Sam's control over the petty cash fund. However, she had not followed up on her concern because Sam was well liked and she regarded him as hard working and loyal.

Required

1. What should April do?

2. Would you change your answer to the previous question in each of the following situations?

   a. Sam has worked for Caltronics Ltd. for ten years, and is now only six months from retirement. If April reports the theft, Sam will probably be fired and lose a portion of his pension.

   b. Sam has worked at Caltronics Ltd. for only eight months.

Challenge Exercise

Exercise 19-15   *Flow of costs through manufacturing companies*   *(Obj. 4, 5)*

Coverup Inc. manufactures and sells a new line of sun-protection clothing. Unfortunately, Coverup suffered serious storm damage in October. The storm partially destroyed—and completely jumbled—the accounting records for that month. Coverup Inc. has hired you to calculate the missing pieces of the accounting puzzle.

Accounts payable, October 1	$6,000	Work in process inventory, October 31	$2,000
Direct materials used in October	16,000	Finished goods inventory, October 1	8,000
Accounts payable, October 31	9,600	Direct labour in October	6,000
Accounts receivable, October 31	12,000	Purchases of direct materials in October	18,000
Direct materials inventory, October 31	4,000	Work in process inventory, October 1	0
Manufacturing overhead in October	14,000	Revenues in October	54,000
Gross margin in October	18,600	Accounts receivable, October 1	4,000

Required

Find the following amounts:

a. Cost of goods sold in October

b. Beginning direct materials inventory

c. Ending finished goods inventory

(*Hint*: You may find Panel B of Exhibit 19-10 helpful.)

Beyond the Numbers

Beyond the Numbers 19-1   *Inventoriable costs*   *(Obj. 3)*

Utility expenses and property taxes on Coca-Cola's Canadian headquarters in North York are not directly traceable to individual containers of Coca-Cola syrup produced by a plant in Don Mills. Are these property taxes part of manufacturing overhead? Is amortization on the automobiles used by the sales force part of manufacturing overhead? How about interest expense on long-term debt issued primarily to finance the construction of a new plant?

Ethical Issue

Link back to Chapter 7. ComDigital Inc. designs and manufactures chips used in digital cell phones. ComDigital is currently developing the next generation of computer chips that will allow users to receive e-mail and surf the Net using voice commands over a cell phone. Because of competition to be the first to perfect the first chip, ComDigital is investing heavily in development. Work is going slowly, and revenue growth from older chips is starting to drop. With year-end approaching, ComDigital's CEO, Jim Mann, has called a meeting with the Vice-President of

Marketing, Joan Peters, the Vice-President of Finance, Tammy Myers, and Larry Case, the Controller. Larry Case asks that as assistant controller, you also attend the meeting.

The CEO starts the meeting by expressing concern that with the slowdown in revenue growth and the heavy investment in new chip development, ComDigital may not meet financial analysts' earnings predictions this year. The conversation eventually turns to the development of the new chip. Mann says the company cannot slow its research and development efforts but, since the new chip will be so profitable when it goes into production, some of the costs should be capitalized now, and then expensed later when the chip is generating revenue. VP of Finance Tammy Myers suggest capitalizing some of these costs and charging them against revenues of the chips currently being produced and sold. She argues that the new chip's research and development efforts must be providing some insights that improve the production process for existing chips. You are surprised by Controller Larry Case's silence during this discussion, as you believe these are research and development costs that GAAP requires to be expensed as incurred. The meeting ends without any resolution.

Later, you learn that the CEO has told your boss to capitalize a large amount of this year's development costs for the new chip. Before talking to anyone, you decide to work through this ethical dilemma, using the following framework from Chapter 7.

1. List the facts.
2. Identify the ethical issues.
3. Specify the alternatives.
4. Identify the people involved.
5. Assess the possible consequences.
6. Make a decision

Complete the framework.

Problems (Group A)

Problem 19-1A   *Value chain, direct versus indirect costs, inventoriable product costs*
(Obj. 2, 3, 4)

B & R, Inc. produces small batches of super-premium ice cream. The ice cream base is prepared, special ingredients such as nuts and fruit are added, and the mixture is frozen. Because milk and cream naturally vary in salt content, the amount of salt added varies from batch to batch.

B & R, Inc. incurs the following costs:

Sales salaries	$9,000	Freight-in	$ 3,200
Customer hotline for quality problems	700	Amortization on delivery van	500
Redesign the production process to keep		Milk	10,000
nuts in bigger chunks	1,500	Wages of production-line workers	20,000
Replacements for products past expiration		Wages of plant maintenance workers	1,800
date (upon customer complaint)	150	Sales force salaries	800
Salt	20	Cream	16,000
Payment to food scientist for developing		Cost of advertisements	700
new recipe with much longer shelf life	3,000	Delivery drivers' wages	900
Amortization expense on plant and		Nuts and fruits	7,000
equipment	3,600	Total	$80,470
Insurance on plant	1,600		

Required

1. Use the following format to classify each of these costs according to its place in the value chain.

(Hint: You should have at least one cost in each value-chain function.)

| | Design of Products, Services, or Processes | Production | | | | | Customer Service |
R&D		Direct Materials	Direct Labour	Manufacturing Overhead	Marketing	Distribution	

2. Compute the total costs for each category.

3. How much are the total inventoriable product costs?

Problem 19-2A *Preparing financial statements for merchandising and manufacturing companies* *(Obj. 4, 5)*

Part One: On January 1, 2002, Kelly Neudorf opened Neudorf's Auto Care Products, a small retail store dedicated solely to selling car polish, bug cleaner, chamois, and other auto care accessories. On December 31, 2002, his accounting records show the following:

Store rent	$9,000	Store utilities	$ 3,900
Sales salaries	7,000	Purchases of merchandise	84,000
Freight-in	1,500	Inventory on January 1, 2002	25,400
Inventory on December 31, 2002	17,500	Advertising expense	4,600
Sales revenue	148,000		

Required

Prepare an income statement for Neudorf's Auto Care Products, a merchandiser.

Part Two: Neudorf's Auto Care Products became so successful that Kelly Neudorf decided to manufacture his own special brand of bug cleaner—Ultracleen. He incorporated a company and on December 31, 2003, his accounting records for Ultracleen Manufacturing Corp. showed:

Finished goods inventory, December 31, 2003	$10,000	Rent on manufacturing plant	$22,500
Work in process inventory, December 31, 2003	6,875	Finished goods inventory, December 31, 2002	0
Direct materials inventory, December 31, 2003	19,375	Amortization expense on delivery trucks	6,250
R&D for plastic squirt container	9,250	Amortization expense on manufacturing equipment	11,750
Sales commissions	16,250	Work in process inventory, December 31, 2002	0
Utilities for factory	7,250	Sales revenue	316,125
Factory janitorial services	4,375	Customer warranty refunds	3,750
Direct labour	58,750	Direct materials inventory, December 31, 2002	37,500
Direct material purchases	92,500		

Required

1. Prepare a schedule of cost of goods manufactured for Ultracleen Manufacturing Corp.

2. Prepare an income statement for Ultracleen Manufacturing Corp.

3. How does the format of the income statement for Ultracleen Manufacturing Corp. differ from the income statement of Neudorf's Auto Care Products?

Part Three: Show the ending inventories that would appear on the balance sheet of

1. Neudorf's Auto Care Products at December 31, 2002.

2. Ultracleen Manufacturing Corp. at December 31, 2003.

Problem 19-3A *Completing a manufacturer's income statement* *(Obj. 4, 5)*

Certain item descriptions and amounts are missing from the income statement of FirstNet Systems Inc.

FIRSTNET SYSTEMS INC.
Income Statement
For the Month Ended March 31, 2003

Sales revenue			$462,000
Cost of goods sold:			
Beginning _____ inventory		$?	
Cost of goods _____:			
Beginning _____ inventory	$?		
Direct _____:			
Beginning materials inventory	$ 68,000		
Purchases of materials	140,000		
Materials available for use	?		
Ending materials inventory	(52,000)		
Direct _____		$?	
Direct _____		160,000	
_____		38,000	
Total _____ costs _____		?	
Total _____ costs _____		?	
Ending _____ inventory		(90,000)	
Cost of goods _____		326,000	
Goods available for sale		384,000	
Ending _____ inventory		(104,000)	
Cost of goods _____			?
Gross margin			182,000
Operating expenses:			
Marketing		46,000	
General		52,000	
Total operating expenses			?
Income before income tax			?
Income tax expense (30%)			?
Net income			$?

Supply the missing item descriptions (_____) and the missing amounts (?).

Problem 19-4A *Preparing financial statements for a manufacturer* *(Obj. 5)*

Certain item descriptions and amounts are missing from the monthly schedule of cost of goods manufactured and income statement of Hardy Manufacturing Corporation. Fill in the missing items.

_____ MANUFACTURING CORPORATION

_____ April 30, 2003

_____ work in process inventory		$ 22,500
Direct materials used:		
_____ materials _____	$?	
_____ of materials	93,000	
_____	112,500	
_____ materials _____	(34,500)	
Direct _____	$?	
Direct _____	102,000	

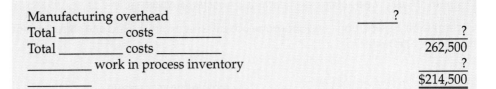

Manufacturing overhead	?
Total _____ costs _____	?
Total _____ costs _____	262,500
_____ work in process inventory	?
_____	$214,500

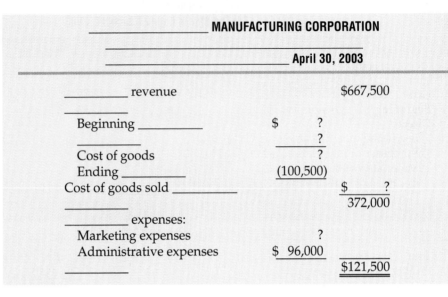

_____ **MANUFACTURING CORPORATION**

_____ **April 30, 2003**

_____ revenue		$667,500
Beginning _____	$?	
_____	?	
Cost of goods	?	
Ending _____	(100,500)	
Cost of goods sold _____		$?
		372,000
_____ expenses:		
Marketing expenses	?	
Administrative expenses	$ 96,000	
_____		$121,500

Problem 19-5A   *TQM, cost-benefit analysis, expected value*   *(Obj. 6)*

Quantx Inc. manufactures computer disk drives. It sells these disk drives to other manufacturers, which use them in assembling computers. Quantx Inc. is having trouble with its new DVD drive. If the parts are not engineered to exact specifications, the drive will not operate. About half the time, Quantx Inc. employees find these defects while the disk drive is still on the production line. These drives are immediately reworked in the plant. Otherwise, Quantx Inc.'s customers do not identify the problem until they are installing the disk drives they've purchased from Quantx Inc. Customers return defective disk drives for replacement under warranty, and they have also complained that after they install the disk drive, the drive's connector (which plugs into the computer system board) often shakes loose while the computer is assembled. The customer must then reassemble the computer after fixing the loose connection.

Quantx Inc. CEO Fred Metcalfe has just returned from a seminar on total quality management (TQM). He forms a team to attack these quality problems. The team includes the plant engineer, the production foreperson, a customer service representative, the marketing director, and the management accountant.

Three months later the team proposes a major project to *prevent* these quality problems. Quantx Inc.'s accountant Beth Wilson reports that implementing the team's proposal will require Quantx Inc. to spend the following over the next three months:

a. $252,000 for Quantx Inc. research scientists to develop a completely new disk drive that still operates even with small deviations from specified part sizes

b. $98,000 for company engineers to redesign the connector so that it is more tolerant of rough treatment

The project team is unsure whether this investment will pay off. If the effort fixes the problem, Wilson expects

a. A reputation for higher quality will increase sales, which in turn will increase the present value of profits by $280,600.

b. Fewer disk drives will fail after customer installation. The present value of the savings from fewer warranty repairs is $229,600.

c. The plant will have fewer defective disk drives to rework. The present value of this savings is $140,300.

However, if this project is not successful, there will be no cost savings and no additional sales. The team predicts a 70 percent chance that the project will succeed, and a 30 percent chance it will fail.

Required

1. If the quality improvement project succeeds, what is the dollar amount of the benefits?
2. Should Quantx Inc. undertake this project? Why or why not? Show supporting calculations.

Problem 19-6A   *Value chain, TQM*   *(Obj. 2, 6)*

Problem 19-5A provided both quantitative and qualitative information about Quantx Inc.'s quality project, and asked you to perform a *quantitative* analysis to help Quantx Inc.'s managers decide whether to embark on the quality project. Now consider some *qualitative* factors in Quantx Inc.'s quality improvement project.

Required

1. Why did Fred Metcalfe create a team to attack this quality problem, rather than assigning the task to one person? Consider each piece of cost-benefit information reported by management accountant Beth Wilson. Which person on the team is most likely to have contributed each item?

   (*Hint*: Which team member is likely to have the most information about each cost or benefit?)

2. Classify the following amounts into one of the six value-chain business functions.

   a. $252,000 cost to develop the completely new disk drive that still operates even with small deviations from specified part sizes

   b. $98,000 cost to redesign the connector so that it is more tolerant of rough treatment

   c. Warranty repairs on disk drives that customers have returned as defective

   d. Disk drives identified as defective while still in the factory that are re-worked

3. This problem illustrates how Quantx Inc. can make trade-offs across different business functions in the value chain. Which of the six value-chain functions are involved in the trade-offs proposed by the quality improvement team? What specific trade-offs do they propose? In what other situations are these trade-offs likely to be effective?

Problem 19-7A   *Globalization, cost-benefit analysis*   *(Obj. 6)*

Cost-benefit analysis applies to many kinds of decisions. This problem applies cost-benefit analysis to a decision about international expansion, similar to the chapter summary review problem on page 1111.

International Chocolates Inc. is a new chain that sells premium chocolates. CEO Abbe Fraser is trying to decide whether to expand into Europe. She has contacted Arabella Grimaldi in Brussels to estimate the costs and benefits of an initial store in Brussels. Grimaldi's market research indicates that European consumers love chocolate. Her initial taste tests show they very much enjoyed International Chocolates' products.

Excluding the one-time up-front costs outlined below, Grimaldi estimates that

International Chocolates could sell enough chocolates to earn profit with a present value of $350,000. Grimaldi believes that within two months a store could be ready in Brussels, at a cost of $165,000. Fraser would have to go to Brussels for two months to acquire the licence to operate, and to oversee renovation of the store and hiring of the employees. Grimaldi estimates that Fraser's expenses for these two months will amount to $50,000. International Chocolates will also have to advertise at an estimated total cost of $127,000. Finally, if International Chocolates expands into Belgium, Fraser will retain Arabella Grimaldi's consulting service, for a fee of $16,000.

Required

Would you recommend that International Chocolates Inc. expand into Europe? Give your reason, showing supporting calculations.

Problem 19-8A   *Globalization, cost-benefit analysis, expected value*   *(Obj. 6)*

Consider International Chocolates Inc.'s proposed expansion into Europe in Problem 19-7A. Arabella Grimaldi revises her estimates of the profits International Chocolates is likely to earn. Specifically, Grimaldi sees a 40 percent chance that International Chocolates will earn $350,000 in profit. She now thinks there is a 60 percent chance that International Chocolates will earn $635,000 in profit.

Required

1. Compute the expected value of the benefits (profits) from the proposed expansion.
2. Would you recommend that International Chocolates Inc. expand into Europe? Why or why not? Show your calculations.
3. What other factors should Abbe Fraser consider when making this decision?

Problem 19-9A   *Ethics (Obj. 7)*

Kristen Hohman is the new controller for Ultrawear, a designer and manufacturer of trendy women's casual wear. Shortly before the December 31 fiscal year end, Liz Kaye (the company president) asks Kristen how the year-end numbers look. Liz is not happy to learn that earnings growth may be below 10 percent for the first time in the company's five-year history. Liz explains that financial analysts have again predicted a 10 percent earnings growth for the company and that she does not intend to disappoint them. She suggests that Kristen talk to the assistant controller, who could explain how the previous controller dealt with this situation. The assistant controller suggests the following strategies:

a. Change the dates on January's shipping documents to December so that they can be recorded in this year's sales.
b. Reduce the allowance for bad debts, given the company's continued strong performance.
c. Ultrawear has very limited warehouse space. It regularly ships finished goods to public warehouses across the country for temporary storage, until Ultrawear receives firm orders from customers. As Ultrawear receives orders, it directs the warehouse to ship the goods to the nearby customer. The assistant controller suggests recording goods sent to the public warehouses as sales.
d. Postpone planned advertising expenditures from December to January.
e. Persuade retail customers to accelerate January orders to December.

Which of these suggested strategies are inconsistent with CMA standards? What should Kristen Hohman do if Liz Kaye insists that she follow all of these suggestions?

Problems Group B

Problem 19-1B   *Value chain, direct and indirect costs, inventoriable product costs* **(Obj. 2, 3, 4)**

Dell Computer Corporation assembles personal computers (PCs) to order. Assume Dell reported the following costs last month. (All costs are in millions.)

Payment to UPS for delivering PCs to customer..	$ 250	Amortization on factory and equipment.........	$ 250
Cost of hard drives used	3,300	Salaries of scientists working on next generation laptops	30
Cost of Internet banner ads	400	Insurance and taxes on factory property.........	40
Factory janitors' wages.......................................	10	Cost of oil used for conveyor belt and other factory equipment..................................	5
Wages of workers who assemble the PCs........	1,000		
Cost of customer hotline for troubleshooting problems..............................	30	Payment to engineers redesigning the exterior case	15
Wages of forklift drivers moving parts and completed computers around the factory floor...	20	Wages of sales associates taking phone orders...	50
Factory utilities..	35	Cost of circuit boards used	4,000
Cost of software loaded on computers	25	Total..	$9,460

Required

1. Use the following format to classify each of these costs according to its place in the value chain.

   (*Hint:* You should have at least one cost in each value chain function.)

Design of Products, Services, or R&D Processes	Production			Marketing	Distribution	Customer Service
	Direct Materials	Direct Labour	Manufacturing Overhead			

2. Compute the total costs for each category.

3. How much are the total inventoriable product costs?

4. Suppose the managers of the R&D and Design functions receive year-end bonuses based on meeting their own unit's target cost reductions. What are they likely to do? How might this affect costs incurred in other elements of the value chain?

Problem 19-2B   *Preparing financial statements for merchandising and manufacturing companies* **(Obj. 4, 5)**

Part One: In 2002, Courtney Wilcox opened Boarder Haven, a small retail store dedicated solely to selling snowboards. On December 31, 2002, her accounting records show the following:

Inventory on December 31, 2002	$10,000
Inventory on January 1, 2002	11,000
Sales revenue	60,000
Utilities	3,000
Rent...	8,000
Sales commissions	3,000
Purchases of merchandise	35,000

Required

Prepare an income statement for Boarder Haven, a merchandiser.

Part Two: Boarder Haven became so successful that Courtney Wilcox decided to manufacture her own brand of snowboards—the Ultimate. She incorporated a company, Ultimate Snowboards Inc., and on December 31, 2003, the accounting records show the following:

Sales salaries	$9,000	
Factory janitorial services	2,500	
Direct labour	35,000	
Direct material purchases	60,000	
Rent on manufacturing factory	18,000	
Direct materials inventory,		
December 31, 2002	24,000	
Direct materials inventory		
December 31, 2003	17,500	
Work in process inventory,		
December 31, 2002	0	

Work in process inventory,	
December 31, 2003	$ 700
Finished goods inventory,	
December 31, 2002	0
Finished goods inventory,	
December 31, 2003	11,400
Sales revenue	194,900
Customer service hotline	2,000
Utilities for factory	6,800
Delivery expense	3,000

Required

1. Prepare a schedule of cost of goods manufactured for Ultimate Snowboards Inc.

2. Prepare an income statement for Ultimate Snowboards Inc.

3. How does the format of the income statement for Ultimate Snowboards Inc. differ from the income statement of Boarder Haven?

Part Three: Show the ending inventories that would appear on the balance sheet of

1. Boarder Haven at December 31, 2002.

2. Ultimate Snowboard Inc. at December 31, 2003.

Problem 19-3B   *Completing a manufacturer's income statement*   **(Obj. 4, 5)**

Certain item descriptions and amounts are missing from the income statement of Union Bay Manufacturing Corp.

UNION BAY MANUFACTURING CORP.
Income Statement
For the Month Ended June 30, 2002

Sales revenue				$?
Cost of goods sold:				
Beginning _____ inventory			$202,000	
Cost of goods _____ :				
Beginning _____ inventory		$ 56,000		
Direct _____ :				
Beginning materials inventory ...	$?			
Purchases of materials	124,000			
Available for use	158,000			
Ending materials inventory	(46,000)			
Direct _____		$?		
Direct_____		?		
_____		80,000		
Total _____ costs _____			332,000	
Total _____ costs _____			?	
Ending _____ inventory			(60,000)	
Cost of goods _____				328,000
Goods available for sale				?
Ending _____ inventory				(?)
Cost of goods _____				$336,000
Gross margin				460,000
Operating expenses:				
Marketing				198,000
General				?
Total operating expenses				288,000
Income before income tax				?
Income tax expense (40%)				?
Net income				$?

Required

Supply the missing item descriptions (_____) and the missing amounts (?).

Problem 19-4B *Preparing financial statements for a manufacturer* *(Obj. 5)*

Certain item descriptions and amounts are missing from the monthly schedule of cost of goods manufactured and income statement of Hirai Manufacturing Corp. Fill in the missing items.

_____ MANUFACTURING CORP.			
_____ June 30, 2003			
Beginning _____			$ 27,000
Direct _____:			
Beginning inventory of materials	$?		
Purchases of materials	93,000		
_____	123,000		
Ending materials inventory	(34,500)		
Direct _____		$?	
Direct _____		?	
Manufacturing overhead		60,000	
Total _____ costs _____			249,000
Total _____ costs _____			?
Ending _____			(45,000)
			$?

_____ MANUFACTURING CORP.			
_____ June 30, 2003			
Sales revenue			$?
Cost of goods sold:			
Beginning _____	$151,500		
_____	?		
Cost of goods _____	?		
Ending _____	?		
Cost of goods sold		295,500	
Gross margin		345,000	
_____expenses:			
Marketing expense	148,500		
Administrative expense	?	231,000	
_____income		$?	

Problem 19-5B *TQM, cost-benefit analysis, expected value* *(Obj. 6)*

Pentium Inc. manufactures fine watches. The company is having trouble with one of its watches. If the parts are not engineered to exact specifications, the watch will not operate. Even a speck of dust under the crystal causes the watch to stop. About half the time, Pentium employees find the defects while the watch is still on the production line. These watches are immediately reworked in the plant. When a defect escapes detection until the customer complains, Pentium repairs the watch. Pentium CEO Pardeep Sandhu has just returned from a seminar on total quality management (TQM). He forms a team to attack this quality problem. The team includes the factory engineer, the production foreman, the factory's watch repair specialist, the marketing director, and the management accountant.

Three months later, the team proposes a major project to prevent these quality problems. Pentium accountant Jennifer Thompson reports that implementing the team's proposal will require Pentium to spend the following over the next six months:

a. $52,500 to redesign the watch so it still operates even with small deviations from specified part sizes

b. $80,000 for Pentium scientists to develop a completely new watch mechanism that is tolerant of dust particles

The project team is unsure whether this investment will pay off. If the effort fixes the problem, Thompson expects the following to occur:

a. The factory will have no defective watches to rework. The present value of this savings is $47,450.

b. Fewer watches will fail after customer purchase. The present value of the savings from fewer warranty repairs is $101,440.

c. A reputation for higher quality will increase sales, which in turn will increase the present value of profits by $126,800.

However, if this project is not successful, there will be no cost savings and no additional sales. The team predicts that there is a 60 percent chance that the project will succeed, and a 40 percent chance that it will fail.

Required

1. If the quality improvement project succeeds, what is the dollar amount of the benefits?

2. Should Pentium undertake this project? Why or why not? Show supporting calculations.

Problem 19-6B   *Value chain, TQM*   *(Obj. 2, 6)*

Problem 19-5B provided both quantitative and qualitative information about Pentium's quality project, and asked you to perform a *quantitative* analysis to help Pentium managers decide whether to embark on the quality project. Now consider some *qualitative* factors in Pentium's quality improvement project.

Required

1. Why did Pardeep Sandhu create a team to attack this quality problem, rather than assigning the task to one person? Consider each piece of cost-benefit information reported by management accountant Jennifer Thompson. Which person on the team is most likely to have contributed each item?

   (*Hint*: Which team member is likely to have the most information about each cost or benefit?)

2. Classify the following costs into one of the six value-chain business functions:
   a. $52,500 cost to redesign the watch so it still operates even with small deviations from specified part sizes
   b. $80,000 cost to develop a completely new watch mechanism that is more tolerant of dust particles
   c. Costs incurred to rework watches identified as defective while still in the factory
   d. Costs incurred to make warranty repairs on the watches that customers have returned as defective

3. The Pentium problem illustrates how managers make trade-offs across different business functions in the value chain. Which of the six value chain functions are involved in the trade-offs proposed by the quality improvement team? What specific trade-offs do they propose? In what other situations are these trade-offs likely to be effective?

Problem 19-7B *E-commerce, cost-benefit analysis* *(Obj. 6)*

Western Central Credit Union (WCCU) is a company in British Columbia that processes cheques for all credit unions in Western Canada. This results in mounds of paperwork, because WCCU keeps track of which cheques have been deposited and which accounts have been debited or credited. When a customer questions that a cheque was not deposited to its account, a WCCU clerk takes the complaint over the phone and fills out a paper form. The complaint form triggers a long search through piles of cancelled cheques in a warehouse to find the cheque in question. WCCU then compares this cheque to its computer and paper records.

WCCU is considering moving this process to the Web. When a customer has a question, its employee simply uses a Web browser and a password to access WCCU's databases. The employee can get access to a computerized image of the cheque in question to verify the amount and then query WCCU's databases to see where the mistake was made. If required, a credit to the customer's account can be issued immediately.

The Web-based system will require WCCU to invest $74,000 in a new server and cheque-scanning equipment. Consultants will charge $110,000 for the software and consulting fees to get the system running. The system will also require increasing WCCU's Internet capacity. The present value of this cost is $20,000.

WCCU has identified two benefits of this project. First, several clerks freed from searching through stacks of cancelled cheques will be reassigned to other more responsible and interesting tasks, which will lead to cost savings with a present value of $156,000. Second, the new system's additional capacity will enable WCCU to expand its cheque-processing business, which should lead to additonal profits with a present value of $39,600.

Required

Does a cost-benefit analysis justify the Web-based system? Explain why, showing supporting calculations.

Problem 19-8B *E-commerce, cost-benefit analysis, expected value* *(Obj. 6)*

Consider the WCCU project described in Problem 19-7B. WCCU has revised its estimates of additional profits the bank is likely to earn. There is a 50% chance that the bank will earn $39,600 in extra profits, but also a 50% chance the bank will earn $75,000 in extra profits.

Required

1. Compute the expected value of the benefits from the additional growth.
2. Would you recommend that WCCU accept the proposal? Give your reason, showing supporting calculations.
3. Are there other potential benefits not listed in Problem 19-7B or Problem 19-8B that may make the proposal more attractive to WCCU?

Problem 19-9B *Ethics* *(Obj. 7)*

Angela Raffan is the new controller for Thundertech Software, Inc., which develops and sells computer software. Shortly before the December 31 fiscal year end, Jason French, the company president, asks Raffan how the year-end numbers look. He is not happy to learn that earnings growth may be below 20 percent for the first time in the company's five-year history. French explains that financial analysts have again predicted a 20 percent earnings growth for the company and that he does not intend to disappoint them. He suggests that Raffan talk to the assistant controller, who could explain how the previous controller dealt with this situation. The assistant controller suggests the following strategies:

a. Delay the year-end closing a few days into January of the next year, so that some of next year's sales are included as this year's sales.

b. Reduce the allowance for bad debts (and bad debts expense), given the company's continued strong performance.

c. Record as sales certain goods awaiting sale that are held in a public warehouse.

d. Postpone routine monthly maintenance expenditures from December to January.

e. Persuade suppliers to postpone billing Thundertech Software, Inc. until January 1.

Which of these suggested strategies are inconsistent with CMA standards? What should Raffan do if French insists that she follow all of these suggestions?

Challenge Problem

Problem 19-1C *Allocating overhead or not* **(Obj. 4, 5)**

There is a school of thought that believes that all overhead should be treated as a period cost and charged to expense when incurred.

Required

1. State the effect on the financial statements of a growing company of charging overhead to expense when incurred. Do the same for a steady-state company.

2. State the potential effect on management decision making of charging overhead costs to expense as incurred.

Extending Your Knowledge

Decision Problem

Effects of adopting JIT (Obj. 6)

Link Back to Chapter 18 (Current Ratio). Paulo San Marco, president of Pasta Products Inc. (a manufacturer of pasta products and sauces), has attended a seminar on the just-in-time (JIT) management philosophy. Paulo returned to his factory in Toronto full of enthusiasm for making the switch to JIT. Maria San Marco, the factory controller, is not as enthusiastic as her brother Paulo. Maria is concerned that adopting JIT might reduce inventory so much that the company may violate its loan covenants. In exchange for loaning the company $20,000, the long-term note payable agreement with First Commercial Bank lists several requirements, or covenants. One requirement is that Pasta Products Inc. maintain a current ratio of at least 2.0. Both the company (Pasta Products Inc.) and the San Marco family have had a long-standing relationship with the bank—particularly with their loan officer, Michael Magee.

Maria San Marco prepares two separate projected balance sheets for the end of the 2003 fiscal year, under the assumptions that

• Pasta Products Inc. does not adopt JIT

• Pasta Products Inc. does adopt JIT

These two highly summarized balance sheets collapse the materials inventory, work in process inventory, and finished goods inventory under the single "Inventory" heading:

PASTA PRODUCTS INC.
Projected Balance Sheet If JIT Is Not Adopted
December 31, 2003

Assets		Liabilities	
Current assets:		Current liabilities:	
Cash....................................	$ 20,000	Accounts payable............	$ 39,000
Accounts receivable........	34,000	Long-term liabilities:	
Inventories	30,000	Note payable....................	40,000
Total current assets.............	84,000	Total liabilities......................	79,000
Capital assets	194,000		
		Shareholders' equity	
		Common stock.....................	128,000
		Retained earnings...............	71,000
		Total shareholders'	
		equity	199,000
		Total liabilities and	
Total assets	$278,000	shareholders' equity	$278,000

PASTA PRODUCTS INC.
Projected Balance Sheet If JIT Is Adopted
December 31, 2003

Assets		Liabilities	
Current assets:		Current liabilities:	
Cash....................................	$ 20,000	Accounts payable............	$ 28,600
Accounts receivable........	34,000	Long-term liabilities:	
Inventories	2,000	Note payable....................	40,000
Total current assets.............	56,000	Total liabilities......................	68,600
Capital assets	194,000		
		Shareholders' equity	
		Common stock.....................	128,000
		Retained earnings...............	53,400*
		Total shareholders'	
		equity	181,400
		Total liabilities and	
Total assets	$250,000	shareholders' equity	$250,000

*Retained earnings are expected to temporarily decline in the year Pasta Products Inc. adopts JIT, because of up-front costs that will reduce income in the transition year. However, a cost-benefit analysis (not shown) indicates that adopting JIT should lead to future benefits that outweigh JIT's up-front transition costs.

Required

1. Compute Pasta Products Inc.'s current ratio if

   a. The company does not adopt JIT

   b. The company adopts JIT

(Chapter 18 covers the current ratio.) If Pasta Products Inc. adopts JIT, will the company violate the loan covenant?

2. As a consultant to Pasta Products Inc., would you recommend that the company adopt JIT?

a. If you recommend against adopting JIT, take the role of Maria San Marco and write a memo to CEO Paulo San Marco explaining why Pasta Products Inc. should *not* adopt JIT this year.

Your memo should take the following form:

Date: _____ To: Paulo San Marco, CEO, Pasta Products Inc. From: Maria San Marco, Controller Subject: Adopting JIT

b. If you recommend that Pasta Products Inc. adopt JIT, write a memo to Michael Magee of First Commercial Bank explaining the situation. Regardless of whether you expect Pasta Products Inc. to violate the loan covenant this year, adopting JIT will increase the likelihood that Pasta Products Inc. will violate the covenant in the future. Write a memo asking Michael Magee to work with Pasta Products Inc. to reduce the likelihood that the company will violate its loan covenant in the future because of the switch to JIT. Your memo should explain why reducing the minimum required current ratio is in everyone's interests. Your memo should take the form shown in part a, with the appropriate changes.

Job Costing

How did Michael Dell turn Dell Computer Corporation around from losses in 1993 to record profits of $1.9 billion for the fiscal year ended January 31, 2000? Most companies can increase gross margin either by increasing selling prices or by reducing costs. But computer prices were falling throughout the industry, so Dell could not increase selling prices. There was no choice—Dell had to reduce manufacturing costs.

Recent estimates indicate that Dell now enjoys a 10 to 15 percent cost advantage over its competitors in the personal computer market. How did it develop this advantage? Management accounting information helped Dell and his managers decide which costs could be cut. The first step was to determine how much it cost the company to assemble a computer.

To determine the manufacturing cost of its products, Dell uses a *job costing* system. Each computer is built to a specific customer order, called a *job*. Dell's job costing system traces direct materials (such as CD-ROMs and hard drives) and direct labour (such as assembly-line labour) to each job. Then Dell allocates indirect manufacturing overhead costs (such as amortization on the plant) to each job. The sum of the job's direct materials, direct labour, and manufacturing overhead is its total cost.

Dell needs to know how much a product—for example, a particular computer model—costs for two main reasons:

1. *To help managers plan and control business operations; so they can*
   - Control costs
   - Identify the most profitable products
   - Develop financial plans
   - Set selling prices for products

2. *To help managers gather information for external reporting:*
   - Cost of goods manufactured and cost of goods sold for the income statement
   - Inventory for the balance sheet

Source: McWilliams, G. "Mimicking Dell, Compaq to Sell its PCs Directly," *Wall Street Journal*, November 11, 1998, p. B1.

IN THIS chapter, we will explain how Dell Computer Corporation and other companies use a job cost system to measure the cost of producing a product or a service. But before we get started on the details, let's pause to see where job costing fits in the big picture of cost determination for management decisions and external reporting.

In Chapter 19 you learned that managers make certain business decisions based on *full product costs* from all elements of the value chain: research and development, design, production, marketing, distribution, and customer service. Managers need to know full product costs because they must, for example, set the long-run average sale price of the products higher than the full product costs if the company is to make a profit.

Recall that full product costs have two components: inventoriable product costs and period costs (also called noninventoriable costs). Inventoriable product costs are from the third element of the value chain in Exhibit 19-3: production for manufacturers and purchases for merchandisers. They are called inventoriable costs because, in addition to serving as building blocks for computing full product costs, these are the costs GAAP requires companies to use in computing inventory and cost of goods sold for the balance sheet and income statement. Most of Chapter 20 focuses on how companies determine these inventoriable product costs. The chapter concludes with a discussion of assigning noninventoriable costs (period costs) to products and services. By adding noninventoriable costs to the inventoriable costs, managers can build up full product costs to guide internal decisions, like setting long-run average sale prices that cover all the costs of the product.

As you read this chapter, keep in mind that *products* are not the only cost objects. For example, managers use costs of *manufacturing processes* to identify inefficiencies and to cut costs. Knowing the costs of serving different *customers* allows managers to identify their most profitable (valuable) customers. Knowing the costs of doing business in different *geographic regions* can help managers decide which regions are more profitable and thus better candidates for expansion.

This chapter focuses on assigning costs to products and services because: (1) products and services are the most common cost objects, and (2) managers use the costs of individual products and services to cut costs and to build costs of customers, geographic regions, and other cost objects.

Two Approaches to Product Costing: Process Costing and Job Costing

It is difficult for companies like Dell to determine how much it costs to manufacture a particular computer. Dell can trace the cost of direct materials like hard drives to the individual computers in which they are installed. But indirect costs such as amortization on the manufacturing plant cannot be traced directly to an individual computer because Dell cannot determine exactly how much amortization a particular computer "caused." Also, Dell makes many different computer models, and each requires different resources. How can Dell accurately measure product costs?

Unfortunately, it is impossible to determine the precise costs of producing a specific individual product. Instead, companies use product costing systems that *average* costs across products. There are two broad types of product costing systems.

- Process costing
- Job costing

Process costing systems accumulate costs for each production process. *Job costing* systems accumulate costs for each individual job. Process costing and job costing also differ in the extent to which they average costs. The type of system a company uses depends on the nature of its production operations.

Process Costing

Process costing is used by companies that produce large numbers of similar or identical product units in a continuous fashion through a series of uniform production steps or processes. Industries in which process costing is common include oil refining, food and beverage, and pharmaceuticals. Petro-Canada produces thousands of litres of each grade of gasoline at a time; Bayer manufactures millions of aspirin tablets— about 158 million in one month. In process costing systems, the cost object is a manufacturing process. Costs of individual units—litres or tablets—are computed by averaging the total costs of the process across the total number of units produced.

Exhibit 20-1 provides examples of different types of companies that use process costing systems. Note that not only manufacturers use process costing, but it is also used by many service companies. For example, banks use process costing to determine the cost of processing customer transactions. We discuss process costing in Chapter 21.

Job Costing

Job costing (sometimes called *job order costing*) is used by companies that manufacture products as individual units or in small batches that vary considerably in terms of resources consumed, time required, or complexity. These companies, which often produce goods according to customer specifications, are found in a wide range of industries, including aircraft, furniture, construction, and machinery. For example, a *job* may be production of a single bridge by a construction contractor or an order for five Canadair SE jets by Bombardier Inc.

In a job costing system, the job is the primary cost object. To assign costs to jobs accurately, accountants seek to determine the *drivers* of job costs. A **cost driver** is any factor that causes costs. When a cost driver changes, the total cost of the job (or other cost object) changes. For example, direct labour *hours* are cost drivers of direct labour *costs*. When the number of direct labour hours increases, the total direct labour cost of, say, a Dell computer increases. Because each job is distinct, the assignment of costs to jobs involves little averaging of costs across jobs.

Job costing is becoming more common in manufacturing industries like electronics. Dell Computer's made-to-order assembly process is one example. Another example is contract manufacturing, where manufacturing plants (often in Mexico and Asia) produce electronic goods for a variety of customers, including Cisco Systems, Hewlett-Packard, and Sony. Most contract manufacturers make goods for several well-known companies. For example, the Flextronics plant in Guadalajara, Mexico, makes Sony Web TV set-top boxes, PalmPilots, Hewlett-Packard printers, and Johnson & Johnson blood glucose monitors. Clearly, the plant must carefully track the costs of each of these separate jobs.

Job costing is not confined to manufacturers. Exhibit 20-1 shows that service organizations such as law firms and physicians also use job costing. A law firm might consider each legal case a different job, while a doctor considers each individual patient a job. Professional service providers such as architects and accountants use job costing to determine the costs of jobs for individual clients. Merchandisers like Indigo.ca can use job costing to determine the cost of meeting each customer order.

Job costing is most complex for manufacturers, so this chapter focuses on job costing in a manufacturing setting. The last section of the chapter applies the same job costing principles to nonmanufacturing companies.

Job Costing Illustrated

In a job costing system, managers are concerned with both inventory valuation and planning and control. Careful planning and cost control are keys to earning a profit on each job. If costs are too high, profit is reduced or eliminated. Managers must monitor the progress of each job to ensure that its costs stay within budgeted limits.

Consider the La-Z-Boy Furniture Company. For this company, each individual customer order can be treated as a different job. Suppose that La-Z-Boy has a job order costing system with the following inventories on December 31, 2002:

Materials inventory (many kinds)	$20,000
Work in process inventory (5 jobs)	29,000
Finished goods inventory (unsold units from 2 jobs)	12,000

La-Z-Boy Furniture Company
www.lazboy.com

EXHIBIT 20-1

Job and Process Costing in Service, Merchandising, and Manufacturing Companies

	Service	Merchandising	Manufacturing
Job Costing	Law firms (cases) Health care (diagnoses, procedures, or patients) Public relations (campaigns)	e-tailers such as Indigo.ca	Commercial building construction Custom furniture Aircraft manufacturers
Process Costing	Banks and other financial institutions (processing customer deposit transactions)	Granaries (redistribute tonnes of identical grains)	Paper mills Breweries Textile mills

The following is a summary of transaction data for the year 2003. We will explain the accounting for these transactions step by step.

1. Materials purchased on account.. $320,000
2. Direct materials used for manufacturing.. 285,000
   Indirect materials used for manufacturing... 40,000
3. Manufacturing wages incurred.. 335,000
4. Direct labour on jobs.. 250,000
   Indirect labour to support manufacturing activities.......................... 85,000
5. Manufacturing overhead (amortization on plant and equipment)... 50,000
6. Manufacturing overhead (factory utilities)... 20,000
7. Manufacturing overhead (factory insurance)...................................... 5,000
8. Manufacturing overhead (property taxes—factory)........................... 10,000
9. Manufacturing overhead assigned to jobs.. 200,000
10. Cost of goods manufactured.. 740,000
11. Sales on account.. 996,000
    Cost of goods sold 734,000

Job Cost Record

The document used to accumulate the costs of a job is called a **job cost record**. A completed job cost record for La-Z-Boy Furniture Company is shown in Exhibit 20-2. It has separate sections for the costs of direct materials, direct labour, and manufacturing overhead charged to Job 293. The total cost of the job is $1,490. The average cost of each recliner chair is $149 ($1,490 ÷ 10).

Managers use job cost data to plan and control manufacturing operations. Suppose $450 was the budgeted direct materials cost of Job 293. Then the $500 actual cost exceeds the budget by more than 10 percent. Production managers may investigate this cost overrun to gain insights that will help them improve their budgeting procedures or future performance, depending on the cause of the overrun.

Companies that use job costing initiate a job cost record when work on a job begins. Records of jobs in process (begun but not yet completed) form a subsidiary ledger for the general ledger account Work in Process Inventory. As costs are incurred on a job, they are added to its job cost record in the subsidiary ledger and the Work

EXHIBIT 20-2

Job Record

Job Cost Record

La-Z-Boy

Job No. 293

Customer Name and Address Brick Furniture, Edmonton

Job Description 10 recliner chairs

Date Promised 31-7		Date Started 24-7		Date Completed 29-7		

| Date | Direct Materials | | Direct Labour | | Manufacturing Overhead Costs | | |
	Requisition Numbers	Amount	Time Record Numbers	Amount	Date	Rate	Amount
2003 24-7 25-7 28-7	334 338 347	$ 90 180 230	236, 251, 258 264, 269, 273, 291 305	$300 200 50	29-7	80% of direct labour	$440

Overall Cost Summary

Direct materials .... $ 500
Direct labour 550
Manufacturing overhead . 440

| Totals | | $500 | | $550 | Total Job Cost .... $1,490 | | |

in Process Inventory in the general ledger. When the job is complete its costs are totaled and transferred out of Work in Process Inventory into Finished Goods Inventory. When the job's output is sold, its costs are moved out of Finished Goods Inventory into Cost of Goods Sold.

We now illustrate accounting procedures for a job costing system. As we do so, you will learn how management accountants assigned the direct materials, direct labour, and manufacturing overhead costs to Job 293.

Accounting for Materials in a Job Costing System

Accounting for Purchases   Manufacturing companies that use job costing tend to have relatively low inventories. They purchase materials as needed to fill orders. Suppose that La-Z-Boy Furniture Company receives an order for ten recliner chairs. If the company needs to buy additional lumber, La-Z-Boy sends a *purchase order* to a lumber supplier.

In practice, general ledger entries are made frequently. To offer a sweeping overview, however, we use a summary entry for the entire year 2003. Our first entry is for purchases of materials (data from page 1137):

1.	Materials Inventory	320,000	
	Accounts Payable		320,000

La-Z-Boy receives the lumber and stores it. Control over materials in storage is established with a subsidiary **materials ledger**. This ledger holds perpetual inventory records, which list the quantity and cost of all manufacturing materials on hand. Exhibit 20-3 shows a materials ledger record for the lumber that goes into the manufacture of recliner chairs.

La-Z-Boy's materials received are logged in by receiving report number (abbreviated as *Rec. Report No.* in Exhibit 20-3). Materials used in the product are recorded by materials requisition number *(Mat. Req. No.)*. Management can use these underlying data to follow the flow of materials into the production process and thereby control the amount of material used in various jobs on a day-to-day basis.

The materials ledger includes a separate record for each raw material. Exhibit 20-4 illustrates the general ledger Materials Inventory account and the materials ledger for La-Z-Boy. The balance of Materials Inventory in the general ledger equals the sum of the balances in the subsidiary materials ledger.

A company manufacturing hundreds of items may have a materials ledger with thousands of accounts. It is little wonder that so many manufacturers have computerized their accounting systems.

After materials are purchased and stored, the manufacturing process begins with a document called a **materials requisition.** That document is a request for materials

EXHIBIT 20-3

Materials Ledger Record

Materials Ledger Record

Item No. B-220   **Description** Lumber/Recliner chairs

	Received				Used				Balance		
Date	Rec. Report No.	Units	Price	Total Price	Mat. Req. No.	Units	Price	Total Price	Units	Price	Total Price
2003 20-7									30	$9.00	$270
23-7	678	20	$9.00	$180					50	9.00	450
24-7					334	10	$9.00	$90	40	9.00	360

EXHIBIT 20-4

Materials Inventory Accounts

General Ledger	Subsidiary Ledger
Materials Inventory	Materials Ledger

Materials Inventory

1,170

Lumber			
Date	Received	Used	Balance
24-7			$360

Padding			
Date	Received	Used	Balance
24-7			$160

Upholstery Fabric			
Date	Received	Used	Balance
24-7			$390

Nails			
Date	Received	Used	Balance
24-7			$40

Thread			
Date	Received	Used	Balance
24-7			$20

Other Materials			
Date	Received	Used	Balance
24-7			$200

$1,170

Total balances equal the balance
in the general ledger account.

and it is prepared by manufacturing personnel. In effect, they ask that the lumber be moved from storage to the factory so work can begin. Exhibit 20-5 illustrates a materials requisition for the lumber needed to manufacture the ten recliner chairs in Job 293. Similar requisitions are used for nails and other indirect materials.

The "Direct Materials" section in the job cost record (Exhibit 20-2) shows how the details of the materials requisitions are posted to the individual job cost records. Be sure to follow the $90 cost of the lumber from materials requisition 334 (Exhibit 20-5) to the materials ledger record (Exhibit 20-3) to the job cost record (Exhibit 20-2) Note that all

EXHIBIT 20-5

Materials Requisition

Materials Requisition No. 334

La-Z-Boy

Date 24-7-2003   **Job No.** 293

Item No.	Item	Quantity	Unit Price	Amount
B-220	Lumber/Recliner chairs	10	$9.00	$90

the dollar amounts in Exhibits 20-2 through 20-11 show La-Z-Boy's *costs*—not the prices at which La-Z-Boy *sells* its products

Technology simplifies the collection of data, including direct material costs. Companies such as Dell Computer Corporation use electronic bar codes to track material costs, tracing materials to individual computers by scanning bar codes on the component parts as they are installed.

Direct and Indirect Materials   Materials Inventory is debited for the costs of all materials purchased—both direct materials and indirect materials. The Materials Inventory account in Exhibit 20-4 includes the costs of direct materials—lumber, padding, and upholstery fabric—and the costs of indirect materials—nails and thread. When either direct or indirect materials are requisitioned from storage, Materials Inventory and the accompanying account in the subsidiary materials ledger are credited.

What account is debited? The answer depends on the type of materials. For direct materials, the debit is to Work in Process Inventory. Recall that Work in Process Inventory is a control account whose balance equals the total cost of jobs in process. Exhibit 20-5 indicates that the $90 cost of requisition 334 is for Job 293. La-Z-Boy accountants enter this cost directly on the job cost record (Exhibit 20-6).

The costs of indirect materials are part of overhead. Actual manufacturing overhead costs are *neither* entered on job cost records *nor* added to Work in Process Inventory. Instead, these costs are accumulated in a separate account called Manufacturing Overhead.

La-Z-Boy Furniture Company works on many jobs over the course of the year. At regular intervals (commonly a month, but for our illustration, a year), accountants collect the data from materials requisitions to make a single journal entry for all the materials that have been used. The 2003 entry for La-Z-Boy is (data are from page 1137):

2.	Work in Process Inventory	285,000	
	Manufacturing Overhead	40,000	
	Materials Inventory		325,000

The flow of materials costs may be diagrammed as follows:

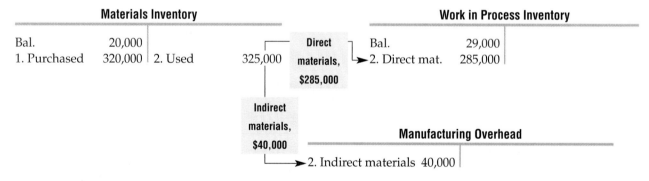

Accounting for Labour in a Job Costing System

Control over labour costs in a job costing system is established through payroll registers and time records. A **labour time record** identifies the employee, the amount of time spent on a particular job, and the labour cost charged to the job. Time records are accumulated for each job to determine its total direct labour cost. Exhibit 20-7 illustrates a labour time ticket used in a job costing system.

Technology can simplify the collection of data such as direct labour cost. Companies can set up computer terminals on the production floor. At various stages in the manufacturing process of Saturn automobiles, for example, employees insert

Job Cost Record

La-Z-Boy

Job No. 293
Customer Name and Address Brick Furniture, Edmonton
Job Description 10 recliner chairs

Date Promised	31-7	Date Started	24-7	Date Completed	

Date	Direct Materials		Direct Labour		Manufacturing Overhead Costs		
	Requisition Numbers	Amount	Time Record Numbers	Amount	Date	Rate	Amount
2003							
24-7	334	$90					

Overall Cost Summary

Direct materials . . . . $
Direct labour . . . .
Manufacturing overhead .

| Totals | | | | | Total Job Cost . . . . $ | | |

EXHIBIT 20-6

Job Cost Record Entry for Direct Materials

WORKING IT OUT

Prepare the journal entry for the following materials-related transactions. (1) Purchased raw materials on account, $25,000. (2) Materials requisitions for the month show that $20,000 was requisitioned for jobs and that $3,000 of indirect materials were used.

A:

(1) Materials Inventory......... 25,000
    Accounts Payable 25,000

(2) Work in Process
    Inv. 20,000
    Manufacturing
    Overhead.................... 3,000
       Materials
       Inventory.............. 23,000

their magnetically imprinted identification cards into the terminals. This system captures direct labour time and cost without detailed labour records.

La-Z-Boy's entry for 2003 for all manufacturing wages for all jobs (data are from page 1137) is:

3.	Manufacturing Wages...	335,000	
	Wages Payable...		335,000

This entry *accumulates* and records the actual labour costs incurred.

Direct and Indirect Labour Similar to the distinction between direct and indirect materials costs, direct and indirect labour costs are *assigned* separately. Direct labour is debited directly to Work in Process Inventory. Indirect labour cannot be traced to a specific job, so it is added to the Manufacturing Overhead account. The transfer of labour cost to production results in a credit to Manufacturing Wages. The following entry assigns manufacturing wages to Work in Process Inventory and Manufacturing Overhead (data are from page 1137):

4.	Work in Process Inventory	250,000	
	Manufacturing Overhead...	85,000	
	Manufacturing Wages..		335,000

Labour Time Record **No.** 251

EMPLOYEE Jay Barlow **Date** 24-7

JOB 293

Time:		Rate $16.00
Started	1:00	Cost of labour
Stopped	8:30	charged to job $120.00
Elapsed	7:30	

Employee _Jay Barlow_
Supervisor _Dean Childres_

EXHIBIT 20-7

Labour Time Record

This entry brings the balance in Manufacturing Wages to zero, its transferred balance now divided between Work in Process Inventory (direct labour) and Manufacturing Overhead (indirect labour), as shown in the following diagram.

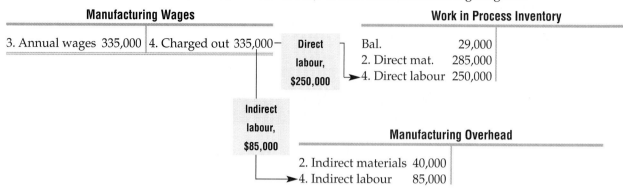

WORKING IT OUT

Prepare the general journal entries for the following labour-related transactions. Labour time records for the month show direct labour of $17,000 and indirect labour of $4,000.

A:

Manufacturing Wages 21,000
  Wages Payable 21,000

Work in Process Inv 17,000
Manufacturing Overhead 4,000
  Manufacturing Wages 21,000

Assume that $300 of one day's direct labour cost is for Job 293. La-Z-Boy Furniture enters Job 293's direct labour on the job cost record. The $300 amount in the Direct Labour section of Exhibit 20-8 includes Jay Barlow's wages of $120 (from labour time record 251, Exhibit 20-7) and the labour costs entered on time tickets 236 and 258 (not shown).

The Work in Process Inventory account now contains the costs of direct materials and direct labour charged to Job 293—and the costs of many other jobs as well. Work in Process Inventory serves as a control account, with the job cost records giving the supporting details for each job.

How Has Information Technology Changed Job Costing?

The flow of costs through the T-accounts and the journal entries applies to systems ranging from simple manual costing to sophisticated automated database systems. The main difference is in the source of data underlying the costs. In traditional systems, the sources of data include source documents like material requisitions and labour time records, and job cost records like those we have described. These documents can be paper-based or automated.

STOP & THINK

How can the materials inventory subsidiary ledger (Exhibit 20-4), labour time records (Exhibit 20-7), and job cost records (Exhibits 20-6 and 20-8) help managers run the company more effectively and efficiently?

Answer: Managers can look at the materials inventory subsidiary ledger to see when inventories of individual materials like lumber, padding, upholstery fabric, nails, and thread are running low, so they can decide when to reorder.

Managers can use the labour time records in two ways: (1) to control employees, and (2) to control labour costs incurred on individual jobs. First, suppose an employee is paid for $7\frac{1}{2}$ hours of work per day. Adding her labour time records for each job she worked on during the day should yield a total of $7\frac{1}{2}$ hours worked. If not, the manager should find out how the employee spent any time unaccounted for. Second, managers can use labour time records to track how much time employees spend on a particular job. Managers need to ensure that employees work efficiently—if they spend longer than expected on a job, the job may not yield a profit.

The job cost record tallies materials, labour, and manufacturing overhead as they are assigned to the job. Managers monitor these costs to ensure that jobs are completed as efficiently as possible. If costs exceed budget, managers must do a better job of controlling costs in the future, or else they may need to raise the sale price on similar jobs to ensure that the company remains profitable.

EXHIBIT 20-8

Job Cost Record Entry for
Direct Labour

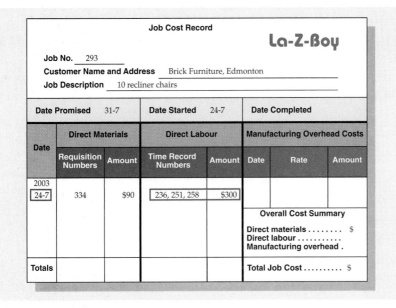

In highly automated systems, there may be no physical source documents. Employees use bar codes to record materials used and scan their identification cards to record their labour time. The software immediately tracks these material and labour costs to the specific job, and updates the general ledger accounts (for example, Materials Inventory, Work in Process Inventory, Manufacturing Wages, and Manufacturing Overhead). Automated database systems may not store data in the form of separate job cost records. But when employees enter the job number, the system quickly tallies the costs that have been assigned to the job so far.

Advances in information technology may:

1. Eliminate the physical source documents
2. Hasten the speed with which:
    a. Materials and labour costs are linked to specific jobs
    b. The general ledger accounts are updated.

However, the cost flows and journal entries are identical to those we have described for La-Z-Boy.

You may also have noticed that La-Z-Boy is a traditional manufacturer: it holds materials, work in process, and finished goods inventories. However, the concepts underlying the flow of costs also apply to companies that use a just-in-time (JIT) philosophy. The main difference is that JIT adopters minimize their inventory levels. In extreme cases where inventory is virtually zero, companies sometimes simplify the accounting and bypass some or all of the inventory accounts. (Chapter 25 explains the simplifications of just-in-time costing in more detail.)

Mid-Chapter Summary Problem
for Your Review

Ecosphere Associates Ltd. in Calgary, Alberta, produces ecospheres—self-sustaining enclosed glass spheres that include water, algae, tiny shrimp, and snails. Suppose Ecosphere has the following transactions:

a. Purchased raw materials on account, $35,000.

b. Materials costing $30,000 were requisitioned for production. Of this total, $3,000 were indirect materials.

c. Labour time records for the month show direct labour of $22,000, and indirect labour of $4,000.

Required

Prepare journal entries for each transaction.

Solution to Review Problem

a. Materials Inventory................... 35,000
        Accounts Payable   35,000

When materials are purchased on account;

- Debit (increase) the Materials Inventory asset for the *cost* of the materials, and
- Credit (increase) Accounts Payable to record the liability for the cost of the materials.

b. Work in Process Inventory........ 27,000
    Manufacturing Overhead..........   3,000
        Materials Inventory...............   30,000

When materials are requisitioned (used) in production, we record the movement of materials out of materials inventory and into production:

- Debit (increase) Work in Process Inventory for the cost of the *direct* materials (in this case, $27,000—the $30,000 total materials requisitioned less the $3,000 indirect materials),
- Debit (increase) Manufacturing Overhead for the cost of the *indirect* materials, and
- Credit (decrease) Materials Inventory for the cost of both direct and indirect materials moved out of the materials storage area and into production.

c. Manufacturing Wages................ 26,000
        Wages Payable........................   26,000

To record total labour costs actually incurred ($22,000 + $4,000):

- Debit (increase) Manufacturing Wages, and
- Credit (increase) Wages Payable to record the liability for wages incurred, but not paid

Work in Process Inventory........ 22,000
Manufacturing Overhead..........   4,000
        Manufacturing Wages.......   26,000

To assign the labour costs:

- Debit (increase) Work in Process Inventory for the cost of the *direct* labour,
- Debit (increase) Manufacturing Overhead for the cost of the *indirect* labour, and
- Credit (decrease) Manufacturing Wages for the cost of both direct and indirect labour

Accounting for Manufacturing Overhead in a Job Costing System

OBJECTIVE 3
Account for manufacturing overhead in a manufacturer's job costing system

Manufacturing overhead costs are debited to a single general ledger account—Manufacturing Overhead. In addition to the entries already recorded for indirect materials and indirect labour, entries 5 through 8 below complete the recording of La-Z-Boy Furniture's overhead costs given on page 1137. The account titles in parentheses indicate the specific records that are debited in an overhead subsidiary ledger. Budgeting these individual items and then analyzing the differences between budgeted and actual amounts helps managers control these overhead costs.

5.	Manufacturing Overhead		
	(Amortization—Plant and Equipment)	50,000	
	Accumulated Amortization—Plant and Equipment		50,000
6.	Manufacturing Overhead (Factory Utilities)	20,000	
	Cash		20,000
7.	Manufacturing Overhead (Factory Insurance)	5,000	
	Prepaid Insurance—Factory		5,000
8.	Manufacturing Overhead (Property Taxes—Factory)	10,000	
	Property Taxes Payable		10,000

The actual manufacturing overhead costs (such as indirect material, indirect labour, and amortization, utilities, insurance, and property taxes related to the factory) are debited to the Manufacturing Overhead account as they occur throughout the year. The Manufacturing Overhead account now contains all the overhead costs:

Manufacturing Overhead

2. Indirect materials	40,000
4. Indirect labour	85,000
5. Amortization—plant and equipment	50,000
6. Factory utilities	20,000
7. Factory insurance	5,000
8. Property taxes—factory	10,000
Total overhead cost	210,000

KEY POINT

Review the flow of costs in a job costing system:

Materials Inventory

Materials purchased	Transferred to WIP (direct materials) and MOH (indirect materials)

Manufacturing Wages

Total wages	Charged out (transferred) to WIP (direct labour) and MOH (indirect labour)

Manufacturing Overhead

Total actual overhead costs	Applied MOH transferred to WIP

Notice that only actual costs are debited to these accounts. When the costs are transferred to Work in Process or Manufacturing Overhead, these accounts are credited.

STOP & THINK

How can managers use the manufacturing overhead subsidiary ledger to control overhead costs?

Answer: Managers plan the expected amount of each individual manufacturing overhead cost, such as amortization, utilities, and insurance. They then investigate why actual costs differ from planned costs. For example, if factory utilities are higher than expected, managers will want to know why. Did utility rates increase? Did workers waste electricity or water? Was there a delay in installing more energy-efficient machinery? Answers to these questions can help managers control (reduce) utility costs and develop more accurate estimates of future utility costs.

How are overhead costs *assigned* to jobs? Materials requisitions and labour time records make it relatively easy to identify direct materials and direct labour costs with individual jobs. But manufacturing overhead includes a variety of costs that cannot be linked to particular orders. For example, it is virtually impossible to say that a specific amount of the cost incurred to cool the factory is related to Job 293. Yet manufacturing overhead costs are as essential as direct materials and direct labour to the production of goods, so we must find some way to assign these costs to specific jobs.

Allocating Overhead Costs to Jobs

Managers want to know the costs incurred in each job, including both direct and indirect costs. Accountants use **cost tracing** to assign direct costs (such as direct materials and direct labour) to cost objects such as jobs. They use **cost allocation** to assign manufacturing overhead and other indirect costs to cost objects. The general term **cost assignment** refers to the process of tracing direct costs and allocating indirect costs to cost objects (jobs, in a job costing system).

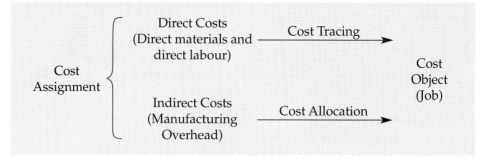

Choosing an Allocation Base   Direct material and direct labour costs are traced directly to each job, as we've seen. But managers also want to know the *total* manufacturing costs incurred on each job, including manufacturing overhead costs. Somehow, the company must allocate to each individual job its share of the wide variety of indirect manufacturing costs like amortization and insurance on the plant and equipment, indirect materials, and indirect labour.

The key to assigning indirect manufacturing costs to jobs is to identify a manufacturing overhead allocation base. The **allocation base** is a common denominator that links indirect manufacturing overhead costs to the cost objects. Ideally, the allocation base is the primary cost driver of manufacturing overhead costs. For example, in many companies, manufacturing overhead costs rise and fall with direct labour costs. In this case, accountants can use either direct labour costs or direct labour hours as the manufacturing overhead allocation base. The more direct labour a job uses, the more manufacturing overhead cost the job is allocated. This is a wise choice if direct labour is a driver of manufacturing overhead costs.

But direct labour is not always the best allocation base. Labour is less important in companies that have automated production processes, like Saturn. Saturn's manufacturing overhead costs are primarily machine-related. Factory amortization, maintenance, and utilities are likely to fluctuate with the number of machine hours used. Companies with automated operations often use machine hours as the manufacturing overhead allocation base. The important point is that the cost allocation base should be the primary driver of the manufacturing overhead costs.

For simplicity, we'll assume the company uses only one allocation base to assign manufacturing overhead costs to jobs. Chapter 25 relaxes this assumption. There, we will see how many companies use a method called *activity-based costing* to identify several different allocation bases that more accurately link indirect costs with the jobs that caused those costs. Because activity-based costing is a straightforward extension of the single allocation base method, it is important to begin by developing a solid understanding of the simpler system we describe here.

The most accurate allocation cannot be made until the total amount of the manufacturing overhead costs is known, at the end of the year. But that would be much too late. Managers making decisions today cannot wait until the end of the year for product cost information. To solve this timing problem, accountants develop an estimated manufacturing overhead allocation rate at the beginning of the year.

This **predetermined manufacturing overhead rate** (sometimes called the **budgeted manufacturing overhead rate**) is computed as follows:

$$\text{Predetermined manufacturing overhead rate} = \frac{\text{Total estimated manufacturing overhead costs}}{\text{Total estimated quantity of the manufacturing overhead allocation base}}$$

Both the numerator and the denominator of the predetermined manufacturing overhead rate are based on *estimated* amounts. These are estimated before the year begins. They cannot be actual amounts because actual overhead costs and the actual quantity of the allocation base are not known until after the end of the period. Companies use the predetermined manufacturing overhead rate to allocate overhead to individual jobs.

Six Steps in Allocating Manufacturing Overhead to Jobs A company generally follows six steps in allocating its manufacturing overhead cost to jobs:

1. Estimate the total overhead cost for the planning period, which is ordinarily a year. Assume that late in 2002 La-Z-Boy personnel predicted overhead costs for 2003 of $220,000.

2. Identify a cost allocation base. As the Manufacturing Overhead section of Exhibit 20-2 shows, La-Z-Boy's accountants selected direct labour cost.

3. Budget the total units of the cost application base. La-Z-Boy production managers expected to incur $275,000 of direct labour cost during 2003.

4. Compute the predetermined manufacturing overhead application rate as follows:

$$\begin{aligned}\text{Predetermined manufacturing overhead rate} &= \frac{\text{Total estimated manufacturing overhead costs}}{\text{Total estimated quantity of the manufacturing overhead allocation base}} \\[2mm] &= \frac{\text{Total estimated manufacturing overhead costs}}{\text{Total estimated direct labour cost}} \\[2mm] &= \frac{\$220,000}{\$275,000} = 0.80, \text{ or } 80\% \end{aligned}$$

Thus the predetermined manufacturing overhead rate is computed as the total *estimated* manufacturing overhead cost (estimated *before* the year starts) divided by the total estimated quantity of the allocation base (also estimated *before* the year starts). Because the numerator and the denominator are both based on amounts that are *estimated before* the year starts, this overhead rate is *predetermined*.

5. Obtain actual quantities of the overhead application base, on a job-by-job basis, as the year unfolds. The total direct labour cost of Job 293 is $550.

6. Allocate manufacturing overhead to jobs by multiplying the *predetermined* manufacturing overhead rate (computed in step 4) by the *actual* quantity of the allocation base used by each job (from step 5). The same predetermined rate is used to allocate manufacturing overhead to all jobs worked on throughout the year. After the direct material and direct labour costs have been traced to a job, the manufacturing overhead is allocated, as shown in the job cost record for Job 293 (Exhibit 20-9). Recall that the total direct labour cost for Job 293 is $550. Because the predetermined overhead allocation rate is 80 percent of direct labour cost, the manufacturing overhead allocated to Job 293 is $440 ($550 × 0.80).

The job cost record of Job 293 now is complete. It provides the details that support the $1,490 total cost and the $149 ($1,490 ÷ 10) unit cost of the Brick's order.

WORKING IT OUT

The Winslow Co. budgeted its manufacturing overhead and direct labour to be $90,000 and $60,000, respectively. The actual costs for the year are:

Indirect labour	$40,000
Factory supplies	20,000
Machinery repair	15,000
Advertising	6,000
Rent on factory	15,000
Factory utilities	10,000
Selling expenses	30,000
Direct labour	64,000

(1) Calculate the predetermined overhead rate, using direct labour as the allocation base.
(2) Calculate actual overhead.
(3) Calculate applied overhead.

A:
(1) Manufacturing Overhead rate = 150% of direct labour ($90,000/$60,000)
(2) Actual Manufacturing Overhead = $100,000 ($40,000 + $20,000 + $15,000 + $15,000 + $10,000)
(3) Applied Manufacturing Overhead = $96,000 ($64,000 × 150%)

EXHIBIT 20-9

Job Cost Record Entry for
Manufacturing Overhead

Job Cost Record

La-Z-Boy

Job No.   293

Customer Name and Address   Brick Furniture, Edmonton

Job Description   10 recliner chairs

Date Promised 31-7			Date Started 24-7		Date Completed 29-7		
Date	**Direct Materials**		**Direct Labour**		**Manufacturing Overhead Costs**		
	Requisition Numbers	Amount	Time Record Numbers	Amount	Date	Rate	Amount
2003 24-7 25-7 28-7	334 338 347	$ 90 180 230	236, 251, 258 264, 269, 273, 291 305	$300 200 50	29-7	80% of direct labour	$440
					Overall Cost Summary		
					Direct materials . . . . $ 500 Direct labour . . . . 550 Manufacturing overhead . 440		
Totals		$500		$550	Total Job Cost $1,490		

Management accountants say that the assignment of costs to a job is accurate if the costs assigned represent the additional (incremental) costs incurred to produce the job—that is, the costs that are incurred only because the job is produced. In general, which do you believe is more accurate: the tracing of direct costs to jobs or the allocation of indirect costs? Why?

Answer: In general, the tracing of direct costs is more accurate. No averaging is required to determine, for example, that Saturn's cost of a car tire is $30 or that the cost of an hour of assembly line labour is $30. In contrast, the allocation of indirect costs often involves substantial averaging. Consider La-Z-Boy's predetermined manufacturing overhead rate. The total budgeted cost of $220,000 includes indirect labour, indirect materials, amortization, and utilities. It is unlikely that direct labour cost, the selected application base, is the only driver of each of those costs. Therefore, it is unlikely that the ratio of additional overhead costs to direct labour costs is exactly the same for every job. Rather, the 80-percent rate is an average for all jobs. Using a broadly averaged application rate to allocate indirect costs results in some jobs being overcosted and others undercosted.

Overhead costs applied to jobs are debited to Work in Process Inventory and credited to Manufacturing Overhead. For 2003, the total overhead allocated to all jobs worked on is 80 percent of the $250,000 direct labour cost, or $200,000 (data are from page 1137). The summary journal entry to allocate manufacturing overhead costs to Work in Process Inventory is:

9.	Work in Process Inventory	200,000	
	Manufacturing Overhead		200,000

La-Z-Boy's application of manufacturing overhead may be diagrammed in this way:

Manufacturing Overhead

2. Indirect materials	40,000	9. Applied	200,000
4. Indirect labour	85,000		
5. Amortization—			
plant and equip.	50,000		
6. Factory utilities	20,000		
7. Factory insurance	5,000		
8. Property taxes—			
factory	10,000		
Actual costs	210,000		
Bal.	10,000		

Work in Process Inventory

Bal.	29,000
2. Direct materials	285,000
4. Direct labour	250,000
9.	200,000

Manufacturing Overhead Applied →

Note that after allocation, there is still a $10,000 debit balance in the Manufacturing Overhead account. This means that La-Z-Boy's actual overhead costs exceed the amount of overhead allocated to Work in Process Inventory. We say that La-Z-Boy's Manufacturing Overhead is *underallocated*. We will discuss how accountants correct this problem on page 1150. First, however, we demonstrate accounting for finished goods and for the sale of inventory.

Accounting for Finished Goods, Sales, and Cost of Goods Sold

As each job is completed, its total cost is transferred from Work in Process Inventory to Finished Goods Inventory. Sales of finished goods are recorded as they occur.

The $740,000 cost of goods manufactured (from the data on page 1137) is the cost of the jobs that La-Z-Boy finished this year. La-Z-Boy credits Work in Process Inventory as the jobs leave the factory floor. The debit is to Finished Goods Inventory because the completed products are moving into the finished goods storage area. A summary entry for La-Z-Boy Furniture's goods completed in 2003 follows:

10.	Finished Goods Inventory	740,000	
	Work in Process Inventory		740,000

In turn, La-Z-Boy makes the usual entries for sales and cost of goods sold:

11.	Accounts Receivable	996,000	
	Sales Revenue		996,000
	Cost of Goods Sold	734,000	
	Finished Goods Inventory		734,000

The second entry is needed to maintain the perpetual inventory records. Only the first entry is needed in a periodic inventory system.

The key accounts for La-Z-Boy's manufacturing costs now show:

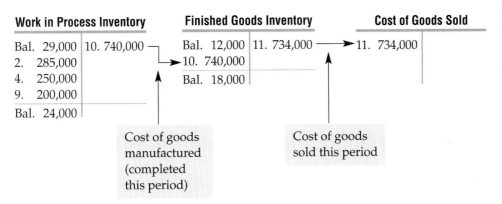

Work in Process Inventory				Finished Goods Inventory				Cost of Goods Sold		
Bal.	29,000	10. 740,000		Bal.	12,000	11. 734,000	→	11. 734,000		
2.	285,000			10. 740,000						
4.	250,000			Bal. 18,000						
9.	200,000									
Bal.	24,000									

Cost of goods manufactured (completed this period)

Cost of goods sold this period

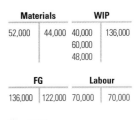

Disposing of Underallocated or Overallocated Overhead

During the year, Manufacturing Overhead is debited for actual overhead costs incurred and credited for applied amounts (amounts allocated to Work in Process Inventory). The total debits rarely equal the total credits. Why? Because overhead is applied to jobs at a *predetermined* rate that represents the *expected* relationship between overhead costs and application base units. In our example, La-Z-Boy's accountants expected to incur 2003 overhead at the rate of 80 percent of direct labour costs ($220,000 ÷ $275,000, page 1147). But the *actual* rate was 84 percent of direct labour costs ($210,000 ÷ $250,000, pages 1145 and 1137). Thus, less overhead was applied to jobs than was actually incurred. Every job worked on in 2003 was undercosted—that is, was allocated less overhead cost than if the 84 percent rate had been accurately forecasted and used.

The $10,000 debit balance of Manufacturing Overhead shown on page 1149 is called **underallocated overhead** because the allocated cost was less than (under) the actual cost. If the actual overhead had been less than 80 percent of direct labour, a credit balance of Manufacturing Overhead, called **overallocated overhead**, would have resulted. Accountants usually ignore under- and overallocated overhead during the year and dispose of it at year end, when the Manufacturing Overhead account is closed.

When overhead is underallocated, as in our example, a credit to Manufacturing Overhead brings the account balance to zero. What account(s) is (are) debited? Ideally, La-Z-Boy would go back and increase the cost of each individual job. Many companies have computer programs that automatically correct each job at the end of the year. Alternatively, accountants could prorate, or apply in proportion to their balances, the difference among the affected inventory accounts (Work in Process Inventory and Finished Goods Inventory) and Cost of Goods Sold. In practice, however, most companies close the amount directly to Cost of Goods Sold, as shown below, unless the amount is so material that this method would materially misstate the affected account balances.

12.	Cost of Goods Sold	10,000	
	Manufacturing Overhead		10,000

With or without proration, the entry to close Manufacturing Overhead ensures that the total actual overhead cost incurred—$210,000 in this case—eventually will be expensed as part of Cost of Goods Sold.

The Manufacturing Overhead balance now is zero, concluding our job order costing example:

Manufacturing Overhead				Cost of Goods Sold	
Actual	210,000	Applied	200,000	734,000	
		Closed	10,000 ──────►	10,000	
				744,000	

Exhibit 20-10 summarizes the accounting for manufacturing overhead:

- before the period
- during the period
- at the end of the period.

EXHIBIT 20-10

Summary of Accounting for Manufacturing Overhead

Before the Period:

Compute predetermined manufacturing overhead rate $=\dfrac{\text{Total estimated manufacturing overhead cost}}{\text{Total estimated quantity of allocation base}}$

During the Period:

Allocate the overhead $=$ Actual quantity of the manufacturing overhead allocation base $\times$ Predetermined manufacturing overhead rate

At the end of the Period:

Close the Manufacturing Overhead account:

If actual > allocated

Underallocated manufacturing overhead
Jobs are *undercosted*
Need to *increase* Cost of Goods Sold
  Cost of Goods Sold XXX
    Manufacturing Overhead XXX

If actual < allocated

Overallocated manufacturing overhead
Jobs are *overcosted*
Need to *reduce* Cost of Goods Sold
  Manufacturing Overhead XXX
    Cost of Goods Sold XXX

Overview of La-Z-Boy Furniture Company Example

The accompanying illustration provides an overview of the La-Z-Boy Furniture Company job costing example. The ending balance sheet account balances are:

Materials Inventory	$15,000
Work in Process Inventory	24,000
Finished Goods Inventory	18,000

La-Z-Boy's condensed income statement for 2003 reports the following through gross margin:

Sales	$996,000
Cost of goods sold	744,000
Gross margin (or gross profit)	$252,000

As mentioned in the text, the remainder of the manufacturer's income statement (operating expenses, other revenues and expenses, and net income) is the same as for a merchandising company.

Job Costing, General Flow of Costs for La-Z-Boy *(in thousands)*

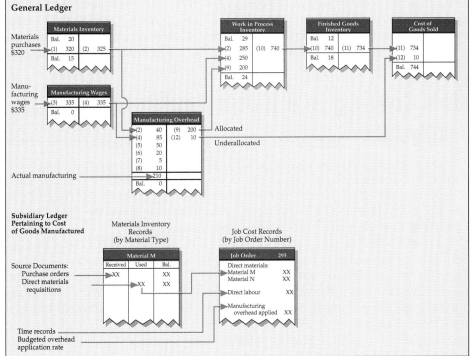

Inventoriable Costs, Noninventoriable Costs, and Job Costing

Job costing can be complex for manufacturers, because manufacturers have

1. The most complex business operations—they use labour and overhead to transform raw materials into different finished goods
2. Three different kinds of inventory—materials, work in process, and finished goods

Job costing in manufacturing companies has traditionally focused on assigning *manufacturing costs (inventoriable costs)* to jobs. This is why the La-Z-Boy illustration in this chapter focuses on assigning only manufacturing costs to jobs. We have not considered costs incurred in other elements of the value chain, such as R&D or marketing.

The focus on manufacturing costs stems from external reporting requirements. GAAP requires that the accounting records treat only inventoriable costs (manufacturing costs, for a manufacturer) as assets. Costs incurred in other elements of the value chain are treated as expenses for financial accounting. For this reason, the general ledger entries in this chapter have been limited to manufacturing costs.

As we noted in Chapter 19, however, managers often want to know the full (total) cost of a product or a job, not just the inventoriable cost. The same principles of tracing direct costs and allocating indirect costs (using predetermined allocation rates) apply to noninventoriable period costs incurred in other elements of the value chain: R&D, design, marketing, distribution, and customer service. Managers can add these noninventoriable (period) costs to the inventoriable costs to build the cost of the product or job to guide internal decisions, such as setting long-run average sale prices. However, these noninventoriable costs are assigned to products (or jobs) *only for internal decision making*. No journal entries assign noninventoriable costs to individual jobs, because noninventoriable costs are not assigned to products for external reporting.

Management accounting is becoming increasingly important to service firms. Recall that a service firm has no inventoriable costs because it has no inventory. Service firms incur only noninventoriable costs. Nevertheless, managers of service companies still need to know the (noninventoriable) costs of different jobs to make decisions such as setting selling prices, or fees. Thus we shift our focus to illustrate the assignment of noninventoriable costs to jobs in a service firm. However, a manufacturer such as La-Z-Boy or a merchandiser such as Future Shop could use the same approach to assign noninventoriable costs to individual jobs.

Job Costing in a Nonmanufacturing Company

We now illustrate how companies that are not manufacturers can use job costing. Barnett and Company is a legal practice that specializes in employment law. Each client is considered a separate job. As with most service firms, Barnett's most significant cost is direct labour—the cost of lawyers' time spent on the clients' cases. How do service firms trace direct labour to individual jobs?

For services like Web site design, information technology consulting, and external auditing, the automated nature of the service means that the employee simply enters the client number to start on the client's job. The software then records the time elapsed until the employee signs off on that job. When the service itself is not automated, employees typically fill out a computerized weekly **time record**. The software tallies the weekly total time spent on each client. Lawyer Teresa Fox's time record appears in Exhibit 20-11 (page 1154). Fox's time record shows that she devoted 14 hours to client 367 during the week of June 6, 2003.

LEARNING TIP

Another term used for inventoriable costs is product costs. These include all costs of a product that are regarded as an asset for financial reporting under GAAP. If a cost is associated with manufacturing, it must be treated as an inventoriable cost.

KEY POINT

Inventoriable costs flow through the balance sheet (they are capitalized as WIP Inventory) and then to the income statement as part of COGS. Other costs (sometimes referred to as period costs) flow immediately to the income statement as expense. All nonmanufacturing expenses are noninventoriable or period costs.

Job Costing in Small- and Medium-Sized Businesses

Rick Montgomery is the general manager of West Coast Alloys Limited. Located in Richmond, British Columbia, the company manufactures specialized pipe products, mainly for the forestry sector.

Job costing is a major focus for West Coast. "We are producing specialized products," Rick explains. "Each order that we receive is slightly different. The market is very competitive and we don't have a lot of room for error. We compete on the basis of price, quality of our product, and on-time deliveries. If we don't perform all of these tasks equally well, we will be out of business."

When West Coast Alloys Limited receives an order, a job order is initiated. The materials required for the job are either ordered or transferred into Work in Process Inventory from Raw Materials Inventory. The exact quantities and the costs of the material are recorded manually on the job order form. As different employees complete the job of transforming the raw material into the finished product, their time is recorded on the job order form.

When the job is completed, the product is given a final inspection and sent to the customer. However, the paperwork is not yet completed. Rick reviews the job order form for the material and direct labour costs that were incurred, and determines how much to invoice the customer.

"A lot of the time, we have had to bid for the work, which means that the amount of the invoice is predetermined. When we bid for the work, we estimate our material and labour cost, and provide a mark-up for our manufacturing overheads, operating costs, and profit. If we do a good job of managing production, we should be OK. If we don't, we run a great risk of losing money on any particular job.

"If a customer has given us a purchase order (where we have not had to bid for the work), we review the actual time and material charges, then apply a standard mark-up for manufacturing overheads, operating costs, and profit."

In a job costing system, it appears that the approach described in this chapter is used by most companies, regardless of company size. Why? Companies using job costing systems typically produce specialized products or provide specialized services. As a result, company size is not an issue. The principles of costing jobs apply to small and large companies.

Fox's salary and benefits total $100,000 per year. Assuming a 40-hour workweek and 50 workweeks in each year, Fox has 2,000 available workhours per year (50 weeks × 40 hours per week). Barnett and Company's hourly (cost) rate of employing Teresa Fox is:

$$\text{Hourly cost rate to the employer} = \frac{\$100,000 \text{ per year}}{2,000 \text{ hours per year}}$$

$$= \$50 \text{ per hour}$$

Fox is the only lawyer who served client 367, so the direct labour cost traced to the client is 14 hours × $50 per hour = $700.

Founding partner John Barnett wants to know the total costs of serving clients, not just the direct labour cost. Barnett also allocates indirect costs to individual jobs (clients). The law firm develops a predetermined indirect cost allocation rate, following the same six-step approach that La-Z-Boy (page 1147) used to develop its indirect manufacturing (overhead) cost rate:

EXHIBIT 20-11

Time Record

Barnett and Company Time Record					
Name			Teresa Fox		
Week of			June 6, 2003		
	M	**T**	**W**	**Th**	**F**
8:00–8:30	367	520	415	367	415
8:30–9:00					
9:00–9:30					
9:30–10:00					
10:00–10:30			367		
10:30–11:00					
11:00–11:30	520				
11:30–12:00	520				
12:00–12:30					
12:30–1:00					
1:00–1:30	520	367	367	520	415
1:30–2:00			367		
2:00–2:30			415		
2:30–3:00					
3:00–3:30					
3:30–4:00					
4:00–4:30					
4:30–5:00					

Weekly Summary:

Client #	Total Hours
367	14
415	13
520	13

1. *Estimate the total indirect costs.*

   In December 2002, Barnett estimates that the following indirect costs will be incurred in 2003:

Maintaining and updating law library for case research...	$ 25,000
Advertisements in the yellow pages....................................	2,000
Sponsorship of the symphony	3,000
Office rent..	200,000
Office support staff	70,000
Total indirect costs	$300,000

2. *Identify a cost allocation base.*

   Barnett uses direct labour hours as the allocation base, because the number of hours that lawyers work on clients' cases is the main driver of indirect costs.

3. *Estimate the total quantity of the indirect cost allocation base.*

   Barnett estimates that its lawyers will work 10,000 direct labour hours in 2003.

4. *Compute the predetermined indirect cost allocation rate. (Divide step 2 by step 3.)*

$$\text{Predetermined indirect cost allocation rate} = \frac{\$300{,}000 \text{ expected indirect costs}}{10{,}000 \text{ expected direct labour hours}}$$

$$= \$30 \text{ per direct labour hour}$$

5. *Obtain the actual quantity of the indirect cost allocation base used by individual jobs, as the year unfolds.*
   Exhibit 20-11 shows that client 367 required 14 direct labour hours.

6. *Allocate indirect costs to jobs by multiplying the predetermined indirect cost rate (step 4) by the actual quantity of the allocation base used by each job (step 5).* Client 367 is allocated indirect costs as follows:

   $$14 \text{ direct labour hours} \times \$30/\text{hour} = \$420$$

   To summarize, the total costs assigned to client 367 are

Direct labour: 14 hours × $50/hour	=	$ 700
Indirect costs: 14 hours × $30/hour	=	420
Total costs		$1,120

STOP & THINK

Would John Barnett want to know the total cost of each job for each of the following purposes? Why or why not?

a. Inventory valuation
b. External financial reporting
c. To determine fees charged to clients

Answers:
a. No. Service firms like Barnett and Company have no inventories.
b. No. Costs need not be assigned to individual clients to prepare Barnett and Company's financial statements.
c. Yes. Fees charged to clients must be high enough to cover indirect costs (and profits) as well as direct labour costs.

In summary: Noninventoriable costs are assigned to jobs only for internal decision making, not for external financial reporting.

You have now learned how to use a job cost system to assign costs to jobs. Review the Job Costing Decision Guidelines to solidify your understanding.

DECISION GUIDELINES Job Costing

Decision	Guidelines
Should I use job costing or process costing?	• *Job costing* for unique products produced in small batches • *Process costing* for identical products produced in large batches, often in a continuous flow

(continued)

Decision	Guidelines

How to record:
- Purchase and use of materials?

Purchase:

Materials Inventory	XX	
Accounts Payable (or Cash)		XX

Use:

Work in Process (direct materials)	XX	
Manufacturing Overhead (indirect materials)........	XX	
Materials Inventory...		XX

- Incurrence and assignment of labour?

Incurred:

Manufacturing Wages	XX	
Wages Payable (or Cash)................................		XX

Assigned:

Work in Process (direct labour)	XX	
Manufacturing Overhead (indirect labour)............	XX	
Manufacturing Wages.....................................		XX

How to determine whether utilities, insurance, property taxes, amortization, and so on are
- Manufacturing overhead?

Utilities, insurance, property taxes, and amortization expense are part of manufacturing overhead only if they are incurred in the manufacturing factory or plant.

- Operating expenses?

If not related to manufacturing, such expenses are operating expenses. For example, if related to a sales office or store, such expenses are marketing expenses. If related to executive headquarters, they are administrative expenses. If related to delivery vehicles or distribution centres, they are distribution expenses. These are all operating expenses, not manufacturing overhead.

How to record *actual* manufacturing overhead costs?

Manufacturing Overhead	XXX	
Accumulated Amortization—Plant		
and Equipment...		XX
Prepaid Insurance—Plant and Equipment		XX
Utilities Payable (or Cash)...............................		XX
and so on...		XX

How to compute a predetermined manufacturing overhead rate?

$$\frac{\text{Total estimated manufacturing overhead cost}}{\text{Total estimated quantity of allocation base}}$$

How to allocate manufacturing overhead?

Work in Process Inventory.....................................	XX	
Manufacturing Overhead..................................		XX

What is the *amount* of the allocated manufacturing overhead?

Actual quantity of the manufacturing overhead allocation base	$\times$	Predetermined manufacturing overhead rate

How to close Manufacturing Overhead at the end of the period?

Close directly to Cost of Goods Sold.

Which T-account summarizes the schedule of cost of goods manufactured?

Work in Process Inventory

How do service companies' employees trace direct labour to individual jobs?

Automated software directly captures the time employee spends on a client's job, or employee fills out a (usually computerized) time record.

When do companies allocate noninventoriable costs to jobs?

When they need total product costs for internal decisions (such as setting selling prices). For external reporting, companies assign only inventoriable costs to jobs.

for Your Review

Dawson Incorporated had the following inventories at the end of 2002:

Materials	$20,000
Work in Process	17,000
Finished Goods	11,000

During January 2003, Dawson Corporation actually used 300 machine hours and recorded the following transactions:

a. Purchased materials on account, $31,000.
b. Requisitioned (placed into production) direct materials, $39,000.
c. Manufacturing labour cost, $40,000.
d. Allocated manufacturing labour as follows: direct labour, 90 percent; indirect labour, 10 percent.
e. Requisitioned indirect materials, $3,000.
f. Incurred other manufacturing overhead, $13,000 (credit Accounts Payable).
g. Allocated manufacturing overhead to production at $60 per machine hour.
h. Completed production, $99,000.
i. Sold goods on account, $172,000; cost of goods sold, $91,400.
j. Closed ending balance of Manufacturing Overhead to Cost of Goods Sold.

Required

1. Record the transactions in the general journal.
2. Determine the ending balances in the three inventory accounts and Cost of Goods Sold.

Solution to Review Problem

Requirement 1 (Journal entries)

a.	Materials Inventory	31,000	
	Accounts Payable		31,000
b.	Work in Process Inventory	39,000	
	Materials Inventory		39,000
c.	Manufacturing Wages	40,000	
	Wages Payable		40,000
d.	Work in Process Inventory ($40,000 × 0.90)	36,000	
	Manufacturing Overhead ($40,000 × 0.10)	4,000	
	Manufacturing Wages		40,000
e.	Manufacturing Overhead	3,000	
	Materials Inventory		3,000
f.	Manufacturing Overhead	13,000	
	Accounts Payable		13,000
g.	Work in Process Inventory (300 hours × $60.00)	18,000	
	Manufacturing Overhead		18,000
h.	Finished Goods Inventory	99,000	
	Work in Process Inventory		99,000
i.	Accounts Receivable	172,000	

Sales Revenue		172,000	
Cost of Goods Sold	91,400		
Finished Goods Inventory		91,400	
j. Cost of Goods Sold	2,000		
Manufacturing Overhead		2,000	

Balance in Manufacturing Overhead for entry (j):

Manufacturing Overhead

(d)	4,000	(g)	18,000
(e)	3,000		
(f)	13,000		
Bal.	2,000		

Requirement 2 (Ending balances)

Materials Inventory

Bal.	20,000	(b)	39,000
(a)	31,000	(e)	3,000
Bal.	9,000		

Work In Process Inventory

Bal.	17,000	(h)	99,000
(b)	39,000		
(d)	36,000		
(g)	18,000		
Bal.	11,000		

Finished Goods Inventory

Bal.	11,000	(i)	91,400
(h)	99,000		
Bal.	18,600		

Cost of Goods Sold

(i)	91,400		
(j)	2,000		
Bal.	93,400		

Summary

1. Distinguish between job costing and process costing.
Process costing is used by companies that produce large numbers of identical products. Costs are accumulated for each production process, and then averaged over the many (identical) units passing through that process.

Companies that use job costing usually produce individual products or small batches of products that pass through production steps as a distinct, identifiable job lot. Jobs can differ greatly from one another in terms of materials, labour, and overhead. Costs are accumulated for each individual job. The *job cost record* includes direct materials, direct labour, and manufacturing overhead costs of producing the job.

2. Account for materials and labour in a manufacturer's job costing system. *Direct materials* costs are traced to individual jobs. They are added (debited) to Work in Process Inventory. *Indirect materials* cannot be easily traced to specific jobs, so their costs are added (debited) to the Manufacturing Overhead account. *Direct labour* costs are traced to jobs, and added (debited) to Work in Process

Inventory. *Indirect labour* such as maintenance and janitorial labour, is difficult to trace to individual jobs. Its costs are added (debited) to Manufacturing Overhead.

3. Account for manufacturing overhead in a manufacturer's job costing system. *Manufacturing overhead* is all manufacturing costs except direct materials and direct labour. Actual manufacturing overhead costs are accumulated as debits in the Manufacturing Overhead account. Manufacturing Overhead is allocated to jobs using a predetermined rate per unit of a *cost allocation base*. Ideally, the allocation base is the driver of the manufacturing overhead costs. Allocating manufacturing overhead requires a debit to Work in Process Inventory and a credit to Manufacturing Overhead. At the end of the period, any underallocated or overallocated manufacturing overhead is closed directly to Cost of Goods Sold in most circumstances.

4. Account for noninventoriable costs in job costing. For a service company, direct labour is traced to individual jobs (clients) using software or time records. Indirect costs such as marketing, office rent, and support staff salaries are allocated to jobs using predetermined indirect cost allocation rates. Service companies have no inventoriable costs, so they use job costing only for internal decisions, such as setting fees.

Self-Study Questions

Test your understanding of the chapter by marking the best answer for each of the following questions.

1. Job costing would be an appropriate system to account for the manufacture of (*p. 1135*)
   a. Aircraft
   b. Matches
   c. Zippers
   d. Cardboard boxes

2. What purpose does a job cost record serve? (*p. 1137*)
   a. Lists total material, labour, and overhead costs charged to a job
   b. Is management's basic internal document that helps to control costs in a job costing system
   c. Both a and b
   d. Neither a nor b

3. Using direct materials in production and charging direct labour costs to a job result in debits to (*pp. 1138–1142*)
   a. Direct Materials and Direct Labour
   b. Work in Process Inventory
   c. Finished Goods Inventory
   d. Materials Inventory and Manufacturing Wages

4. Which documents serve as a subsidiary ledger for the general ledger balance of Work in Process Inventory? (*p. 1138*)
   a. Job cost records
   b. Material requisitions
   c. Labour time records
   d. Materials ledger accounts

5. Why might direct labour be used as a manufacturing cost allocation base? Because overhead (*p. 1146*)
   a. Is very similar to direct labour
   b. Includes direct labour
   c. Occurs before direct labour is charged to a job
   d. Occurs in proportion to direct labour cost

6. At the end of a period, after overhead has been allocated to all jobs, Manufacturing Overhead has a credit balance of $900. We say that overhead is (*pp. 1150–1151*)
   a. Misstated
   b. Incorrectly allocated
   c. Overallocated
   d. Underallocated

7. Ideally, the allocation base for allocating manufacturing overhead costs should be (*p. 1147*)
   a. Direct Labour
   b. Purchases
   c. Direct materials
   d. The primary cost driver that causes the cost to be incurred

8. Actual overhead costs are (*p. 1150*)
   a. Debited to cost of goods sold directly
   b. Debited to manufacturing overhead
   c. Debited to materials inventory
   d. Credited to materials overhead

9. The numerator for the determination of the predetermined manufacturing overhead rate is (*p. 1147*)
   a. Total actual manufacturing overhead costs
   b. Total estimated manufacturing overhead costs
   c. Total direct material costs
   d. Total direct labour costs

10. In job costing (*p. 1153*)
   a. Costs are accumulated for each job
   b. Indirect costs are ignored
   c. Costs are accumulated for each production process
   d. Actual indirect costs are used to calculate the predetermined overhead rate.

Answers to the Self-Study Questions follow the Similar Accounting Terms.

Accounting Vocabulary

allocation base (*p. 1146*)
budgeted manufacturing overhead rate (*p. 1147*)
cost allocation (*p. 1146*)
cost assignment (*p. 1146*)
cost driver (*p. 1136*)
cost tracing (*p. 1146*)
job cost record (*p. 1137*)
job costing (*p. 1135*)
labour time record (*p. 1140*)

materials ledger (*p. 1138*)
materials requisition (*p. 1138*)
overallocated (manufacturing) overhead (*p. 1150*)
predetermined manufacturing overhead rate (*p. 1147*)
process costing (*p. 1135*)
time record (*p. 1152*)
underallocated (manufacturing) overhead (*p. 1150*)

Similar Accounting Terms

Cost allocation base   Cost application base; cost driver

Inventoriable costs   Product costs; manufacturing costs

Job costing   Job order costing

Overallocated overhead   Overapplied overhead

Predetermined manufacturing   Budgeted manufacturing
   overhead rate   overhead rate

Underallocated overhead   Underapplied overhead

Answers to Self-Study Questions

1. a	5. d	8. b
2. c	6. c	9. b
3. b	7. d	10. a
4. a		

Assignment Material

Questions

1. Explain the basic difference between job costing and process costing.

2. Give three examples of companies that would use job costing rather than process costing, and explain why.

3. How can information technology simplify tracing direct materials and direct labour to specific jobs?

4. What source document requests that raw materials be brought to the production floor? What journal entry does this source document support?

5. What is the essential nature of a job costing system? How can companies that use a job costing system operate with low levels of inventories?

6. Distinguish direct materials from indirect materials and direct labour from indirect labour. Direct materials and direct labour are debited to what inventory account when placed in production? To what account are indirect materials and indirect labour debited?

7. Give examples of direct materials and indirect materials for a caterer.

8. Is Manufacturing Overhead a temporary or permanent account? Explain how the account operates. What do the debits represent? What do the credits represent?

9. What document is used to trace direct manufacturing labour cost to specific jobs? Briefly describe how the document is used.

10. What document is used to charge materials cost to specific jobs? Briefly describe how the document is used.

11. Is manufacturing overhead cost allocated to jobs by a precise identification of the overhead cost of each job or by an estimation process? Briefly discuss the process.

12. What source document acts as the subsidiary ledger for the Work in Process Inventory control account?

13. Explain the distinctions among cost tracing, cost allocation, and cost assignment.

14. Would a heavily automated manufacturing plant be more likely to use machine hours or direct labour hours as the manufacturing overhead allocation base? Explain.

15. Why do companies use predetermined rather than actual manufacturing overhead rates?

16. When is manufacturing overhead underallocated? When is it overallocated?

17. Cost of goods sold is just one line in the income statement. What kinds of costs are included in cost of goods sold?

18. Which of the following accounts have their balances brought to zero at the end of the period, and which keep their ending balances to start the next period? Materials Inventory, Manufacturing Overhead, Finished Goods Inventory, Manufacturing Wages.

19. Why would an international professional services firm like Deloitte Consulting use job costing?

20. How do professional service firms such as law firms and management consulting firms trace direct labour to individual jobs?

Exercises

Exercise 20-1 *Distinguishing between job and process costing* **(Obj. 1)**

A Petro-Canada refining plant incurs $90,000 to refine 450,000 litres of unleaded gasoline. What is the cost per litre? Would Petro-Canada use job costing or process costing? Why?

Exercise 20-2 *Distinguishing between job and process costing* **(Obj. 1)**

Job costing and process costing differ in (a) the cost object, and (b) the number of units over which costs are averaged. Explain these two differences.

Exercise 20-3 *Analyzing job cost data* **(Obj. 2)**

Quicktech Printing Company Ltd. job cost records yielded the following information:

| Job | Date | | | Total Cost of |
No.	Started	Finished	Sold	Job at July 31
1	June 19	July 14	July 15	$ 2,000
2	June 29	July 21	July 26	20,000
3	July 3	Aug. 11	Aug. 13	7,000
4	July 7	July 29	Aug. 1	6,500
5	July 9	July 30	Aug. 2	1,500
6	July 22	Aug. 11	Aug. 13	1,200
7	July 23	July 27	July 29	2,800

Required

Compute Quicktech Printing Company Ltd.'s cost of (a) work in process inventory at July 31, (b) finished goods inventory at July 31, and (c) cost of goods sold for July.

Exercise 20-4 *Journalizing manufacturing transactions* **(Obj. 2, 3)**

Record the following transactions in the general journal:

a. Purchased materials on account, $22,000.

b. Paid manufacturing wages, $28,000.

c. Used in production: direct materials, $18,000; indirect materials, $4,000.

d. Applied manufacturing labour to jobs: direct labour, 80 percent; indirect labour, 20 percent.

e. Recorded manufacturing overhead: amortization, $26,000; insurance, $3,400; property tax, $8,400 (credit Property Tax Payable).

f. Applied manufacturing overhead to jobs, at a rate of 200 percent of direct labour.

g. Completed production, $54,000.

h. Sold inventory on account, $44,000; cost of goods sold, $28,000.

i. Paid marketing expenses, $4,000.

Exercise 20-5 *Identifying manufacturing transactions* **(Obj. 2)**

Describe the lettered transactions in the following manufacturing accounts:

Materials Inventory		Work in Process Inventory		Finished Goods Inventory	
(a)	(b)	(b)	(h)	(h)	(i)
	(e)	(d)	(j)		(j)
		(g)			

Manufacturing Wages		Manufacturing Overhead		Cost of Goods Sold	
(c)	(d)	(d)	(g)	(i)	(j)
		(e)			
		(f)			
		(j)			

Exercise 20-6 *Using the Work in Process Inventory account* **(Obj. 2)**

August production generated the following activity in the Work in Process Inventory account of Keremeos Manufacturing Company Inc.:

Work in Process Inventory

August 1 Bal.	15,000
Direct materials used	35,000
Direct labour charged to jobs	44,000
Manufacturing overhead applied to jobs	16,000

Completed production, not yet recorded, consists of jobs B-78, G-65, and Y-11, with total costs of $22,000, $29,000, and $44,000, respectively.

Required

1. Compute the cost of work in process at August 31.
2. Journalize completed production for August.
3. Journalize the credit sale of job G-65 for $61,000. Also make the cost-of-goods-sold entry.

Exercise 20-7 *Accounting for overhead cost* **(Obj. 3)**

Selected cost data for Senko Corp. are presented below:

Budgeted manufacturing overhead cost for the year	$112,500
Budgeted direct labour cost for the year	90,000
Actual manufacturing overhead cost for the year	105,000
Actual direct labour cost for the year	82,000

Required

1. Compute the predetermined manufacturing overhead rate per direct labour dollar.
2. Journalize the application of overhead cost for the year.
3. By what amount is manufacturing overhead overallocated or underallocated?
4. On the basis of your answer to requirement 3, journalize disposition of the manufacturing overhead balance.

Exercise 20-8 *Accounting for manufacturing overhead* **(Obj. 3)**

Bell Packaging Corp. uses a predetermined manufacturing overhead rate to allocate overhead to individual jobs, based on the direct labour hours. At the beginning of 2002, the company expected to incur the following:

Manufacturing overhead costs	$ 800,000
Direct labour cost	$2,000,000
Machine hours	100,000 hours
Direct labour hours	200,000 hours

At the end of 2002, the company had actually incurred:

Direct labour cost	$2,420,000
Amortization on manufacturing property, plant, and equipment	700,000
Property taxes on factory	40,000
Factory utility expense	30,000
Sales salaries	50,000
Delivery drivers' wages	30,000
Factory janitors' wages	20,000
Machine hours	90,000 hours
Direct labour hours	220,000 hours

Required

1. Compute Bell Packaging Corp.'s predetermined manufacturing overhead rate.

2. Record the summary journal entry for *allocating* manufacturing overhead.

3. Post the manufacturing overhead transactions to the Manufacturing Overhead T-account. Is manufacturing overhead underallocated or overallocated? By how much? Is cost of goods sold understated or overstated?

4. Close the Manufacturing Overhead account to Cost of Goods Sold. Does your entry increase or decrease cost of goods sold?

Exercise 20-9 *Prorating underallocated or overallocated manufacturing overhead (Obj. 3)*

Refer to the data in Exercise 20-8. The Bell Packaging Corp. accountant found an error in her 2002 expense records. Amortization on manufacturing property, plant, and equipment was actually $1,000,000, not the $700,000 she had originally reported. Unadjusted balances at the end of 2002 include

Materials Inventory	$400,000
Work in Process Inventory	140,000
Finished Goods Inventory	260,000
Cost of Goods Sold	1,200,000

Required

1. Is manufacturing overhead underallocated or overallocated? By how much?

2. Record the entry to prorate the underallocated or overallocated manufacturing overhead.

3. What are the adjusted ending balances of Materials Inventory, Work in Process Inventory, Finished Goods Inventory, and Cost of Goods Sold?

Exercise 20-10 *Job costing in a service company (Obj. 4)*

Eco-Systems Inc., an environmental consulting firm, specializes in advising electric utilities on compliance with recent environmental regulations. Eco-Systems uses a job cost system with a predetermined indirect cost allocation rate, computed as a percentage of expected direct labour costs.

At the beginning of 2003, manager Paul Watson prepared the following plan, or budget, for 2003:

| Direct labour hours (professionals) | 20,000 hours |
| Direct labour costs (professionals) | $1,400,000 |

Office rent	312,500
Support staff salaries	695,000
Utilities	182,500

North Island Light & Gas Ltd. is inviting several consultants to bid for its work. Paul Watson estimates that this job will require about 275 direct labour hours.

Required

1. Compute Eco-System Inc.'s (a) hourly direct labour cost rate, and (b) indirect cost allocation rate.

2. Compute the predicted cost of the North Island Light & Gas Ltd. job.

3. If Paul Watson wants to earn a profit that equals 20 percent of the job's cost, how much should the company bid for the North Island Light & Gas Ltd. job?

Challenge Exercise

Exercise 20-11 *Prorating manufacturing overhead* *(Obj. 3)*

At the end of the 2003 fiscal year, Mission Industries Ltd.'s manufacturing inventory and expense accounts show the following unadjusted account balances:

	Work in Process Inventory	Finished Goods Inventory	Cost of Goods Sold
Direct materials	$150,000	$ 255,000	$ 540,000
Direct labour	120,000	375,000	900,000
Manufacturing overhead	90,000	450,000	720,000
Total	$360,000	$1,080,000	$2,160,000

Mission's accountants applied overhead during the year using a predetermined rate of $50 per machine hour. At year end, they computed the actual rate of $55 per machine hour. The beginning balances of both Work in Process Inventory and Finished Goods Inventory were zero.

Required

1. How many machine hours were worked in 2003?

2. Was manufacturing overhead overallocated or underallocated for the year? By how much?

3. Prepare the general journal entry required to dispose of the overallocated or underallocated overhead.

Beyond the Numbers

Beyond the Numbers 20-1 *Accounting for manufacturing overhead* *(Obj. 3)*

The predetermined rate used to allocate manufacturing overhead usually turns out to be inaccurate (different from the actual overhead rate). As a result, accountants have to make adjusting entries at the end of the year to correct this error in allocating the manufacturing overhead. Because this predetermined overhead rate usually turns out to be "wrong" aren't these allocated costs misleading? Why don't accountants just use the actual manufacturing overhead rate?

Beyond the Numbers 20-2 *Accounting for manufacturing overhead* *(Obj. 3)*

McKenzie Preserves Ltd. is a small manufacturer of fruit preserves. The factory operates 50 weeks a year, and closes for the holidays during the last two weeks of December. McKenzie's manufacturing overhead cost is mostly straight-line amortization on the manufacturing plant and equipment. This cost is constant from month to month. The company allocates manufacturing overhead to products based on direct labour hours.

If McKenzie uses a monthly predetermined manufacturing overhead rate, will the December rate be higher or lower than in the other months? Why?

Now suppose that air-conditioning costs are a significant component of manufacturing overhead. McKenzie expects to incur much higher air-conditioning costs in July than in other months. If McKenzie uses monthly predetermined overhead rates, will the July manufacturing overhead rate be higher or lower than the rate in other months?

Should McKenzie compute its predetermined manufacturing overhead rate on an annual basis or a monthly basis? Explain.

Ethical Issue

Quebec has the greatest concentration of furniture manufacturers in Eastern Canada. These companies dominate furniture sales in the East. To break into this market, Charest Furniture Company Inc. is considering several options. Under one plan, Charest would charge no overhead cost to products destined for the Eastern market. This plan would enable Charest to offer its furniture at lower prices than its competitors charge and still show adequate profits on Eastern sales.

Required

1. Is Charest's pricing strategy ethical? Explain your answer.
2. Can Charest expect to follow this strategy indefinitely? Give your reason.

Problems (Group A)

Problem 20-1A   *Analyzing job cost data*   *(Obj. 2, 3)*

O'Shea Manufacturing Corp. job cost records yielded the following information. The company has a perpetual inventory system.

Job No.	Date Started	Date Finished	Sold	Total Cost of Job at June 30	Total Manufacturing Costs Added in July
1	26-5	7-6	9-6	$ 1,400	
2	3-6	12-6	13-6	2,800	
3	3-6	30-6	1-7	560	
4	17-6	24-7	27-7	400	$ 1,000
5	29-6	29-7	3-8	800	3,200
6	8-7	12-7	14-7		1,500
7	23-7	6-8	9-8		1,000
8	30-7	22-8	26-8		5,800

Required

1. Compute O'Shea Manufacturing Corp.'s cost of (a) work in process inventory at June 30 and July 31, (b) finished goods inventory at June 30 and July 31, and (c) cost of goods sold for June and July.
2. Make summary journal entries to record the transfer of completed units from work in process to finished goods for June and July.
3. Record the sale of Job 4 for $1,800.
4. What is the gross margin for Job 4? What other costs must this gross margin cover?

Problem 20-2A *Accounting for manufacturing transactions* *(Obj. 2, 3)*

Chinook Homes Inc. is a home builder in Medicine Hat, Alberta. Chinook Homes Inc. uses a perpetual inventory system and a job cost system in which each house represents a job. Because it constructs houses, the company uses accounts titled Construction Wages, Construction Overhead, and Supervisory Salaries (for indirect labour). The following transactions and events were completed during August:

a. Purchased materials on account, $296,700.
b. Requisitioned direct materials and used direct labour in construction:

	Direct Materials	Direct Labour
House 302............	$27,600	$14,325
House 303............	36,825	13,050
House 304............	34,200	15,375
House 305............	20,550	9,000
House 306............	47,925	25,275
House 307............	39,600	20,625

c. Amortization of equipment used in construction, $4,350.
d. Other overhead costs incurred on houses 302–307:

Supervisory salaries......................	$14,250
Equipment rentals paid................	12,975
Liability insurance expired..........	3,825

e. Applied overhead to jobs at the predetermined overhead rate of 35 percent of direct labour.
f. Houses completed: 302, 304, 305, 307.
g. Houses sold: 305 for $38,625; 307 for $86,250.

Required

1. Record the foregoing transactions and events in the general journal.

2. Open T-accounts for Work in Process Inventory and Finished Goods Inventory. Post the appropriate entries to these accounts, identifying each entry by letter. Determine the ending account balances, assuming that the beginning balances were zero.

3. Add the costs of unfinished houses, and show that this total amount equals the ending balance in the Work in Process Inventory account.

4. Add the costs of completed houses that have not yet been sold, and show that this total amount equals the ending balance in the Finished Goods Inventory account.

5. Compute the gross margin on each house that was sold. What costs must the gross margin cover for Chinook Homes Inc.?

Problem 20-3A *Preparing and using a job cost record* *(Obj. 2, 3)*

Digital Reproductions Inc. manufactures CDs & DVDs for computer software and entertainment companies. The company uses job costing and has a perpetual inventory system.

On November 2, 2003, the company began production of 5,000 DVDs, job number 378, for Alliance Pictures for $1.20 each. The company incurred the following costs:

Date	Materials Requisition No.	Description	Amount
Nov. 2	36	31 kg polycarbonate plastic @ $12	$372
Nov. 2	37	14 kg acrylic plastic @ $50	700
Nov. 3	42	3 kg refined aluminum @ $48	144

Date	Time Record No.	Description	Amount
Nov. 2	556	12 hours @ $20	$240
Nov. 3	557	25 hours @ $18	450

Digital Reproductions Inc. charges overhead to jobs on the basis of the relationship between budgeted overhead ($537,600) and budgeted direct labour ($448,000). Job 378 was completed and shipped on November 3.

Required

1. Prepare a job cost record, similar to that in Exhibit 20-2, for Job 378.
2. Journalize in summary form the requisition of direct materials and the application of direct labour and manufacturing overhead to Job 378.
3. Journalize completion of the job and the sale of the DVDs to Alliance Pictures.
4. How will what you learned from this problem help you manage a business?

Problem 20-4A *Comprehensive accounting treatment of manufacturing transactions (Obj. 2, 3)*

Y-Tech Inc. manufactures specialized parts used in its business. Initially, the company manufactured the parts for its own use, but it gradually began selling them to other companies as well. Y-Tech Inc.'s trial balance on April 1, 2002, the beginning of the current fiscal year, follows.

April 1 balances in the subsidiary ledgers were:

Materials ledger: circuit boards, $3,160; electronic parts, $3,920; indirect
materials, $860.
Work in process ledger: Job 145, $71,760.
Finished goods ledger: relays, $10,620; transmission lines, $9,560;
switches, $17,740.

Y-TECH INC.
Trial Balance
April 1, 2002

Cash	$ 38,320	
Accounts receivable	148,580	
Inventories:		
Materials	7,940	
Work in process	71,760	
Finished goods	37,920	
Capital assets	489,140	
Accumulated amortization		$207,360
Accounts payable		47,920
Wages payable		7,340
Common stock		240,000
Retained earnings		291,040
Sales revenue		—
Cost of goods sold	—	
Manufacturing wages	—	
Manufacturing overhead	—	
Marketing and general expenses	—	—
	$793,660	$793,660

April transactions are summarized as follows:

a. Materials purchased on credit: circuit boards, $13,080; electronic parts, $31,660; indirect materials, $7,180.

b. Materials used in production (requisitioned):
Job 145: circuit boards, $680
Job 146: circuit boards, $7,140; electronic parts, $9,960.
Job 147: circuit boards, $3,940; electronic parts, $7,460.
     Indirect materials, $5,160.

c. Manufacturing wages incurred during April, $64,860, of which $61,040 was paid. Wages payable at March 31 were paid during April, $7,340.

d. Labour time records for the month: Job 145, $7,000; Job 146, $22,100; Job 147, $21,880; Indirect labour, $13,880.

e. Manufacturing overhead incurred on account, $9,260.

f. Amortization recorded on factory plant and equipment, $6,900.

g. Payments on account, $72,080.

h. Manufacturing overhead was applied at the budgeted rate of 70 percent of direct labour.

i. Jobs completed during the month: Job 145, 400 relays at total cost of $84,340; Job 146, 200 switches at total cost of $54,670.

j. Marketing and general expenses paid, $54,940.

k. Credit sales on account: all of Job 145 for $195,280 (cost $84,340); Job 146, 120 switches for $70,200 (cost, $32,802).

l. Collections on account, $254,940.

m. Close the manufacturing overhead account balance to cost of goods sold.

Required

1. Open T-accounts for the general ledger, the materials ledger, the work in process ledger, and the finished goods ledger. Insert each account balance as given, and use the reference *Bal.*

2. Record the April transactions directly in the accounts, using the letters as references. Y-Tech has a perpetual inventory system.

3. Prepare a trial balance at April 30 of the current year.

4. Prepare a multiple-step income statement through operating income for April 2002. Take amounts directly from the trial balance.

Problem 20-5A   *Job costing in a service company   (Obj. 4)*

Oneclick Inc. is a Web site design and consulting firm. The firm uses a job cost system, where each client is a different "job." Oneclick Inc. traces direct labour, licensing costs, and travel costs directly to each job (client). It allocates indirect costs to jobs based on a predetermined indirect cost allocation rate, computed as a percentage of direct labour costs.

At the beginning of 2003, manager Laura Schwartz prepared the following plan, or budget:

Direct labour hours (professional)	6,000 hours
Direct labour costs (professional)..................	$600,000
Support staff salaries......................................	70,000
Computer lease	34,000
Office supplies...	11,000
Office rent	35,000

In November 2003, Oneclick Inc. served several clients. Records for two clients appear here:

	Planet Foods	Deception Fragrances
Direct labour hours	675 hours	25 hours
Licensing costs	$1,325	$100
Travel costs	$12,000	—

Required

1. Compute Oneclick Inc.'s predetermined indirect cost allocation rate for 2003.

2. Compute the total cost of each of the two jobs detailed above.

3. If Oneclick Inc. wants to earn profits equal to 30 percent of sales revenue, how much (what total fee) should it charge each of these two clients?

4. Why does Oneclick Inc. assign costs to jobs?

Problems (Group B)

Problem 20-1B *Analyzing job cost data* **(Obj. 2, 3)**

Weyburn Cabinets Inc.'s job cost records yielded the following information. The company has a perpetual inventory system.

Job No.	Date Started	Date Finished	Date Sold	Total Cost of Job at March 31	Total Manufacturing Costs Added in April
1	26-2	7-3	9-3	$3,300	
2	3-2	12-3	13-3	2,400	
3	29-3	31-3	3-4	450	
4	31-3	1-4	1-4	750	$ 600
5	17-3	24-4	27-4	2,250	3,750
6	8-4	12-4	14-4		1,050
7	23-4	6-5	9-5		1,800
8	30-4	22-5	26-5		900

Required

1. Compute Weyburn's cost of (a) work in process inventory at March 31 and April 30, (b) finished goods inventory at March 31 and April 30, and (c) cost of goods sold for March and April.

2. Make summary journal entries to record the transfer of completed units from work in process to finished goods for March and April.

3. Record the sale of Job 5 for $9,000.

4. Compute the gross margin for Job 5. What costs must the gross margin cover?

Problem 20-2B *Accounting for manufacturing transactions* **(Obj. 2, 3)**

Oceanside Homes Inc. builds prefabricated cottages in a factory. The company uses a perpetual inventory system and a job cost system in which each cottage represents a job. The following transactions and events were completed during May:

a. Purchased materials on account, $422,000.
b. Requisitioned direct materials and used direct labour in manufacturing:

	Direct Materials	Direct Labour
Cottage 613	$52,200	$23,200
Cottage 614	83,400	45,000
Cottage 615	102,000	30,000
Cottage 616	108,000	47,600

Cottage 617	87,800	41,400	
Cottage 618	65,600	35,200	

c. Amortization of manufacturing equipment used on different cottages, $28,600.

d. Other overhead costs incurred on cottages 613–618:

Manufacturing wages...................	$43,200
Equipment rentals paid................	16,000
Liability insurance expired	7,800

e Applied overhead to jobs at the predetermined rate of 30 percent of direct labour.

f. Cottages completed: 613, 615, 616.

g. Cottages sold: 615 for $158,000; 616 for $207,800.

Required

1. Record the foregoing transactions and events in the general journal.

2. Open T-accounts for Work in Process Inventory and Finished Goods Inventory. Post the appropriate entries to these accounts, identifying each entry by letter. Determine the ending account balances, assuming that the beginning balances were zero.

3. Add the costs of unfinished cottages, and show that this total amount equals the ending balance in the Work in Process Inventory account.

4. Add the costs of completed cottages that have not yet been sold, and show that this total amount equals the ending balance in the Finished Goods Inventory account.

5. Compute the gross margin on each house that was sold. What cost must the gross margin cover for Oceanside Homes Inc.?

Problem 20-3B   Preparing and using a job cost record   (Obj. 2, 3)

Precision Manufacturing Corp. manufactures assembly-line equipment that is used by other companies in their manufacturing processes. Precision Manufacturing Corp. has a job cost system and a perpetual inventory system.

On September 22, 2002, Precision Manufacturing Corp. received an order for 50 industrial-grade transmission belts from Lance Corporation at a price of $80 each. The job, assigned number 449, was promised for October 15. After purchasing the materials, Precision Manufacturing Corp. began production on September 30 and incurred the following costs in completing the order:

Date	Materials Requisition No.	Description	Amount
Sept. 30	593	20 kg rubber @ $13	$260
Oct. 2	598	30 m polyester fabric @ $14	420
Oct. 3	622	12 m steel cord @ $15	180

Date	Time Record No.	Description	Amount
Sept. 30	1754	10 hours @ $14	$ 140
Oct. 3	1805	40 hours @ $12	480

Precision Manufacturing Corp. charges manufacturing overhead to jobs on the basis of the relationship between expected overhead ($450,000) and direct labour ($300,000). Job 449 was completed on October 3 and shipped to Lance Corporation on October 5.

Required

1. Prepare a job cost record, similar to that in Exhibit 20-2, for Job 449.

2. Journalize in summary form the requisition of direct materials and the application of direct labour and manufacturing overhead to Job 449.

3. Journalize completion of the job and sale of the goods.

4. How will what you learned from this problem help you manage a business?

Problem 20-4B *Comprehensive accounting treatment of manufacturing transactions (Obj. 2, 3)*

Central Electric Company Ltd. manufactures specialized parts used in the generation of power. Initially, the company manufactured the parts for its own use, but it gradually began selling them to other public utilities as well. The trial balance of Central Electric's manufacturing operation on January 1, 2003, follows:

CENTRAL ELECTRIC COMPANY LTD.—MANUFACTURING OPERATIONS Trial Balance January 1, 2003		
Cash	$ 66,000	
Accounts receivable	130,000	
Inventories:		
Materials	28,000	
Work in process	87,000	
Finished goods	158,000	
Capital assets	686,000	
Accumulated amortization		$292,000
Accounts payable		168,000
Wages payable		12,000
Common stock		400,000
Retained earnings		283,000
Sales revenue		—
Cost of goods sold	—	
Manufacturing wages	—	
Manufacturing overhead	—	
Marketing and general expenses	—	—
	$1,155,000	$1,155,000

January 1 balances in the subsidiary ledgers were:

> Materials ledger: petrochemicals, $10,000; electronic parts, $16,000; indirect materials, $2,000.
> Work in process ledger: Job 86, $87,000.
> Finished goods ledger: transformers, $71,000; transmission lines, $45,000; switches, $42,000.

January transactions are summarized as follows:

a. Materials purchased on credit: petrochemicals, $40,000; electronic parts, $57,000; indirect materials, $12,000.

b. Materials used in production (requisitioned):
Job 86: petrochemicals, $8,000.
Job 87: petrochemicals, $20,000; electronic parts, $12,000.
Job 88: petrochemicals, $15,000; electronic parts, $60,000.
Indirect materials, $11,000.

c. Manufacturing wages incurred during January, $104,000, of which $100,000 was paid. Wages payable at December 31 were paid during January, $12,000.

d. Labour time records for the month: Job 86, $8,000; Job 87, $41,000; Job 88, $33,000; indirect labour, $22,000.

e. Manufacturing overhead incurred on account, $55,000.

f. Amortization recorded on manufacturing plant and equipment, $13,000.

g. Payments on account, $160,000.

h. Manufacturing overhead was applied at the predetermined rate of 120 percent of direct labour.

i. Jobs completed during the month: Job 86, one transformer at total cost of $112,600; Job 87, 400 switches at total cost of $122,200.

j. Marketing and general expenses paid, $43,000.

k. Credit sales on account: all of Job 86 for $182,000 (cost $112,600); Job 87, 300 switches for $176,000 (cost, $91,650).

l. Collections on account, $375,000.

m. Close the manufacturing overhead account balance to cost of goods sold.

Required

1. Open T-accounts for the general ledger, the materials ledger, the work in process ledger, and the finished goods ledger. Insert each account balance as given, and use the reference *Bal*.

2. Record the January transactions directly in the accounts, using the letters as references. Central Electric has a perpetual inventory system.

3. Prepare a trial balance at January 31, 2003.

4. Prepare a multiple-step income statement through operating income for January 2003. Take amounts directly from the trial balance.

Problem 20-5B   *Job costing in a service company*   **(Obj. 4)**

Banner.com is an Internet advertising agency. The firm uses a job cost system in which each client is a different "job." Banner.com traces direct labour, licensing costs, and travel costs directly to each job (client). The company allocates indirect costs to jobs based on a predetermined indirect cost allocation rate, computed as a percentage of direct labour costs.

At the beginning of 2003, manager Michael Whitehead prepared the following plan, or budget:

Direct labour hours (professional)	30,000 hours
Direct labour costs (professional)..................	$3,000,000
Support staff salaries.......................................	1,000,000
Utilities..	200,000
Art supplies	40,000
Office rent	400,000
Leased computer equipment	160,000

In January 2003, Banner.com served several clients. Records for two clients appear here:

	Port Angeles Tennis and Golf Resort	Woo's Cuisine
Direct labour hours..............................	400 hours	50 hours
Licensing costs	$ 1,250	$150
Travel costs	$10,000	—

Required

1. Compute Banner.com's predetermined indirect cost allocation rate for 2003.

2. Compute the total cost of each of the two jobs detailed above.

3. If the company wants to earn profits equal to 20 percent of sales revenue, how much (what total fee) should the company charge each of these two clients?

4. Why does Banner.com assign costs to jobs?

Challenge Problems

Problem 20-1C *Allocating overhead or not* *(Obj. 3, 4)*

There is a school of thought that believes that all overhead should be treated as a period cost and charged to expense when incurred.

Required

1. State the effect on the financial statements of charging overhead to expense when incurred of a growing company. Of a steady-state company.
2. State the potential effect on management decision making of charging overhead costs to expense as incurred.

Problem 20-2C *Allocating costs to products in a job order costing system* *(Obj. 2, 3)*

Stratford Manufacturing Corp. has manufactured furniture for the past 60 years. When the company first started, the ratio of costs was: material—20 percent; direct labour—70 percent; and machine labour—10 percent. Now the company is automated and while material is still 20 percent, machine labour is 60 percent.

Required

1. How did the company allocate overhead in 1940? Why?
2. How should the company allocate overhead in 2002? Why?

Extending Your Knowledge

Decision Problems

1. Costing and pricing identical products *(Obj. 2, 3)*

GiftPak Chocolate Ltd. is located in Regina. The company prepares gift boxes of chocolates for private parties and corporate promotions. Each order contains a selection of chocolates determined by the customer, and the box is designed according to the customer's specifications.

One of GiftPak's largest customers is Webtech Inc., a provider of Internet services. This organization sends chocolates to its clients each Christmas and also provides them to employees at the firm's gatherings. Webtech Inc.'s manager, Andrew Kirkham, placed the client gift order in September for 500 boxes of cream-filled dark chocolates. But Webtech Inc. did not place its December staff-party order until the last week of November. This order was for an additional 100 boxes of chocolates identical to the ones to be distributed to clients.

The cost per box for the original 500-box order was budgeted as follows:

Chocolate, filling, wrappers, box	$16.00
Employee time to fill and wrap the box (10 min.)	2.00
Manufacturing overhead	1.00
Total manufacturing cost	$19.00

Joan Davison, the president of GiftPak Chocolate Ltd., priced the order at $24 per box.

In the past few months, GiftPak Chocolate Ltd. has experienced price increases for both dark chocolate and employee time. All other costs have remained the same. The cost per box for the second order was predicted to be:

Chocolate, filling, wrappers, box	$17.00
Employee time to fill and wrap the box (10 min.)	2.20
Manufacturing overhead	1.10
Total manufacturing cost	$20.30

Required

1. Do you agree with the cost analysis for the second order? Explain your answer.
2. Should the two orders be accounted for as one job or two in GiftPak Chocolate Ltd.'s system?
3. What sale price per box should Joan Davison set for the second order? What are the advantages and disadvantages of this price?

2. Costing jobs and using job cost information to bid on contracts   (Obj. 2, 3)

National Electronics Systems Ltd. (NES) is a government contractor that specializes in electronics systems for military applications. The company's job costing system has two direct cost categories: direct materials and direct labour. NES uses direct labour hours as its manufacturing overhead cost application base. For the current fiscal year, budgeted total manufacturing overhead cost was $4,600,000. Budgeted direct labour hours for all production totaled 200,000.

NES bids on government contracts (jobs) by adding 80 percent to the predicted total manufacturing cost of the contract. The 80-percent markup covers the other value chain costs of the contract and provides the company's profit.

NES is preparing to bid on two new contracts. If the bids are accepted, the contracts will be produced as Job A and Job B. Budget data relating to the contracts are as follows:

	Job A	Job B
Direct materials cost...........	$60,000	$420,000
Direct labour cost................	$24,000	$320,000
Total direct labour hours ...	1,200	16,000
Number of output units	100	1,000

Required

1. Compute NES's manufacturing overhead cost application rate for the current year.
2. Compute the budgeted (predicted) total manufacturing cost and the unit cost of Job A and of Job B.
3. Determine the amount per output unit that NES should bid on each contract.
4. Suppose that the government awards both contracts to NES. What factors will determine the actual profit that NES will earn?

21

Process Costing

CHAPTER OBJECTIVES

After studying this chapter, you should be able to

1 Distinguish between the flow of costs in process costing and job costing

2 Record process costing transactions

3 Compute equivalent units of production

4 Assign costs to units completed and to units in ending work in process inventory

5 Account for a second processing department by the FIFO method

6 Account for a second processing department by the weighted-average method

A regional producer and distributor of premium quality specialty beers (also known as "craft" beers), Big Rock Brewery Ltd. is committed to developing its business by following three sound business fundamentals:

- Consistently brewing distinctive, premium quality craft beers;
- Constantly providing superior personalized customer service; and
- Creating and sustaining strong community relationships within each core market area.

Big Rock Brewery Ltd. is a fast-growing regional micro-brewery located in Calgary. It ranks as one of the top five draft beer producers in North America. It was founded in 1985 and markets its products in Alberta, British Columbia, and Manitoba, as well as in the United States.

As well as being noted for the high quality of its products, Big Rock is noted for the names of its products,

which include "Warthog Ale," "Grasshopper Wheat Ale," and "Chinook Pale Ale."

Brewing beer is a three-stage process that involves the steeping, boiling, and fermenting of malted barley, hops, water, and yeast. The purity of the inputs, especially the water, is considered to be quite important. Big Rock Brewery's management considers its use of innovative brewing technology and unfailing attention to quality control to be important factors in its success.

Despite intense competition from Canada's two major breweries, other regional breweries, and U.S. breweries, Big Rock's growth in net sales and net income has been significant. Net sales increased by over 130 percent from 1994 to 2000. The company and its workers are concerned with continuous improvement in quality and productivity in an attempt to continue Big Rock Brewery's amazing growth.

Source: Big Rock Brewery Ltd. Annual Report for the year ended March 31, 2000.

HOW MUCH does it cost Big Rock Brewery to make a batch of Warthog Ale? What is the value of the inventory of malted barley, hops, and yeast? How efficient was the brewing and bottling process last week? Much like their counterparts in other manufacturing companies, managers at Big Rock Brewery use accounting information to answer these questions.

OBJECTIVE 1
Distinguish between the flow of costs in process costing and job costing

Big Rock Brewery Ltd.
www.bigrockbrewery.com

General Mills, Inc.
www.generalmills.com

Petro-Canada
www.petro-canada.ca

Sony of Canada Ltd.
www.sony.ca

Palm, Inc.
www.palm.com

Process Costing: An Overview

Manufacturers develop product costing systems to assign direct materials, direct labour, and overhead costs to their products. The two basic types of product costing systems are *job costing* and *process costing*. We saw in Chapter 20 that job costing is a system used to determine the cost to produce custom goods and services. In contrast, companies like Big Rock Brewery, General Mills, and Petro-Canada use process costing to assign costs to goods that are mass produced in a continuous sequence of steps, called processes. Process industries produce large numbers of identical units, such as CDs, Sony Playstations®, PalmPilots™ and cases of salsa sauce. Companies that use process costing are in the petroleum, food and beverage, pharmaceutical, and chemical industries, to name a few. Exhibit 21-1 summarizes key differences between job costing and process costing.

Whether a company uses job costing or process costing depends on the products it produces and the nature of its production operations. Companies in custom industries typically divide their operations into jobs. Companies in mass-production industries typically divide their operations into departments—one for each

EXHIBIT 21-1

Differences between Job and Process Costing

	Job Costing	Process Costing
Cost object	Job	Process
Outputs	Single units or small batches, with large differences between jobs	Large quantities of identical units
Extent of averaging	Less averaging—costs are averaged over the small number of units in a batch (often 1 unit)	More averaging—costs are averaged over the many identical units in the large batch

manufacturing process. The flow of goods through the departments is continuous and repetitive. For example, to produce Kellogg's Corn Flakes, Kellogg's has one department for forming and toasting the flakes and a second department for packaging. The company does not use job cost records to keep track of costs. Instead, it accumulates costs in each department for each production period. Unit cost is computed by dividing total cost by the number of units produced. For example, if it costs $400,000 to produce 1,000,000 boxes of corn flakes, the unit cost is $0.40 ($400,000/1,000,000).

Kelloggs's
www.kelloggs.ca

STOP & THINK

Why are job cost records used in job costing systems but not in process costing systems?

Answer: Job cost records are used to keep track of the costs of custom goods because the unit costs of the goods differ. For example, a 750-square-metre house built by a contractor for one customer does not cost the same to build as a 750-square-metre house for another customer. The contractor uses job cost records to keep track of the costs of each house. But companies in process industries sell identical goods—with identical unit costs—to different customers. Schneider may sell 10,000 packages of hot dogs to one customer and 5,000 packages to another. Job cost records are not needed to determine the costs of the two orders. The company's accountants simply multiply the order quantities by the unit cost.

Schneider's
www.schneiders.ca

Suppose that Enesco Corp., the manufacturing company at the bottom of Exhibit 21-2, produces ceramic figurines in three steps. It mixes materials to produce liquid ceramic, injects the liquid ceramic into moulds, and heats the moulded figurines for hardness. The company has a Mixing Department, a Moulding Department, and a Heating Department. To account for the costs that make up the finished products, Enesco accountants use three Work in Process Inventory accounts—one for mixing, one for moulding, and one for heating.

In Exhibit 21-2, mixing costs accumulate in the Work in Process Inventory—Mixing account. After mixing is completed, the liquid ceramic is transferred to the Moulding Department, and the costs are transferred to Work in Process—Moulding. When moulding is completed, product costs flow to Work in Process—Heating and then to Finished Goods Inventory. When the figurines are sold, the cost of the inventory is transferred to Cost of Goods Sold. In contrast, a job costing system has only one Work in Process Inventory account.

Exhibit 21-3 on page 1180 uses dollar amounts to illustrate how costs flow through a process system. Each Enesco Work in Process Inventory account lists direct materials, direct labour, and manufacturing overhead. All amounts are assumed.

EXHIBIT 21-2

Comparison of Job Costing and Process Costing

Job Costing:
(Examples include aircraft, construction, furniture, auditing, jewellery, and machinery)

Direct Materials
Direct Labour
Manufacturing
Overhead
→ Job 100, Job 101, Job 102 → Finished Goods → Cost of Goods Sold

Work in Process Inventory		Finished Goods Inventory		Cost of Goods Sold
xx	xx →	xx	xx →	xx

Process Costing:
(Example: Enesco Corp., manufacturer of ceramic figurines)

Direct Materials
Direct Labour
Manufacturing
Overhead
→ Mixing Process → Moulding Process → Heating Process → Finished Goods → Cost of Goods Sold

Work in Process Inventory—Mixing		Work in Process Inventory—Moulding		Work in Process Inventory—Heating		Finished Goods Inventory		Cost of Goods Sold
xx	xx →	xx	xx →	xx	xx →	xx	xx →	xx

Recording Costs

The journal entries for process costing are similar to those for job costing. Direct materials, direct labour, and manufacturing overhead are recorded as follows (all amounts are in thousands and are assumed):

Materials Inventory	11	
Accounts Payable		11
Manufacturing Wages	4	
Wages Payable		4
Manufacturing Overhead	10	
Accumulated Amortization		2
Property Tax Payable		2
Accounts Payable, and so on		6

To purchase materials and incur direct labour and manufacturing overhead.

The main difference between job costing and process costing is in assigning the costs of direct materials, direct labour, and manufacturing overhead. (Chapter 20, page 1135, distinguishes between *accumulating* actual costs and *assigning* costs to jobs and processes.) Job costing assigns costs to individual *jobs* that are transferred from Work in Process Inventory directly to Finished Goods Inventory. Process costing assigns costs to *processes*. There is a separate Work in Process Inventory account for each process. As products move from one process to the next, their costs flow from one Work in Process Inventory account to the next.

The following entries detail the flow of costs through the process costing system in Exhibit 21-3.

KEY POINT

The journal entries for a process costing system are essentially the same as the entries for a job costing system. The main difference is that in a job costing system, goods are transferred from the Work in Process Inventory to the Finished Goods Inventory. In a process costing system, goods are transferred from one Work in Process Inventory account to another.

Work in Process Inventory—Mixing	7	
Materials Inventory		7
Work in Process Inventory—Mixing	2	
Manufacturing Wages		2
Work in Process Inventory—Mixing	3	
Manufacturing Overhead		3

To requisition materials, assign direct labour cost, and assign manufacturing overhead cost to the Mixing Department.

Work in Process Inventory—Moulding	10	
Work in Process Inventory—Mixing		10

To transfer cost from the Mixing Department to the Moulding Department.

Work in Process Inventory—Moulding	1	
Manufacturing Wages		1
Work in Process Inventory—Moulding	2	
Manufacturing Overhead		2

To record the additional labour and overhead cost of the Moulding Department.

Work in Process Inventory—Heating	9	
Work in Process Inventory—Moulding		9

To transfer cost from the Moulding Department to the Heating Department.

Entries for the Heating Department parallel those for the Moulding Department:

Work in Process Inventory—Heating	1	
Manufacturing Wages		1
Work in Process Inventory—Heating	5	
Manufacturing Overhead		5

To record the additional labour and overhead cost of the Heating Department.

Finished Goods Inventory	12	
Work in Process Inventory—Heating		12

To transfer the cost of goods completed from the Heating Department to Finished Goods Inventory.

Cost of Goods Sold	8	
Finished Goods Inventory		8

To account for the cost of goods sold.

Notice that in process costing

- Direct materials, direct labour, and manufacturing overhead costs are assigned to separate Work in Process Inventory accounts *for each process*.

- Costs are transferred, along with the units, from one Work in Process Inventory account to the next. Costs are not transferred to Finished Goods Inventory *until the last process is completed.*

Building Blocks of Process Costing

Exhibit 21-3 shows that the total cost of the first process, mixing, was $12,000 ($7,000 direct materials + $2,000 direct labour + $3,000 manufacturing overhead). Where did these costs of $12,000 go? The exhibit shows that $10,000 was transferred out of Work in Process—Mixing and into Work in Process—Moulding, leaving a $2,000 ending balance in Work in Process—Mixing. How de we know how much of the $12,000 to assign to the ceramic figurines transferred out to the Moulding Department versus those still in ending Work in Process Inventory—Mixing? This is a key question in process costing. But before we can answer it, we must first learn about two building blocks of process costing:

- Conversion costs
- Equivalent units

Conversion Costs

Conversion costs are all manufacturing costs *other than* direct materials costs. Chapter 19 introduced three kinds of manufacturing costs: direct materials, direct labour, and indirect manufacturing costs (manufacturing overhead). Many companies, particularly those using automated production processes, have found that

EXHIBIT 21-3

Flow of Costs Through a Process Costing System (amounts in thousands)

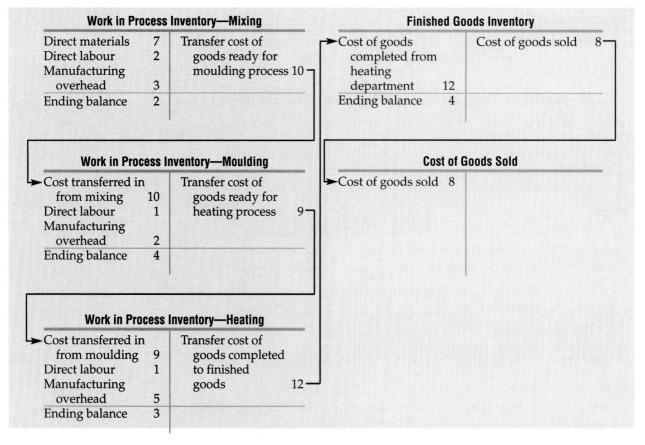

direct labour costs are only a small part of total manufacturing costs. Thus, such companies increasingly use only two categories:

- Direct materials
- Conversion costs (direct labour plus manufacturing overhead)

Collapsing direct labour and manufacturing overhead into a single category simplifies the accounting. We call this category *conversion costs* because it is the cost (direct labour and manufacturing overhead) to *convert* raw materials into new finished products.

Tracking the Flow of Costs

In process costing, the accounting task is to track the flow of costs through the production process. This task has two parts:

1. Account for the cost of goods that have been completed in one department and transferred out to the next department.
2. Account for the cost of incomplete units that remain as a department's ending work in process inventory.

Let's examine Recreational Divers Ltd., a sporting goods company that manufactures swim masks. This company's Shaping Department shapes the body of the swim masks. The Shaping Department's direct material is the plastic that is formed into Recreational Divers' masks. The partially completed masks are then moved to the Finishing Department, where the mask bodies are finished and the clear faceplates are inserted and sealed in place.

Assume that during October 2003, the Shaping Department incurs the following costs in processing 50,000 masks:

Direct materials		$140,000
Conversion costs:		
Direct labour	$21,250	
Manufacturing overhead	46,750	68,000
Costs to account for		$208,000

If the shaping process is complete for all 50,000 masks, the costs to be transferred to Work in Process Inventory—Finishing are the full $208,000. The unit cost is $4.16 ($208,000/50,000 units). But suppose that shaping is complete for only 40,000 units. At October 31, 2003, the Shaping Department still has 10,000 masks in process. How do we compute unit cost when the total cost applies to finished units *and* unfinished units? Accountants answer this question by using the concept of *equivalent units of production*.

Equivalent Units of Production

OBJECTIVE 3
Compute equivalent units of production

Equivalent units is a measure of the amount of work done during a production period, expressed in terms of fully complete units of output.

Assume that the 10,000 unfinished units still in the Shaping Department of Recreational Divers Ltd. are one-quarter complete as to conversion work. For costs that are incurred evenly throughout the production process, the number of partially complete units times the percentage of completion equals the number of conversion equivalent units:

Number of partially complete units	×	Percentage of process completed	=	Number of conversion equivalent units
10,000 units	×	**25% complete**	=	**2,500 equivalent units**

This formula holds only for costs that are incurred evenly throughout the production process. This is usually true for conversion costs (direct labour and manufacturing overhead). For the Shaping Department, the number 2,500 tells us how many whole units of conversion work are represented by the incomplete units. We add the 2,500 units to the number of finished units—40,000—to arrive at the period's equivalent units of production regarding conversion: 42,500.

Be careful to distinguish the *end of the production process* from the *end of the accounting period.* Goods at the end of the production process are transferred to the next process or to finished goods. For example, Recreation Divers Ltd.'s completed swim masks proceed to the finished goods warehouse. By contrast, at the end of the accounting period, goods that are only partway through the production process are the ending work in process inventory. In our example, Recreational Divers Ltd.'s ending work in process inventory includes swim masks that have been shaped but not yet been through the Finishing Department.

STOP & THINK

The idea of equivalent units is not confined to manufacturing situations. It is a basic common denominator for measuring activities, output, and workload. For example, colleges and universities measure student enrollments in "full-time equivalents." Suppose that a full-time class load is 12 hours per term. Assume that 1,000 students are taking a full load and that 1,000 other students are taking an average of six hours in classes. What is the full-time equivalent enrollment?

Answer: 1,500 students [$1,000 + (1,000 \times 6/12)$].

WORKING IT OUT

Data for the next few Working it Outs are summarized below.

A company using a process cost system has two departments—mixing and packaging. For the Mixing Department:

Units:

WIP, May 1	–0–
Started production	5,000
Transferred out—May	4,500
WIP, May 31 (45% complete as to direct materials; 10% complete as to conversion costs)	500

Costs:

WIP, May 1	$ –0–
Costs added during May:	
Direct Materials	15,120
Conversion Costs:	
Direct Labour	$11,102
Man. Overhead	16,653 27,755
Total costs added during May	$42,875

Compute the equivalent units.

A:	Equiv. Units	
	Dir. Mtls.	Conv. Costs
Trans. out	4,500	4,500
WIP, May 31	225*	50**
Equiv. units	4,725	4,550

*500 × 0.45 = 225
**500 × 0.10 = 50

Steps in Process Cost Accounting

Using the data from the swim mask example, we discuss a five-step application of process costing to each production department. Our example is the Shaping Department of Recreational Divers Ltd.

Step 1: Summarize the Flow of Physical Units

Exhibit 21-4 tracks the movement of swim masks into and out of the Shaping Department. We assume for simplicity that work began October 1, 2003, so the Work in Process Inventory account had a zero balance at September 30, 2003. Of the 50,000 masks started in October, 40,000 were completely shaped and transferred out to the Finishing Department during the month. The remaining 10,000 partially shaped masks are in the Shaping Department's ending work in process inventory on October 31, 2003.

Step 2: Compute Output in Terms of Equivalent Units

We compute equivalent units separately for the two types of costs incurred in manufacturing—direct materials and conversion costs—because work progresses differently for materials and for conversion. For instance, in the Shaping Department, all direct materials are added at the beginning of the process, but conversion costs are incurred evenly throughout the process.

The Shaping Department has 10,000 units unfinished at October 31, 2003. We assume that all direct materials have been added (the chemicals have been added to begin shaping the bodies of the masks) but that three-quarters of the conversion work remains to be done. Thus, all 50,000 units are finished in terms of direct materials. We must compute equivalent units for conversion costs. Because 25 percent of conversion work has been done, we multiply the 10,000 unfinished units by 0.25, which gives 2,500 equivalent units. We add that to the 40,000 finished units, so equivalent units for conversion costs total 42,500.

RECREATIONAL DIVERS LTD.
Shaping Department
For the Month Ended October 31, 2003

| | Step 1 | Step 2 Equivalent Units | |
| | Flow of Physical | Direct | Conversion |
Flow of Production	Units	Materials	Costs
Units to account for:			
Work in process, September 30	0		
Started in production during October	50,000		
Total physical units to account for.....................	50,000		
Units accounted for:			
Completed and transferred out			
during October	40,000	40,000	40,000
Work in process, October 31	10,000	10,000*	2,500**
Total physical units accounted for.....................	50,000		
Equivalent units		50,000	42,500

*10,000 units each 100% complete = 10,000 equivalent units.
**10,000 units each 25% complete = 2,500 equivalent units.

Exhibit 21-4 combines the data for steps 1 and 2. Note that the numbers of equivalent units for direct materials and conversion costs are different. This often is the case.

Step 3: Summarize Total Costs to Account For

Exhibit 21-5 summarizes the total costs to account for in the Shaping Department (cost data are from page 1181). These costs are the total debits in Work in Process Inventory—Shaping, including any beginning balance. The Shaping Department has 50,000 units and $208,000 of costs to account for. Our next task is to assign these costs to the 40,000 masks completed and transferred out to the Finishing Department and to the 10,000 masks that remain in the Shaping Department's ending work in process inventory.

WORKING IT OUT

Using the data from the previous Working It Out, compute the unit cost in the Mixing Dept.

A:

	Dir. Mtls.	Conv. Costs
WIP, 5/1	$ –0–	$ –0–
Costs added		
during May.......	15,120	27,755
÷ equiv. units........	÷ 4,725	÷ 4,550
Cost per equiv.		
unit..................	$ 3.20	$ 6.10

EXHIBIT 21-5

Step 3: Summarize Total
Costs to Account For

RECREATIONAL DIVERS LTD.
Shaping Department
For the Month Ended October 31, 2003

	Physical Units	Dollars		Physical Units	Dollars
Inventory, September 30	0	$ 0	Transferred out	40,000	$?
Production started:	50,000				
Direct materials		140,000			
Conversion costs:					
Direct labour		21,250			
Manufacturing overhead		46,750			
Total to account for	50,000	$208,000			
Ending inventory	10,000	$?			

EXHIBIT 21-6

Step 4: Compute Equivalent-
Unit Costs

RECREATIONAL DIVERS LTD.
Shaping Department
For the Month Ended October 31, 2003

	Direct Materials	Conversion Costs
Work in process, September 30	$ 0	$ 0
Costs added during October (from Exhibit 21-5)	$140,000	$68,000
Divide by equivalent units (from Exhibit 21-4)	÷ 50,000	÷ 42,500
Cost per equivalent unit......................................	$2.80	$1.60

WORKING IT OUT

Compute the total costs of mixing department units completed and ending work in process for the Working It Out on page 1183.

A:

Compl. (4,500 ×	
$9.30)..........................	$41,850
End. WIP	
Direct Mat. (225 ×	
$3.20).....................	720
Conv. Costs	
(50 × $6.10)...........	305
Total End. WIP	1,025
Total Acc. for..................	$42,875

"Total [cost] accounted for" of $42,875 agrees with the amount in the previous Working It Out for "Total costs added during May." You must account for all manufacturing costs.

OBJECTIVE 4
Assign costs to units completed and to units in ending work in process inventory

Step 4: Compute the Cost per Equivalent Unit

In step 2, we computed the number of equivalent units for direct materials (50,000) and conversion costs (42,500). Because their equivalent units differ, a separate cost per unit must be computed for each category. Exhibit 21-5 provides the data. The direct materials cost is $140,000. Conversion cost is $68,000, which is the sum of direct labour ($21,250) and manufacturing overhead ($46,750).

We now have all the data we need to compute the Shaping Department unit costs. We divide the direct materials cost by the equivalent units for direct materials: $140,000/50,000 = $2.80. This amount is the unit cost for direct materials. We compute unit conversion cost in a similar manner: $68,000/42,500 = $1.60. Exhibit 21-6 shows the computation of equivalent-unit costs.

In addition to using the cost per equivalent unit in the five-step process-costing procedure, managers also use this information to determine how well they have controlled costs. If the cost per equivalent unit of conversion (or direct materials) meets or beats the target cost per equivalent unit based on planned or historical data, then the manager has successfully controlled the conversion (or direct materials) costs.

Step 5: Assign Costs to Units Completed and to Units in Ending Work in Process Inventory

Exhibit 21-7 shows how the equivalent units computed in step 2 (Exhibit 21-4) are costed at the cost per equivalent unit computed in step 4 (Exhibit 21-6) to cost the 50,000 physical units (swim mask bodies) worked on in the Shaping Department during October.

RECREATIONAL DIVERS LTD.
Shaping Department
For the Month Ended October 31, 2003

	Direct Materials	Conversion Costs	Total
Units completed and transferred out (40,000)...	40,000 × $4.40		= $176,000
Units in ending work in process inventory (10,000):			
Direct materials...................................	10,000 × $2.80		= $ 28,000
Conversion costs.................................		2,500 × $1.60 =	4,000
Total cost of ending work in process inventory............................			$ 32,000
Total cost accounted for			$208,000

First consider the 40,000 units completed and transferred out (that is, transferred into the Finishing Department). Exhibit 21-4 reveals 40,000 equivalent units of work for both direct materials and conversion costs. Thus, the total cost of these completed units is (40,000 × $2.80) + (40,000 × $1.60), or simply 40,000 × $4.40 = $176,000.

Next consider the 10,000 units still being shaped at the end of the month. These swim masks have 10,000 equivalent units of direct materials (at $2.80 per unit) and 2,500 equivalent units of conversion work (at $1.60 per unit). Exhibit 21-7 uses these amounts to compute the total cost of the ending inventory units as of October 31— $32,000.

The total cost accounted for in step 5, $208,000, is equal to the total cost to account for in step 3.

Recording the Costs   Journal entries to record October production in the Shaping Department is recorded as follows (data are from Exhibit 21-5):

Work in Process Inventory—Shaping	140,000	
Materials Inventory		140,000
Work in Process Inventory—Shaping	21,250	
Manufacturing Wages		21,250
Work in Process Inventory—Shaping	46,750	
Manufacturing Overhead		46,750

To requisition materials and apply labour and overhead cost to the Shaping Department.

The entry to transfer the cost of the 40,000 completed swim masks from the Shaping Department to the Finishing Department is as follows (data are from Exhibit 21-7):

Work in Process Inventory—Finishing	176,000	
Work in Process Inventory—Shaping		176,000

After these entries are posted, the Work in Process Inventory—Shaping account appears as follows:

Work in Process Inventory—Shaping

Balance, September 30	0	Transferred to Finishing	176,000
Direct materials	140,000		
Direct labour	21,250		
Manufacturing overhead	46,750		
Balance, October 31	32,000		

Before continuing, review the Process Costing Decision Guidelines to make sure you understand equivalent units and the flow of costs in process costing.

WORKING IT OUT

Using the data in the previous few Working It Outs, (1) prepare journal entries summarizing these transactions, and (2) prepare the T-account for Work in Process Inventory—Mixing.

A:

a. To requisition materials:
WIP Inventory—
　Mixing.............. 15,120
　Materials
　　Inventory .... 　　15,120
b. To apply labour:
WIP Inventory—
　Mixing.............. 11,102
　Man. Wages... 　　11,102
c. To apply overhead:
WIP Inventory—
　Mixing.............. 16,653
　Man. Overhead 　　16,653
d. To transfer the cost of completed units from the Mixing Dept. to the Packaging Dept.:
WIP Inventory—
　Packaging 41,850
　WIP Inventory—
　　Mixing........ 　　41,850

Work in Process Inventory— Mixing

Bal., May 1	0	Trans. to	
Dir. mtls.	15,120	Packaging	
Dir. labour	11,102		41,850
Man. over.	16,653		
Bal, May 31	1,025		

DECISION GUIDELINES   *Process Costing—First Process (No Beginning Inventory)*

Decision	Guidelines
How do costs flow from Work in Process Inventory to Finished Goods Inventory?	Job costing → Costs flow from Work in Process Inventory directly to Finished Goods Inventory. Process costing → Costs flow from one Work in Process Inventory account to the next, until the last process. Costs flow from Work in Process Inventory of the last process into Finished Goods Inventory.
How many Work in Process Inventory accounts in a process costing system?	There is one Work in Process Inventory account for each separate manufacturing process.

(continued)

Decision	Guidelines
How to account for partially completed goods?	Use equivalent units. • If cost is incurred evenly throughout the production process: $$\text{Equivalent units} = \text{Number of partially complete units} \times \text{Percentage of process completed}$$ • If cost is added at a specific point in the production process: If physical units have passed the point where cost is added → units are complete with respect to that cost, so equivalent units = physical units If physical units have *not* passed the point where cost is added → units have not incurred any of that cost, so equivalent units = 0
Which costs require separate equivalent-unit computations?	Perform separate equivalent-unit computations for each input added at a different point in the production process. Often this requires separate equivalent-unit computations for (1) direct materials, and (2) conversion costs.
How to compute the cost per equivalent unit?	Divide the cost by the number of equivalent units
How to split the costs of a process between: • Units completed and transferred out? • Units in ending work in process inventory?	Multiply the cost per equivalent unit by • Number of equivalent units of work in the physical units completed and transferred out • Number of equivalent units of work in the ending work in process inventory
How to evaluate whether a manager controlled a department's costs?	If direct material and conversion cost per equivalent unit meets or beats target unit costs, the manager has controlled costs.

Mid-Chapter Summary Problem
for Your Review

Use the five steps of process costing to identify the missing amounts X and Y in the following production cost report prepared by Oxford Manufacturing Inc. for May. (A production cost report summarizes the operations of a processing department for a period.)

OXFORD MANUFACTURING INC.
Assembly Department
Production Cost Report
For the Month Ended May 31, 2003

	Physical Units	Total Costs
Work in process, April 30...	0	$ 0
Started in production during May	20,000	43,200*
Total to account for...	20,000	$43,200
Completed and transferred to Finishing Department during May..	16,000	$ X
Work in process, May 31 (25% complete as to direct materials, 55% complete as to conversion cost)	4,000	Y
Total accounted for...	20,000	$43,200

*Includes direct materials of $6,800 and conversion costs of $36,400.

Solution to Review Problem

Step 1: Summarize the flow of physical units.
Step 2: Compute output in terms of equivalent units of production.

OXFORD MANUFACTURING INC.
Assembly Department
For the Month Ended May 31, 2003

	Step 1	Step 2 Equivalent Units	
	Flow of Physical	Direct	Conversion
Flow of Production	**Units**	**Materials**	**Costs**
Units to account for:			
Work in process, April 30....................................	0		
Started in production during May	20,000		
Total physical units to account for......................	20,000		
Units accounted for:			
Completed and transferred out during May	16,000	16,000	16,000
Work in process, May 31	4,000	1,000*	2,200*
Total physical units accounted for......................	20,000		
Equivalent units		17,000	18,200

*Direct materials: 4,000 units each 25% complete = 1,000 equivalent units.
Conversion costs: 4,000 units each 55% complete = 2,200 equivalent units.

Step 3: Summarize total costs to account for.

OXFORD MANUFACTURING INC.
Assembly Department
For the Month Ended May 31, 2003

	Direct Materials	Conversion Costs	Total
Work in process, April 30	$ 0	$ 0	$ 0
Costs added during May	$6,800	$36,400	43,200
Total cost to account for.............................			$43,200

Step 4: Compute the cost per equivalent unit.

OXFORD MANUFACTURING INC.
Assembly Department
For the Month Ended May 31, 2003

	Direct Materials	Conversion Costs
Work in process, April 30	$ 0	$ 0
Costs added during May..	$ 6,800	$ 36,400
Divide by equivalent units of production................	÷ 17,000	÷ 18,200
Cost per equivalent unit	$ 0.40	$ 2.00

Step 5: Assign costs to units completed and to units in ending work in process inventory.

OXFORD MANUFACTURING INC.
Assembly Department
For the Month Ended May 31, 2003

	Direct Materials	Conversion Costs	Total
X: Units completed and transferred out (16,000)	16,000 × ($0.40 + $2.00)		= $38,400
Units in ending work in process inventory (4,000):			
Direct materials..................	1,000 × $0.40=		400
Conversion costs................		2,200 × $2.00 =	4,400
Y: Total cost of ending work in process inventory			4,800
Total cost accounted for.............			$43,200

From Process Costing to Job Costing?

Canadians will soon be able to pick out a fully custom-built car and drive it away in the same time it takes to tailor a three-piece suit—15 days from order to delivery.

Ford Motor Co. of Canada Ltd. expects to have the technology to make this option available within five years. And these are true custom cars: a mix-and-match design to suit your needs and tastes from about 70,000 permutations and combinations of options. The cost will be based on a list price plus options.

The driver that will make this possible is technology. Car makers are among the first to recognize that technology can turn mass production into true custom crafting on a huge scale.

This is how it would work. Computers capture the specifics of an individual order. Glass-fibre networks relay the order to an assembly plant, where other computers translate it into instructions for building the vehicle on the assembly line. These instructions are programmed into wireless transponders or bar codes that instruct robots and humans on what to add, and when and where.

At each stage, computers track progress, and inventory is counted and ordered, with parts arriving as they are needed, often trucked from factories 1,000 kilometres away.

The wonder is not so much the use of new technology, but the ability to use many different technologies so seamlessly and in concert. "A decade ago, we didn't have things like transponders and radio-scanning systems," says assembly plant manager Rich Wagner. "But now that we have them, they are giving us the ability to do custom production on a mass-production scale."

Source: Terrence Belford, "Dream Car on Fast Track," *Globe and Mail*, February 23, 2001, p. T3.

Process Costing for a Second Department—FIFO Method

OBJECTIVE 5
Account for a second processing department by the FIFO method

Most products require a series of processing steps. In this section, we introduce a second department—the Finishing Department of Recreational Divers Ltd.—to complete the picture of process costing. We also introduce beginning inventories of work in process, a complicating factor that was not present in our examples up to this point.

As in many areas of accounting, there are alternative methods of accounting for process costs. We discuss two: the first-in, first-out (FIFO) method and the weighted-average method. (A third method, standard costing, is covered in cost accounting and advanced managerial accounting texts.) FIFO and weighted-average differ only in their treatment of beginning work in process inventory. When there is no beginning inventory, the two methods are identical. They use the same five steps that we applied earlier to Recreational Divers Ltd.'s Shaping Department.

The **first-in, first-out (FIFO) method** of process costing assigns to each period's equivalent units of production that period's costs per equivalent unit. Consider swim masks that are transferred to the Finishing Department of Recreational Divers Ltd. and partially processed in September and then are completed in October. The total Finishing Department cost of the masks is the sum of

- September's equivalent units of the Finishing Department's work on these swim masks, costed at September's cost per equivalent unit, *plus*
- October's equivalent units of the Finishing Department's work on these swim masks, costed at October's cost per equivalent unit.

The Finishing Department smoothes and polishes the shaped swim mask bodies and adds the faceplates to them. The faceplate is the direct material added in the finishing process. Keep in mind that the label *direct materials* in the Finishing Department refers to the faceplates added *in that department* and not to the materials (the plastic) added in the previous department, Shaping. Likewise, *conversion cost* in the Finishing Department refers to all manufacturing costs (other than direct materials) of that department only.

Steps 1 and 2: Summarize the Flow of Physical Units and Compute Output in Terms of Equivalent Units

We assume that 5,000 units were in process in the Finishing Department on October 1. These units were 60 percent complete as to Finishing Department conversion costs but 0 percent complete as to direct materials because the faceplates are added near the end of the finishing process. These facts, used throughout our discussion of the Finishing Department, are summarized in Exhibit 21-8.

A major task in accounting for a second department is the computation of equivalent units. Exhibit 21-9 summarizes the flow of physical units (step 1) and tabulates equivalent units (step 2) for the Finishing Department. There are three categories of equivalent units. In addition to equivalent units for direct materials (faceplates) and conversion costs added in the Finishing Department, we must compute equivalent units for the shaped swim masks that are *transferred in* from the Shaping Department. The cost ($176,000 in our example) of these transferred-in units—referred to as **transferred-in costs**—must be accounted for by the Finishing Department. In general, all second and later departments will have transfered-in costs that are transferred in from the preceding department and must be accounted for.

The FIFO method of process costing is used in Exhibits 21-9 through 21-13. With FIFO, the focus is on the current period—October in this example. The FIFO method determines October equivalent units of work and costs those units with October unit costs. A major advantage of the FIFO method is that with these current amounts, the efficiency of October production can be judged independently of production efficiency in other months. Current-month data are important for planning and control.

Units:	
Work in process, September 30 (0% complete as to direct materials, 60% complete as to conversion work)	5,000 units
Transferred in from Shaping Department during October...	40,000 units
Completed during October and transferred to Finished Goods Inventory...	38,000 units
Work in process, October 31 (0% complete as to direct materials, 30% complete as to conversion work)	7,000 units

Costs:		
Work in process, September 30		$ 24,000
(Transferred-in cost $22,900; conversion costs, $1,100)		
Transferred in from Shaping Department during October...		176,000
Direct materials added during October in Finishing Department		19,000
Conversion costs added during October in Finishing Dep:		
Direct labour..	$ 3,710	
Manufacturing overhead...	11,130	14,840

EXHIBIT 21-8

Finishing Department Data for October

RECREATIONAL DIVERS LTD.
Finishing Department
For the Month Ended October 31, 2003

| | Step 1 | Step 2 Equivalent Units | | |
| | Flow of Physical Units | Transferred In | Direct Materials | Conversion Costs |
Flow of Production				
Units to account for:				
Work in process, September 30	5,000			
Transferred in during October	40,000			
Total physical units to account for................................	45,000			
Units accounted for:				
Completed and transferred out during October:				
From beginning inventory..	5,000	—	5,000*	2,000*
Transferred in and completed during October				
(38,000 – 5,000)...	33,000	33,000	33,000	33,000
Work in process, October 31	7,000	7,000	0†	2,100†
Total physical units accounted for................................	45,000			
Equivalent units		40,000	38,000	37,100

*Direct materials: 5,000 units each 100% completed in Finishing Department during October = 5,000 equivalent units.
  Conversion costs: 5,000 units each 40% completed in Finishing Department during October = 2,000 equivalent units.
†Direct materials: 7,000 units each 0% completed in Finishing Department during October = 0 equivalent units.
  Conversion costs: 7,000 units each 30% completed in Finishing Department during October = 2,100 equivalent units.

EXHIBIT 21-9

FIFO Method, Step 1: Summarize the Flow of Physical Units; Step 2: Compute Output in Terms of Equivalent Units

As Exhibit 21-9 shows, the FIFO method distinguishes between two categories of swim masks completed during October: the 5,000 units already in the Finishing Department on October 1 and the 33,000 units that were both transferred in and completed during that month. This distinction is due to FIFO's current-month orientation. All the Finishing Department work on the 33,000 units was done in October, but some of the work on the beginning inventory units was done in September. This key difference in the timing of work affects the equivalent-unit computations in step 2.

The Transferred In column of Exhibit 21-9 shows that 40,000 shaped swim masks were transferred from the Shaping Department to the Finishing Department in October. Of these, 33,000 were completed and 7,000 remain in Finishing on October 31. The Direct Materials column shows that faceplates were added to the 38,000 units completed and transferred out during the month. These completed units include the 5,000 that were in the Finishing Department on October 1 and the 33,000 that were both transferred in and completed. Ending inventory has no direct materials equivalent units.

The equivalent-unit total for conversion costs has three components: beginning work in process inventory, units transferred in and completed during the month, and ending work in process inventory. The beginning inventory of 5,000 units was 60 percent complete as to conversion work when September ended. During October, the Finishing Department completed these 5,000 units by doing the remaining 40 percent of conversion work. For beginning inventory, equivalent production is 2,000 units (5,000 × 0.40). Units transferred in and completed during the month (33,000 units) are the second component of equivalent production. Ending inventory is the third component. At October 31 the inventory of 7,000 units still in process is 30 percent complete as to conversion work, so equivalent production is 2,100 units (7,000 × 0.30). Altogether, October equivalent production for Finishing Department conversion totals 37,100 units (2,000 + 33,000 + 2,100).

RECREATIONAL DIVERS LTD.
Finishing Department
For the Month Ended October 31, 2003

	Transferred-In Costs	Direct Materials	Conversion Costs	Total
Work in process, September 30 (from Exhibit 21-8)....	$ 22,900	0	$ 1,100	$ 24,000
Costs added during October (from Exhibit 21-8)........	$176,000	$19,000	$14,840	209,840
Divide by equivalent units (from Exhibit 21-9)...........	÷ 40,000	÷ 38,000	÷ 37,100	
Cost per equivalent unit	$ 4.40	$ 0.50	$ 0.40	
Total cost to account for				$233,840

EXHIBIT 21-10

FIFO Method, Steps 3 and 4: Summarize Total Costs to Account for and Compute the Cost per Equivalent Unit

Steps 3 and 4: Summarize Total Costs to Account For and Compute the Cost per Equivalent Unit

Exhibit 21-10 accumulates the Finishing Department's October costs. The exhibit shows how to use equivalent units to compute the cost per equivalent unit. The $24,000 beginning balance of work in process is kept separate from the costs incurred during the current period. That is, the $24,000 is not included in computing the cost per equivalent unit for work done in October. The work in process beginning balance is the cost incurred in *September* on the 5,000 physical units in process on October 1. Under FIFO, each *October* cost per equivalent unit is computed by dividing an October cost by the number of equivalent units of work performed in October.

(**WORKING IT OUT**)

Using the data in the previous Working It Outs, compute the unit costs in the Packaging Dept.

A:

	Trans. In	Dir. Mtls.	Conv. Costs
Costs added, May	$41,850	$1,890	$15,400
	÷	÷	÷
equiv. units	4,500	4,200	5,600
Cost/equiv. unit	$ 9.30	$ 0.45	$ 2.75

Step 5: Assign Costs to Units Completed and to Units in Ending Work in Process Inventory

Exhibit 21-11 shows how to apply the costs of the Finishing Department of Recreational Divers Ltd. to

- Units completed and transferred to Finished Goods Inventory
- Units still in process in the Finishing Department at the end of the period.

The Finishing Department's journal entries are similar to those for the Shaping Department. The entries for the Shaping Department were recorded on page 1185. The following entries record Finishing Department activity during October.

(**WORKING IT OUT**)

Apply unit costs to (a) units completed and (b) units in ending work in process, for the previous Working It Out.

A:

(a) Units completed and transferred out to FG:	
From WIP, May 1.........................	$43,100
Costs added—May	
Dir. mtls.	0[a]
Conv. costs	5,500[b]
Total completed from May 1 inventory.......................	48,600
Units trans. in and completed—May	37,500[c]
Total costs trans. out	86,100
(b) WIP, May 31	
Trans.-in costs..........................	13,950[d]
Dir. materials	540[e]
Conv. costs................................	1,650[f]
Total WIP, May 31	16,140
Total cost acc. for	$102,240

[a] 0 × $0.45
[b] 2,000 × $2.75
[c] 3,000 × [$9.30 + $0.45 + $2.75]
[d] 1,500 × $9.30
[e] 1,200 × $0.45
[f] 600 × $2.75

Work in Process Inventory—Finishing	176,000	
Work in Process Inventory—Shaping		176,000

To transfer in the cost of shaped swim masks from the Shaping Department.

Work in Process Inventory—Finishing	19,000	
Materials Inventory		19,000
Work in Process Inventory—Finishing	3,710	
Manufacturing Wages		3,710
Work in Process Inventory—Finishing	11,130	
Manufacturing Overhead		11,130

To requisition materials and apply conversion costs to the Finishing Department (amounts from Exhibit 21-8).

The entry to transfer the cost of completed units from the Finishing Department to Finished Goods Inventory is based on the dollar amount in Exhibit 21-11:

Finished Goods Inventory	202,200	
Work in Process Inventory—Finishing.......................		202,200

RECREATIONAL DIVERS LTD.
Finishing Department
For the Month Ended October 31, 2003

	Transferred-In Costs	Direct Materials	Conversion Costs	Total
Units completed and transferred to Finished Goods Inventory:				
From work in process, September 30	$ 22,900		$ 1,100	$ 24,000
Costs added during October:				
Direct materials (5,000 × $0.50)		2,500		2,500
Conversion costs (2,000 × $0.40)			800	800
Total completed from September 30 inventory.......	22,900	2,500	1,900	27,300
Units transferred in and completed during October .				
(33,000 × $4.40), (33,000 × $0.50), (33,000 × $0.40)	145,200	16,500	13,200	174,900
Total cost transferred out				202,200
Work in process, October 31:				
Transferred-in costs (7,000 × $4.40)............................	30,800			30,800
Direct materials (0 × $0.50)		0		0
Conversion costs (2,100 × $0.40)			840	840
Total work in process, October 31...............................	30,800	0	840	31,640
Total cost accounted for...................................				$233,840

EXHIBIT 21-11

FIFO Method, Step 5: Assign Costs to Units Completed and to Units in Ending Work in Process Inventory

After posting, the key accounts appear as follows. Observe the accumulation of costs as debits to Work in Process Inventory and the transfer of costs from one account to the next.

Work in Process Inventory—Shaping

(Exhibit 21-5)		(Exhibit 21-7)	
Balance, September 30	0	Transferred to Finishing	176,000
Direct materials	140,000		
Direct labour	21,250		
Manufacturing overhead	46,750		
Balance, October 31	32,000		

Work in Process Inventory—Finishing

(Exhibit 21-8)		(Exhibit 21-11)	
Balance, September 30	24,000	Transferred to Finished	
Transferred in from		Goods Inventory	202,200
Shaping	176,000		
Direct materials	19,000		
Direct labour	3,710		
Manufacturing overhead	11,130		
Balance, October 31	31,640		

Finished Goods Inventory

Balance, September 30	0		
Transferred in from			
Finishing	202,200		

WORKING IT OUT

Prepare the journal entries for the Working It Outs on pages 1190 and 1192.

1. To requisition materials:
WIP Inventory—
Pkg 1,890
Materials Inventory 1,890
2. To apply labour:
WIP Inventory—
Pkg 10,800
Manufacturing
Wages 10,800
3. To apply overhead:
WIP Inventory—
Pkg 4,600
Man. Over. 4,600
4. To transfer complete units:
Finished Goods
Inventory................. 86,100
WIP Inventory—
Pkg....................... 86,100

Production Cost Report

A **production cost report** summarizes the operations of a processing department for the period. Exhibit 21-12 is a FIFO production cost report for the Finishing Department of Recreational Divers Ltd. for October. It shows the department's beginning inventory, the number of units and the cost transferred in during the month, and the costs added. These amounts make up the totals to account for. The report also shows the units completed, the costs transferred out of the department, and the ending inventory.

Production cost reports vary from company to company, depending on the level of detail desired by the managers. If managers want more detail, some or all of the additional information in Exhibits 21-9, 21-10, and 21-11 can be included. For example, Exhibit 21-13 provides more detail about costs than does Exhibit 21-12.

How do managers use the production cost report? Recreational Divers Ltd. managers compare actual direct materials and conversion costs—particularly the unit costs in Exhibit 21-13—with budgeted amounts for the department. If these costs are too high, managers will investigate with the goal of finding a way to reduce the costs. If costs are below budget, employees may receive a bonus.

Managers also compare the number of units produced with budgeted production. Production that is too low can be investigated and corrected. If production in excess of the budget is welcomed, such performance may lead to rewards for high-achieving employees.

OBJECTIVE 6
Account for a second processing department by the weighted-average method

Process Costing for a Second Department—Weighted-Average Method

We now rework Recreational Divers Ltd.'s Finishing Department example to demonstrate the second process costing method, weighted-average.

We learned that the FIFO method assigns costs to (1) physical units completed and transferred out and (2) work in process ending inventory by costing equivalent units of work done each period with that period's unit costs. In contrast, the **weighted-average method** costs all equivalent units of work for each period with a weighted average of that period's and the previous period's costs per equivalent

EXHIBIT 21-12

FIFO Method Production Cost Report

	Physical Units	Total Costs
RECREATIONAL DIVERS LTD. Finishing Department Production Cost Report For the Month Ended October 31, 2003		
Work in process, September 30	5,000	$ 24,000
Transferred in from Shaping Department during October	40,000	176,000
Costs added in Finishing Department during October:		
Direct materials	0	19,000
Conversion costs ($3,710 + $11,130)	0	14,840
Total to account for	45,000	$233,840
Completed and transferred to finished goods during October	38,000	$202,200
Work in process, October 31	7,000	$ 31,640
Total accounted for	45,000	$233,840

RECREATIONAL DIVERS LTD.
Finishing Department
Production Cost Report (Expanded)
For the Month Ended October 31, 2003

	Transferred-In Costs	Direct Materials	Conversion Costs	Total
Work in process, September 30				$ 24,000
Costs added during October	$176,000	$19,000	$14,840	209,840
Total cost to account for				$233,840
Equivalent units	÷ 40,000	÷ 38,000	÷ 37,100	
Cost per equivalent unit	$ 4.40	$ 0.50	$ 0.40	
Assignment of total costs:				
Units completed during October:				
From work in process, September 30				$ 24,000
Costs added during October		5,000 × $0.50 = $2,500	2,000 × $0.40 = $800	3,300
Total completed from September 30 inventory........				27,300
Units transferred in and completed				
during October	33,000 × ($4.40 + $0.50 + $0.40)			174,900
Total completed and transferred out........................				202,200
Work in process, October 31:				
Transferred-in costs	7,000 × $4.40			30,800
Direct materials		0		0
Conversion costs.			2,100 × $0.40	840
Total work in process, October 31				31,640
Total cost accounted for				$233,840

EXHIBIT 21-13

FIFO Method Production Cost Report (Expanded)

unit. Exhibits 21-14 through 21-18 are the weighted-average equivalents of Exhibits 21-9 through 21-13. We apply the weighted-average method with the same five steps that we used with FIFO.

Steps 1 and 2: Summarize the Flow of Physical Units and Compute Output in Terms of Equivalent Units

The weighted-average method is simpler than the FIFO method because it does not require us to separate the work and costs for beginning inventory from the units started and completed this period. Instead, all the units completed and transferred out—whether from beginning inventory or units started and completed this period—are treated identically and are assigned the same cost per equivalent unit, using

- All costs incurred for the physical units in process this period, whether those costs were incurred this period or last period, and
- All work performed on the physical units in process this period, whether that work was performed this period or last period.

Exhibit 21-14 shows that 38,000 units were completed and transferred out of the Finishing Department in October. The full 38,000 equivalent units of production are assigned to these physical units in each step 2 cost category. Why? Because by October 31, all these units had been transferred into Finishing from Shaping, faceplates had been added to all of them, and all the finishing conversion work had been done. The equivalent units for ending inventory of work in process are the same with the weighted-average method as with FIFO. All the Finishing Department

WORKING IT OUT

Using the data from the previous Working It Outs, apply the weighted-average method to a second department. Compute equivalent units.

A:	Trans. In	Dir. Mat.	Conv. Costs
Trans. out........	7,000	7,000	7,000
WIP, end..........	1,500	1,200	600
Equiv. units	8,500	8,200	7,600

RECREATIONAL DIVERS LTD.
Finishing Department
For the Month Ended October 31, 2003

| | Step 1 | Step 2 | | |
| | | Equivalent Units | | |
Flow of Production	Flow of Physical Units	Transferred In	Direct Materials	Conversion Costs
Units to account for:				
Work in process, September 30	5,000			
Transferred in during October	40,000			
Total physical units to account for................................	45,000			
Units accounted for:				
Completed and transferred out during October:	38,000	38,000	38,000*	38,000*
Work in process, October 31	7,000	7,000	0†	2,100†
Total physical units accounted for................................	45,000			
Equivalent units		45,000	38,000	40,100

*Direct materials: 38,000 units each 100% completed in Finishing Department by October 31 = 38,000 equivalent units.
 Conversion costs: 38,000 units each 100% completed in Finishing Department by October 31 = 38,000 equivalent units.
†Direct materials: 7,000 units each 0% completed in Finishing Department by October 31 = 0 equivalent units.
 Conversion costs: 7,000 units each 30% completed in Finishing Department by October 31 = 2,100 equivalent units.

EXHIBIT 21-14

Weighted-Average Method, Step 1: Summarize the Flow of Physical Units; Step 2: Compute Output in Terms of Equivalent Units

work done on these 7,000 units by October 31 was done in October, because they were among the 40,000 units transferred in from Shaping during that month.

Step 3: Summarize Total Costs to Account For

The total cost to account for (Exhibit 21-15) is the sum of work in process beginning inventory cost ($24,000) and the costs added to the Work in Process—Finishing account during October ($209,840). The total is $233,840.

Suppose that you know the weighted-average equivalent-unit totals in Exhibit 21-14. How can you use these amounts to compute FIFO equivalent units for October?

Answer: Weighted-average equivalent units of work are the sum of the current-month (FIFO) equivalent units and equivalent units already in the process when the current month began. The Finishing Department inventory on October 1 consisted of 5,000 physical units that were 0 percent complete as to direct materials and 60 percent complete as to conversion work. Thus, on October 1, 5,000 transferred-in equivalent units, zero direct-materials equivalent units, and 3,000 (5,000 × 0.60) conversion equivalent units were in the finishing process. FIFO equivalent units can be computed as follows:

| | Equivalent Units | | |
	Transferred In	Direct Materials	Conversion Costs
Weighted-average totals....................................	45,000	38,000	40,100
October 1 work in process inventory	5,000	0	3,000
FIFO totals..	40,000	38,000	37,100

The FIFO totals can be seen in Exhibit 21-9.

WORKING IT OUT

Assume that the beginning inventory for the previous Working It Outs consisted of $1,800 of materials, $4,100 of conversion costs, and $37,200 of transferred-in costs. Compute unit costs.

A:

	Trans. In	Dir. Mat.	Conv. Costs
Beg. WIP	$37,200	$1,800	$ 4,100
Costs added	41,850	1,890	15,400
Total cost.........	$79,050	$3,690	$19,500
Equiv. units......	8,500	8,200	7,600
Unit cost..........	$ 9.30	$ 0.45	$2.5658

	Total
Beg. WIP	$ 43,100
Costs added	59,140
Total cost.........	$102,240

RECREATIONAL DIVERS LTD.
Finishing Department
For the Month Ended October 31, 2003

	Transferred-In Costs	Direct Materials	Conversion Costs	Total
Work in process, September 30 (from Exhibit 21-8) ...	$ 22,900	$ 0	$ 1,100	$ 24,000
Costs added during October (from Exhibit 21-8)	176,000	19,000	14,840	209,840
Total cost..	$198,900	$19,000	$ 15,940	
Divide by equivalent units (from Exhibit 21-14).........	÷ 45,000	÷ 38,000	÷ 40,100	
Cost per equivalent unit..	$ 4.42	$ 0.50	$ 0.3975	
Total cost to account for...				$233,840

EXHIBIT 21-15

Weighted-Average Method, Step 3: Summarize Total Costs to Account For; Step 4: Compute the Cost per Equivalent Unit

Step 4: Compute the Cost per Equivalent Unit

The numerators and denominators of the weighted-average unit-cost calculations include both current-month amounts and amounts from October's beginning work in process inventory. In our example, the resulting unit costs are weighted averages of September unit costs and October unit costs. The computations are shown in Exhibit 21-15. Consider conversion costs. The Finishing Department incurred $1,100 of conversion costs in September to get the 5,000 masks in beginning inventory 60% of the way through the production process by the end of September. This $1,100 is added to the $14,840 total Finishing Department conversion cost incurred in October. We divide the sum, $15,940, by the total number of (weighted-average) equivalent units, 40,100, to obtain a weighted-average conversion cost per equivalent unit of $0.3975. The transferred-in cost per equivalent unit and the direct materials cost per equivalent unit are computed in the same way.

Step 5: Assign Costs to Units Completed and to Units in Ending Work in Process Inventory

With the weighted-average method, the 38,000 physical units completed and transferred out of the Finishing Department of Recreational Divers Ltd. are costed in one step. The 38,000 equivalent units are multiplied by the full equivalent-unit cost of $5.3175 ($4.42 + $0.50 + $0.3975). The result is $202,065 (Exhibit 21-16). Equivalent units in October 31 work in process inventory also are costed at the appropriate unit amounts.

EXHIBIT 21-16

Weighted-Average Method, Step 5: Assign Costs to Units Completed and to Units in Ending Work in Process Inventory

RECREATIONAL DIVERS LTD.
Finishing Department
For the Month Ended October 31, 2003

	Transferred-In Costs	Direct Materials	Conversion Costs	Total
Units completed and transferred out to Finished Goods Inventory..	38,000 × ($4.42 + $0.50 + $0.3975)			$202,065
Work in process, October 31:				
Transferred-in costs..	7,000 × $4.42			30,940
Direct materials..		0		0
Conversion costs...			2,100 × $0.3975	835
Total work in process, October 31				31,775
Total cost accounted for				$233,840

The weighted-average production cost reports in Exhibit 21-17 and 21-18 are similar to their FIFO counterparts, Exhibits 21-12 and 21-13. They too may signal the need for action if actual costs or production quantities differ materially from budgeted amounts. But weighted-average costs per equivalent unit are not as useful for evaluating the efficiency of October production because they are affected by the costs incurred in September. Even so, managers may use the weighted-average method because (1) the computations are simpler than those of the FIFO method, and (2) the differences in costs assigned to units often are immaterial.

EXHIBIT 21-17

Weighted-Average Method
Production Cost Report

RECREATIONAL DIVERS LTD.
Finishing Department
Production Cost Report
For the Month Ended October 31, 2003

	Physical Units	Total Costs
Work in process, September 30	5,000	$ 24,000
Transferred in from Shaping Department during October........	40,000	176,000
Costs added in Finishing Department during October:		
Direct materials	0	19,000
Conversion costs ($3,710 + $11,130)	0	14,840
Total to account for	45,000	$233,840
Completed and transferred to finished goods during October	38,000	$202,065
Work in process, October 31	7,000	31,775
Total accounted for	45,000	$233,840

EXHIBIT 21-18

Weighted-Average Method
Production Cost Report
(Expanded)

RECREATIONAL DIVERS LTD.
Finishing Department
Production Cost Report (Expanded)
For the Month Ended October 31, 2003

	Transferred-In Costs	Direct Materials	Conversion Costs	Total
Work in process, September 30	$ 22,900	$ 0	$ 1,100	$ 24,000
Costs added during October	176,000	19,000	14,840	209,840
Total cost to account for	$198,900	$19,000	$15,940	$233,840
Equivalent units	÷ 45,000	÷ 38,000	÷ 40,100	
Cost per equivalent unit...	$ 4.42	$ 0.50	$0.3975	
Assignment of total costs:				
Units completed during October............................	38,000 × ($4.42 + $0.50 + $0.3975)			$202,065
Work in process, October 31:				
Transferred-in costs...	7,000 × $4.42			30,940
Direct materials		0		0
Conversion costs			2,100 × $0.3975	835
Total work in process, October 31......................				31,775
Total cost accounted for..				$233,840

When will the FIFO and weighted-average methods give significantly different results?

Answer:

FIFO and weighted-average methods give different results when

- There is beginning inventory. If there is no beginning inventory, FIFO and weighted-average yield identical numbers. This is why we did not need to specify whether Recreational Divers Ltd.'s Shaping Department used FIFO or weighted-average—Shaping had no beginning inventory.
- The cost per unit changes from one period to the next. If the cost per unit in the current period is the same as in the prior period, then FIFO and weighted-average methods yield identical results.

FIFO and weighted-average yield significantly different results only when there are large beginning inventories *and* costs change dramatically from one period to the next. This could happen, for example, in the wine-making industry, where there are significant work in process inventories, and where the cost of grapes fluctuates depending on weather and other crop conditions.

The following Decision Guidelines review key issues arising in process costing systems with multiple processes and beginning work in process inventories.

DECISION GUIDELINES   *Process Costing—Second Process (with Beginning Inventory)*

Decision	Guidelines
At what point in a second process are transferred-in costs incurred?	Transferred-in costs are typically incurred at the *beginning* of the second (or subsequent) process.
When do FIFO and weighted-average methods of process costing yield different results?	When there is beginning work in process inventory *and* cost per unit changes from one period to the next.
Which periods' costs are included in the cost per equivalent unit computation?	• *FIFO* → Only costs incurred in current period • *Weighted average* → Cost of work done in prior period to start the beginning inventory, plus all costs incurred in the current period
How to compute equivalent units using • FIFO method?	*FIFO* equivalent units of work done in current period equals work done to • *Complete* beginning inventory, plus • *Start and complete* additional units, plus • *Start* ending inventory
• Weighted-average method?	*Weighted-average* equivalent units of all work done on units in process equals • All work ever done on units completed and transferred out this period (whether work was done this period or last period), plus • Work done to *start* the ending inventory

This problem extends the Mid-Chapter Summary Problem on page 1186 to a second processing department. During May, Oxford Manufacturing Inc. has the following activity in its Finishing Department:

Finishing Department Facts for May

Units:

Work in process, April 30 (20% complete as to direct materials, 70% complete as to conversion work)	4,000 units
Transferred in from Assembly Department during May	16,000 units
Completed during May	15,000 units
Work in process, May 31 (36% complete as to direct materials, 80% complete as to conversion work)	5,000 units

Costs:

Work in process, April 30 (Transferred-in costs, $11,982; direct materials costs, $488; conversion costs, $5,530)	$18,000
Transferred in from Assembly Department during May	38,400
Direct materials added during May	6,400
Conversion costs added during May	24,300

Required

Show the allocation of total cost to units completed and to units in ending work in process inventory for the Finishing Department in May. Use

1. The FIFO method.
2. The weighted-average method.

Solution to Review Problem

1. The FIFO method

Step 1: Summarize the flow of physical units.
Step 2: Compute output in terms of equivalent units.

OXFORD MANUFACTURING INC.
Finishing Department
For the Month Ended May 31, 2003

Flow of Production	Step 1 — Flow of Physical Units	Step 2 Equivalent Units — Transferred In	Direct Materials	Conversion Costs
Units to account for:				
Work in process, April 30	4,000			
Transferred in during May	16,000			
Total physical units to account for	20,000			
Units accounted for:				
Completed and transferred out during May:				
From beginning inventory	4,000	0	3,200*	1,200*
Transferred in and completed during May				
(16,000 – 5,000)	11,000	11,000	11,000	11,000
Work in process, May 31	5,000	5,000	1,800†	4,000†
Total physical units accounted for	20,000			
Equivalent units		16,000	16,000	16,200

*Direct materials: 4,000 units each 80% completed = 3,200 equivalent units.
Conversion costs: 4,000 units each 30% completed = 1,200 equivalent units.
†Direct materials: 5,000 units each 36% completed = 1,800 equivalent units.
Conversion costs: 5,000 units each 80% completed = 4,000 equivalent units.

Step 3: Summarize total costs to account for; Step 4: Compute the cost per equivalent unit.

OXFORD MANUFACTURING INC.
Finishing Department
For the Month Ended May 31, 2003

	Transferred-In Costs	Direct Materials	Conversion Costs	Total
Work in process, April 30				$18,000
Costs added during May	$38,400	$ 6,400	$24,300	69,100
Divide by equivalent units	÷ 16,000	÷ 16,000	÷ 16,200	
Cost per equivalent unit	$ 2.40	$ 0.40	$ 1.50	
Total costs to account for				$87,100

Step 5: Apply costs to units completed and to units in ending work in process inventory.

OXFORD MANUFACTURING INC.
Finishing Department
For the Month Ended May 31, 2003

	Transferred-In Costs	Direct Materials	Conversion Costs	Total
Units completed and transferred to Finished Goods Inventory:				
From work in process, April 30.............................				$18,000
Costs added during May:				
Direct materials.....................................		3,200 × $0.40		1,280
Conversion costs....................................			1,200 × $1.50	1,800
Total completed from April 30 inventory............				21,080
Units transferred in and completed during May....	11,000 × ($2.40 + $0.40 + $1.50)			47,300
Total cost transferred out..........................				68,380
Work in process, May 31:				
Transferred-in costs.................................	5,000 × $2.40			12,000
Direct materials.....................................		1,800 × $0.40		720
Conversion costs....................................			4,000 × $1.50	6,000
Total work in process, May 31........................				18,720
Total cost accounted for............................				$87,100

2. The weighted-average method

Step 1: Summarize the flow of physical units.
Step 2: Compute output in terms of equivalent units.

OXFORD MANUFACTURING INC.
Finishing Department
For the Month Ended May 31, 2003

	Step 1	Step 2 Equivalent Units		
Flow of Production	Flow of Physical Units	Transferred In	Direct Materials	Conversion Costs
Units to account for:				
Work in process, April 30.................................	4,000			
Transferred in during May	16,000			
Total physical units to account for...................	20,000			
Units accounted for:				
Completed and transferred out during May	15,000	15,000	15,000	15,000
Work in process, May 31..................................	5,000	5,000	1,800*	4,000*
Total physical units accounted for......................	20,000			
Equivalent units..		20,000	16,800	19,000

*Direct materials: 5,000 units each 36% completed = 1,800 equivalent units.
Conversion costs: 5,000 units each 80% completed = 4,000 equivalent units.

Step 3: Summarize total costs to account for; Step 4: Compute the cost per equivalent unit.

OXFORD MANUFACTURING INC.
Finishing Department
For the Month Ended May 31, 2003

	Transferred-In Costs	Direct Materials	Conversion Costs	Total
Work in process, April 30	$11,982	$ 488	$ 5,530	$18,000
Costs added during May	38,400	6,400	24,300	69,100
Total cost	$50,382	$ 6,888	$29,830	
Divide by equivalent units	÷ 20,000	÷ 16,800	÷ 19,000	
Cost per equivalent unit	$2.5191	$ 0.41	$ 1.57	
Total costs to account for				$87,100

Step 5: Assign costs to units completed and to units in ending work in process inventory.

OXFORD MANUFACTURING INC.
Finishing Department
For the Month Ended May 31, 2003

	Transferred-In Costs	Direct Materials	Conversion Costs	Total
Units completed and transferred to Finished Goods Inventory	15,000 × ($2.5191 + $0.41 + $1.57)			$67,486
Work in process, May 31:				
Transferred-in costs	5,000 × $2.5191			12,596
Direct materials		1,800 × $0.41		738
Conversion costs			4,000 × $1.57	6,280
Total work in process, May 31				19,614
Total costs accounted for				$87,100

Summary

1. **Distinguish between the flow of costs in process costing and job costing.** In process costing systems, costs are accumulated by processing departments and flow from one department to another until the product is completed. In contrast, in job cost systems, costs are accumulated on job cost records and the cost of a completed job flows directly to finished goods inventory.
2. **Record process costing transactions.** Journal entries in a process costing system are like those in a job cost system, with one key exception: A job cost system typically uses one Work in Process Inventory account, but a process costing system uses one such account for each processing department. As goods move from one department to the next, the Work in Process Inventory account of the receiving department is debited and the account of the transferring department is credited. After processing is completed, the cost of the goods moves with them into Finished Goods Inventory and Cost of Goods Sold.
3. **Compute equivalent units of production.** Because goods in process may be in various stages of completion, we compute *equivalent units*—the amount of work expressed in terms of fully completed units of output. Equivalent units are computed for each input cost category.
4. **Assign costs to units completed and to units in ending work in process inventory.** Accounting for a department's costs is a five-step procedure. First, the flow of physical (output) units is determined. Second, we compute equivalent units. Third, the total cost to account for is determined. Fourth, costs per equivalent unit are computed for each input category. Fifth, physical units are costed by multiplying equivalent units of production from step 2 by equivalent-unit costs from step 4.
5. **Account for a second processing department by the FIFO method.** *FIFO*, one of two methods that are widely used for process costing, focuses on current-period work. With this method, equivalent units of work performed in the current month are costed at current-month unit costs.

6. **Account for a second processing department by the weighted-average method.** The *weighted-average method* costs all work to account for each month—work in process at the beginning of the month and the current month's work—with unit costs that are a weighted average of cur- rent-month and prior-month costs. In both methods, the operations of processing departments are summarized in monthly *production cost reports*. Managers compare the actual costs in the reports with budgeted costs to evaluate the efficiency of production.

Self-Study Questions

Test your understanding of the chapter by marking the best answer to each of the following questions.

1. For which of the following products is a process costing system most appropriate? (*p. 1176*)
   a. Breakfast cereal   c. Houses
   b. Automobiles   d. Furniture

2. A key difference between job costing and process costing is that (*pp. 1176–1178*)
   a. Costs are assigned to direct materials in job cost- ing and to indirect materials in process costing
   b. Job costing uses a single Work in Process Inventory account and process costing uses a separate Work in Process Inventory account for each department
   c. Job costing, but not process costing, accounts for conversion costs
   d. Manufacturing overhead is accounted for in process costing but not in job costing

3. During August, the Assembly Department of Damask Manufacturing Corp. completed and transferred 20,000 intercom units to the Finishing Department. The Assembly Department's August 31 inventory included 6,000 units, 90 percent com- plete as to direct materials and 75 percent com- plete as to conversion work. August equivalent units of the Assembly Department total (*p. 1181*)
   a. 20,000
   b. 24,500
   c. 25,400
   d. 25,400 for direct materials and 24,500 for conversion costs

4. The concept of equivalent units is useful for (*p. 1181*)
   a. Measuring the total costs of direct materials and conversion incurred in a processing department
   b. Measuring the unit costs of direct materials and conversion to compute the cost of goods trans- ferred from one processing department to the next
   c. Separating the cost of a manufacturing *process* from the cost of a manufacturing *activity*
   d. Dividing ending inventory between finished goods and work in process

5. The entry to record the transfer of goods from the Heating Department to the Drying Department is (*p. 1185*)

   a. Finished Goods XXX
         Work in Process—Drying   XXX
   b. Work in Process—Heating.......XXX
         Work in Process—Drying   XXX
   c. Work in Process—Heating....... XXX
         Finished Goods   XXX
   d. Work in Process—Drying XXX
         Work in Process—Heating...   XXX

6. The costs to account for in a second processing de- partment include those associated with (*p. 1189*)
   a. Beginning work in process and goods trans- ferred in during the period
   b. Beginning work in process and costs added dur- ing the period
   c. Beginning work in process, goods transferred in, and goods transferred out
   d. Beginning work in process and ending work in process

7. Refer to the production cost report in Exhibit 21-12. The unit cost of goods completed and transferred to finished goods during October was (*p. 1194*)
   a. $4.40   c. $4.90
   b. $4.80   d. $5.32

8. If you already know equivalent units for trans- ferred-in costs, direct materials costs, and conver- sion costs under FIFO, what is the easiest way to compute equivalent units under the weighted-av- erage method? (*p. 1196*)
   a. Add the difference between the physical units in beginning work in process inventory and equiv- alent units in beginning work in process in- ventory to the FIFO equivalent units.
   b. Subtract the equivalent units in beginning work in process inventory from the FIFO equivalent units
   c. Add the equivalent units in ending work in process inventory to the FIFO equivalent units
   d. Subtract the equivalent units in ending work in process inventory from the FIFO equivalent units

9. If direct materials are added at the beginning of a second processing department, direct materials equivalent units for that department are (*p. 1191*)
   a. Less than transferred-in equivalent units
   b. Equal to transferred-in equivalent units
   c. Greater than transferred-in equivalent units
   d. Always less than the number of physical units

transferred in currently, regardless of whether FIFO or weighted-average is used

10. An advantage of the FIFO method over the weighted-average method is that (p. 1198)
   a. Its computations are simpler
   b. It is more useful for income determination
   c. It is more useful for inventory valuation
   d. It is more useful for evaluating manufacturing performance

Answers to the Self-Study Questions follow the Similar Accounting Terms.

Accounting Vocabulary

Conversion costs *(p. 1180)*
Equivalent units *(p. 1181)*
First-in, first-out (FIFO) process costing method *(p. 1189)*
Production cost report *(p. 1194)*
Transferred-in costs *(p. 1190)*
Weighted-average process costing method *(p. 1194)*

Similar Accounting Terms

Equivalent units	Equivalent units of production
FIFO	First-in, First-out
Job costing	Job order costing

Answers to Self-Study Questions

1. a
2. b
3. d   Direct materials: 20,000 + (6,000 × 0.90) = 25,400
      Conversion costs: 20,000 + (6,000 × 0.75) = 24,500
4. b
5. d
6. b
7. d $202,200/38,000 = $5.32
8. a
9. b
10. d

Assignment Material

Questions

1. Distinguish a process cost accounting system from a job cost system.

2. Which type of costing system—job or process— would be better suited to account for the manufacture of each of the following products: (a) chemicals, (b) automobiles, (c) lumber, (d) hand-held calculators, (e) custom lampshades?

3. Why does a process costing system use multiple Work in Process Inventory accounts but a job cost system use only one such account?

4. Give the entries (accounts only) to record the following: (a) purchase of materials; (b) incurrence of labour; (c) incurrence of manufacturing over-head cost; (d) requisition of materials and appli-cation of labour and overhead to Work in Process Inventory—Department 1 (combine in one entry); (e) transfer of cost of work in process inventory from Department 1 to Department 2; (f) transfer of cost of completed units to finished goods in-ventory; (g) cost of goods sold.

5. What is an equivalent unit? Give an example of equivalent units.

6. Capplett Manufacturing Ltd. completed and trans-ferred 35,000 units of its product to a second de-partment during the period. At the end of the period, another 10,000 units were in work in process inventory, 20 percent complete. How many equivalent units did Capplett Manufacturing Ltd. produce during the period?

7. Outline the five steps of process cost accounting.

8. How are equivalent units used in Exhibits 21-6 and 21-7?

9. Why might a company have different numbers of equivalent units for direct materials and conversion costs?

10. What information does a production cost report give? Why does the format of the report differ from company to company?

11. What is the major accounting challenge in a process costing system that has more than one processing department? Why is this such a challenge?

12. Using the FIFO method, compute the equivalent units of production for Department 2 during July:

> Units:
> Work in process, June 30 (10% complete as to direct materials, 40% complete as to conversion costs)............ 1,000 units

> Transferred in from Department 1
> during July .... 25,000 units
> Completed during July.............. 22,000 units
> Work in process, July 31 (20% complete as to direct materials, 70% complete as to conversion costs)............... 4,000 units

13. Repeat Question 12, using the weighted-average method.

14. Under what conditions are FIFO equivalent-unit costs equal to weighted-average equivalent-unit costs?

15. "Unit costs in process costing are averages, but that is not true in job costing." Do you agree or disagree? Explain.

Exercises

Exercise 21-1 *Diagramming flows through a process costing system* **(Obj. 1)**

Century Furniture Corp. manufactures oak furniture in a three-stage process that includes milling, assembling, and finishing, in that order. Direct materials are added in the Milling and Finishing Departments. Direct labour and overhead are applied in those two departments and in the Assembling Department. The company's general ledger includes the following accounts:

Cost of Goods Sold	Work in Process Inventory—Finishing
Manufacturing Wages	Materials Inventory
Work in Process Inventory—Milling	Finished Goods Inventory
Work in Process Inventory—Assembling	Manufacturing Overhead

Outline the flow of costs through the company's accounts. Include a T-account for each account title given.

Exercise 21-2 *Computing equivalent units in a single department* **(Obj. 3)**

Insert the missing values:

		Equivalent Units	
Flow of Production	**Flow of Physical Units**	**Direct Materials**	**Conversion Costs**
Units to account for:			
Work in process, November 30	21,000		
Started in production during December......	?		
Total physical units to account for...............	100,500		
Units accounted for:			
Completed and transferred out during December:			
From beginning inventory.........................	21,000	?*	?*
Started and completed during December	70,500	?	?
Work in process, December 31	?	?†	?†
Total physical units accounted for................	100,500		
Equivalent units of production		?	?

*Direct materials: 40% completed during Dec.
Conversion costs: 50% completed during Dec.

†Direct materials: 20% completed during Dec.
Conversion costs: 30% completed during Dec.

Exercise 21-3 *Computing equivalent units and applying costs to completed units and to work in process inventory* **(Obj. 3, 4, 5)**

Cambie Industries, Inc. experienced the following activity in its Finishing Department during December.

Units:
Work in process, November 30 (60% complete as to
direct materials, 80% complete as to conversion work)............... 16,000 units
Transferred in from Heating Department during December.......... 62,000 units
Completed during December .... 52,000 units
Work in process, December 31 (60% complete as to
direct materials, 80% complete as to conversion work)............... 26,000 units
Costs:
Work in process, November 30 .... $ 118,000
Transferred in from Heating Department during December.......... 204,600
Direct materials added during December... 145,000
Conversion costs added during December....................................... 204,000

Required

1. Compute the number of equivalent units produced by the Finishing Department during December. Use the FIFO method.
2. Compute unit costs, and apply total cost to (a) units completed and transferred to finished goods and (b) units in December 31 work in process inventory.

Exercise 21-4 *Computing equivalent units and applying costs to completed units and to work in process inventory* **(Obj. 3, 4, 6)**

Repeat Exercise 21-3, using the weighted-average method. Assume that the November 30 balance of Work in Process—Finishing Department ($118,000) is composed of the following amounts: transferred-in costs, $52,100; direct materials costs, $25,352; and conversion costs, $40,548.

Exercise 21-5 *Transferring costs between processing departments* **(Obj. 2, 3, 4)**

The Forming Department of a chemical company began February with no work in process inventory. During the month, production that cost $73,100 (direct materials, $17,100, and conversion costs, $56,000) was started on 42,000 units. A total of 34,000 units were completed and transferred to the Heating Department. The ending work in process inventory was 50 percent complete as to direct materials and 75 percent complete as to conversion work.

Required

1. Journalize the transfer of cost from the Forming Department to the Heating Department.
2. What is the balance in Work in Process Inventory—Forming on February 28?
3. Account for the total cost incurred during February.

Exercise 21-6 *Computing processing costs and journalizing cost transfers* **(Obj. 2, 3)**

The following information was taken from the ledger of High River Products, Inc. Ending inventory is 70 percent complete as to direct materials but 40 percent complete as to conversion work.

Work in Process—Forming

	Physical Units	Dollars		Physical Units	Dollars
Inventory, Nov. 30	–0–	$ –0–	Transferred		
Production started:	160,000		to Finishing	144,000	$?
Direct materials		814,800			
Conversion costs		714,240			
Ending Inventory	16,000	?			

Required

Journalize the transfer of cost to the Finishing Department.

Exercise 21-7   *Computing equivalent units in two departments*   *(Obj. 3, 5)*

Selected production and cost data of Sanchez Inc. follow for May 2003:

	Flow of Physical Units	
	Sanding	Finishing
Flow of Production	Department	Department
Units to account for:		
Work in process, April 30.....................................	24,000	7,200
Transferred in during May	84,000	96,000
Total physical units to account for..................	108,000	103,200
Units accounted for:		
Completed and transferred out during May:		
From beginning inventory............................	24,000*	7,200‡
Transferred in and completed during May .	72,000	90,000
Work in process, May 31	12,000†	6,000§
Total physical units accounted for..................	108,000	103,200

*Direct materials: 20% completed during May.   ‡Direct materials: 2/3 completed during May.
Conversion costs: 30% completed during May.   Conversion costs: 40% completed during May.
†Direct materials: 50% completed during May.   §Direct materials: 50% completed during May.
Conversion costs: 40% completed during May.   Conversion costs: 60% completed during May.

Use the FIFO method to compute equivalent units for transferred-in cost, direct materials, and conversion costs for each department.

Exercise 21-8   *Computing equivalent units in a second department*   *(Obj. 3, 6)*

Repeat Exercise 21-7 for the Finishing Department, using the weighted-average method.

Exercise 21-9   *Journalizing process costing transactions*   *(Obj. 2)*

Record the following process cost accounting transactions in the general journal:

a. Purchase of raw materials on account, $4,500.

b. Requisition of direct materials to Processing Department 1, $2,000.

c. Payment of manufacturing labour, $12,000.

d. Incurrence of manufacturing overhead costs: amortization, $700; insurance, $600; utilities paid, $1,000.

e. Application of conversion costs to Processing Department 1: direct labour, $2,000; manufacturing overhead, $3,000.

f. Transfer of cost from Processing Department 1 to Department 2, $5,500.

g. Application of conversion costs to Processing Department 2: direct labour, $900; manufacturing overhead, $1,200.

h. Transfer of cost from Processing Department 2 to finished goods inventory, $6,000.

Exercise 21-10 *Using a production cost report* **(Obj. 2)**

Cost accountants for Wellington Manufacturing Ltd. prepared the following production cost report for February:

WELLINGTON MANUFACTURING LTD.
Finishing Department
Production Cost Report
For the Month Ended February 28, 2003

	Physical Units	Total Costs
Work in process, January 31..	14,000	$ 123,000
Transferred in from Grinding Department during February..	90,000	600,000
Costs added in Finishing Department during February:		
Direct materials...	0	87,000
Conversion costs:...		
Direct labour..	0	126,000
Manufacturing overhead..	0	124,500
Total to account for..	104,000	$1,060,500
Completed and transferred to finished goods inventory during February...	95,000	$987,000
Work in process, February 28	9,000	73,500
Total accounted for..	104,000	$1,060,500

Journalize all February activity in the Finishing Department.

Challenge Exercise

Exercise 21-11   *Using equivalent units to determine the flow of physical units*   **(Obj. 5, 6)**

The following data pertain to the Packaging Department of Chemproducts Inc. for the month of April 2002:

	Equivalent Units		
Method	Transferred In	Direct Materials	Conversion Costs
Weighted-average	630,000	630,000	626,250
FIFO	600,000	640,000	618,750

Direct materials are added when conversion is 50-percent complete in the packaging process. The number of physical units completed and transferred out during April was 615,000.

Required

1. How many physical units were transferred in to the Packaging Department in April?

2. How many physical units were in the month's beginning work in process inventory?

3. How many physical units were both transferred in and completed in April?
4. How many physical units were in the ending work in process inventory?
5. What fraction of the total required conversion work was done on the beginning work in process inventory in March? That is, at what percentage of completion were the beginning inventory units on April 1?
6. What fraction of the total required conversion work was done on the ending work in process inventory in April?

Beyond the Numbers

Beyond the Numbers 21-1 *FIFO versus weighted-average costs; first department (Obj. 1, 5, 6)*

The first part of this chapter considers Recreational Divers Ltd.'s first department—the Shaping Department. In that discussion, we did not worry about whether Recreational Divers Ltd. used the FIFO or weighted-average method. Why? Would the choice of FIFO versus weighted average ever matter in a first department? If so, under what circumstances?

Beyond the Numbers 21-2 *FIFO versus weighted-average costs; second department (Obj. 5, 6)*

Link Back to Chapter 9 (difference between FIFO and weighted average). Compare Recreational Divers Ltd.'s Finishing Department's cost per equivalent unit under the FIFO versus weighted-average method (Exhibit 21-10 and 21-15). Consider transferred-in costs, direct materials, and conversion costs separately. Did the cost per equivalent unit increase or decrease during October? How do you know?

Ethical Issue

Opscan Manufacturing Corp. produces component parts for laser optic equipment. Customers include civilian companies and the Canadian government. Under most government contracts, Opscan receives reimbursement for its manufacturing costs plus a specified profit. For most civilian contracts, Opscan bids a fixed price and either earns a profit or incurs a loss, depending on how well the company controls costs. Opscan accountants allocate to government contracts any overhead whose proper allocation to a particular product is questionable.

Required

1. Is Opscan's overhead allocation practice ethical? Give your reason.
2. Who benefits and who is harmed by the Opscan practice?

Problems (Group A)

Problem 21-1A *Computing equivalent units and applying cost to completed units and work in process inventory; no beginning inventory or cost transferred in (Obj. 3, 4)*

Find-It Inc. prints textbooks. Production occurs in three processes: engraving, printing, and binding. The Engraving Department was idle on May 31. In mid-June, Find-It Inc. started production on 50,000 books. Of this number, 40,500 books were engraved during June. The June 30 work in process in the Engraving Department was 20 percent complete as to direct materials and 50 percent complete as to conversion work. Direct materials costing $106,000 were placed in production in Engraving during June, and direct labour of $33,225 and manufacturing overhead of $61,800 were applied in that department.

Required

1. Compute the number of equivalent units and the unit costs in the Engraving Department for June.

2. Show the application of total cost in the Engraving Department to (a) units completed and transferred to Printing during June and (b) units still in process at June 30.

3. Prepare a T-account for Work in Process Inventory—Engraving to show its activity during June, including the June 30 balance.

Problem 21-2A *Computing equivalent units, applying cost to completed units and work in process inventory, and journalizing transactions; no beginning inventory or cost transferred in* **(Obj. 2, 3, 4)**

Commercial Paper Inc. produces the paper on which newspapers are printed by a four-stage process that includes mixing, cooking, rolling, and cutting. In the Mixing Department, wood pulp and chemicals, the basic raw materials, are blended. The resulting mix is heated in the Cooking Department in much the same way food is prepared. Then the cooked mix is rolled to produce sheets. The final process, cutting, divides the sheets into large rolled units.

Cost accumulation in the Mixing Department during August is summarized in this account:

Work in Process Inventory—Mixing

Direct materials	26,000
Direct labour	7,400
Manufacturing overhead	18,340

August activity in the Mixing Department consisted of completion of the mixing process for 5,000 rolls of newsprint plus partial completion of 600 additional rolls. These in-process units were one-third complete with respect to both direct materials and conversion work.

Required

1. Compute the equivalent units of production and unit costs in the Mixing Department for August.

2. Prove that the sum of (a) cost of goods transferred out of the Mixing Department and (b) ending Work in Process Inventory—Mixing equals the total cost accumulated in the department during August.

3. Journalize all transactions affecting the company's mixing process during August, including those already posted.

Problem 21-3A *Computing equivalent units for a second department with beginning inventory; applying cost to completed units and work in process inventory; FIFO method* **(Obj. 3, 4, 5)**

Avalon Mills Inc. manufactures broadloom carpet in seven processes: spinning, dyeing, plying, spooling, tufting, latexing, and shearing. First, fluff nylon purchased from a company such as DuPont or Monsanto is spun into yarn that is dyed the desired colour. Then two or more threads of the yarn are joined together, or plied, for added strength. The plied yarn is spooled for use in actual carpet making. Tufting is the process by which yarn is added to burlap backing. After the backing is latexed to hold it together and make it skid-resistant, the carpet is sheared to give it an even appearance and feel.

At March 31, before recording the transfer of costs among departments, the Avalon Mills general ledger included the following account for one of its lines of carpet:

Work in Process Inventory—Dyeing

Feb. 28 Balance	32,700	
Transferred in from Spinning	67,200	
Direct materials	37,170	
Direct labour	21,621	
Manufacturing overhead	128,700	

Work in process inventory of the Dyeing Department on February 28 consisted of 75 rolls that were 60 percent complete as to direct materials and conversion work. During March, 560 rolls were transferred in from the Spinning Department. The Dyeing Department completed 500 rolls of the carpet in March, and 135 rolls were still in process on March 31. The ending inventory was 100 percent complete as to direct materials and 80 percent complete as to conversion work.

Required

1. Compute the equivalent units, unit costs, and total costs to account for in the Dyeing Department for March. Use the FIFO method.
2. Show the assignment of total Dyeing Department cost to (a) goods transferred from Dyeing to Plying and (b) Work in Process Inventory—Dyeing on March 31.

Problem 21-4A *Preparing a production cost report and recording transactions on the basis of the information in the report* **(Obj. 2)**

Refer to Problem 21–3A.

Required

1. Prepare the March production cost report for the Dyeing Department.
2. Journalize all transactions affecting the Dyeing Department during March, including the entries that have already been posted.

Problem 21-5A *Computing equivalent units for a second department with beginning inventory and applying cost to completed units and work in process inventory; FIFO method* **(Obj. 3, 4, 5)**

The manufacture of snow blowers by Snow Equipment Inc. includes two processes: forming the blade housing from steel and assembling the parts of the blower. Two additional operations, lubricating the moving parts and testing the completed blowers, complete their manufacture. The blowers are transferred to finished goods before being shipped to Canadian Tire, Pro Hardware, and other hardware stores.

Process costing information for the Assembling Department of Snow Equipment Inc. for a period follows. No direct materials are required.

Units:	
Work in process, beginning (60% complete as to conversion work)	3,000 units
Transferred in from the Forming Department during the period	13,500 units
Completed during the period	9,000 units
Work in process, ending (70% complete as to conversion work)	7,500 units
Costs:	
Work in process, beginning	$ 276,000
Transferred in from the Forming Department during the period	918,000
Conversion costs added during the period	199,200

The cost transferred in to the lubricating phase is the cost of the blowers transferred out of the Assembling Department. The lubricating operation is entirely automated and takes 30 seconds per blower. Testing each completed blower requires an average of five minutes of a technician's time. Conversion costs are $30 per machine hour for lubricating and $50 per labour hour for testing. There is only one work order for the blowers in each production run.

Required

1. Compute the number of equivalent units produced by the Assembling Department during the period, unit costs, and total costs to account for. Use the FIFO method.

2. Show the application of total cost to (a) units completed and transferred to the lubricating operation and (b) units in ending work in process inventory.

3. Compute the total manufacturing cost of the 6,000 blowers completed and transferred to finished goods. Also compute the unit cost of each complete blower.

4. You are the production manager of Snow Equipment Inc. Do you want periodic production cost reports in the condensed format of Exhibit 21-12 or the expanded format of Exhibit 21-13? Why?

5. How will what you learned from this problem help you manage a business?

Problem 21-6A *Computing equivalent units for a second department with beginning inventory and applying cost to completed units and work in process inventory; weighted-average method (Obj. 3, 4, 6)*

Repeat Problem 21-5A, using the weighted-average method. Assume that the $276,000 balance of Work in Process—Assembling Department at the beginning of the period was composed of $213,750 of transferred-in cost and $62,250 of conversion cost.

Problem 21-7A *Record process costing transactions; compute equivalent units, apply cost to units completed and to units in ending work in process inventory; account for a second processing department by the weighted-average method (Obj. 2, 3, 4, 6)*

Annapolis Valley Canning Inc. purchases fruit and vegetables from the local area and cans them for the wholesale market. The production process consists of two departments: the Food Processing Department, where the raw fruit and vegetables are sliced and prepared for canning, and the Canning Department, where the materials from the Food Processing Department are put into the cans, sealed, and labels applied.

The Canning Department has four types of inputs: transferred-in costs from the Food Processing Department, canning materials, labels, and conversion costs. Processing information for the canning department for the month of July follows:

Units:	
Work in process—July 1	9,000 units
(100 percent complete as to transferred-in and canning materials, zero percent complete as to labels, and 40 percent complete as to conversion)	
Transferred in from the Food Processing Department in July	45,000 units
Completed during the period	30,000 units
Work in process—July 31	? units
(100 percent complete as to transferred-in, 80 percent complete as to canning materials, zero percent complete as to labels, and 40 percent complete as to conversion)	

Costs:
Work in process—July 1:

Transferred-in costs	$22,500	
Canning materials	11,460	
Conversion costs	3,600	$ 37,560

Costs incurred in July:

Transferred-in costs	$112,500	
Canning materials	40,200	
Labeling materials	1,500	
Conversion costs	36,000	$190,200

Conversion costs consist of direct labour (80 percent) and manufacturing overhead (20 percent).

Required

1. Compute the number of equivalent units produced by the Canning Department during July, including the number of units in the July 31 work in process. Use the weighted-average method.

2. Compute the total costs to account for the unit costs and the application of total costs to (a) units completed and transferred to finished goods inventory and (b) units in July 31 work in process. Use the expanded format of Exhibit 21-18.

3. Prepare all general journal entries required in the Canning Department for the month of July.

Problem 21-8A   *Record process costing transactions; compute equivalent units, apply cost to units completed and to units in ending work in process inventory; account for a second processing department by the FIFO method*
(Obj. 2, 3, 4, 5)

Repeat Problem 21-7A, using the FIFO method.

Problems (Group B)

Problem 21-1B   *Computing equivalent units and applying cost to completed units and work in process inventory; no beginning inventory or cost transferred in*
(Obj. 3, 4)

Quickcomm Inc. produces component parts for the telecommunications industry. One part, a laser diode, is manufactured in a single processing department. No laser diodes were in process on May 31, and Quickcomm Inc. started production on 15,000 units during June. Completed production for June totaled 12,375 units. The June 30 work in process was 20 percent complete as to direct materials and 30 percent complete as to conversion work. Direct materials costing $6,600 were placed in production during June, and direct labour of $5,100 and manufacturing overhead of $2,271 were applied to the process.

Required

1. Compute the number of equivalent units and the unit costs for June.

2. Show the application of total cost to (a) units completed and transferred to finished goods inventory and (b) units still in process at June 30.

3. Prepare a T-account for Work in Process Inventory to show its activity during June, including the June 30 balance.

Problem 21-2B *Computing equivalent units, applying cost to completed units and work in process inventory, and journalizing transactions; no beginning inventory or cost transferred in* **(Obj. 2, 3, 4)**

The Aberdeen Wool Company Ltd. produces wool fabric by a three-stage process: cleaning, spinning, and weaving. Costs incurred in the Cleaning Department during September are summarized as follows:

Work in Process Inventory—Cleaning

Direct materials	140,800
Direct labour	5,160
Manufacturing overhead	17,400

September activity in the Cleaning Department included completion of 23,100 kg of wool, which was transferred to the Spinning Department. Also, work began on 4,050 kg of wool, which on September 30 was 100 percent complete as to direct materials and 60 percent complete as to conversion work.

Required

1. Compute the equivalent units of production and unit costs in the Cleaning Department for September.
2. Prove that the sum of (a) cost of goods transferred out of the Cleaning Department and (b) ending Work in Process Inventory—Cleaning equals the total cost accumulated in the department during September.
3. Journalize all transactions affecting the company's cleaning process during September, including those already posted.

Problem 21-3B *Computing equivalent units for a second department with beginning inventory; applying cost to completed units and work in process inventory; FIFO method* **(Obj. 3, 4, 5)**

Autorack Manufacturing Corporation manufactures auto roof racks in a two-stage process that includes shaping and plating. Steel alloy is the basic raw material of the shaping process. The steel is moulded according to the design specifications of automobile manufacturers. The Plating Department then adds an anodized finish.

At March 31, before recording the transfer of cost from the Plating Department to Finished Goods Inventory, the Autorack Manufacturing Corporation general ledger included the following account:

Work in Process Inventory—Plating

Feb. 28 Balance	36,900
Transferred in from Shaping	54,000
Direct materials	36,300
Direct labour	25,650
Manufacturing overhead	58,140

Work in process of the Plating Department on February 28 consisted of 600 racks that were 40 percent complete as to direct materials and conversion work. During March, 3,000 racks were transferred in from the Shaping Department. The Plating Department transferred 2,200 racks to finished goods in March, and 1,400 racks were still in process on March 31. This ending inventory was 40 percent complete as to direct materials and 70 percent complete as to conversion work.

Required

1. Compute the equivalent units, unit costs, and total costs to account for in the Plating Department for March. Use the FIFO method.

2. Show the assignment of total Plating Department cost to (a) goods transferred out of the Plating Department and (b) Work in Process Inventory—Plating on March 31.

Problem 21-4B *Preparing a production cost report and recording transactions on the basis of the information in the report* *(Obj. 2)*

Refer to Problem 21–3B.

Required

1. Prepare the March production cost report for the Plating Department.
2. Journalize all transactions affecting the Plating Department during March, including the entries that have already been posted.

Problem 21-5B *Computing equivalent units for a second department with beginning inventory and applying cost to completed units and work in process inventory; FIFO method* *(Obj. 3, 4, 5)*

The forming of hand-tool parts at Craftmaster Tool Company Ltd. occurs in four departments. Consider screwdrivers with plastic handles. The forming of the handles includes mixing the raw materials, heating the mix, shaping the mix by pouring it into moulds, and drying. Production of the screwdrivers is then completed in two operations: assembling the handles and shanks and packaging for shipment to retail outlets.

Process costing information for the Drying Department of Craftmaster Tool Company Ltd. for a period follows. No direct materials are required.

Units:	
Work in process, beginning (30% complete as to conversion work)	14,000 units
Transferred in from the Moulding Department during the period	64,000 units
Completed during the period	32,000 units
Work in process, ending (20% complete as to conversion work)	46,000 units
Costs:	
Work in process, beginning	$1,690
Transferred in from the Moulding Department during the period	7,680
Conversion costs added during the period	3,330

The cost transferred in to the assembling phase is the cost of the plastic handles transferred out of the Drying Department. Assembling operation direct materials are the metal shanks, which cost $2,888 for the period. The assembling and packaging operations are automated. Assembling occurs at the rate of 8,000 units per hour and packaging at 4,000 units per hour. Conversion cost is allocated to the assembling operation at the predetermined rate of $25.00 per machine hour and to packaging at the rate of $30.00 per machine hour. There is only one work order for the screwdrivers.

Required

1. Compute the number of equivalent units produced by the Drying Department during the period, the unit costs, and the total costs to account for. Use the FIFO method.
2. Show the application of total cost to (a) units completed and transferred to the assembly operation and (b) units in ending work in process inventory.

3. Compute the total manufacturing cost of the 32,000 screwdrivers completed and transferred to finished goods. Also compute the unit cost of each complete screwdriver.

4. You are the production manager of Craftmaster Tool Company Ltd. Do you want periodic production cost reports in the condensed format of Exhibit 21-12 or the expanded format of Exhibit 21-13? Why?

5. How will what you learned from this problem help you manage a business?

Problem 21-6B *Computing equivalent units for a second department with beginning inventory and applying cost to completed units and work in process inventory; weighted-average method (Obj. 3, 4, 6)*

Repeat Problem 21-5B, using the weighted-average method. Assume that the $1,690 balance of Work in Process—Drying Department at the beginning of the period was composed of $900 of transferred-in cost and $790 of conversion cost.

Problem 21-7B *Record process costing transactions; compute equivalent units, apply cost to units completed and to units in ending work in process inventory; account for a second processing department by the weighted-average method (Obj. 2, 3, 4, 6)*

Okanagan Canning Inc. purchases fruit and vegetables from the local area and cans them for the wholesale market. The production process consists of two departments: the Food Processing Department, where the raw fruit and vegetables are sliced and prepared for canning, and the Canning Department, where the materials from the Food Processing Department are put into the cans, sealed, and labels applied.

The Canning Department has four types of inputs: transferred-in costs from the Food Processing Department, canning materials, labels, and conversion costs. Processing information for the Canning Department for the month of July follows:

Units:
    Work in process—July 1 .... 18,000 units
        (100 percent complete as to transferred-in and canning materials, zero
          percent complete as to labels, and 60 percent complete as to conversion)
    Transferred in from the Food Processing Department in July...... 90,000 units
    Completed during the period... 84,000 units
    Work in process—July 31 .... ? units
        (100 percent complete as to transferred-in, 70 percent complete as to
        canning materials, zero percent complete as to labels, and 50 percent
        complete as to conversion)
Costs:
    Work in process—July 1:
        Transferred-in costs... $ 45,000
        Canning materials.. 10,800
        Conversion costs ....   5,400 $ 61,200
    Costs incurred in July:
        Transferred-in costs... $225,000
        Canning materials.. 124,200
        Labeling materials.. 4,200
        Conversion costs 42,600 $396,000

Conversion costs consist of direct labour (90 percent) and manufacturing overhead (10 percent).

Required

1. Compute the number of equivalent units produced by the Canning Department during July, including the number of units in the July 31 work in process. Use the weighted-average method.
2. Compute the total costs to account for the unit costs and the application of total costs to (a) units completed and transferred to finished goods and (b) units in July 31 work in process. Use the expanded format of Exhibit 21-18.
3. Prepare all general journal entries required in the canning department for the month of July.

Problem 21-8B *Record process costing transactions; compute equivalent units, apply cost to units completed and to units in ending work in process inventory; account for a second processing department by the FIFO method* **(Obj. 2, 3, 4, 5)**

Repeat Problem 21-7B, using the FIFO method.

Challenge Problems

Problem 21-1C *Utilizing process costs in decision making* **(Obj. 1, 2, 3)**

Dereck Eng has just joined Fastblade Corp., a maker of ice skates and in-line skates, as executive vice president. Fastblade Corp. has a complete process costing system and monitors cost at each stage of the multiple-stage production processes for the two kinds of skates.

Eng thinks the process costing record keeping and the related employees are unnecessary and in a cost-cutting move proposes to consolidate all cost accounting so that Fastblade Corp. will know only the total cost by finished product.

Required

Write a memo to Peter Fast, president of Fastblade Corp., explaining the value of controlling costs at each step of the production process (moulded boot, blade production, assembly) rather than at the end of the process.

Problem 21-2C *Allocating costs to completed units* **(Obj. 4)**

Carol Gallagher has the responsibility for calculating the equivalent units at each stage of production for each of the ten products produced by Windsor Brands Ltd. There are, on average, five stages of production for each product.

Required

The estimating process is subject to error in the Windsor Brands Ltd. processing of its products.

1. What would be the impact if Carol's estimates were random across all 50 estimating opportunities per month and averaged out to zero?
2. What would be the impact if Carol's estimates of the amount of conversion was consistently underestimated (i.e., the degree of conversion was greater than Carol estimated)?

Extending Your Knowledge

Decision Problems

1. Preparing a production cost report and evaluating production efficiency (Obj. 5)

Montgomery Manufacturing Company Ltd. makes automobile parts. The following cost data for the company's Finishing Department are available for October:

Flow of Production	Flow of Physical Units	Equivalent Units Transferred In	Direct Materials	Conversion Costs
Units to account for:				
Beginning work in process inventory	24,000			
Transferred in during October	56,000			
Total units to account for	80,000			
Units accounted for:				
Completed and transferred out to finished goods inventory during October:				
From beginning inventory	24,000	0	14,400	12,000
Transferred in from Moulding and completed during October	48,000	48,000	48,000	48,000
Work in process, October 31	8,000	8,000	1,600	2,400
Total physical units accounted for	80,000			
Equivalent units of production		56,000	64,000	62,400

Unit costs:	Transferred-In Costs	Direct Materials	Conversion Costs	Total
Work in process, September 30				$118,000
Costs added during October	$128,800	$70,400	$99,840	299,040
Divide by equivalent units	÷ 56,000	÷ 64,000	÷ 62,400	
Cost per equivalent unit	$ 2.30	$ 1.10	$ 1.60	
Total cost to account for				$417,040

Allocation of total cost:	Transferred-In Costs	Direct Materials	Conversion Costs	Total
Units completed and transferred out to finished goods:				
From work in process, September 30				$ 118,000
Costs added during October:				
Direct materials		[14,400 × $1.10]		15,840
Conversion costs			[12,000 × $1.60]	19,200
Total completed from September 30 inventory				153,040
Units transferred in from Moulding and completed during October		[48,000 × ($2.30 + $1.10 + $1.60)]		240,000
Total cost transferred out				393,040
Work in process, October 31:				
Transferred-in costs	[8,000 × $2.30]			18,400
Direct materials		[1600 × $1.10]		1,760
Conversion costs			[2,400 × $1.60]	3,840
Total work in process, October 31				24,000
Total cost accounted for				$417,040

Required

1. Prepare a basic production cost report for the Finishing Department for the month of October.

2. Suppose that the budgeted cost per completed unit of output in October was $5.05. Were Montgomery's costs during October higher or lower than budgeted? Why might the company's production managers want more information than is revealed in the basic production cost report?

2. Using process costing information to make an outsourcing decision   (Obj. 5)

Refer to the data for Decision Problem 1. Suppose that the Montgomery Manufacturing Company Ltd. is approached by another manufacturer that offers to finish Montgomery's products for $2.50 per unit. If Montgomery accepts the offer to "outsource" the finishing operation, it will shut down its Finishing Department.

Required

1. What process costing information is useful in deciding whether to make or buy finishing operations?

2. What other factors should be considered by Montgomery's management before it accepts or rejects the other company's offer?

Comprehensive Problem
for Part Five

Using and Evaluating a Product Costing System

Keon Corporation has a machine shop that specializes in the production of aircraft components. Its primary manufacturing activities are materials handling, lathe work, milling, grinding, and testing completed units of product. The milling and grinding operations are automated.

Keon Corporation's job costing system traces direct materials and direct labour costs directly to jobs. The system applies manufacturing overhead costs to jobs at a budgeted percentage of direct labour cost. For 2003, the company expected to incur $500,000 of direct labour cost. Keon Corporation's budgeted manufacturing overhead totaled $2,250,000.

Keon Corporation bids on jobs in order to generate business. The company's bid prices are determined in two steps. First, the full cost of each job is budgeted by adding the costs of direct materials, direct labour, and manufacturing overhead to the budgeted operating cost. Operating cost is budgeted at 10 percent of manufacturing cost. Second, the budgeted full cost of the job is marked up by 25 percent. That is, the bid price of each job is 125 percent of the job's budgeted full cost.

Keon Corporation recently won two bids from long-time customers. Budget data for the jobs are:

	Job 1	Job 2
Direct materials cost	$50,000	$300,000
Direct labour cost	$4,000	$56,000
Number of parts	500	2,000
Number of machine hours	150	250
Number of product units (all of which are tested)	10	200

Required

1. Compute Keon Corporation's 2003 budgeted manufacturing overhead cost application rate.

2. Compute Keon Corporation's
   a. Budgeted manufacturing product cost of Jobs 1 and 2
   b. Budgeted full product cost of Jobs 1 and 2
   c. Bid (sale) price of each job

3. Evaluate Keon Corporation's costing system. Do you believe that the manufacturing overhead cost *applied* to individual jobs is an accurate estimate of the manufacturing overhead cost *incurred* on the jobs? Why or why not?

4. On the basis of your analysis for requirement 3, which of the two jobs is likely to be less profitable than Keon Corporation's managers believe? Which is likely to be more profitable?

5. Suppose that Job 2 is the only job that Keon Corporation worked on in June 2003. On June 30, the company had charged $28,000 of direct labour to the job. Estimate the equivalent units of direct labour that were worked on during the month.

Cost-Volume-Profit Analysis

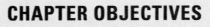

CHAPTER OBJECTIVES

After studying this chapter, you should be able to

1 Identify different cost behaviour patterns

2 Use a contribution margin income statement to make business decisions

3 Compute breakeven sales and perform sensitivity analysis

4 Compute the sales level needed to earn a target operating income

5 Graph a set of cost-volume-profit relationships

6 Compute a margin of safety

7 Use the sales mix in CVP analysis

8 Compute income using variable costing and absorption costing

The Great Canadian Railtour Company Ltd. operates the Rocky Mountaineer Railtours. The company was established in 1990 to provide rail tours through the Rocky Mountains along rail lines procured from the Canadian Pacific and Canadian National railways.

During the summer season of operation, the company offers rail tours between Vancouver and Jasper, and between Vancouver and Banff and Calgary. Passengers ride in refurbished coaches purchased from VIA Rail, in a luxury bi-level dome coach, or in luxury "Goldleaf Dome" coaches.

Peter Armstrong is the president of The Great Canadian Railtour Company Ltd. "Generally speaking, rail is no longer a cheap, efficient way to transport people over long distances. However, this kind of rail experience, where the scenery, service, and history are the attractions—more of an enjoyable excursion rather than a means of transportation—can still be marketed successfully."

The company invested in the restoration of the tracks, locomotives, and coaches. Few of the railway's costs vary with the number of passengers because most costs are *fixed*. Track maintenance, insurance, and amortization stay the same whether one or 1,000 passengers travel the scenic route. However, food and beverage costs are *variable*. They rise and fall with the number of passengers on board.

Peter Armstrong and his managers have to find a delicate balance. They must set the ticket prices high enough to cover their costs and earn a profit, but low enough to attract passengers. Because most of the railway's costs are fixed, the extra costs to serve each additional passenger are low. Once the fixed costs are covered, most of the revenue from an extra guest goes towards providing a profit.

HOW DO The Great Canadian Railtour Company Ltd. managers ensure that revenues will cover costs and provide profits? How do the managers decide on the price to charge for tickets? How many seats must the railway fill to cover its costs? As we shall see in this chapter, managers perform cost-volume-profit analysis to answer these important questions.

Cost-volume-profit (CVP) analysis expresses the relationships among costs, volume, and profit or loss. It is a key tool for short-term business decisions. In the first half of this chapter, you will learn how to compute *profit* in a way that is tailor-made for CVP analysis. To do this, we first need to discuss the different types of *costs*.

Rocky Mountaineer Railtours
www.rkymtnrail.com

Canadian Pacific
www.cp.ca

Via Rail
www.viarail.ca

Types of Costs

OBJECTIVE 1
Identify different cost behaviour patterns

In Chapter 19, we defined a *cost driver* as any factor that affects costs. Many cost drivers exist. The most prominent cost driver is volume, which often is expressed in physical *units* produced or sold, or in sales *dollars*. For example, the more jackets Roots produces—that is, the greater its production volume—the greater the costs the company incurs. Nonvolume factors also act as cost drivers. An example is weight, which may affect freight costs. To emphasize basic concepts in this chapter, we focus on volume as the cost driver. **Cost behaviour** describes how costs change—indeed, if they change at all—in response to a change in a cost driver. We examine three basic types of costs: variable, fixed, and mixed.

Variable Costs

A **variable cost** is a cost that changes in total in direct proportion to a change in volume of activity. For example, sales commissions are variable costs; the higher the sales, the higher the sales commissions. Variable costs also include direct materials costs and delivery costs. These costs rise or fall directly with an increase or decrease in production or sales volume.

Exhibit 22-1 shows the graphs of three different variable costs. The slope of each line is the variable cost per unit (here, Warrenknit athletic socks purchased by Zellers or the Bay). The higher the variable cost per unit, the steeper the slope. Every line passes through the origin, because at zero volume the total variable cost is zero.

The left-hand graph of Exhibit 22-1 is for socks that cost $2 per pair. We see that 3,000 pairs of socks cost $6,000 (3,000 × $2) and that 4,500 pairs of socks cost $9,000 (4,500 × $2). A 50-percent increase in volume (4,500 − 3,000 = 1,500; 1,500/3,000 = 50%) results in a 50-percent increase in total cost ($9,000 − $6,000 = $3,000; $3,000/$6,000 = 50%). But the unit variable cost is $2 for both (and all other) volume levels.

The middle graph in Exhibit 22-1 has a steeper slope. It is for socks that cost $3 per pair. This graph shows that 2,000 of these pairs of socks cost $6,000 (2,000 × $3) and that 4,000 pairs of socks cost $12,000 (4,000 × $3). When volume doubles, total cost doubles.

The right-hand variable cost graph relates to designer socks that cost $10 per pair. Total cost increases much more rapidly with volume than it does for the less-expensive socks. This graph has the steepest slope.

> The higher the variable cost per unit, the steeper the slope of the line in the total variable cost graph.

Fixed Costs

A **fixed cost** is a cost that does not change in total despite wide changes in volume. For example, office rent usually does not change with the volume of business. A real estate company pays the same monthly rent for a real estate office regardless of whether sales volume rises, falls, or stays the same. Other examples of fixed costs include amortization, property taxes, and many executive salaries. These costs occur even if the company makes no sales. Exhibit 22-2 graphs a fixed cost, which is a horizontal line intersecting the cost axis at the level of the total cost. In such a graph, total fixed cost is the same for any volume. However, the *fixed cost per unit*

EXHIBIT 22-1

Variable Cost Pattern—Pairs of Warrenknit Athletic Socks

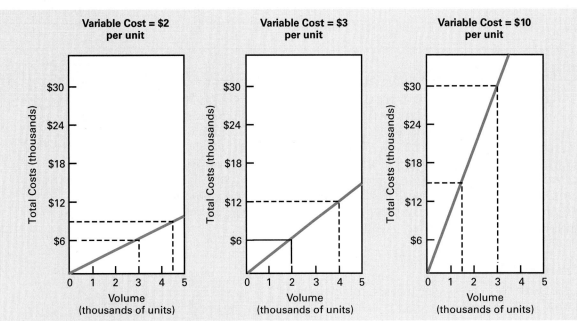

The Contribution Margin Income Statement

OBJECTIVE 2
Use a contribution margin income statement to make business decisions

Earlier chapters presented the conventional income statement. That format, illustrated for Jones Manufacturing Inc. in Panel A of Exhibit 22-5, classifies expenses by value-chain function. Manufacturing costs are expensed as cost of goods sold. Sales revenue minus cost of goods sold equals gross margin. Most other costs (for example, costs of marketing and administration) are grouped as "operating expenses." As explained in Chapter 5, gross margin minus operating expenses equals operating income.

Cost of goods sold on a conventional income statement includes both variable and fixed manufacturing costs. Among the variable costs are direct materials, direct labour, and the cost of electricity used by production equipment. In contrast, such manufacturing costs as amortization, factory rent, and property taxes are fixed. As Panel A shows, conventional income statements do not distinguish between variable and fixed expenses.

Companies use conventional income statements to report the results of operations to external parties. Managers also use the statements for budgeting and other internal purposes. But for decision making, many managers demand a different income format. To see why, let's suppose that executives want to predict the operating income that Jones Manufacturing Inc. will earn if sales volume increases by 10 percent.

The conventional income statement does not help Jones's managers predict how the change in volume will affect income. This is because the conventional income statement does not separate variable costs from fixed costs. To solve this problem, the **contribution margin income statement** in Panel B of Exhibit 22-5 groups variable and fixed expenses separately. It highlights the **contribution margin**, which is the excess of sales revenues over variable expenses.

The contribution margin is so named because the excess of revenues over variable expenses is the amount that contributes to "covering" fixed expenses and to providing operating income. Think about fixed expenses. Many fixed costs are incurred *before* any production or sales take place. For instance, machines must be purchased before goods can be produced. Their cost becomes amortization expense. As goods are produced and sold, the contribution margin grows and covers the expense. In effect, the company recoups its machine investment. After all fixed costs are recouped by the contribution margin, additional sales provide operating income. The contribution margin is useful for decision making as well as for reporting income.

WORKING IT OUT

(1) Allen Corp. has fixed expenses of $100,000, variable expenses of $5 per unit, and a selling price of $20 per unit. Prepare a contribution margin (CM) income statement at a sales level of 15,000 units. (2) By how much would operating income increase if 25,000 units were sold?

A: (1)

Sales	$300,000
Var. expenses	75,000
CM	225,000
Fixed expenses	100,000
Operating income	$125,000

(2) Operating income would increase by the contribution margin of the additional units sold—$150,000 (10,000 units × $15 CM).

EXHIBIT 22-5

Alternative Income Statement Formats

Panel A—Conventional Format

JONES MANUFACTURING INC.
Conventional Income Statement
For the Year Ended December 31, 2003

Sales revenue		$2,100,000
Cost of goods sold		1,320,000
Gross margin		780,000
Operating expenses:		
Marketing	$310,000	
Other	290,000	600,000
Operating income		$ 180,000

Panel B—Contribution Margin Format

JONES MANUFACTURING INC.
Contribution Margin Income Statement
For the Year Ended December 31, 2003

Sales revenue		$2,100,000
Variable expenses:		
Manufacturing	$840,000	
Marketing	150,000	
Other operating	210,000	1,200,000
Contribution margin		900,000
Fixed expenses:		
Manufacturing	480,000	
Marketing	160,000	
Other operating	80,000	720,000
Operating income		$ 180,000

REAL WORLD EXAMPLE

The contribution margin (CM) income statement is often used by managers to evaluate different departments or product lines. By looking at the CM of a department that is operating at a loss, management can decide whether or not to close that department. A good general rule of thumb: If the department shows a positive CM, then the company as a whole will be more profitable (in the short run) if the department is kept operating.

Compare the conventional income statement in Exhibit 22-5, Panel A, with the contribution margin income statement in Panel B. The conventional income statement subtracts cost of goods sold (including both variable and fixed manufacturing costs) from sales to obtain gross margin. In contrast, the contribution margin income statement subtracts all variable costs (both manufacturing and nonmanufacturing) to obtain contribution margin. The following chart highlights the differences between gross margin and contribution margin:

Conventional Income Statement	Contribution Margin Income Statement
Sales revenue	Sales revenue
deduct Cost of Goods Sold:	deduct Variable Expenses:
Variable manufacturing cost of goods sold	Variable manufacturing cost of goods sold
Fixed manufacturing cost of goods sold	Variable marketing expenses Other variable expenses
= Gross margin	= Contribution margin

The two major differences are

- Fixed manufacturing cost of goods sold is subtracted from sales to compute gross margin, but not to compute contribution margin.
- Variable marketing expenses and other variable nonmanufacturing expenses are subtracted from sales to calculate contribution margin, but not to compute gross margin.

Managers use the contribution margin for planning and decision making, because the contribution margin distinguishes between variable and fixed costs. As an example, let's examine how Jones Manufacturing Inc.'s managers can use the contribution margin income statement to predict the company's operating income if sales volume increases by 10 percent. If sales volume increases by 10 percent, then variable costs (expenses) should also increase by 10 percent. Fixed costs (expenses), however, should remain the same, assuming Jones Manufacturing Inc. remains in the same relevant range:

Increase in sales (10% × $2,100,000).....................................	$210,000
Increase in variable expenses (10% × $1,200,000)...............	(120,000)
Increase in contribution margin..	90,000
Increase in fixed expenses	0
Increase in operating income	$ 90,000

Now suppose that Jones Manufacturing Inc. could achieve the same 10 percent increase in sales only by spending an additional $20,000 on a new advertising campaign. Should Jones undertake the advertising campaign?

Increase in contribution margin (from above).....................		$ 90,000
Increase in marketing expenses		(20,000)
Increase in operating income		$ 70,000

The increased profits from higher sales outweigh the increased costs of the new advertising campaign, so Jones Manufacturing should undertake the campaign.

This analysis cannot be performed using the conventional income statement, because that statement's format does not show which expenses are variable and which are fixed.

Mid-Chapter Summary Problem
for Your Review

The 2003 contribution margin income statement of Prestige Shirt Company Inc. is shown below. The average selling price of Prestige's shirts is $45.

PRESTIGE SHIRT COMPANY INC.
Contribution Margin Income Statement
For the Year Ended December 31, 2003

Sales revenue		$900,000
Variable expenses:		
Manufacturing	$280,000	
Operating	120,000	400,000
Contribution margin		500,000
Fixed expenses:		
Manufacturing	225,000	
Operating	75,000	300,000
Operating income		$200,000

Required

1. How many shirts did Prestige Shirt Company Inc. sell in 2003?

2. What operating income will the company earn in 2003 if sales volume increases by 20 percent and all sale prices, unit variable costs, and total fixed costs do not change? There are no beginning and ending inventories.

3. Recast the 2003 income statement in the conventional format.

Solution to Review Problem

Requirement 1

Prestige Shirt Company Inc. sold 20,000 shirts in 2003

$$\text{Shirts sold} = \frac{\text{Sales revenue}}{\text{Sale price per shirt}} = \frac{\$900,000}{\$45} = 20,000$$

Requirement 2

Increase in sales revenue ($900,000 × 20%)......................	$180,000
Increase in variable expenses:	

$$\frac{\text{Increase in sales}}{\text{Current sales}} \times \text{Current variable expenses}$$

$\dfrac{\$180,000}{\$900,000}$	×	$400,000	80,000
Increase in contribution margin......................................			100,000
Increase in fixed expenses...			0
Increase in operating income..			100,000
2003 operating income..			200,000
2004 operating income..			$300,000

Requirement 3

PRESTIGE SHIRT COMPANY INC.
Conventional Income Statement
For the Year Ended December 31, 2003

Sales revenue	$900,000
Cost of goods sold*..	505,000
Gross margin..	395,000
Operating expenses[†]...	195,000
Operating income..	$200,000

*$280,000 variable manufacturing expense + $225,000 fixed manufacturing expense from contribution margin statement.
[†]$120,000 variable operating expense + $75,000 fixed operating expense.

Cost-Volume-Profit (CVP) Analysis

The Jones Manufacturing Inc. example illustrated how changes in volume affect costs and profit—this is one type of cost-volume-profit (CVP) analysis. The example also showed that CVP analysis is closely tied to the format of the contribution margin approach.

KEY POINT

For CVP analysis, mixed costs must be broken down into their fixed and variable components.

Assumptions Underlying CVP Analysis

Cost-volume-profit analysis is based on the following assumptions:

1. Expenses are either variable or fixed.
2. Cost-volume-profit relationships are linear over a wide range of production and sales. Linear relationships appear on graphs as straight lines (such as in Exhibits 22-1 and 22-2).
3. Sale prices, unit variable costs, and total fixed expenses will not change during the period.
4. Volume is the only cost driver. Other possible cost drivers (such as weight or size) are held constant or are insignificant.
5. The relevant range of volume is specified.
6. Inventory levels will not change.
7. The *sales mix* of products will not change during the period. **Sales mix** is the

combination of products that make up total sales. For example, the sales mix of a Leon's Furniture store may be 70 percent household furniture and 30 percent office furniture.

When these conditions are met, CVP analysis is accurate. But most business conditions do not perfectly correspond to these assumptions. That is why managers often regard CVP analysis as approximate rather than exact.

Basic CVP Analysis—The Breakeven Point

The easiest way to learn more about CVP analysis is with an example. Suppose Kay Pak is thinking of renting a booth at a trade fair for travel agents. She plans to sell international travel posters for $3.50 each. Pak can purchase the posters for $2.10 each and can return all unsold items for a full refund. The booth rents for $700. Using this information, let's answer six questions about Pak's business.

> **Question 1: What is Pak's breakeven sales level?**

The **breakeven point** is the sales level at which operating income is zero: Total revenues equal total expenses. Sales below the breakeven point result in a loss. Sales above breakeven provide a profit.

Breakeven analysis is only one component of CVP analysis. The breakeven point often is only incidental to managers of ongoing operations because their focus is on the sales level needed to earn a target profit. When managers are evaluating a new product or market opportunity, however, or when demand for an established product is declining, the breakeven point becomes even more important. Many managers view the breakeven point as a useful place to start the analysis of a new product's sales potential.

Let's use two different methods to determine the breakeven point.

The Income Statement Equation Approach   To determine the breakeven point, we start by separating total expenses into variable expenses and fixed expenses. For Kay Pak, the variable cost is her cost to purchase the posters. Her total variable expense equals the number of posters sold multiplied by her cost of $2.10 to purchase each poster. Her fixed cost is the rent expense, $700. A large company has many more variable expenses and fixed expenses. Such a business combines all variable expenses into a single total and computes a single total for fixed expenses.

Our next step is to express income in equation form:

$$\text{Sales} - \text{Variable expenses} - \text{Fixed expenses} = \text{Operating income}$$

At the breakeven point, sales revenue equals expenses, so operating income is zero. Sales revenue equals the unit sale price multiplied by the number of units sold. Variable expenses equals variable cost per unit times the number of units sold. We substitute these terms into the equation and enter the dollar amounts:

Sales	−	Variable expenses	−	Fixed expenses	=	Operating income
$\left(\dfrac{\text{Sales price}}{\text{per unit}} \times \text{Units sold}\right)$	−	$\left(\dfrac{\text{Variable cost}}{\text{per unit}} \times \text{Units sold}\right)$	−	Fixed expenses	=	Operating income
($3.50 × Units sold)	−	($2.10 × Units sold)	−	$700	=	$0
($3.50	−	$2.10) × Units sold	−	$700	=	$0
		$1.40 × Units sold			=	$700
		Units sold			=	$700/$1.40
		Breakeven sales in units			=	500 posters

Kay Pak must sell 500 posters to break even. Her breakeven sales level in dollars is $1,750 (500 units × $3.50) for the travel posters.

It is wise to check your calculations by "proving" the breakeven point with a contribution margin income statement:

Sales revenue (500 × $3.50)		$1,750
Less:		
Variable expenses (500 × $2.10)	$1,050	
Fixed expenses	700	(1,750)
Operating income		$ 0

WORKING IT OUT

The following data will be used in the next several Working It Outs. (1) Compute the breakeven point in units. (2) Prove this by preparing an income statement.

Unit sale price .... $ 250
Unit variable exp. 150
Total fixed
    expenses 35,000

A:

(1) Let *x* = units sold at breakeven:

$250*x* − $150*x* = $35,000 + $0
$100*x* = $35,000
x = $35,000/$100
    = 350 units

(2) Revenue (350 units ×
    $250) $87,500
Less Expenses:
    Variable expenses
    (350 units ×
    $150) 52,500
    Fixed
    expenses...... 35,000
                        87,500
Operating
    income .... $ 0

The Contribution Margin CVP Formula: A Shortcut Method   There is a shortcut method for CVP analysis. To use the shortcut, we first need to understand more about Pak's contribution margin. Each unit sold has a **contribution margin per unit**, which is the excess of the sale price over the variable expense per unit.

$$\begin{matrix} \text{Contribution} \\ \text{margin} \\ \text{per unit} \end{matrix} = \begin{matrix} \text{Sales} \\ \text{revenue} \\ \text{per unit} \end{matrix} - \begin{matrix} \text{Variable} \\ \text{expense} \\ \text{per unit} \end{matrix}$$

Contribution margin can be expressed on a per-unit basis or as a ratio computed as a percentage of sales revenue. For Kay Pak's business:

	Per Unit	**Percent**	**Ratio**
Sale price	$3.50	100%	1.00
Variable expense	(2.10)	(60)%	(0.60)
Contribution margin	$1.40	40%	0.40

Contribution margin ratio is the ratio of contribution margin to sales revenue:

$$\text{Contribution margin ratio} = \frac{\text{Contribution margin}}{\text{Sales revenue}}$$

For Kay Pak's poster business, the contribution margin ratio is 40% ($1.40/$3.50). The contribution margin ratio tells how much a dollar of sales revenue contributes to contribution margin. Kay Pak's 40% contribution margin ratio means that each dollar of sales revenue contributes $0.40 toward fixed costs and profit, as shown in Exhibit 22-6.

Computing the Breakeven Point in Number of Units Sold   We now rearrange the income statement equation and use the contribution margin to develop a shortcut method of finding the breakeven point. Our goal is to find the number of posters that Pak must sell to break even. Consequently, we solve the equation for the number of units sold:

Sales revenue   −   **Variable expenses**   −   **Fixed expenses** = **Operating income**

$$\left(\begin{matrix} \text{Sales price} \\ \text{per unit} \end{matrix} \times \text{Units sold} \right) - \left(\begin{matrix} \text{Variable} \\ \text{cost} \\ \text{per unit} \end{matrix} \times \text{Units sold} \right) - \text{Fixed expenses} = \text{Operating income}$$

(Sales price per unit − Variable cost per unit) × **Units Sold**   =   **Fixed expenses + Operating income**

Contribution margin per unit

The sale price per unit minus the variable cost per unit equals the contribution margin per unit, so

Contribution margin per unit × **Units sold** = **Fixed expenses** + **Operating income**

Variable costs consume 60¢ of each dollar of revenue.

Contribution Margin 40¢ of each dollar of revenue contributed to fixed costs and profit.

Breakdown of $1 of Revenue

Dividing both sides of the last equation by the unit contribution margin per unit yields:

$$\text{Units sold} = \frac{\text{Fixed expenses} + \text{Operating income}}{\text{Contribution margin per unit}}$$

Kay Pak can use this contribution margin CVP formula to find her breakeven point. The contribution margin per poster is $1.40 ($3.50 sale price – $2.10 variable cost). Operating income is zero at the breakeven point. Pak's breakeven computation is

$$\text{Units sold} = \frac{\text{Fixed expenses} + \text{Operating income}}{\text{Contribution margin per unit}}$$

$$= \frac{\$700 + \$0}{\$1.40}$$

$$= 500 \text{ posters}$$

The contribution margin CVP formula is derived from the income statement equation, so the two approaches are mathematically equivalent. Both approaches always give the same answer (500 posters, in Pak's case).

Why does this shortcut method work? The formula shows that each poster Pak sells provides $1.40 of contribution margin. To break even, Pak must generate enough contribution margin to cover her $700 of fixed expenses. At the rate of $1.40 per poster, Pak will have to sell 500 posters ($700/$1.40) to cover her $700 of fixed expenses.

Computing the Breakeven Point in Sales Dollars Using the Contribution Margin Ratio It is easy to compute the breakeven point for a simple business, like Kay Pak's, that has only one product. The sale price per poster and the variable cost per poster are readily available. But what about companies that have hundreds of products, like Bombardier and Roots?

Large companies often use the contribution margin ratio to compute breakeven points in terms of *sales dollars*, without detailed information on individual products. The contribution margin ratio approach differs from the contribution margin CVP formula we've just seen in only one way—fixed expenses plus operating income are divided by the *contribution margin ratio* to yield sales in *dollars*.

$$\text{Sales in dollars} = \frac{\text{Fixed expenses} + \text{Operating income}}{\text{Contribution margin ratio}}$$

Using this formula, Kay Pak's breakeven point in sales dollars is

$$\text{Sales in dollars} = \frac{\$700 + 0}{0.40}$$

$$= \$1,750$$

This is the same breakeven sales revenue as shown in the proof on page 1232.

 **WORKING IT OUT**

Refer to the Working It Out on page 1232. Calculate the contribution margin per unit, contribution margin ratio, and the breakeven point in units.

A:

	Per Unit	Ratio
Sale price	$250	1.00
Variable expense	(150)	(0.60)
Contribution margin	$100	0.40

$$= \frac{\$35,000 \text{ Fixed expenses}}{\$100 \text{ Contribution margin}}$$

$$= 350 \text{ units}$$

$$= \text{Breakeven point}$$

WORKING IT OUT

Using the contribution margin ratio in the previous Working It Out, calculate sales in dollars at the breakeven point.

A:

$$\text{Breakeven sales} = \frac{\$35,000}{0.4}$$

$$= \$87,500$$
$$[350 \text{ units}$$
$$\times \$250]$$

Why does the contribution margin ratio formula work? Each dollar of Kay Pak's sales contributes $0.40 to fixed expenses and profit. To break even, she must generate enough contribution margin at the rate of $0.40 per sales dollar to cover the $700 fixed expenses ($700 ÷ 0.40 = $1,750).

Large companies find it easier to compute breakeven points in sales dollars using the contribution margin ratio approach because it does not require detailed information on individual products. The only information required is total fixed expenses and the contribution margin ratio. Suppose Bombardier's total fixed expenses are $4 billion and its contribution margin ratio is 50 percent. Then the breakeven point in sales dollars would be

$$\text{Breakeven sales in dollars} \ = \ \frac{\$4 \text{ billion}}{0.50}$$

$$= \ \$8 \text{ billion}$$

CVP Sensitivity Analysis

Sensitivity analysis is a "what if" technique that asks what a result will be if a predicted amount is not achieved or if an underlying assumption changes. Let's use sensitivity analysis to see how changes in the sale price, variable costs, and fixed costs affect CVP analysis and the breakeven point.

> **Question 2: If the sale price per unit is changed, what will the new breakeven sales be?**

Now suppose that the sale price per poster is $3.85 rather than $3.50. Variable expense per poster remains at $2.10, and fixed expenses stay at $700. What is the revised breakeven point in units and in dollars? The unit contribution margin becomes $1.75 ($3.85 – $2.10), and the new contribution margin ratio is 0.4545 ($1.75 ÷ $3.85).

Using the contribution margin CVP formula:

$$\text{Sales in units} \ = \ \frac{\text{Fixed expenses } + \text{ Operating income}}{\text{Contribution to margin per unit}}$$

$$= \ \frac{\$700 + 0}{\$1.75}$$

$$= \ 400 \text{ posters}$$

Observe that

- Sale price per unit increased, so
- Contribution margin per unit increased, and as a result,
- Fewer posters had to be sold to break even

Proof:

Sales revenue ($3.85 × 400)		$1,540
Deduct:		
Variable expenses (400 × $2.10)..........	$840	
Fixed expenses	700	(1,540)
Operating income		$ 0

The proof shows that Pak needs sales revenue of $1,540 to break even with a $3.85 sales price. Alternatively, we could directly compute the breakeven sales in dollars using the contribution margin ratio form of the CVP formula:

$$\text{Sales in dollars} \ = \ \frac{\text{Fixed expenses } + \text{ Operating income}}{\text{Contribution margin ratio}}$$

$$= \ \frac{\$700 + 0}{0.4545}$$

$$= \ \$1,540$$

This example shows that an increase in sale price reduces breakeven sales, both in units and dollars. With a higher sale price, each poster contributes more toward fixed expenses, so Pak can break even with fewer sales. Conversely, cutting the sale price would decrease the contribution margin. Then Kay Pak would have to increase the number of units sold just to break even.

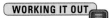

WORKING IT OUT

Kay Pak believes she could dominate the travel poster business if she cut the sale price to $2.00. Would this be a good idea?

A: No. The variable cost per poster is $2.10. If Pak sold posters for $2.00 each, she would lose $0.10 on each poster. There can be no profit if sale price does not even cover variable expenses.

Question 3: If variable costs change, what will breakeven sales be?

Suppose Pak's variable expense per poster is $2.38 instead of $2.10. The sale price per poster remains $3.50, and fixed expenses stay at $700. What is the breakeven point in units and in dollars?

The new contribution margin per unit drops to $1.12 ($3.50 – $2.38), and the new contribution margin ratio declines to 0.32 ($1.12/$3.50). Breakeven sales are

$$\text{Sales in units} = \frac{\text{Fixed expenses} + \text{Operating income}}{\text{Contribution margin per unit}}$$

$$= \frac{\$700 + 0}{\$1.12}$$

$$= 625 \text{ posters}$$

$$\text{Sales in dollars} = \frac{\text{Fixed expenses} + \text{Operating income}}{\text{Contribution margin ratio}}$$

$$= \frac{\$700 + 0}{0.32}$$

$$= \$2,187.50$$

As these numbers make clear, an increase in variable expense per unit

- Reduces the contribution margin, and as a result,
- More posters must be sold to break even

Pak must increase sales in units and in dollars to break even. Conversely, a decrease in variable cost per unit would lower the breakeven point.

Question 4: If fixed costs change, what will breakeven sales be?

Suppose the booth rental costs $1,050 instead of the original $700. Variable expense per poster remains at $2.10, and sale price stays at $3.50. What is Kay Pak's breakeven point in units and dollars?

Using the contribution margin CVP formula:

$$\text{Sales in units} = \frac{\text{Fixed expenses} + \text{Operating income}}{\text{Contribution margin per unit}}$$

$$= \frac{\$1,050 + 0}{\$1.40}$$

$$= 750 \text{ posters}$$

$$\text{Sales in dollars} = \frac{\text{Fixed expenses} + \text{Operating income}}{\text{Contribution margin ratio}}$$

$$= \frac{\$1,050 + 0}{0.40}$$

$$= \$2,625.00$$

For the Working It Out on
page 1233: If the sale price is
decreased from $250 to $240
while unit variable expenses are
$150 and total fixed expenses are
$35,000, what is the new
breakeven point in units and in
dollars?

A:

$$\frac{\$35,000}{\$90} = 389 \text{ units}$$

The new contribution margin is
$90 ($240 – $150). The new
contribution margin ratio is 37.5%
($90/$240).

$$\frac{\$35,000}{0.375} = \$93,333$$

The $1,050 in fixed expenses is an increase of $350, or 50%, over the original fixed cost of $700. Note that

- Fixed expenses increased by 50%, and
- Breakeven sales also increased by 50% [(750 – 500) ÷ 500]

Pak must sell more posters to cover the higher fixed costs. However, if fixed expenses had declined, she could have sold fewer posters and still covered these (lower) costs.

In general, managers prefer a lower breakeven point to a higher one. But do not overemphasize this one aspect of CVP analysis. Managers are more interested in profits than in breakeven sales levels. In our example, Kay Pak may be willing to pay an extra $350 ($1,050 – $700) for a better location if the expected increase in sales volume provides enough contribution margin to cover the extra rent expense and to provide extra operating income.

Exhibit 22-7 summarizes the effects on the breakeven point of various changes to sale price or to costs.

Using CVP Analysis to Plan Profits

Managers of ongoing operations with established products and services are more interested in the sales level needed to earn a target profit than in the breakeven point. We now show how managers can use CVP analysis to plan profits.

OBJECTIVE 4
Compute the sales level
needed to earn a target
operating income

Question 5: How many units must be sold to earn a target operating income?

WORKING IT OUT

Use the data in the Working It Out
on pages 1232 and 1233. Calculate
how many units must be sold to
earn a target operating income of
$40,000. What is the total sales
revenue?

A:

Target unit sales
$$= \frac{\$35,000 + \$40,000}{\$100} = 750 \text{ units}$$

Target dollar sales
$$= \frac{\$35,000 + \$40,000}{0.40} = \$187,500$$

You can verify this by preparing an
income statement.

Suppose that Kay Pak hopes to earn operating income of $490. Assuming fixed expenses of $700, variable expenses of $2.10 per poster, and a $3.50 per poster sale price, how many posters must she sell to earn a profit of $490?

Until now, we have concentrated on breakeven sales, the point at which operating income is zero. How should we consider a target operating income greater than zero? The contribution margin must be high enough to cover the fixed expenses *and* provide the profit. We can still use the contribution CVP formula. The only difference is that the target operating income is $490, compared to zero when we computed breakeven sales.

With a $1.40 contribution margin per unit and a 0.40 contribution margin ratio:

$$\text{Sales in units} = \frac{\text{Fixed expenses} + \text{Target operating income}}{\text{Contribution margin per unit}}$$

$$= \frac{\$700 + \$490}{\$1.40} \qquad = \frac{\$1,190}{\$1.40} = 850 \text{ units}$$

Proof:

Sales revenue (850 × $3.50)		$2,975
Less:		
Variable expenses (850 × $2.10)..........	$1,785	
Fixed expenses	700	(2,485)
Target operating income		$ 490

EXHIBIT 22-7

**Effects of Changes on
Breakeven Sales**

Change in Factor	Change in Breakeven Sales
Increase in sale price	Decrease
Decrease in sale price	Increase
Increase in variable expenses	Increase
Decrease in variable expenses	Decrease
Increase in fixed expenses	Increase
Decrease in fixed expenses	Decrease

This proof shows that Pak needs sales revenue of $2,975 to earn a profit of $490. Alternatively, we could directly compute the dollar sales necessary to earn a $490 profit by using the contribution margin ratio form of the CVP formula:

$$\text{Sales in dollars} = \frac{\text{Fixed expenses } + \text{ Target operating income}}{\text{Contribution margin ratio}}$$

$$= \frac{\$700 + \$490}{0.40} = \frac{\$1,190}{0.40} = \$2,975$$

Question 6: What operating income is expected at various sales levels?

OBJECTIVE 5
Graph a set of cost-volume-profit relationships

A convenient way to determine expected operating income at various sales levels is to graph the cost-volume-profit relationships, as shown in Exhibit 22-8. As in the cost behaviour graphs earlier in the chapter (Exhibits 22-1 through 22-4), we place units on the horizontal axis and dollars on the vertical axis. We use Kay Pak's data (as originally given on page 1231) and follow five steps:

Step 1. Choose a sales volume, such as 1,000 units. Plot the point for sales dollars at that volume: 1,000 units × $3.50 per unit = sales of $3,500. Draw the *sales revenue line* from the origin through the $3,500 point.

Step 2. Draw the *fixed expense line*, a horizontal line that intersects the Dollars axis at $700.

Step 3. Draw the *total expense* line. Total expense is the sum of variable expense plus fixed expense. Compute variable expense at the chosen sales volume: 1,000 units × $2.10 per unit = variable expense of $2,100. Add variable expense to fixed expense: $2,100 + $700 = $2,800. Plot the total expense point ($2,800) for 1,000 units. Then draw a line through this point from the $700 fixed expense intercept on the Dollars axis. This is the *total expense line*.

Step 4. Identify the *breakeven point*. The breakeven point is the spot where the sales line intersects the total expense line. The equations we used earlier told us that Pak's breakeven point is 500 units, or $1,750 in sales. The graph gives us the same information visually.

Step 5. Mark the *operating income* and the *operating loss* areas on the graph. To the left of the breakeven point, the total expense line lies above the sales revenue line. Expenses exceed sales revenue, leading to an operating loss. For example, Exhibit 22-8 shows that if Pak sells only 300 posters, she will incur an operating loss. The amount of the loss is the vertical difference between the total expense line and the sales revenue line:

Sales revenue (300 × $3.50)		$1,050
Less:		
Variable expenses (300 × $2.10)	$630	
Fixed expenses	700	(1,330)
Operating loss		$ (280)

To the right of the breakeven point in Exhibit 22-8, Pak's business earns a profit. The vertical distance between the sales line and the total expense line equals the amount of operating income. For example, the graph shows that if Kay Pak sells 1,000 posters, she will earn operating income of $700 ($3,500 sales revenue – $2,800 total expense).

Why bother with a graph like Exhibit 22-8? Why don't managers use the equation approach or the contribution margin CVP formula? Graphs like Exhibit 22-8 help managers quickly estimate the profit or loss earned at different levels of sales. In contrast, the equation or formula approaches only indicate income or loss from a single sales amount.

Computer spreadsheets are ideally suited for cost-volume-profit analysis.

KEY POINT

Remember these features of a CVP graph:
(1) The revenue line always passes through the origin because when no units are sold, there is no revenue.
(2) The fixed expense line is flat and parallel to the horizontal axis because fixed expenses in the relevant range do not change with changes in number of units sold.
(3) The total expense line and the fixed expense line intersect the vertical axis in the same place.
(4) The point at which the total expense line intersects the sales revenue line is the breakeven point.

Managers can use these spreadsheets to answer what-if questions such as: What will variable expenses be if sales rise by $1,000? By 200 units? If we cut fixed expenses by $20,000, how many units must we sell to earn a profit of $100,000? Spreadsheets allow managers to analyze the results of any one change or the results of several changes in the business's operations. Most software also displays graphs of CVP relationships similar to the one in Exhibit 22-8.

Other CVP Applications

Margin of Safety

OBJECTIVE 6
Compute a margin of safety

The **margin of safety** is the excess of expected sales over breakeven sales. In other words, the margin of safety is the drop in sales that the company can absorb before incurring an operating loss. A high margin of safety serves as a cushion. A low margin of safety is a warning. Managers use the margin of safety to evaluate current operations or to measure the risk of a new business plan. The lower the margin, the higher the risk. The higher the margin, the lower the risk.

Kay Pak's breakeven point in our original data is 500 posters. Suppose she expects to sell 950 posters during the period. Her margin of safety is computed as follows:

Margin of safety in units	=	Expected sales in units	−	Breakeven sales in units		
	=	950	−	500	=	450 units
Margin of safety in dollars	=	**Margin of safety in units** ×		**Sale price per unit**		
	=	450	×	$3.50	=	$1,575

Sales can drop by 450 posters, or $1,575, before Pak incurs a loss.

EXHIBIT 22-8

Cost-Volume-Profit Graph

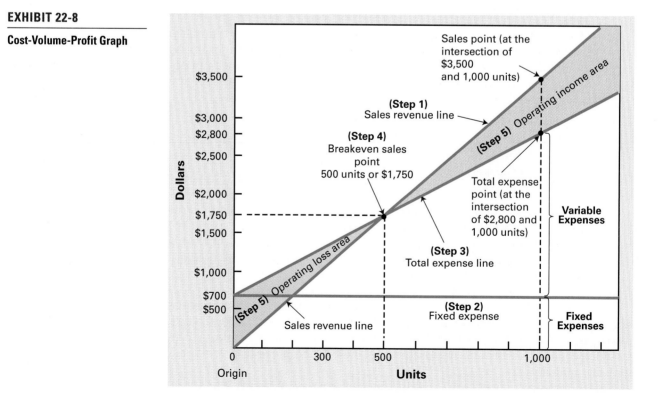

For any level of sales, managers can compute the margin of safety as a percentage. Simply divide the margin of safety by sales. We obtain the same percentage whether we perform this computation in terms of units or dollars.

In units:

$$\text{Margin of safety as a percentage} = \frac{\text{Margin of safety in units}}{\text{Expected sales in units}}$$

$$= \frac{450 \text{ units}}{950 \text{ units}}$$

$$= 47.4\%$$

In dollars:

$$\text{Margin of safety as a percentage} = \frac{\text{Margin of safety in dollars}}{\text{Expected sales in dollars}}$$

$$= \frac{450 \text{ units} \times \$3.50}{950 \text{ units} \times \$3.50}$$

$$= \frac{\$1,575}{\$3,325}$$

$$= 47.4\%$$

Sales Mix

Our example thus far has focused on a single product, travel posters. Companies that sell more than one product must consider sales mix in determining CVP relationships. Sales mix has an important effect on profits. A company earns more income by selling high-margin products than by selling an equal number of low-margin items.

For example, Air Canada has focused on attracting more business-class and full-fare economy business travellers. These passengers pay more for their seats than travellers taking advantage of a seat sale or traveling on frequent-flyer points. Improving sales mix by selling a greater proportion of high-margin tickets reduces Air Canada's breakeven point.

In contrast, the annual report of Deere and Company, manufacturer of John Deere farm equipment, stated that profits decreased because of "a less favourable mix of products sold." What is a *less favourable mix* of products? It is a mix with a higher percentage of items that have below-average contribution margins.

We can perform CVP analysis for a company that sells more than one product by using the same equations that we used for a company with a single product. But first, we must compute the weighted-average contribution margin of all products. The sales mix provides the weights.

Suppose that Kay Pak plans to sell two types of posters instead of one. Recall that the regular poster costs $2.10 and sells for $3.50. Its contribution margin is $1.40 ($3.50 − $2.10). The second, larger poster costs $4.00 and sells for $7.00. Its contribution margin is $3.00 ($7.00 − $4.00).

An established business estimates its sales mix based on experience. Kay Pak, however, is starting a new venture. Suppose she estimates that she will sell 500 regular posters and 300 large posters. This is a 5:3 sales mix. For every 5 regular posters, Pak expects to sell 3 large posters. In other words, she expects 5/8 of the posters sold to be regular posters and 3/8 to be large posters. To compute breakeven sales in units, Pak arranges the data as follows:

OBJECTIVE 7
Use the sales mix in CVP analysis

WORKING IT OUT

Assume that Levy Sales, Inc. sells two products, A and B:

	A	B
Sale price	$100	$80
Variable cost	60	50
Contribution margin (CM)	$ 40	$30

Levy estimates that it will sell 190 of A and 280 of B. Total fixed costs are $3,810. How many units of each product must Levy sell to break even?

A: 45 of A and 67 of B:

	A	B	Total
Sale price	$ 100	$ 80	
Variable cost	60	50	
CM per unit	$ 40	$ 30	
Est. sales in units	190	280	470
Est. CM	$7,600	$8,400	$16,000

Wtd. avg. CM/unit	=	$16,000/470
	=	$34.04
Breakeven sales	=	$3,810/$34.04
	=	112 units
Breakeven sales of A	=	112 × 190/470
	=	45 units
Breakeven sales of B	=	112 × 280/470
	=	67 units

You can prove that this is correct by preparing an income statement.

	Regular Posters	Large Posters	Total
Sale price per unit...................................	$3.50	$7.00	
Deduct: Variable expense per unit.......	(2.10)	(4.00)	
Contribution margin per unit...............	$1.40	$3.00	
Sales mix in units...................................	× 5	× 3	8
Contribution margin	$7.00	$9.00	$ 16
Weighted-average contribution margin per unit ($16/8)....................			$2.00

$$\begin{array}{c} \text{Sales in} \\ \text{total units} \end{array} = \frac{\text{Fixed expenses + Operating income}}{\begin{array}{c}\text{Weighted-average contribution} \\ \text{margin per unit}\end{array}}$$

$$= \frac{\$700 + 0}{\$2.00} = 350 \text{ units}$$

Breakeven sales of regular posters (350 × 5/8) .... 219 regular posters
Breakeven sales of large posters (350 × 3/8) .... 131 large posters

The overall breakeven point in sales dollars is $1,684 (amounts round to the nearest dollar):

219 regular posters at $3.50 each	$ 767
131 large posters at $7.00 each	917
Total revenues	$1,684

We can check these amounts by preparing a contribution margin income statement (amounts rounded to the nearest dollar):

	Regular Posters	Large Posters	Total
Sales revenue:			
Regular (219 × $3.50)........................	$767		
Large (131 × $7.00)............................		$917	$1,684
Variable expenses:			
Regular (219 × $2.10)........................	460		
Large (131 × $4.00)............................		$524	$ 984
Contribution margin.............................	$307	$393	$ 700
Fixed expenses.....................................			(700)
Operating income.................................			$ 0

Let's review our approach:

- First, compute the weighted-average contribution margin per unit. This figure expresses both types of posters in terms of a single hypothetical product that has a contribution margin of $2.00. From here on, the contribution margin approach follows the usual pattern.
- Second, divide fixed expenses (plus operating income) by the weighted-average contribution margin per unit to determine the required sales in total units.
- Third, separate total units (350) into regular posters (219) and large posters (131).

The breakeven point proof shows that Pak's breakeven sales are $1,684. Kay Pak could use an alternative approach to estimating breakeven sales in dollars—the contribution margin ratio formula. But first, Pak must estimate her contribution margin ratio:

Total expected contribution margin:

Regular posters (500 × $1.40)	$700	
Large posters (300 × $3.00)	$900	$1,600

Divided by total expected sales:

Regular posters (500 × $3.50)	$1,750	
Large posters (300 × $7.00)	$2,100	3,850
Contribution margin ratio..		41.56%

Second, Pak uses the contribution margin ratio form of the CVP formula to estimate breakeven sales in dollars:

$$\text{Sales in dollars} = \frac{\text{Fixed expenses} + \text{Operating income}}{\text{Contribution margin ratio}}$$

$$= \frac{\$700 + \$0}{0.4156}$$

$$= \$1,684$$

If Pak's actual sales mix is not 5 regular posters to 3 large posters, her actual operating income will differ from the budgeted amount, even if she sells exactly the 800 total units she predicts. For each total number of units sold, there are as many different operating incomes as there are unique sales mixes. Similarly, there are as many different breakeven points—in total units and in sales dollars—as there are sales mixes. Therefore, the sales-mix factor greatly complicates planning.

STOP & THINK

Suppose that Kay Pak *budgets* the sale of 800 total posters in the 5:3 sales mix (5 regular posters sold for every 3 large posters). She *actually* sells 800 posters—375 regular and 425 large. The unit sale prices and variable expenses are exactly as predicted, and the fixed expense is the budgeted $700. Can you tell, without computations, whether Pak's actual operating income is greater than, less than, or equal to the budgeted amount?

Answer: Pak sold more of the higher-margin large posters. This favourable change in the sales mix increased her operating income.

Companies can use CVP analysis to motivate their sales force. Salespeople who know the contribution margin of each product they sell can generate more profit by emphasizing high-margin products. To motivate the sales force, many companies base all or part of their sales commissions on the contribution margins produced by sales rather than on sales revenue alone.

The next section uses building blocks of CVP analysis (contributed margin, the distinction between variable and fixed costs) to explain a costing approach that many managers find useful for internal decision making. Before continuing, stop and review the CVP Analysis Decision Guidelines to make sure you understand these basic concepts.

Decision	Guidelines
How do changes in the number of units affect	
• total costs?	Total variable costs → change in proportion to changes in volume Total fixed costs → no change

• cost per unit?	Variable cost per unit → no change
	Fixed cost per unit:
	  Increases when volume decreases
	  (Fixed costs are spread over fewer units)
	  Decreases when volume increases
	  (Fixed costs are spread over more units)

What is the difference between gross margin and contribution margin?	Gross margin = Sales − Cost of goods sold Contribution margin = Sales − Total variable expenses
How to compute sales needed to break even or earn a target operating income	
• in units?	$\dfrac{\text{Fixed expense} + \text{Operating income}}{\text{Contribution margin per unit}}$
• in dollars?	$\dfrac{\text{Fixed expense} + \text{Operating income}}{\text{Contribution margin ratio}}$
How to use CVP analysis to measure risk?	Margin of safety = Expected sales − Breakeven sales

OBJECTIVE 8
Compute income using variable costing and absorption costing

KEY POINT

Absorption costing is the same as full costing: With this method of assigning costs, *all* manufacturing costs (direct materials, direct labour, variable overhead, *and* fixed overhead) are included in inventoriable cost.

KEY POINT

Variable costing is the same as direct costing: With this method of assigning costs, *only* direct materials, direct labour, and variable overhead are included in inventoriable cost.

Variable Costing and Absorption Costing

Thus far, we have assigned both variable and fixed manufacturing costs to products. This approach is called **absorption costing** because products *absorb* fixed manufacturing costs as well as variable manufacturing costs. Supporters of absorption costing argue that products cannot be produced without fixed manufacturing costs, so these costs are an important part of product costs.

For planning and decision making, many managers prefer a different costing approach. **Variable costing** assigns only variable manufacturing costs to products. Under variable costing, fixed manufacturing costs are considered period costs, and are expensed in the period when they are incurred. Supporters of variable costing argue that fixed manufacturing costs (such as amortization on the factory) provide the capacity to produce during a period. These fixed expenses are incurred whether or not the company produces any products or services. Thus, they argue, these fixed manufacturing expenses are period costs, not product costs. However, GAAP allows only absorption costing for external reporting. Consequently, published financial statements are based on absorption costing. While variable costing often provides a more useful basis for management decisions, companies can only use variable costing for internal reports. Exhibit 22-9 clarifies the difference between variable costing and absorption costing.

The only difference between absorption costing and variable costing is that absorption costing considers fixed manufacturing costs as inventoriable product costs, while variable costing considers fixed manufacturing costs as period costs (expenses). All other costs are treated the same way under both absorption and variable costing:

- Variable manufacturing costs are inventoriable product costs.
- All nonmanufacturing costs are period costs.

To see the difference between absorption costing and variable costing, let's consider the following example. Sportade Inc. manufactures a sports beverage in both liquid and powdered form. Sportade Inc. incurs the following costs for its powdered mix in March 2002:

Direct material cost per case	$6.00
Direct labour cost per case	3.00
Variable manufacturing overhead cost per case	2.00
Sales commission per case	2.50
Total fixed manufacturing overhead expenses	50,000
Total fixed marketing and administrative expenses	25,000

Sportade Inc. produced 10,000 cases of powdered mix as planned, but sold only 8,000 cases, at a price of $30 per case. There were no beginning inventories. So Sportade has 2,000 (10,000–8,000) cases of powdered mix in ending finished goods inventory.

What is Sportade Inc.'s product cost per case under absorption costing and variable costing?

	Absorption Costing	Variable Costing
Direct materials	$ 6.00	$ 6.00
Direct labour	3.00	3.00
Variable manufacturing overhead	2.00	2.00
Fixed manufacturing overhead	5.00*	—
Total cost per unit	$16.00	$11.00

$$*\frac{\$50,000 \text{ fixed manufacturing overhead}}{10,000 \text{ cases}} = \$5 \text{ per case}$$

The only difference between absorption costing and variable costing is that fixed manufacturing overhead is a product cost under absorption costing, but a period cost under variable costing. This is why the cost per case is $5 higher under absorption costing (total cost of $16) than under variable costing ($11).

Exhibit 22-10, Panel A, shows that absorption costing income statements are typically presented using the conventional format from Chapters 1–19. As usual, cost

EXHIBIT 22-9

Differences Between Absorption Costing and Variable Costing

	Absorption Costing	Variable Costing
Product Costs (Capitalized as Inventory until expensed as Cost of Goods Sold)	Direct materials Direct labour Variable manufacturing overhead Fixed manufacturing overhead	Direct materials Direct labour Variable manufacturing overhead
Period Costs (Expensed in period incurred)	Variable nonmanufacturing costs Fixed nonmanufacturing costs	Fixed manufacturing overhead Variable nonmanufacturing costs Fixed nonmanufacturing costs
Focus	External reporting—required by GAAP	Internal reporting only
Typical Income Statement Format	Conventional income statement as in Chapters 1–19	Contribution margin income statement

EXHIBIT 22-10

Absorption and Variable Costing Income Statements

Panel A—Conventional Income Statement (Absorption Costing)

SPORTADE INC.
Income Statement (Absorption Costing)
For the Month Ended March 31, 2002

Sales (8,000 × $30)..		$240,000
Deduct: Cost of goods sold:		
Beginning finished goods inventory	$ 0	
Cost of goods manufactured (10,000 × $16)	160,000	
Cost of goods available for sale.............................	160,000	
Ending finished goods inventory (2,000 × $16)	(32,000)	
Cost of goods sold		(128,000)
Gross Margin...		112,000
Deduct: Operating expenses		
[(8,000 × $2.50) + $25,000)]		(45,000)
Operating income..		$67,000

Panel B—Contribution Margin Income Statement (Variable Costing)

SPORTADE INC.
Income Statement (Variable Costing)
For the Month Ended March 31, 2002

Sales (8,000 × $30)..		$240,000
Deduct: Variable expenses:		
Variable cost of goods sold:		
Beginning finished goods inventory	$ 0	
Variable cost of goods manufactured		
(10,000 × $11)...	110,000	
Variable cost of goods available for sale	110,000	
Ending finished goods inventory (2,000 × $11).	(22,000)	
Variable cost of goods sold	88,000	
Sales commission expense (8,000 × $2.50)	20,000	(108,000)
Contribution margin..		132,000
Deduct: Fixed expenses:		
Fixed manufacturing overhead...............................	50,000	
Fixed marketing and administrative expenses	25,000	(75,000)
Operating income...		$ 57,000

of goods sold is deducted from sales to obtain gross margin. Chapter 19 showed that manufacturers compute cost of goods sold by starting with beginning finished goods inventory (zero in Sportade's case) and adding the cost of goods *manufactured*. The cost of goods *manufactured* is computed by multiplying the number of units *produced* by the absorption costing product cost per unit.

Sportade Inc. produced 10,000 cases at an absorption costing cost per case of $16, so the cost of goods manufactured is $160,000 (10,000 cases × $16 per case). This cost of goods manufactured plus beginning inventory of finished goods is the cost of goods available for sale. We then subtract the ending finished goods inventory—the number of units multiplied by the absorption costing product cost per unit (2,000 cases × $16 per case in our example)—to obtain the cost of goods sold.

From gross margin we subtract operating expenses (nonmanufacturing expenses) to find absorption costing operating income. The data on page 1243 indicate that Sportade Inc. paid $2.50 per case sales commission for each case *sold*, so the total sales commission is $20,000 (8,000 cases sold × $2.50 per case). Fixed marketing and administrative costs are $25,000, so marketing and administrative expenses total $45,000 ($20,000 + $25,000).

Exhibit 22-10, Panel B shows that variable costing income statements are presented using the contribution margin income statement format illustrated earlier in Exhibit 22-5 (Panel B). All the variable expenses are deducted from sales to get contribution margin. First notice that the details of the (variable) cost of goods sold computation parallel those in the absorption costing income statement, *except we use the $11 variable costing product cost per case rather than the $16 absorption costing product cost per case.* To the beginning finished goods inventory, we add the variable cost of goods manufactured (10,000 cases produced × $11 variable costing product cost per case). This yields the variable cost of goods available for sale, from which we subtract ending finished goods inventory (2,000 cases × $11 per case) to obtain variable cost of goods sold.

To get the contribution margin, we subtract from sales both the variable cost of goods sold and variable operating expenses like the sales commission (8,000 cases sold × $2.50 sales commission per case). Finally, to obtain variable costing operating income, we subtract all the fixed expenses ($50,000 fixed manufacturing overhead + $25,000 fixed marketing and administrative expenses) from contribution margin.

Panel A of Exhibit 22-10 shows that Sportade Inc. absorption costing operating income is $67,000. However, Panel B shows that variable costing yields only $57,000 of operating income. Why is operating income $10,000 lower under variable costing? To answer this question, we need to understand what happened to the $160,000 ($110,000 variable + $50,000 fixed) total manufacturing costs under each costing method.

The total manufacturing costs incurred in March are either

- Expensed in March, or
- Held back in inventory (an asset)

Exhibit 22-11 shows that of the $160,000 manufacturing costs incurred during March, absorption costing holds back $32,000 (2,000 × $16) as inventory. This $32,000 assigned to inventory is not expensed until next month, when the units are sold. Thus only $160,000 − $32,000 = $128,000 of the manufacturing costs are expensed during March.

Variable costing holds back in ending inventory only $22,000 (2,000 × $11) of the total manufacturing costs. This is $10,000 *less* ($22,000 − $32,000) than absorption costing holds back in inventory. The difference arises because absorption costing assigns the $5 per case fixed manufacturing overhead costs to the 2,000 cases in ending inventory, while variable costing does not—it expenses all the fixed manufacturing overhead in the current month.

Costs that are not held back in inventory are expensed in the current period, so variable costing expenses $138,000 ($160,000 − $22,000) in March. (This $138,000 also equals the $88,000 variable cost of goods sold plus the $50,000 fixed manufacturing overhead.) This is $10,000 *more* than absorption costing expenses during March. *Variable costing has $10,000 more expense in March, so its income is $10,000 lower than absorption costing income.*

The Sportade Inc. example shows that when the quantity of inventory on hand increases, absorption costing reports higher operating income than variable costing. This is because absorption costing holds back some of the fixed manufacturing overhead in inventory (an asset), whereas variable costing expenses all the fixed manufacturing cost immediately. Because absorption costing expenses less fixed manufacturing overhead, it has higher income in the current period.

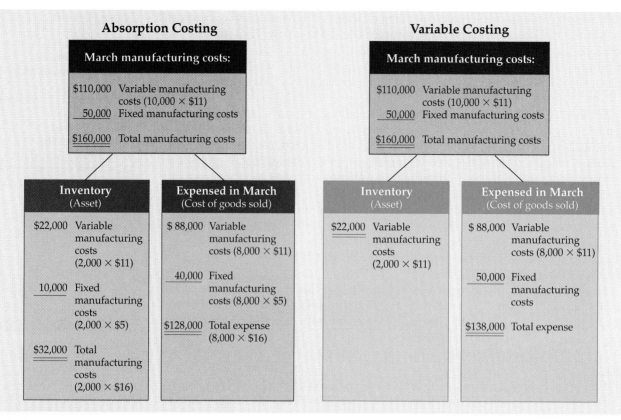

EXHIBIT 22-11

Inventory versus Expenses
under Absorption and
Variable Costing

Absorption Costing and Managers' Incentives

The general rule is this: When inventories increase (more units are produced than sold), absorption costing income is higher than variable costing income. When inventories decline (when fewer units are produced than sold), absorption costing income is lower than variable costing income. Managers can use this relationship to their own advantage. Suppose the Sportade Inc. manager receives a bonus based on absorption costing income. Will the manager want to increase or decrease production?

The manager knows that absorption costing assigns each case of Sportade $5 of fixed manufacturing overhead.

- For every case that is produced but not sold, absorption costing "hides" $5 of fixed overhead in ending inventory (an asset).

- The more cases added to inventory, the more fixed overhead is "hidden" in ending inventory at the end of the month.

- The more fixed overhead in ending inventory, the smaller the cost of goods sold, and the higher the operating income.

To maximize the bonus under absorption costing, the manager will want to increase production to build up inventory.

This incentive directly conflicts with the just-in-time philosophy (introduced in Chapter 19), which emphasizes minimal inventory levels. Companies that have adopted just-in-time should either (1) evaluate their managers based on variable costing income, or (2) implement strict controls to prevent inventory build-up.

Before continuing, take time to study the Absorption and Variable Costing Decision Guidelines to make sure you understand the differences between absorption and variable costing.

Decision	Guidelines
When to use absorption costing? Variable costing?	Absorption costing must be used for external reporting. Variable costing is used only for internal costing.
What is the difference between absorption and variable costing?	Fixed manufacturing costs are treated as • inventoriable product costs under absorption costing • period costs under variable costing

How to compute product costs under absorption and variable costing?

Absorption Costing	Variable Costing
Direct materials	Direct materials
+ Direct labour	+ Direct labour
+ Variable overhead	+ Variable overhead
+ Fixed overhead	—
= Total product cost	= Total product cost

Decision	Guidelines

How to determine whether absorption costing income is higher, lower, or the same as variable costing income?	If units produced > units sold:
	    Absorption costing income > Variable costing income
	
	If units produced < units sold:
	    Absorption costing income < Variable costing income
	
	If units produced = units sold:
	    Absorption costing income = Variable costing income

Summary Problem
for Your Review

PART A. Runner's Corp. buys jogging shorts for $6 and sells them for $10. Management budgets monthly fixed costs of $10,000 for sales volumes between zero and 12,000 pairs of shorts.

Required

1. Use both the income statement equation approach and the shortcut contribution margin approach to compute the company's breakeven monthly sales in units.
2. Use the contribution margin ratio approach to compute the breakeven point in sales dollars.
3. Compute the monthly sales level (in units) that is needed to earn a target operating income of $14,000. Use either the income statement equation approach or the contribution margin approach.
4. Prepare a graph of Runner Corp.'s CVP relationships similar to Exhibit 22-8. Draw the sales revenue line, the fixed expense line, and the total expense line. Label the axes, the breakeven point, the operating income area, and the operating loss area.

PART B. Suppose that Runner's Corp. sells a second product—sweatpants. Each pair costs $7 and sells for $15. Fixed costs are unchanged.

Required

1. If the company sells 2 pairs of jogging shorts for every 3 pairs of sweatpants, what is the company's breakeven sales in units? Use the contribution margin approach.

2. If expected sales total 11,000 units, what is Runner's Corp.'s margin of safety in units?

3. In a sales mix of 2:3 (2 pairs of jogging shorts sold for every 3 pairs of sweatpants), what operating income will Runner's Corp. earn if it sells a total of 11,000 items? Use the contribution margin method.

Solution to Review Problem

PART A—Requirement 1

Income statement equation approach:

Sales		−	Variable expenses		−	Fixed expenses	= Operating income
$\left(\begin{array}{c}\text{Sale price} \\ \text{per unit}\end{array} \times \begin{array}{c}\text{Sales} \\ \text{in units}\end{array}\right)$		−	$\left(\begin{array}{c}\text{Variable cost} \\ \text{per unit}\end{array} \times \begin{array}{c}\text{Sales} \\ \text{in units}\end{array}\right)$		−	Fixed expenses	= Operating income
($10 × Sales in units)	−		($6 × Sales in units)	−		$10,000	= $0
($10	−		$6) × Sales in units	=		$10,000	
			$4 × Sales in units	=		$10,000	
			Sales in units	=		$10,000/$4	
			Breakeven sales in units	=		2,500 units	

Contribution margin approach:

$$\text{Sales in units} = \frac{\text{Fixed expenses} + \text{Operating income}}{\text{Contribution margin per unit}}$$

$$\text{Breakeven sales in units} = \frac{\$10,000 + 0}{(\$10 - \$6)} = \frac{\$10,000}{\$4} = 2,500 \text{ units}$$

Requirement 2

$$\text{Breakeven sales in dollars} = \frac{\text{Fixed expenses} + \text{Operating expenses}}{\text{Contribution margin ratio}}$$

$$= \frac{\$10,000 + \$0}{0.40^*} = \$25,000$$

$$^*\text{Contribution margin ratio} = \frac{\text{Contribution margin per unit}}{\text{Sales price per unit}} = \frac{\$4}{\$10} = 0.40$$

Requirement 3

Income statement equation approach:

Sales		−	Variable expenses		−	Fixed expenses	=	Operating income
$\left(\begin{array}{c}\text{Sale price}\\\text{per unit}\end{array} \times \begin{array}{c}\text{Sales}\\\text{in units}\end{array}\right)$		−	$\left(\begin{array}{c}\text{Variable cost}\\\text{per unit}\end{array} \times \begin{array}{c}\text{Sales}\\\text{in units}\end{array}\right)$		−	Fixed expenses	=	Operating income

$$(\$10 \times \text{Sales in units}) - (\$6 \times \text{Sales in units}) - \$10,000 = \$14,000$$
$$(\$10 - \$6) \times \text{Sales in units} = \$10,000 + \$14,000$$
$$\$4 \times \text{Sales in units} = \$24,000$$
$$\text{Sales in units} = \$24,000/\$4$$
$$\text{Sales in units} = 6,000 \text{ units}$$

Contribution margin approach:

$$\text{Sales in units} = \frac{\text{Fixed expenses} + \text{Operating income}}{\text{Contribution margin per unit}}$$

$$\text{Sales in units} = \frac{\$10,000 + \$14,000}{(\$10 - \$6)}$$

$$\text{Sales in units} = \frac{\$24,000}{\$4}$$

$$\text{Sales in units} = 6,000 \text{ units}$$

Requirement 4

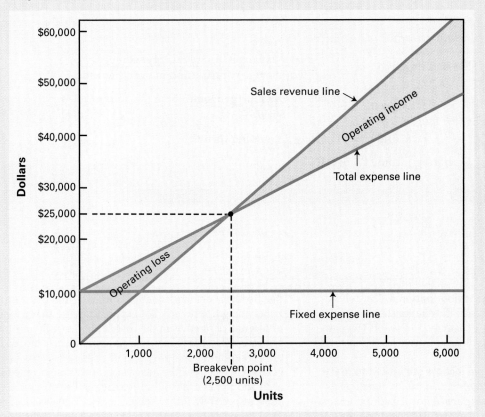

	Jogging Shorts	Sweatpants	Total
Sale price per unit	$10	$15	
Variable cost per unit.......................................	6	7	
Contribution margin per unit.......................	$ 4	$ 8	
Sales mix in units	×2	×3	5
Contribution margin.......................................	$ 8	$24	$ 32
Weighted-average contribution margin per unit ($32/5 units)....................			$6.40

$$\text{Breakeven sales in units} \quad = \quad \frac{\text{Fixed expenses} + \text{Operating income}}{\text{Weighted-average contribution margin per unit}}$$

$$= \quad \frac{\$10,000 + \$0}{\$6.40} \quad = \quad 1,563 \text{ units}$$

Breakeven sales of jogging shorts (1,563 × 2/5)   =   625 units

Breakeven sales of sweatpants (1,563 × 3/5)   =   938 units

Requirement 2

Margin of safety in units = Expected sales in units − Breakeven sales

= 11,000 − 1,563

= 9,437 units

Requirement 3

Sales in units $\quad = \quad \dfrac{\textbf{Fixed expenses} + \textbf{Operating income}}{\textbf{Weighted-average contribution margin per unit}}$

$$11,000 \; = \; \frac{\$10,000 + \text{Operating income}}{\$6.40}$$

$$\$70,400 \; = \; \$10,000 + \text{Operating income}$$

Operating income = $60,400

Summary

1. **Identify different cost behaviour patterns.** *Cost-volume-profit (CVP) analysis* expresses the relationships among a company's costs, volume of activity, and profit. These relationships depend on *cost behaviour.* We classify costs as *variable, fixed,* or *mixed.*

2. **Use a contribution margin income statement to make business decisions.** A *contribution margin income statement* reports variable expenses and fixed expenses separately. It features the total *contribution margin,* the excess of sales revenues over variable expenses. This format helps managers predict the operating income that will result from various decisions.

3. **Compute breakeven sales and perform sensitivity analysis.** Two popular ways to perform CVP analysis are

the income statement equation approach and the contribution margin approach. Both approaches use an equation or formula derived from the contribution margin income statement. The contribution margin approach uses the product's contribution margin per unit or its *contribution margin ratio,* which give the increase in operating income for each additional unit sold or for each dollar of sales revenue, respectively. Either approach to CVP analysis can be used to compute a company's *breakeven point*—the sales level at which operating income is zero. We also perform sensitivity analysis to determine how changes in sales price, variable costs, or fixed costs affect the breakeven point.

4. **Compute the sales level needed to earn a target operating income.** CVP analysis also can show how many

units must be sold to earn a target operating income. The target operating income is added to the total fixed expense to determine the total contribution margin required to earn the income. That amount is divided by the unit contribution margin to give the number of units that must be sold.

5. **Graph a set of cost-volume-profit relationships.** Graphic displays of CVP relationships present information over a *relevant range* of sales levels. CVP graphs show the breakeven point and the ranges of sales volume that yield operating incomes and operating losses.

6. **Compute a margin of safety.** The *margin of safety* is the excess of expected sales over breakeven sales. The larger the margin, the lower the risk of a given plan.

7. **Use the sales mix in CVP analysis.** *Sales mix* is the combination of products that make up total sales. There is a unique breakeven point for each different sales mix—the greater the proportion of higher margin items, the lower the breakeven point. Companies with multiple products use the weighted average contribution margin per unit in computing the breakeven point.

8. **Compute income using variable costing and absorption costing.** Variable and absorption costing differ only in the way they treat fixed manufacturing costs. Variable costing considers fixed manufacturing costs as period costs that are expensed in the period incurred. In contrast, absorption costing considers fixed manufacturing costs as inventoriable product costs. Variable and absorption costing yield different income figures when the number of units in inventory changes. This is because absorption costing assigns some of the current period's fixed manufacturing costs to ending inventory, so this portion of current period fixed manufacturing cost is not expensed until future periods when the units are sold. In contrast, variable costing always expenses all fixed manufacturing costs in the current period. GAAP requires companies to use absorption costing for external reporting. However, many managers prefer a variable costing income statement for internal use because the separation of variable and fixed costs is helpful in making business decisions.

Self-Study Questions

Test your understanding of the chapter by marking the best answer for each of the following questions.

1. Cost-volume-profit analysis is most directly useful to (*p. 1223*)
   a. Managers to help them predict the outcome of their decisions
   b. Investors for deciding how much to pay for a company's stock
   c. Lenders for analyzing a loan request
   d. Tax authorities for setting income tax rates

2. The graph of a mixed cost (*p. 1225*)
   a. Passes through the origin and slopes upward
   b. Is horizontal from the point marking the level of fixed costs
   c. Has a steeper slope than the graph of a fixed cost or a variable cost
   d. Slopes upward from the point marking the level of fixed costs

3. Refer to Exhibit 22-5, page 1227. What will operating income be if sales increase by 10 percent? (*p. 1227*)
   a. $198,000   c. $390,000
   b. $270,000   d. $60,000

4. Refer to Exhibit 22-10, page 1244. If sales are 9,000 units, the business can expect fixed expenses of (*pp. 1227–1228*)
   a. $183,000   c. $75,000
   b. $108,000   d. $100,000

5. At the breakeven point (*p. 1231*)
   a. Sales equal fixed expenses
   b. Sales equal variable expenses
   c. Sales equal total expenses
   d. Sales exactly equal operating income

6. Variable expenses consume 70 percent of sales, and fixed expenses total $420,000. The breakeven point in dollars of sales is (*p. 1231*)
   a. $140,000   c. $1,260,000
   b. $600,000   d. $1,400,000

7. What happens to the breakeven point if both variable expenses and fixed expenses increase? (*p. 1236*)
   a. Breakeven sales increase
   b. Breakeven sales decrease
   c. Breakeven sales are unchanged because the two changes offset each other
   d. The effect on breakeven cannot be determined from the information given

8. William Thomas Corporation's monthly sales have averaged $480,000 for the past year. The monthly breakeven point is $400,000. The company's margin of safety percentage is (*p. 1238*)
   a. $16\frac{2}{3}$%   c. $62\frac{1}{2}$%
   b. 20%   d. 100%

9. Raj Mujadeen sells handmade Oriental rugs for $1,000 each and machine-made rugs for $300 each. Customers buy five times as many machine-made rugs as handmade rugs. Variable expenses consume 80 percent of sales, and monthly fixed expenses total $2,000. How many of each type of rug must Mujadeen sell to earn a target operating income of $3,000? (*p. 1239*)
   a. 8 handmade and 40 machine-made rugs
   b. 10 handmade and 50 machine-made rugs
   c. 12 handmade and 60 machine-made rugs
   d. 20 handmade and 100 machine-made rugs

Answers to the Self-Study Questions follow the Similar Accounting Terms

Accounting Vocabulary

Absorption costing *(p. 1242)*
Breakeven point *(p. 1231)*
Contribution margin *(p. 1227)*
Contribution margin income statement *(p. 1227)*
Contribution margin per unit *(p. 1232)*
Contribution margin ratio *(p. 1232)*
Cost behaviour *(p. 1223)*
Cost-volume-profit (CVP) analysis *(p. 1223)*
Fixed cost *(p. 1227)*
Margin of safety *(p. 1238)*
Mixed (semivariable) cost *(p. 1225)*
Relevant range *(p. 1225)*
Sales mix *(p. 1230)*
Sensitivity analysis *(p. 1234)*
Variable cost *(p. 1223)*
Variable costing *(p. 1242)*

Similar Accounting Terms

Mixed cost	Semivariable cost
Variable costing	Direct costing
Absorption costing	Full costing

Answers to Self-Study Questions

1. a

2. d

3. b
Increase in contribution margin ($900,000 × 0.10)	$ 90,000
Operating income before sales increase	180,000
Operating income after sales increase	$270,000

4. c

5. c

6. d Sales − 0.70 Sales = $420,000; 0.30 Sales = $420,000;
Breakeven sales = $420,000/0.30 = $1,400,000

7. a

8. a Margin of safety in dollars = $80,000 ($480,000 − $400,000)
Margin of safety as a percentage = $16\frac{2}{3}\%$ ($80,000/$480,000)

9. b calculated as follows:

	Handmade	Machine-Made	Total
Sale price per unit	$1,000	$300	
Variable expense per unit (80%)	800	240	
Contribution margin per unit	$ 200	$ 60	
Expected sales mix	× 1	× 5	6
Contribution margin	$ 200	$300	$ 500
Weighted-average contribution margin per unit ($500/6 units)			$83.333

$$\frac{\text{Sales}}{\text{in units}} = \frac{\text{Fixed expenses } + \text{ Target operating income}}{\text{Weighted-average contribution margin per unit}} = \frac{\$2,000 \ + \ \$3,000}{\$83.333} = 60 \text{ units}$$

| Target sales of handmade rugs (60 units × ⅙) | 10 units |
| Target sales of machine-made rugs (60 units × ⅚) | 50 units |

Assignment Material

Questions

1. How do managers use cost-volume-profit analysis in planning?
2. Define the three types of cost behaviour patterns.
3. Draw graphs of the three types of costs.
4. What are three questions cost-volume-profit analysis can answer?
5. How does a contribution margin income statement differ from a conventional income statement? Which income statement is more useful for predicting the income effect of a change in sales? Why?
6. Why is the relevant range important to cost-volume-profit analysis?
7. Draw a graph of fixed expenses from 0 to 50,000 units. The relevant range lies between 20,000 and 35,000 units, where fixed expenses are $300,000. Below the relevant range, fixed expenses are $200,000. Above the relevant range, fixed expenses are $400,000.
8. What is the breakeven point? What is its significance to a business?
9. Give the contribution margin cost-volume-profit formulas for breakeven sales in units and in dollars.
10. How does an increase in fixed expenses affect the breakeven point? How does a decrease in fixed expenses affect breakeven sales? Give the reason for each answer.
11. How does an increase in variable expenses affect the breakeven point? How does a decrease in variable expenses affect breakeven sales? Give the reason for each answer.
12. How does an increase in sale price affect the breakeven point? How does a decrease in sale price affect breakeven sales? Give the reason for each answer.
13. Briefly outline two ways to compute the sales in dollars needed to earn a target operating income.
14. Give the cost-volume-profit formula for sales in units needed to earn a target operating income. Do the same for sales in dollars.
15. Identify the steps in the preparation of a CVP graph.
16. What advantages does a CVP graph have over the equation approach and the contribution margin approach?
17. How does the margin of safety serve as a measure of risk?
18. Give the assumptions underlying CVP analysis.
19. Briefly describe how to perform CVP analysis when a company sells more than one product.
20. How is fixed overhead cost expensed under absorption costing? Under variable costing?

Exercises

Exercise 22-1 *Graphing cost behaviours* *(Obj. 1)*

Graph each of the following cost behaviour patterns over a relevant range from 0 to 10,000 units:

a. Fixed expenses of $25,000
b. Mixed expenses made up of fixed costs of $10,000 and variable costs of $3 per unit
c. Variable expenses of $10 per unit

Exercise 22-2 *Preparing a contribution margin income statement* *(Obj. 2, 3)*

Timmins Apparel Ltd.'s accounting records indicate that cost of goods sold is a variable expense. Selling expense is 20 percent fixed and 80 percent variable. General and administrative expense is 60 percent fixed and 40 percent variable. Prepare Timmins Apparel Ltd.'s contribution margin income statement for April. Compute the expected increase in operating income to the nearest $100 if sales increase by $50,000.

Timmins Apparel Ltd.'s April income statement appears on the next page.

TIMMINS APPAREL LTD.
Income Statement
For the Month Ended April 30, 2003

Sales revenue		$650,000
Cost of goods sold		448,000
Gross margin		202,000
Operating expenses:		
Selling	$80,000	
General and administrative	42,000	122,000
Operating income		$ 80,000

Exercise 22-3 *Using a contribution margin income statement* *(Obj. 2, 3)*

For its top managers, Coast Refining Corp. formats its income statement as follows:

COAST REFINING CORP.
Contribution Margin Income Statement
For the Three Months Ended March 31, 2002

Sales revenue	$450,000
Variable expenses	180,000
Contribution margin	270,000
Fixed expenses	190,000
Operating income	$ 80,000

Coast Refining's relevant range is between sales of $360,000 and $480,000. Prepare contribution margin income statements at those volume levels. Also, compute breakeven sales in dollars.

Exercise 22-4 *Computing breakeven sales by the contribution margin approach* *(Obj. 3)*

Curtains by Maria Ltd. has fixed expenses of $72,000 and variable expenses of $60.00 per unit of its product, which it sells for $100.00 per unit.

Required

1. Compute the company's contribution margin per unit and its contribution margin ratio.

2. Determine the breakeven point in units and in dollars, using the contribution margin approach.

Exercise 22-5 *Computing a change in breakeven sales* *(Obj. 3)*

For several years, Fran's Family Restaurant Ltd. has offered a lunch special for $5.00. Monthly fixed expenses have been $4,500. The variable cost of a meal has been $2.50. Fran Dunn, the owner, believes that by remodeling the restaurant and upgrading the food services, she can increase the price of the lunch special to $6.00. Monthly fixed expenses would increase to $5,600 and the variable expenses would increase to $3.25 per meal. Use the contribution margin approach to compute Fran's Family Restaurant Ltd.'s monthly breakeven sales in dollars before and after remodeling.

Exercise 22-6 *Computing breakeven sales and operating income or loss under different conditions* **(Obj. 3, 4)**

Praire Motor Freight Ltd. delivers freight throughout Manitoba and Saskatchewan. The company has monthly fixed expenses of $540,000 and a contribution margin of 60 percent of revenues.

Required

1. Compute Praire's monthly breakeven sales in dollars. Use the contribution margin approach.
2. Compute Praire's monthly operating income or operating loss if revenues are $600,000 and if they are $1,100,000.

Exercise 22-7 *Computing breakeven sales and sales needed to earn a target operating income; sales-mix considerations* **(Obj. 3, 4, 7)**

Consider the following cases.

a. Whitelaw Tire Supply Inc. has fixed monthly expenses of $11,200 and a contribution margin ratio of 40 percent. What must monthly sales be for the business to break even? To earn operating income of $5,800?

b. Henri's Bikes sells two product lines, one with a contribution margin ratio of 50 percent, the other with a contribution margin ratio of 55 percent. Each product line makes up half of sales. If monthly fixed expenses are $8,100 what must monthly sales be for the business to break even? To earn operating income of $7,200?

Exercise 22-8 *Cost-volume-profit analysis with a sales mix* **(Obj. 3, 4, 7)**

Three college friends open an off-campus shop named P.A.S. T-Shirts Ltd. They plan to sell a standard T-shirt for $7.00 and a fancier version for $9.00. The $7.00 shirt costs them $4.00, and the $9.00 shirt costs them $5.00. The friends expect to sell two fancy T-shirts for each standard T-shirt. Their monthly fixed expenses are $3,600. How many of each type of T-shirt must they sell monthly to break even? To earn $1,200?

Exercise 22-9 *Graphing cost-volume-profit relationships* **(Obj. 5)**

Suppose that Marineland in Niagara Falls earns total revenue that averages $18 for every ticket sold. Annual fixed expenses are $12 million, and variable expenses are $3 per ticket. Prepare the amusement park's CVP graph under these assumptions. Show the breakeven point in dollars and in tickets. Label fixed expenses, variable expenses, the operating loss area, and the operating income area on the graph.

Exercise 22-10 *Analyzing a cost-volume-profit graph* **(Obj. 5)**

The top managers of Atwater Ltd. are planning the budget for 2003. The accountant who prepared the CVP graph shown on the next page forgot to label the lines.

Required

Answer the following questions asked by the managers:
1. What do the lines mean?
2. Where is the operating income area? The operating loss area?
3. What is breakeven sales in units and in dollars?
4. What will be operating income (or operating loss) if sales are 6,800 units?

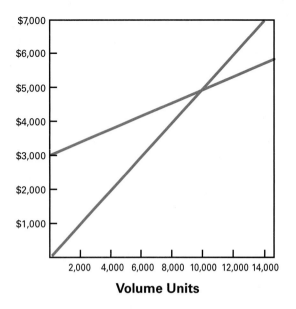

$7,000$
$6,000$
$5,000$
$4,000$
$3,000$
$2,000$
$1,000$

2,000 4,000 6,000 8,000 10,000 12,000 14,000

Volume Units

Exercise 22-11 *Computing a margin of safety (Obj. 6)*

Shoppers' Choice Ltd. convenience store has a monthly operating income target of $7,000. Variable expenses are 60 percent of sales, and fixed monthly expenses are $9,000. Compute the monthly margin of safety in dollars if the store achieves its income goal. Express Shoppers' Choice Ltd.'s margin of safety as a percentage of target sales.

Exercise 22-12 *Conventional (absorption costing) and contribution margin (variable costing) income statements; business decisions (Obj. 8)*

The 2003 data that follow pertain to Pilote Inc., manufacturer of a single product:

Sale price: $105	Fixed operating cost: $250,000
Variable manufacturing cost per unit: $70	Units produced: 120,000
Variable operating cost per unit: $5	Units sold: 90,000
Fixed manufacturing cost: $480,000	

Required

1. Prepare both conventional (absorption costing) and contribution margin (variable costing) income statements for Pilote Inc. The company's year end is December 31.

2. Which statement shows the higher operating income? Why?

3. Pilote Inc.'s marketing vice-president believes that a sales promotion that costs $85,000 would increase sales to 100,000 units. Should the company go ahead with the promotion? Give your reason.

Challenge Exercise

Exercise 22-13 *Computing contribution margin for one of two products (Obj. 7)*

Highpeak Inc. manufactures two styles of climbing shoe—the Mountaineer and the Pro Mountaineer. The following data pertain to the Mountaineer:

Sale price	$80
Variable manufacturing cost....................................	35
Variable operating cost...	10

Highpeak Inc. monthly fixed expenses total $80,000. When Mountaineers and Pro Mountaineers are sold in the mix of 7:3, respectively, the sale of 2,000 total units results in an operating income of $35,000. Compute the unit contribution margin of Pro Mountaineers.

Beyond the Numbers

Beyond the Numbers 22-1 *Breakeven point* *(Obj. 3)*

Your best friend, who is majoring in marketing, has just opened a small business selling T-shirts with your school's logo. Variable expenses include buying and printing the T-shirts, and sales commissions. Fixed expenses include rent for space at the student activities centre.

Your friend has excellent sales skills, but he knows little about accounting. He is surprised that even though he is selling 200 T-shirts per month, he seems to be losing money. After studying this chapter, you realized that part of his problem is that his breakeven point is too high. What steps can your friend take to reduce the breakeven point?

Beyond the Numbers 22-2 *Absorption and variable costing incentives* *(Obj. 8)*

Link Back to Chapter 19 (Just-in-Time Production). You serve on the board of directors of Norco Ltd., a medium-size manufacturing company that has recently adopted a just-in-time production philosophy. Part of your responsibility is to develop a compensation contract for Lisa Chin, the Vice President of Manufacturing Operations. To give her the incentive to make decisions that will increase the company's profits, the board decides to give Chin a year-end bonus if Norco meets a target operating income.

Write a memo to the chairman of the board, Hans Theil, explaining your view on whether the bonus contract should be based on absorption or variable costing.

Ethical Issue

In recent years, professional sports teams have considered shifting from paying stars salaries only to paying them lower salaries but adding a bonus that is based on team revenues. That way, a star is motivated to play harder. The more the team wins, the greater the team revenues as more and more fans purchase tickets and as television companies increase payments for the rights to broadcast games. If the star has a bad year, the team may win fewer games and revenues could drop, and the star's compensation would be lower. By shifting player compensation from only salary to a lower salary plus bonus that is based on team revenues, these player contracts increase the team's percentage of variable costs and decrease its percentage of fixed costs.

Required

1. Why would team owners favour these contracts?
2. Would star players favour these contracts?
3. Are team owners taking advantage of stars? Are these contracts ethical?

Problems (Group A)

Problem 22-1A *Explaining the contribution margin approach and the margin of safety to decision makers* *(Obj. 2, 6)*

Hunt Club Clothiers Inc. is managed as traditionally as the button-down shirts that have made it famous. Arch Huntington founded the business in 1952 and has directed operations "by the seat of his pants" ever since. Approaching retirement, he must turn the business over to his daughter, Sarah. Recently Arch and Sarah had this conversation:

Sarah: Dad, I am convinced that we can increase sales by advertising. I think we can spend $700 monthly on advertising and increase monthly sales by $8,000. With our contribution margin, operating income should increase by $4,500.

Arch: You know how I feel about advertising. We've never needed it in the past. Why now?

Sarah: Two new shops have opened near us this year, and those guys are getting lots of business. I've noticed our profit margin slipping as the year has unfolded. Our margin of safety is at its lowest point ever.

Arch: Profit margin I understand, but what is the contribution margin that you mentioned? And what is this "margin of safety"?

Required

Explain for Arch Huntington the contribution margin approach to decision making. Show how Sarah Huntington computed the $4,500. (Advertising is a fixed cost.) Also, describe what Sarah means by margin of safety, and explain why the business's situation is critical.

Problem 22-2A *Computing contribution margin and breakeven analysis* **(Obj. 2, 3)**

The budgets of four companies yield the following information:

	A	B	C	D
Target sales...............................	$	$340,000	$500,000	$
Variable expenses	100,000	120,000		104,000
Fixed expenses	80,000	138,000		
Operating income (loss).........	$	$	$110,000	$ 35,000
Units sold	5,000		125,000	
Unit contribution margin.......		$100	$2	$14
Contribution margin ratio	0.20			0.60

Fill in the blanks for each company. Which company has the lowest breakeven point? What causes the low breakeven point?

Problem 22-3A *Computing breakeven revenue and the revenue needed to earn a target operating income; preparing a contribution margin income statement* **(Obj. 2, 3, 4)**

The *Tam O'Shanter* is a schooner that sails from Halifax, Nova Scotia, during the spring and fall. During the summer the ship leaves from Charlottetown, P.E.I. The average cruise has 50 tourists on board, and each person pays $80 for a day's sail. The ship sails 80 days each year.

The *Tam O'Shanter* has a crew of eight. Each crew member earns an average of $100 per cruise. The crew is paid only when the ship sails. The other variable expense is for refreshments, which average $15 per passenger per cruise. Annual fixed expenses total $132,000.

Required

1. Compute revenue and variable expenses for each cruise.
2. Use the equation approach to compute the number of cruises the *Tam O'Shanter* must make each year to break even.
3. Use the contribution margin approach to compute the number of cruises needed each year to earn $110,000. Is this profit goal realistic? Give your reason.
4. Prepare the *Tam O'Shanter's* contribution margin income statement for 80 cruises for the year. Report only two categories of expenses: variable and fixed.

Problem 22-4A   *Analyzing CVP relationships*   *(Obj. 2, 3, 4)*

Suppose that Specialty Pens Inc. imprints ballpoint pens with company logos. The company has fixed expenses of $360,000 per year plus variable expenses of $1.80 per box of pens. For each box of pens sold, the company earns revenue of $3.30.

Required

1. Use the equation approach to compute the number of boxes of pens Specialty Pens Inc. must sell each year to break even.

2. Use the contribution margin approach to compute the dollar sales Specialty Pens Inc. needs in order to earn $40,000 in operating income.

3. Prepare Specialty Pens Inc.'s contribution margin income statement for 2003 for sales of 240,000 boxes of pens. Cost of goods sold is 80 percent of variable expenses. Operating expenses make up the rest of variable expenses and all of fixed expenses.

4. The company is considering an expansion that will increase fixed expenses by 30 percent and variable expenses by 10 cents per box of pens. Compute the new breakeven point in units and in dollars. Use either the equation approach or the contribution margin approach.

5. How will what you learned from this problem help you manage a business?

Problem 22-5A   *Using a contribution margin income statement for breakeven analysis; sales mix, margin of safety, and changes in CVP relationships*   *(Obj. 2, 3, 6, 7)*

The contribution margin income statement of Monical's Pizzeria Ltd. for May 2003 follows:

MONICAL'S PIZZERIA LTD.
Contribution Margin Income Statement
For the Month Ended May 31, 2003

Sales revenue		$150,000
Variable expenses:		
Cost of goods sold	$40,000	
Selling	17,000	
General and administrative	3,000	60,000
Contribution margin		90,000
Fixed expenses:		
Selling	20,750	
General and administrative	8,500	29,250
Operating income		$ 60,750

Monical's Pizzeria Ltd. sells three small pizzas for every large pizza. A small pizza sells for $10, with a variable expense of $4.25. A large pizza sells for $18, with a variable expense of $6.

Required

1. Determine Monical's Pizzeria Ltd.'s monthly breakeven point in the numbers of small pizzas and large pizzas. Prove the correctness of your computation by preparing a summary contribution margin income statement at breakeven. Show only two categories of expenses: variable and fixed.

2. Compute Monical's Pizzeria Ltd.'s margin of safety in dollars.

3. If Monical's Pizzeria Ltd. can increase monthly sales by 15 percent above $150,000, what will operating income be?

4. Monical's Pizzeria Ltd. hopes to decrease monthly fixed expenses by $10,000. Use the contribution margin approach to determine the new breakeven sales in dollars.

Problem 22-6A   *Computing breakeven sales and sales needed to earn a target operating income; graphing CVP relationships   **(Obj. 3, 4, 5)***

West Coast Travel Ltd. is opening an office in White Rock, B.C. Fixed monthly expenses are office rent ($3,000), amortization of office furniture ($200), utilities ($110), a special telephone line ($520), a connection with computerized reservation service ($380), and the salary of a travel agent ($3,440). Variable expenses include incentive compensation for the employee (5 percent of sales), advertising (6 percent of sales), supplies and postage (1 percent of sales), and a usage fee for the telephone line and computerized reservation service (3 percent of sales).

Required

1. Use the contribution margin approach to compute West Coast Travel Ltd.'s breakeven sales in dollars. If the average commission for arranging a holiday tour is $900, how many tours must be sold to break even?

2. Use the equation approach to compute the dollar sales needed to earn a target monthly operating income of $6,800.

3. Graph the travel agency's CVP relationships. Assume that an average sale is a $900 commission. Show the breakeven point, fixed expenses, variable expenses, operating loss area, operating income area, and the sales in units and dollars when monthly operating income of $6,800 is earned. The graph should range from 0 to 25 units.

4. Assume that the average tour commission decreases to $740. Use the contribution margin approach to compute the new breakeven point in tours sold. What is the effect of the sale price decrease on the breakeven point?

Problem 22-7A   *Identify different cost behaviour patterns; use a contribution margin income statement to make business decisions; compute breakeven sales; compute the sales needed to earn a target operating income*
(Obj. 1, 2, 3, 4)

Elite Deck Products Ltd. produces a kit for cleaning backyard decks with the following results budgeted for the production and sales of 50,000 units:

Sales (50,000 units)...		$1,500,000
Cost of goods sold:		
Direct materials...	390,000	
Direct labour (hourly wages)	240,000	
Variable manufacturing overhead.....................................	120,000	
Fixed manufacturing overhead*..	360,000	
Total cost of goods sold...		1,110,000
Gross margin		390,000
Operating expenses:		
Sales commissions ($3 per unit)..	150,000	
Head office salaries..	240,000	
Total operating expenses...		390,000
Net operating income..		$ 0

*Fixed overhead costs give a production capacity of 110,000 units.

Required

1. Reformat the budgeted income statement into one in the contribution margin format.

2. How many units would the company have to produce and sell if it desired operating income of $120,000?

3. The company is considering reducing the kit's selling price to $27 per unit and using a new production process. The new production process would reduce variable manufacturing costs by 40 percent but increase fixed manufacturing costs by 30 percent.

   a. What would be the new breakeven point?
   b. Should the company make the changes if sales are expected to be 90,000 units next period?

Problem 22-8A *Identify different cost behaviour patterns; use a contribution margin income statement to make business decisions; compute breakeven sales; compute a margin of safety; compute the sales needed to earn a target operating income; use the sales mix in CVP analysis* **(Obj. 1, 3, 4, 6)**

The Outdoors Company Inc. produces and sells two lines of snowboards with the following results based on the production and sale of 3,000 units of each:

	Champion	Champion Plus
Sales...	$210,000	$330,000
Cost of goods sold:		
Direct materials	60,000	90,000
Direct labour..	45,000	30,000
Variable overhead	15,000	30,000
Fixed overhead...	30,000	60,000
Total cost of goods sold	150,000	210,000
Gross margin...	60,000	120,000
Fixed selling and administrative	36,000	79,000
Operating income	$ 24,000	$ 41,000

Required

1. Calculate the contribution margin per unit for each of the product lines. What is their weighted-average contribution margin?

2. What is the company's breakeven point with its current sales mix? What is the company's margin of safety (in units)?

3. How many units of each product line would the company have to produce and sell if it decided to change the sales mix to a 3:1 ratio (Champion:Champion Plus) and if it desired operating income of $100,000?

Problem 22-9A *Preparing absorption and variable costing income statements and explaining the difference in income* **(Obj. 8)**

Precision Optics Ltd. manufactures binoculars, which it sells for $60 each. The company uses the FIFO inventory costing method, and it computes a new monthly fixed manufacturing overhead rate based on the actual number of binoculars produced that month. All costs and production levels are exactly as planned. The following data are from Precision Optics Ltd.'s first two months in business during 2002.

Required

1. Compute the product cost per pair of binoculars under absorption costing and under variable costing. Do this first for October and then for November.

2. Prepare separate income statements for October and November, using
   a. Absorption costing
   b. Variable costing

3. Is operating income higher under absorption costing or variable costing in

October? In November? Explain the pattern of differences in operating income based on absorption costing versus variable costing.

	October, 2002	November, 2002
Sales	2,000 units	2,200 units
Production	2,500 units	2,000 units
Variable manufacturing expense per pair of binoculars.................................	$25	$25
Variable marketing and administrative costs per pair of binoculars.................................	$8	$8
Total fixed manufacturing overhead expenses..	$12,000	$12,000
Total fixed marketing and administrative expenses..	$5,000	$5,000

Problems (Group B)

Problem 22-1B   *Explaining the effects of different cost behaviour patterns on the breakeven point and on likely profits   (Obj. 1)*

Manjuris Restaurant Supply Ltd. is opening early next year. The owner is considering two plans for obtaining the capital assets and employee labour needed for operations. Under plan 1, Manjuris would lease equipment month by month and pay employees low salaries but give them a big part of their pay in commissions on sales. Plan 2 calls for purchasing all equipment outright and paying employees straight salaries. Discuss the effects of the two plans on variable expenses, fixed expenses, breakeven sales, and likely profits for a new business in the start-up stage. Indicate which plan you favour for Manjuris Restaurant Supply Ltd.

Problem 22-2B   *Computing contribution margin and breakeven analysis   (Obj. 2, 3)*

The budgets of four companies yield the following information:

	A	B	C	D
Target sales.............................	$600,000	$300,000	$250,000	$ ____
Variable expenses			100,000	$135,000
Fixed expenses	312,000	130,000		
Operating income (loss).........	$ ____	$ ____	$ 7,000	$140,000
Units sold	84,000	11,000		8,000
Unit contribution margin.......		$12	$6	$40
Contribution margin ratio	0.30			

Fill in the blanks for each company. Which company has the lowest breakeven point? What causes the low breakeven point?

Problem 22-3B   *Computing breakeven revenue and the revenue needed to earn a target operating income; preparing a contribution margin income statement (Obj. 2, 3, 4)*

Tradewinds Cruises Ltd. sails a schooner from Vancouver. The average cruise has 90 tourists on board. Each person pays $100 for a day's sail in the Pacific. The ship sails 85 days each year.

The schooner has a crew of 12. Each crew member earns an average of $115 per cruise. The crew is paid only when the ship sails. Other variable expenses are for refreshments, which average $14 per passenger per cruise. Annual fixed expenses total $172,600.

Required

1. Compute revenue and variable expenses for each cruise.

2. Use the equation approach to compute the number of cruises needed annually to break even.

3. Use the contribution margin approach to compute the number of cruises needed annually to earn $193,000. Is this profit goal realistic? Give your reason.

4. Prepare Tradewinds' contribution margin income statement for 85 cruises each year. Report only two categories of expenses: variable and fixed.

Problem 22-4B   *Analyzing CVP relationships*   *(Obj. 2, 3, 4)*

Saville Advertising Ltd. imprints calendars with company names. The company has fixed expenses of $420,000 each month plus variable expense of $2.40 per carton of 12 calendars. For each carton of calendars sold, Saville Advertising Ltd. earns revenue of $3.80.

Required

1. Use the equation approach to compute the number of cartons of calendars Saville Advertising Ltd. must sell each month to break even.

2. Use the contribution margin approach to compute the dollar amount of monthly sales Saville Advertising Ltd. needs in order to earn $70,000 in operating income.

3. Prepare Saville Advertising Ltd.'s contribution margin income statement for June for sales of 500,000 cartons of calendars. Manufacturing costs are 70 percent of variable expenses. Operating expenses make up the rest of the variable expenses and all of the fixed expenses.

4. The company is considering an expansion that will increase fixed expenses by 30 percent and variable expenses by 10 percent. Compute the new breakeven point in units and in dollars. Use either the equation approach or the contribution margin approach.

5. How would this expansion affect Saville Advertising Ltd.'s risk?

Problem 22-5B   *Using a contribution margin income statement for breakeven analysis; sales mix, margin of safety, and changes in CVP relationships*
(Obj. 2, 3, 6, 7)

The contribution margin income statement of Modern Man's Accessories Ltd. for November 2002 is as follows:

MODERN MAN'S ACCESSORIES LTD.
Contribution Margin Income Statement
For the Month Ended November 30, 2002

Sales revenue		$60,000
Variable expenses:		
Manufacturing	$22,000	
Selling	13,000	
General and administrative	7,000	42,000
Contribution margin		18,000
Fixed expenses:		
Selling	11,000	
General and administrative	3,000	14,000
Operating income		$ 4,000

Modern Man's Accessories Ltd. sells two ties for every belt. The ties sell for $10, with a variable expense of $4 per unit. The belts sell for $12, with a variable unit cost of $5.

Required

1. Determine Modern Man's Accessories Ltd.'s monthly breakeven point in the numbers of ties and belts. Prove the correctness of your computation by preparing a summary contribution margin income statement at breakeven. Show only two categories of expenses: variable and fixed.

2. Compute Modern Man's Accessories Ltd.'s margin of safety in dollars.

3. Suppose that Modern Man's Accessories Ltd. increases monthly sales by 20 percent above $60,000. Compute operating income.

4. Modern Man's Accessories Ltd. may expand the store and increase monthly fixed expenses by $5,600. Use the contribution margin approach to determine the new breakeven sales in dollars.

Problem 22-6B *Computing breakeven sales and sales needed to earn a target operating income; graphing CVP relationships* **(Obj. 3, 4, 5)**

Executive Travel Inc. is opening an office in Montreal. Fixed monthly expenses are office rent ($4,600), amortization of office furniture ($190), utilities ($140), a special telephone line ($390), a connection with computerized reservation service ($480), and the salary of two travel agents ($7,000). Variable expenses include incentive compensation of the employees (6 percent of sales), advertising (6 percent of sales), supplies and postage (1 percent of sales), and a usage fee for the telephone line and computerized reservation service (7 percent of sales).

Required

1. Use the contribution margin approach to compute the travel agency's breakeven sales in dollars. If the average commission for arranging a package tour is $800, how many tours must be sold to break even?

2. Use the income statement equation approach to compute dollar sales needed to earn monthly operating income of $4,000.

3. Graph the travel agency's CVP relationships. Assume that an average commission is $800. Show the breakeven point, fixed expenses, variable expenses, operating loss area, operating income area, and the sales in units and dollars when monthly operating income of $4,000 is earned. The graph should range from 0 to 40 units.

4. Assume that the average tour commission decreases to $500. Use the contribution margin approach to compute the new breakeven point in units. What is the effect of the sale price decrease on the breakeven point?

Problem 22-7B *Identify different cost behaviour patterns; use a contribution margin income statement to make business decisions; compute breakeven sales, compute the sales needed to earn a target operating income* **(Obj. 1, 2, 3, 4)**

Svenson Marine Products Inc. produces a kit for cleaning fiberglass boats with the results shown on page 1265 budgeted for the production and sale of 50,000 units.

Required

1. Reformat the budgeted income statement into one in the contribution margin format.

2. How many units would the company have to produce and sell if it desired operating income of $90,000?

3. The company is considering reducing the kit's selling price to $18 per unit and using a new production process. The new production process would reduce variable manufacturing costs by 30 percent but increase fixed manufacturing costs by 35 percent.

a. What would be the new breakeven point?

b. Should the company make the changes if sales are expected to be 70,000 units next period?

Sales (50,000 units)		$1,000,000
Cost of goods sold:		
Direct materials	200,000	
Direct labour (hourly wages)	160,000	
Variable manufacturing overhead	80,000	
Fixed manufacturing overhead*	240,000	
Total cost of goods sold		680,000
Gross margin		320,000
Operating expenses:		
Sales commissions ($2 per unit)	100,000	
Head office salaries	220,000	
Total operating expenses		320,000
Net operating income		$ 0

*Fixed overhead costs give a production capacity of 80,000 units.

Problem 22-8B *Identify different cost behaviour patterns; use a contribution margin income statement to make business decisions; compute breakeven sales, compute a margin of safety, compute the sales needed to earn a target operating income; use the sales mix in CVP analysis* **(Obj. 1, 3, 4, 6)**

The Burnaby Boot Company Inc. produces and sells two lines of hiking boots with the following results based on the production and sale of 12,000 units of each:

	Hiker	Expert
Sales	$480,000	$780,000
Cost of goods sold:		
Direct materials	90,000	210,000
Direct labour	60,000	60,000
Variable overhead	120,000	120,000
Fixed overhead	60,000	70,000
Total cost of goods sold	330,000	460,000
Gross margin	150,000	320,000
Sales commissions	42,000	78,000
Fixed selling and administrative	30,000	40,000
Total selling and administrative	72,000	118,000
Operating income	$ 78,000	$202,000

Required

1. Calculate the contribution margin per unit for each of the product lines. What is their weighted-average contribution margin?

2. What is the company's breakeven point with its current sales mix? What is the margin of safety (in units)?

3. How many units of each product line would the company have to produce and sell if it decided to change the sales mix to a 3:2 ratio (Hiker:Expert) and if the company desired an operating income of $120,000?

Problem 22-9B *Preparing absorption and variable costing income statements and explaining the difference in income* **(Obj. 8)**

Recycall Corporation manufactures plastic recycling bins, which it sells for $7 each. The company uses the FIFO inventory costing method, and it computes a new monthly fixed manufacturing overhead rate based on the actual number of bins produced that month. All costs and production levels are exactly as planned. The following data are from Recycall Corporation's first two months in business:

	January 2003	February 2003
Sales	1,000 bins	1,200 bins
Production	1,400 bins	1,000 bins
Variable manufacturing expense per bin	$2	$2
Variable marketing and administrative expenses per bin	$1	$1
Total fixed manufacturing overhead	$700	$700
Total fixed marketing and administrative expenses	$500	$500

Required

1. Compute the product cost per bin under absorption costing and under variable costing. Do this first for January and then for February.

2. Prepare separate income statements for January and February, using
   a. Absorption costing
   b. Variable costing

3. Is operating income higher under absorption costing or variable costing in January? In February? Explain the pattern of differences in operating income based on absorption costing versus variable costing.

Challenge Problems

Problem 22-1C *Explaining relevant range* *(Obj. 1)*

It is important that management recognize the concept of relevant range when performing cost-volume-profit analysis.

Required

Explain the concept of relevant range and why it must be considered in cost-volume-profit analysis.

Problem 22-2C *Understanding breakeven sales* *(Obj. 3)*

While companies would like to operate at breakeven, or better, sometimes they are prepared to operate at a loss in the short run.

Required

Under what conditions would a company consider operating below the breakeven level of sales? Why would a company operate at such a level when management knows that a loss will be incurred?

Extending Your Knowledge

Decision Problems

1. Using CVP analysis to make business decisions *(Obj. 1, 3, 4)*

Richard and Lani Strom live in Calgary. Two years ago, they visited Thailand. Lani, a professional chef, was impressed with the cooking methods and the spices used in the Thai food. The Stroms are contemplating opening a Thai restaurant in Calgary.

Lani would supervise the cooking, and Richard would leave his current job to be the maitre d'. The restaurant would serve dinner Tuesday through Saturday.

Richard has noticed a restaurant for lease. The restaurant has seven tables, each of which can seat four. Tables can be moved together for a large party. Lani is planning two seatings per evening.

The Stroms have drawn up the following estimates:

Average revenue, including beverages and dessert..................	$45 per meal
Average cost of the food, including preparation	$15.75 per meal
Chef's and dishwasher's salaries	$49,600 per year
Rent (premises, equipment)	$3,500 per month
Cleaning (linen and premises)	$500 per month
Replacement of dishes, cutlery, glasses....................................	$300 per month
Utilities, advertising, telephone	$1,400 per month

Compute breakeven revenue for the restaurant. Also compute the amount of revenue needed to earn operating income of $70,000 for the year. How many meals must the Stroms serve each night to earn their target income of $70,000? Should the couple open the restaurant?

2. Using a contribution margin income statement to make business decisions (Obj. 2, 3)

Funtime Toy Company Ltd. makes three lines of toys. Each line is manufactured in a different plant, and each line has a different set of CVP relationships. Budgeted income statements for 2003 are:

	Newborn	Toddler	Preschooler
Sales..	$320,000	$160,000	$240,000
Variable expenses	64,000	80,000	108,000
Contribution margin..........................	256,000	80,000	132,000
Fixed expenses....................................	188,000	126,000	118,000
Operating income (loss)	$ 68,000	$(46,000)	$ 14,000

Average sale prices are $2 for toys for newborns, $4 for toys for toddlers, and $6 for preschoolers' toys.

Required

1. Which product line is the least profitable?

2. How many toddler toys must be sold to break even?

3. Prepare a contribution margin income statement for 2003 assuming that sales of toddler toys are eliminated altogether. Also assume that $120,000 is the toddler line's fixed cost for all volumes in the range of zero to 100,000 toys.

4. Would it be wise to drop the toddler toy line immediately? What would you recommend to Funtime's management regarding the future of the line?

23

The Master Budget and Responsibility Accounting

CHAPTER OBJECTIVES

After studying this chapter, you should be able to

1 Identify the benefits of budgeting

2 Prepare an operating budget for a company

3 Prepare the components of a financial budget

4 Use sensitivity analysis in budgeting

5 Distinguish among different types of responsibility centres

6 Prepare a performance report for management by exception

7 Allocate indirect costs to departments

Everyone in the world should have a simple, decent, affordable place to live. That's the mission of Habitat for Humanity International, a world-wide nonprofit organization with nearly 2,000 local affiliates that oversee construction of homes in their own communities. Habitat for Humanity International and its affiliates solicit donations of building materials, and families who will become the homeowners invest "sweat equity" alongside volunteers. The total now is more than 90,000 homes built in over 60 countries across the globe, from Australia, Bangladesh, and Canada, to Uganda, the U.S., and Zimbabwe.

Habitat plans to build 100,000 new houses over the next five years—a tall order since it took 24 years to build the first 100,000. Founder and president Millard Fuller must plan carefully to meet this lofty goal:

- How much will it cost to support construction of 100,000 houses over the next five years?
- How can Habitat raise enough revenue to pay these expenses?
- Can Habitat raise contributions in time to fund these expenses, or will it have to borrow to finance a cash shortfall?

Fuller and his management team use *budgets* to help answer these questions. The budget is Habitat's financial roadmap: it spells out how it will obtain and spend its resources. To develop the expense budget, managers predict the funds that headquarters will transfer to affiliates for house-building, the money to be spent on educational programs, and administrative expenses like fundraising. The revenue budget predicts the contributions individuals, corporations, and government grants will offer Habitat. After developing the revenue budget, Habitat's managers realized that they would not have enough money to fund the ambitious house-building goal. So Habitat is embarking on a five-year fundraising campaign, and is using its Web site to encourage additional on-line donations.

Habitat also uses budgets to control revenues and costs. Simply preparing the expense budget helps managers identify cost-cutting opportunities. And the budget is a benchmark for assessing actual results. Reports compare:

- actual revenues to budgeted revenues for each type of donor (individuals, corporations, governments)
- actual expenses to budgeted expenses for each type of expense (funds transferred to affiliates for house-building, technology upgrades, fundraising).

MANAGERS investigate differences between actual and budgeted figures. For example, if actual revenues from individuals fall short of the budget, managers may redouble efforts to solicit funds from individuals, or they may decide to focus elsewhere, perhaps on obtaining larger donations from corporations.

Why Managers Use Budgets

Managers of for-profit companies as well as nonprofit companies like Habitat for Humanity play several key roles. First, they develop strategies—overall business goals like Habitat's goal to build 100,000 houses over the next five years. Next, they plan and take specific actions to achieve those goals. Finally, managers control operations by comparing actual results with plans or budgets. This performance evaluation provides valuable feedback. For example, if Habitat's expenses are higher than budgeted, managers must either cut costs or increase revenues, and these decisions will affect their future strategies and plans.

Exhibit 23-1 shows that managers develop budgets to implement the organization's strategy, and then use these budgets to plan, act, and control business operations. The process is continuous: determine strategy, develop plans and budgets to implement the strategy, act to implement the strategy, control by comparing actual

Habitat for Humanity International
www.habitat.org

THINKING IT OVER

Assume that a business does not budget sales. The production department produces at 100 percent of capacity. However, sales decline due to a foreseeable economic recession. What happens?

A: Excess inventory is produced. The business will either keep the inventory that cannot be sold or sell it at a discount to move it. Either way the business loses money.

Bombardier
www.bombardier.com

EXHIBIT 23-1

Budgets, Performance Evaluation, and the Management Cycle

results to the budget or plan, and then use feedback from the control step to start the process again.

Budget Timeframes

In Chapter 19, we defined a *budget* as a quantitative expression of a plan that helps managers coordinate and implement the plan. Budgets can focus on the short-term or long-term. Habitat developed a long-term budget to predict the costs required to reach its goal of building 100,000 houses over the next five years. Bombardier's long-term budgets forecast demand for its planes for the next twenty years!

Other budgets have a short-term focus. Many companies budget their cash flows monthly, weekly, and daily to ensure that they have enough cash to meet their needs. They also budget revenues and expenses—and thus operating income—for months, quarters, and years. This chapter focuses on shorter-term budgets of a year or less. Chapter 26 focuses on budgets for large capital expenditures (property, plant, and equipment, for example) that naturally have a longer-term focus.

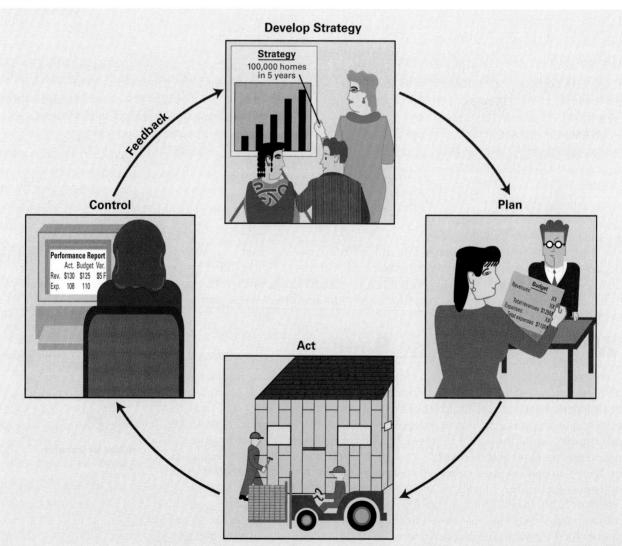

The Importance of Budgeting

Rick Montgomery, the general manager of West Coast Alloys Limited, has been preparing budgets for the upcoming year.

"Budgeting is essential in a company our size," Rick explains. "We need to be able to forecast our sales and profitability in order to make other decisions. Our target market is the forest products industry and we have to follow the economics of that industry in order to forecast our sales."

Once a sales forecast has been developed, material, labour, and overhead costs are determined. "We have to estimate our material costs closely due to the competitiveness of our business," according to Rick. "Labour costs are estimated based on anticipated rates and estimated hours. Manufacturing overheads are developed based on last year's numbers and trends in the economy."

Perhaps the most important aspect of the budgeting process for a small- or medium-sized business is the cash budget. "Cash flow is extremely important to a company like ours," Rick says. "We have to monitor our cash on a day-to-day basis. The operating budget helps us to identify the pattern of our cash collections and payments."

Finally, Rick explained the importance of budgeting for controlling ongoing operations. "We review our operating results on a monthly basis and compare them to what we had anticipated in the operating budget. It is important that we identify areas of concern as quickly as possible in order to do what is necessary to maintain profitability."

Budgeting for a Service Company

Let's begin by considering a budget for a small service company. Ram Dharan started a small business—an online service that provides travel itineraries for leisure travellers. Dharan wants to earn $240 per month to help cover his college expenses. He develops a budget to determine whether he can expect to meet this goal.

Dharan expects to sell 100 itineraries per month at a price of $3 each. Over the last six months, he paid his Internet service provider an average of $60 per month, and he spent an additional $20 per month on reference materials. He expects these monthly costs to remain about the same. Finally, he spends 5 percent of his sales revenues for Internet banner advertising.

To prepare the budget, Dharan computes his total budgeted revenues and subtracts his total budgeted expenses:

RAM DHARAN TRAVEL ITINERARIES Budget for May 2003		
Budgeted sales revenue ($3 × 100)......		$300
Less budgeted expenses:		
Internet access expense.....................	$60	
Reference materials expense............	20	
Advertising expense (5% × $300)...	15	95
Budgeted operating income.................		$205

The budget shows that if business goes according to plan, Ram Dharan will not meet his $240 per month operating income goal. Dharan will have to increase revenue (by using word-of-mouth advertising) or cut expenses (by finding a less expensive Internet access provider) to meet his income goal.

Ram Dharan is the sole proprietor of a simple business, so his budget covers the entire company's operations. While managers of large companies also prepare budgets for the organization as a whole, individual subunits prepare their own budgets, as well. For example, each of Habitat's Regional Support Centres across Canada and the U.S., and Area offices in Costa Rica, Thailand, and South Africa prepares a budget. Headquarters in Americus, Georgia, uses the individual budgets to prepare the organization-wide budget.

The Budget as a Management Tool

Budgets are key management tools that help large organizations like Habitat for Humanity, Bombardier, and TELUS just as much as sole proprietors like Ram Dharan. Exhibit 23-2 summarizes budgeting's benefits.

Benefits of Budgeting

Budgeting requires planning   Ram Dharan discovered that his expected income fell short of his target. The sooner he learns of the expected shortfall, the more time he has to plan how to increase revenues or cut expenses. The better his plan and the more time he has to execute the plan, the more likely he will meet his income target. In the chapter opening story, Habitat for Humanity's budget prompted managers to immediately initiate a major fundraising campaign.

Budgeting helps managers set realistic goals by requiring them to plan specific actions to meet their goals. Budgeting also leads managers to ask what-if questions and to plan for contingencies. Suppose that Toyota assigns a plant with 3 million units of capacity to production of Camry cars. What if expected demand for a year is 2.6 million cars but actual demand turns out to be 3.2 million? To satisfy demand, Toyota must add 600,000 units of capacity. If Toyota considered the possibility of such a high demand in the budgeting process, the adjustments probably will be smoother and less costly than if Toyota is forced to "manage by crisis."

EXHIBIT 23-2

Benefits of Budgeting

1. Budgets compel managers to plan.

2. Budgets promote coordination and communication.

3. Budgets aid performance evaluation by providing a benchmark for performance.

4. Budgets motivate employees to help achieve the company's goals.

Budgeting promotes coordination and communication The master budget coordinates the activities of the organization. It forces managers to consider relationships among operations across the entire value chain. Consider Magna International, a manufacturer of parts for the automotive industry. Sales managers at Magna, who are evaluated on the basis of sales volume, prefer to accept all special orders for unique parts. But some special orders cost the company more than the customer is willing to pay. The budget promotes coordination by encouraging sales managers to accept orders only for parts that Magna can design, manufacture, and deliver at a profit.

Coordination requires effective communication. Budgets are effective tools to communicate a consistent set of plans throughout the company. Suppose Toyota's engineers plan to redesign the Camry's brake system. By participating in the budgeting process alongside engineers, the manufacturing vice-president can see how to change the production process. He or she communicates the plan to plant managers and production supervisors to enable them to make changes in an orderly way.

Budgets provide a benchmark that helps managers evaluate performance A department or activity can be evaluated by managers who compare its actual results with either its budget or its past performance. In general, the budget is a better benchmark. One problem with comparisons with past results is that changes may have taken place in the company's operations or its markets. Comparing this year's results with last year's may be like comparing apples with oranges. In contrast, the budget considers all changes from past conditions.

Suppose that RE/MAX's real estate agents sell 10 percent more houses in the third quarter of 2003 than in the third quarter of 2002. Is this good performance? Not necessarily. If nationwide sales are up 20 percent for the quarter, RE/MAX's results may be disappointing. If the overall market has declined, the 10 percent increase may be excellent.

Another problem with past results is that they may represent inefficient performance. Suppose that difficulties obtaining donations of material or land drove Habitat For Humanity's cost per house in Mexico to $3,500. An average cost of $3,200 the following year is better, but may still fall short of expectations if the budgeted cost is $3,000 per house.

A budget motivates employees Budgets affect behaviour. The budgeting process prompts managers to look into the future. Doing so helps them foresee and avoid problems. Budgets also motivate employees to achieve the business's goals. Motivation is especially strong when employees accept budget goals as fair. For this reason, companies often ask employees to participate in preparing budgets that will be used to judge their performance.

Unrealistic budgets can hurt employee morale. Suppose RE/MAX's management imposed a budgeted increase of 15 percent in house sales for each territory. That budget may be acceptable to agents in areas with strong economies. They may work hard to achieve the increase. Agents in depressed areas may consider it impossible to meet the budget. They may become resentful and not attempt to meet the budget. Management should allow agents in each territory a voice in the budget so budgets will be tailored to local conditions.

Magna International Inc.
www.magnaint.com

RE/MAX
www.remax.ca

The Performance Report

We have seen how budgets can help managers plan. However, budgets are just as useful for controlling. To control operations, managers prepare performance reports that compare actual results to the budget. These reports help managers

- Evaluate operations
- Decide how to fix problems
- Prepare next period's budget

Suppose that a division of Magna International has the performance report in Exhibit 23-3.

Actual sales in Exhibit 23-3 are $550,000, which is $50,000 less than budgeted sales. The actual net income is half the budgeted amount. The vice-president of sales will have to explain why sales revenue was so far below the budgeted amount. The vice-president, in turn, will meet with the sales staff to learn why they failed to meet the budget. Three possible explanations exist in this example: (1) The budget was unrealistic; (2) the division did a poor job of selling during the period; or (3) uncontrollable factors (such as a sluggish economy) reduced sales. Of course, all of these factors may have contributed to the poor results.

Managers use performance reports like the one in Exhibit 23-3 to decide how to fix problems. If the sales department did not perform well, perhaps sales staff compensation should be tied more closely to sales revenue in order to increase the incentive to sell. Or a new advertising campaign may be needed. Managers must decide whether to reduce budgeted sales for the next period—a decision that directly affects next period's budgeted net income.

STOP & THINK

The performance report of Exhibit 23-3, shows that actual sales revenue is 8.33 percent less than budgeted sales revenue ($50,000/$600,000). However, actual expenses are only 1.9 percent less than budgeted expenses ($10,000/$520,000). Why is the percentage shortfall in expenses so much lower than the percentage shortfall in revenue?

Answer: One reason why expenses did not fall as far short of the budget is that some expenses do not increase or decrease with revenue (sales volume). For example, the vice-president of sales may be paid a salary of $100,000 regardless of the revenue generated by the company. Expenses such as amortization, rent, property taxes, and insurance are *fixed*. When revenue and variable expenses decrease, fixed expenses remain the same. Thus total expense does not decrease as rapidly as revenue.

Preparing the Master Budget

The **master budget** is the set of budgeted financial statements and supporting schedules for the entire organization. This comprehensive budget includes (1) the operating budget, (2) the capital expenditures budget, and (3) the financial budget. The **operating budget** sets the expected revenues and expenses—and thus operating income—for the period. The **capital expenditures budget** presents the company's plan for purchases of capital assets and other long-term assets. The **financial budget** projects cash inflows and outflows and the period-ending balance sheet. This chapter discusses components of the operating budget and the financial budget. Chapter 26 covers budgeting for capital expenditures.

The components of the master budget are summarized as follows:

1. Operating budget
   a. Sales or revenue budget
   b. Inventory budget, and purchases and cost of goods sold budget

EXHIBIT 23-3

Summary Income Statement Performance Report

	Actual	Budget	Variance (Actual − Budget)
Sales revenue..........................	$550,000	$600,000	$(50,000)
Total expenses	510,000	520,000	10,000
Net income	$ 40,000	$ 80,000	$(40,000)

   c. Operating expenses budget
   d. Budgeted income statement
2. Capital expenditures budget
3. Financial budget
   a. Cash budget: statement of budgeted cash receipts and payments
   b. Budgeted balance sheet
   c. Budgeted cash flow statement

The end result of the *operating* budget is the budgeted income statement, which shows expected revenues, expenses, and operating income for the period. The *financial* budget results in the budgeted cash flow statement, which shows budgeted cash flows for operating, investing, and financing activities. The budgeted financial statements look exactly like ordinary statements. The only difference is that they list budgeted rather than actual figures. Exhibit 23-4 diagrams the various sections of the master budget for a merchandising company such as Sobeys or Zellers.

The sales budget is the cornerstone of the master budget. Every element on the budgeted income statement depends on sales activity. After projecting sales and expenses, management can prepare the budgeted income statement. The income statement, the capital expenditures budget, and plans for raising cash and paying debts provide information for the cash budget, which feeds into the budgeted balance sheet. The budgeted cash flow statement usually is the last step in the process. The best way to learn about budgeting is to prepare a master budget.

···········
····· (**THINKING IT OVER**)

(1) Which budget is prepared first, and why? (2) What factors influence the estimated sales volume?

A: (1) The sales budget, because sales determines the purchases budget, the cost of goods sold budget, and so on. (2) Prior years' sales, general economic conditions, the trend of sales in that particular industry, competition, and the business' expected place in the market should be considered.

Sobeys Inc.
www.sobeys.ca

Zellers
www.hbc.com/zellers

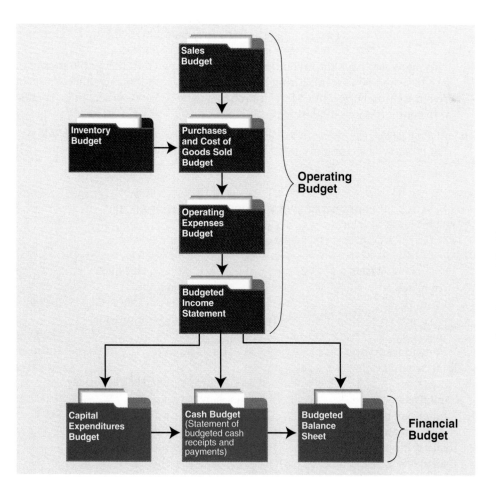

EXHIBIT 23-4

Master Budget for a Merchandising Company

LEARNING TIP

After the sales budget is prepared, the cost of goods sold, purchases, and inventory budget can be prepared. The cost of goods sold will be a part of the budgeted income statement, and inventory will appear on the budgeted balance sheet.

Data for Example

1. *You manage Whitewater Sporting Goods Ltd. Store No. 18, which carries a complete line of outdoor recreation equipment.* You are to prepare the master budget for your store for April, May, June, and July, the main selling season. The division manager and the assistant controller (head of the Accounting Department) of the company will arrive from headquarters next week to review the budget with you.

2. *Cash collections follow sales because the company sells on account.* When extra cash is needed, the company borrows on six-month installment notes payable.

3. *The balance sheet of your store at March 31, 2003, is shown in Exhibit 23-5.*

4. *Sales in March were $40,000.* Monthly sales are projected by sales personnel:

April	$50,000
May	80,000
June	60,000
July	50,000

Sales are 60 percent cash and 40 percent on credit. Whitewater collects all credit sales in the month following the sale. The $16,000 of accounts receivable at March 31 arose from credit sales made in March (40 percent of $40,000). Uncollectible accounts are insignificant.

5. *Whitewater maintains inventory equal to $20,000 plus 80 percent of the budgeted cost of goods sold for the following month.* Target ending inventory on July 31 is $42,400. Cost of goods sold averages 70 percent of sales. These percentages are drawn from the business's past experience. Inventory on March 31 is $48,000:

$$\text{March 31 inventory} = \$20,000 + 0.80 \times (0.70 \times \text{April sales of } \$50,000)$$
$$= \$20,000 + (0.80 \times \$35,000)$$
$$= \$20,000 + \$28,000 = \$48,000$$

Whitewater pays for inventory as follows: 50 percent during the month of purchase and 50 percent during the next month. Accounts payable consists of inventory purchases only. March purchases were $33,600, so accounts payable at the end of March total $16,800 ($33,600 X 0.50).

6. *Monthly payroll has two parts: a salary of $2,500 plus sales commissions equal to 15 percent of sales.* The company pays half this amount during the month and half

---

EXHIBIT 23-5

Balance Sheet

WHITEWATER SPORTING GOODS LTD. STORE NO. 18
Balance Sheet
March 31, 2003

Assets		Liabilities	
Current assets:		Current liabilities:	
Cash	$ 15,000	Accounts payable	$ 16,800
Accounts receivable	16,000	Salary and commissions	
Inventory	48,000	payable	4,250
Prepaid insurance	1,800	Total liabilities	21,050
Total current assets	80,800		
		Shareholders' Equity	
Capital assets:		Share capital	40,000
Equipment and fixtures	32,000	Retained earnings	38,950
Accumulated amortization	(12,800)		78,950
Total capital assets	19,200	Total liabilities	
Total assets	$100,000	and shareholders' equity	$100,000

early in the following month. Therefore, at the end of each month Whitewater reports salary and commissions payable equal to half the month's payroll. The $4,250 liability on the March 31 balance sheet is half the March payroll of $8,500:

March payroll = Salary of $2,500 + Sales commissions of $6,000 (0.15 × $40,000)
 = $8,500
March 31 salary and commissions payable = 0.50 × $8,500 = $4,250

7. *Other monthly expenses are as follows:*

Rent expense	$2,000, paid as incurred
Amortization expense, including truck	500
Insurance expense	200 expiration of prepaid amount
Miscellaneous expenses	5% of sales, paid as incurred

8. *A used delivery truck will be purchased in April for $3,000 cash.*

9. *Whitewater requires each store to maintain a minimum cash balance of $10,000 at the end of each month.* The store can borrow money on 6–month notes payable of $1,000 each at an annual interest rate of 12 percent. Management borrows no more than the amount needed to maintain the $10,000 minimum. Notes payable require six equal monthly payments consisting of principal plus monthly interest on the entire unpaid principal. Borrowing, and all principal and interest payments occur at the end of the month.

10. *Income taxes are the responsibility of corporate headquarters, so you can ignore tax for budgeting purposes.*

You have studied the company guidelines on how to prepare a budget. The directions instruct you to prepare the following:

Title

Sales budget (Exhibit 23–7)
Inventory, purchases, and cost of goods sold budget (Exhibit 23–8)
Operating expenses budget (Exhibit 23–9)
Budgeted income statement for the four months ending July 31, 2003
    (see Exhibit 23-6)
Budgeted cash collections from customers (Exhibit 23–10)
Budgeted cash payments for purchases (Exhibit 23–11)
Budgeted cash payments for operating expenses (Exhibit 23–12)
Cash budget for the four months ending July 31, 2003 (see Exhibit 23-13)
Budgeted cash flow statement for the four months ending July 31, 2003 (see
    Exhibit 23-15)
Budgeted balance sheet at July 31, 2003 (see Exhibit 23-14)

Preparing the Operating Budget

OBJECTIVE 2
Prepare an operating budget for a company

As you prepare the master budget, remember that you are developing the company's operating and financial plan for the next four months. The steps in this process may seem mechanical, but remember that budgeting stimulates thoughts about pricing, product lines, job assignments, needs for additional equipment, and negotiations with banks. Successful managers use this opportunity to make decisions that affect the future course of business. The operating budget—consisting of the sales budget; the inventory purchases and cost of goods sold budgets; and the operating expenses budget—results in the budgeted income statement.

Preparing the Budgeted Income Statement   There are four steps to preparing the budgeted income statement shown in Exhibit 23–6.

Step 1. **The sales budget**. Sales is the key business activity. Budgeted total sales for each product is the sale price multiplied by the predicted unit sales. The overall sales

EXHIBIT 23-6

Budgeted Income Statement

·········· **THINKING IT OVER**

Look at Exhibit 23-6. Assume that the budgeted income statement projects a net loss instead of net income. What can be done?

A: Since the sales budget is the starting point, we must first evaluate sales. Can the sale price be raised? Can we begin an advertising campaign to boost sales?

Next we evaluate cost of goods sold. Can we buy the units at a lower price from another supplier or save by buying in larger quantities?

Finally we analyze each of the operating expenses. Where can costs be cut?

The budgeted income statement often is revised and reworked until net income is an acceptable amount.

WORKING IT OUT

In a series of Working It Out exercises, we are going to prepare parts of a budget for Coleman Corporation for January and February. Unit sales for January are expected to be 3,000 at $13.50 each, and for February, 4,500 at $13.75 each. Prepare the sales budget for Jan. and Feb.

A:

Budgeted Sales

Jan.	Feb.
3,000	4,500
× $13.50	× $13.75
$40,500	$61,875

WHITEWATER SPORTING GOODS LTD. STORE NO. 18
Budgeted Income Statement
For the Four Months Ending July 31, 2003

	Amount		Source
Sales		$240,000	Sales Budget (Exhibit 23-7)
Cost of goods sold		168,000	Inv., Pur., and COGS Budget
Gross margin		72,000	(Exhibit 23-8)
Operating expenses:			
Salary and commissions ...	$46,000		Op. Exp. Budget (Ex. 23-9)
Rent......................................	8,000		Op. Exp. Budget (Ex. 23-9)
Amortization	2,000		Op. Exp. Budget (Ex. 23-9)
Insurance............................	800		Op. Exp. Budget (Ex. 23-9)
Miscellaneous	12,000	68,800	Op. Exp. Budget (Ex. 23-9)
Operating income		3,200	
Interest expense......................		225*	Cash Budget (Ex. 23- 13)
Net income............................		$ 2,975	

* $90 + $75 + $60

---

budget is the sum of the budgets for individual products. Trace the April through July total sales ($240,000) to the budgeted income statement in Exhibit 23-6.

Step 2. **Inventory, purchases, and cost of goods sold budget.** This schedule determines cost of goods sold for the budgeted income statement, ending inventory for the budgeted balance sheet, and purchases for the cash budget. The familiar cost-of-goods-sold computation specifies the relation among these items:

Beginning inventory + Purchases – Ending inventory = Cost of goods sold

Beginning inventory is known from last month's balance sheet, budgeted cost of goods sold is a fixed percentage of sales, and budgeted ending inventory is a computed amount. You must solve for the budgeted purchases figure. To do this, take the cost-of-goods-sold computation and then move beginning inventory and ending inventory to the right side of the equation, isolating purchases on the left side:

Beginning inventory + Purchases – Ending inventory = Cost of goods sold
Purchases = Cost of goods sold + Ending inventory – Beginning inventory

This second equation also makes sense. How much does Whitewater have to purchase? Enough to cover sales and desired ending inventory, less the amount of beginning inventory already on hand at the start of the period. Exhibit 23-8 shows Whitewater's inventory, purchases, and cost of goods sold budget.

EXHIBIT 23-7

Sales Budget

WHITEWATER SPORTING GOODS LTD. STORE NO. 18
Sales Budget (item 4)

	April	May	June	July	April–July Total
Cash sales, 60%	$30,000	$48,000	$36,000	$30,000	
Credit sales, 40%..........	20,000	32,000	24,000	20,000	
Total sales, 100%	$50,000	$80,000	$60,000	$50,000	$240,000

WHITEWATER SPORTING GOODS LTD. STORE NO. 18
Inventory, Purchases, and Cost of Goods Sold Budget (item 5)

	April	May	June	July	April–July Total
Cost of goods sold (0.70 × sales, from Sales budget in Exhibit 23–7)	$35,000	$56,000	$42,000	$35,000	$168,000
+ Desired ending inventory ($20,000 + 0.80 × Cost of goods sold for the next month)	64,800*	53,600	48,000	42,400‡	
= Total inventory required	99,800	109,600	90,000	77,400	
– Beginning inventory	(48,000)†	(64,800)	(53,600)	(48,000)	
= Purchases	$51,800	$44,800	$36,400	$29,400	

*$20,000 + (0.80 × $56,000) = $64,800   ‡Given in item 5 on page 1276
†Balance at March 31 (Exhibit 23-5)

EXHIBIT 23-8

Inventory, Purchases, and
Cost of Goods Sold Budget

WORKING IT OUT

Now we can prepare Coleman's Inventory, Purchases, and Cost of Goods Sold Budget. Refer to the Sales Budget that we prepared in the previous Working It Out exercise. Assume that Coleman's cost of goods sold percentage is 65% of sales, and sales for March are predicted to be 4,300 units at $13.75, or $59,125. Coleman desires each month's ending inventory to be $10,000 plus 50% of the next month's cost of goods sold.

A:
COGS (65% × ea. month's sales):
Jan. $26,325*   Feb. $40,219†
+ Desired End. Inv. ($10,000 + 50% of next month's COGS):
Jan. +30,110**   Feb. +29,216††
– Beg. Inv.:
Jan. –23,163***   Feb. –30,110
= Purchases:
Jan. $33,272   Feb. $39,325

*$40,500 × 65% = $26,325
†$61,875 × 65% = $40,219
**$40,219 × 50% + $10,000
  = $30,110
††($59,125 × 65% × 50%)
  + $10,000 = $29,216
***$26,325 × 50% + $10,000
  = $23,163

To see how this information fits into the operating budget, trace the total budgeted cost of goods sold from Exhibit 23–8 ($168,000) to the budgeted income statement in Exhibit 23-6. We will use the budgeted inventory and purchases amounts later.

Step 3. **Operating expenses budget** Budgeted operating expenses such as sales commissions fluctuate with sales (variable). Other expenses, such as rent and insurance, are the same each month (fixed).

Trace the April through July totals from the operating expenses budget in Exhibit 23–9 (salary and commissions of $46,000, rent of $8,000, and so on) to the budgeted income statement in Exhibit 23-6.

Step 4. **Budgeted income statement.** Use steps 1 through 3 to prepare the budgeted income statement in Exhibit 23-6. We explain the computation of interest expense as part of the cash budget in the next section.

EXHIBIT 23-9

Operating Expense Budget

WHITEWATER SPORTING GOODS LTD. STORE NO. 18
Operating Expenses Budget (items 6 and 7)

	April	May	June	July	April–July Total
Salary, fixed amount (item 6, page 1276)	$ 2,500	$ 2,500	$ 2,500	$ 2,500	
Commission, 15% of sales from Sales Budget (Item 6, page 1276 and Exhibit 23-7)	7,500	12,000	9,000	7,500	
Total salary and commissions	10,000	14,500	11,500	10,000	$46,000
Rent expense, fixed amount (item 7, page 1277	2,000	2,000	2,000	2,000	8,000
Amortization expense, fixed amount (item 7, page 1277)	500	500	500	500	2,000
Insurance expense, fixed amount (item 7, page 1277)	200	200	200	200	800
Miscellaneous expenses, 5% of sales from Sales Budget (item 7, page 1277 and Exhibit 23-7)	2,500	4,000	3,000	2,500	12,000
Total operating expenses	$15,200	$21,200	$17,200	$15,200	$68,800

EXHIBIT 23-10

Budgeted Cash Collections

Preparing the Financial Budget

The second major section of the master budget that we will discuss is the financial budget. This includes the cash budget, the budgeted balance sheet, and the budgeted cash flow statement. The **cash budget,** or **statement of budgeted cash receipts and payments,** details how the business expects to go from the beginning cash balance to the desired ending balance. Cash receipts and payments depend on revenues and expenses, which appear in the budgeted income statement. This is why the cash budget is not prepared until after the budgeted income statement.

Preparing the Cash Budget   The cash budget has four major parts:

- Cash collections from customers (Exhibit 23-10)
- Cash payments for purchases (Exhibit 23-11)
- Cash payments for operating expenses (Exhibit 23-12)
- Capital expenditures (for example, the $3,000 capital expenditure to acquire the delivery truck)

Exhibit 23-10 shows how to compute budgeted cash collections. April's cash collections consist of two parts: (1) April's cash sales from the sales budget in Exhibit 23-7 ($30,000), plus (2) March's credit sales ($16,000 from the March 31 balance sheet, Exhibit 23-5). Trace April's $46,000 ($30,000 + $16,000) total cash collections to the cash budget in Exhibit 23-13 on page 1282.

Exhibit 23-11 uses the inventory, purchases, and cost of goods sold budget from Exhibit 23-8 and payment information from item 5 to compute budgeted cash payments for purchases of inventory. April's cash payments for purchases consists of two parts: (1) payment of 50% of March's purchases ($16,800 accounts payable balance from the March 31 balance sheet, Exhibit 23-5), plus (2) payment for 50% of April's pruchases ($25,900 = 50% x $51,800 from Exhibit 23-8). Trace April's $42,700 ($16,800 + $25,900) cash outlay for purchases to the cash budget in Exhibit 23-13 on page 1282.

Exhibit 23-12 uses items 6 and 7 and the operating expenses budget (Exhibit 23-9) to compute cash payments for operating expenses. April's cash payments for operating expenses consists of four items:

Payment of 50% of March's salary and commissions (from March 31 balance sheet, Exhibit 23-5)	$ 4,250
Payment of 50% of April's salary and commissions (50% × $10,000, Exhibit 23-9)	5,000
Payment of rent expense (Exhibit 23-9)	2,000
Payment of miscellaneous expenses (Exhibit 23-9)	2,500
Total April cash payments for operating expenses	$13,750

Follow April's $13,750 cash payments for operating expenses from Exhibit 23-12 to the cash budget in Exhibit 23-13 on page 1282.

WHITEWATER SPORTING GOODS LTD. STORE NO. 18
Budgeted Cash Collections from Customers

	April	May	June	July	April–July Total
Cash sales from Sales Budget (Exhibit 23-7)	$30,000	$48,000	$36,000	$30,000	
Collections of last month's credit sales, from Sales Budget (Exhibit 23-7)	16,000*	20,000	32,000	24,000	
Total collections	$46,000	$68,000	$68,000	$54,000	$236,000

*March 31 accounts receivable, Exhibit 23-5.

WHITEWATER SPORTING GOODS LTD. STORE NO. 18
Budgeted Cash Payments for Purchases

	April	May	June	July	April–July Total
50% of last month's purchases from Inventory, Purchases, and Cost of Goods Sold Budget (Exhibit 23-8)	$16,800*	$25,900	$22,400	$18,200	
50% of this month's purchases from Inventory, Purchases, and Cost of Goods Sold Budget (Exhibit 23-8)	25,900	22,400	18,200	14,700	
Total payments for purchases	$42,700	$48,300	$40,600	$32,900	$164,500

*March 31 accounts receivable, Exhibit 23-5.

EXHIBIT 23-11

Budgeted Cash Payments for Purchases

STOP & THINK

Why are amortization expense and insurance expense from the operating expense budget (Exhibit 23-9) *excluded* from the budgeted cash payments for operating expenses in Exhibit 23-12?

Answer: These expenses do not require cash outlays in the current period. Amortization is the periodic write-off of the cost of the equipment and fixtures that Whitewater acquired previously. Insurance expense is the expiration of prepaid insurance.

EXHIBIT 23-12

Budgeted Cash Payments for Operating Expenses

WHITEWATER SPORTING GOODS LTD. STORE NO. 18
Budgeted Cash Payments for Operating Expenses

	April	May	June	July	April–July Total
Expense amounts, from Operating Expenses Budget (Exhibit 23-9)					
Salary and commissions:					
50% of last month's expenses, from Operating Expenses Budget (Exhibit 23-9)	$ 4,250*	$ 5,000	$ 7,250	$ 5,750	
50% of this month's expenses, from Operating Expenses Budget (Exhibit 23-9)	$ 5,000	7,250	5,750	5,000	
Total salary and commissions	9,250	12,250	13,000	10,750	
Rent expense, from Operating Expenses Budget (Exhibit 23-9)	2,000	2,000	2,000	2,000	
Miscellaneous expenses, from Operating Expenses Budget (Exhibit 23-9)	2,500	4,000	3,000	2,500	
Total payments for operating expenses	$13,750	$18,250	$18,000	$15,250	$65,250

*March 31 salary and commissions payable, Exhibit 23-5.

To prepare the cash budget in Exhibit 23-13, start with the beginning cash balance and add the budgeted cash collections from Exhibit 23-10 to determine the cash available. Then subtract cash payments for purchases (Exhibit 23-11), operating expenses (Exhibit 23-12), and any capital expenditures. This yields the ending cash balance before financing. For April, we have:

Beginning cash balance (March 31 balance sheet, Exhibit 23-5)		$15,000
Plus April cash collections (Exhibit 23-10)		46,000
Cash available in April		61,000
Deduct April cash payments:		
April cash payments for purchases (Exhibit 23-11)....	$42,700	
April cash payments for operating expenses (Exhibit 23-12)	13,750	
April cash payment to purchase delivery truck (item 8)	3,000	
Total April cash payments		59,450
Ending cash balance before financing		$ 1,550

EXHIBIT 23-13

Cash Budget

WHITEWATER SPORTING GOODS LTD. STORE NO. 18
Cash Budget
For the Four Months Ending July 31, 2003

	April	May	June	July
Beginning cash balance	$15,000*	$10,550	$10,410	$18,235
Cash collections from customers (Exhibit 23–10)	46,000	68,000	68,000	54,000
Cash available before financing	$61,000	$78,550	$78,410	$72,235
Cash payments:				
Purchases of inventory (Exhibit 23–11)	$42,700	$48,300	$40,600	$32,900
Operating expenses (Exhibit 23–12)	13,750	18,250	18,000	15,250
Purchase of delivery truck (Item 8, page 1277)	3,000	—	—	—
Total cash payments	59,450	66,550	58,600	48,150
(1) Ending cash balance before financing	1,550	12,000	19,810	24,085
Minimum cash balance desired	10,000	10,000	10,000	10,000
Cash excess (deficiency)	$(8,450)	$ 2,000	$ 9,810	$14,085
Financing of cash deficiency (see notes a–c):				
Borrowing (at end of month)	$ 9,000			
Principal payments (at end of month)		$ (1,500)	$ (1,500)	$ (1,500)
Interest expense (at 12% annually)		(90)	(75)	(60)
(2) Total effects of financing	9,000	(1,590)	(1,575)	(1,560)
Ending cash balance (1) + (2)	$10,550	$10,410	$18,235	$22,525

*March 31 cash balance, Exhibit 23-5

Notes:

a. Borrowing occurs in multiples of $1,000 and only for the amount needed to maintain a minimum cash balance of $10,000.

b. Monthly principal payments: $9,000/6 = $1,500

c. Interest expense:
  May: $9,000 \times (0.12 \times 1/12) = $90
  June: ($9,000 - $1,500) $\times (0.12 \times 1/12) = $75
  July: ($9,000 - $1,500 - $1,500) $\times (0.12 \times 1/12) = $60
  Total: $90 + $75 + $60 = $225

Item 9 states that Whitewater requires a minimum cash balance of $10,000. The $1,550 budgeted cash balance before financing falls $8,450 short of the minimum required ($10,000–$1,550). Because Whitewater borrows in $1,000 notes, the company will have to borrow $9,000 to cover April's expected shortfall. The budgeted ending cash balance equals the "ending cash balance before financing," adjusted for the total effects of the financing (a $9,000 inflow in April). Exhibit 23-13 shows that Whitewater expects to end April with $10,550 of cash ($1,550 + $9,000). The exhibit also shows the cash balance at the end of May, June, and July.

Item 9 states that Whitewater must repay the notes in six equal installments. Thus May through July show principal repayments of $1,500 ($9,000 ÷ 6) per month. Whitewater also pays interest expense on the outstanding notes payable, at 12% per year. The June interest expense is $75 [($9,000 principal–$1,500 repayment at the end of May) × 12% × 1/12]. Interest expense for the four months totals $225 ($90 + $75 + $60). This interest expense appears on the budgeted income statement in Exhibit 23-6.

Notice that the cash balance at the end of July is $22,525. This becomes the cash balance in the July 31 budgeted balance sheet in Exhibit 23-14 on page 1284.

Preparing the Budgeted Balance Sheet   The next step in preparing the master budget is to complete the balance sheet. Project each asset, liability, and shareholders' equity account based on the plans outlined in the previous exhibits. Exhibit 23-14 presents the budgeted balance sheet. Study Exhibit 23-14 carefully to make certain you understand the computation of each figure. For example, on the budgeted balance sheet as of July 31, 2003, budgeted cash equals the ending cash balance from the cash budget in Exhibit 23-13 ($22,525). Accounts receivable as of July 31 equal July's credit sales of $20,000, shown in the sales budget (Exhibit 23-7). July 31 inventory of $42,400 is taken from July's desired ending inventory in the inventory, puchases, and cost of goods sold budget displayed in Exhibit 23-8. Detailed computations for each of the other accounts appear in Exhibit 23-14.

Preparing the Budgeted Cash Flow Statement   The final step in preparing the master budget is completing the budgeted cash flow statement. Use the information from the schedules of cash collections and payments, the cash budget, and the beginning balance of cash to project cash flows from operating, investing, and financing activities. Take time to study Exhibit 23-15, and make sure you understand the origin of each figure.

Now the *master budget* is complete. It consists of the budgeted financial statements and all supporting schedules.

STOP & THINK

Many companies allow the manager of each department to participate in setting the budget for his or her own department. Such participation can help employees accept the budget and motivate them to achieve the budget. What is the *disadvantage* of allowing managers to set budgets for their own departments? (*Hint*: Superiors often use the budget as a benchmark against which to compare actual performance.)

Answer: Managers who are evaluated by comparing their department's actual results to the budget have incentives to build *slack* into their budgets. For example, the manager might budget sales to be less than she really expects, and budget purchases costs higher than she expects. This increases the chance that her department's actual performance will be better than the budget, and that she will receive a favourable evaluation. Consequently, higher-level managers usually negotiate with lower-level managers to remove at least part of the slack lower-level managers might add to the budget.

EXHIBIT 23-14

Budgeted Balance Sheet

WHITEWATER SPORTING GOODS LTD. STORE NO. 18
Budgeted Balance Sheet
July 31, 2003

Assets

Current assets:

Cash (Exhibit 23-13)..	$22,525	
Accounts receivable (Sales Budget, Exhibit 23-7)	20,000	
Inventory (Inventory, Purchases, and Cost of Goods Sold Budget, Exhibit 23-8)	42,400	
Prepaid insurance (beginning balance of $1,800 – $800 for four months' expiration; Operating Expenses Budget, Exhibit 23-9)	1,000	
Total current assets		$ 85,925

Capital assets:

Equipment and fixtures (beginning balance of $32,000 + $3,000 truck acquisition; Item 8, page 1277)	$35,000	
Accumulated amortization (beginning balance of $12,800 + $500 amortization for each of four months; Operating Expenses Budget, Exhibit 23-9)..........................	(14,800)	
Total capital assets		20,200
Total assets		$106,125

Liabilities

Current liabilities:

Accounts payable (0.50 × July purchases of $29,400)	$14,700	
Short-term note payable ($9,000 – $4,500 paid back; Exhibit 23-13)...	4,500	
Salary and commissions payable (0.50 × July expenses of $10,000; Operating Expenses Budget, Exhibit 23-9)...........	5,000	
Total liabilities		$ 24,200

Shareholders' Equity

Share capital	$40,000	
Retained earnings (beginning balance of $38,950 + $2,975 net income; Exhibit 23-6)	41,925	
Total shareholders' equity		81,925
Total liabilities and shareholders' equity		$106,125

WORKING IT OUT

Assume that Coleman has $8,300 cash on hand on January 1 and requires a minimum cash balance of $7,500. January cash collections are $39,508. Total cash payments for January are $48,320. What is the cash excess or the cash deficiency at the end of January?

A:

Beginning cash	$ 8,300
+ Cash collections	39,508
= Cash available	47,808
– Cash payments	48,320
= Ending balance before financing	(512)
– Minimum cash bal. required	7,500
= Cash deficiency ($7,500 + $512)	$ 8,012

Coleman must borrow $8,012 to bring ending cash for January up to the required $7,500.

EXHIBIT 23-15

Budgeted Cash Flow
Statement

WHITEWATER SPORTING GOODS LTD. STORE NO. 18
Budgeted Cash Flow Statement
For the Four Months Ending July 31, 2003

Cash flows from operating activities:
  Receipts:
    Collections from customers (Exhibit 23–10) .... $ 236,000
    Total cash receipts $236,000
  Payments:
    Purchases of inventory (Exhibit 23–11) .... $(164,500)
    Operating expenses, excluding interest expense
      (Exhibit 23–12) .... (65,250)
    Payment of interest expense
      (Exhibits 23-13 and 23-6) .... (225)
    Total cash payments..................................... (229,975)
    Net cash inflow from operating activities 6,025

Cash flows from investing activities:
  Acquisition of delivery truck
    (Item 8, page 1277) .... $ (3,000)
  Net cash outflow from investing activities............. (3,000)

Cash flows from financing activities:
  Proceeds from issuance of notes payable
    (Exhibit 23-13) .... $ 9,000
  Payment of notes payable (Exhibit 23-13) .... (4,500)
  Net cash inflow from financing activities............... 4,500
Net increase in cash.. $ 7,525
Cash balance, April 1, 2003 (Exhibit 23-5)................. 15,000
Cash balance, July 31, 2003 (Exhibit 23-13 and 23-14) $ 22,525

Budgeting, Sensitivity Analysis, and Information Technology

The master budget models the organization's *planned* activities. The most important budget documents are the budgeted income statement (Exhibit 23-6), the cash budget (Exhibit 23-13), and the budgeted balance sheet (Exhibit 23-14). Top management analyzes these statements to ensure that all the budgeted figures are consistent with the company's goals or strategies.

Sensitivity Analysis

Actual results often differ from plans, however, so managers conduct *sensitivity analyses* to plan for various possibilities. Recall that Chapter 22 defined **sensitivity analysis** as a *what-if* technique that asks *what* a result will be *if* a predicted amount is not achieved or *if* an underlying assumption changes. *What if* the stock market crashes? How will this affect contributions to Habitat for Humanity? Will it have to postpone the planned expansion in Eastern Europe? *What* will be Whitewater Store No. 18's cash balance on July 31 *if* the period's sales are 45% cash, not 60% cash? Will Whitewater have to borrow more cash?

Many companies use computer spreadsheet programs to prepare master budget schedules and statements. In fact, one of the earliest spreadsheet programs was developed by graduate business students specifically to perform master budget sensitivity analyses. The students realized that computers could take the drudgery out of hand-computed master budget sensitivity analyses. Managers and accountants could answer what-if questions simply by changing a number. At the press of a key, the spreadsheet prepares a revised budget that includes all the effects of the change. The nearly instant display of changes makes sensitivity analysis a powerful planning tool.

Budget Management Software

Suppose the manager of Whitewater Store No. 18 uses a spreadsheet to develop the store's master budget. Then Whitewater's headquarters must somehow "roll up" the budget data from Store No. 18, along with budgets for each of the other individual stores, to prepare the company-wide master budget. This roll-up can be difficult for companies with far-flung operations, whose units may use different types of spreadsheets. Companies like Sunoco are beginning to use budget management software. Often designed to work with the company's Web-based Intranet and enterprise resource planning (ERP) databases, this software provides a company-wide system that helps managers develop and analyze budgets. Across the globe, managers can sit at their desks, log into the company's budget system, and enter their numbers. The software allows them to conduct sensitivity analyses on their own unit's data—for example, how a change in oil prices would affect the unit's budget. When the unit manager is satisfied with her budget, she can enter it in the company-wide budget with the click of a mouse, and her unit's budget automatically "rolls up" with budgets from all other units around the world. Whether at headquarters or on the road, top executives can log into the budget system and conduct their own sensitivity analyses on individual units' budgets or on the company-wide budget. The new technology allows managers to spend less time compiling and summarizing data, and more time analyzing it to ensure that the budget leads the company toward achieving the strategic goals identified at the beginning of the budget process.

STOP & THINK

Consider two budget situations: (1) Whitewater Sporting Goods' marketing analysts produce a near-certain forecast for four-month sales of $4,500,000 for the company's 20 stores. (2) Much uncertainty exists about the period's sales. The most likely amount is $4,500,000, but the analysts consider any amount between $3,900,000 and $5,100,000 to be possible. How will the budgeting process differ in these two circumstances?

Answer: Whitewater will prepare a master budget for the expected sales level of $4,500,000 in either case. Because of the uncertainty about sales in situation 2, the company's executives will want a set of budgets covering the entire range of volume rather than a single level. Whitewater's managers may use a spreadsheet program to prepare budgets based on sales of, say, $3,900,000, $4,200,000, $4,500,000, $4,800,000, and $5,100,000. These budgets help managers plan actions for sales levels throughout the forecasted range.

ERP: Enterprise Resource Planning or Enterprise Ruins Plans?

Most accountants know—though few will admit—that at least three-quarters of the best-laid budgets and corporate plans gather dust. Now some pioneering Fortune 1000 companies are reengineering their budgeting process to favour top-down strategic plans budgeted by department managers. To make it happen, they are replacing spreadsheet software with Enterprise Resource Planning (ERP) software.

ERP software links corporate data across the entire enterprise. At Fujitsu Computer Products of America, an Oracle ERP program tracks the entire supply chain, including data on shipments of materials and supplies, purchases, inventory, accounts receivable, and accounts payable. An enterprise application system (EAS) program links to the ERP to provide a planning database and an analytical tool. While the ERP system is the repository of information, the Hyperion Pillar EAS is the user-interface planning tool that allows managers to create what-if scenarios.

Reengineering the budget using ERP is not cheap. Fujitsu invested $40 million. Allstate Insurance invested $60 million. But, implemented correctly, the savings can be enormous. Allstate saved roughly $100 million in processing costs in just 18 months.

Yet well-publicized ERP fiascoes have kept many companies from taking this route. In 1999, Hershey Foods Corp. installed an ERP system, squeezing what was originally supposed to be a four-year project into just 30 months. Hershey began its new ERP system just when retailers began ordering large amounts of candy for back-to-school and Halloween; profits fell 19% due to disrupted delivery of its chocolate and candies, and Hershey is still trying to regain market share. Consultants caution that implementation alone takes at least one to two years. And the reengineering process must start well before the technology is in place, with clear business goals for the ERP system.

Based on: Russ Banham, "Better Budgets," *Journal of Accountancy,* February 2000, pp. 37-40. J. W. Dysart, "Planning for Real-Time Information," *Banking Strategies,* May/June 2000, pp. 6-10. Louisa Wah, "Give ERP a Chance," *Management Review,* March 2000, pp. 20-24. Craig Stedman, "Failed ERP Haunt's Hershey," *Computerworld*, November 1, 1999, pp. 1, 89.

Mid-Chapter Summary Problem
for Your Review

Review the Whitewater Sporting Goods Ltd. example in the chapter. You now think that July sales might be $40,000 instead of the projected $50,000 in Exhibit 23-7. You want to perform a sensitivity analysis to see how this change in sales affects the budget.

Required

1. Revise the sales budget (Exhibit 23-7), the inventory, purchases, and cost of goods sold budget (Exhibit 23-8), and the operating expenses budget (Exhibit 23-9). Prepare a revised budgeted income statement for the four months ended July 31, 2003.

2. Revise the schedule of budgeted cash collections (Exhibit 23-10), the schedule of budgeted cash payments for purchases (Exhibit 23-11), and the schedule of budgeted cash payments for operating expenses (Exhibit 23-12). Prepare a revised cash budget, a revised budgeted balance sheet at July 31, 2003, and a revised budgeted cash flow statement for the four months ended July 31, 2003. Note: You need not repeat the parts of the revised schedules that do not change.

Solution to Review Problem

Although not required, this solution repeats the budgeted amounts for April, May, and June. Revised figures appear in boldface type for emphasis.

Requirement 1

WHITEWATER SPORTING GOODS LTD. STORE NO. 18
REVISED Sales Budget

	April	May	June	July	Total
Cash sales, 60%.........................	$30,000	$48,000	$36,000	**$24,000**	
Credit sales, 40%......................	20,000	32,000	24,000	**16,000**	
Total sales, 100%......................	$50,000	$80,000	$60,000	**$40,000**	**$230,000**

WHITEWATER SPORTING GOODS LTD. STORE NO. 18
REVISED Inventory, Purchases, and Cost of Goods Sold Budget

	April	May	June	July	Total
Cost of goods sold (0.70 × sales, from Revised Sales Budget.............................	$35,000	$ 56,000	$42,000	**$28,000**	**$161,000**
+ Desired ending inventory ($20,000 + 0.80 × cost of goods sold for next month)..........	64,800	53,600	**42,400**	42,400†	
= Total inventory required	99,800	109,600	**84,400**	**70,400**	
− Beginning inventory	(48,000)*	(64,800)	**(53,600)**	**(42,400)**	
= Purchases..	$51,800	$ 44,800	**$30,800**	**$28,000**	

*Balance at March 31, Exhibit 23-5
†Given in item 5, page 1276

WHITEWATER SPORTING GOODS LTD. STORE NO. 18
REVISED Operating Expenses Budget

	April	May	June	July	Total
Salary, fixed amount	$ 2,500	$ 2,500	$ 2,500	$ 2,500	
Commission, 15% of sales from Revised Sales Budget	7,500	12,000	9,000	**6,000**	
Total salary and commissions	10,000	14,500	11,500	**8,500**	$44,500
Rent expense, fixed amount	2,000	2,000	2,000	2,000	8,000
Amortization expense, fixed amount......................	500	500	500	500	2,000
Insurance expense, fixed amount	200	200	200	200	800
Miscellaneous expense, 5% of sales from Revised Sales Budget..	2,500	4,000	3,000	**2,000**	**11,500**
Total operating expenses..	$15,200	$21,200	$17,200	**$13,200**	**$66,800**

WHITEWATER SPORTING GOODS LTD. STORE NO. 18
REVISED Budgeted Income Statement
For the Four Months Ending July 31, 2003

	Amount	Source
Sales	$230,000	Revised Sales Budget
Cost of goods sold	161,000	Revised Inv., Pur., and
Gross margin	69,000	COGS Budget
Operating expenses:		
Salary and commissions ...	$44,500	Revised Op. Exp. Budget
Rent......................................	8,000	Revised Op. Exp. Budget
Amortization	2,000	Revised Op. Exp. Budget
Insurance.............................	800	Revised Op. Exp. Budget
Miscellaneous.....................	11,500	66,800	Revised Op. Exp. Budget
Operating income		2,200	
Interest expense....................	225	Revised Cash Budget
Net income............................	$ 1,975	

Requirement 2

WHITEWATER SPORTING GOODS LTD. STORE NO. 18
REVISED Budgeted Cash Collections From Customers (2003)

	April	May	June	July	Total
Cash sales, from Revised Sales Budget..................	$30,000	$48,000	$36,000	$24,000	
Collections of last month's credit sales, from Revised Sales Budget	16,000*	20,000	32,000	24,000	
Total collections	$46,000	$68,000	$68,000	$48,000	$230,000

*March 31 accounts receivable, Exhibit 23–5

WHITEWATER SPORTING GOODS LTD. STORE NO. 18
REVISED Budgeted Cash Payments for Purchases (2003)

	April	May	June	July	Total
50% of last month's purchases, from Revised Inventory, Purchases, and Cost of Goods Sold Budget	$16,800*	$25,900	$22,400	$15,400	
50% of this month's purchases, from Revised Inventory, Purchases, and Cost of Goods Sold Budget	25,900	22,400	15,400	14,000	
Total payments for purchases	$42,700	$48,300	$37,800	$29,400	$158,200

*March 31, accounts payable, Exhibit 23–5.

WHITEWATER SPORTING GOODS LTD. STORE NO. 18
REVISED Budgeted Cash Payments for Operating Expenses (2003)

	April	May	June	July	Total
Expense amounts, from Revised Operating Expenses Budget					
Salary and commissions:					
50% of last month's expenses, from Revised Operating Expenses Budget	$ 4,250*	$ 5,000	$ 7,250	$ 5,750	
50% of this month's expenses, from Revised Operating Expenses Budget	5,000	7,250	5,750	4,250	
Total salary and commissions	9,250	12,250	13,000	10,000	
Rent expense, from Revised Operating Expenses Budget	2,000	2,000	2,000	2,000	
Miscellaneous expenses, from Revised Operating Expenses Budget)	2,500	4,000	3,000	2,000	
Total payments for operating expenses	$13,750	$18,250	$18,000	$14,000	$64,000

*March 31 salary and commissions payable, Exhibit 23–5.

WHITEWATER SPORTING GOODS LTD. STORE NO. 18
REVISED Cash Budget
For the Four Months Ending July 31, 2003

	April	May	June	July
Beginning cash balance	$15,000*	$10,550	$10,410	$21,035
Cash collections from customers (Revised Budgeted Cash Collections)	46,000	68,000	68,000	48,000
Cash available before financing	$61,000	$78,550	$78,410	$69,035
Cash payments:				
Purchases of inventory (Revised Budgeted Cash Payments for Purchases)	$42,700	$48,300	$37,800	$29,400
Operating expenses (Revised Budgeted Cash Payments for Operating Expenses)	13,750	18,250	18,000	14,000
Purchase of delivery truck (Item 8, page 1277)	3,000	—	—	—
Total cash payments	59,450	66,550	55,800	43,400
(1) Ending cash balance before financing	1,550	12,000	22,610	25,635
Minimum cash balance desired	10,000	10,000	10,000	10,000
Cash excess (deficiency)	$ (8,450)	$2,000	$12,610	$15,635
Financing of cash deficiency (see notes a–c):				
Borrowing (at end of month)	$ 9,000			
Principal payments (at end of month)		$ (1,500)	$ (1,500)	$ (1,500)
Interest expense (at 12% annually)		(90)	(75)	(60)
(2) Total effects of financing	9,000	(1,590)	(1,575)	(1,560)
Ending cash balance (1) + (2)	$10,550	$10,410	$21,035	$24,075

*March 31 cash balance, Exhibit 23–5

Notes
a. Borrowing occurs in multiples of $1,000 and only for the amount needed to maintain a minimum cash balance of $10,000.
b. Monthly principal payments: $9,000 ÷ 6 = $1,500
c. Interest expense:
   May: $9,000 × (0.12 × 1/12) = $90
   June: ($9,000 − $1,500) × (0.12 x 1/12) = $75
   July: ($9,000 − $1,500 − $1,500) × (0.12 × 1/12) = $60
   Total: $90 + $75 + $60 = $225

WHITEWATER SPORTING GOODS LTD. STORE NO. 18
REVISED Budgeted Balance Sheet
July 31, 2003

Assets

Current assets:

Cash (Revised Cash Budget)	$24,075	
Accounts receivable (Revised Sales Budget)	16,000	
Inventory	42,400	
Prepaid insurance	1,000	
Total current assets		$ 83,475

Capital assets:

Equipment and fixtures	$35,000	
Accumulated amortization	(14,800)	
Total capital assets		20,200
Total assets		$103,675

Liabilities

Current liabilities:

Accounts payable (0.50 × July purchases of **$28,000**; Revised Inventory, Purchases, and Cost of Goods Sold Budget)	$14,000	
Short-term note payable	4,500	
Salary and commissions payable (0.50 × July expenses of **$8,500**; Revised Operating Expenses Budget)	4,250	
Total liabilities		$ 22,750

Shareholders' Equity

Share capital	$40,000	
Retained earnings (beginning balance of $38,950 + **$1,975** net income; Revised Budgeted Income Statement)	40,925	
Total shareholders' equity		80,925
Total liabilities and shareholders' equity		$103,675

WHITEWATER SPORTING GOODS LTD. STORE NO. 18
REVISED Budgeted Cash Flow Statement
For the Four Months Ending July 31, 2003

Cash flows from operating activities:		
Receipts:		
Collections from customers (Revised Budgeted Cash Collections)	$ 230,000	
Total cash receipts		230,000
Payments:		
Purchases of inventory (Revised Budgeted Cash Payments for Purchases)	$(158,200)	
Operating expenses, excluding interest expense (Revised Budgeted Cash Payments for Operating Expenses)	(64,000)	
Payment of interest expense	(225)	
Total cash payments		(222,425)
Net cash inflow from operating activities		7,575
Cash flows from investing activities:		
Acquisition of delivery truck (item 8, page 1277)	$ (3,000)	
Net cash outflow from investing activities		(3,000)
Cash flows from financing activities:		
Proceeds from issuance of notes payable	$ 9,000	
Payment of notes payable	(4,500)	
Net cash inflow from financing activities		4,500
Net increase in cash		$ 9,075
Cash balance, April 1, 2003 (Exhibit 23-5)		15,000
Cash balance, July 31, 2003 (Revised Cash Budget)		$ 24,075

OBJECTIVE 5
Distinguish among different types of responsibility centres

LEARNING TIP

A responsibility accounting system divides a business into subunits called responsibility centres. A manager is assigned to each responsibility centre and is evaluated on how well the responsibility centre performs.

Responsibility Accounting

You've now seen how managers set strategic goals, and then develop plans and budget resources for activities that will help reach those goals. Each manager is responsible for planning and controlling some part of the firm's activities. A **responsibility centre** is a part or subunit of the organization whose manager is accountable for specific activities. At lower levels, managers are often responsible for budgeting and controlling costs of a single value chain function. For example, one manager is responsible for planning and controlling the *production* of Ski-Doos at the factory, while another is responsible for planning and controlling the *distribution* of the Ski-Doos to customers. Lower level managers report to higher level managers who have broader responsibilities. For example, managers in charge of production and distribution report to senior managers responsible for profits (revenues minus costs) earned by the entire product line.

Types of Responsibility Centres

Responsibility accounting is a system for evaluating the performance of each responsibility centre and its manager. Responsibility accounting reports compare plans (budgets) with actions (actual results) for each responsibility centre. Superiors then evaluate how well each manager: (1) used the budgeted resources to achieve the responsibility centre's strategic goals, and thereby (2) controlled the operations for which he or she is responsible. Exhibit 23-16 illustrates four common types of responsibility centres: cost centres, revenue centres, profit centres, and investment centres.

1. *Cost centre: A responsibility centre where managers are accountable for cost (expenses) only.* Manufacturing operations like the Ski-Doo production lines are cost centres. The line manager is charged with controlling costs by ensuring that employees work efficiently with minimal waste of raw materials. The line manager is *not* responsible for generating revenues, because he is not involved in selling the Ski-Doos. The factory manager evaluates the line manager on his ability to control *costs* by comparing actual costs to budgeted costs. All else being equal (for example, holding quality constant), the line manager is likely to receive a more favourable performance evaluation if actual costs are less than budgeted costs.

2. *Revenue centre: A responsibility centre where managers are primarily accountable for revenues.* Examples include the Prairie sales regions of businesses like Bombardier and Roots. Managers of revenue centres are primarily responsible for generating sales revenue, although they may also be responsible for the costs of their own sales operations. Revenue centre performance reports compare actual with bud-

EXHIBIT 23-16

Four Common Types of Responsibility Centres

(a) A cost centre, such as a production line for Ski-Doos—where managers are responsible for costs

(b) A revenue centre, such as Bombardier's prairie sales region—where managers are responsible for generating sales revenue

(c) A profit centre, such as Bombardier's Ski-Doo product line—where managers are responsible for generating income

(d) An investment centre, such as Bombardier's Aerospace division—where managers are responsible for income and invested capital

geted revenues, and may also include the costs incurred by the revenue centre itself. All else being equal, the manager is likely to receive a more favourable performance evaluation if actual revenues exceed the budget.

3. *Profit centre: A responsibility centre where managers are accountable for revenues and costs (expenses), and therefore profits.* The (higher-level) manager responsible for the entire Ski-Doo product line would be accountable for increasing sales revenue and controlling costs to achieve the profit goals. Profit centre reports include both revenues and expenses to show the profit centre's income. Superiors evaluate the manager's performance by comparing actual revenues, expenses, and profits to the budget. All else being equal, the manager is likely to receive a more favourable performance evaluation if actual profits exceed the budget. Other examples of profit centres include a Swiss Chalet restaurant and the housewares department of a Canadian Tire store.

4. *Investment centre: A responsibility centre where managers are accountable for investments, revenues, and costs (expenses).* Examples include Zellers, which is owned by Hudson's Bay Co., Day + Ross Inc., the trucking company owned by McCain Foods, and Union Gas, which is owned by Westcost Energy. Managers of investment centres are responsible for: (1) generating sales, (2) controlling expenses, and (3) managing the amount of investment required to earn the income (revenues minus expenses).

Top management often evaluates investment centre managers based on return on investment. Chapter 18 introduced a common return on investment measure—the rate of return on total assets:

$$\frac{\text{Net income plus interest}}{\text{Average total assets}}$$

When evaluating a division rather than the entire company, however, the return on investment is often computed as:

$$\frac{\text{Division's operating income}}{\text{Division's average total assets}}$$

All else being equal, the manager will receive a more favourable performance evaluation if the division's actual return on investment exceeds the budgeted return on investment.

Responsibility Accounting: An Example

.... **THINKING IT OVER**

Name the four types of responsibility centres, and give an example of each one in a department store.
A: (1) Cost centre—payroll, accounting, and personnel departments; (2) revenue centre— shoes, electronics, and men's clothing. (These are considered revenue centres because the manager has only limited responsibility for costs). (3) profit centre—the store itself if the manager has responsibility to purchase merchandise; (4) investment centre—the store itself.

The simplified organization chart in Exhibit 23-17 shows how a company may assign responsibility in the fast-food industry. At the top level of Casey's Restaurant Corporation, a district manager oversees the branch managers, who supervise the managers of the individual restaurants (called stores). Store managers have limited freedom to make operating decisions. They may decide the quantities of food items to order, the number of employees and their schedules, and store hours. Branch managers oversee several stores, evaluate store managers' performance, and set store managers' compensation levels. In turn, district managers oversee several branches, evaluate branch managers' performance and compensation, set food prices, and approve sales promotions. District managers are accountable to regional managers, who answer to home-office vice-presidents.

Exhibit 23-18 on page 1296 provides a more detailed view of how managers use responsibility accounting to evaluate profit centres. At each level, the reports compare results with the budget. Examine the lowest level and move to the top. Follow how the reports are related through the three levels of responsibility.

Trace the $54,000 budgeted operating income from the Casey's Yorkdale store manager's report to the Toronto branch manager's report. The branch manager's

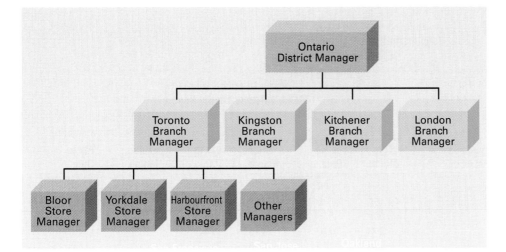

report summarizes the results of the stores under his supervision. This report also includes charges incurred by the branch manager's office.

Now trace the $465,000 total from the Toronto branch manager's report to the Ontario district manager's report. The report of the district manager includes costs from her own district office plus a summary of each branch's operating performance.

Casey's Restaurant Corporation
www.primerestaurants.com/
caseysgrillhouse/default.asp

STOP & THINK

Casey's store managers do not have authority to set sale prices or control advertising. Both factors affect store revenues. But despite the lack of store-manager authority, the corporation evaluates each store as a profit centre instead of as a cost centre. Why?

Answer: If each store were a cost centre, then store managers would be motivated to cut costs in order to keep actual costs below the budget. Excessive cost cutting can hurt quality and service. By evaluating each store as a profit centre, executives give store managers the incentive to keep stores clean and to ensure that employees provide fast and friendly service. Store managers thus are more likely to work hard to increase customer value, the foundation of long-run profitability.

Management by Exception

OBJECTIVE 6
Prepare a performance report for management by exception

Exhibit 23-18 stresses variances. This reporting format aids **management by exception,** the practice of directing executive attention to important differences between actual and budgeted amounts. Look at the district manager's report, and consider the Toronto branch. Its actual operating income of $460,000 is very close to its budget for the current month. Under management by exception, the district manager will not waste time investigating such a small variance. In contrast, both the Kingston and Kitchener branches substantially exceeded budgeted performance. Their large favourable variances probably will be investigated to determine their causes. For example, suppose that the Kitchener manager believes that a local sales promotion was especially effective. That promotion may be repeated, and also used in other cities.

Managers investigate large favourable variances as well as large unfavourable variances. A large favourable variance could reflect good performance. But a large

CASEY'S RESTAURANT CORPORATION
Responsibility Accounting at Various Levels
(in thousands of dollars)

Ontario District Manager
Monthly Responsibility Report

Operating income of branches and district manager office expense:	Budget		Actual		Variance Favourable (Unfavourable)	
	This Month	Year to Date	This Month	Year to Date	This Month	Year to Date
District manager office expense..............	$ (150)	$ (600)	$ (154)	$ (620)	$ (4)	$ (20)
Toronto branch	465	1,730	460	1,780	(5)	50
Kingston branch..	500	1,800	560	1,994	60	194
Kitchener branch.......................................	390	1,540	475	1,855	85	315
London branch	520	2,240	468	2,061	(52)	(179)
Operating income	$1,725	$6,710	$1,809	$7,070	$84	$360

Toronto Branch Manager
Monthly Responsibility Report

Operating income of stores and branch manager office expense:	Budget		Actual		Variance Favourable (Unfavourable)	
	This Month	Year to Date	This Month	Year to Date	This Month	Year to Date
Branch manager office expense	$ (20)	$ (306)	$ (25)	$ (302)	$(5)	$ 4
Bloor restaurant	48	148	40	136	(8)	(12)
Yorkdale restaurant	54	228	61	244	7	16
Harbourfront restaurant.............................	38	160	42	170	4	10
Others	345	1,500	342	1,532	(3)	32
Operating income	$465	$1,730	$460	$1,780	$(5)	$50

Yorkdale Restaurant Manager
Monthly Responsibility Report

Revenues and expenses:	Budget		Actual		Variance Favourable (Unfavourable)	
	This Month	Year to Date	This Month	Year to Date	This Month	Year to Date
Revenues	$170	$690	$178	$702	$8	$12
Food expense	50	198	45	184	5	14
Paper	15	62	18	64	(3)	(2)
Wages...	24	98	28	103	(4)	(5)
Repairs	5	19	4	20	1	(1)
General..	12	45	12	47	—	(2)
Amortization...	10	40	10	40	—	—
Total expenses..	116	462	117	458	(1)	4
Operating income.......................................	$ 54	$228	$ 61	$244	$7	$16

EXHIBIT 23-18

Responsibility Accounting Performance Report

favourable variance for costs such as food or wages could indicate that the store manager is skimping on the food or service.

The Ontario district manager will concentrate her efforts this month on improving the London branch. Its actual income of $468,000 is 10 percent ($52,000/$520,000) lower than its budget. The district manager may ask to see the London branch manager's monthly responsibility report. That report reveals whether the income shortfall is due to excessively high office expenses, below-budget performance by individual restaurants, or both. The two managers will work together to identify and correct problems.

Exhibit 23-18 also shows that summarized data may hide problems. Although the Toronto branch as a whole performed well, the Bloor restaurant did not. Its actual income of $40,000 is 16.7 percent ($8,000/48,000) below its budgeted amount. This shortfall is offset by excellent performances by the Yorkdale and Harbourfront restaurants. If the district manager receives only the condensed report at the top of the exhibit, she must rely on branch managers to spot and correct problems with individual restaurants. Some upper-level executives prefer to receive the more-detailed middle-level reports in order to keep tighter control over their responsibility centres.

Not a Question of Blame

Responsibility accounting helps top executives delegate decisions. Responsibility accounting assigns lower-level managers responsibility for their unit's actions and provides a way to evaluate the manager's and unit's performance. By allowing top managers to delegate decisions, responsibility accounting and management by exception free them to concentrate on strategic issues that affect the entire business.

Managers should not misuse responsibility accounting systems to find fault or to place blame. The question is not, Who should be blamed for an unfavourable variance? Instead, the question is, Who is in the best position to explain why a specific variance occurred? Consider again the performance of the London branch in Exhibit 23-18. Suppose that a month of unusually nasty weather resulted in a 15-percent drop in restaurant volume. It may be that only efficient operations by the branch's restaurants kept the income variance as low as $52,000. Therefore, the London branch manager may have done a good job despite the unfavourable variance.

Departmental Accounting

OBJECTIVE 7
Allocate indirect costs to departments

Wal-Mart
www.walmart.com

Responsibility centres are often called *departments*. Consider a department store such as Zellers, The Bay, or Wal-Mart. Top managers of a department store want more information than just the net income of the store as a whole. At a minimum, they want to know each department's gross margin (sales minus cost of goods sold). They also usually want to know each department's operating income. These data can help identify the most profitable departments, so managers can decide whether to expand some departments and phase out others.

It is easy to measure gross margin for each department because the department keeps records for sales and cost of goods sold. However, it is more difficult to measure a department's operating income (gross margin minus operating expenses). Why? Many operating expenses are indirect costs that are not directly traceable to the department.

As we discussed in Chapter 19, *direct costs* are traceable to a particular department or product. Consider The Bay's Shoe Department. Clerks' wages, the cost of ads for shoes, and amortization on display racks are all directly traceable to the Shoe Department. *Indirect costs*—all expenses other than direct costs—are not traceable to a single department. For example, The Bay's Receiving Department and Stockroom serve all departments. How should The Bay allocate the cost of its Receiving Department and its Stockroom?

THINKING IT OVER

What are some examples of direct departmental costs?

A: Department manager's salary, amortization of furniture and equipment in the department, and delivery expense that can be traced directly to the department.

THINKING IT OVER

What are some examples of indirect departmental costs?

A: Insurance, utilities, accounting, rent, and so on. These costs usually are incurred for the benefit of the business as a whole and, therefore, must be allocated to each department.

Allocation of Indirect Costs

Chapters 20 and 21 explained how indirect costs are allocated to *products*. Indirect costs are allocated to *departments* or responsibility centres using a similar process.

- Choose an allocation base for the indirect cost
- Compute an indirect cost allocation rate:

Total indirect cost ÷ Total quantity of the allocation base

THINKING IT OVER

What is a reasonable basis for allocating the following costs? (1) Rent, (2) utilities, (3) advertising, and (4) purchasing department costs.

A: (1) Square metres of floor space, (2) number of machine hours worked, (3) sales, and (4) number of orders placed.

REAL WORLD EXAMPLE

Weyerhaeuser Company has developed an interesting procedure for assigning corporate overhead. Rather than allocate overhead as an indirect cost, the costs of corporate services are traced directly to the departments that consume the services. Managers are free to purchase services from outsiders or from corporate service departments. Each service department must carefully price its service (preparation of payroll cheques, for example) to be competitive with outside companies that can also provide that service.

LEARNING TIP

Remember that only indirect costs, which benefit more than one department, must be allocated. Indirect costs must be allocated on some basis that is fair to all departments that benefit from them.

- Allocate the indirect cost:

Quantity of the allocation base used by the department
× Indirect cost allocation rate

As we discussed in Chapter 20, the ideal cost allocation base is also a cost driver. Because different costs have different cost drivers, a company can use several different allocation bases to allocate different indirect costs to the various departments. Exhibit 23-19 lists common allocation bases for different indirect costs. There is no single "correct" allocation base for each indirect cost. Managers use their experience and judgment to choose these bases. If managers help identify cost allocation bases, they will be more confident that the indirect cost allocations are reasonable.

Consider The Bay's receiving costs. Suppose The Bay decides that these costs are driven by the number of orders placed to purchase inventory. If 15 percent of the orders are for the Shoe Department and 20 percent are for the Menswear Department, then The Bay will allocate 15 percent of the Receiving Department costs to the Shoe Department and 20 percent to the Menswear Department. (The remaining Receiving Department costs will be allocated to other departments in proportion to the number of orders each issued.)

Allocating Indirect Costs to Departments: An Example

Exhibit 23-20 shows a departmental income statement for WorldPC, a retail computer store. We focus on the allocation of indirect operating expenses to the store's two departments: Hardware and Software.

Salaries and Wages WorldPC traces salespersons' salaries and department managers' salaries directly to each department.

Rent WorldPC allocates the $600,000 rent expense based on the square metres occupied by each department. The Hardware and Software Department occupy 2,000 square metres and 500 square metres, respectively. The allocation of rent is com-

EXHIBIT 23-19

Bases for Allocating Costs to Departments

Cost or Expense	Base for Allocating Cost
Direct materials	Separately traced
Merchandise inventory purchases	Separately traced
Direct labour	Separately traced
Other labour	Time spent in each department
Supervision	Time spent, or number of employees, in each department
Equipment amortization	Separately traced, hours used by each department
Building amortization, property taxes	Square metres of space
Heat, light, and air conditioning	Square metres or cubic metres of space
Janitorial services	Square metres of space
Advertising	Separately traced if possible; otherwise, in proportion to sales
Materials Handling Department	Number or weight of items handled for each department
Payroll Department	Number of employees in each department
Personnel Department	Number of employees in each department
Purchasing Department	Number of purchase orders placed for each department

puted as follows:

Rent for entire store	$600,000
Total square metres (2,000 + 500)	÷ 2,500
Rent per square metre ($600,000 ÷ 2,500)	$ 240

Hardware Department: 2,000 square metres × $240 per square metre = $480,000
Software Department: 500 square metres × $240 per square metre = 120,000
Total rent expense = $600,000

Purchasing Department WorldPC found that it takes just as long to complete a purchase order for inexpensive modems as for expensive "loaded" notebook computers. Consequently, the company allocates the $48,000 costs of the Purchasing Department based on the number of purchase orders processed. Hardware had 300 purchase orders, while Software had 100 purchase orders.

Purchasing Department costs	$48,000
Total number of purchase orders (300 + 100)	÷ 400
Cost per purchase order ($48,000 ÷ 400)	$ 120

Hardware Department: 300 purchase orders × $120 per purchase order = $36,000
Software Department: 100 purchase orders × $120 per purchase order = $12,000
Total Purchase Department Cost = $48,000

WorldPC's top executives can use the departmental income statements in Exhibit 23-20 to evaluate how well each department and its manager performed in 2003. The Hardware Department's profit margin (income divided by sales) was $1,324,000 ÷ $7,000,000 = 18.9 percent, while Software's profit margin was only $128,000 ÷ $3,000,000 = 4.3 percent. However, it is usually better to compare a department's actual results to its budget, rather than to another department's results. For example, if WorldPC has just added the Software Department, performance may have exceeded expectations.

The Decision Guidelines on the following page review budgets and how they are used in responsibility accounting. Take a moment to study these guidelines before beginning the summary review problem on page 1301.

WORKING IT OUT

Departments A and B occupy a building with 2,000 square metres. Department A uses 800 square metres, and Department B uses 1,200 square metres.

Q: How would the utilities cost of $36,000 be allocated to the two departments?

A:

Dept. A	
($36,000 x 800/2,000)	$14,400
Dept. B	
($36,000 x 1,200/2,000)	21,600
Total	$36,000

WORKING IT OUT

Department A produces a product with five different raw materials, while Department B produces a product with only three different raw materials. The purchasing department costs for the year totalled $64,000.

Q: How would these costs be allocated to the two departments?

A:

Department A	
($64,000 x 5/8)	$40,000
Department B	
($64,000 x 3/8)	24,000
Total	$64,000

EXHIBIT 23-20

Departmental Income Statement

WORLDPC
Departmental Income Statement
For the Year Ended December 31, 2003
(In Thousands)

	Total	Department Hardware	Software
Sales revenue	$10,000	$7,000	$3,000
Cost of goods sold	6,500	4,500	2,000
Gross margin	3,500	2,500	1,000
Operating expenses:			
Salaries and wages expense	1,400	660	740
Rent expense	600	480	120
Purchasing department expense	48	36	12
Total operating expenses	2,048	1,176	872
Operating income	$ 1,452	$1,324	$ 128

Decision	Guidelines
Why should a company develop a budget?	• Requires managers to plan • Promotes organization and communication • Provides a benchmark to help managers evaluate performance • Motivates employees
In what order should you prepare the components of the master budget?	Begin with the *operating budget*. • Start with the *sales budget*, which feeds into all other budgets. • The sales and *ending inventory budgets* determine the *purchases and cost of goods sold budget*. • The sales, cost of goods sold, and *operating expense budgets* determine the *budgeted income statement*. Next, prepare the *capital expenditures budget*. Finally, prepare the *financial budget*. • Start with the *cash budget*. • The cash budget provides the ending cash balance for the *budgeted balance sheet*, and the details for the *budgeted cash flow statement*.
What if the sales forecast is uncertain?	Prepare a *sensitivity analysis* and project budgeted results at different sales levels.
How to compute budgeted purchases?	$$\text{Beginning Inventory} + \text{Purchases} - \text{Ending inventory} = \text{Cost of goods sold}$$ $$\text{Purchases} = \text{Cost of goods sold} + \text{Ending inventory} - \text{Beginning inventory}$$
What kind of a responsibility centre does a given manager supervise?	Cost centre: Manager is responsible for costs. Revenue centre: Manager is responsible for revenues. Profit centre: Manager is responsible for both revenues and costs, and therefore profits. Investment centre: Manager is responsible for revenues, costs, and managing the amount of the investment required to earn the income.
How to evaluate managers?	Compare actual performance with the budget for the manager's responsibility centre. *Management by exception* focuses only on large differences between budgeted and actual results.
How to identify the most profitable departments or product lines?	Departmental or product line income statements.
How to allocate indirect costs to departments or product lines?	1. Choose an allocation base for each indirect cost. 2. Compute an indirect cost allocation rate: $$\frac{\text{Total indirect cost (\$)}}{\text{Total quantity of allocation base}}$$ 3. Allocate the indirect cost: $$\text{Quantity of allocation base used by the department} \times \text{Indirect cost allocation rate}$$

Summary Problem
for Your Review

Canadian Pacific operates an exclusive "hotel within a hotel" that provides an even more luxurious atmosphere than the hotel's regular accommodations. Access is limited to guests residing on the hotel's top floor. The private lounge serves complimentary continental breakfast, afternoon snacks, and evening cocktails and chocolates. It also has its own concierge staff that provides personal service to preferred guests. Guests staying in regular accommodations do not receive complimentary snacks and beverages, nor do they have a private concierge.

The exclusive floors are considered one department, and regular accommodations are considered a separate department.

Suppose the general manager of a new Canadian Pacific hotel wants to know the costs for her hotel's Prestige Accommodations Department and Regular Accommodations Department. Housekeeping costs are allocated based on the number of occupied room-nights, utilities are allocated based on the number of cubic metres, and building amortization is allocated based on the number of square metres. Assume each department reports the following information for March:

	Prestige Accommodations	Regular Accommodations
Number of occupied room-nights	540	7,560
Cubic metres	7,111	53,333
Square metres	1,778	16,000

Required

1. Given the following (assumed) total costs, what are the costs assigned to the Prestige Accommodations and the Regular Accommodations Departments?

Food and beverage expense.............	$12,000
Housekeeping expense.....................	194,400
Utilities expense................................	97,920
Building amortization expense........	480,000
Concierge staff salaries	15,000
Total	$799,320

2. What is the cost per occupied room in Prestige Accommodations? In Regular Accommodations?

Solution to Review Problem

Requirement 1

Cost assignment

	Prestige Accommodations	Regular Accommodations	Total
Food and beverage expense[a]	$12,000	$ —	$ 12,000
Housekeeping expense[b]	12,960	181,440	194,400
Utilities expense[c]	11,520	86,400	97,920
Building amortization expense[d]	48,000	432,000	480,000
Concierge staff salaries[a]	15,000	—	15,000
Total	$99,480	$699,840	$799,320

[a]Food and beverage expenses and concierge staff salaries are directly traced to the Prestige Accommodations Department.

[b]Housekeeping expense

$$\text{Cost per occupied room} = \frac{\$194,400}{540 + 7,560}$$

$$= \$24/\text{room}$$

Prestige Accommodations: 540 rooms × \$24/room = \$ 12,960
Regular Accommodations: 7,560 rooms × \$24/room = 181,440
Total housekeeping expense = \$194,400

[c]Utilities expense

$$\text{Cost per cubic metre} = \frac{\$97,920}{7,111 + 53,333}$$

$$= \$1.62/\text{m}^3$$

Prestige Accommodations: 7,111 m^3 × \$1.62/m^3 = \$11,520
Regular Accommodations: 53,333 m^3 × \$1.62/m^3 = 86,400
Total utilities expense = \$97,920

[d]Building amortization expense

$$\text{Cost per square metre} = \frac{\$480,000}{1,778 + 16,000}$$

$$= \$27/\text{m}^2$$

Prestige Accommodations: 1,778 m^2 × \$27/m^2 = \$ 48,000
Regular Accommodations: 16,000 m^2 × \$27/m^2 = 432,000
Total building amortization expense = \$480,000

Requirement 2

Cost per occupied room

	Prestige Accommodations	Regular Accommodations
Total costs	\$99,480	\$699,840
÷ Occupied rooms	÷ 540	÷ 7,560
= Cost per occupied room	\$184.22	\$ 92.57

Summary

1. **Identify the benefits of budgeting.** A budget is a quantitative expression of a plan of action that helps managers coordinate and implement the plan. Budgets require managers to plan, coordinate activities, and communicate plans throughout the company. Budgets also help managers evaluate performance and motivate employees to achieve goals.

2. **Prepare an operating budget for a company.** The *operating budget* sets the target revenues and expenses—and thus operating income—for the period. To budget income, accountants must budget sales, inventory, purchases, cost of goods sold, and operating expenses. Sales revenue is budgeted first because all other income statement elements depend on sales volume.

3. **Prepare the components of a financial budget.** A *capital expenditures budget* presents plans for purchasing long-term capital assets. This budget and the budgeted income statement provide data for the *cash budget*. All three are used to prepare the budgeted balance sheet and budgeted cash flow statement.

4. **Use sensitivity analysis in budgeting.** Managers should make contingency plans in case actual results differ from predictions. *Sensitivity analysis* asks *what* a result will be *if* a predicted amount is not achieved or *if* an underlying assumption changes. Many managers use spreadsheets or special Web-based software to study a broad range of budget possibilities.

5. **Distinguish among different types of responsibility centres.** Most companies are organized by *responsibility centres* to establish authority for planning and controlling business operations. Four types of responsibility centres are: cost centres, revenue centres, profit centres, and investment centres.

6. **Prepare a performance report for management by exception.** Performance reports show differences between budgeted and actual amounts. By focusing on important variances, managers can direct their attention to areas that need improvement. This practice is called *management by exception*.

7. **Allocate indirect costs to departments.** Indirect costs are allocated to responsibility centres called departments. The process is similar to the allocation of indirect costs to products, as explained in Chapter 20. First, choose an allocation base, which ideally should be a cost driver. Second, calculate an indirect cost allocation rate: Divide the total amount of the indirect cost by the total quantity of the allocation base. Third, use this indirect cost allocation rate to allocate indirect costs to departments. Multiply the quantity of the allocation base used by the department times the indirect cost allocation rate.

Self-Study Questions

Test your understanding of the chapter by marking the correct answer to each of the following questions:

1. Which of the following is *not* a benefit of budgeting? *(pp. 1269–1270)*
   a. Coordinates activities
   b. Automatically leads to underachieving employees being fired
   c. Aids performance evaluation
   d. Compels managers to plan

2. Chewning Corporation's actual revenues are $90,000, and operating expenses are $50,000. Budgeted revenues were $86,000 and budgeted expenses were $51,000. What is the variance in operating income? *(p. 1274)*
   a. $40,000 favourable
   b. $35,000 unfavourable
   c. $5,000 favourable
   d. $5,000 unfavourable

3. The master budget starts with *(p. 1274)*
   a. Budgeted cash
   b. Shareholders' equity
   c. Budgeted sales
   d. Inventory

4. The operating budget ends with *(p. 1275)*
   a. Budgeted sales
   b. The budgeted income statement
   c. The cash budget
   d. The budgeted balance sheet

5. The master budget usually ends with *(p. 1275)*
   a. Budgeted sales
   b. The budgeted income statement
   c. The cash budget
   d. The budgeted balance sheet

6. Managers can use a computer spreadsheet program along with a master budget to *(p. 1285)*
   a. Plan for various possibilities
   b. Eliminate uncertainty in the business environment
   c. Prepare the budget correctly on the first attempt
   d. Set ideal goals for the company

7. Which responsibility centre is most likely to be a cost centre? *(p. 1292)*
   a. Personnel department
   b. Housewares department of a department store
   c. Audit department of a public accounting firm
   d. Manufacturing plant

8. Under management by exception, which of the following variances should be investigated? *(p. 1295)*
   a. Small favourable variance
   b. Small unfavourable variance
   c. Large favourable variance
   d. Large unfavourable variance

9. Responsibility accounting systems *(p. 1295)*
   a. Help top managers to delegate decision making
   b. Assign responsibility for activities to managers
   c. Provide a way to evaluate performance
   d. All of the above

10. The most important step in allocating indirect costs to departments is *(p. 1297)*
    a. Tracing direct costs to departments
    b. Choosing the appropriate allocation base for each indirect cost
    c. Determining one allocation base for all indirect costs
    d. Multiplying the quantity of the allocation base by the indirect cost rate

Answers to the Self-Study Questions follow the Similar Accounting Terms.

Accounting Vocabulary

Capital expenditures budget *(p. 1274)*
Cash budget *(p. 1280)*
Financial budget *(p. 1274)*
Management by exception *(p. 1295)*
Master budget *(p. 1274)*

Operating budget *(p. 1274)*
Responsibility accounting *(p. 1292)*
Responsibility centre *(p. 1292)*
Sensitivity analysis *(p. 1285)*
Statement of budgeted cash receipts and payments *(p. 1280)*

Similar Accounting Terms

Allocation base   Application base
Cash budget   Cash flow budget
Master budget   Static budget

Assignment Material

Questions

1. What are four benefits of budgeting?

2. How does a manager use a performance report?

3. List the components of a master budget.

4. A Ford dealer sets a goal of selling more Ford automobiles than any other dealer in the city. Is this goal a budget? Give your reason.

5. Duck Lake Corporation installs a budgeting system in which the president sets all the goals for the company. The vice-president oversees all 90 employees to ensure that they are meeting the president's budget goals. What is the weakness in this budgeting system? How can the system be improved?

6. Why should the capital expenditures budget be prepared before the cash budget, the budgeted balance sheet, and the budgeted cash flow statement?

7. How does a company budget inventory purchases? In your answer, show the relationships among purchases, cost of goods sold, and inventory.

8. Outline the four steps in preparing an operating budget.

9. Is revenue forecasting important only to a profit-seeking business, or is it used by nonprofit organizations such as colleges and hospitals? Give your reason.

10. Why are computer spreadsheets and budget management software well suited for budgeting?

11. What three amounts are combined in the "total effects of financing" on the cash budget statement?

12. Which manager will control expenses better: Grant, whose performance is measured by his department's sales, or Burns, whose performance is gauged by her department's income? Why?

13. Identify four types of responsibility centres, and give examples of each. State the information they report.

14. A company owns eight Burger King restaurants in Moncton, Fredericton, and St. John, New Brunswick. In each city, a local manager oversees operations. Starting at the individual store level, describe the likely flow of information in a responsibility accounting system. What data are reported?

15. What is the objective of management by exception?

16. What question about unfavourable variances is a responsibility accounting system designed to answer? How can managers abuse such a system?

17. Distinguish between direct expenses and indirect expenses of a department in a department store. Give examples of each type.

18. Name a reasonable allocation base for the following indirect expenses: heating expense, amortization of manufacturing equipment used by three departments, and advertising expense.

19. Suppose that supplies expense is allocated to departments at the end of each period on the basis of the period's sales. In a recent month, departments X, Y, and Z had sales of $5,000, $12,000, and $8,000, respectively. How much of the month's $1,200 supplies expense was charged to each department?

20. Why do managers want to allocate indirect costs to departments?

Exercises

Exercise 23-1   *Budgeting and performance evaluation*   **(Obj. 1)**

Miranda Low owns a store that sells athletic shoes. Last year, her sales staff sold 7,500 pairs of shoes at an average sale price of $65. Variable expenses were 60 percent of sales revenue, and the total fixed expense was $100,000. This year the store sold more expensive shoe lines. Sales were 7,000 pairs at an average price of $80. The variable expense rate and the total fixed expense were the same both years. Low evaluates the store manager by comparing this year's income with last year's income.

Prepare a performance report for this year. Use the format of Exhibit 23-3. How would you improve Low's performance evaluation system to analyze this year's results better?

Exercise 23-2   *Budgeting purchases, cost of goods sold, and inventory*   *(Obj. 2)*

The sales budget of Euston Ltd. for the nine months ended September 30, 2002, is as follows:

	Quarter Ended			Nine-Month Total
	March 31	June 30	Sept. 30	
Cash sales, 30%	$ 27,000	$ 45,000	$ 37,500	$109,500
Credit sales, 70%	63,000	105,000	87,500	255,500
Total sales, 100%.......	$90,000	$150,000	$125,000	$365,000

In the past, cost of goods sold has been 70 percent of total sales. The director of marketing, the production manager, and the financial vice-president agree that each quarter's ending inventory should not be below $15,000 plus 10 percent of cost of goods sold for the following quarter. Euston Ltd. expects sales of $100,000 during the fourth quarter. The January 1 inventory was $22,000.

Prepare an inventory, purchases, and cost of goods sold budget for each of the first three quarters of the year. Compute cost of goods sold for the entire nine-month period. (Use Exhibit 23–8 as a model.)

Exercise 23-3   *Budgeting quarterly income for a year*   *(Obj. 2)*

RE/MAX is a nationwide real estate firm. Suppose that the St. John's, Newfoundland, office of the firm projects that 2003 quarterly sales will increase by 4 percent in quarter one, 3 percent in quarter two, 5 percent in quarter three, and 4 percent in quarter four. Management expects operating expenses to be 85 percent of revenues during each of the first two quarters, 86 percent of revenues during the third quarter, and 80 percent during the fourth. The office manager expects to borrow $100,000 on July 1, with quarterly principal payments of $10,000 beginning on September 30 and interest paid at the annual rate of 10 percent. Last-quarter sales in 2002 were $2,000,000.

Prepare a budgeted income statement for each of the four quarters of 2003 and for the entire year. Present the 2003 budget as follows:

Quarter 1	Quarter 2	Quarter 3	Quarter 4	Full Year

Exercise 23-4   *Computing cash receipts and payments*   *(Obj. 3)*

For each of items (a) through (d), compute the amount of cash receipts or payments Jasper Ltd. will budget for December. A solution to one item may depend on the answer to an earlier item.

a. Management expects to sell 8,000 units in November and 8,400 in December. Each unit sells for $7. Cash sales average 30 percent of total sales, and credit sales make up the rest. Two-thirds of credit sales are collected in the month of sale, with the balance collected the following month.

b. Management has budgeted inventory purchases of $30,000 for November and $32,000 for December. Jasper Ltd. pays for 50 percent of its inventory at the time of purchase in order to get a 2-percent discount. The business pays the balance the following month, with no discount.

c. Management expects to sell equipment that cost $14,100 at a gain of $2,000. Accumulated amortization on this equipment is $8,000.

d. The company pays rent and property taxes of $4,000 each month. Commissions and other selling expenses average 20 percent of sales. Jasper Ltd. pays two-thirds of selling expenses in the month incurred, with the balance paid in the following month.

Exercise 23-5 *Budgeting cash receipts and payments; sensitivity analysis* *(Obj. 3, 4)*

Cassell's Inc., a family-owned gardening store, began October 2002 with $8,000 cash. Management forecasts that collections from credit customers will be $9,500 in October and $12,200 in November. The store is scheduled to receive $5,000 cash on a business note receivable in November. Projected cash payments include inventory purchases ($10,200 in October and $13,000 in November) and operating expenses ($3,000 each month).

Cassell's bank requires a $7,500 minimum balance in the store's chequing account. At the end of any month when the account balance goes below $7,500, the bank automatically extends credit to the store in multiples of $1,000. Cassell's borrows as little as possible and pays back these loans in quarterly installments of $3,000, plus 10 percent interest on the entire unpaid principal. The first payment occurs three months after the loan.

Required

1. Prepare the store's cash budget for October and November.

2. How much cash will Cassell's borrow in November if collections from customers that month total $9,200 instead of $12,200?

Exercise 23-6 *Preparing a budgeted balance sheet* *(Obj. 3)*

Use the following information to prepare a budgeted balance sheet for Scarrow's Shoes Ltd. at March 31, 2003. Show computations for the cash and shareholders' equity amounts.

a. March 31 inventory balance, $18,000.

b. March payments for inventory, $5,900.

c. March payments of accounts payable and accrued liabilities, $7,600.

d. March 31 accounts payable balance, $4,900.

e. February 28 furniture and fixtures balance, $34,800; accumulated amortization balance, $27,700.

f. March capital expenditures of $3,200 budgeted for cash purchase of furniture.

g. March operating expenses, including income tax, total $4,500; paid in cash.

h. March amortization, $300.

i. Cost of goods sold, 50 percent of sales.

j. February 28 shareholders' equity: Common stock, $5,000, and Retained earnings, $20,700.

k. February 28 cash balance, $10,300.

l. March budgeted sales, $16,400.

m. March 31 accounts receivable balance, one-fourth of March sales.

n. March cash receipts, $12,800.

Exercise 23-7 *Identifying different types of responsibility centres* *(Obj. 5)*

Identify each responsibility centre as a cost centre, a revenue centre, a profit centre, or an investment centre.

a. The accounting department of a law office prepares its budget and subsequent performance report on the basis of its expected expenses for the year.

b. The manager of a Tim Hortons donut store is evaluated on the basis of the store's revenues and expenses.

c. The manager of the British Columbia sales territory is evaluated based on a comparison of current period sales against budgeted sales.

d. A college cafeteria unit reports both revenues and expenses.

e. A charter airline records revenues and expenses for each airplane each month. The airplane's performance report shows its ratio of operating income to average book value.

f. Accountants compile the cost of surgical supplies for evaluating the purchasing department of a hospital.

g. A division manager's performance is judged by the ratio of the division's operating income to the corporation's investment in the division.

Exercise 23-8 *Using responsibility accounting to evaluate profit centres* **(Obj. 6)**

C*Books.com Ltd. is a Calgary company that sells discount books on the Web. C*Books.com has assistant managers for its adult-fiction and adult-nonfiction operations. These assistant managers report to the manager of adult books, who with the manager of children's books report to the manager for all book sales, Beth Beverly. Beverly received the following data for November 2002 operations.

| | **Adult** | | |
	Non-Fiction	**Fiction**	**Children**
Revenues, budget	$520,000	$600,000	$1,100,000
Expenses, budget	350,000	390,000	750,000
Revenues, actual	550,000	620,000	1,000,000
Expenses, actual	340,000	400,000	690,000

Arrange the data in a performance report similar to Exhibit 23-18. Show November results, in thousands of dollars, for adult non-fiction, adult, and books as a whole. Should Beverly investigate the performance of adult non-fiction operations?

Exercise 23-9 *Preparing a departmental income statement* **(Obj. 7)**

Saraste Products Ltd. has two departments, electronics and industrial. The company's income statement for the year ended December 31, 2002, appears as follows:

Net sales	$360,000
Cost of goods sold	126,000
Gross margin	234,000
Operating expenses:	
Salaries...	$ 75,000
Amortization	15,000
Advertising..	6,000
Other..	10,000
Total operating expenses	106,000
Operating income	$128,000

Sales are: electronics, $136,000; industrial, $224,000. Cost of goods sold is distributed $42,000 to electronics and $84,000 to industrial products. Salaries are traced directly to departments: electronics, $33,000; industrial, $42,000. Seventy percent of advertising is spent on electronics. Amortization is allocated on the basis of square metres: Electronics has 7,000 square metres; industrial has 14,000 square metres. Other expenses are allocated on the basis of number of employees. An equal number work in the two departments.

Required

1. Prepare a departmental income statement that shows revenues, expenses, and operating income for the company's two departments.

2. In a departmental performance report, which are the most important of Saraste Products Ltd.'s expenses for evaluating department managers? Give your reason.

Exercise 23-10 *Allocating indirect expenses to departments* **(Obj. 7)**

Edmonton Fabricating Inc. incurred the following indirect costs in January, 2003:

Indirect labour expense......................	$16,000
Equipment amortization expense......	22,500
Marketing expense..............................	20,000

Data for cost allocations:

	Department		
	Priming	**Welding**	**Custom**
Sales revenue	$70,000	$50,000	$80,000
Indirect labour hours..................................	400	500	100
Machine hours...	300	450	150
Building square metres................................	3,000	1,000	1,000

Marketing expense is allocated to departments in proportion to sales.

Required

1. Allocate Edmonton Fabricating Inc.'s January indirect expenses to the three departments.
2. Compute total indirect expenses for each department.

Challenge Exercise

Exercise 23-11 *Preparing a cash budget* **(Obj. 3)**

You recently began a job as an accounting co-op student at Trailblazers Ltd. Your first task was to help prepare the cash budget for May and June, 2002. Unfortunately, the computer with the budget file crashed, and you did not have a backup or even a hard copy. You ran a program to salvage bits of data from the budget file. After entering the following data in the budget, you may have just enough information to reconstruct the budget.

Trailblazers Ltd. eliminates any cash deficiency by borrowing the exact amount needed from First Provincial Bank, where the current interest rate is 12 percent. Trailblazers repays all borrowed amounts at the end of the month, as cash becomes available.

Complete the following cash budget.

TRAILBLAZERS LTD.
Cash Budget
May and June, 2002

	May	**June**
Beginning cash balance..	$10,900	$?
Cash collections from customers.............................	?	74,800
Cash from sale of capital assets	0	1,800
Cash available before financing	90,900	?
Cash payments:		
Purchases of inventory	$?	$41,400

Operating expenses	31,900	?
Total payments	82,500	?
(1) Ending cash balance before financing	?	19,500
Minimum cash balance desired	15,000	15,000
Cash excess (deficiency)	?	?
Financing of cash deficiency:		
Borrowing (at end of month)	$?	$?
Principal repayments (at end of month)	?	?
Interest expense	?	?
(2) Total effects of financing	?	?
Ending cash balance (1) + (2)	$?	$?

Beyond the Numbers

Beyond the Numbers 23-1   *Using a budgeted income statement*   *(Obj. 1)*

Kate Fawcett is the accountant for Paperie Ltd., a Regina retailer of handmade paper products. Paperie president Carrie Bewly asked Fawcett to prepare a budgeted income statement for 2003. Fawcett's budget follows:

PAPERIE LTD.
Budgeted Income Statement
For the Year Ending July 31, 2003

Sales revenue		$250,000
Costs of goods sold		172,000
Gross margin		78,000
Operating expenses:		
Salary and commission expense	$56,000	
Rent expense	8,000	
Amortization expense	2,000	
Insurance expense	800	
Miscellaneous expenses	12,000	78,800
Operating income		(800)
Interest expense		225
Net Loss		$ (1,025)

Kate Fawcett does not want to give Bewly this budget without making constructive suggestions for steps Paperie could take to improve expected performance. Write a memo to Bewly outlining your suggestions. Your memo should take the following form:

Date:	Today's date
To:	Ms. Carrie Bewly, President
From:	Kate Fawcett
Subject:	Paperie Ltd.'s 2003 budgeted income statement

Beyond the Numbers 23-2   *Responsibility Accounting*   *(Obj. 5, 6)*

Lakota Machine Tool Corp. has not been performing well. Production has fallen to a ten-year low. The company has several skilled machinists who would be diffi-cult to replace if demand picks up. To avoid laying off these skilled workers, three have been temporarily transferred to the Janitorial Services Department. The machinists continue to earn their regular wages of $27 per hour, which were charged to the Janitorial Services Department. Supervisor of janitorial services Jill Carter is dismayed to receive the following performance report:

	Actual Results	Budget	Variance
Wages expense	$10,080	$4,032	$6,048 Unfavourable

Carter confronts the controller, "This unfavourable wage expense variance is not my fault. Lakota Machine Tool laid off my regular workers who earned $9 per hour, and transferred these highly paid machinists into my department. Instead of charging my department $27 per hour for these workers, you should charge us $9."

Who is reponsible for the unfavourable wage expense variance? As the controller, how would you respond to Carter's request?

Ethical Issue

Link Back to Chapter 7, Ethics Guidelines Hotels B.C. Ltd. operates a regional motel chain. Each motel is operated by a manager and an assistant manager/controller. Many of the staff who run the front desk, clean the rooms, and prepare the breakfast buffet work part-time or have a second job, so turnover is high.

An accounting student recently accepted the bookkeeper's position at the local Hotels B.C. Motel. Assistant manager/controller May Johnson asked the new bookkeeper to help prepare the motel's master budget. The master budget is prepared once a year and submitted to company headquarters for approval. Once approved, the master budget is used to evaluate the motel's performance. These performance evaluations affect motel managers' bonuses and they also affect company decisions on which motels deserve extra funds for capital improvements.

When the budget was almost complete, Johnson asked the bookkeeper to increase amounts budgeted for labour and supplies by 20 percent. When asked why, Johnson responded that motel manager John Hetter told her to do this when she began working at the motel. Hetter explained that this budgetary cushion gave him flexibility in running the motel. For example, since company headquarters tightly controls capital improvement funds, Hetter can use the extra money budgeted for labour and supplies to replace broken televisions or pay "bonuses" to keep valued employees. Johnson accepted this explanation because she had observed similar behaviour at the motel where she worked previously.

Put yourself in Johnson's position. Use the ethical judgment decision guidelines in Chapter 7 (page 378) to decide how Johnson should deal with the situation.

Problems (Group A)

Problem 23-1A *Budgeting income for two months* **(Obj. 2)**

Representatives of the various departments of Victoria Athletics Co. Ltd. have assembled the following data. You are the business manager, and you must prepare the budgeted income statements for August and September 2003.

a. Sales in July were $200,000. You forecast that monthly sales will increase 2 percent in August, and 2 percent in September.

b. Victoria tries to maintain inventory of $50,000 plus 30 percent of sales budgeted for the following month. Monthly purchases average 60 percent of sales. Actual inventory on July 31 is $80,000. Sales budgeted for October are $212,000.

c. Monthly salaries amount to $14,000. Sales commissions equal 6 percent of sales. Combine salaries and commissions into a single figure.

d. Other monthly expenses are:

Rent expense.................................	$14,000, paid as incurred
Amortization expense	3,000
Insurance expense.......................	1,000, expiration of prepaid amount
Income tax....................................	25% of operating income

Prepare Victoria Athletics Co. Ltd.'s budgeted income statements for August and September. Show cost of goods sold computations. Round *all* amounts to the nearest $1,000. For example, budgeted August sales are $204,000 ($200,000 × 1.02) and September sales are $208,000 ($204,000 × 1.02).

Problem 23-2A   *Budgeting cash receipts and disbursements*   (Obj. 3)

Refer to Problem 23-1A. Victoria Athletics Co. Ltd.'s sales are 50 percent cash and 50 percent credit. Credit sales are collected in the month after sale. Inventory purchases are paid 60 percent in the month of purchase and 40 percent the following month. Salaries and sales commissions are paid half in the month earned and half the next month. Income tax is paid at the end of the year.

The July 31, 2003, balance sheet showed the following balances:

Cash	$20,000
Accounts payable.......................................	48,000

Required

1. Prepare schedules of (1) budgeted cash collections from customers, (2) budgeted cash payments for purchases, and (3) budgeted cash payments for operating expenses. Show amounts for each month and totals for August and September.

2. Prepare a cash budget in the format of Exhibit 23-13. Assume that no financing activity took place. What is the budgeted cash balance on September 30, 2003?

Problem 23-3A   *Preparing a budgeted balance sheet; sensitivity analysis*   (Obj. 3, 4)

Con-Nix Ltd. has applied for a loan. The Royal Bank has requested a budgeted balance sheet at June 30, 2002, and a budgeted cash flow statement for June. As the controller (chief accounting officer) of Con-Nix, you have assembled the following information:

a. May 31 equipment balance, $60,600; accumulated amortization, $11,700.

b. June capital expenditures of $15,800 budgeted for cash purchase of equipment.

c. June operating expenses, including income tax, total $40,800, 75 percent of which will be paid in cash and the remainder accrued at June 30.

d. June amortization, $500.

e. Cost of goods sold, 45 percent of sales.

f. May 31 shareholders' equity: Common stock, $10,000, and Retained earnings, $95,500.

g. May 31 cash balance, $40,900.

h. June budgeted sales, $90,000, 40 percent of which is for cash. Of the remaining 60 percent, half will be collected in June and half in July.

i. June cash collections on May sales, $16,000.

j. June cash payments of May 31 liabilities, $10,700.

k. May 31 inventory balance, $10,400.

l. June purchases of inventory, $11,000 for cash and $27,400 on credit. Half the credit purchases will be paid in June and half in July.

Required

1. Prepare the budgeted balance sheet of Con-Nix Ltd. at June 30, 2002. Show separate computations for cash, inventory, and retained earnings balances.
2. Prepare the budgeted cash flow statement for June.

Problem 23-4A   *Budgeted balance sheet, sensitivity analysis*   *(Obj. 3, 4)*

Refer to Problem 23-3A. Before granting a loan to Con-Nix Ltd., the Royal Bank asks for a sensitivity analysis assuming that sales are only $70,000 rather than the $90,000 originally budgeted.

Required

1. Prepare a revised budgeted balance sheet for Con-Nix Ltd. showing separate computations for cash, inventory, and retained earnings balances.
2. Suppose Con-Nix has a minimum desired cash balance of $15,000. Will the company borrow cash in June?

Problem 23-5A   *Identifying different types of responsibility centres*   *(Obj. 5)*

Identify each of the following as being most likely a cost centre, a revenue centre, a profit centre, or an investment centre.

a. Ontario sales territory of Empire Company
b. A small clothing boutique
c. Century 21 Real Estate Co.
d. Different product lines of Dorel Industries
e. European subsidiary of Magna International
f. Proposed new office of a public accounting firm
g. Lighting department of The Bay
h. Children's nursery in a church or synagogue
i. Harveys restaurants under the supervision of a regional manager
j. Personnel department of Coca-Cola, Canada
k. Consumer Complaint Division of McCain Foods
l. Service department of a Ford dealership
m. Maritimes region of Pizza Inns, Inc.
n. Payroll department of the University of Prince Edward Island
o. Top management of Future Shop
p. Editorial department of *The National Post*
q. Westjet Airlines
r. Police department of Red Deer
s. Quality-control department of Nortel Networks
t. Job superintendents of a home builder

Problem 23-6A   *Preparing a profit-centre performance report for management by exception; benefits of budgeting*   *(Obj. 1, 6)*

Clear Vision Ltd. is a chain of optical shops. Each store has a manager who reports to a city manager, who in turn reports to a province-wide manager. The actual income statements of Store No. 8, all stores in the Calgary area (including Store No. 8), and all stores in the province of Alberta (including all Calgary stores) are summarized as follows for April, 2002:

	Store No. 8	Calgary	Alberta
Revenues and expenses:			
Sales...	$89,000	$496,000	$3,100,000
Expenses:			
City/province manager office.	$ —	$ 16,000	$ 44,000
Cost of goods sold....................	31,000	171,300	1,205,800
Salary expense	5,000	37,500	409,700
Amortization.............................	3,000	26,100	320,000
Utilities	2,700	19,300	245,600
Rent	2,000	16,400	186,000
Total expenses.............................	43,700	286,600	2,411,100
Operating income	$45,300	$209,400	$ 688,900

Budgeted amounts for April were as follows:

	Store No. 8	Calgary	Alberta
Revenues and expenses:			
Sales...	$92,000	$468,000	$3,043,000
Expenses:			
City/province manager office.	$ —	$ 17,000	$ 43,000
Cost of goods sold....................	32,000	172,800	1,202,000
Salary expense	5,600	37,900	412,000
Amortization..........................	3,500	25,400	320,000
Utilities....................................	2,100	17,000	240,000
Rent	2,000	15,700	181,000
Total expenses...........................	45,200	285,800	2,398,000
Operating income.....................	$46,800	$182,200	$ 645,000

Required

1. Prepare a report for April that shows the performance of Store No. 8, all the stores in the Calgary area, and all the stores in the province of Alberta. Follow the format of Exhibit 23-18.

2. As the city manager of Calgary, would you investigate Store No. 8 on the basis of this report? Why or why not?

3. Briefly discuss the benefits of budgeting. Base your discussion on Clear Vision Ltd.'s performance report.

4. How will what you learned from this problem help you manage a business?

Problem 23-7A *Allocating indirect costs; departmental income statements* **(Obj. 7)**

Insti-Print Ltd. has a Printing Department and a Copy Services Department. At May 31, 2003, the end of Insti-Print's fiscal year, the bookkeeper prepared the adjusted trial balance shown on the next page.

Insti-Print owns its printing equipment and leases a high-speed copier from Xerox. Insti-Print performs print jobs on a credit basis for established customers, but copy services are cash only. The store manager spends 70 percent of her time on Printing Services and 30 percent on Copy Services. The bookkeeper spends approximately two-thirds of his time on accounts receivable and other Printing Department transactions, and the remainder on Copy Services transactions. Insurance expense is evenly divided between the two departments. The company allocates all other expenses based on relative service revenues.

Cash	$2,400	
Accounts receivable	3,600	
Prepaid expenses	1,100	
Building and office furniture	84,900	
Accumulated amortization—building and furniture..		$25,800
Other assets	4,700	
Accounts payable		3,200
Unearned service revenue		2,200
Common stock		5,000
Retained earnings		14,600
Printing service revenue		90,000
Copy service revenue		60,000
Salary expense—machine operators	32,000	
Salary expense—store manager	30,000	
Salary expense—bookkeeper	21,300	
Lease expense—copy equipment	12,000	
Property tax expense	2,800	
Amortization expense—building	1,500	
Amortization expense—printing equipment	2,600	
Insurance expense	1,600	
Bad debt expense	300	
	$200,800	$200,800

Required

1. Prepare departmental income statements.
2. Which department is more profitable? What factor contributes most to the profit differences between the two departments?

Problem 23-8A *Identify the benefits of budgeting; prepare the components of a financial budget* **(Obj. 1, 3)**

The soccer/football boot division of Thunderbirds Company Ltd., a sporting goods retailer, had the following budgeted income statement for November, 2002:

Sales (10,000 units)		$400,000
Cost of goods sold		220,000
Gross margin		180,000
Operating costs:*		
Rent expense	$ 12,000	
Insurance expense	2,400	
Amortization expense	5,000	
Salaries expense	60,000	
Bad debt expense	3,600	
Interest expense on funds borrowed by the division	1,400	
Total operating expenses		84,400
Net operating income		$ 95,600

*Disregard income taxes in this question.

Other information:

1. Actual and budgeted sales were (no change in selling price is expected):
   - September, 2002 .... $240,000
   - October, 2002 .... $320,000
   - December, 2002 .... $480,000
   - January, 2003 .... $400,000

2. Company policy is to always maintain Merchandise Inventory equal to 2,000 units plus 20 percent of the following month's budgeted sales (units).

3. The company expects the following results from sales and collections of accounts receivable:
   - 10 percent of all sales are for cash.
   - All credit sales are on terms of 2/10, n/30.
   - 80 percent of all credit sales are collected in the month of the sale, with 60 percent of these qualifying for the discount.
   - 15 percent of all credit sales are collected in the month after the sale (no discounts).
   - 4 percent of all credit sales are collected two months after the sale.
   - The remainder of credit sales are uncollectible.

4. The following information is available regarding cash payments:
   - The insurance is an annual policy purchased on October 1, 2002.
   - Interest is on a $140,000, 12 percent note payable dated August 16, 2002, with principal and interest due in 3 months from that date.
   - The company had a cash balance of $35,000 on November 1, 2002, and always maintains a minimum cash balance of at least $10,000.
   - All purchases are paid for in the month they are made.

Required

1. Prepare a merchandise purchases budget for November, 2002, to show the total payments for purchases in the month.

2. Prepare a cash budget for the month of November, 2002.

3. How many units would the company have to sell in November in order to maintain its desired cash level?

4. How might the cash budget help managers of the division?

Problems (Group B)

Problem 23-1B   *Budgeting income for two months*   *(Obj. 2)*

The budget committee of Voltex Ltd. has assembled the following data. You are the business manager, and you must prepare the budgeted income statements for May and June 2002.

a. Sales in April were $30,000. You forecast that monthly sales will increase 1.4 percent in both May and June.

b. The company maintains inventory of $8,000 plus 25 percent of sales budgeted for the following month. Monthly purchases average 55 percent of sales. Actual inventory on April 30 is $12,000. Sales budgeted for July are $31,200.

c. Monthly salaries amount to $4,000. Sales commissions equal 5 percent of sales. Combine salaries and commissions into a single figure.

d. Other monthly expenses are:

Rent expense.................................	$2,700, paid as incurred
Amortization expense	500
Insurance expense........................	100, expiration of prepaid amount
Income tax.....................................	20% of operating income

Prepare Voltex's budgeted income statements for May and June. Show cost of goods sold computations. Round *all* amounts to the nearest $100. For example, budgeted May sales are $30,400 ($30,000 × 1.014).

Problem 23-2B   *Budgeting cash receipts and payments*   *(Obj. 3)*

Refer to Problem 23-1B. Voltex's sales are 60 percent cash and 40 percent credit. Credit sales are collected in the month after sale. Inventory purchases are paid 70 percent in the month of purchase and 30 percent the following month. Salaries and sales commissions are paid half in the month earned and half the next month. Income tax is paid at the end of the year.

The April 30, 2002, balance sheet showed the following balances:

Cash	$12,000
Accounts payable.......................................	5,100

Required

1. Prepare schedules of (1) budgeted cash collections from customers, (2) budgeted cash payments for purchases, and (3) budgeted cash payments for operating expenses. Show amounts for each month and totals for May and June.
2. Prepare a cash budget in the format of Exhibit 23-13. If no financing activity took place, what is the budgeted cash balance on June 30, 2002?

Problem 23-3B   *Preparing a budgeted balance sheet and income statement*   *(Obj. 3)*

Chalmers Auto Parts Ltd. has applied for a loan. The Toronto-Dominion Bank has requested a budgeted balance sheet at April 30, 2003. As the controller (chief accounting officer) of Chalmers you have assembled the following information:

a. March 31 equipment balance, $35,200; accumulated amortization, $22,800.
b. April capital expenditures of $44,000 budgeted for cash purchase of equipment.
c. April operating expenses, including income tax, total $13,600, 25 percent of which will be paid in cash and the remainder accrued at April 30.
d. April amortization, $700.
e. Cost of goods sold, 60 percent of sales.
f. March 31 shareholders' equity: Common stock, $10,000, and Retained earnings, $68,900.
g. March 31 cash balance, $26,200.
h. April budgeted sales, $100,000, 60 percent of which is for cash. Of the remaining 40 percent, half will be collected in April and half in May.
i. April cash collections on March sales, $31,200.
j. April cash payments of March 31 liabilities, $19,300.
k. March 31 inventory balance, $28,400.
l. April purchases of inventory, $9,000 for cash and $40,600 on credit. Half of the credit purchases will be paid in April and half in May.

Required

1. Prepare the budgeted balance sheet of Chalmers Auto Parts Ltd. at April 30, 2003. Show separate computations for cash, inventory, and retained earnings balances.
2. Prepare the budgeted cash flow statement for April.

Problem 23-4B   *Budgeted balance sheet; sensitivity analysis*   *(Obj. 3, 4)*

Refer to Problem 23-3B. Before granting a loan to Chalmers Auto Parts Ltd., the Toronto-Dominion Bank asks for a sensitivity analysis assuming that sales are only $80,000 rather than the $100,000 originally budgeted.

Required

1. Prepare a revised budgeted balance sheet for Chalmers Auto Parts Ltd., showing separate computations for cash, inventory, and retained earnings balances.

2. Suppose Chalmers has a minimum desired cash balance of $21,000. Will the company need to borrow cash in April?

3. In this sensitivity analysis, sales declined by 20 percent ($20,000 ÷ $100,000). Is the decline in expenses and income more or less than 20 percent? Explain why.

Problem 23-5B   *Identifying different types of responsibility centres*   *(Obj. 5)*

Identify each of the following as being most likely a cost centre, a revenue centre, a profit centre, or an investment centre.

a. Work crews of a painting contractor
b. The CN Tower in Toronto
c. Accounting department of HMV
d. Canadian subsidiary of Toyota
e. Service department of Steve's TV
f. Eastern district of a salesperson's territory
g. Assembly-line supervisors at Bombardier
h. Accounts payable section of the accounting department of Jean Coutu
i. Surgery unit of a dental clinic
j. Marineland
k. Music director of a church or synagogue
l. Catering operation of a restaurant
m. Executive director of a United Way agency
n. Men's clothing in a The Bay department store
o. Proposed new office of Century 21 Real Estate Co.
p. Personnel department of the city of Dartmouth, Nova Scotia
q. Different product lines of a gift shop
r. Typesetting department of a printing company
s. Investments department of a credit union
t. Branch warehouse of a carpet manufacturer

Problem 23-6B   *Preparing a profit-centre performance report for management by exception; benefits of budgeting*   *(Obj. 1, 6)*

Audio and Video Ltd. is organized with store managers reporting to a province-wide manager, who in turn reports to the vice-president of marketing. The *actual* income statements of the Saskatoon store, all stores in Saskatchewan (including the Saskatoon store), and the company as a whole (including Saskatchewan stores) are summarized as follows for July 2003:

	Saskatoon	Saskatchewan	Companywide
Revenues and expenses:			
Sales...................................	$144,800	$1,647,000	$4,500,000
Expenses:			
Provincial manager/vice-president's office...............	$ —	$ 59,000	$ 116,000
Cost of goods sold.................	59,000	671,900	1,507,000
Salary expense	39,100	415,500	1,019,000
Amortization..........................	7,200	91,000	435,000
Utilities..................................	4,200	46,200	260,000
Rent	2,400	34,700	178,000
Total expenses......................	111,900	1,318,300	3,515,000
Operating income..................	$ 32,900	$ 328,700	$ 985,000

Budgeted amounts for July were as follows:

	Saskatoon	Saskatchewan	Companywide
Revenues and expenses:			
Sales	$151,300	$1,769,700	$4,400,000
Expenses:			
Provincial manager/vice-president's office	$ —	$ 65,600	$ 118,000
Cost of goods sold	61,500	763,400	1,522,000
Salary expense	38,800	442,000	1,095,000
Amortization	7,200	87,800	449,000
Utilities	4,700	54,400	271,000
Rent	2,400	32,300	174,000
Total expenses	114,600	1,445,500	3,629,000
Operating income	$ 36,700	$ 324,200	$ 771,000

Required

1. Prepare a report for July 2003 that shows the performance of the Saskatoon store, all the stores in Saskatchewan, and the company as a whole. Follow the format of Exhibit 23-18.

2. As Saskatchewan manager, would you investigate the Saskatoon store on the basis of this report? Why or why not?

3. Briefly discuss the benefits of budgeting. Base your discussion on Audio and Video's performance report.

Problem 23-7B *Allocating indirect costs; departmental income statements* *(Obj. 7)*

Adanac Travel Ltd. has a Custom Travel Department and a Group Travel Department. At August 31, 2002, the end of Adanac's fiscal year, the bookkeeper prepared the following adjusted trial balance:

Cash	$ 7,800	
Receivables	34,600	
Prepaid expenses	1,700	
Building and office furniture	128,600	
Accumulated amortization—building and furniture		$ 28,200
Other assets	5,300	
Accounts payable		11,400
Accrued liabilities		6,900
Unearned service revenue		5,800
Common stock		5,000
Retained earnings		23,200
Custom travel service revenue		90,000
Group travel service revenue		180,000
Salary expense—travel agents	60,000	
Commission expense—travel agents	36,000	
Salary expense—office manager	30,000	
Salary expense—bookkeeper	16,800	
Computerized reservation system expense	20,000	
Property tax expense	2,200	
Amortization expense—building and furniture	4,600	
Insurance expense	1,700	
Advertising expense	1,200	
	$350,500	$350,500

Last September, Adanac hired a specialist in group travel, at an annual salary of $35,000. Remaining agent salaries of $25,000 are for part-time agents who handle custom travel plans. The office manager spends 70 percent of her time on group travel plans and 30 percent on custom travel planning. The bookkeeper spends approximately two-thirds of his time on accounting for custom travel and the remainder on group travel plans. Adanac uses a computerized reservation system. About 80 percent of the time spent on the system is for custom travel, and the remaining 20 percent is for group travel packages. Insurance expense is evenly divided between the two departments. The company allocates commissions and all other expenses based on relative service revenue.

Required

1. Prepare departmental income statements.
2. Which department is more profitable? Was the decision to hire the group specialist wise? Give your reason.

Problem 23-8B   *Identify the benefits of budgeting; prepare the components of a financial budget*   **(Obj. 1, 3)**

Bill Gardhouse Ltd., a men's shirt importer and retailer, had the following budgeted income statement for December, 2002:

Sales (40,000 units)		$600,000
Cost of goods sold		360,000
Gross margin		240,000
Operating costs:		
Rent expense	$18,000	
Insurance expense	5,200	
Amortization expense	12,000	
Salaries expense	45,000	
Bad debt expense	5,600	
Interest expense	1,200	
Total operating expenses		87,000
Net operating income		153,000
Income taxes (40%)		61,200
Net income after taxes		$ 91,800

Other information:

1. Actual and budgeted sales were (no change in selling price is expected):
   - October, 2002 .... $450,000
   - November, 2002 .... $525,000
   - January, 2003 .... $660,000
   - February, 2003 .... $500,000

2. Bill Gardhouse Ltd.'s policy is to always maintain Merchandise Inventory equal to 5,000 units plus 25 percent of the following month's budgeted sales (units).

3. Bill Gardhouse Ltd. expects the following results from sales and collections of accounts receivable:
   - 10 percent of all sales are for cash.
   - All credit sales are on terms of 2/10, n/30.
   - 80 percent of all credit sales are collected in the month of the sale, with 70 percent of these qualifying for the discount.
   - 12 percent of all credit sales are collected in the month after the sale (no discounts).
   - 7 percent of all credit sales are collected two months after the sale.
   - The remainder of credit sales are uncollectible.

4. The following information is available regarding cash payments:
   - The insurance is an annual policy purchased on November 1, 2002.

- The salaries payable account is expected to decrease by $4,000 in the month of December, 2002.
- Interest is on a $120,000, 12 percent note payable dated August 16, 2002, with principal and interest due in 4 months from that date.
- The company had a cash balance of $20,000 on November 30, 2002, and always maintains a minimum cash balance of at least $20,000.
- All purchases are paid for in the month they are made.
- Dividends of $50,000 were declared on October 15, 2002, and were payable on December 15, 2002.

Required

1. Prepare a merchandise purchases budget for December, 2002, to show the total payments for purchases in the month.
2. Prepare a cash budget for the month of December, 2002.
3. How many units would Bill Gardhouse Ltd. have to sell in November in order to maintain its desired cash level?
4. How might the cash budget help management?

Challenge Problems

Problem 23-1C *Identifying the benefits of budgeting* *(Obj. 1)*

The text explains why budgets are beneficial to management and lists four specific benefits that accrue from the budgeting process. However, only some organizations such as not-for-profit organizations (for example, hospitals) provide budgets in their annual report.

Required

1. Explain why you think external users of financial statements would find budget information to be useful in their assessment of an organization's activities.
2. Select an organization, such as a company or not-for-profit organization, and explain how budget information would be helpful specifically to the users of financial statements provided by that organization.

Problem 23-2C *Understanding responsibility accounting* *(Obj. 5)*

Organizational theory states that an employee who is held responsible for an activity must have the requisite authority over the activity.

Required

Explain how the principle stated above applies in the case of responsibility accounting.

Extending Your Knowledge

Decision Problems

1. Projecting cash flows and financial statements to analyze alternatives (Obj. 2, 3)

Chantal Le Doux is a librarian in a Regina library. Each autumn, as a hobby, she weaves cotton placemats for sale through a local craft shop. The mats sell for $25 per set of four. The shop charges 10-percent commission and remits the net proceeds to

Le Doux at the end of December. Le Doux has woven and sold 25 sets each of the last two years. She has enough cotton in inventory to make another 25 sets. She paid $11 per set for the cotton. Le Doux uses a four-harness loom that she purchased for cash exactly two years ago (August 31, 2000). It is amortized at the rate of $10 per month.

Le Doux is considering buying an eight-harness loom immediately so that she can weave more intricate patterns in linen. The new loom costs $1,000; it would be amortized at $20 per month. Her bank has agreed to lend her $1,000 at 12-percent interest, with $200 principal plus accrued interest payable each December 31. Le Doux believes that she can weave 15 linen placemat sets in time for the Christmas rush if she does not weave any cotton mats. She predicts that each linen set will sell for $60. Linen costs $25 per set. Le Doux's supplier will sell her linen on credit, payable December 31.

Le Doux plans to keep her old loom whether or not she buys the new loom. The balance sheet for her weaving business at August 31, 2002, is as follows:

Chantal Le Doux, Weaver
Balance Sheet
August 31, 2002

Current assets:		Current liabilities:	
Cash	$ 65		
Inventory of cotton	275	Accounts payable	$ 74
	340		74
Capital assets:			
Loom	500	Owner's equity	526
Accumulated amortization	(240)		
	260	Total liabilities	
Total assets	$600	and owner's equity	$600

Required

1. Prepare a cash budget for the four months ending December 31, 2002, for two alternatives: weaving the placemats in cotton and weaving the placemats in linen. For each alternative, prepare a budgeted income statement for the four months ending December 31, 2002, and a budgeted balance sheet at December 31, 2002. Round all numbers to the nearest dollar.

2. On the basis of financial considerations only, what should Le Doux do? Give your reason.

3. What nonfinancial factors might Le Doux consider in her decision?

2. Allocating indirect costs (Obj. 7)

Extreme Sports Ltd. designs, manufactures, and sells wakeboards through watersports specialty stores and sports superstores. In 2003, Extreme incurred the following costs that are directly traceable to its Airadical product line:

Production—Moulding (direct materials and direct labour)	$338,000
Production—Graphics (direct materials and direct labour)	430,000
Advertising for Airadical	150,000

In addition to these direct costs, Extreme also incurred other costs that cannot be traced directly to individual product lines. These indirect costs are allocated to the different product lines. For 2003, Extreme reports the information on the next page about its indirect costs.

During 2003, the whole Airadical product line required a total of one new product design, 1,000 machine hours, 3,500 labour hours, and 140 shipments. There were no beginning inventories of any kind.

	Total Indirect Costs	Allocation Base for Indirect Costs	Total Quantity of Allocation Base
Product design	$ 240,000	New designs	4 new designs
Production—Moulding	1,200,000	Machine hours	4,000 machine hours
Production—Graphics	1,800,000	Labour hours	18,000 labour hours
Distribution	400,000	Shipments	1,000 shipments

Required

1. Compute an indirect cost allocation rate for each of the four indirect costs.
2. Use the indirect cost allocation rates from requirement 1 to compute the *total costs* for the Airadical wakeboard product line, including all direct and indirect costs. Assuming Extreme Sports Ltd. produced 7,000 Airadical wakeboards, what is the total cost per wakeboard?
3. At the end of 2003, Extreme's ending inventory consists solely of 500 Airadical wakeboards. What inventory value would appear on Extreme's December 31, 2003 balance sheet?
4. A snow ski manufacturer has asked Extreme to produce snowboards, which the ski manufacturer would sell under its own name. Suppose Extreme decides to produce the snowboards for the snow ski manufacturer on a cost-plus-fixed-fee basis. (That is, the sale price is Extreme's cost to make the snowboards plus a fixed fee of $50,000.) The rest of Extreme's business is at fixed sales prices—for example, $300 for Airadical wakeboards. What cost allocation incentives would this give Extreme's managers? When there are difficult allocation decisions, will Extreme Sports be tempted to allocate a bigger or smaller share of indirect costs to the snowboards? Why?
5. Extreme's top management knows that the sale price of Airadical wakeboards may change over the product's life. But management wishes to identify a target sale price they should receive on average, over the life of the product. Which of Extreme Sports' costs are relevant in setting the long-run average sale price for Airadical wakeboards? Give your reason.

Flexible Budgets and Standard Costs

CHAPTER OBJECTIVES

After studying this chapter, you should be able to

1 Prepare a flexible budget for the income statement

2 Prepare an income statement performance report

3 Identify the benefits of standard costs

4 Compute standard cost variances for direct materials and direct labour

5 Analyze manufacturing overhead in a standard cost system

6 Record transactions at standard cost

7 Prepare a standard cost income statement for management

How does McDonald's ensure that its 26,000 restaurants deliver quality, service, cleanliness, and value to 43 million customers worldwide daily? How do McDonald's managers use management accounting to earn a profit?

The answers are budgets, standards, and variances. McDonald's managers budget sales for each hour. The manager schedules just enough workers to handle the budgeted level of sales. During the day, the manager computes variances for sales (for example, actual sales minus budgeted sales) and for direct labour. These variances are computed *hourly*. If actual sales fall short of the budget, the manager quickly sees an unfavourable sales variance. If sales are less than budgeted, the manager can send employees home early. This helps control direct labour cost.

McDonald's also sets budgets and standards for direct materials. From Beijing to Winnipeg, the standards for a regular McDonald's hamburger are the same: 1 bun, 1 hamburger patty, 1 pickle slice, 1 mL (1/8 teaspoon) dehydrated onion, 1 mL (1/8 teaspoon) mustard and 10 mL (1/3 ounce) of ketchup. To control direct material costs, the manager compares the number of, say, hamburger patties actually used with the number of patties that should have been used.

McDonald's uses budgets, standards, and variances to control costs so prices remain low enough that customers believe McDonald's provides good *value*. McDonald's also uses standards and variances to motivate employees to focus on *quality*, *service*, and *cleanliness*:

- Quality—sandwiches unsold within 10 minutes are thrown away.
- Service—customers should receive food within 90 seconds of placing an order.
- Cleanliness—visiting inspectors score restaurants on cleanliness.

IN CHAPTER 23 we saw how managers quantify their plans.

Executives compare actual revenues and expenses with budgeted amounts in order to evaluate the performance of responsibility centres and managers. This chapter explores budgeting in greater depth. The first half of the chapter shows how flexible budgets and variances help managers learn *why* actual results differed from planned performance. The second half of the chapter discusses standard costs, which companies like McDonald's use to build flexible budgets.

McDonald's
www.mcdonalds.com

OBJECTIVE 1
Prepare a flexible budget for the income statement

Static versus Flexible Budgets

The **master budget** in Chapter 23 is a **static budget**—it is prepared for only one level of volume. The static budget does not change after it is developed, regardless of changes in volume, sale prices, or costs.

Consider Kool-Time Pools Ltd., a company that makes residential swimming pools. Kool-Time buys direct materials—gunite (a concrete derivative). It then uses labour and equipment to convert the gunite into finished outputs—installed pools. Kool-time's static master budget forecasts that the company will install eight pools in June. However, due to an early heat wave, Kool-time actually installed ten pools.

The comparison of June's actual results with the static budget in Exhibit 24-1 shows that Kool-Time's actual operating income is $3,000 higher than originally expected. This is a $3,000 favourable difference, or variance, in Kool-Time's June operating income. A **variance** is the difference between an actual amount and the corresponding budgeted amount. The variances in the third column of Exhibit 24-1 are favourable (F) if a higher actual amount increases operating income, and

EXHIBIT 24-1

Actual Results versus Static Budget

KOOL-TIME POOLS LTD.
Comparison of Actual Results with Static Budget
For the Month Ended June 30, 2002

	Actual Results	Static Budget	Variance	
Output units (pools installed)	10	8	2	F
Sales revenue	$120,000	$96,000	$24,000	F
Expenses	(105,000)	(84,000)	21,000	U
Operating income	$ 15,000	$12,000	$ 3,000	F

unfavourable (U) if a higher actual amount decreases operating income. The variance for the number of pools installed is favourable because higher volume (ten rather than eight pools) tends to increase income.

The report in Exhibit 24-1 is hard to analyze because the static budget is based on eight pools, but actual results are for ten pools. Why did the $21,000 unfavourable expense variance occur? Did workers waste materials? Did the cost of gunite suddenly increase? How much of the additional expense arose because Kool-Time built ten rather than eight pools? Exhibit 24-1's simple comparison of actual results with the static budget does not give managers enough information to answer these questions.

Flexible budgets help managers to answer such questions. Exhibit 24-2 illustrates the difference between static and flexible budgets. A static master budget—like the Whitewater Sporting Goods Ltd. store budget developed in Chapter 23—is computed for a single level of sales volume. In contrast, **flexible budgets** are summarized budgets that can easily be computed for several different volume levels.

Exhibit 24-3 uses flexible budgets to show how Kool-Time's revenues and expenses should vary as sales increase from five pools to eight pools to eleven pools. The budgeted sale price per pool is $12,000. The condensed flexible budget shows two costs or expenses: variable and fixed. The *flexible budget formula for total cost* is:

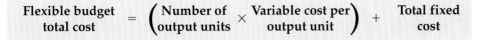

$$\text{Flexible budget total cost} = \left(\text{Number of output units} \times \text{Variable cost per output unit} \right) + \text{Total fixed cost}$$

Budgeted total variable costs (such as the cost of gunite and labour) increase at the rate of $8,000 per pool installed. It is these variable costs that put the "flex" in the flexible budget, because budgeted total monthly fixed costs (such as administrative salaries and amortization of equipment) remain constant at $20,000 throughout the range of five to eleven pools. For example, Kool-time's flexible budget cost for installing 11 pools is $108,000:

$$
\begin{aligned}
\text{Flexible budget total cost} &= \left(\text{Number of output units} \times \text{Variable cost per output unit} \right) + \text{Total fixed cost} \\
&= (11 \text{ pools} \times \$8,000 \text{ per pool}) + \$20,000 \\
&= \$88,000 + \$20,000 \\
&= \$108,000
\end{aligned}
$$

Kool-Time's managers could prepare a more detailed flexible budget that lists individual variable and fixed costs separately. Each of the variable costs would behave like the total variable costs in Exhibit 24-3 (increase with the number of pools installed), and each of the fixed costs would behave like the total fixed costs (remain constant over the relevant range).

Managers develop flexible budgets like that in Exhibit 24-3 for any number of out-

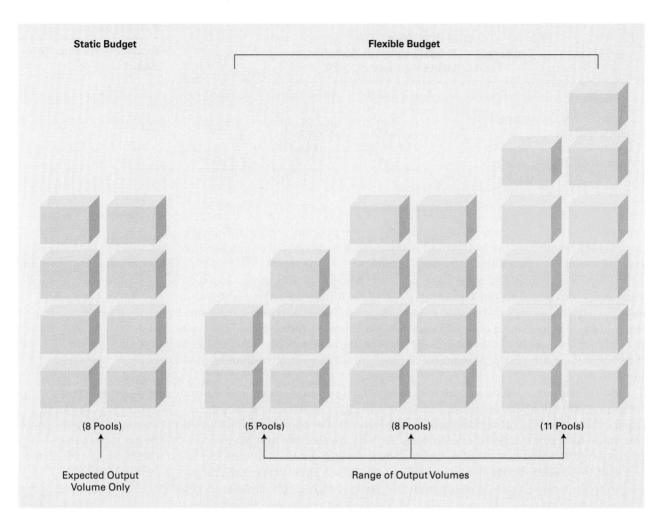

Static Budget

Flexible Budget

(8 Pools)

(5 Pools) (8 Pools) (11 Pools)

Expected Output
Volume Only

Range of Output Volumes

EXHIBIT 24-2

**Static versus Flexible
Budgets**

puts, using a simple spreadsheet or more sophisticated Web-based budget management software. Kool-Time's flexible budget could include additional columns for seven, nine, or any other number of pools for which management wants to know budgeted sales revenues, costs, and profits.

However, managers must be wary: *The flexible budget total cost formula applies only to a specific relevant range.* Why? Because total monthly fixed costs and the variable cost per pool change outside this range. Kool-Time's relevant range is 0–11 pools. If the company installs 12 pools, it will have to rent additional equipment, so fixed costs will exceed $20,000. Kool-Time will also have to pay workers an overtime premium, so the variable cost per pool will be more than $8,000.

Managers prepare flexible budgets like those in Exhibit 24-3

- *Before* the period, or
- At the *end* of the period

Flexible budgets prepared *before* the period help managers *plan*. They can estimate revenues, costs, and profits, and plan for alternative levels of sales. Flexible budgets prepared at the *end* of the period help managers *control* operations. They can compare actual costs to the costs that *should have been* incurred for that level of output. For example, Kool-time can compare the actual costs to install 10 pools with the budgeted costs (the costs that should have been incurred) to install 10 pools. Managers use flexible budget graphs to budget total costs at various output levels for both planning and control.

EXHIBIT 24-3

Flexible Budget

KOOL-TIME POOLS LTD.
Flexible Budget
For the Month Ended June 30, 2002

	Flexible Budget Formula per Unit	Level of Volume		
		5	8	11
Units		5	8	11
Sales..	$12,000	$60,000	$96,000	$132,000
Variable expenses	8,000	40,000	64,000	88,000
Fixed expenses*		20,000	20,000	20,000
Total expenses		60,000	84,000	108,000
Operating income.................		$ 0	$12,000	$ 24,000

* Fixed expenses are given as a total amount rather than as a cost per unit.

WORKING IT OUT

A company's master budget was prepared for a volume of 50,000 units per month. The actual volume for May was 48,500 units. In the master budget, variable expenses and fixed overhead were budgeted at $50,000 and $15,000, respectively. What amounts should appear in May's flexible budget for variable expenses and fixed overhead?

A: Variable expenses: $48,500 [($50,000/50,000) × 48,500]; fixed overhead: $15,000.

Graphing the Flexible Budget

Exhibit 24-4 shows budgeted total costs for the entire relevant range of 0 to 11 pools. The flexible budget total cost line in Exhibit 24-4 intersects the vertical axis at the amount of the total fixed cost ($20,000) Kool-Time will incur whether it installs 0 or 11 pools. The flexible budget's total cost line slopes upward at the rate of $8,000 per pool, which is Kool-Time's variable cost per pool. For example, the cost for one pool is $28,000 [(1 pool × $8,000 variable cost per pool) + $20,000 fixed cost]. But the *extra* cost of installing a second pool is only the additional $8,000 variable cost. The cost to install two pools is therefore $36,000 [(2 pools × $8,000 variable cost per pool) + $20,000 fixed cost].

Kool-Time's managers initially expected to install eight pools per month ($84,000). The graph also shows the flexible budget costs for 5 pools ($60,000) and 11 pools

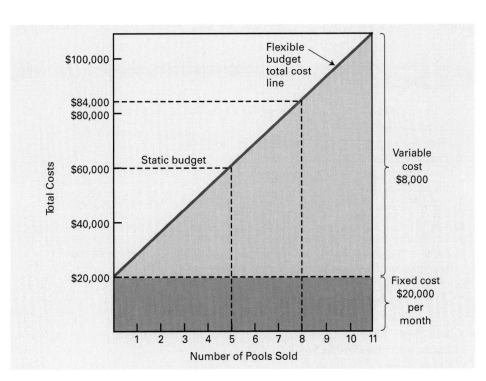

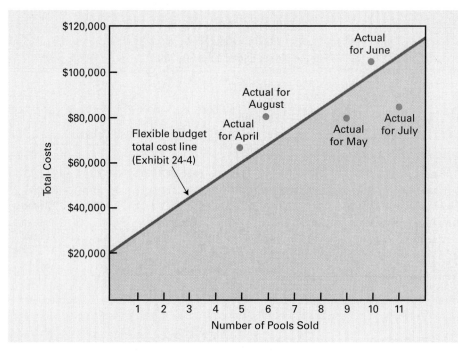

($108,000). Managers can use the flexible budget graph in Exhibit 24-4 to plan costs for anywhere from zero to 11 pools.

At the end of the period, managers can also use the flexible budget to help control costs. They plot actual costs on the graph, as shown in Exhibit 24-5. Consider the month of June, when Kool-Time actually installed ten pools. The flexible budget graphs in Exhibit 24-4 and 24-5 show the *budgeted* total costs for ten pools are

Variable costs (10 × $8,000)....................	$ 80,000
Fixed costs	20,000
Total costs	$100,000

June's *actual* costs, or expenses, were $105,000 (Exhibit 24-1). Consequently, Exhibit 24-5 shows that June's actual costs for ten pools ($105,000) exceed the bud-

---

STOP & THINK

Use the graph in Exhibit 24-5 and Kool-Time's flexible budget formula (page 1325) to answer the following questions:

1. How many pools did Kool-Time install in July?
2. What were Kool-Time's actual costs in July?
3. Using Kool-Time's flexible budget formula, what is the flexible budget total cost for the month of July?
4. Is Kool-Time's variance for total costs favourable or unfavourable in July?

Answers:
1. Exhibit 24-5 shows that Kool-Time installed 11 pools in July.
2. Exhibit 24-5 shows that Kool-Time's actual costs in July were about $80,000.
3. Using Kool-Time's flexible budget total cost formula:

Variable costs (11 × $8,000)............................	$ 88,000
Fixed costs	20,000
Total costs	$108,000

4. Kool-Time's July variance for total costs is $28,000 ($80,000 − $108,000) favourable, since actual costs are less than the budget.

---

get for ten pools ($100,000). Managers use graphs of actual versus budgeted costs to see at a glance whether actual costs are

- Higher than budgeted for the actual level of output, as in April, June, and August, or
- Lower than budgeted for the actual level of output, as in May and July

The Flexible Budget and Variance Analysis

OBJECTIVE 2
Prepare an income statement performance report

Managers also use flexible budgets at the *end* of the period to help explain why actual results differ from budgeted results. Let's step back for a moment and consider managers' planning and controlling activities:

1. Quantify the company's goals in a static master budget.
2. Take actions to achieve the goals.
3. Analyze the variance between actual results and static budget amounts (the static budget variance).
4. Change actions (or plans) so that future results conform to the plan.

The flexible budget is an important tool in step 3. To analyze the variance (step 3), managers begin by asking

- How many units did we actually sell?
- How much sales revenue *should* we have received from selling this number of outputs?
- How much *should* this number of output units have cost us?

The *flexible budget for the number of units that were actually sold* helps answer the second question. Of course, the number of units actually sold is not known until the end of the period. Why calculate a budget for a period that is already over? Because *the flexible budget for the number of units actually sold shows how much the company should have spent to obtain that level of output.* Exhibit 24–6 shows how managers use this

LEARNING **TIP**

A sales volume variance is the difference between a flexible budget amount and a static budget amount; it is caused by a difference between the predetermined static budget volume and the actual volume. A flexible budget variance is the difference between a flexible budget amount and the actual result—that is, the difference between what the results should have been and what the results actually are.

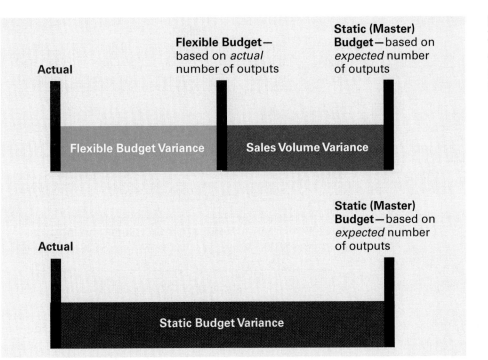

EXHIBIT 24-6

The Static Budget Variance, the Sales Volume Variance, and the Flexible Budget Variance

flexible budget for the number of units actually sold to divide the static budget variance into two broad categories:

- **Sales volume variance**—arises only because the number of units actually sold differs from the static budget sales.
- **Flexible budget variance**—arises because the company actually earned more or less revenue, or incurred more or less cost, than expected at the actual level of output.

Exhibit 24-6 shows that the sales volume variance is the difference between

1. the *static* (master) budget—for the number of units *expected* to be sold (8 pools, for Kool-Time Pools Ltd.), and
2. the *flexible* budget—for the number of units *actually* sold (10 pools in June).

Consider Kool-Time Pools Ltd.'s performance report in Exhibit 24-7. The static budget amounts in column 5 are based on the static budget sales forecast developed at the *beginning* of the period—the eight pools Kool-Time Pools Ltd. *expected* to install. For these eight pools, Kool-Time Pools Ltd.'s

- Budgeted sales revenue is $96,000 (8 × $12,000).
- Budgeted variable expenses (costs) are $64,000 (8 × $8,000).
- Budgeted fixed expenses (costs) are $20,000.

In contrast to the static budget, which is developed *before* the period, the flexible budget used in the performance report is not developed until the *end* of the period. Why? Because *flexible budgets used in performance reports are based on the actual number of outputs, which is not known until the end of the period.* For Kool-Time Pools Ltd.,

LEARNING TIP

Refer to Exhibit 24-7. Actual Results (column 1) comes from the June 30, 2002, income statement. Flexible Budget for Actual Volume (column 3) is prepared based on the volume shown in column 1. Static Budget (column 5) was prepared before the period began. Determining the variances (columns 2 and 4) is the final step in preparing the performance report.

EXHIBIT 24-7

Income Statement Performance Report

KOOL-TIME POOLS LTD.
Income Statement Performance Report
For the Month Ended June 30, 2002

	(1) Actual Results at Actual Prices	(2) (1) – (3) Flexible Budget Variance	(3) Flexible Budget for Actual Number of Output Units*	(4) (3) – (5) Sales Volume Variance	(5) Static (Master) Budget*
Output units (pools installed)	10	–0–	10	2 F	8
Sales revenue	$120,000	$ –0–	$120,000	$24,000 F	$96,000
Variable expenses	83,000	3,000 U	80,000	16,000 U	64,000
Fixed expenses	22,000	2,000 U	20,000	–0–	20,000
Total expenses	105,000	5,000 U	100,000	16,000 U	84,000
Operating income	$ 15,000	$ 5,000 U	$ 20,000	$ 8,000 F	$12,000

Flexible budget variance, $5,000 U   Sales volume variance, $8,000 F

Static budget variance, $3,000 F

*Budgeted sales price is $12,000 per pool, budgeted variable expense is $8,000 per pool, and budgeted total monthly fixed expenses are $20,000.

the flexible budget used in the performance report (column 3 of Exhibit 24-7) is based on the 10 pools actually installed. For these 10 pools actually installed, Kool-Time Pools Ltd.'s

- Budgeted sales revenue is $120,000 (10 × $12,000).
- Budgeted variable expenses are $80,000 (10 × $8,000).
- Budgeted fixed expenses are $20,000.

The only difference between the static budget and the flexible budget used in the performance report is the number of outputs on which the budget is based (eight pools versus ten pools in the Kool-Time Pools Ltd. example). Both budgets use the same

- Budgeted sale price per unit ($12,000 per pool)
- Budgeted variable cost per unit ($8,000 per pool)
- Budgeted total fixed costs ($20,000 per month)

Holding selling price per unit, variable cost per unit, and total fixed costs constant at their budgeted amounts highlights the effects of differences in sales volume—the variance in column 4. This variance captures the effects of differences in the number of units sold, which is typically the responsibility of the marketing staff. Exhibit 24-7 shows that by installing two more pools than initially expected, Kool-Time Pools Ltd.'s

- Sales revenue should increase from $96,000 (8 × $12,000) to $120,000 (10 × $12,000)—a $24,000 favourable sales volume variance.
- Variable costs should increase from $64,000 (8 × $8,000) to $80,000 (10 × $8,000)—a $16,000 unfavourable sales volume variance.

Budgeted total fixed expenses are unaffected because eight pools and ten pools are within the relevant range where fixed expenses total $20,000 (0–11 pools). Consequently, installing two more pools should increase operating income by $8,000 ($24,000 F − $16,000 U).

STOP & THINK

When is there a sales volume variance for fixed expenses?

Answer: Only when the number of units actually sold falls within a different relevant range than the static budget sales volume. When actual and expected number of units sold fall within the same relevant range, there is no sales volume variance for fixed expenses.

Exhibits 24-6 and 24–7 show that the second piece of the static budget variance is the flexible budget variance—the difference between

- Actual amounts (column 1 in Exhibit 24-7) and
- Flexible budget amounts that should have been incurred *for the actual number of output units* (column 3 in Exhibit 24-7)

Kool-Time Pools Ltd. actually incurred $83,000 of variable costs to install the ten pools. This is $3,000 more than the $80,000 (10 pools × $8,000 per pool) budgeted variable cost for ten pools. The company also spent $2,000 more than budgeted on fixed expenses ($22,000 – $20,000). Consequently, the flexible budget variance for total expenses is $5,000 unfavourable ($3,000 U + $2,000 U). The $5,000 unfavourable flexible budget variance offsets much of the $8,000 favourable sales volume variance, resulting in a $3,000 favourable static budget variance (Exhibits 24-1 and 24-7).

We have now shown why simply comparing the static budget with actual results (like Exhibit 24-1) does not explain much. This is because the *actual* number of units sold may differ from the *expected* sales used to prepare the static budget. The flexible budget provides part of the information managers need to understand why actual revenues, expenses, and income differ from the budget.

Exhibit 24-7 shows how the flexible budget splits the static budget variance into the sales volume variance and the flexible budget variance. How would Kool-Time's managers use the information in these variances? Variance information can help managers decide which business operations deserve praise or need improvement. The favourable sales volume variance reveals that strong sales caused actual income to exceed the budget by $8,000. Kool-Time's managers may therefore reward their sales staff. On the other hand, the performance report in Exhibit 24-7 shows a $5,000 unfavourable flexible budget variance for expenses. Management will want to find out why expenses were too high.

Kool-Time's higher-than-expected expenses might have resulted from an uncontrollable increase in the cost of gunite. Or higher costs might have resulted from more controllable factors such as employees wasting materials or working inefficiently. If so, managers can take action to reduce waste or inefficiency. The second half of this chapter explains how Kool-Time Pools Ltd.'s managers can further analyze flexible budget variances to identify the reason for the cost overrun.

Volvo
www.volvo.com

Before proceeding, take some time to test your understanding of the flexible budget, static budget, and variances by reviewing the Decision Guidelines and then completing the mid-chapter review problem.

Decision	Guidelines
How to estimate sales revenues, costs, and profits over the range of likely output levels?	Prepare a set of flexible budgets for different output levels.
How to prepare a flexible budget for total costs?	$$\text{Flexible budget total cost} = \left(\begin{array}{c}\text{Number of output units}\end{array} \times \begin{array}{c}\text{Variable cost per output units}\end{array}\right) + \begin{array}{c}\text{Fixed cost}\end{array}$$
How to use budgets to help control costs?	• Graph actual costs versus flexible budget costs, as in Exhibit 24-5. • Prepare an income statement performance report, as in Exhibit 24-7.
On which output level is the budget based?	Static (master) budget—*expected* number of outputs, estimated before the period Flexible budget (made at the end of the period)—*actual* number of outputs, not known until the end of the period
Why does actual income differ from budgeted income?	Prepare income statement performance report comparing actual results, flexible budget for actual number of outputs, and static (master) budget.

How much of the difference occurs because the actual number of output units sold does not equal budgeted sales?	Compute the sales volume variance (SVV) by comparing the flexible budget with the static budget.
	• Favourable SVV—Income effect if
	  Flexible budget sales revenue > Static budget sales revenue
	  Flexible budget expenses < Static budget expenses
	• Unfavourable SVV—Income effect if
	  Flexible budget sales revenue < Static budget sales revenue
	  Flexible budget expenses > Static budget expenses

How much of the difference occurs because actual revenues and costs are not what they should have been for the actual number of outputs?	Compute the flexible budget variance (FBV) by comparing actual results with the flexible budget.
	• Favourable FBV—Income effect if
	  Actual sales revenue > Flexible budget sales revenue
	  Actual expenses < Flexible budget expenses
	• Unfavourable FBV—Income effect if
	  Actual sales revenue < Flexible budget sales revenue
	  Actual expenses > Flexible budget expenses

Mid-Chapter Summary Problem
for Your Review

Exhibit 24-7 indicates that Kool-Time Pools Ltd. sold and installed ten swimming pools during June. Suppose that June sales were seven pools instead of ten and that the actual sales price of the pools averaged $12,500 instead of $12,000. Actual variable expenses were $57,400, and actual fixed expenses were $19,000.

Required

1. Prepare a revised income statement performance report using Exhibit 24-7 as a guide.
2. Show that the sum of the flexible budget variance and the sales volume variance for operating income equals the static budget variance for operating income.
3. As the company owner, what specific employees would you praise or criticize after you analyze this performance report?

Solution to Review Problem

Requirements 1 and 2

KOOL-TIME POOLS LTD.
Income Statement Performance Report—Revised
For the Month Ended June 30, 2002

	(1) Actual Results at Actual Prices	(2) (1) – (3) Flexible Budget Variances	(3) Flexible Budget for Actual Volume Achieved	(4) (3) – (5) Sales Volume Variances	(5) Static (Master) Budget
Units	7	–0–	7	1 U	8
Sales...............................	$87,500	$3,500 F	$84,000	$12,000 U	$96,000
Variable expenses	57,400	1,400 U	56,000	8,000 F	64,000
Fixed expenses.............	19,000	1,000 F	20,000	—	20,000
Total expenses..............	76,400	400 U	76,000	8,000 F	84,000
Operating income........	$11,100	$3,100 F	$ 8,000	$ 4,000 U	$12,000

Flexible budget variance, $3,100 F

Sales volume variance, $4,000 U

Static budget variance, $900 U

Requirement 3

As the company owner, you should determine the *causes* of the variances before deciding who deserves praise or criticism. It is especially important to determine who is responsible for the variance and whether the variance is due to factors the manager can control. For example, the unfavourable sales volume variance could be due to an ineffective sales staff. On the other hand, it could also be due to an uncontrollable long period of heavy rain that brought work to a standstill. Similarly, the $1,000 favourable flexible budget variance for fixed expenses could be due to an employee finding a lower-cost source of rented equipment. Or the savings may have come from delaying a needed overhaul of equipment that could increase the company's costs in the long run. The key point is that smart managers use variances to raise questions and direct attention, not to fix blame.

Standard Costing

KEY POINT

A standard cost is a cost that should be incurred under normal conditions to produce a specific product. A standard is determined by examining past experience and incorporating anticipated changes. Usually two standards are set—a price standard and a quantity standard.

Many companies—especially those that routinely produce similar or identical products—use standard costs for budgeting and control. A **standard cost** is a carefully predetermined cost that usually is expressed on a per-unit basis. In contrast, the term *budgeted cost* usually refers to a total amount. To budget a variable cost, accountants multiply a number of output units by a standard or budgeted cost per unit. Continuing our Kool-Time Pools Ltd. example, the $8,000 budgeted variable cost of an installed pool is made up of *inputs*, including direct materials, direct labour, and variable overhead costs. Suppose the variable expenses in Exhibit 24-3 include direct materials costs as follows:

	Flexible Budget Formula per Unit (Standard Cost)	Output Units (Pools Installed)		
		5	8	11
Direct materials	$2,000	$10,000	$16,000	$22,000

The standard cost of direct materials is $2,000 *per pool*. Budgeted cost is the expected total cost of all pools sold during the month. As volume increases from five to eleven pools, the budgeted direct materials cost increases from $10,000 to $22,000. But the standard direct materials cost is $2,000 per pool at all three flexible budget output levels. Think of a standard cost as *a budget for a single unit of output*.

In a standard cost system, each input has both a quantity standard and a price standard. McDonald's has a standard for the amount of beef per hamburger and for the price paid per kilogram of beef. Likewise, Kool-Time Pools Ltd. has a standard for the cubic metres of gunite per pool and for the price per cubic metre of gunite.

Setting Standards

Accountants help managers set price standards. For direct labour, they take into account payroll costs and benefits as well as hourly wage rates. And for overhead, accountants help identify the overhead application bases and then compute the overhead application rates.

In setting direct materials price standards, accountants consider early-payment discounts, freight-in, and receiving costs, in addition to the base purchase price. World-class businesses set continuous improvement standards for direct material prices. Companies work with suppliers to cut direct material costs. For example, Toyota sent its own engineers to one of its bumper suppliers' factories to help the supplier cut costs. Toyota expected the supplier to pass on much of the savings in lower prices for the bumpers. E-commerce also helps managers to continuously improve direct material price standards. Purchasing managers use the Internet to solicit price quotes from suppliers throughout the world. Major Canadian automakers are collaborating on an electronic market linking the automakers with their suppliers. The automakers expect price reductions from suppliers not only on their own purchases, but also on purchases the suppliers make from each other through the electronic marketplace. Automakers expect these efforts to reduce costs throughout the supply chain to yield substantially lower direct material price standards.

Engineers and production managers usually set direct material and direct labour quantity standards, often following the continuous improvement philosophy. For example, groups of managers and workers in Westinghouse Air Brake's Chicago factory analyzed every moment in the production of brakes. The goal was to: (1) eliminate unnecessary work, (2) reduce the time and effort required for necessary work, and (3) set a time standard for the work. To eliminate unnecessary work, the company rearranged machines in tight U-shaped cells so production wasn't spread over a vast expanse of the factory floor. Workers no longer had to move parts all over the factory. The team conducted time-and-motion studies to streamline and reduce the physical demands of the various tasks. For example, the factory installed a conveyor at waist height to minimize bending and lifting. The result? By 2000, workers had slashed the standard time to produce the slack adjustor component by 90%.

STOP & THINK

General Motors had cut average labour time per vehicle to 45.6 hours by 2000. But this is much higher than Toyota's average of 30.4 labour hours per vehicle. If General Motors workers earn an average of $45 per hour, how much cost does this extra labour add to each General Motors car?

Answer: $684. On average, General Motors workers put in an extra 15.2 hours (45.6 − 30.4) per car at an average rate of $45 per hour.

Many companies set currently attainable standards that allow for normal amounts of waste and spoilage. These standards represent very good performance that can be achieved, but with difficulty. However, more and more companies, such as Schneiders and McNeil Consumer Products, a division of Johnson & Johnson, are using standards based on the "best practice" level of performance. This is often called **benchmarking.**

Best practice may be an internal benchmark or an external benchmark from other companies. Internal benchmarks are easy to obtain. Companies can purchase external benchmark data from consulting firms. Consider a consulting firm that develops reports comparing the costs of treating specific diagnoses (say an appendectomy) across hospitals. Your local hospital can compare its cost of an appendectomy with the "best practice" cost from the report.

OBJECTIVE 3
Identify the benefits of standard costs

Benefits of Standard Costs

Carefully set standard costs yield several benefits (Exhibit 24-8):

1. They help managers plan by providing the unit amounts—the building blocks—for budgeting.
2. They help managers control by setting target levels of operating performance. *Management by exception* suggests that managers focus attention where actual results differ significantly from standards.
3. They help motivate employees by serving as benchmarks against which their performance is measured.
4. They provide unit costs that are useful in setting the sale prices of products or services.
5. They help simplify record keeping and so reduce clerical costs.

Standard cost systems might appear to be expensive. Indeed, the company must invest in developing the standards. But standards can save data-processing costs. It is more economical to value all inventories at standard costs rather than at actual costs. With standard costs, accountants avoid the expense of tracking actual unit costs and of making LIFO, FIFO, or average-cost computations.

Given these benefits, it is not surprising that companies around the globe use standard costing. Canadian surveys have shown that more than 50 percent of responding companies use standard costing. International surveys suggest that over half the responding companies in Ireland, the United Kingdom, Sweden, and Japan use standard costing, primarily because it helps managers control costs.

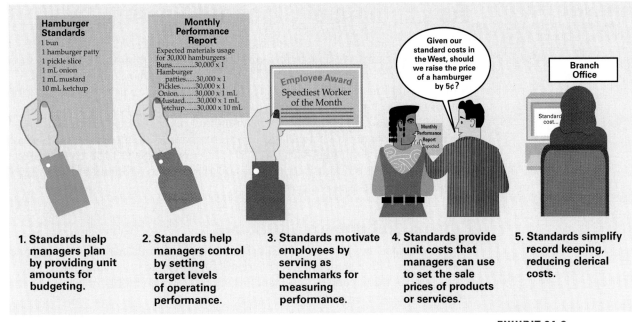

1. **Standards help managers plan by providing unit amounts for budgeting.**

2. **Standards help managers control by setting target levels of operating performance.**

3. **Standards motivate employees by serving as benchmarks for measuring performance.**

4. **Standards provide unit costs that managers can use to set the sale prices of products or services.**

5. **Standards simplify record keeping, reducing clerical costs.**

EXHIBIT 24-8

The Benefits of Standard Costs

Accounting and the *e*-World

"It's 10:00. Do You Know What Your Suppliers Are Doing?"

These days it's not enough for companies to continuously improve their own standards. Shrinking product cycles and increased pressure to reduce overhead have made it imperative for vendors to collaborate with their suppliers to cut costs while maintaining or improving product quality. Companies are transferring the responsibility for crafting more of their product to suppliers or outside contractors. Nortel Networks Corp. has seen the supplier content in its networking systems increase from 30 percent to 60 percent in just the past few years. The Internet enables vendors to keep close tabs on their suppliers.

Buzzwords abound for Web-enabled collaboration between suppliers and vendors: "seamless integration," "Web-based modeling," "electronic *keiretsu*." It is all made possible by Internet-based software such as Extranets (secure environments for the interchange of critical data with approved business partners) or Web-based-design, project-management, and data-management tools.

Companies must meld product design and development all along the supply chain. The Milwaukee-based motorcycle company, Harley-Davidson, Inc., manages interaction with its supply base through a Supplier Advisory Council (SAC). Sixteen top suppliers sit on the council and each member communicates with about ten other top-level suppliers, giving Harley-Davidson access to some 200 suppliers. In 1999 one of the key issues SAC addressed was understanding the cost drivers of the suppliers' production. Suppliers bidding on jobs give Harley the details behind cost breakdowns, such as process flow, run times, yield, and overhead. Says Greg Smith, a Harley-Davidson purchasing director, "But we want to understand their cost drivers because they can have a huge [effect] on how we design our products."

Based on: Tim Stevens, "Designs in Sync," http://www.iwvaluechain.com, June 12, 2000. Alorie Gilbert, "Online Collaboration Tools Help Simplify Product Design," *Informationweek*, April 24, 2000, pp. 130–136. Richard Vlosky and Renee J. Fontenot, "Learning to Love Extranets," *Marketing Management*, Fall 1999, pp. 33–55. Richard W. Oliver, "Killer KEIRETSU," *Management Review*, September 1999, pp. 10–11.

OBJECTIVE 4
Compute standard cost
variances for direct
materials and direct labour

An Example of Standard Costing

Let's return to our Kool-Time Pools Ltd. example. To focus on the main aspects of standard costing, we assume that Kool-Time Pools Ltd.'s standard costing system pertains to direct materials (gunite), direct labour, and manufacturing overhead but not design, marketing, or administrative expenses. We assume also that the quantity of direct materials purchased equals the quantity used.

Recall that Kool-Time installed ten swimming pools during June. Exhibit 24-9 provides cost data for this actual level of output. Exhibit 24-9 also shows Kool-Time Pools Ltd.'s flexible budget variances for direct materials ($3,100 U) and direct labour ($200 F). Accountants separate these variances into two components: a price variance and an efficiency variance.

Price and Efficiency Variances

A **price variance** measures how well the business keeps unit prices of material and labour inputs within standards. As the name suggests, the price variance is the *difference in prices* (actual unit price – standard unit price) of an input, multiplied by the *actual quantity* of the input:

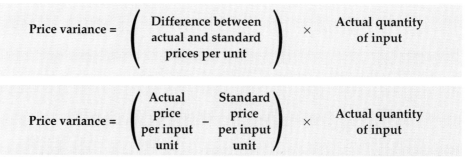

The standard price per input unit is the *price that should have been paid per unit* of the input (per cubic metre of gunite or per direct labour hour). If the company actually pays less, then the price variance is favourable. Conversely, if the company actually pays more than the standard price, then the price variance is unfavourable. The manager in charge of purchasing the input is responsible for the price variance. For example, the Kool-Time employee who buys the gunite is responsible for the difference between the actual and standard price for all the gunite he purchased, so the difference in price is multiplied by the *actual quantity* purchased.

An **efficiency variance** measures whether the quantity of materials or labour actually used to make the *actual number of outputs* is within the standard allowed for that number of outputs. The efficiency variance is the *difference in quantities* (actual quantity of input used – standard quantity of input allowed for the actual number of outputs), multiplied by the *standard price per unit* of the input.

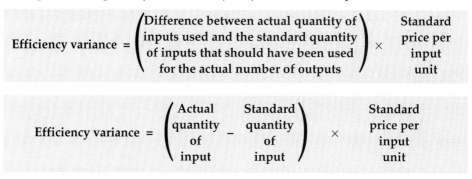

The standard quantity of inputs is the *quantity that should have been used*, or the standard quantity *allowed*, for the actual output. If the company actually uses less

EXHIBIT 24-9

Data for Standard Costing Example

KOOL-TIME POOLS LTD.
Data for Standard Costing Example
For the Month of June 2002

PANEL A—Computation of Flexible Budget for Direct Materials, Direct Labour, and Variable Overhead for 10 Swimming Pools

	(1) Standard Quantity of Inputs Allowed for 10 Pools	(2) Standard Price per Unit of Input	(1) × (2) Flexible Budget for 10 Pools
Direct materials	37.03 cubic metres per pool × 10 pools = 370.3 cubic metres	$54.01	$20,000
Direct labour	400 hours per pool × 10 pools = 4,000 hours	10.50	42,000
Variable overhead	400 hours per pool × 10 pools = 4,000 hours	2.00	8,000

PANEL B—Computation of Actual Costs for Direct Materials and Direct Labour for 10 Swimming Pools

	(1) Actual Quantity of Inputs Used for 10 Pools	(2) Actual Price per Unit of Input	(1) × (2) Actual Cost for 10 Pools
Direct materials	445 cubic metres actually used	$51.91 actual cost/cubic metre	$23,100
Direct labour	3,800 hours actually used	$11.00 actual cost/hour	41,800

PANEL C—Comparison of Actual Results with Flexible Budget for 10 Swimming Pools

	Actual Results at Actual Prices	Flexible Budget for 10 Pools	Flexible Budget Variances
Variable expenses:			
Direct materials	$ 23,100*	$ 20,000‡	$3,100 U
Direct labour	41,800*	42,000‡	200 F
Variable overhead	9,000	8,000‡	1,000 U
Marketing and administrative expenses	9,100	10,000	900 F
Total variable expenses	83,000	80,000	3,000 U
Fixed expenses:			
Fixed overhead	12,300	12,000++	300 U
Marketing and administrative expenses	9,700	8,000	1,700 U
Total fixed expenses	22,000	20,000	2,000 U
Total expenses	$105,000	$100,000	$5,000 U

*See Panel B.
‡See Panel A.
++Fixed overhead was budgeted at $12,000 per month.

than the standard quantity of inputs allowed to produce the output, the efficiency variance is favourable. If the company uses more than the standard quantity, the efficiency variance is unfavourable.

Price variances show how changes in prices of raw materials and labour affect the company's profit. But price variances that reflect changes in the market prices of materials and labour are largely beyond the company's control. Because managers generally have limited control over changes in prices, *efficiency* variances are computed by multiplying the difference in quantity by the *standard* price per unit of the input. Efficiency variances thus capture the controllable aspect of how the company's *use* of materials and labour affects profits.

We now turn our attention to computing Kool-Time Pools Ltd.'s standard cost variances for direct materials and direct labour.

Direct Materials Variances

We begin our analysis of direct materials variances by compiling the relevant data from Exhibit 24-9, as follows:

Direct Materials	Actual	Flexible Budget	Flexible Budget Variance
Cubic metres......................	445	370.3	
Unit price.........................	× $ 51.91	× $ 54.01	
Total	$23,100	$20,000	$3,100 U

We use these data to compute the price and efficiency variances:

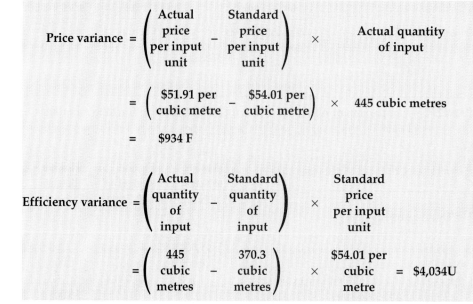

WORKING IT OUT

Use the following data for the next few Working It Outs.

Actual costs for 60,000 units:
Direct mats.   1.1 kg @ $0.30/kg
Direct labour   1/4 hr. @ $12/hr.
Variable over. $92,000
Fixed over. $10,000

Standard costs:
Direct mats.   1 kg @ $0.25/kg
Direct labour   1/5 hr. @ $13/hr.
Variable over.   1/5 hr. @ $6/hr.

Fixed over. $\frac{\$20,000 \text{ budgeted}}{10,000 \text{ hours}}$ = $2/hr.

Compute the materials variances.

A:
Price variance
= ($0.30 − $0.25)
× (60,000 × 1.1) = $3,300 U

Efficiency variance
= (66,000 − 60,000)
× $0.25 = $1,500 U

Total
= $3,300 U + $1,500 U
= $4,800 U

The price variance indicates that Kool-Time Pools Ltd.'s operating income will be $934 higher because the company paid less than the standard price for gunite in June. The efficiency variance indicates that Kool-Time Pools Ltd.'s operating income will be $4,034 lower because its workers used more gunite than the standard allowance for 10 pools.

Exhibit 24-10 summarizes the direct materials variance computations. Variance analysis begins with a total variance to be explained—in this example, the $3,100 unfavourable flexible budget variance for direct materials. This variance is the sum of the price and efficiency variances:

Direct materials price variance	$ 934 F
Direct materials efficiency variance	4,034 U
Direct materials flexible budget variance	$3,100 U

Splitting the $3,100 unfavourable direct materials flexible budget variance into price and efficiency variances explains why Kool-Time actually spent $3,100 more than it should have for gunite:

- A good price for the gunite increased profits by $934, but
- Inefficient use of the gunite reduced profits by $4,034

Who is most likely responsible for the direct materials price variance? For the direct materials efficiency variance?

- Purchasing personnel are typically responsible for the direct materials price variance, because they should know why the actual price differs from the standard price. Purchasing personnel may have negotiated a good price for gunite, thus obtaining the favourable variance. Should the gunite supplier raise prices, purchasing personnel will know why an unfavourable price variance occurred.
- Production personnel are generally responsible for the direct materials efficiency variance. Perhaps their equipment malfunctioned, causing them to use more than the standard quantity of gunite.

Common Pitfalls: Price and Efficiency Variances

Make sure you avoid three common pitfalls in computing price and efficiency variances:

1. *Static budgets like column 5 of Exhibit 24-7 play no role in computing the flexible budget variance or how it is split into the price and efficiency variances.* Exhibit 24-11 shows that the static budget is used *only* in computing the sales volume variance—never in computing the flexible budget variance (or its component price and efficiency variances).

   As Exhibit 24-11 shows, the price variance and the efficiency variance are components of the flexible budget variance—the difference between actual amounts and flexible budget amounts. The $934F + $4,034U = $3,100U direct materials flexible budget variance is part of the $3,000U flexible budget variance for variable expenses shown in column 2 of Exhibit 24-7. (The rest of the variable cost flexible budget variance is comprised of flexible budget variances for other variable expenses, as shown in Exhibit 24-9.)

EXHIBIT 24-10

Kool-Time Pools Ltd. Direct Materials Variances

Actual Cost Incurred: Actual quantity of inputs × Actual price per input unit	**Standard Cost of Actual Inputs:** Actual quantity of inputs × Standard price per input unit	**Flexible Budget:** Standard quantity of *inputs* for actual number of *outputs* × Standard price per input unit
445 × $51.91 = $23,100	445 × $54.01 = $24,034	370.3 × $54.01 = $20,000

(b) Price variance, $934 F   (c) Efficiency variance, $4,034 U

(a) Flexible budget variance, $3,100 U

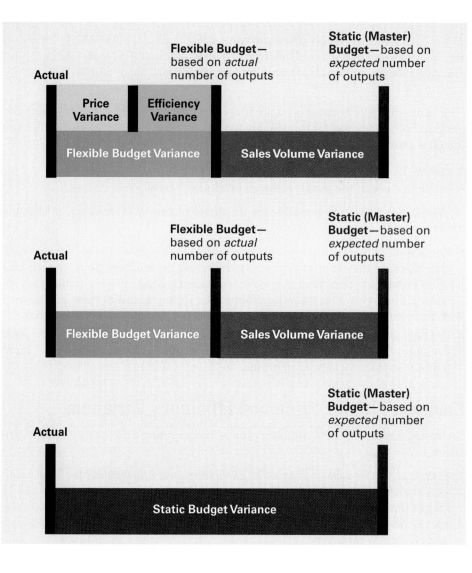

2. In the efficiency variance, the standard quantity is the *standard quantity of inputs allowed for the actual number of outputs*—the basis for the flexible budget. To compute the standard quantity of inputs allowed, first determine the actual number of outputs. For Kool-Time Pools Ltd., the actual number of outputs is ten pools. Next, compute how many inputs should have been used to produce the actual number of outputs (ten pools). Each pool should use 370.3 cubic metres of gunite, so the standard quantity of gunite allowed for ten pools is 10×370.3 cubic metres = 3,703 cubic metres.

Notice that the standard quantity of inputs is *not* based on the budgeted number of outputs (eight pools). That number is the basis for the static budget, which is not used to compute price and efficiency variances.

3. In the direct materials price variance, the difference in prices is multiplied by the *actual quantity* of materials. In the direct materials efficiency variance, the difference in quantities is multiplied by the *standard price* of the materials. The following explanation can help you remember this difference.

- The materials price variance is usually the responsibility of purchasing personnel; they purchase the actual quantity used, not just the amount of materials that should have been used (the standard quantity). So the price variance is the difference in prices multiplied by the *actual quantity* of materials they purchased.

- The materials efficiency variance is usually the responsibility of production personnel; they have no influence over the actual price paid. So the efficiency variance is computed as the difference in quantities multiplied by the *standard* price (the price that should have been paid).

Direct Labour Variances

We begin our analysis of direct labour variances by compiling the relevant data from Exhibit 24-9, as follows:

Direct Labour	Actual	Flexible Budget	Flexible Budget Variance
Hours..................................	3,800	4,000	
Hourly rate	× $11.00	× $10.50	
Total	$41,800	$42,000	$200 F

We then use the data from this table to compute the price and efficiency variances:

$$\text{Price variance} = \begin{pmatrix} \text{Actual} \\ \text{price per} \\ \text{input unit} \end{pmatrix} - \begin{pmatrix} \text{Standard} \\ \text{price per} \\ \text{input unit} \end{pmatrix} \times \begin{pmatrix} \text{Actual quantity} \\ \text{of input} \end{pmatrix}$$

$$= (\$11.00 - \$10.50) \times 3{,}800 \text{ hours} = \$1{,}900 \text{ U}$$

$$\text{Efficiency variance} = \begin{pmatrix} \text{Actual} \\ \text{quantity} \\ \text{of} \\ \text{input} \end{pmatrix} - \begin{pmatrix} \text{Standard} \\ \text{quantity} \\ \text{of} \\ \text{input} \end{pmatrix} \times \begin{pmatrix} \text{Standard} \\ \text{price per} \\ \text{input unit} \end{pmatrix}$$

$$(3{,}800 \text{ hours} - 4{,}000 \text{ hours}) \times \$10.50 \text{ per hour} = \$2{,}100 \text{ F}$$

Had they looked only at the $200 favourable direct labour flexible budget variance, Kool-Time's managers may have concluded that direct labour costs were close to expectations. But this illustrates the danger in ending the analysis after computing only the flexible budget variance. "Peeling the onion" to examine the price and efficiency variances yields more insight:

- The unfavourable direct labour price variance means that Kool-Time Pools Ltd.'s operating income will be $1,900 lower because the company paid its employees an average of $11.00 per hour in June instead of the standard rate of $10.50. But this unfavourable variance was more than offset by:

  - The favourable direct labour efficiency variance. Kool-Time's operating income is $2,100 higher than expected because workers completed installing ten pools in 3,800 hours instead of the budgeted 4,000 hours.

As with direct materials, the direct labour price and efficiency variances sum to the flexible budget variance.

Direct labour price variance	$1,900	U
Direct labour efficiency variance	2,100	F
Direct labour flexible budget variance	$ 200	F

Exhibit 24-12 summarizes the direct labour variance computations.

WORKING IT OUT

Compute the direct labour variances for the previous Working It Out.

A:

Price Variance
$= (\$12 - \$13) \times (1/4 \times 60{,}000)$
$= \$15{,}000 \text{ F}$

Efficiency Variance
$= (15{,}000 - 12{,}000) \times \$13$
$= \$39{,}000 \text{ U}$

Total Variance
$= \$15{,}000 \text{ F} + \$39{,}000 \text{ U}$
$= \$24{,}000 \text{ U}$

EXHIBIT 24-12

Kool-Time Pools Ltd. Direct
Labour Variances

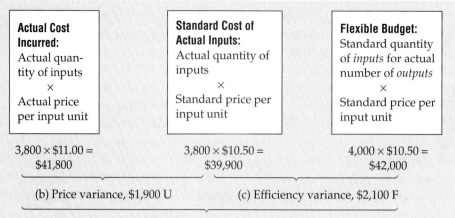

Actual Cost Incurred: Actual quantity of inputs × Actual price per input unit	Standard Cost of Actual Inputs: Actual quantity of inputs × Standard price per input unit	Flexible Budget: Standard quantity of *inputs* for actual number of *outputs* × Standard price per input unit
3,800 × $11.00 = $41,800	3,800 × $10.50 = $39,900	4,000 × $10.50 = $42,000

(b) Price variance, $1,900 U   (c) Efficiency variance, $2,100 F

(a) Flexible budget variance, $200 F

STOP & THINK

Why might an auto assembly factory experience a favourable direct labour efficiency variance? Should managers investigate favourable as well as unfavourable efficiency variances? Why?

Answer:

1. The factory may have redesigned the manufacturing process to avoid wasted motion. For example, a Dodge van factory in Windsor, Ontario, significantly reduced direct labour by reorganizing production so employees reach for raw materials as needed rather than carry armloads of materials across the factory floor.

2. Employees may have worked harder or more intensely than budgeted.

3. Employees may have rushed through the work and skimped on quality.

There are two reasons why managers should investigate favourable efficiency variances. First, managers want to maximize improvements that increase profits. For example, can managers capitalize on 1 and 2 to further improve labour efficiency at this or other factories? Second, managers want to prevent employees from achieving favourable variances at the expense of long-run profits through strategies like 3, which hurt the company in the long run.

Using Variance Information

How often should companies compute variances? Many firms monitor sales, materials quantities, and direct labour hours on a day-to-day or even hour-to-hour basis. For example, McDonald's restaurants compute variances for sales and direct labour each hour. Material efficiencies are computed for each shift. The Brass Products Division of Parker Hannafin computes variances for each job the day after workers finish the job. This allows managers to ask questions about any large variances while the job is still fresh in workers' minds. The division also prepares weekly reports showing variances by product line. The resulting database allows managers to examine variances by product (part number), by job, or by dollar amount of the variance, with just a few keystrokes. Technology like bar coding and computerized data entry allows companies like McDonald's and Parker Hannafin to quickly compute efficiency variances. In contrast to efficiency variances, monthly computations of material and labour price variances may be sufficient if long-term contracts with suppliers or labour unions makes large price variances unlikely.

Variances by themselves do not identify problems or opportunities. But large variances raise questions that deserve attention. When is a variance "large" or "significant"? The answer depends on the manager's judgment. Many managers use rules of thumb such as "investigate all variances over $10,000 or 8%, whichever is greater." For example, Parker Hannafin's Brass Products Division requires managers to investigate all variances over 5% of sales revenue, and to develop a plan of action to correct any problems.

Returning to our Kool-Time Pool example, in June, Kool-Time Pools Ltd. bought gunite for $51.91 per cubic metre (less than the standard price of $54.01). Kool-Time's 3.9-percent [($51.91 – $54.01)/$54.01] favourable direct materials price variance could arise because the purchasing officer did a good job negotiating prices with suppliers, or because the officer purchased lower-quality gunite. (Many managers consider a 3.5 percent variance insignificant and not worth investigating.)

Favourable direct materials price variances can also arise when purchasing personnel buy materials in larger lot sizes to get a lower price per unit. Because Kool-Time purchased only the quantity of gunite needed for June, there was no buildup of inventory. But a manager who is evaluated on price variance may place large orders to receive lower unit costs.

Purchasing more materials than currently needed violates the just-in-time philosophy introduced in Chapter 19. Purchasing too large a quantity of materials increases inventory, which increases inventory carrying costs, obsolescence, theft, and damage costs. Thus, as explained earlier, smart managers interpret variances carefully—even a "favourable" variance can hurt long-run profits.

Kool-Time's 20.1-percent [(445 – 370.3)/370.3] unfavourable direct materials efficiency variance may indicate that the gunite used was of low quality. Poor quality materials spoil, break, or crack more often, requiring replacement. Or perhaps an uncontrollable event led to excess usage. For example, the settling of the pools may have cracked several pools after the gunite had hardened but before all work was completed. Workers may have used extra gunite to repair the damage.

Now consider Kool-Time's direct labour variances. While this variance is only $200, as indicated earlier, dividing it into its two components is revealing. The 4.8-percent [($11.00 – $10.50)/$10.50] unfavourable price variance reveals that the company used more expensive labour than was budgeted. But those workers were more efficient. The average number of hours worked per pool (3,800 hours/10 pools = 380) was 5 percent less than the standard of 400 hours per pool. Kool-Time's managers may have decided to hire more-experienced workers and *trade off* an unfavourable price variance for favourable efficiency variance. If so, the strategy was successful—the overall effect of their decision was favourable.

The preceding examples lead to two conclusions:

1. *Executives should be careful in using standard cost variances to evaluate performance.* First, some variances are caused by factors managers cannot control. Second, managers often make tradeoffs among variances. Daimler-Chrysler intentionally accepted a large order for customized Dodge vans because it expected the favourable sales volume variance to more than offset the unfavourable direct labour price variance from the overtime premium and the unfavourable sales revenue price variance from extra rebates offered to the customer. Similarly, managers often trade off price variances against efficiency variances. Purchasing personnel may decide to buy higher quality (but more expensive) direct materials to reduce waste and spoilage. The unfavourable price variance may be more than offset by a favourable efficiency variance.

2. *Executives should consider using several measures to evaluate managers' performance.* Evaluations based on only one variance sometimes inadvertently encourage managers to take actions that make the variance look good, but hurt the company in the long run. For example, Kool-Time's managers could

   • Buy more gunite than needed when the price is below standard to get a favourable price variance

   • Purchase low-quality gunite or hire less-experienced labour to get favourable price variances

- Use less gunite or less labour (resulting in lower-quality installed pools) to get favourable efficiency variances

How can upper management discourage such actions? One approach is to base performance evaluation on *nonfinancial* measures as well, such as the difference between the quantities of materials purchased and materials used, and quality indicators like variances in the grade of gunite or labour used, or variances in the thickness or smoothness of the pool walls, and customer satisfaction measures.

McDonald's faces similar challenges (see the chapter-opening story). McDonald's discourages skimping on labour by evaluating nonfinancial measures such as the difference between actual and standard time to serve drive-through customers. If the McDonald's shift manager does not have enough workers, drive-through customers may have to wait too long to get their french fries. They may take their business to Harvey's or Burger King.

OBJECTIVE 5
Analyze manufacturing overhead in a standard cost system

Manufacturing Overhead Variances

Ideally, manufacturing overhead cost variances should be computed and monitored for individual overhead costs like factory-related property taxes, utilities, and insurance. However, many companies compute variances on total overhead costs. These companies often split the variances on total manufacturing overhead cost into two parts: a *flexible budget variance* and a *production volume variance.*

The *flexible budget variance* for manufacturing overhead shows whether managers are keeping total overhead cost within the budgeted amount, given the actual number of outputs during the period. The *production volume variance* arises when the actual number of outputs differs from the expected numbr of outputs used in the static (master) budget. The two variances combine to explain the difference between actual overhead cost and the standard overhead cost that has been allocated to production (underallocated or overallocated overhead). Before discussing how companies compute overhead variances, let's see how they allocate manufacturing overhead.

Applying Manufacturing Overhead to Production in a Standard Costing System

In a standard costing system, the amount of the manufacturing overhead allocated to production is

Manufacturing overhead allocated to production	=	Standard predetermined manufacturing overhead rate	×	Standard quantity of the allocation base allowed for the *actual* number of outputs

Let's begin by computing the first term on the right-hand side, the standard predetermined manufacturing overhead rate. Kool-Time allocates manufacturing overhead based on direct labour hours. Thus, we want to compute Kool-Time's standard predetermined manufacturing overhead rate per direct labour hour. As explained in Chapter 20, the predetermined overhead rate is the budgeted manufacturing overhead cost, divided by the budgeted quantity of the allocation base.

But which budget? Exhibit 24-13 shows Kool-Time's budgeted overhead costs and direct labour hours for:

- The flexible budget for actual output, which is based on actual output of ten pools (not known until the end of the period)
- The static budget, which is based on expected output of eight pools (known at the beginning of the period)

KOOL-TIME POOLS LTD.
Budget Data for the Month Ended June 30, 2002

	Flexible Budget for Actual Output	Static Budget for Expected Output
Output units (pools installed)...	10	8
Standard direct labour hours (400 hours per pool)	4,000	3,200
Budgeted manufacturing overhead cost:		
Variable	$ 8,000	$ 6,400
Fixed	12,000	12,000
Total	$20,000	$18,400
Standard variable manufacturing overhead rate per direct labour hour		$ 6,400/3,200 = $2.00
Standard fixed manufacturing overhead rate per direct labour hour.............................		$12,000/3,200 = 3.75
Standard total manufacturing overhead rate per direct labour hour		$18,400/3,200 = $5.75

EXHIBIT 24-13

Budgeted Manufacturing Overhead Costs and Allocation Rates

Notice that the $12,000 budgeted *fixed* manufacturing overhead is the same in both the static budget for eight pools and the flexible budget for ten pools. Why? Because fixed costs do not change throughout the relevant range of 0–11 pools. In contrast, the budgeted *variable* manufacturing overhead is higher in the flexible budget for ten pools than in the static budget for eight pools. Why? Because variable costs vary (in total) with the number of outputs, so Kool-Time expects to use more variable overhead items (indirect materials, indirect labour) for ten pools than for eight pools.

Keep in mind that managers use predetermined overhead rates because they cannot wait until the end of the year to determine the overhead costs of products. Thus, *predetermined* overhead rates use data that are available at the *beginning* of the year. Most companies base their predetermined overhead rates on amounts from the static (master) budget, which is known at the beginning of the year. (The predetermined manufacturing overhead rate cannot be based on the flexible budget for actual production, because the actual number of outputs is not known until the end of the year.)

Exhibit 24-13 shows that Kool-Time's standard manufacturing overhead rates are

- Variable—$2.00 per direct labour hour ($6,400 static budget variable manufacturing overhead divided by 3,200 static budget standard direct labour hours),

- Fixed—$3.75 per direct labour hour ($12,000 static budget fixed manufacturing overhead divided by 3,200 static budget standard direct labour hours),

- Total—$5.75 per direct labour hour ($2.00 + $3.75). This is the standard predetermined manufacturing overhead rate Kool-Time uses to allocate manufacturing overhead to products.

Now that we have computed the standard predetermined manufacturing overhead rate, the next step is to identify the standard quantity of the allocation base allowed for the *actual* number of outputs. Kool-Time allocates manufacturing overhead based on direct labour hours. Kool-Time actually installed ten pools during June. Thus, the standard quantity of the allocation base (direct labour hours) allowed for the actual number of outputs (ten pools) is 4,000 direct labour hours (400 direct labour hours per pool x 10 pools actually installed). Notice that the 4,000 direct labour hours is the standard number of direct labour hours for the flexible budget at the actual output level of ten pools in Exhibit 24-13, and for the direct labour efficiency variance computation (Exhibit 24-12).

Thus, Kool-Time allocates manufacturing overhead as follows:

Manufacturing overhead allocated to production	=	Standard predetermined manufacturing overhead rate	×	Standard quantity of the allocation base allowed for the *actual* number of outputs
	=	$5.75 per hour	×	4,000 hours
	=	$23,000		

The total manufacturing overhead variance is the amount of underallocated or overallocated manufacturing overhead. This is the difference between actual and allocated manufacturing overhead, as explained in Chapter 20. Exhibit 24-14 shows that actual manufacturing overhead is $21,300.

Given $21,300 of actual manufacturing overhead and $23,000 of allocated manufacturing overhead, Kool-Time has *overallocated* overhead of $1,700. Overallocated overhead is considered a favourable variance because actual overhead costs are less than allocated costs. We now will see how Kool-Time splits this total $1,700 favourable manufacturing overhead variance into the overhead flexible budget variance and the production volume variance.

KEY POINT

The computation of overhead variances is different from the computation of direct materials and labour variances. Materials and labour are strictly variable, but overhead has both fixed and variable components.

Overhead Flexible Budget Variance

The **overhead flexible budget variance** is the difference between the actual overhead cost and the flexible budget overhead for the actual number of outputs. Kool-Time Pools Ltd.'s overhead flexible budget variance for June is computed as follows (data from Exhibit 24-14):

Actual overhead cost..	$21,300
Flexible budget overhead for actual outputs (10 pools)	20,000
Overhead flexible budget variance	$ 1,300 U

EXHIBIT 24-14

Data for Computing Overhead Cost Variances

KOOL-TIME POOLS LTD.
Data for Computing Manufacturing Overhead Variances

	Actual Overhead Cost (Exhibit 24-9)	Flexible Budget Overhead for Actual Number of Outputs (Exhibits 24-9 and 24-13)	Standard Overhead Allocated to Production (Rates from Exhibit 24-13)
Variable overhead.........	$ 9,000	$ 8,000	4,000 direct labour hours × $2.00 = $ 8,000
Fixed overhead..............	12,300	12,000	4,000 direct labour hours × $3.75 = 15,000
Total overhead...............	$21,300	$20,000	4,000 direct labour hours × $5.75 = $23,000

Overhead flexible budget variance, $1,300 U

Production volume variance, $3,000 F

Total manufacturing overhead cost variance
$1,700 F

Kool-Time actually spent $21,300 on manufacturing overhead, when the flexible budget indicated that installing ten pools should have required only $20,000 of overhead. The unfavourable variance raises questions regarding managers' control of overhead costs.

Production Volume Variance

The **production volume variance** is the difference between: (1) the manufacturing overhead cost in the flexible budget for actual outputs, and (2) the standard overhead allocated to production. Kool-Time computes its production volume variance using data from Exhibit 24-14:

Flexible budget overhead for actual outputs (10 pools)	$20,000
Standard overhead allocated to (actual) production ...	23,000
Production volume variance	$ 3,000 F

The production volume variance is favourable whenever actual output (ten pools) exceeds expected output (eight pools, Exhibit 24-13). By installing ten pools instead of eight, Kool-Time used its production capacity more fully than originally planned. If Kool-Time had installed seven or fewer pools, the production volume variance would have been unfavourable because the company would have used less production capacity than expected.

Exhibit 24-14 reveals that the *variable* overhead cost in the flexible budget is always the same as the standard variable overhead allocated (standard predetermined variable overhead rate × the standard quantity of the allocation base allowed for the actual number of outputs). Thus the production volume variance is due only to fixed overhead.

WORKING IT OUT

Use the overhead flexible budget variance and production volume variance methods and the data from the Working It Out on page 1340 to compute the overhead variances.

A:

Actual over. cost	$102,000
Flex. budget over.	92,000*
Flex. budget var.	$ 10,000 U
Flex. budget over.	$92,000
Standard over. applied	96,000[†]
Prod. volume var.	$ 4,000 F

*$20,000 + ($6 × 12,000)
[†]$8 × 12,000

The flexible budget variance is unfavourable because actual costs were more than the budgeted costs. The production volume variance is favourable because the predetermined volume was 10,000 hours needed to produce 50,000 units. More capacity was utilized: 60,000 units were actually produced.

STOP & THINK

How did the increase in Kool-Time's "production volume," from eight pools (the expected static budget amount) to ten pools (actually installed) affect June's profit? Is this amount equal to the production volume variance?

Answer: To see how the increase from eight to ten pools affected Kool-Time's June profits, use the contribution margin income statement approach from Chapter 22:

Increase in sales revenue (2 × $ 12,000)	$24,000
Increase in variable expenses (2 × $8,000)	16,000
Increase in contribution margin	8,000
Increase in fixed expenses..	–0–
Increase in operating income	$ 8,000

Installing two more pools than initially expected increased Kool-Time's profits by $8,000, not by the favourable "production volume variance." Thus, the production volume variance does *not* reveal how changes in production volume affect profits. The production volume variance only captures the difference between the flexible budget manufacturing overhead and the allocated manufacturing overhead. Companies use the term "production volume variance" because this variance arises only when actual production differs from expected (static budget) production.

Accounting for Standard Costs

Standard Costs in the Accounts

Recall that manufacturing companies have three inventory accounts: Materials Inventory, Work in Process Inventory, and Finished Goods Inventory. Firms with standard cost accounting systems assign costs to these accounts in various ways but most companies record individual variances in separate accounts.

We use Kool-Time Pools Ltd.'s June 2002 transactions to demonstrate standard cost accounting in a job costing context. Our entries are based on an important assumption: Kool-Time recognizes variances from standards as soon as possible. This means that Kool-Time records direct materials price variances when materials are purchased. It also means that Work in Process Inventory is debited (swimming pools are costed) at standard input quantities and prices. June's entries follow:

1. Materials Inventory (445 × $54.01)	24,034	
Direct Materials Price Variance		934
Accounts Payable (445 × $51.91)		23,100
To record purchases of direct materials.		

The credit to Accounts Payable is for the *actual quanity* of gunite purchased (445 cubic metres) costed at the *actual price* ($51.91 per cubic metre). In contrast, the debit to Materials Inventory is for the *actual quantity* purchased (445 cubic metres) costed at the *standard price* ($54.01 per cubic metre). By maintaining Materials Inventory at the *standard* price ($54.01), Kool-Time accountants can record the direct materials price variance at time of purchase. Recall that Kool-Time's direct materials price variance was $934 favourable (page 1340). A favourable variance has a credit balance in the accounts, and is a contra expense, or a reduction in expense. Consequently, the $934 favourable direct materials price variance is a contra expense that increases Kool-Time's June profits.

2. Work in Process Inventory (370.3 × $54.01)	20,000	
Direct Materials Efficiency Variance	4,034	
Materials Inventory (445 × $54.01)		24,034
To record use of direct materials.		

Kool-Time's direct materials efficiency variance was $4,034 unfavourable (page 1340). An unfavourable variance has a debit balance, which increases expense. Consequently, Kool-Time's $4,034 unfavourable direct materials efficiency variance is an expense that decreases June profits. Work in Process is debited for the *standard price × standard quantity* of direct materials that should have been used for the actual output of ten pools. This maintains Work in Process Inventory at standard cost. Of course, Materials Inventory is credited for the *actual quantity* of material put into production (445 cubic metres) costed at the *standard price* at which journal entry 1 entered them into Materials Inventory account.

3. Manufacturing Wages (3,800 × $10.50)	39,900	
Direct Labour Price Variance	1,900	
Wages Payable (3,800 × $11.00)		41,800
To record direct labour costs incurred.		

By maintaining Manufacturing Wages at the *standard* price for direct labour ($10.50), Kool-Time Pools Ltd. can record the direct labour price variance at the time work is performed. Of course, Wages Payable is credited for the *actual* hours worked at the *actual* wage rate.

4. Work in Process Inventory (4,000 × $10.50)	42,000	
Direct Labour Efficiency Variance		2,100
Manufacturing Wages (3,800 × $10.50)		39,900
To assign direct labour costs.		

Work in Process is debited for the standard price × standard quantity of direct labour that should have been used for ten pools, similar to the (earlier) direct materials entry #2. This maintains Work in Process Inventory at standard cost.

5. Manufacturing Overhead.. 21,300
    Accounts Payable, Accumulated Amortization,
      and so on 21,300
    To record actual overhead costs incurred. (See Exhibit 24-14.)

6. Work in Process Inventory (4,000 × $5.75) 23,000
    Manufacturing Overhead 23,000
    To allocate overhead. (See Exhibit 24-14.)

In standard costing, the overhead allocated to Work in Process Inventory is computed as: the standard predetermined overhead rate × standard quantity of the allocation base that should have been used for the actual output (ten pools, in this case).

7. Finished Goods Inventory.. 85,000
    Work in Process Inventory.. 85,000
    To record completion of 10 pools ($20,000 of materials + $42,000 of labour + $23,000 of manufacturing overhead).

8. Cost of Goods Sold.. 85,000
    Finished Goods Inventory 85,000
    To record the cost of sales of 10 pools.

9. Manufacturing Overhead.. 1,700
    Overhead Flexible Budget Variance 1,300
    Production Volume Variance... 3,000
    To record overhead variances and close the Manufacturing Overhead account. (See Exhibit 24–14.)

Entry 9 closes Manufacturing Overhead. Many companies wait until the end of the fiscal year to close this account.

Exhibit 24-15 shows selected Kool-Time Pools Ltd. accounts, after posting the preceding journal entries.

Standard Cost Income Statement for Management

OBJECTIVE 7
Prepare a standard cost income statement for management

Exhibit 24-16 shows Kool-Time's standard cost income statement. After sales revenue, the statement shows the cost of goods sold at standard cost. Then the statement separately lists each variance, followed by the cost of goods sold at actual cost. (Recall that since Kool-Time had no raw materials, work in process, or finished goods inventories, all the variances related to June's sales.) At the end of the period, all the variance accounts are closed to zero-out their balances. The net amount is closed to Income Summary.

The income statement shows that the net effect of this adjustment is $1,200 unfavourable. Thus, June's operating income is $1,200 lower than it would have been if all actual costs had been equal to standard amounts. Management can prepare statements with similar detail for research and development, design, marketing, distribution, customer service, and administrative costs, if they are subject to standard cost analysis.

Take a moment to review standard costing by studying the Decision Guidelines, then complete the summary problem.

WORKING IT OUT

Prepare journal entries to record the material and labour variances for the data in the Working It Out on page 1340.

A:

Materials Inv.
  (66,000 × $0.25) 16,500
Direct Materials
  Price Var...................... 3,300
    Accounts Pay.
    (66,000 × $0.30).... 19,800

WIP Inv.
  (60,000 × $0.25) 15,000
Direct Materials
  Efficiency Var................ 1,500
    Materials Inv.
    (66,000 × $0.25).... 16,500

Manufacturing Wages
  (15,000 × $13)........... 195,000
    Direct Labour
    Price Var.............. 15,000
    Wages Payable
    (15,000 × $12)....... 180,000

WIP Inv.
  (12,000 × $13) 156,000
Direct Labour
  Efficiency Var............. 39,000
    Manufacturing Wages
    (15,000 × $13)....... 195,000

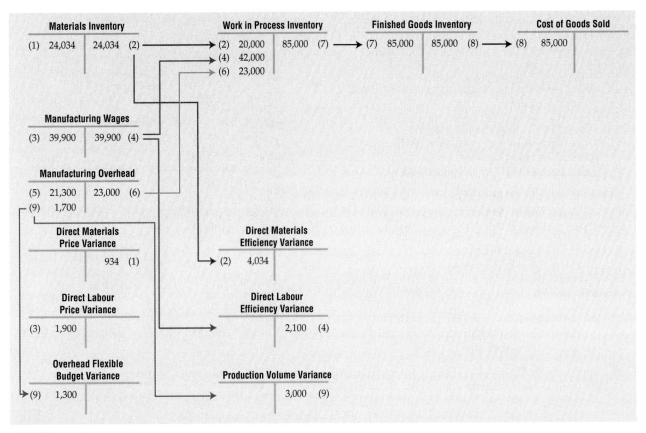

EXHIBIT 24-15

Kool-Time Pools Ltd. Flow of
Costs in Standard Costing
System

EXHIBIT 24-16

Standard Cost Income
Statement

KOOL-TIME POOLS LTD.
Standard Cost Income Statement
For the Month Ended June 30, 2002

Sales revenue		$120,000
Cost of goods sold at standard cost........................		$85,000
Manufacturing cost variances:		
Direct materials price variance	$ (934)	
Direct materials efficiency variance	4,034	
Direct labour price variance	1,900	
Direct labour efficiency variance	(2,100)	
Overhead flexible budget variance	1,300	
Production volume variance	(3,000)	
Total manufacturing variances............................		1,200
Cost of goods sold at actual cost.............................		86,200
Gross margin..		33,800
Selling and administrative expenses*		18,800
Operating income		$ 15,000

*$9,100 + $9,700 from Exhibit 24-9.

Decision	Guidelines
How to set standards?	Historical performance data Engineering analysis/time-and-motion studies Continuous improvement standards Benchmarking
How to compute a price variance for materials or labour?	$\text{Price variance} = \left(\begin{array}{c} \text{Actual} \\ \text{price per} \\ \text{input unit} \end{array} - \begin{array}{c} \text{Standard} \\ \text{price per} \\ \text{input unit} \end{array} \right) \times \begin{array}{c} \text{Actual} \\ \text{quantity} \\ \text{of input} \end{array}$
How to compute an efficiency variance for materials or labour?	$\text{Efficiency variance} = \left(\begin{array}{c} \text{Actual} \\ \text{quantity} \\ \text{of input} \end{array} - \begin{array}{c} \text{Standard} \\ \text{quantity of} \\ \text{input for actual} \\ \text{number} \\ \text{of outputs} \end{array} \right) \times \begin{array}{c} \text{Standard} \\ \text{price per} \\ \text{input unit} \end{array}$

Who is most likely responsible for
  Sales volume variance?
  Sales revenue flexible budget variance?
  Direct material price variance?
  Direct material efficiency variance?
  Direct labour price variance?
  Direct labour efficiency variance?
	
	Marketing Department
	Marketing Department
	Purchasing Department
	Production Departments
	Personnel Department or Production Department
	Production Department

How to allocate manufacturing overhead to production in a standard costing system?	$\begin{array}{c} \text{Manufacturing} \\ \text{overhead} \\ \text{allocated} \end{array} = \left(\begin{array}{c} \text{Standard} \\ \text{predetermined} \\ \text{manufacturing} \\ \text{overhead rate} \end{array} \right) \times \left(\begin{array}{c} \text{Standard} \\ \text{quantity of} \\ \text{allocation base} \\ \text{allowed for} \\ \text{actual outputs} \end{array} \right)$
How to analyze overallocated or underallocated manufacturing overhead?	Split overallocated or underallocated overhead into • $\begin{array}{c}\text{Flexible budget} \\ \text{variance}\end{array} = \begin{array}{c}\text{Actual} \\ \text{overhead}\end{array} - \begin{array}{c}\text{Flexible budget} \\ \text{overhead}\end{array}$ • $\begin{array}{c}\text{Production} \\ \text{volume variance}\end{array} = \begin{array}{c}\text{Flexible budget} \\ \text{overhead}\end{array} - \begin{array}{c}\text{Standard overhead} \\ \text{allocated to} \\ \text{actual outputs}\end{array}$
How to record standard costs in the accounts?	Materials Inventory: Actual quantity at standard price Work in Process Inventory (and Finished Goods Inventory and Cost of Goods Sold): Standard quantity of inputs allowed for actual outputs, at standard price of inputs

Exhibit 24-9 indicates that Kool-Time Pools Ltd. installed ten swimming pools during June. Suppose that June sales and installations were seven pools instead of ten and that actual expenses were:

Direct materials	274.04 cubic metres @ $54.01 per cubic metre
Direct labour	2,740 hours @ $10.00 per hour
Variable overhead..........................	$5,400
Fixed overhead	$11,900

Required

1. Given these new data, prepare two exhibits similar to Exhibits 24-9 and 24-13. Ignore selling and administrative expenses in your first exhibit.

2. Compute price and efficiency variances for direct materials and direct labour.

3. Compute the total variance, the flexible budget variance, and the production volume variance for overhead.

4. Prepare a June income statement through operating income for the president of Kool-Time Pools Ltd. Report all standard cost variances; assume that selling and administrative expenses for the month were $17,700.

Solution to Review Problem

Requirement 1

KOOL-TIME POOLS LTD.
Revised Data for Standard Costing Example
For the Month Ended June 30, 2002

Panel A—Computation of Flexible Budget for Direct Materials, Direct Labour, and Variable Overhead for 7 Swimming Pools

	(1) Standard Quantity of Inputs Allowed for 7 Pools	(2) Standard Price per Unit of Input	(1) × (2) Flexible Budget for 7 Pools
Direct materials	37.03 cubic metres × 7 = 259.21 cubic metres	$ 54.01	$14,000
Direct labour	400 hours × 7 = 2,800 hours	10.50	29,400
Variable overhead	400 hours × 7 pools = 2,800 hours	2.00	5,600

Panel B—Computation of Actual Budget Costs for Direct Materials and Direct Labour for 7 Swimming Pools

	(1) Actual Quantity of Inputs Used for 7 Pools	(2) Actual Price per Unit of Input	(1) × (2) Actual Cost for 7 Pools
Direct materials	274.04 cubic metres actually used	$54.01 actual cost/cubic metre	$14,800
Direct labour..................	2,740 hours actually used	$10.00 actual cost/hour	27,400

Panel C—Comparison of Actual Results with Flexible Budget for 7 Swimming Pools

	Actual Results at Actual Prices	Flexible Budget for 7 pools	Flexible Budget Variance
Variable expenses:			
Direct materials.....................................	$14,800*	$14,000‡	$ 800 U
Direct labour...	27,400*	29,400‡	2,000 F
Variable overhead................................	5,400	5,600‡	200 F
Total variable expenses....................	47,600	49,000	1,400 F
Fixed expenses:			
Fixed overhead	11,900	12,000 ‖	100 F
Total expenses	$59,500	$61,000	$1,500 F

*See Panel B
‡See Panel A.
‖Fixed overhead was budgeted at $12,000 per month.

KOOL-TIME POOLS LTD.
Budget Data for the Month Ended June 30, 2002

	Flexible Budget for Actual Production	Static (Master) Budget
Number of pools installed	7	8
Standard direct labour hours	2,800	3,200
Budgeted overhead cost:		
Variable...	$ 5,600*	$ 6,400
Fixed	12,000†	12,000
Total	$17,600	$18,400
Standard variable overhead rate per direct labour hour	$ 6,400/3,200 = $2.00	
Standard fixed overhead rate per direct labour hour ...	$12,000/3,200 = 3.75	
Standard total overhead rate per direct labour hour....	$18,400/3,200 = $5.75	

*Flexible budget variable overhead is computed as the standard quantity of the allocation base
  allowed for actual outputs (2,800 direct labour hours = 7 pools × 400 direct labour hours per
  pool) multiplied by the $2.00 standard variable manufacturing overhead rate per direct labour
  hour: 2,800 hours × $2.00 per hour = $5,600.
†Budgeted fixed overhead is *fixed* within the relevant range, so flexible budget fixed overhead
  is $12,000, the same as static budget fixed overhead.

Requirement 2

$$\text{Price variance} = \left(\begin{array}{c} \text{Actual} \\ \text{price} \\ \text{per} \\ \text{input unit} \end{array} - \begin{array}{c} \text{Standard} \\ \text{price} \\ \text{per} \\ \text{input unit} \end{array} \right) \times \begin{array}{c} \text{Actual quantity} \\ \text{of input} \end{array}$$

Direct materials:

| Price variance | = | ($54.01 – $54.01) | × | 274.04 cu. metres | = | $ 0 |

Direct labour:

| Price variance | = | ($10.00 – $10.50) | × | 2,740 hours | = | $1,370 F |

$$\text{Efficiency variance} = \left(\begin{array}{c} \text{Actual} \\ \text{quantity} \\ \text{of} \\ \text{input} \end{array} - \begin{array}{c} \text{Standard} \\ \text{quantity} \\ \text{of} \\ \text{input} \end{array} \right) \times \begin{array}{c} \text{Standard} \\ \text{price per} \\ \text{input unit} \end{array}$$

Direct materials:

| Efficiency variance | = | (274.04 cubic metres – 259.21 cubic metres) | × | $54.01 per cubic metre | = | $800 U |

Direct labour:

| Efficiency variance | = | (2,740 hours – 2,800 hours) | × | $10.50 per hour | = | $630 F |

Requirement 3

Total overhead variance:

Actual overhead cost (variable, $5,400 + fixed, $11,900)	$17,300
Standard overhead applied to production	
(2,800 standard direct labour hours × $5.75)...........................	16,100
Total overhead variance...	$ 1,200 U

Overhead Flexible Budget Variance:

Actual overhead cost ($5,400 + $11,900)	$17,300
Flexible budget overhead for	
actual outputs ($5,600 + $12,000)	17,600
Overhead flexible budget variance	$ 300 F

Production Volume Variance:

Flexible budget overhead for actual outputs	
($5,600 + $12,000)	$17,600
Standard overhead allocated to (actual) production	
(2,800 direct labour hours × $5.75)..	16,100
Production volume variance...	$ 1,500 U

Requirement 4

KOOL-TIME POOLS LTD.
Revised Standard Cost Income Statement
For the Month Ended June 30, 2002

Sales revenue		$84,000
Cost of goods sold at standard cost*		59,500
Manufacturing cost variances:		
Direct materials price variance...	$ 0	
Direct materials efficiency variance...................................	800	
Direct labour price variance	(1,370)	
Direct labour efficiency variance	(630)	
Overhead flexible budget variance....................................	(300)	
Production volume variance	1,500	
Total manufacturing variances..		0
Cost of goods sold at actual cost..		59,500
Gross margin...		24,500
Marketing and administrative expenses...............................		17,700
Operating income...		$ 6,800

*Cost of goods sold at standard cost:	
Direct materials (37.03 cubic metres × $54.01 per cubic metre)	$14,000
Direct labour (2,800 direct labour hours × $10.50 per direct labour hour)	29,400
Standard overhead allocated (2,800 direct labour hours	
× $5.75 per direct labour hour)	16,100
Cost of goods sold at standard cost	$59,500

Summary

1. **Prepare a flexible budget for the income statement.** A *flexible budget* is a summarized budget that can easily be computed for several different volume levels. Flexible budgets separate variable costs from fixed costs. These budgets show how revenues and costs vary—if at all—as the number of outputs varies within the budget range.

2. **Prepare an income statement performance report.** Static budget variances are differences between actual amounts and corresponding amounts (revenues and expenses) in the static budget. At the end of the period, accountants prepare an after-the-fact flexible budget for the actual number of outputs. Accountants use this flexible budget to divide static budget variances into two broad categories: *Sales volume variances* and *flexible budget variances*.

3. **Identify the benefits of standard costs.** *Standard costs* are carefully predetermined costs that usually are expressed on a per-unit basis. Standards help managers plan and control, motivate employees, provide unit costs, and simplify record keeping.

4. **Compute standard cost variances for direct materials and direct labour.** Companies divide flexible budget variances for direct materials and direct labour into price and efficiency (quantity) variances. A *price variance* reveals the effect on total cost—and thus the effect on operating income—of paying more or less for an input than

the standard allows. An *efficiency variance* reveals the effect on total cost of using more or less input than the quantity allowed by the flexible budget for the actual number of outputs.

5. **Analyze manufacturing overhead in a standard cost system.** The total variance between actual manufacturing overhead cost incurred and standard overhead cost allocated to production has two components: the *overhead flexible budget variance* and the *production volume variance*. Overhead flexible budget variance is the difference between actual overhead and flexible budget overhead that should have been incurred given the actual number of outputs. Production volume variance is the difference between flexible budget overhead for actual outputs and standard overhead allocated to production.

6. **Record transactions at standard cost.** Many companies record standard costs in their inventory and expense accounts. They also record standard cost variances. At year's end, all variance accounts are closed out.

7. **Prepare a standard cost income statement for management.** The statement shows cost of goods sold at standard cost, lists all variances, and then shows the adjusted cost of goods sold—at actual cost. Operating expenses are treated similarly if they are part of the company's standard cost system.

Self-Study Questions

Test your understanding of the chapter by marking the best answer for each of the following questions.

1. A flexible budget shows (p. 1325)
   a. Expected results over a range of volume levels
   b. A single target level of volume
   c. Price variances
   d. Volume variances

2. Which is the most useful formula for budgeting expenses? (p. 1325)
   a. Expenses = Sales − Income
   b. Expenses = Fixed + Variable
   c. Expenses = Fixed + (Variable per unit × Number of units)
   d. Expenses = Standard + Variances

3. Flexible budget variances are differences between (p. 1331)
   a. Actual results and the static (master) budget
   b. Actual results and flexible budget amounts
   c. The static (master) budget and the flexible budget
   d. None of the above

4. Accountants play a major role in setting (p. 1335)
   a. Price standards   c. Both a and b
   b. Quantity standards   d. None of the above

5. Flexible budget variances for direct materials and direct labour are divided into (p. 1338)
   a. Flexible budget effects and production volume effects
   b. Efficiency effects and flexible budget effects
   c. Controllable effects and master budget effects
   d. Price effects and efficiency effects

6. Krakow Inc. paid $3 per kilogram for 10,000 kilograms of direct materials purchased and used. The standard price was $2.80 per kilogram, and standard usage for actual production was 11,000 kilograms. The price variance is (p. 1340)

a. $800 favourable   c. $2,800 favourable
b. $2,000 unfavourable   d. $3,000 unfavourable

7. The efficiency variance in Self-Study Question 6 is (p. 1340)
   a. $800 favourable   c. $2,800 favourable
   b. $2,000 unfavourable   d. $3,000 unfavourable

8. Actual overhead of Roma Supply Company Ltd. is $540,000. Overhead for static (master) budget volume is $500,000, and flexible budget overhead for actual production is $510,000. The production volume variance is (p. 1349)
   a. $10,000 unfavourable
   b. $30,000 unfavourable
   c. $40,000 unfavourable
   d. Not determinable. Why?

9. If direct labour hours are used to apply overhead to output produced, the sign (favourable or unfavourable) of the overhead variance is the same as that of the (pp. 1346–1349)
   a. Direct materials efficiency variance
   b. Direct labour efficiency variance
   c. Overhead spending variance
   d. Overhead flexible budget variance

10. Martinez Manufacturing Inc. made the following entry for the use of direct materials in production:

    Work in Process Inventory 380,000
    Direct Materials Efficiency Variance   29,000
        Materials Inventory   409,000

    Which of the following statements is true? (p. 1350)
    a. The actual cost of direct materials used is $380,000.
    b. The actual cost of direct materials purchased is $409,000.
    c. The actual cost of direct materials used is $409,000.
    d. The efficiency variance is unfavourable.

Answers to the Self-Study Questions follow the Similar Accounting Terms.

Accounting Vocabulary

Benchmarking (p. 1336)
Efficiency variance (p. 1338)
Flexible budget (p. 1325)
Flexible budget variance (p. 1330)
Master budget (p. 1324)
Overhead flexible budget variance (p. 1348)

Price variance (p. 1338)
Production volume variance (p. 1349)
Sales volume variance (p. 1330)
Standard cost (p. 1335)
Static budget (p. 1324)
Variance (p. 1324)

Similar Accounting Terms

Flexible budget   Variable budget
Master budget   Static budget
Standard cost per unit   Budgeted unit cost

Assignment Material

Questions

1. How does a static budget differ from a flexible budget?

2. What is the relevant range, and why must it be considered in preparing a flexible budget?

3. Identify how managers use variance information from a performance report.

4. McLaren Inc. prepared its static (master) budget for a sales level of 35,000 for the month. Actual sales totaled 46,000. Describe the problem of using the static budget to evaluate company performance for the month. Propose a better way to evaluate McLaren Inc.'s performance.

5. What advantage does a flexible budget graph offer over a columnar flexible budget with four levels of volume?

6. What do the sales volume variance and the flexible budget variance for operating income measure?

7. Describe the benefits of a standard cost system.

8. Identify the similarities and differences between a standard cost and a budgeted cost.

9. Your company is installing a standard cost system. What sort of standard cost is most popular?

For employees, what purpose does a standard cost fulfill?

10. What does a price variance measure? How is it computed?

11. What does an efficiency variance measure? How is it computed?

12. How are the price variance and the efficiency variance related to the flexible budget variance for direct materials and direct labour?

13. Describe a trade-off a manager might make for labour cost.

14. When should a cost variance be investigated?

15. What causes an overhead flexible budget variance? What information does this variance provide?

16. Scott & White, Inc. enters standard costs in the company accounts. The standard cost of actual direct materials used to manufacture inventory was $21,600. The direct materials efficiency variance was $1,400 favourable. Make the journal entry to charge materials to production.

17. How does a standard cost income statement for management differ from an income statement reported to the public?

Exercises

Exercise 24-1   *Preparing a flexible budget for the income statement*   *(Obj. 1)*

Target Manufacturing Ltd. sells its main product for $7.50 per unit. Its variable cost is $3.00 per unit. Fixed expenses are $200,000 per month for volumes up to 60,000 units of output. Above 60,000 units, monthly fixed expenses are $220,000.

   Prepare a monthly flexible budget for the product, showing sales, variable expenses, fixed expenses, and operating income or loss for volume levels of 30,000, 50,000, and 70,000 units.

Exercise 24-2   *Graphing expense behaviour*   *(Obj. 1)*

Graph the expense behaviour of Target Manufacturing Ltd. in Exercise 24-1. Show total expenses for volume levels of 30,000, 50,000, and 70,000 units.

Exercise 24-3 *Completing a performance report* *(Obj. 2)*

Girrard Inc. managers received the following incomplete performance report:

GIRRARD INC.
Income Statement Performance Report
For the Year Ended April 30, 2003

	Actual Results at Actual Prices	Flexible Budget Variances	Flexible Budget for Actual Volume Achieved	Sales Volume Variances	Static (Master) Budget
Units	24,000		24,000	4,000 F	
Sales...........................	$192,000		$192,000	$32,000 F	
Variable expenses......	84,000		72,000	12,000 U	
Fixed expenses...........	94,000		90,000	–0–	
Total expenses............	178,000		162,000	12,000 U	
Operating income	$ 14,000		$ 30,000	$20,000 F	

Complete the performance report. Identify the employee group that may deserve praise and the group that may be subject to criticism. Give your reasons.

Exercise 24-4 *Preparing an income statement performance report* *(Obj. 2)*

Top managers of Arc Industries Inc. predicted 2002 sales of 150,000 units of its product at a unit price of $6.00. Actual sales for the year were 140,000 units at $7.00. Variable expenses were budgeted at $2.20 per unit, and actual variable expenses were $2.30 per unit. Actual fixed expenses of $420,000 exceeded budgeted fixed expenses by $10,000. Prepare Arc's income statement performance report in a format similar to Exhibit 24-7. The bracketed amounts are not required. What variance contributed most to the year's favourable results? What caused this variance?

Exercise 24-5 *Computing price and efficiency variances for direct materials* *(Obj. 4)*

The following direct materials variance computations are incomplete:

$$\text{Price variance} = (\$? - \$15) \times 14{,}500 \text{ kilograms} = \$5{,}075 \text{ F}$$
$$\text{Efficiency variance} = (? - 14{,}200 \text{ kilograms}) \times ? = ?$$
$$\text{Direct materials flexible budget variance} = \$?$$

Fill in the missing values, and identify the flexible budget variance as favourable or unfavourable.

Exercise 24-6 *Computing price and efficiency variances for materials and labour* *(Obj. 4)*

Sapawe Wood Products Ltd., which uses a standard cost accounting system, manufactured 400,000 picture frames during the year, using 450,000 board metres of lumber purchased at $4.70 per metre. Production required 9,500 direct labour hours that cost $11.00 per hour. The materials standard was 1 board metre of lumber per frame, at a standard cost of $4.80 per metre. The labour standard was 0.0275 direct labour hour per frame, at a standard cost of $10.00 per hour. Compute the price and efficiency variances for direct materials and direct labour.

Exercise 24-7 *Journalizing standard cost transactions* *(Obj. 6)*

Make the journal entries to record the purchase and use of direct materials and direct labour in Exercise 24-6.

Exercise 24-8 *Explaining standard cost variances* **(Obj. 4, 5)**

Leven Corporation managers are seeking explanations for the variances in this report:

LEVEN CORPORATION
Income Statement for Managers
For the Year Ended December 31, 2003

Sales revenue..		$1,200,000
Cost of goods sold—standard.......................................		$700,000
Manufacturing cost variances:		
Materials: Price..	8,000 F	
Efficiency..................................	12,000 F	
Labour: Price..	14,000 F	
Efficiency.....................................	8,000 U	
Overhead: Flexible budget...........................	28,000 U	
Production volume.................................	10,000 U	
Net variance		12,000U
Cost of goods sold—actual...		712,000
Gross profit...		488,000
Selling and administrative expenses		418,000
Operating income...		$ 70,000

Explain the meaning of each of Leven Corporation's labour and overhead variances.

Exercise 24-9 *Computing overhead cost variances* **(Obj. 5)**

Millbank Manufacturing Company Ltd. manufactures plastic shovels. The company charges the following standard unit costs to production on the basis of master budget volume of 30,000 shovels per month:

Direct materials	$5.00
Direct labour	2.00
Overhead...	1.50
Standard unit cost	$8.50

Millbank Manufacturing Company Ltd. uses the following overhead flexible budget:

	Monthly Volume		
Number of shovels.....................................	27,000	30,000	33,000
Standard machine hours...........................	2,700	3,000	3,300
Budgeted manufacturing overhead cost:			
Variable...	$13,000	$15,000	$17,000
Fixed	30,000	30,000	30,000

Actual values: monthly production, 33,000 shovels; overhead costs, variable, $15,700, and fixed, $29,000; machine hours worked, 3,250. Compute: total overhead variance, overhead flexible budget variance, and production volume variance.

Exercise 24-10 *Preparing a standard cost income statement for management* **(Obj. 7)**

Victor Corp. revenue and expense information for the month of March, 2002, follows.

Sales revenue..	$440,000
Cost of goods sold (standard)...	272,000
Information regarding:	
Direct materials price variance	2,000F
Direct materials efficiency variance	5,000U
Direct labour price variance...	1,000U
Direct labour efficiency variance.................................	3,000F
Overhead flexible budget variance	2,500F
Production volume variance..	6,000U

Prepare a standard cost income statement through gross margin. Report all standard cost variances for management's use.

Challenge Exercise

Exercise 24-11   *Two-variance analysis of overhead*   *(Obj. 5)*

Klassen Electric Ltd. repairs appliances. The company measures "production output" in terms of appliances repaired. The company allocates overhead at the rate of $30 per television, VCR, or stereo repaired:

	Per Unit
Variable overhead rate............................	$10
Fixed overhead rate................................	20

In November, 2002, Klassen "produced" 5,200 repaired televisions, VCRs, and stereos. Its production volume variance was $6,000 U. Compute Klassen's budgeted fixed overhead cost per month. What monthly capacity level was used to compute the fixed overhead rate of $20 per unit?

Beyond the Numbers

Beyond the Numbers 24-1   *Explaining benefits of flexible budgets*   *(Obj. 1, 2)*

You recently accepted a management trainee position with Creative Barriers Inc., a company that installs residential fencing. At the end of your first month on the job, July 2002, your boss asks you to prepare a flexible budget for July's actual output of 228,000 metres of fencing. You are delighted to be assigned a task that uses your management accounting knowledge. Upon returning home that evening, you tell your roommate about your new task. Your roommate, a health sciences major, replies:

> Making a budget for a period that is already over reminds me of the round-the-world hot-air ballooner who lost track of his location. He landed in a meadow in a remote wilderness. Just as he was landing a hiker happened by:
>
> | Ballooner: | Can you tell me where I am? |
> |---|---|
> | Hiker: | Standing in a hot-air balloon basket in a meadow. |
> | Ballooner: | You must be an accountant. |
> | Hiker: | Yes! How in the world did you know that? |
> | Ballooner: | Because what you told me was precisely correct and utterly useless! |
>
> Why are you wasting time preparing an accurate budget for *last* month? Wouldn't it be more useful to develop a budget for *next* month?

Explain to your roommate how a budget for a period that has already finished can be useful.

Beyond the Numbers 24-2   *Explaining benefits of standard costing*   *(Obj. 3)*

One of your fellow classmates who is frustrated by the details of variance analysis complains:

> Our textbook says that standard costing is easier than actual costing. But if it's so much easier, why does the book need an extra half chapter just to explain it? I don't get it...

Use the Kool-Time Pools Ltd. example to explain why standard costing can simplify record-keeping in real companies.

Beyond the Numbers 24-3 *Explaining materials and labour variances* *(Obj. 4)*

You have a summer internship at the Quaker Oats Company of Canada factory in Peterborough, Ontario. Part of your job is to help the factory manager interpret accounting reports. One day the manager says:

> I can see that the direct materials price variance is based on the difference in prices. And I can see that the direct materials efficiency variance is based on the difference in quantities. What I've never understood is why we
>
> - Multiply the difference in prices by the *actual* quantity for the price variance, but
> - Multiply the difference in quantities by the *standard* price for the efficiency variance

Respond to the factory manager.

Ethical Issue

Better Living Products Inc. budgets from the bottom up. Production workers prepare departmental goals, which are coordinated by supervisors. Top managers combine the departmental budgets into the company's overall master budget. Standard costs developed from the budget amounts are used for the full year.

Production workers have observed that the standard costs correspond closely to their own budget amounts. Accordingly, they have built a cushion for themselves by overestimating the quantities of materials and labour needed to manufacture products.

Required

1. Are Better Living Products Inc.'s cost variances likely to be favourable or unfavourable? Why?
2. Whose behaviour is unethical, and whose behaviour is lax?
3. If this situation persists over several years, what is the likely outcome?

Problems (Group A)

Problem 24-1A *Preparing a flexible budget income statement and graphing cost behaviour* *(Obj. 1)*

Cellular Technologies Ltd. manufactures capacitors for cellular base stations. The company's master budget income statement for March 2003 follows. It is based on expected sales volume of 9,000 units.

Cellular Technologies Ltd.'s factory capacity is 9,500 units. If actual volume exceeds 9,500 units, the company must rent additional space. In that case, salaries will increase by 20 percent, rent will double, insurance expense will increase by $500, and amortization will increase by 30 percent.

Required

1. Prepare a flexible budget income statement for 7,500, 9,000, 10,000, and 11,000 units.
2. Graph the total operating expense behaviour of the company.

CELLULAR TECHNOLOGIES LTD.
Master Budget Income Statement
For the Month Ended March 31, 2003

Sales	$198,000
Variable expenses:	
Cost of goods sold	79,200
Sales commissions	9,450
Shipping	4,500
Fixed expenses:	
Salaries	27,500
Amortization	13,250
Rent	11,250
Insurance	2,750
Total operating expenses	147,900
Operating income	$ 50,100

Problem 24-2A *Preparing an income statement performance report* *(Obj. 2)*

Refer to Cellular Technologies Ltd., Problem 24-1A. The company sold 11,000 units during March 2003, and its actual income statement was as reported below.

CELLULAR TECHNOLOGIES LTD.
Income Statement

For the Month Ended March 31,	2003
Sales	$245,000
Variable expenses:	
Cost of goods sold	98,000
Sales commissions	11,250
Shipping	6,750
Fixed expenses:	
Salaries	34,000
Amortization	17,225
Rent	22,000
Insurance	3,500
Total operating expenses	192,725
Operating income	$ 52,275

Required

1. Prepare an income statement performance report for March 2003.

2. What was the effect on Cellular Technologies Ltd.'s operating income of selling 2,000 units more than the master budget level of sales?

3. What is Cellular Technologies Ltd.'s static budget variance? Explain why the income statement performance report provides more useful information to Cellular Technologies Ltd.'s managers than the simple static budget variance. What insights can Cellular Technologies Ltd.'s managers draw from this performance report?

Problem 24-3A *Preparing a flexible budget and computing standard cost variances* *(Obj. 1, 3, 4, 5)*

Preformed Fabricating Inc. manufactures molded plastic chairs, and uses flexible budgeting and a standard cost system. The company's performance report includes the following selected data:

	Static Budget 10,000 units	Actual Results 9,800 units
Sales (10,000 units × $21)	$210,000	
(9,800 units × $21.50)		$210,700
Variable expenses:		
Direct materials (40,000 kilograms × $0.80)	32,000	
(41,000 kilograms × $0.78)		31,980
Direct labour (5,000 hours × $6.00)...................	30,000	
(4,825 hours × $6.20)...................		29,915
Variable overhead (40,000 kilograms × $0.50)	20,000	
(41,000 kilograms × $0.64)		26,240
Fixed expenses:		
Fixed overhead..	28,000	28,500
Total cost of goods sold..	$110,000	$116,635
Gross margin...	$100,000	$94,065

Required

1. Prepare a flexible budget based on actual volume.
2. Compute the price variance and the efficiency variance for direct materials and for direct labour. For manufacturing overhead, compute the total variance, the flexible budget variance, and the production volume variance.
3. Show that the price variance plus the efficiency variance equals the flexible budget variance for direct materials and for direct labour. Use Exhibit 24-10 as a guide.
4. What are the benefits of standard costs? Refer to the Preformed Fabricating data.

Problem 24-4A   *Using incomplete cost and variance information to determine the number of direct labour hours worked*   *(Obj. 4)*

The province of Alberta has a shop that manufactures road signs used throughout the province. The manager of the shop uses standard costs to judge performance. Recently a clerk mistakenly threw away some of the records, and the manager has only partial data for July. The manager knows that the direct labour flexible budget variance for the month was $450 U and that the standard labour price was $6.00 per hour. The shop experienced an unfavourable labour price variance of $0.25 per hour. The standard direct labour hours for actual July output were 3,500.

Required

1. Find the actual number of direct labour hours worked during July. First, find the actual direct labour price per hour. Then, determine the actual number of direct labour hours by setting up the computation of the direct labour flexible budget variance of $450 U.
2. Compute the direct labour price and efficiency variances.

Problem 24-5A   *Computing and journalizing standard cost variances*   *(Obj. 4, 5, 6)*

Linghorn Cotton Mills Ltd. manufactures T-shirts that it sells to other companies for customizing with their own logos. Linghorn prepares flexible budgets and uses a standard cost system to control manufacturing costs. The standard unit cost of a basic white T-shirt is based on master budget volume of 30,000 T-shirts per month. The unit cost is computed as follows:

Direct materials (2 sq. metres at $0.21 per sq. metre)		$0.42
Direct labour (3 minutes at $0.12 per minute)		0.36
Overhead:		
Variable (3 minutes at $0.09 per minute).......................	$0.27	
Fixed (3 minutes at $0.14 per minute)	0.42	0.69
Total unit cost		$1.47

Transactions during May 2002 included the following:

a. Actual production and sales were 33,000 units.

b. Actual direct materials usage was 1.80 square metres per unit at cost of $0.17 per square metre.

c. Actual direct labour usage of 102,000 minutes cost $14,790.

d. Actual overhead cost was $21,970.

Required

1. Compute the price and efficiency variances for direct materials and direct labour.

2. Journalize the usage of direct materials and the application of direct labour, including the related variances.

3. Compute the total overhead variance, the flexible overhead budget variance, and the production volume variance for overhead.

4. Evaluate the performance of the factory managers in controlling overhead cost in May.

Problem 24-6A   *Computing standard cost variances and reporting to management*
           (Obj. 4, 5, 7)

Marco School Products Ltd. manufactures plastic rulers among other school products. During August 2002, the company produced and sold 104,000 rulers and recorded the following cost data:

	Standard Unit Cost	Actual Total Cost
Direct materials:		
Standard (1 unit at $0.28 per unit)	$0.28	
Actual (102,800 units at $0.30 per unit)..................		$30,840
Direct labour:		
Standard (0.02 hour at $5.00 per hour)...................	0.10	
Actual (1,560 hours at $5.75 per hour)		8,970
Overhead:		
Standard:		
Variable (0.03 machine hour at $6.00 per hour) .$0.18		
Fixed ($24,000 for static budget volume of		
100,000 units and 3,000 machine hours) 0.24 0.42		
Actual...		45,800
Total..	$0.80	$85,610

Required

1. Compute the price and efficiency variances for direct materials and direct labour.

2. For overhead, compute the total variance, the flexible budget variance, and the production volume variance.

3. Prepare a standard cost income statement through gross profit to report all variances to management. Sale price of the rulers to school supply stores was $1.25 each.

4. Marco's management used more-experienced workers during August. Discuss the trade-off between the two direct labour variances.

Problem 24-7A   *Computing standard cost variances and reporting to management*
           (Obj. 4, 5, 7)

The Halifax Flyrods Company Inc. produces a high quality graphite fly-fishing rod.

The company uses a standard costing system with the following standards based on the production of 5,000 units per year:

Direct materials (800 grams at $0.15 per gram)	$ 120.00 per unit
Direct labour (3 hours at $27.00 per hour)	81.00 per unit
Variable overhead (3 hours at $9.00 per hour)	27.00 per unit
Fixed overhead (3 hours at $15.00 per hour)	45.00 per unit
Total standard cost	$273.00 per unit

Actual results for 2003 included:

- Produced and sold 5,650 units at $425.00 per unit in the year.
- Purchased and used 4,550,000 grams of materials at a cost of $614,250.
- Actual direct labour costs were $448,875 for 17,100 hours.
- Actual variable overhead was $174,000 and the fixed overhead was $231,000.

Required

1. Compute the price and efficiency variances for direct materials and direct labour.
2. For overhead, compute the total overhead variance, the flexible budget variance, and the production volume variance.
3. Prepare a standard cost income statement through gross profit to report all variances to management.
4. During the year, management hired less-experienced workers at a lower wage rate. Evaluate management's decision.

Problem 24-8A *Computing standard cost variances, recording transactions at standard, and reporting to management* *(Obj. 4, 5, 6, 7)*

Empire Stove Company Ltd. uses a standard costing system in reporting on its production of wood stoves. The following standards were developed based on the production of 8,000 stoves:

Direct materials (100 kg at $3 per kg)	$300.00 per unit
Direct labour (15 hours at $15.00 per hour)	225.00 per unit
Variable overhead (6 machine hours at $18.00 per hour)	108.00 per unit
Fixed overhead (6 machine hours at $42.00 per hour)	252.00 per unit
Total standard cost	$885.00 per unit

The company had the following results for 2002:

- Produced and sold 7,800 stoves at an average selling price of $1,350 per stove.
- Purchased and used in production 793,000 kg of direct materials at an average cost of $2.925 per kilogram.
- Direct labour costs for the year were $1,680,000 for 112,000 hours.
- Production required 48,200 machine hours.
- Actual overhead costs were $3,045,000 (of which $845,000 was variable).

Required

1. Compute the price and efficiency variances for direct materials and direct labour.
2. For overhead, compute the total variance, the flexible budget variance, and the production volume variance.
3. Journalize all transactions for the year.
4. Prepare a brief explanation to management as to what in general is indicated by each of the two overhead variances.

Problems (Group B)

Problem 24-1B *Preparing a flexible budget income statement and graphing cost behaviour* *(Obj. 1)*

HomeAlert Inc. produces and sells prepackaged tests for radon gas. The company's master budget income statement for June 2002 follows. It is based on expected sales volume of 50,000 units.

HOMEALERT, INC.
Master Budget Income Statement
For the Month Ended June 30, 2002

Sales	$250,000
Variable expenses:	
Cost of goods sold	68,750
Sales commissions	18,750
Utilities	5,500
Fixed expenses:	
Salaries	40,000
Amortization	24,000
Rent	11,500
Insurance	8,850
Utilities	6,200
Total operating expenses	183,550
Operating income	$ 66,450

HomeAlert Inc.'s factory capacity is 65,000 units. If actual volume exceeds 65,000 units, the company must expand the factory. In that case, salaries will increase by 10 percent, amortization by 20 percent, rent by $5,500, and insurance by $1,400. Fixed utilities will be unchanged by the volume increase.

Required

1. Prepare a flexible budget income statement for the company, showing volume levels of 50,000, 60,000, and 70,000 units.
2. Graph the total operating expense behaviour of the company.

Problem 24-2B *Preparing an income statement performance report* *(Obj. 2)*

Refer to HomeAlert Inc. of Problem 24-1B. The company sold 52,000 units during June 2002, and its actual income statement was as follows:

HOMEALERT, INC.
Income Statement
For the Month Ended June 30, 2002

Sales	$263,500
Variable expenses:	
Cost of goods sold	74,600
Sales commissions	19,850
Utilities	6,000
Fixed expenses:	
Salaries	41,000
Amortization	24,000
Rent	11,500
Insurance	8,850
Utilities	6,200
Total operating expenses	192,000
Operating income	$ 71,500

Required

1. Prepare an income statement performance report for June 2002.
2. What accounts for most of the difference between actual operating income and master budget operating income?
3. What is HomeAlert's static budget variance? Explain why the income statement performance report provides more useful information than the simple static budget variance. What insights can HomeAlert's managers draw from this performance report?

Problem 24-3B *Preparing a flexible budget and computing standard cost variances (Obj. 1, 3, 4, 5)*

Apex Products Ltd. assembles VCRs and uses flexible budgeting and a standard cost system. Apex allocates overhead based on the number of direct material parts. The company's performance report includes the following selected data:

	Static Budget 20,000 VCRs	Actual Results 22,000 VCRs
Sales (20,000 units × $200)	$4,000,000	
(22,000 units × $210)		$4,620,000
Variable expenses:		
Direct materials (200,000 parts at $8.20)	1,640,000	
(214,200 parts at $7.90)		1,692,180
Direct labour (40,000 hours at $10.00)	400,000	
(42,500 hours at $10.50)		446,250
Variable overhead (200,000 parts at $2.00)	400,000	
(214,200 parts at $1.90)		406,980
Fixed expenses:		
Fixed overhead	650,000	660,000
Total cost of goods sold	3,090,000	3,205,410
Gross margin	$ 910,000	$1,414,590

Required

1. Prepare a flexible budget based on actual volume.
2. Compute the price variance and the efficiency variance for direct materials and for direct labour. For manufacturing overhead, compute the total variance, the flexible budget variance, and the production volume variance.
3. Show that the price variance plus the efficiency variance equals the flexible budget variance for direct materials and for direct labour. Use Exhibit 24-10 as a guide.
4. What are the benefits of standard costs? Refer to the Apex Products data in your answer.

Problem 24-4B *Using incomplete cost and variance information to determine the number of direct labour hours worked (Obj. 4)*

The city of Windsor, Ontario, has a shop that manufactures lampposts. The manager of the shop uses standard costs to judge performance. Recently, a clerk mistakenly threw away some of the records, and the manager has only partial data for October. The manager knows that the direct labour flexible budget variance for the month was $840 F and that the standard labour price was $7.50 per hour. A recent pay raise caused an unfavourable labour price variance of $0.50 per hour. The standard direct labour hours for actual October output were 3,200.

Required

1. Find the actual number of direct labour hours worked during October. First, find the actual direct labour price per hour. Then, determine the actual number of direct labour hours by setting up the computation of the direct labour flexible budget variance of $349 F.

2. Compute the direct labour price and efficiency variances.

Problem 24-5B *Computing and journalizing standard cost variances* **(Obj. 4, 5, 6)**

JKW Ltd. manufactures running shoes under licence. The company prepares flexible budgets and uses a standard cost system to control manufacturing costs. The following standard unit cost of a pair of shoes is based on the master budget volume of 12,000 pairs per month:

Direct materials (0.311 sq. metres at $18.00 per sq. metre)		$ 5.60
Direct labour (2 hours at $9.50 per hour)		19.00
Overhead:		
Variable (2 hours at $0.65 per hour)	$1.30	
Fixed (2 hours at $2.50 per hour)	5.00	6.30
Total unit cost		$30.90

Data for August 2002 include:

a. Actual production was 12,600 units.
b. Actual direct materials usage was 0.30 square metres per pair of shoes at actual cost of $17.60 per square metre.
c. Actual direct labour usage of 24,480 hours cost $235,008.
d. Total actual overhead cost was $78,500.

Required

1. Compute the price and efficiency variances for direct materials and direct labour.

2. Journalize the usage of direct materials and the application of direct labour, including the related variances.

3. For overhead, compute the total variance, the flexible budget variance, and the production volume variance.

4. JKW Ltd. management intentionally purchased less expensive materials for August production. How did this decision affect the other cost variances? Overall, was the decision wise?

Problem 24-6B *Computing standard cost variances and reporting to management* (Obj. 4, 5, 7)

Melrose Manufacturing Corp. produces industrial plastics. During April 2003, the company produced and sold 42,000 sheets of plastic and recorded the cost data on the following page.

Required

1. Compute the price and efficiency variances for direct materials and direct labour.

2. For overhead, compute the total variance, the flexible budget variance, and the production volume variance.

3. Prepare a standard cost income statement through gross profit to report all variances to management. Sale price of the plastic was $10.75 per sheet.

4. Melrose Manufacturing Corp. intentionally purchased more expensive materials during April. Was the decision wise? Discuss the trade-off between the two materials cost variances.

	Standard Unit Cost	Actual Total Cost
Direct materials:		
Standard (3 kg at $1.25 per kg).................................	$3.75	
Actual (124,400 kg at $1.30 per kg)		$161,720
Direct labour:		
Standard (0.1 hour at $7.00 per hour)......................	0.70	
Actual (4,400 hours at $6.80 per hour)		29,920
Overhead:		
Standard:		
Variable (0.2 machine hour at $6.00 per hour) ... $1.20		
Fixed ($64,000 for master budget volume of		
40,000 units and 8,000 machine hours) 1.60 2.80		
Actual...		118,900
Total..	$7.25	$310,540

Problem 24-7B *Computing standard cost variances and reporting to management (Obj. 4, 5, 7)*

Regina Storage Products Ltd. uses a standard costing system with the following standards based on the production of 4,000 canvas car tents per year:

Direct materials (6 square metres at $6.00 per square metre) .	$ 36.00 per unit
Direct labour (3 hours at $18.00 per hour)................................	54.00 per unit
Variable overhead (3 hours at $8.00 per hour)..........................	24.00 per unit
Fixed overhead (3 hours at $14.00 per hour).............................	42.00 per unit
Total standard cost	$156.00 per unit

Actual results for the year ended December 31, 2002, included:

- Produced and sold 3,000 units at $290.00 per car tent in the year.
- Purchased and used 19,800 square metres of materials at a cost of $124,760.
- Actual direct labour costs were $197,160 for 12,000 hours.
- Actual variable overhead was $94,200 and the fixed overhead was $166,000.

Required

1. Compute the price and efficiency variances for direct materials and direct labour.
2. For overhead, compute the total variance, the flexible budget variance, and the production volume variances.
3. Prepare a standard cost income statement through gross profit to report all variances to management.
4. During the year, management cut the workers' pay in hopes of increasing profits. Evaluate management's decision.

Problem 24-8B *Computing standard cost variances, recording transactions at standard, and reporting to management (Obj. 4, 5, 6, 7)*

The Lakehead Canoe Company Ltd. uses a standard costing system in reporting on its production of canoes. The following standards were developed based on the production of 4,000 canoes:

Direct materials (40 kg at $4.60 per kg)......................................	$184.00 per unit
Direct labour (12 hours at $12.00 per hour)..............................	144.00 per unit
Variable overhead (10 machine hours at $10.50 per hour)......	105.00 per unit
Fixed overhead (10 machine hours at $14.50 per hour)...........	145.00 per unit
Total standard cost	$578.00 per unit

The company had the following results for 2003:

- Produced and sold 4,200 canoes at an average selling price of $1,215 per canoe.
- Purchased and used in production 175,000 kg of direct materials at an average cost of $4.575 per kilogram.
- Direct labour costs for the year were $625,200 for 52,100 hours.
- Production required 42,200 machine hours.
- Actual overhead costs were $1,008,000 (of which $457,500 was variable).

Required

1. Compute the price and efficiency variances for direct materials and direct labour.
2. For overhead, compute the total variance, the flexible budget variance, and the production volume variances.
3. Journalize all transactions for the year.
4. Prepare a brief explanation to management indicating what, in general, is indicated by each of the two overhead variances.

Challenge Problems

Problem 24-1C   *Explaining a flexible budget*   *(Obj. 1, 2)*

Herman Jaworski, the production manager at Standard Tool and Die Inc., is very much opposed to flexible budgets. He believes that a budget should be set for the year and that the budget targets should be met. He has stated that if the budget is allowed to vary with sales and production and other factors, the value of the budget is lost.

Required

Explain to Mr. Jaworski why his firm should consider flexible budgets as a way of better understanding the company's operations.

Problem 24-2C   *Identify the benefits of standard costs*   *(Obj. 3)*

Many companies use standard costs for internal decision making as well as in the preparation of their financial statements.

Required

Because standard costs are used widely by manufacturing companies, great care must be taken in their determination. Discuss how standard costs would be used both internally and externally and indicate the problems that would arise if the standard costs were not accurate.

Extending Your Knowledge

Decision Problems

1. *Preparing a performance report and using it to evaluate performance* *(Obj. 2)*

The board of directors of ProGolf Distributors Ltd., a distributor of mid-range golf clubs, is meeting to evaluate the company's performance for the year just ended. The accompanying report has been prepared for the meeting.

PROGOLF DISTRIBUTORS LTD.
Income Statement Performance Report
For the Year Ended September 30, 2003

	Actual Results	Static Budget	Variances
Sales	$1,998,000	$2,520,000	$522,000 U
Variable expenses:			
Cost of goods sold	891,750	1,162,000	270,250 F
Sales commissions	87,675	124,500	36,825 F
Shipping	48,000	62,250	14,250 F
Fixed expenses:			
Salaries	331,200	320,250	10,950 U
Amortization	229,500	234,750	5,250 F
Rent	128,250	128,250	–0–
Advertising	95,100	82,500	12,600 U
Total operating expenses	1,811,475	2,114,500	303,025 F
Operating income	$ 186,525	$ 405,500	$218,975 U

The directors are disappointed by the operating income results. Further, they are puzzled by the presence of so many favourable variances. After all, actual operating income for the year is only 46.0 percent of the master (static) budget amount.

In response to the directors' initial questions, ProGolf's controller revealed that the actual sale price of $180 per unit was equal to the budgeted price. Also, there were no changes in inventories for the year.

Required

1. Prepare a more informative performance report than the one provided. Be sure to include a flexible budget for the actual quantity of golf clubs purchased and sold.

2. A downturn in the market for mid-range clubs was responsible for the company's inability to sell more golf clubs. In light of this information, how would you rate the company's performance? As a member of ProGolf Distributors Ltd.'s top management, which variances would you want investigated? Why?

2. Variance analysis and reporting in a nonprofit organization (Obj. 1, 2)

The Community Church is a congregation in suburban Halifax. At the end of 2001, the church's membership was 400 families. Each family donated an average of $600 per year to the church's operating fund and $1,000 to its mission and service fund.

For 2002, Community Church's Membership Committee budgeted a 10-percent increase in the number of families. Its Finance Committee planned a campaign to increase average donations to $625 for the operating fund and $1,100 for missions and service. On the first Sunday in 2002, the chairperson of the Finance Committee presented a budget to the congregation that incorporated the goals of the two committees. The budget called for operating receipts of $275,000.

During 2002, Community Church actually lost 10 families. The congregation's operating receipts totaled $252,000. The missions and service givings at $472,000 were close to the amount budgeted. The pastor has asked the Finance Committee if a sermon on giving is in order.

Required

1. As chairperson of the Finance Committee, prepare a thorough analysis of the congregation's donations in 2002.

2. Write a one-paragraph report to the pastor that addresses the question of a sermon on giving.

Comprehensive Problem

for Part Six

Planning for and assessing a new line of products

Fermi Manufacturing Co. Ltd. is in the process of deciding whether or not to introduce a new product line. The company manufactures recliners and is thinking of introducing two new styles: a standard model and a deluxe model. The company believes that, to be competitive, the selling price of the standard chair must be $425 and the deluxe chair must be $850. The company is unsure whether there will be sufficient profit at these prices.

The company determined that the costs to produce the chairs are:

	Standard	Deluxe
Direct materials	$120	$250
Direct labour	30	120
Variable overhead	15	60

The company anticipates that it will incur $1,200,000 of fixed manufacturing costs for the new product line.

The company analyzed the cost of activities in the other value chain areas and determined that it would incur $625,000 of fixed costs and the following variable costs in the nonmanufacturing activities:

Standard Model $ 60 per chair
Deluxe Model   100 per chair

Required

1. Compute the unit contribution margins for the standard model and the deluxe model.

2. Suppose that Fermi Manufacturing Co. Ltd.'s sales mix is six standard models for every two deluxe models. How many chairs must the company sell to break even?

3. The company will not undertake production of these products unless an operating income of $200,000 can be made. How many chairs must the company sell to achieve this level of income?

4. The company decided to introduce these two new products and budgeted sales of 6,000 standard units and 2,000 deluxe units at the sale price and costs presented above. Prepare the master budget for the two products. (Hint: the budgeted operating income of the two products is $15,000).

5. At the end of the first year, management wished to review the results for the two models. The company actually sold 5,600 standard units and 2,300 deluxe units. The selling prices were as anticipated, as were all costs except material costs, which were 10 percent higher for both models. Prepare a flexible budget and complete a performance report, analyzing the year's activities. Did the company achieve its budgeted net income? Why or why not?

25

Activity–Based Costing and Other Tools for Cost Management

CHAPTER OBJECTIVES

After studying this chapter, you should be able to

1 Describe and develop activity-based costs (ABC)

2 Use ABC data and activity-based management (ABM) to make business decisions

3 Use ABM and value engineering to achieve target costs for target pricing

4 Decide when ABC is most likely to pass the cost-benefit test.

5 Compare a traditional production system to a just-in-time (JIT) production system

6 Record manufacturing costs for a just-in-time costing system

7 Contrast the four types of quality costs and use these costs to make decisions

Mobil Oil Corporation was a worldwide leader in petroleum and derivative products prior to its merger with Exxon in 1999. The new combined company reported revenues of $233 billion and net income of almost $18 billion for the year ending December 31, 2000.

Prior to the merger, Mobil Oil had been implementing an activity-based costing approach in its product categories. One of Mobil's major categories was lubricants, which contains readily recognizable products such as Mobil 1 passenger vehicle lubricant and thousands of other industrial and commercial grade lubricants. Mobil continues to be an integrated supplier of lubricants, meaning that it possesses the technology and infrastructure for producing lubricants from base components and delivering finished products to end customers through both the Mobil and Exxon distribution networks.

After Mobil's 1996 fiscal year, the company's chairman, Lou Noto, announced a strategic goal of becoming the most profitable company in lubricants worldwide. The goal was to achieve a 33 percent increase in after-tax profits by the year 2000 through the broad strategies of growth, cost reduction, and stronger competitive position. In the complex product category of lubricants, cost reduction strategies were difficult to implement.

Fortunately for Mobil, the U.S. Lubricants division had previously embarked on a project of cost analysis. The general manager of the division suspected that the high degree of complexity was adding cost to the business. An analysis of the situation revealed that the cost accounting system in place at the time had no way of reflecting the cost of complexity, because it treated all products equally. Indirect manufacturing costs were volumetrically applied to the lubricants manufactured. This method could not address the cost to produce each product individually. The consultants involved in the study, A.D. Little, recommended using Activity-Based Costing (ABC) to better reflect the real costs of producing the multiple product and package combinations within Mobil's lubricant network.

ABC proved to be the perfect tool for identifying the cost of complexity in the lubricant business. By using activity drivers instead of volume drivers, ABC could expose fundamental differences in costs of producing thousands of product and package combinations.

Did the switch to ABC pay off? The results were startling. In the years since adopting ABC, every business indicator has become more positive—profits, return on common equity, and manufacturing expense reduction. This turnaround made Mobil a more attractive investment in its merger with Exxon.

Source: "ABC Gathers Speed at Mobil" by Tom Kang, Mobil Oil Corporation, from the Internet Web site ABC Technologies (http://www.abctech.com/successes/successes.dsp?Mode= DisplayArticle&ArticleID=71)

Mobil Oil Corporation
www.mobil.com

T O T H R I V E in a globally competitive market, Mobil Oil Corporation must provide customers with goods or services at an attractive price, while managing costs so the company still earns a profit. This is called delivering value to the customer. This chapter will show you several methods managers use to control costs so the company can deliver value to the customer at a profit:

- Activity-based costing
- Activity-based management and target costing
- Just-in-time systems
- Costs of quality

These methods, largely unheard of 15 years ago, are now routinely used by companies like Mobil Oil Corporation, General Motors Corporation, and Dell Computer Corporation. Before discussing activity-based costing and activity-based management, we first consider why companies need more detailed and accurate cost systems.

Refining Cost Systems

The Need for Refined Cost Systems

To allocate indirect costs to cost objects like departments or products, companies use average allocation rates. The broader the indirect cost pool used in the numerator of the allocation rate, and the broader the allocation base used in the denominator, the less accurate the resulting cost allocation. Similarly, the narrower the cost pools and cost allocation bases, the more refined the average rates and the more accurate the cost allocation. A simple example shows that organizations from Mobil Oil Corporation to Dell Computer are developing more refined costing systems like ABC. Why? Because simple systems that do not match costs with the consumption of resources can assign costs inaccurately and inequitably.

Suppose David Larmer, Matt Sewell, and Marc Bryan are three college friends who decide to room together during their second year. They agree to share on an equal basis the following monthly costs:

Rent and utilities	$570
Cable TV	50
High-speed Internet access	40
Groceries	240
Total monthly costs	$900

Each roommate's share is $300 ($900/3).

Things go smoothly for the first few months. But then David calls a meeting. "Since I started having dinner at Amy's each night, I shouldn't have to chip in for the groceries." Matt then pipes in: "I'm so busy studying and surfing the Net that I never have time to watch TV. I don't want to pay for the cable TV anymore." And, he continues, "Marc, since your friend Jennifer eats here most evenings, you should pay a double share of the grocery bill." Marc retorts, "If that's the way you feel, Matt, then you should pay for the Internet access, since you're the only one around here who uses it!"

What happened? The friends originally agreed to share the costs equally. But they soon discover that they are not participating equally in three costly activities: watching cable TV, surfing the Net, and eating. Equal assignment of the costs is therefore not equitable.

The roommates could use a refined approach that better matches the costs with the people who participate in each activity. This means splitting the cable TV costs between David and Marc, assigning the Internet access cost to Matt, and allocating the grocery bill 1/3 to Matt and 2/3 to Marc. Exhibit 25-1 compares the results of this refined system with the original system.

No wonder David called a meeting! The original system allocated him $300 a month, but the refined system shows that a more equitable share would be only

	David Larmer	Matt Sewell	Marc Bryan	Total
More refined cost allocation system:				
Rent and utilities	$190	$190	$190	$570
Cable TV	25	—	25	50
High-speed Internet access	—	40	—	40
Groceries	—	80	160	240
Total costs allocated	$215	$310	$375	$900
Less refined original cost allocation system	$300	$300	$300	$900
Difference	$ (85)	$ 10	$ 75	$ 0

EXHIBIT 25-1

More Refined versus Less Refined Cost Allocation System

$215. On the other hand, the new system allocates Marc $375 a month instead of $300. David was paying for resources he did not consume (Internet access and groceries), while Marc was not paying for all the resources (groceries) he and his guest consumed. We could say that David was "overcosted" and Marc was "undercosted."

Notice, however, that the total monthly costs are the same ($900) under both systems. The only difference is how that $900 is allocated among the three roommates. The amount by which David is "overcosted" ($85) must exactly equal the amounts by which Matt and Marc are "undercosted" ($10 + $75).

In a highly competitive, globally wired marketplace, companies from Coca-Coca to Dell Computer need to know how much it costs to bring each product to market. Dell needs to know what it costs to assemble and deliver a customized laptop to a client in Edmonton, Alberta. Why? So Dell can set a price that covers the costs of all the resources required to assemble and deliver that specific laptop (and provide some profit), yet remain competitive with prices charged by its competitors.

Sharpening the Focus: From Business Functions, to Departments, to Activities

Refining the cost system requires drilling down from the six broad business functions that compose the value chain, to individual departments in each function, to specific activities in those departments.

Panel A of Exhibit 25-2 lists these six broad value-chain functions for a manufacturer like Dell Computer Corporation: research and development, design, production, marketing, distribution, and customer service. In Chapter 19, we showed that companies need to know the full costs (from all elements of the value chain) to set sale prices that cover all these costs, and to determine the profitability of different products. However, remember that under GAAP, only costs incurred in the

EXHIBIT 25-2

Overview of Business Functions, Departments, and Activities

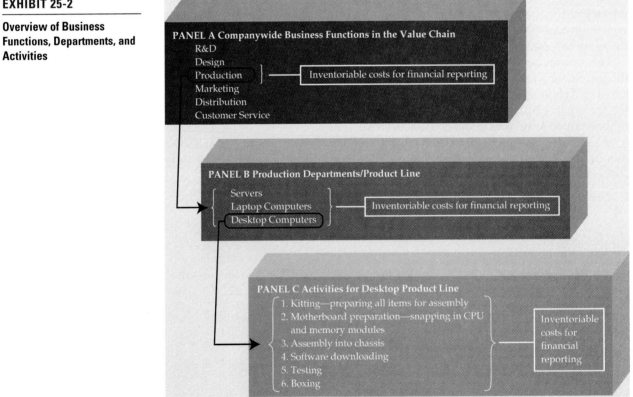

production element of the value chain are inventoriable for financial reporting. Since most companies begin refining their cost systems in the production/manufacturing function, our discussion and examples focus on this function. But managers in companies like Dell and Mobil Oil can apply the same principles to costs incurred in other elements of the value chain.

Panel B of Exhibit 25-2 shows that the production function is divided into departments (servers, laptop computers, and desktop computers). Panel C then focuses on the desktop computer production department, and lists six common activities in assembling desktop computers. Managers need to know the costs of cost object at each level.

- Business functions—such as Dell Computer's production function
- Departments—such as Dell's desktop product line
- Activities—such as Dell's assembly or software downloading activities in the desktop production department

Exhibit 25-3 shows that when managers limited their focus to broad business functions, simple cost systems that allocated indirect costs using broad-based averages were often good enough to meet their needs. As increasing competition forced managers to drill down to individual departments within a function, companies often developed separate indirect cost allocation rates for each individual department. Rather than using a factory-wide manufacturing overhead rate, for example, the company could develop one overhead rate for the server production department and another for the desktop production department.

Now managers are drilling down farther to focus on specific activities within individual departments. Exhibit 25-3 shows that companies further refine their cost systems to develop separate indirect cost allocation rates for each activity within a department. For example, rather than using one manufacturing overhead rate for the entire desktop production department, they may develop separate indirect cost allocation rates for each activity in the desktop production department. See Panel C of Exhibit 25-2: There is one allocation rate for the kitting activity, another for the motherboard preparation activity, and so on. Such a refined system is called an *activity-based costing system.*

Managers Focus on:	Indirect Cost Allocation System:
Broad business functions such as production	Single functionwide indirect cost allocation rate—for example, a factory-wide manufacturing overhead rate
↓	↓
Departments within a function, such as the server, laptop, and desktop computer production departments	Separate indirect cost allocation rates for each different department—for example, separate manufacturing overhead rates for the server, laptop, and desktop production departments
↓	↓
Activities within a department, such as the kitting, motherboard preparation, and assembly activities in the desktop computer production department	Specific indirect cost allocation rates for each activity within a department—for example, one indirect cost allocation rate for kitting, a separate rate for motherboard preparation, and so on. The indirect cost allocation rate for each activity uses a different cost driver.

EXHIBIT 25-3

Sharpening the Business Focus

Dell Canada Online
www.dell.ca

General Motors
www.gmcanada.com

Johnson & Johnson
www.johnsonandjohnson.com

REAL WORLD EXAMPLE

A recent survey indicated that 62 percent of companies still use direct labour as their primary cost driver.

LEARNING TIP

Exhibit 25-2 shows that *only* production (manufacturing) costs are assigned to products for financial reporting. However, companies need to know the full costs (from all elements of the value chain) to set a sale price that covers all their costs, and to determine the profitability of different products. Many companies use ABC to assign costs from the entire value chain.

Activity-Based Costing

Chapter 24 showed how managers use standard costing and variance analysis to control direct material and direct labour costs. But most managers need more than the aggregate manufacturing overhead flexible budget variance to control indirect manufacturing costs. Over the past several years, companies like General Motors Corporation and Johnson & Johnson have developed refined systems like activity-based costing to help control indirect costs.

Activity-based costing (ABC) focuses on *activities* as the fundamental cost objects. The costs of those activities become building blocks for compiling costs, as ABC links costs to the activities that cause those costs. Activity-based costing can be used with job costing or process costing, and it is used by many banks and hospitals as well as by manufacturers.

ABC systems trace direct materials and direct labour to cost objects, as described in Chapter 20. The only difference is the allocation of indirect costs. While direct materials and direct labour are easy to trace, it is more difficult to allocate *indirect* costs—such as manufacturing overhead—to the products that caused these costs.

Many companies start out using a simple system and combine all the indirect costs into a single cost pool, and then allocate those costs using a single allocation base—often direct labour. However, inaccurate product costs can result if:

1. *The allocation base is not a cost driver.* Recall that a *cost driver* is any factor whose change causes a change in a related total cost. For example, if the production process is highly automated, most overhead costs are not related to direct labour, so direct labour is not the main driver of overhead costs.

2. *One allocation base is insufficient.* In most companies, no *single* factor drives all manufacturing overhead costs, much less all indirect costs in the value chain.

In either case, allocation bases that are not cost drivers lead to inaccurate product costs.

Activity-based costing reduces these problems by separately estimating the indirect costs of each activity, and then allocating the costs of each activity based on what caused those costs. This means that each activity's indirect cost has its own (usually unique) cost allocation base, or cost driver. For example, Dell Computer Corporation's ABC system allocates indirect assembly labour costs based on the number of times workers touch a computer as it moves through the assembly process. A computer that requires more touches is allocated more of the indirect assembly labour activity cost than a different model that requires fewer touches.

Exhibit 25-4 lists common activities and related cost drivers. By using cost drivers that capture causal relationships, ABC systems yield more accurate product costs than systems that use a single allocation base. Hence, managers can make wiser decisions about what sale price to charge customers, and which products to push.

Accountants have long known that product costs would be more accurate if companies allocated indirect costs using several cost drivers rather than a single allocation base. Until recently, however, it was too expensive to develop multiple-cost-driver costing systems. This is why most companies started out using direct

EXHIBIT 25-4

Activities and Cost Drivers

Activity	Cost Driver
Materials purchasing	Number of purchase orders
Materials handling	Number of parts
Production scheduling	Number of batches
Quality inspections	Number of inspections
Photocopying	Number of pages copied
Warranty services	Number of service calls
Shipping	Number of kilograms

labour as their only allocation base. However, "data warehouses" and other information technology have made ABC feasible. Optical scanning and bar coding reduce the cost of collecting activity costs and cost driver information. Powerful enterprise resource planning (ERP) systems like SAP, Oracle, and Peoplesoft now contain ABC applications. Companies can buy ABC software or develop their own ABC software. For example, Dell Computer Corporation began its ABC system using Excel spreadsheets.

Dell builds the manufacturing cost of each computer from the direct costs plus the indirect costs of the specific activities required to produce it. This buildup of *manufacturing costs* determines the inventoriable product cost used for *financial reporting* purposes. However, for internal decisions such as pricing and product profitability analysis, Dell also assigns the costs of nonmanufacturing activities to products. For example, Dell assigns the costs of the warranty service activity to product lines based on the number of service calls.

Developing an Activity-Based Costing System

In many ways, ABC systems are similar to traditional systems. The main difference is that ABC systems have separate indirect cost allocation rates for each activity. This means ABC systems have (1) more indirect cost pools, and (2) more indirect cost allocation bases. The greater detail makes ABC systems more accurate but more expensive than traditional costing systems.

ABC requires seven steps. Managers must

1. Identify the activities.
2. Estimate the total indirect costs for each activity.
3. Identify the allocation base for each activity's indirect costs—this is the primary cost driver.
4. Estimate the total quantity of each allocation base.
5. Compute the cost allocation rate for each activity:

$$\text{Cost allocation rate for activity} = \frac{\text{Estimated total indirect costs of activity}}{\text{Estimated total quantity of cost allocation base}}$$

6. Obtain the actual quantity of each allocation base used by the cost object (for example, the quantity of each allocation base used by a particular product).
7. Allocate the costs to the cost object:

$$\text{Allocated activity cost} = \text{Cost allocation rate for activity} \times \text{Actual quantity of cost allocation base used by the cost object}$$

The first step in developing an activity-based costing system is identifying the activities. Analyzing all the activities required to make a product forces managers to think about how each activity might be improved—or whether the activity is necessary at all. It also helps executives manage operations more efficiently.

Steps 2 through 7 are the same approach used to allocate manufacturing overhead, as explained in Chapter 20. The only difference is that ABC systems repeat steps 2 through 7 for each activity.

Traditional versus Activity-Based Costing Systems

We use a streamlined example to emphasize the basic distinctions between activity-based costing systems and traditional costing systems. Our example necessarily simplifies the process that would occur in real companies like Dell Computer

Corporation or Mobil Oil Corporation, which would identify many different activities.

Our example uses the Chemical Manufacturing Department of Chemtech Inc., a company that produces hundreds of different chemicals. Chemtech Inc. has focused on producing mass quantities of "commodity" chemicals for many large customers. But it also manufactures small quantities of specialty chemicals for individual customers.

Last updated in 1992, the Chemical Manufacturing Department's cost system uses a single indirect cost pool and allocates manufacturing overhead at 200 percent of direct labour cost. Chemtech Inc.'s controller, Martha Wise, gathered data for two of the department's many products:

- Aldehyde—a commodity chemical used in producing plastics
- Phenylephrine hydrochloride (PH)—a specialty chemical (A single customer uses PH in manufacturing blood-pressure medications.)

	Aldehyde	Phenylephrine Hydrochloride (PH)
Number of kilograms (kg) per year	7,000 kg	5 kg
Direct materials cost per kg	$ 5	$20
Direct labour cost per kg	$ 1	$10
Sale price per kg	$10	$70

Wise used this information to compute each product's gross margin, as shown in Exhibit 25-5.

The gross margin for the PH (phenylephrine hydrochloride) specialty chemical is $20 per kilogram—ten times as high as the gross margin for the aldehyde commodity chemical ($2). Chemtech Inc. CEO Randy Smith is surprised that PH appears so much more profitable (per kilogram) than aldehyde, so he asks Wise to check 50 of the department's other products. After doing so, Wise confirms that the gross margin per kilogram is ten times as high for specialty chemicals as it is for commodity chemicals. As a result, Smith wonders whether Chemtech Inc. should switch its focus to manufacturing specialty chemicals.

STOP & THINK

1. What is the *total* direct labour cost assigned to
   a. Aldehyde?   b. PH (phenylephrine hydrochloride)?
2. What is the *total* manufacturing overhead allocated to
   a. Aldehyde?   b. PH?

Answers:

1. Total direct labour cost assigned to aldehyde is 7,000 kgs × $1 per kg = $7,000. Total direct labour cost assigned to PH is 5 kg × $10 per kg = $50. Thus Chemtech Inc. assigns to aldehyde 140 times as much total direct labour cost as it does to PH ($7,000 ÷ $50 = 140).

2. **Key Point**: Because Chemtech Inc. uses direct labour cost as its single allocation base, Chemtech Inc. also allocates 140 times as much total overhead to aldehyde as to PH. Total overhead allocated to aldehyde is 7,000 kg × $2 per kg = $14,000. Total overhead allocated to PH is 5 kg × $20 per kg = $100. Thus the original single-allocation-base (direct labour) system allocates 140 times as much total overhead to aldehyde as to PH ($14,000 ÷ $100). This traditional costing procedure is accurate only if aldehyde really does cause 140 times as much overhead as PH. That is, the existing system assumes that direct labour really is the primary overhead cost driver and that total manufacturing overhead really does change in direct proportion to direct labour.

	Aldehyde	PH
Sale price per kg.....................................	$10.00	$70.00
Less: Manufacturing cost per kg		
Direct materials.....................................	5.00	20.00
Direct labour..	1.00	10.00
Manufacturing overhead		
(at 200% of direct labour cost)......	2.00	20.00
Total manufacturing cost per kg..........	8.00	50.00
Gross margin per kg.............................	$ 2.00	$20.00

CEO Randy Smith calls a meeting with the department's foreman Steve Pronai and controller Martha Wise. Smith is perplexed that the accounting numbers show that specialty chemicals like PH are more profitable (on a per-kilogram basis) than commodity chemicals like aldehyde. He expected the department would be more efficient producing a few different commodity chemicals (in very large batches) than producing a wide variety of specialty chemicals (in small batches). Foreman Pronai echoes Smith's concern. Pronai says it takes just as long to mix a small batch of specialty chemicals as a large batch of commodity chemicals. Finally, Smith is puzzled because Chemtech's competitors seem to be earning good profits, even though they usually undercut Chemtech Inc.'s sale prices on commodity chemicals.

After listening to this discussion, Wise fears that the problem could be Chemtech Inc.'s cost accounting system. For years she had tried to get Smith to update the costing system, but Smith ignored accounting and invested in new equipment and in marketing. Now Wise has Smith's attention. Wise suggests that foreman Pronai and the plant engineer work with her to develop a pilot ABC system for part of the Chemical Manufacturing Department's operations. Exhibit 25-6 compares the original direct-labour-single-allocation-base system (Panel A) with the new ABC system (Panel B).

In developing their new ABC system, Chemtech Inc.'s ABC team followed the seven steps:

Step 1. *Identify the activities.*
Wise and her team identify three activities in the Chemical Manufacturing Department: mixing, processing, and testing. See Exhibit 25-7, column 1.

Step 2. *Estimate the total indirect costs of each activity.*
Pronai estimates that total mixing costs for all products will be $600,000. Estimated costs for each activity appear in Exhibit 25-7, column 2.

Step 3. *Identify the allocation base for each activity's indirect costs—the primary cost driver.*
Workers mix ingredients separately for each batch of chemicals, so the number of batches drives mixing costs. Exhibit 25-7, column 3, lists the cost driver (allocation base) for each activity.

Step 4. *Estimate the total quantity of each allocation base.*
Wise and Pronai estimate that the department will produce a total of 4,000 batches of chemicals. Estimated quantities of the cost driver allocation base appear in column 4 of Exhibit 25-7.

Step 5. *Compute the cost allocation rate for each activity.*
Wise computes the allocation rate for mixing, as follows:

$$\text{Cost allocation rate for mixing} = \frac{\$600,000}{4,000 \text{ batches}}$$
$$= \$150 \text{ per batch}$$

Column 5 of Exhibit 25-7 shows the cost allocation rate for each activity.

EXHIBIT 25-6

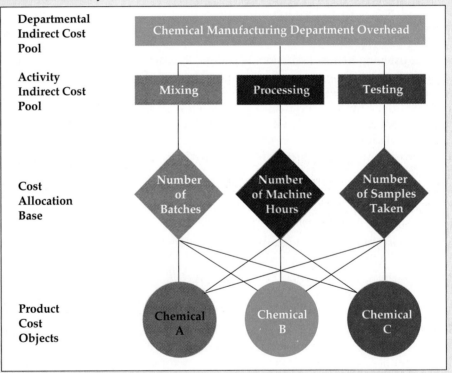

PANEL A—Traditional System

Departmental
Indirect Cost
Pool

Chemical Manufacturing Department Overhead

Cost
Allocation
Base

Direct
Labour
Cost

Product
Cost
Objects

Chemical A — Chemical B — Chemical C

PANEL B—ABC System

Departmental
Indirect Cost
Pool

Chemical Manufacturing Department Overhead

Activity
Indirect Cost
Pool

Mixing — Processing — Testing

Cost
Allocation
Base

Number of Batches — Number of Machine Hours — Number of Samples Taken

Product
Cost
Objects

Chemical A — Chemical B — Chemical C

EXHIBIT 25-7

Chemtech Inc.'s Activity-
Based Costing System

(1)	(2)	(3)	(4)
Activity	**Estimated Costs**	**Cost Allocation Base**	**Estimated Quantity of Cost Allocation Base**
Mixing	$600,000	# Batches	4,000 batches
Processing	$3,000,000	# Machine hours (MH)	50,000 MH
Testing	$600,000	# Samples	3,000 samples

Step 6. *Obtain the actual quantity of each allocation base used by each product.*

During the year, Chemtech produces 60 batches of aldehyde and 1 batch of PH. (This total of 61 batches is only a small fraction of the 4,000 total batches Chemtech produces. The remaining batches consist of Chemtech's other chemicals.) Exhibit 25-7, column 6, shows the actual quantities of each activity's allocation base used by aldehyde and PH.

Step 7. *Allocate the costs to each product.*

Wise allocates mixing costs as follows:

> Aldehyde: 60 batches × $150 per batch = $9,000
> PH: 1 batch × $150 per batch = $ 150

Column 7 of Exhibit 25-7 shows the cost allocation for all three activities.

Wise then recomputes manufacturing overhead costs (Panel A) and gross margins (Panel B), as shown in Exhibit 25-8. For each product, Wise adds the total costs of the three activities to obtain the total manufacturing overhead allocated to each product. Panel A shows that the total ABC overhead is $13,630 for aldehyde and $470 for PH. As in the original direct-labour-single-allocation-base system, this multiple-allocation-base ABC system allocates more *total* overhead to aldehyde, because Chemtech Inc. produces much more aldehyde than PH. However, there is a significant difference in the *ratio* of overhead allocated to aldehyde versus PH. The ABC system allocates only 29 times as much overhead to aldehyde as to PH ($13,630 ÷ $470 = 29). This is much less than in the original direct-labour-based system, which allocated 140 times as much overhead to aldehyde as to PH (see Stop & Think on page 1382).

After totaling the manufacturing overhead costs for each product, Wise computes the overhead cost per kilogram, as shown in Exhibit 25-8, Panel A. For aldehyde, Wise divides the $13,630 total manufacturing overhead by the 7,000 kg of aldehyde produced, to get an overhead cost per kilogram of $1.95 (rounded). For PH, the ABC overhead cost per kilogram is $94.00 ($470 ÷ 5 kg)

Now, let's compare the overhead cost per kilogram under the original direct-labour-based system with the ABC costs:

	Overhead Cost per Kilogram	
	Traditional Direct Labour System (Exhibit 25-5)	**ABC System (Exhibit 25-8)**
Aldehyde	$ 2.00	$ 1.95
PH	20.00	94.00

(5)	(6)		(7)	
	Actual Quantity of Cost Allocation Base Used by:		**Allocated Activity Cost**	
Cost Allocation Rate	**Aldehyde**	**PH**	**Aldehyde**	**PH**
$\frac{\$600,000}{4,000}$ = $150/batch	60 batches	1 batch	$150 × 60 = $9,000	$150 × 1 = $150
$\frac{\$3,000,000}{50,000}$ = $60/MH	30½ MH	2 MH	$60 × 30½ = $1,830	$60 × 2 = $120
$\frac{\$600,000}{3,000}$ = $200/sample	14 samples	1 sample	$200 × 14 = $2,800	$200 × 1 = $200

EXHIBIT 25-8

Chemtech Inc.'s Activity-
Based Costing System

Panel A—Manufacturing Overhead per Kilogram

	Aldehyde	PH
Mixing (from Exhibit 25-7)	$ 9,000	$150
Processing (from Exhibit 25-7)	1,830	120
Testing (from Exhibit 25-7)	2,800	200
Total manufacturing overhead	$13,630	$470
Divided by number of kg	÷ 7,000 kg	÷ 5 kg
Manufacturing overhead per kg	$1.95/kg*	$ 94/kg

*Rounded

Panel B—Gross Margin per Kilogram

	Aldehyde	PH
Sale price	$10.00	$ 70.00
Less: Manufacturing costs:		
Direct materials	$ 5.00	$ 20.00
Direct labour	1.00	10.00
Manufacturing overhead (from Panel A)	1.95	94.00
Total manufacturing cost	7.95	124.00
Gross margin (Loss)	$ 2.05	$ (54.00)

Which cost approach is more accurate? *ABC costs are more accurate because ABC represents the resources (mixing costs, machine time, and testing) that each product actually uses.* The old direct-labour-single-allocation-base system allocated too much overhead to the product that uses more total direct labour (aldehyde) and too little overhead to the product that uses less total direct labour (PH). (The Stop & Think on page 1382 shows that aldehyde uses a total of $7,000 of direct labour cost, while PH uses a total of only $50 of direct labour). The simpler traditional system *overcosted* aldehyde and *undercosted* PH.

With more precise allocations, ABC shifts costs out of aldehyde and into PH where the costs belong. Why? Exhibit 25-7 shows that aldehyde used more of each activity than PH but *not* 140 times as much. Column 6 shows that aldehyde uses 60 times as much mixing, about 15 times as many machine hours (processing costs), and 14 times as much testing as PH.

Although Chemtech Inc. made only five kilograms of PH, this product still required

- Workers to mix a batch, at a mixing cost of $150
- 2 machine hours at $60 per hour
- One sample tested at a cost of $200

Spreading these costs over the five kilograms of PH yields an overhead cost of $94 per kilogram, as shown in Exhibit 25-8, Panel A.

Allocating overhead based on actual *usage* of the resources increases the costs of low-volume products like PH that are produced in small batches. Why? Because costs like mixing and testing a batch are spread over the small number of units in that batch. On the other hand, mixing and testing costs are spread over the larger number of kilograms for high-volume products that are produced in large batches, like aldehyde.

Controller Martha Wise is now ready to recompute product costs and gross margins using the ABC data. Exhibit 25-8, Panel B, shows that the cost per kilogram of aldehyde is $7.95 under the ABC system. Contrast this with the $8.00 cost per kilogram under Chemtech Inc.'s original system (Exhibit 25-5). More important, the ABC data in Exhibit 25-8 show that specialty chemical PH costs $124 per kilogram, rather than $50 per kilogram as indicated by the old direct-labour-single-allocation-base system (Exhibit 25-5). Panel B shows that by selling PH for $70 per kilogram, Chemtech Inc. has been losing $54 on each kilogram—and this is *before* considering nonmanufacturing costs such as R&D, marketing, and distribution. Wise finds that most of Chemtech Inc.'s other specialty chemicals show similar increases in cost under the ABC system.

The Chemtech Inc. example shows that ABC can dramatically affect product costs. In many cases, ABC systems show that companies lose money on their low-volume products, such as Chemtech Inc.'s PH. One business consultant says: "20 percent of a company's products usually produce 80 percent of its profits." ABC spurs many companies to cut their money-losing products.

Activity-Based Management: Using ABC for Decision Making

OBJECTIVE 2
Use ABC data and activity-based management (ABM) to make business decisions

Activity-based management (ABM) refers to using activity-based cost information to make decisions that increase profits while satisfying customers' needs. We consider how Chemtech Inc. can use ABC information in three kinds of decisions: (1) pricing and product mix, (2) cost reduction, and (3) routine planning and control.

Pricing and Product Mix Decisions

Exhibit 25-9 compares key cost and gross profit information for aldehyde and PH, based on Chemtech's original cost system and then on the new ABC system. ABC shows that PH costs Chemtech $124 rather than the $50 reported by the old cost system. Chemtech is losing $54 on every kilogram of PH—*before* considering nonmanufacturing costs!

Chemtech Inc. may be able to use the ABC analysis to find ways to cut costs. If it cannot cut costs enough to earn a profit on PH, then it will have to consider raising the sale price. If customers will not pay a higher price, Chemtech should consider dropping PH. More generally, if the ABC system shows that commodity chemicals are more profitable than Chemtech thought, and specialty chemicals are less profitable, Chemtech Inc. may shift its product mix away from specialty chemicals toward commodity chemicals. This is the exact opposite of the strategy suggested by cost data from the original system.

Cost Reduction Decisions

Most companies adopt ABC to get more accurate product costs for pricing and product mix decisions. But managers often find that they reap even greater benefits by using ABM to pinpoint opportunities to cut costs.

Value Engineering With an ABC system in place, organizations can use value engineering to reduce costs. **Value engineering** means systematically evaluating

	Aldehyde	PH
Original cost system (from Exhibit 25-5)		
Sale price per kilogram.....................	$10.00	$ 70.00
Less: Manufacturing cost per kilogram	8.00	50.00
Gross margin per kilogram..............	$ 2.00	$ 20.00
Activity-based cost system (from Exhibit 25-8)		
Sale price per kilogram.....................	$10.00	$ 70.00
Less: Manufacturing cost per kilogram	7.95	124.00
Gross margin per kilogram..............	$ 2.05	$ (54.00)

EXHIBIT 25-9

Comparison of Chemtech Inc.'s Product Costs Under Original versus ABC Systems

activities in an effort to reduce costs while satisfying customer needs. Companies conduct value engineering using cross-functional teams: marketers identify customer needs, engineers and production personnel design more efficient processes and products, and accountants estimate how proposed changes will affect costs.

Carrier Corporation, the world's largest manufacturer of air conditioning and heating products, assembled a cross-functional team that used ABM in a value engineering drive to minimize complexity or variety in products, component parts, and manufacturing processes. The goal is to cut by half the 280 different circuit breakers and 580 different fasteners used in its products. Slashing the number of different component parts will significantly cut Carrier's ordering costs, since ABC often estimates that purchase orders cost up to $100–$200 each. It will also cut receiving, inspection, and materials-handling costs. Carrier may benefit from quantity discounts on larger orders of the remaining parts. Since experts estimate that 75–90% of a product's costs are locked in when the design is set, design changes usually present the greatest opportunities to slash costs.

Let's return to our illustration. Chemtech Inc. assembles a cross-functional value engineering team that includes marketing manager Liz Smith, plant engineer Edward Michaels, and production foreman Steve Pronai, along with controller Martha Wise. The team analyzes each of Chemtech's three production activities: mixing, processing, and testing. For each activity, the team considers (1) how to cut costs given current production processes, and (2) how to redesign the production process to further cut costs. The team presents the following proposals to the CEO:

Carrier Corporation
www.carrier.com

Accounting and the *e*-World

Point, Click, Buy, Sell: Businesses Cut Costs by Buying and Selling Online

The cost of processing a single purchase order for direct or indirect materials is about $175. Make that same purchase online, however, and the cost drops to as little as $10. With the electronic connection of buyers and suppliers, all authorized users in the buying organization can initiate purchases from their desktops. Companies can automate processes and access critical information across continents, business units, divisions, and departments. This incredible potential for removing excess costs from supply chains is making business-to-business (B2B) e-commerce "the next big killer app" of the World Wide Web. Analysts estimate the B2B e-commerce market will soar to $6.4 trillion in 2004.

The Big Three automakers (Ford, General Motors, and Daimler-Chrysler), recently announced they will move all business—more than $250 billion and 60,000 suppliers—to the Internet. This change will replace a procurement system built on phone calls and faxes. General Motors alone issues over 100,000 purchase orders a year. Suppliers can avoid the costs of sending sales staff to their customers.

So moving B2B commerce to the Internet makes buying and selling more cost efficient. Buyers and sellers get exposure to a worldwide market at the click of a mouse. Buyers conduct real-time trading to get the parts they need. Sellers auction off excess inventory. And now corporate accountants and financial managers can use their time to focus on strategic activities, such as finding the most profitable B2B relationships.

Source: Based on Russ Banham, "The B-to-B Virtual Bazaar," *Journal of Accountancy*, July 2000, pp. 26–30. Don Tapscott, "Manager's Journal: Virtual Webs Will Revolutionize Business," *Wall Street Journal*, April 24, 2000, p. A38. Kevin P. O'Brien, "Value-Chain Report: Should Your Firm Be Using e-Procurement?" June 12, 2000, http://www.iwvaluechain.com.

Mixing activity
- Group raw materials that are frequently used together, to reduce time required to assemble raw materials when mixing each batch.
- Automate the mixing process so workers can use a few mouseclicks to instruct the automated system to pipe chemicals into the mixing vat.

Processing activity
- Schedule preventive maintenance at nights and weekends to reduce emergency repairs while a batch of chemicals is in-process.
- Purchase new equipment that cuts processing time in half.

Testing activity
- Improve quality control to reduce the need for testing.
- Fully automate testing.

Using ABM and Value Engineering to Achieve Target Costs for Target Pricing

OBJECTIVE 3
Use ABM and value engineering to achieve target costs for target pricing

Companies like Carrier Corporation, General Motors, and Compaq are following Japanese automakers like Toyota and Nissan, and setting sale prices based on **target prices**—what customers are willing to pay for the product or service. Instead of starting with the full product cost from all elements of the value chain (as discussed in Chapter 19) and then adding a profit to determine the sale price, Exhibit 25-10 shows that target pricing does just the opposite. Target pricing starts with the price customers are willing to pay, and then subtracts the company's desired profit to determine the **target** (or allowable) **cost** to develop, produce, and deliver the product or service. Target costs are usually less than the (current) full product cost of the product or service. The target cost is really a goal the company must strive for.

Returning to Chemtech Inc.'s ABC analysis, CEO Randy Smith decides to focus on commodity chemicals. The marketing department informs him that the market price of aldehyde is likely to fall to $9.50 per kilogram. Smith wants to earn a target profit equal to 20% of the sale price. In addition to the manufacturing costs in Exhibit 25-8, Chemtech incurs a total of $0.50 per kilogram in nonmanufacturing costs (R&D, design, marketing, distribution, and customer service).

STOP & THINK

What is Chemtech Inc.'s target cost per kilogram of aldehyde? Do Chemtech's current costs meet this target?

Answer:

Target sale price per kilogram of aldehyde	$9.50
Desired profit ($9.50 × 20%)	(1.90)
Target cost per kilogram of aldehyde	$7.60

Chemtech's current costs do not meet the target cost:

Current total manufacturing cost (from Exhibit 25-8)	$7.95
Nonmanufacturing costs	0.50
Current full product cost per kilogram of aldehyde	$8.45

Chemtech's current full product costs ($8.45) exceed the target cost of $7.60.

Target Pricing	Traditional Cost-Based Pricing
Target sale price (based on market research)	Full product cost (from entire value chain)
Less desired profit	Plus desired profit
= Target cost	= Sale price

EXHIBIT 25-10

Target Pricing versus Traditional Cost-Based Pricing

Smith decides to implement three of the cost reduction strategies Chemtech's value engineering team proposed earlier (page 1389):

- Group raw materials that are frequently used together. Total estimated savings is $150,000 and the factory's total number of batches remains unchanged at 4,000.

- Purchase equipment that cuts processing time by half. This will increase total processing costs by $1,000,000. Total machine hours will remain 50,000 but each product will require only half as many machine hours (Chemtech will use the extra machine hours to produce other profitable products).

- Improve quality control to reduce the need to test samples of each product. This action will cut total testing costs by $375,000, and cut the total number of samples tested throughout the factory by half (from 3,000 to only 1,500). Chemtech will now test only 7 (rather than 14) samples of aldehyde.

Will these changes allow Chemtech Inc. to reach the target costs? Exhibit 25-11 shows how Controller Wise starts with the original data summarized in Exhibit 25-7 and adjusts these data for the value engineering changes. Wise first recomputes the cost allocation rates for each activity: She incorporates changes in both the numerator (estimated indirect costs of the activity) and the denominator (estimated total quantity of the activity's allocation base). She then uses these new allocation rates to assign the costs of each activity to aldehyde, based on how much of each allocation base aldehyde uses after the value engineering changes.

Exhibit 25-11 shows that value engineering cuts the total manufacturing overhead costs assigned to aldehyde to $9,020 ($6,750 + $1,220 + $1,050), from $13,630 (in Exhibit 25-8). Spread over 7,000 pounds of aldehyde, this is $1.29 per kilogram ($9,020 ÷ 7,000, rounded). Now Wise totals the revised cost estimates for aldehyde:

Direct materials (from Exhibit 25-8)....................	$5.00
Direct labour (from Exhibit 25-8)........................	1.00
Manufacturing overhead......................................	1.29
Total manufacturing costs	7.29
Nonmanufacturing costs	0.50
Full product cost of aldehyde	$7.79

EXHIBIT 25-11

Rcomputing Activity Costs for Aldehyde after Value Engineering Changes

	Mixing	Processing	Testing
Estimated total indirect costs of activity:			
Mixing ($600,000 − $150,000)	$450,000		
Processing ($3,000,000 + $1,000,000)................................		$4,000,000	
Testing ($600,000 − $375,000)			$225,000
Estimated total quantity of each allocation base	4,000 batches	50,000 MH	1,500 samples
Compute the cost allocation rate for each activity:			
(Divide estimated indirect cost by......................................	$450,000	$4,000,000	$225,000
estimated quantity of the allocation base)	÷ 4,000 batches	÷ 50,000 MH	÷ 1,500 samples
Cost allocation rate for each activity	= $112.50/batch	= $80/MH	= $150/sample
Actual quantity of each allocation base used by aldehyde:			
Mixing...	60 batches		
Processing ($30\frac{1}{2}$ × 50%)		$15\frac{1}{4}$ MH	
Testing...			7 samples
Allocation the costs to aldehyde:			
Mixing (60 batches × $112.50)..	$6,750		
Processing ($15\frac{1}{4}$ MH × $80)		$1,220	
Testing (7 samples × $150)			$1,050

These changes are quite an improvement from the prior full product cost of $8.45 per kilogram. But they are *not* enough to meet the $7.60 target cost. Chemtech Inc. must conduct more value engineering (or accept less profit) to meet the target sale price.

Routine Planning and Control Decisions

In addition to pricing, product mix, and cost reduction decisions, Chemtech Inc. can also use ABC in routine planning and control. Companies using ABC can do activity-based budgeting, where managers budget costs of individual activities to build up the indirect cost schedules in the master budget (discussed in Chapter 23). Chemtech can also analyze manufacturing overhead variances (presented in Chapter 24) in more detail by computing variances for each of the three individual indirect activities (mixing, processing, and testing). Finally, Chemtech's managers can use ABC information to evaluate workers. For example foreman Steve Pronai may receive a bonus if he can cut:

- the cost per sample tested (that is, cut the cost allocation rate for the testing activity) or
- the number of samples tested (that is, cut the consumption of the activity) *while maintaining product quality.*

Activity-Based Costing and the Cost-Benefit Test

OBJECTIVE 4
Decide when ABC is most likely to pass the cost-benefit test

The ABC concept is deceptively simple: Products cause activities, and activities consume resources. However, it is not easy for a company to develop an ABC/ABM system. In the Chemtech Inc. example shown in Exhibit 25-6, ABC triples the number of allocation bases—from the single allocation base (direct labour) in the original system, to three allocation bases (for mixing, processing, and testing) under ABC. ABC systems are even more complex in real-world companies, such as Mobil Corporation, that have many more activities and cost drivers.

The Cost-Benefit Test

Like all other management tools, ABC must pass the cost-benefit test. The system should be refined enough to provide accurate product costs, but simple enough for managers to understand. It is especially important that ABC has the wholehearted support of top management and operating managers, not just accountants. For example, Dell's ABC team included representatives from all areas affected by ABC—from product engineering, to manufacturing, to customer service. Such cross-functional teams increase the chance that ABC will succeed. The ABC system will be more accurate because it incorporates a wider variety of perspectives, and managers of different functions are more likely to understand and believe costs from the ABC system they helped to build.

Activity-based costing and activity-based management pass the cost-benefit test when the benefits of adopting ABC/ABM exceed the costs. Benefits of adopting ABC/ABM are higher for companies in competitive markets because

- Accurate product cost information is essential for setting competitive sale prices that still allow the company to earn a profit.
- ABC can pinpoint opportunities for cost savings, which increase the company's profit, or are passed on to customers in lower sale prices.

ABC's benefits are higher when ABC gives managers new insights by reporting different product costs than the old system. This is likely to happen when

- The company produces many different products that use different amounts of resources. (If all products use similar amounts of resources, then a simple single-allocation-base system works fine.)
- The company has high indirect costs. (If indirect costs are immaterial, it does not matter how they are allocated.)
- The company produces high volumes of some products, and low volumes of other products. (Traditional single-allocation-base systems tend to overcost high-volume products and undercost low-volume products.)

The costs of adopting ABC are lower when the company has

- Accounting and information system expertise to develop the system.
- Information technology like bar coding and optical scanning, or "data warehouse" systems to record and compile cost driver data.

Are real-world companies glad they adopted ABC? Usually, but not always. A recent survey has shown that 89% of the companies using ABC data say it was worth the cost.[1] Adoption is on the rise among financial companies, utilities, and non-profit companies. Organizations adopting ABC and ABM have more diverse product lines and processes, higher overhead costs, and more sophisticated information technology than nonadopters. But ABC is not a cure-all. As the controller for one manufacturer said, "ABC will not reduce cost, it will only help you understand costs better to know what to correct."

Signs That the Cost System May Be Broken

Broken cars or computers simply stop running. But unlike cars and computers, even broken or outdated product cost systems continue to report "product costs." Without flashing lights or ringing bells, how can you tell whether a company's cost system needs repair?

A company's product cost system may need repair when

Managers don't understand costs and profits:

- In bidding for jobs, managers lose bids they expected to win, and win bids they expected to lose.
- Competitors with products similar to our high-volume products price their products below our costs, but still earn good profits.
- Employees do not believe the cost numbers reported by the accounting system.

The cost system is outdated:

- The company uses a single-allocation-base system that was developed long ago.
- The company has reengineered its production process, but has not changed its accounting system.

---

[1]K. Krumwiede, "ABC: Why It's Tried and How It Succeeds," *Management Accounting* (April 1998), pp. 32–38.

Review the Chemtech Inc. example. List the symptoms that indicate Chemtech Inc.'s original cost system may be broken.

Answer:

1. The Chemical Manufacturing Department uses a single allocation base (direct labour cost) in a cost system that was developed over ten years ago.

2. Competitors that focused on high-volume commodity chemicals earned good profits, despite undercutting Chemtech Inc.'s sale prices. This was puzzling because Chemtech Inc. should be especially efficient at producing large batches of commodity chemicals.

3. Cost numbers reported by the accounting system were inconsistent with employees' intuition.

To make sure you understand activity-based costing, take a few minutes to study the Decision Guidelines feature before working on the mid-chapter review problem.

DECISION GUIDELINES — *Activity-Based Costing*

Decision	Guidelines
How to develop an ABC system?	1. Identify the activities. 2. Estimate total indirect costs of each activity. 3. Identify the allocation base (primary cost driver) for each activity's indirect costs. 4. Estimate the total quantity of each allocation base. 5. Compute the cost allocation rate for each activity. 6. Obtain the actual quantity of each allocation base used by cost object. 7. Allocate costs to cost object.
How to compute a cost allocation rate for an activity?	$$\dfrac{\text{Estimated total indirect cost of activity}}{\text{Estimated total quantity of allocation base}}$$
How to allocate an activity's cost to the cost object?	$\dfrac{\text{Cost allocation}}{\text{rate for activity}} \times \dfrac{\text{Actual quantity of allocation}}{\text{base used by cost object}}$
For what kinds of decisions do managers use ABC?	Managers use ABC data in ABM to make decisions on • Pricing and product mix • Cost reduction • Routine planning and control
How to set target costs?	Target sale price (based on market research) $\underline{\text{− less desired profit}}$ = Target cost
How to achieve target costs?	Cross-functional teams use value engineering to cut costs by improving product design or production processes.
What are the main benefits of ABC?	• More accurate product cost information • More detailed information on costs of activities and drivers of those costs helps managers control costs

(continued)

Decision	Guidelines
When is ABC most likely to pass the cost-benefit test?	• Company is in competitive environment and needs accurate product costs. • Company makes different products that use different amounts of resources. • Company has high indirect costs. • Company produces high volumes of some products and lower volumes of other products. • Company has accounting and information system expertise to implement system. • Old cost system appears "broken."
How to tell when a cost system needs revision?	• Managers cannot explain changes in profit. • Managers lose bids they expected to win and win bids they expected to lose. • Competitors earn profits despite pricing high-volume products below our costs. • Employees do not believe cost numbers. • Company uses a single-allocation-base system developed long ago. • Company has reengineered the production process but not the accounting system.

Mid-Chapter Summary Problem
for Your Review

Woodstock Auto Parts Ltd. (WAP) has a Seat Manufacturing Department that uses activity-based costing. WAP's system has the following features:

Activity	Allocation Base	Cost Allocation Base
Purchasing	Number of purchase orders	$60.00 per purchase order
Assembling	Number of parts	0.50 per part
Packaging	Number of finished seats	0.90 per finished seat

Each seat has 20 parts; direct materials cost per seat is $11. Suppose Ford Motor Company has asked for a bid on 50,000 built-in baby seats that would be installed as an option on some Ford vans. WAP will use a total of 200 purchase orders if Ford accepts WAP's bid.

Required

1. Compute the total cost that WAP will incur to purchase needed materials and then assemble and package 50,000 baby seats. Also compute the average cost per seat.

2. For bidding, WAP adds a 30 percent markup to total cost. What price will the company bid for the Ford order?

3. Suppose that instead of an ABC system, WAP has a traditional product costing system that allocates all costs other than direct materials at the rate of $65 per direct labour hour. The baby-seat order will require 10,000 direct labour hours. What price will WAP bid using this system's total cost?

4. Use your answers to requirements 2 and 3 to explain how ABC can help WAP make a better decision about the bid price it will offer Ford.

Solution to Review Problem

Requirement 1

Direct materials, 50,000 × $11.00	$ 550,000
Activity costs:	
Purchasing, 200 × $60.00	12,000
Assembling, 50,000 × 20 × $0.50	500,000
Packaging, 50,000 × $0.90	45,000
Total cost of order	$1,107,000
Divide by number of seats	÷ 50,000
Average cost per seat	$ 22.14

Requirement 2

$1,107,000 × 130% = $1,439,100

Requirement 3

Direct materials, 50,000 × $11.00	$ 550,000
Other product costs, 10,000 × $65	650,000
Total cost of order	$1,200,000
Bid price: $1,200,000 × 130%	$1,560,000

Requirement 4

WAP's bid would be $120,900 higher using the direct-labour-single-allocation-base system than using ABC ($1,560,000 – $1,439,100). Assuming the ABC system more accurately captures the costs caused by the Ford order, the traditional direct labour system overcosts the order. This leads to a higher bid price that in turn reduces WAP's chance of winning the bid. The ABC system shows that WAP can increase its chance of winning the bid by bidding a lower price and still make a profit.

Traditional versus Just-in-Time Production Systems

OBJECTIVE 5
Compare a traditional production system to a just-in-time (JIT) production system

ABC and ABM often reveal the high costs of (1) buying, storing, and moving inventories, and (2) poor quality products and services. So it is not surprising that a recent study of "best practices" companies revealed most had linked their ABC/ABM systems to just-in-time (JIT) or quality initiatives. For example, Carrier Corporation's ABC/ABM system's evidence that materials handling was a major cost driver prompted Carrier to adopt JIT. The rest of the chapter expands on Chapter 19's introduction to JIT and quality.

We begin by contrasting just-in-time production systems with traditional systems.

Traditional Production Systems

Traditional businesses keep large inventories of raw materials, work in process, and finished goods. Why? First, to protect against poor quality. Poor quality raw materials leads companies to purchase more materials than they need strictly for production. Also, machine breakdowns and poor-quality production *within* departments prompt managers to keep extra work in process *between* departments. Consider the sequence of operations shown in Exhibit 25-12 for the production of drill bits from bar stock (the raw material). Work in process inventory between the thread grinding and smoothing operations allows smoothing work to continue even if thread-grinding machines break down.

A second reason for large inventories is long setup times on production equipment. Manufacturing operations can require setup times ranging from a few minutes to several hours, with correspondingly high setup costs. Companies with long set-up times often make products in large batches to spread setup costs over many units of product. This minimizes the cost per unit.

A third reason for stocking large inventories is uncertainty in both deliveries from suppliers and demand from customers. Large amounts of raw materials protect against delays in deliveries; if a supplier is late in delivering materials, the company still has materials to use in production. Large inventories of finished goods protect against lost sales if customer demand is higher than expected.

Why are large inventories a problem? First, inventories tie up cash. Companies either incur interest expense or forgo interest revenue on that cash. Second, inventories often hide problems, production bottlenecks, and obsolescence.

Just-in-Time Production Systems

As the name suggests, companies with just-in-time (JIT) systems buy materials and complete finished goods *just in time* for delivery to customers. **Just-in-time (JIT) production systems** are designed to eliminate waste. Indeed, many people regard JIT as a *general philosophy of waste elimination* instead of a particular type of manufacturing system. Companies that follow JIT have several common characteristics:

1. *Arrangement of production activities.* Companies following JIT arrange their equipment differently than traditional manufacturers. A traditional drill-bit manufacturer would group all the shaping machines in one area, all the grinding machines in another area, and all the smoothing machines in a third area. After switching to JIT, the company would group the machines in self-contained production cells, or production lines. Machines performing sequential steps may even be physically joined. The goal is continuous production without interruptions or work in process inventories.

   Arranging machines in sequential production cells results in great reductions in production time. For example, within six years of adopting JIT, Harley-Davidson reduced the time required to produce a motorcycle by 77 percent.

2. *Setup times.* JIT companies work to reduce setup times on machines that are used to make more than one product. Through a combination of employee training, preparation, and technology, the companies have achieved impressive results. For example, Toyota has reported reductions in setup times from several hours

Harley-Davidson
www.harley-davidson.com

Toyota Canada
www.toyota.ca

EXHIBIT 25-12

Sequence of Operations for Drill-Bit Production

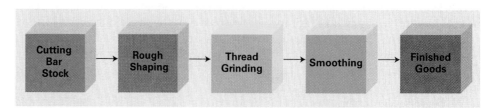

to a few minutes. Such improvements give companies greater flexibility in scheduling production to meet customer requirements. The results are increased customer satisfaction and increased profits.

3. *Employee roles.* Production employees in JIT systems are trained to do more than operate a single machine. They also are trained to conduct routine maintenance, perform setups, inspect their own work, and operate other machines. Cross-training increases flexibility, boosts employee morale, and decreases costs.

4. *Production scheduling.* JIT businesses schedule production in small batches *just in time* to satisfy needs. A customer order triggers manufacturing. The final operation in the production sequence (smoothing, in our drill-bit example) "pulls" parts from the preceding operation (thread grinding). The grinding-machine operator pulls shaped parts from rough shaping, and so on. This "demand-pull" system extends back to suppliers of materials. Suppliers must make frequent deliveries of defect-free materials *just in time* to be placed into production. This arrangement coordinates efforts throughout the value chain.

   Purchasing and producing only what customers demand reduces inventory. As inventory declines, hidden problems are exposed. Production problems are detected quickly and can be corrected before the company produces a large number of defective units. Early detection saves rework and scrap costs. Also, floor space devoted to inventories is freed up for more-productive use. When Hewlett-Packard adopted JIT, the company reduced its work in process inventory by 82 percent and its production floor space by 40 percent.

5. *Supply chain management.* Because there are no inventory buffers, JIT requires close coordination with suppliers who will guarantee on-time delivery of defect-free materials. Chapter 19 defined *supply chain management* as exchanging information with suppliers and customers to reduce costs, improve quality, and speed delivery of goods and services from the company's suppliers, through the company itself, and on to the company's end customers. Consider the following examples.[2]

Chrysler's Brazilian plant, which makes Dakota pickup trucks, buys a partially completed chassis from supplier Dana Corporation's factory three kilometres away. Dana assembles 320 parts onto the truck's frame, including axles, brakes, and wheels, within 108 minutes of receiving an electronic order from the Chrysler factory. Dana then delivers each partially complete chassis to the Chrysler production line, in the sequence that Chrysler specifies, so Chrysler can add the engines, transmissions, and body to complete each truck.

Wal-Mart shares its sales data to help suppliers match their production to Wal-Mart's needs. When Procter & Gamble delivers Crest toothpaste on a just-in-time basis to Wal-Mart's distribution centre, Wal-Mart immediately unloads the toothpaste directly onto trucks headed for Wal-Mart stores. On average, the toothpaste is on the Wal-Mart shelf within 4 hours, and sold within 24 hours. "It is our objective to sell the merchandise before we pay for it" says a Wal-Mart senior vice president.

Often credited for developing JIT, Toyota is not standing still. Toyota recently shocked competitors—who often keep customers waiting 30–60 days for custom ordered cars—by announcing plans to custom-make vehicles within 5 days of receiving an order. How can Toyota meet this goal? By further streamlining and standardizing its production process, and by rolling out its "next generation just-in-time logistics system." Suppliers deliver parts to the assembly lines up to 24 times a day. These changes cut storage requirements by 37% and freed more space for manufacturing. In addition to saving on inventory, warehousing, and production costs,

---

[2]Gregory L. White, "Chrysler Makes Manufacturing Inroads at Plant in Brazil," *Wall Street Journal,* August 3, 1998. Emily Nelson, "Wal-Mart Sets Supply Plan as Net Tops Forecasts," *Wall Street Journal,* November 10, 1999, B12. Robert L. Simison, "Toyota Develops a Way to Make a Car Within Five Days of a Custom Order," *Wall Street Journal,* August 6, 1999, A4. John E. Hillsenrath, "Parts Shortages Hamper Electronics Makers," *Wall Street Journal,* July 7, 2000, B5.

faster make-to-order times mean that Toyota dealers can cut their retail inventories, saving thousands in inventory carrying costs.

While companies like Toyota, Carrier, and Dell credit JIT for saving them millions of dollars, JIT is not without problems. With no inventory buffers, JIT adopters are vulnerable when problems strike suppliers or distributors. The Teamsters' walk-out against UPS in the 1990s left manufacturing plants across the country starved for raw materials. More recently, Ford cut production of its SUVs in response to the tire shortage resulting from the Firestone tire recall. The electronics industry has also suffered from shortages of components. Assemblers who normally obtain capacitors (parts that control the flow of electricity in telecommunications equipment) in 4 weeks are now waiting up to 40 weeks. Companies like Dell that have limited supplies of these components are hurting because their raw materials are scarce. This shortage has led one electronics executive to exclaim that just-in-time has become "just-in-trouble."

Exhibit 25-13 compares traditional production systems with JIT production systems. Now let's see how JIT can simplify cost accounting.

OBJECTIVE 6
Record manufacturing costs for a just-in-time costing system

Just-in-Time Costing

After adopting JIT, many companies simplify their cost accounting systems. **Just-in-time costing**, sometimes called **backflush costing**, is a standard costing system that starts with output completed and works backward to apply manufacturing costs to units sold and to inventories. There are three major differences between JIT costing and the traditional standard costing system we described in Chapter 24:

1. JIT systems do not track the cost of products from raw materials inventory, to work in process inventory, to finished goods inventory, like traditional standard costing systems do. Instead, JIT costing systems wait until the units are completed to record the cost of production.

2. Because JIT systems do not track costs attached to units in the production process, JIT systems do not need a separate Work in Process Inventory account. They combine raw materials and work in process inventories into a single account called Raw and In Process Inventory.

3. Under the JIT philosophy, workers perform many tasks. Since little labour is directly traceable to individual finished products, most companies using JIT costing do not track direct labour separately. They combine labour and manufacturing overhead costs into an account called Conversion Costs (as we saw in Chapter 21 on process costing). The Conversion Cost account is a temporary account that works just like the Manufacturing Overhead account described in Chapter 20. Actual conversion costs accumulate as debits in the Conversion Cost account, and the account is credited when conversion costs are allocated to completed units. Accountants close any underallocated or overallocated conversion costs to Cost of Goods Sold at the end of the year, just like underallocated and overallocated manufacturing overhead in Chapter 20.

EXHIBIT 25-13

Traditional versus Just-in-Time Production Systems

Traditional Production Systems	Just-in-Time Production Systems
Arrange machines by function	Arrange machines in sequence of operations
Long machine setup times	Short machine setup times
Production workers operate a single machine	Cross-trained workers perform many tasks
Produce large batches	Produce small batches
Many suppliers	Fewer, well-coordinated suppliers

Just-in-Time Costing: An Example

To illustrate JIT costing, consider Mintel Corp., which converts silicon wafers into integrated circuits for computers.

Mintel has only one direct manufacturing product cost: silicon wafers, which are labeled "raw." All other manufacturing costs, including labour and various chemicals, are indirect costs of converting the "raw" silicon wafers into the finished integrated circuits. These indirect costs are collected in the "Conversion Costs" account.

Mintel does not use a separate Work in Process Inventory account. Instead, it uses the following two inventory accounts:

- Raw and In Process (RIP) Inventory, which combines direct materials and work in process
- Finished Goods Inventory, which is the usual Finished Goods account

The Mintel Corp. JIT system has two **trigger points**, points in operations that prompt entries in the accounting records. The trigger points are (1) the purchase of direct materials and (2) the transfer of completed units to finished goods.

Mintel has $100,000 of Raw and In Process Inventory and $900,000 of Finished Goods Inventory at July 31. In August, Mintel purchases $3,020,000 of direct materials (silicon wafers), and spends $18,540,000 on labour and overhead to produce 3,000,000 integrated circuits. The standard cost of the circuit is $7 ($1 direct materials and $6 conversion cost). Mintel sells 2,930,000 circuits in August.

Mintel uses JIT costing to record the August transactions.

1. Mintel purchases $3,020,000 of direct materials (silicon wafers) on account. These costs are debited (added) to Raw and In Process Inventory.

    Raw and In Process Inventory 3,020,000
        Accounts Payable 3,020,000

    (RIP Inventory is carried at standard cost. Variances are discussed later.)

2. Record the $18,540,000 actual conversion costs incurred. Mintel debits the Conversion Cost account. It works just like the Manufacturing Overhead account, except conversion costs also include all manufacturing labour costs.

    Conversion Costs 18,540,000
        Various Accounts (such as wages payable and
            accumulated amortization) 18,540,000

3. Record the standard cost of goods completed during the month. Since Mintel completed 3,000,000 circuits at a cost of $7 each, the debit (increase) to finished goods is $21,000,000 (3,000,000 completed circuits × $7). What accounts are credited? There is no work in process inventory in JIT costing, so Mintel credits

    - Raw and In Process Inventory, $3,000,000 (3,000,000 completed circuits × $1 standard raw material cost per circuit) for the raw silicon wafers, and
    - Conversion Costs, $18,000,000 (3,000,000 completed circuits × $6 standard conversion cost per completed circuit) for the labour and other indirect costs allocated to the finished circuits. This credit is similar to the way traditional systems allocate manufacturing overhead to products.

    Finished Goods Inventory 21,000,000
        Raw and In Process Inventory 3,000,000
        Conversion Costs 18,000,000

This is the second trigger point and the essence of JIT costing. The system does not track costs as the integrated circuits move through the various manufacturing operations. Instead, *completion* of the units triggers the accounting system to go back and pull costs from Raw and In Process inventory and to allocate conversion costs to the finished products.

WORKING IT OUT

Ace Corp. manufactures a product at a standard cost of $5/unit ($3 for materials; $2 for conversion costs). In May, when 100 units were completed and 98 were sold, total materials costs were $294 and conversion costs were $210. Beginning RIP inventory was $12 and beginning finished goods inventory was $25. What are (1) the standard cost of units completed in May? (2) COGS for May? (3) the ending balances in the RIP Inventory and Finished Goods Inventory accounts?

A: (1) $500 ($5 × 100 units);
(2) $490 ($5 × 98 units);
(3) RIP Inventory = $6
($12 + $294 − $300);
Finished Goods Inventory = $35
($25 + $500 − $490).

4. Record cost of goods sold in the usual manner. Assume that 2,930,000 units were sold; 2,930,000 units × $7 per unit = $20,510,000:

Cost of Goods Sold	20,510,000	
Finished Goods Inventory		20,510,000

The August 31 inventory balances are:

RIP inventory ($100,000 + $3,020,000 − $3,000,000)	$ 120,000
Finished goods inventory ($900,000 + $21,000,000 − $20,510,000)....	1,390,000
Total inventory	$1,510,000

Exhibit 25-14 shows Mintel Corp.'s major JIT costing accounts. Combining the raw materials inventory with work in process inventory to form the single Raw and In Process Inventory account eliminates detail. Although Mintel tracks the number of physical units in process, the company does not use material requisitions or time records to assign *costs* to circuits as they flow through the production process. Mintel does not assign costs to physical products until the goods are completed, at the second trigger point.

A two-trigger-point system that uses completion of goods as the second trigger point is the most popular version of JIT costing, but other trigger points may be used. For example, Toyota's cost accounting system for its Cambridge plant uses the sale of units, not their completion, as the second trigger point.

The simplest version of JIT costing has only one trigger point, the completion of output. This version's accounting records do not record the purchase of direct materials. This version is appropriate for manufacturing systems that have almost no direct materials inventories and minimal work in process inventories.

Variances in JIT Costing Systems All standard costing systems share the same fundamental approach to accounting for variances. In our Mintel Corp. example, assume that the direct materials were purchased for $3,145,000. Thus the materials had an unfavourable price variance of $125,000. Entry 1 then becomes:

Raw and In Process Inventory	3,020,000	
Direct Materials Price Variance	125,000	
Accounts Payable		3,145,000

Direct materials efficiency variances are measured by working backward from the output units completed. Completed output is the key to determining what should remain in Raw and In Process Inventory (beginning inventory plus purchases, less standard materials used for completed units). What should remain in inventory is compared with what does remain. Suppose that such a comparison for Mintel Corp. reveals an unfavourable efficiency variance of $9,000. The entry, which is linked to entry 3, is:

Direct Materials Efficiency Variance	9,000	
Raw and In Process Inventory		9,000

EXHIBIT 25-14

Mintel Corp.'s Major JIT Costing Accounts

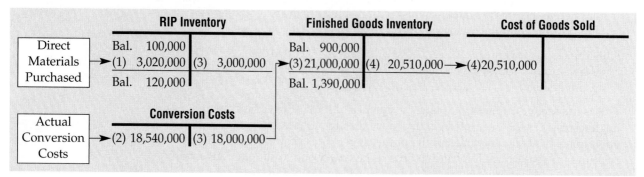

An unfavourable efficiency variance in JIT costing means that more direct materials were used for units *completed* during the month than the standard amount allowed. This entry pulls the cost of that over-standard material out of Raw and In Process Inventory.

Conversion costs may be overapplied or underapplied in any month. Mintel Corp.'s conversion costs are underapplied by $540,000 ($18,540,000 incurred − $18,000,000 applied to production) in August. Companies vary in how they write off underapplied amounts. If Mintel Corp. favours a monthly write-off, the August entry is:

Cost of Goods Sold	540,000	
Conversion Costs		540,000

A company may close its Conversion Costs account annually instead of monthly. In that case, debits and credits accumulate throughout the year. An entry like the one above is made only at year end.

Companies that use JIT costing typically have low inventories. They therefore write off variances directly to Cost of Goods Sold.

STOP & THINK

Activity-based costing (ABC) is a more detailed and complex costing method that provides more accurate product costs. Just-in-time (JIT) costing is simplified and does not track costs through the sequence of manufacturing operations. Are these two costing systems incompatible? Or can they be used together?

Answer: ABC and JIT costing can be compatible. Mintel's $6 standard conversion cost per circuit used in JIT costing could be provided by an ABC system.

Continuous Improvement and the Management of Quality

OBJECTIVE 7
Contrast the four types of quality costs and use these costs to make decisions

Companies with a just-in-time philosophy strive for high-quality production. Because goods are produced only as needed, there are no inventories to hide inefficiencies. Poor quality materials or defective manufacturing processes just shut down production.

Today's competitive marketplace demands ever-higher quality. Managers know that if they fail to satisfy customers' demand for high-quality goods, their competitors will not. As explained in Chapter 19, many companies have adopted *total quality management (TQM)* to meet this challenge. Recall that the goal of total quality management is to provide customers with superior products and services. Companies achieve this goal by improving quality and by eliminating defects and waste throughout the value chain. Each business function in the value chain examines its own activities, and sets higher and higher goals.

Many managers invest in the front end of the value chain (R&D and design) to generate savings in the back end (production, marketing, and customer service). They strive to *design* and *build* quality into the product rather than having to *inspect* and *repair* it later. Carefully designed products reduce manufacturing time inspections, rework, and warranty claims. The theme of total quality management is that superior work benefits the whole organization. We now consider several types of quality costs.

Types of Quality Costs

Business analysts have identified four types of quality-related costs: prevention costs, appraisal costs, internal failure costs, and external failure costs.

1. **Prevention costs** are incurred to *avoid* poor-quality goods or services in the first place. For example, Arthur Andersen and other accounting firms invest heavily in training personnel to use appropriate auditing and consulting procedures. Highly trained accountants are more likely to follow company policies and to make fewer errors. Production workers assigned to quality teams at General Motors carry beepers so line workers can page them when they spot a problem. The quality team then identifies and corrects the cause of the defect (for example, a misaligned robot) right away. The factory does not waste time and materials producing defective cars.

2. **Appraisal costs** are incurred to *detect* poor-quality goods or services. For example, Intel, a manufacturer of integrated circuits, incurs appraisal costs when it tests its products. One procedure, called *burn-in*, heats circuits to a temperature exceeding 2,000 degrees Centigrade. A circuit that fails the burn-in test is also likely to fail when being used by a customer.

3. **Internal failure costs** occur when the company detects and corrects poor-quality goods or services *before* delivery to customers. An example is the labour of a BMW mechanic who reworks a faulty brake job after inspection by a supervisor. It is better to detect the problem in-house than to have it detected by the customer.

4. **External failure costs** occur when the company does not detect poor-quality goods or services until *after* delivery to customers. If the auto-repair shop does faulty work, the customer will discover the flawed brakes. Then the shop may have to repair the body of the car as well as the brakes. External failures can ruin a company's reputation.

Exhibit 25-15 shows some examples of the four quality costs. Study these examples closely and you will see that most prevention costs occur in the R&D and design stages of the value chain. In contrast, most of the appraisal and internal failure costs occur in the production element of the value chain. External failure costs either occur in the customer service stage, or are opportunity costs of lost sales. As mentioned earlier, companies make trade-offs among these costs. Many prevention costs are incurred only periodically, while internal and external failure costs are ongoing. One expert estimates that 8¢ spent on prevention saves most manufacturers $1 in failure costs.

Let's revisit Chemtech Inc., the chemical processing company. Suppose Chemtech Inc. is considering spending the following amounts on a new quality program:

Inspect raw materials	$100,000
Reengineer the production process to improve product quality	750,000
Inspect finished goods	150,000
Supplier screening and certification	25,000
Preventative maintenance of plant and equipment	75,000

Chemtech Inc. expects this quality program to reduce the following costs:

Avoid lost profits from lost sales due to disappointed customers	$800,000
Process fewer sales returns	50,000
Avoid lost profits from lost production time due to rework	250,000
Reduced warranty costs	125,000

Chemtech Inc.'s CEO Randy Smith asks controller Martha Wise to

1. Classify each of these costs into one of the four categories (prevention, appraisal, internal failure, external failure) and total the estimated costs in each category.

2. Recommend whether Chemtech Inc. should undertake the quality program.

Exhibit 25-16 classifies each cost and totals the estimated costs in each of the four categories. Wise uses these results to analyze Chemtech Inc.'s two alternatives:

EXHIBIT 25-15

Example of Quality Costs

Prevention Costs	Appraisal Costs
Training of personnel	Inspection of incoming materials
Evaluating potential suppliers	Costs of overseeing suppliers
Improved materials	Inspection at various stages of production
Preventive maintenance	Inspection of final products or services
Design engineering	Product testing
Improved equipment and processes	

Internal Failure Costs	External Failure Costs
Production loss caused by quality-related downtime	Lost profits from lost customers
Rework	Warranty costs
Scrap	Service costs at customer sites
Rejected product units	Sales returns and allowances due to quality problems
Disposal of rejected units	Product liability claims

- Incur the prevention and appraisal costs to undertake the quality program, or
- Do not undertake the quality program and incur the internal and external failure costs

Undertake the Quality Program		Do Not Undertake the Quality Program	
Prevention costs..............	$ 850,000	Internal failure costs.......	$ 250,000
Appraisal costs...............	250,000	External failure costs......	975,000
Total costs	$1,100,000	Total costs	$1,225,000
See Exhibit 25-16		See Exhibit 25-16	

These estimates suggest that Chemtech Inc. would save $125,000 ($1,225,000 – $1,100,000) by undertaking the quality program.

REAL WORLD EXAMPLE

ISO (International Organization for Standardization) 9000 is a set of five international standards for quality management, adopted by more than 60 countries. Some companies transact business only with ISO-certified suppliers. Before ISO 9000, companies demanding high quality took a risk when they used foreign suppliers that did not have the same quality standards.

EXHIBIT 25-16

Chemtech Inc.'s Quality Costs

Prevention

Reengineer the production process to improve product quality	$750,000
Supplier screening and certification...	25,000
Preventative maintenance of plant and equipment....................	75,000
Total prevention costs...	$850,000

Appraisal

Inspect raw materials	$100,000
Inspect finished goods	150,000
Total appraisal costs	$250,000

Internal Failure

Lost profits from lost production time due to rework...............	$250,000
Total internal failure costs..	$250,000

External Failure

Lost profits from lost sales due to disappointed customers......	$800,000
Sales return processing	50,000
Warranty costs..	125,000
Total external failure costs..	$975,000

These quality costs can be hard to measure. For example, design engineers may spend only part of their time on quality-related projects. Allocating their salaries to various activities is subjective. It is especially hard to measure external failure costs. The biggest external failure cost—profits lost because unhappy customers never return ($800,000)—is not recorded in the accounts at all. Consequently, total quality management programs emphasize nonfinancial performance measures such as number of customer complaints.

Management Accounting in the Real World 🌐

The Importance of Quality Control

Rick Montgomery, the general manager of West Coast Alloys Limited, was discussing the importance of quality control in his company.

"We deal mainly with forest product companies and are producing piping to exact specifications. It is important that we spend sufficient time in the preproduction phase so that we can produce the product as it was intended. We also ensure that we inspect the product at each stage of the process. The last thing we want is to deliver a product that does not conform to specifications, for two reasons. First of all, we have to pay for any rework costs out of our own pocket. Second, we have to worry about our reputation. With the competition in our industry, we have to produce a quality product on time. Otherwise, our customers will look elsewhere for their pipe requirements."

Rick has neatly explained the importance of quality control. Large and small companies that compete in highly competitive industries must continually improve their design and manufacturing techniques, and deliver a quality product on time. It is important to capture any flaws before the product is delivered to the customer. Thus, companies like West Coast Alloys are willing to spend more time and effort in the early stages of production to preserve their reputation as a first-class supplier to their customers.

"I can't stress enough how important it is to establish a reputation as a company that can deliver quality products on time. We want to spend enough time up front to ensure that we avoid as many external failures as possible."

Nonfinancial Performance Measures

Nonfinancial performance measures include number of customer complaints, percentage of defective units, and first-time inspection pass rates. Companies use benchmarking to evaluate their performance on these dimensions. *Benchmarking* is the comparison of current performance with some standard. The standard often is the performance level of a leading outside organization such as a leading competitor.

Exhibit 25-17 lists examples of nonfinancial measures of quality used by the Cummins Engine Company, a manufacturer of diesel engines and trucks. The company's emphasis on continuous improvement of nonfinancial quality measures shows how businesses are broadening the scope of performance measurement. Many companies no longer are concentrating solely on financial measures such as

- Percent of engines passing test first time
- Incoming supplier quality—percent of suppliers with acceptance rate of 98 percent or better
- Average downtime of bottleneck machines
- Number of machine breakdowns
- Number of product failures in the field
- Percent of engines delivered on time
- Average supplier delivery in percent of parts on time
- Training hours as percent of total hours worked

operating income or return on investment. Companies are linking managers' compensation to performance on nonfinancial measures of quality, innovation, speed to market, and customer satisfaction. Nonetheless, the ultimate test is long-term profitability.

More and more managers believe that nonfinancial measures are the keys to profitability. They base a strategy for gaining competitive advantage on links such as those shown in Exhibit 25-18. As the exhibit indicates, continuous improvement of critical nonfinancial performance measures is essential for long-term success.

The Decision Guidelines feature summarizes key points about just-in-time and quality costs. Study these guidelines before working through the summary review problem.

EXHIBIT 25-18

Links among Performance Measures

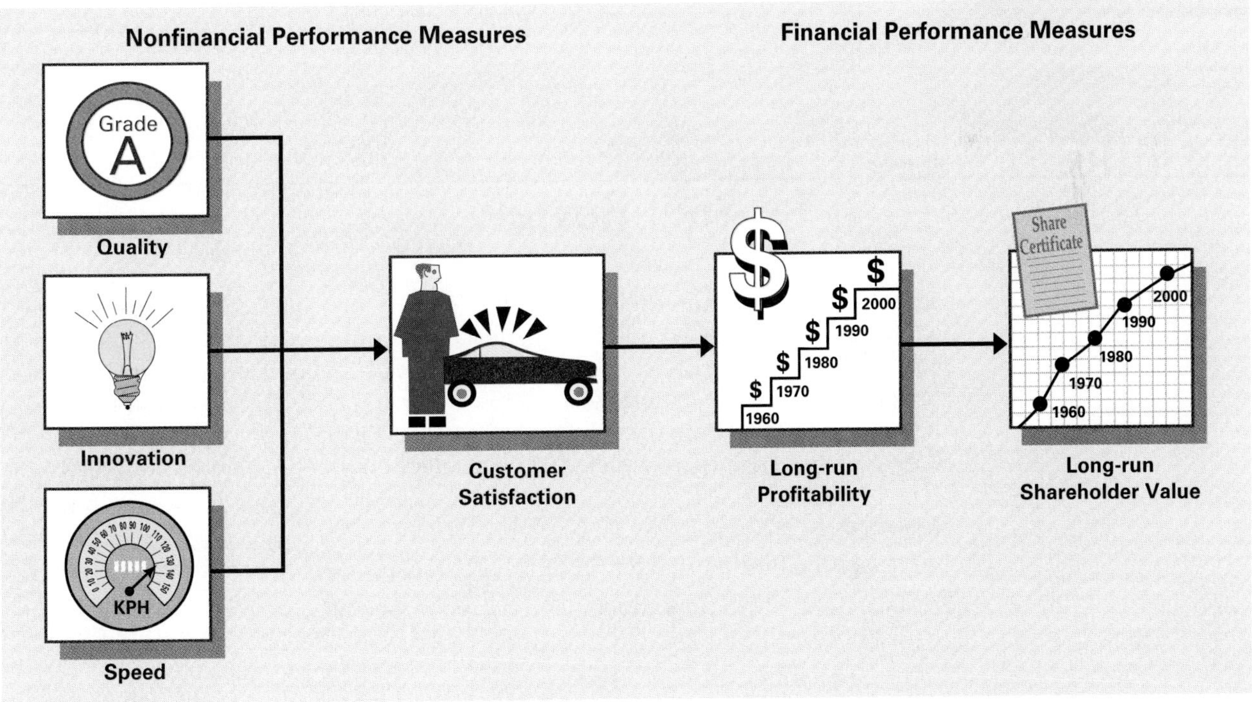

Nonfinancial Performance Measures

Quality

Innovation

Speed

Financial Performance Measures

Customer Satisfaction

Long-run Profitability

Long-run Shareholder Value

Decision	Guidelines	

How to distinguish between just-in-time and traditional production systems?

JIT	Traditional
Production cells	Like machines grouped together
Short setup times	Longer setup times
Smaller batches	Larger batches
Lower inventories	Higher inventories
An individual does wider range of tasks	An individual does fewer tasks
Fewer, but well co-ordinated suppliers	Many suppliers

How does JIT costing differ from traditional costing?

In JIT costing,
1. Summary journal entries are not made until units are completed—costs are not separately tracked as units move through production.
2. Raw materials and work in process are combined into a single Raw and In Process Inventory account.
3. Labour and overhead are combined into a Conversion Cost account.

What are the four types of quality costs?

Prevention costs
Appraisal costs
Internal failure costs
External failure costs

How to make trade-offs among the four types of quality costs?

Investment in prevention costs and appraisal costs reduces later internal failure costs and external failure costs.

Summary Problem
for Your Review

Flores Corp. manufactures telephones. Flores Corp. uses a JIT costing system with two trigger points: (1) when direct materials are purchased, and (2) when completed telephones are transferred to finished goods inventory. The standard unit cost is $37: $24 direct materials and $13 conversion costs. Direct materials purchased on account during June totaled $2,540,000. Actual conversion costs totaled $1,295,000. Flores Corp. completed 102,000 telephones in June, and sold 98,000.

Required

1. Prepare the June journal entries for these transactions.
2. Make the entry to close the underallocated or overallocated conversion costs to Cost of Goods Sold.
3. Some of Flores Corp.'s costs are
   a. Product repairs after sale
   b. Training of supplier personnel
   c. Inspection costs of incoming materials
   d. Rework

   Classify each cost in one of the four categories of quality costs: prevention, appraisal, internal failure, or external failure.

Solution to Review Problem

Requirement 1

Raw and In Process Inventory..................................	2,540,000	
Accounts Payable.....................................		2,540,000
Conversion Costs.......................................	1,295,000	
Various Accounts (such as payables)................		1,295,000
Finished Goods Inventory.......................................	3,774,000	
Raw and In Process Inventory (102,000 × $24)		2,448,000
Conversion Costs (102,000 × $13).....................		1,326,000
Cost of Goods Sold (98,000 × $37).........................	3,626,000	
Finished Goods Inventory................................		3,626,000

Requirement 2

Conversion Costs...	31,000	
Cost of Goods Sold..		31,000

Requirement 3

a. External failure   c. Appraisal
b. Prevention   d. Internal failure

Summary

1. **Describe and develop activity-based costs (ABC).** *Activity-based costing* focuses on activities as the fundamental cost objects. It uses the costs of activities as building blocks for compiling the costs of products and other cost objects. ABC uses multiple cost allocation bases to allocate activity costs.

2. **Use ABC data and activity-based management (ABM) to make business decisions.** In ABM, managers use ABC data to make decisions that increase profits while satisfying customers' needs. Managers use ABC information to make pricing, product mix, cost reduction, and routine planning and control decisions.

3. **Use ABM and value engineering to achieve target costs for target pricing.** Target price is what customers are willing to pay for the product or service. Managers subtract desired profit from target pricing to obtain target cost. Target cost is usually less than the current cost to produce the product or service, so managers use value engineering to improve design or production processes to cut costs to the target.

4. **Decide when ABC is most likely to pass the cost-benefit test.** ABC passes the cost-benefit test when the benefits (more accurate product cost information, better information for cost control) outweigh the costs of implementing the system. Companies (1) in competitive markets with (2) high indirect costs that (3) produce a wide variety of different products that make different demands on resources, and that (4) have accounting and information technology to collect the data and implement the system are most likely to pass the cost-benefit test. This is especially true if the company produces (5) high volumes of some products but low volumes of other products.

5. **Compare a traditional production system to a just-in-time (JIT) production system.** Traditional production systems have functionally arranged clusters of machines, large inventories, long setup times, and relatively inflexible employees. *Just-in-time production systems* are designed to eliminate waste. They have sequentially arranged production activities, "demand-pull" production scheduling, minimal inventories, quick setup times, cross-trained employees, and fewer but better-coordinated suppliers. JIT systems rely on dependable suppliers to deliver perfect quality materials just in time for production.

6. **Record manufacturing costs for a just-in-time costing system.** *Just-in-time costing* is a standard costing system that begins with output completed and then assigns manufacturing cost to units sold and to inventories. This differs from traditional sequential tracking standard costing that moves forward, step by step, from direct materials inventory, to work in process inventory, to finished goods inventory, to cost of goods sold. JIT costing is simpler because it uses a single Raw and In Process Inventory account rather than separate accounts for raw materials and work in process.

7. **Contrast the four types of quality costs and use these costs to make decisions.** The goal of total quality management is to delight customers by providing superior products and services. Companies achieve this goal by improving quality and eliminating defects and waste throughout the value chain. Four types of quality costs

are *prevention, appraisal, internal failure,* and *external failure.* Managers make trade-offs among these costs, often investing more in prevention and appraisal to reduce internal and external failure costs. Because quality costs are hard to measure, many companies use nonfinancial measures to evaluate quality management.

Self-Study Questions

Test your understanding of the chapter by marking the best answer for each of the following questions.

1. Activity-based product costs are likely to be more accurate than product costs computed with *(p. 1380)*
   a. A job order costing system
   b. A process costing system
   c. A single overhead rate
   d. Target costing

2. Activity-based costing is part of an overall process known as *(p. 1387)*
   a. Activity-based management
   b. Total quality management
   c. Just-in-time manufacturing
   d. Just-in-time costing

3. Investments in activity-based costing systems are justified only if they lead to *(p. 1391)*
   a. More-accurate product costs
   b. More-accurate inventory values
   c. Better cost-driver analysis
   d. Better management decisions

4. Just-in-time (JIT) production systems are characterized by *(pp. 1396–1397)*
   a. Long setup times
   b. Small batch sizes
   c. Machines arranged by function
   d. Employee departments that specialize in machine setups

5. In just-in-time costing systems, trigger points are points in operations that prompt *(p. 1398)*
   a. Entries in the internal accounting system
   b. Collections of receivables
   c. Issuances of purchase requisitions
   d. Additions to cost of goods sold

6. Just-in-time costing is noteworthy because it eliminates the use of the following separate account *(p. 1398)*
   a. Work in Process Inventory
   b. Accounts Receivable
   c. Finished Goods Inventory
   d. Cost of Goods Sold

7. Which of the following is an example of an internal failure cost? *(p. 1403)*
   a. Inspection of services
   b. Product liability claims
   c. Rework
   d. Design engineering

8. Which of the following is an example of an external failure cost? *(p. 1403)*
   a. Inspection of services
   b. Design testing
   c. Rework
   d. On-site repairs

9. Which of the following statements about quality control is true? *(pp. 1401–1402)*
   a. Appraisal costs are incurred to detect poor quality goods or services.
   b. Internal failure costs are incurred when poor quality goods or services are detected before delivery to the customer and are reworked or scrapped.
   c. External failure costs can be devastating to a company's reputation.
   d. All of the statements above are true.

10. An example of a non-financial performance measure is *(p. 1404)*
    a. Return on investment
    b. Residual income
    c. Customer complaints
    d. Activity-based costing

Answers to the Self-Study Questions follow the Similar Accounting Terms.

Accounting Vocabulary

Activity-based costing (ABC) *(p. 1380)*
Activity-based management (ABM) *(p. 1387)*
Appraisal costs *(p. 1402)*
Backflush costing *(p. 1398)*
External failure costs *(p. 1402)*
Internal failure costs *(p. 1402)*
Just-in-time (JIT) costing *(p. 1398)*

Just-in-time (JIT) production systems *(p. 1396)*
Prevention costs *(p. 1402)*
Target costing *(p. 1389)*
Target price *(p. 1389)*
Trigger points *(p. 1399)*
Value engineering (VE) *(p. 1387)*

Similar Accounting Terms

Allocation base	Application base
Continuous improvement	Kaizen costing
Just-in-time costing	Backflush costing
Raw and In Process inventory	RIP inventory
Traditional costing	Sequential costing

Answers to Self-Study Questions

1. c	3. d	5. a	7. c	9. d
2. a	4. b	6. a	8. d	10. c

Assignment Material

Questions

1. List three management accounting techniques that managers use to achieve their strategic goal of delivering value to customers.

2. Give two reasons why allocating manufacturing overhead based on direct labour can yield inaccurate product costs.

3. Managers often use standards and variance analysis to control direct material and direct labour costs. What accounting tool can they use to help control manufacturing overhead costs?

4. "Activity-based costing systems provide more accurate information than do traditional systems that use one overhead allocation rate. Every company should adopt ABC." Do you agree? Why or why not?

5. "Activity-based costing systems promote coordination and communication across the various functions within a company." Do you agree? Explain.

6. "For costing-system alternatives, accountants have activity-based costing, job order costing, and process costing." True or false? Explain.

7. Give three examples of technology that have made the gathering of activity-based accounting information less expensive.

8. What kind of decisions do managers make using ABC data?

9. What is target pricing and how does it affect cost management?

10. Contrast the traditional and just-in-time approaches to managing machine setups.

11. Describe "demand-pull" production scheduling.

12. Do companies that implement JIT production systems usually increase or decrease the number of suppliers they use? Why?

13. List three differences between JIT costing and traditional standard costing.

14. The just-in-time costing account Raw and In Process Inventory represents two accounts in a sequential-tracking system. What are they?

15. How do management accountants using a just-in-time costing system compute the amount of a direct materials efficiency variance?

16. "Prevention costs are the most important quality costs." Explain.

17. "Financial performance measures are used almost exclusively in evaluating quality management efforts." Do you agree? Why or why not?

Exercises

Exercise 25-1 *Product costing in an activity-based costing system* **(Obj. 1)**

Sherbrooke Manufacturing Ltd. uses activity-based costing to account for its manufacturing process. Company managers have identified four manufacturing activities: materials handling, machine setup, insertion of parts, and finishing. The budgeted activity costs for 2003 and their cost drivers are as follows:

Manufacturing Activity	Total Budgeted Cost	Cost Driver Chosen as Application Base
Materials handling	$24,000	Number of parts
Machine setup	4,800	Number of setups
Insertion of parts	48,000	Number of parts
Finishing	120,000	Finishing direct labour hours
	$196,800	

Sherbrooke Manufacturing Ltd. expects to produce 2,000 chrome wheels during the year. The chrome wheels are expected to use 12,000 parts, require 6 setups, and consume 1,000 hours of finishing time.

Required

1. Compute the cost allocation rate for each activity.

2. Compute the indirect manufacturing product cost of each chrome wheel (excluding direct materials).

Exercise 25-2 *Product costing in activity-based and traditional systems* **(Obj. 1)**

Several years after reengineering its production process, SEMCO Corp. hired a new controller, Lindsay Bays. She developed an ABC system very similar to the one used by SEMCO's chief rival, Sherbrooke Manufacturing Ltd. of Exercise 25-1. Part of the reason Bays developed the ABC system was that SEMCO's profits had been declining, even though the company had shifted its product mix toward the product that appeared most profitable under the old system. Before adopting the new ABC system, SEMCO had used a direct labour hour single-allocation-base system that was developed 20 years ago. For 2003, SEMCO's budgeted ABC application rates are:

Manufacturing Activity	Cost Driver Chosen as Application Base	Cost per Unit of Application Base
Materials handling	Number of parts	$ 1.75 per part
Machine setup	Number of setups	300.00 per set-up
Insertion of parts	Number of parts	4.00 per part
Finishing	Finishing direct labour hours	70.00 per hour

SEMCO produces two chrome wheel models: standard and deluxe. Budgeted data for 2003 are as follows:

	Standard	Deluxe
Parts per wheel	5.0	7.0
Setups per 1,000 wheels	3.0	3.0
Finishing direct labour hours per wheel	0.2	1.0
Total direct labour hours per wheel	2.0	3.0

The company's managers expect to produce 1,000 units of each model during the year.

Required

1. Compute the total budgeted cost for 2003.

2. Compute the ABC cost per unit of each model.

3. Assume that SEMCO budgets conversion costs in the amount computed in requirement 1. Assume also that SEMCO does not use an ABC system but

instead applies conversion costs to products using a single allocation-base system based on total direct labour hours. Compute the single rate, and use it to determine the cost per wheel for each model.

Exercise 25-3 *Activity-based costing and management decisions* **(Obj. 2)**

Refer to Exercise 25-2. For 2004, SEMCO's managers have decided to use the same conversion costs per wheel that they computed in 2003. In addition to the unit conversion costs, the following data are budgeted for the company's standard and deluxe models for 2004:

	Standard	Deluxe
Sale price	$155.00	$215.00
Direct materials	15.00	25.00
Direct labour	30.00	45.00

Suppose that because of limited machine hour capacity, SEMCO can produce either 2,000 standard wheels or 2,000 deluxe wheels.

Required

1. If the company's managers rely on the ABC unit cost data computed in Exercise 25-2, which model will they decide to manufacture? (Assume that all non-manufacturing costs are the same for both models.)
2. If the managers rely on the single allocation-base cost data, which model will they produce?
3. Which course of action will yield more income for SEMCO?

Exercise 25-4 *Activity-based management and target cost* **(Obj. 3)**

Refer to Exercise 25-2. Controller Lindsay Bays is surprised by the increase in cost of the deluxe model under ABC. Market research shows that to remain a viable product while still providing a reasonable profit, SEMCO will have to meet a target cost of $165 for the deluxe wheel. A value engineering study by SEMCO's employees suggests that modifications to the finishing process could cut finishing cost from $70 to $60 per hour and reduce the finishing direct labour hours per deluxe wheel from 1 hour to 0.8 hour per wheel. Direct materials would remain unchanged at $25 per wheel, as would direct labour at $45 per wheel. The materials handling, machine setups, and insertion of parts activity costs would remain the same as in Exercise 25-2. Would implementing the value engineering recommendation allow SEMCO to achieve its target ABC-based cost for the deluxe wheel?

Exercise 25-5 *Explaining why ABC passes the cost-benefit test* **(Obj. 4)**

Refer to Exercise 25-2. Why might controller Lindsay Bays have expected ABC to pass the cost-benefit test? Were there any warning signs that SEMCO's old direct-labour-based allocation system was "broken"?

Exercise 25-6 *Recording manufacturing costs in a just-in-time costing system* **(Obj. 6)**

Kanata Technologies Inc. (KTI) produces electronic components. KTI uses a JIT costing system with two trigger points: the purchase of direct materials and the transfer of completed units to finished goods. One of the company's products has a standard direct materials cost of $4 per unit and a standard conversion cost of $20 per unit.

During 2002, KTI produced 250,000 units of the component and sold 240,000. It purchased direct materials whose standard cost was $1,050,000 and incurred actual conversion costs totaling $5,475,000.

Required

1. Prepare summary journal entries for 2002.
2. Assume that KTI's January 1, 2002, balance of the Raw and In Process Inventory account was $40,000. What is the December 31, 2002, balance?
3. Is conversion cost overapplied or underapplied for the year? By how much?
4. Give the journal entry to close the conversion cost account.

Exercise 25-7 *Recording variances in a just-in-time costing system* *(Obj. 6)*

Ramius Engineering Inc. produces sonar components that are used on ice breakers. The company uses a JIT costing system with trigger points at direct materials purchase and completion of goods. In 2003, Ramius Engineering Inc. purchased direct materials having a standard cost of $6,000,000.

Required

1. Record the journal entries that correspond to the following variances:
    a. Favourable direct materials price variance of $75,000.
    b. Unfavourable direct materials price variance of $37,500.
    c. Favourable direct materials efficiency variance of $52,500.
    d. Unfavourable direct materials efficiency variance of $30,000.
2. Conversion cost is underallocated by $45,000 in 2003. Record the entry to close the Conversion Costs account to Cost of Goods Sold.

Exercise 25-8 *Recording manufacturing costs in a JIT costing system* *(Obj. 6)*

E-Voice Corp. produces cordless telephones. Suppose that E-Voice's standard cost per phone is $31.20 for materials and $36.00 for conversion costs. The following data apply to July production:

Materials purchased	$6,360,000
Conversion costs incurred	$7,296,000
Number of telephones completed	200,000 telephones
Number of telephones sold	192,000 telephones

Assume that E-Voice Corp. uses JIT costing with trigger points at the purchase of materials and at the completion of finished telephones.

Required

1. Prepare summary journal entries for July, including the entry to close the Conversion Costs account.
2. The beginning balance of Finished Goods Inventory was $120,000. What is the ending balance of Finished Goods Inventory?

Exercise 25-9 *Types of quality costs* *(Obj. 7)*

Total Engineering Ltd. makes electronic components for microwave ovens. James Nixon, the president, recently instructed financial vice-president Monique Smith to develop a total quality control program. "If we don't at least match the quality improvements our competitors are making," he told Smith, "we'll soon be out of business."

Smith began her task by listing various "costs of quality" that Total Engineering Ltd. incurs. The first five items that came to mind were:

a. Costs of inspecting components in one of Total Engineering Ltd.'s production processes.
b. Labour costs of product design engineers who work to design components that will withstand electrical overloads.
c. Costs of reworking defective components after discovery by company inspectors.
d. Costs of electronic components returned by customers.
e. Costs incurred by Total Engineering Ltd. customer representatives in traveling to customer sites to inspect defective products.

Required

Classify each item as a prevention cost, an appraisal cost, an internal failure cost, or an external failure cost.

Exercise 25-10   *Classifying quality costs and using these costs to make decisions*   *(Obj. 7)*

RPP Inc. manufactures radiation shielding glass panels. Suppose RPP is considering spending the following amounts on a new total quality management (TQM) program:

Strength-testing one item from each batch of panels	$50,000
Training employees in TQM	25,000
Training suppliers in TQM...	35,000
Identifying preferred suppliers who commit to on-time delivery of perfect quality materials.....................................	60,000

RPP expects the new program would save costs through the following:

Avoid lost profits from lost sales due to disappointed customers...	$75,000
Avoid rework and spoilage	50,000
Avoid inspection of raw materials	40,000
Avoid warranty costs	15,000

Required

1. Classify each item as a prevention cost, an appraisal cost, an internal failure cost, or an external failure cost.
2. Should RPP implement the new quality program? Give your reasons.

Challenge Exercise

Exercise 25-11   *Using activity-based costing*   *(Obj. 1, 2)*

Patterson Manufacturing Company Ltd. completed two jobs in June 2002. Patterson's accounting records recorded the following costs applied to the jobs by the company's activity-based costing system:

Activity	Application Base	Applied Cost Job BMW	Applied Cost Job BMX
Materials handling	Number of parts	$ 800	$ 400
Lathe work	Number of turns	12,000	4,000
Milling	Number of machine hours	21,000	3,000
Grinding	Number of parts	1,200	400
Testing	Number of output units	3,000	150

Job BMW required 2,000 parts; 60,000 lathe turns; and 1,050 machine hours. All 200 of the job's output units were tested, and all units of the BMX job were tested.

Required

1. How do you know that at least one of the costs recorded for the two jobs is inaccurate?
2. Disregard materials-handling costs. How many parts were used for job BMX? How many lathe turns did job BMX require? How many machine hours? How many units were produced in the job?
3. A nearby company has offered to test all product units for $13 each. On the basis of ABC data, should Patterson accept or reject the offer? Give your reason.

Beyond the Numbers

Beyond the Numbers 25-1   *Using ABC information to make decisions*   *(Obj. 2)*

Laura Taylor is a lawyer who has recently opened her own practice. She is interested in using ABC information to make decisions about her practice. Consider how she could use ABC information in

- Setting fees (prices)
- Responding to client concerns about fees
- Controlling costs

Prepare a memo to Ms. Taylor explaining how she could use ABC in her practice.

Beyond the Numbers 25-2   *Explaining when JIT-costing is most likely to be used*
(Obj. 4)

JIT costing is typically used by businesses that

- Assign standard costs to each product
- Have low inventories

Explain why each of these conditions make JIT costing more feasible.

Ethical Issue

Stoiko Precision Engineering Ltd. manufactures complex metal products used in consumer goods. The company is under extreme pressure to reduce costs. Stoiko's managers have decided to implement a JIT production system in an effort to eliminate waste. Company accountants have decided to design a new ABC system to help identify and reduce manual activities that could be done by robots or computers. The accountants are seeking the help of all operating personnel to identify and modify activities.

The problem? The company's employees do not want to cooperate with the accounting staff. Many believe that the ABC program is just one more way to cut jobs. Specifically, they are afraid that computerized activities will lead to unnecessary employees, who will be fired.

Is it ethical to ask employees to participate in a management initiative that may eliminate some employees' jobs? Why or why not? What can Stoiko's managers do to relieve the fears of employees and gain their cooperation?

Problems (Group A)

Problem 25-1A *Product costing in an activity-based costing system* **(Obj. 1)**

A National Semiconductor Corp. factory assembles and tests electronic components used in high-definition television sets. Consider the following data regarding component J47:

Direct materials cost	$71.00
Activity costs applied	?
Manufacturing product cost	?

The activities required to build the component follow:

Manufacturing Activity	Cost Driver	Activity Costs Applied to Each Unit
1. Start station	Number of raw component chassis	$1 \times \$\ 1.30 = \$1.30$
2. Dip insertion	Number of dip insertions	$? \times\ \ \ 0.60 = 10.20$
3. Manual insertion	Number of manual insertions	$11 \times\ \ \ 0.80 =\ \ \ ?$
4. Wave solder	Number of components soldered	$1 \times\ \ \ 1.50 =\ \ \ 1.50$
5. Backload	Number of backload insertions	$6 \times\ \ \ \ \ ? =\ \ \ 4.80$
6. Test	Standard time each component is in test activity	$0.30 \times\ \ 90.00 =\ \ \ ?$
7. Defect analysis	Standard time for defect analysis and repair	$0.10 \times\ \ \ \ \ ? =\ \ 7.00$
Total		$\$\ \ ?$

Required

1. Fill in the blanks in both the opening schedule and the list of activities.

2. How is labour cost identified with products under this product costing system?

3. Why might managers favour this activity-based accounting system instead of the older system, which applied all conversion costs on the basis of direct labour?

Problem 25-2A *Product costing in an activity-based costing system* **(Obj. 1, 2)**

Hilton Inc. manufactures TV stands and uses an activity-based costing system. Hilton Inc.'s activity areas and related data follow:

Manufacturing Activity	Budgeted Cost of Activity	Cost Driver Used as Application Base	Activity Cost per Unit of Application Base
Materials handling	$ 300,000	Number of parts	$ 0.30
Assembling	4,500,000	Direct labour hours	27.00
Finishing	240,000	Number of finished units	7.50

Two styles of TV stands were produced in April—the standard stand and an unfinished stand, which has fewer parts and requires no finishing. The quantities, direct materials costs, and other data follow:

Product	Units Produced	Direct Materials Costs	Number of Parts	Assembling Direct Labour Hours
Standard TV stand	2,000	$24,000	30,000	3,000
Unfinished TV stand	3,000	27,000	36,000	2,800

Required

1. Compute the manufacturing product cost of each type of stand.

2. Suppose that "upstream" activities, such as product design, were analyzed and applied to the standard TV stands at $4.00 each and to the unfinished stands at $3.00 each. Similar analyses were conducted of "downstream" activities such as distribution, marketing, and customer service. The downstream costs applied were $18.00 per standard stand and $13.00 per unfinished stand. Compute the full product costs per unit.

3. Which product costs are reported in the external financial statements? Which costs are used for management decision making? Explain the difference.

4. What price should Hilton's managers set for unfinished stands to earn a unit profit of $15.00?

Problem 25-3A   *Costing products with ABC rates and comparing to costs from a single-rate system; clues that ABC passes cost-benefit test*   *(Obj. 1, 3)*

LaChance Pharmaceuticals Inc. in Montreal manufactures an over-the-counter allergy medication called Breathe. The company is trying to win market share from Sudafed and Tylenol. LaChance Pharmaceuticals Inc. has developed several different Breathe products tailored to specific markets. For example, the company sells large commercial containers of 1,000 capsules to health-care facilities and travel packs of 15 capsules to shops in airports, train stations, and hotels.

LaChance's controller Michelle Charest has just returned from a conference on activity-based costing. She asks Alain Massicotte, foreperson of the Breathe production line, to help her develop an activity-based costing system. Charest and Massicotte identify the following activities, related costs, and cost drivers:

Activity	Estimated Indirect Activity Costs	Allocation Base	Estimated Quantity of Allocation Base
Materials handling	$180,000	# Kilograms	18,000 kilograms
Packaging	300,000	# Machine hours	2,000 hours
Quality assurance	112,500	# Samples	2,250 samples
Total indirect costs	$592,500		

The commercial container Breathe product line had a total weight of 6,000 kilograms, used 1,000 machine hours, and required 200 samples. The travel pack line had a total weight of 4,000 kilograms, used 200 machine hours, and required 300 samples. LaChance Pharmaceuticals Inc. produced 2,500 commercial containers of Breathe and 50,000 travel packs.

Required

1. Compute the cost allocation rate for each activity.

2. Use the activity-based cost allocation rates to compute the activity costs of the commercial containers and the travel packs. (*Hint*: First compute the total activity costs allocated to each product line, and then compute the cost per unit.)

3. LaChance's original single-allocation-base cost system allocated indirect costs to products at $300 per machine hour. Compute the total indirect costs allocated to the commercial containers and to the travel packs under the original system. Then compute the indirect cost per unit for each product.

4. Compare the activity-based costs to the costs from the original system. How have the unit costs changed? Explain why the costs changed as they did.

5. What are the clues that LaChance Pharmaceutical Inc.'s ABC system is likely to pass the cost-benefit test?

Problem 25-4A   *Activity-based management, target cost, and value engineering*
(Obj. 2, 3)

Continuing Problem 25-3A, LaChance Pharmaceuticals Inc. controller is surprised that ABC reports such a higher indirect production cost per travel pack. She wonders whether LaChance is making the desired profit of $1.25 per unit on this product. The current sale price is $5.75 per travel pack, direct production costs are $2.15 per pack, marketing and distribution costs are $0.90 per pack, and the indirect production costs are $1.70 per pack (from Problem 25-3A). Charest believes that to reach estimated sales of 50,000 units, the sale price cannot exceed $5.75. If the travel pack is not providing the desired profit of $1.25 per unit, Charest decides that the next step should be to establish a cross-functional value engineering team to identify opportunities for cost savings. If this does not provide the desired profit, Charest doubts it will be possible to increase market share to sales of 50,000 travel packs.

Required

1. Determine the sale price that yields a profit of $1.25 per travel pack. Does this meet the $5.75 target price?

2. Charest establishes a value engineering team. The value engineering team finds that improved supply-chain management can cut the travel pack's direct production costs from $2.15 per pack to $2.03 per pack. Further, the team believes it can cut materials-handling costs from $180,000 to $171,000. Changes in the packaging department will save $76,000 in packaging costs and 400 in machine hours. Improvements to quality assurance should reduce costs to $107,500 based on 2,150 samples. Marketing and distribution costs will remain unchanged.

   Given these cost savings, compute the indirect activity cost allocation rates for materials handling, packaging, and quality assurance.

3. If the value engineering team's suggestions are implemented, the travel pack would require 4,000 kilograms, use 180 machine hours, and require 256 samples. Compute the new indirect production cost per travel pack (including all three activities).

4. With these changes, can LaChance set a sale price of $5.75 and still earn a profit of $1.25 per travel pack?

Problem 25-5A   *Recording manufacturing costs for a JIT costing system*   (Obj. 5, 6)

Pilapil Manufacturers Ltd. produces precision hydraulic system components. The company uses JIT costing for its just-in-time production system. Its costing system has two trigger points: the purchase of direct materials and the completion of hydraulic system components.

Pilapil Manufacturers Ltd. has two inventory accounts: Raw and In Process Inventory and Finished Goods Inventory. On December 1, 2003, the account balances were Raw and In Process Inventory, $3,000; Finished Goods Inventory, $5,000.

The standard cost of a component is $45: $15 direct materials plus $30 conversion costs. Data for December's activity follow.

Direct materials purchased	$454,000
Conversion costs incurred	$934,000
Number of components completed	30,000
Number of components sold	29,600

Required

1. What are the major features of a just-in-time production system such as that of Pilapil Manufacturers Ltd.?

2. Prepare summary journal entries for December. Assume that there are no direct

materials variances. Assume also that underapplied or overapplied conversion costs are closed to Cost of Goods Sold monthly.

3. What is the December 31, 2003, balance of Raw and In Process Inventory?

Problem 25-6A   *Recording JIT costs, second trigger point is sale*   *(Obj. 6)*

Pilapil Manufacturers Ltd. of Problem 25-5A has a two-trigger-point JIT costing system, but now suppose that the second trigger point is the sale, not the completion, of hydraulic system components. The company has only one inventory account, labelled simply "Inventory." Only direct materials costs are assigned to Inventory; the account balance is the sum of the costs of materials in the storeroom (if any), in process, and in finished units not yet sold.

Conversion costs are not inventoried. They are applied, at standard, to units sold. Continue to assume that the Conversion Costs account is closed to Cost of Goods Sold monthly.

Required

1. Prepare summary journal entries that correspond to the entries you prepared in Problem 25-5A, requirement 2.

2. Why might a company use the point of sale as the second trigger point instead of the point of completion?

Problem 25-7A   *Analyzing costs of quality*   *(Obj. 7)*

Morishita Electronics Inc. is using a costs-of-quality approach to evaluate design-engineering efforts for a new DVD player. The company's senior managers expect the engineering work to yield sizable savings in the costs of appraisal, internal failure, and external failure activities. The predicted reductions in activities over the two-year life of the player are shown below. Also shown are the budgeted unit activity costs.

Activity	Predicted Reduction in Activity Units	Unit Activity Cost
Inspection of incoming materials	300	$ 35
Inspection of work in process	300	20
Number of defective units discovered in-house	1,000	40
Number of defective units discovered by customers	500	70
Lost sales due to dissatisfied customers	150	100

Required

1. Calculate the predicted quality-cost savings from the design-engineering work.

2. Suppose that Morishita Electronics Inc. spent $103,000 on design engineering for the new DVD player. What is the net benefit of this "preventive" quality activity?

3. What major difficulty would Morishita Electronics Inc. managers have in implementing this costs-of-quality approach? What alternative approach to quality improvement could they use?

4. How will what you learned from this problem help you manage a business?

Problem 25-8A   *Using an activity-based costing system, evaluating whether to change to just-in-time production*   *(Obj. 2, 4)*

The Tremblant Baking Company Ltd. produces and sells two product lines with the following budgeted results for October, 2003:

	Loaves	Rolls
Number of sales orders............................	3,000 orders	7,500 orders
Budgeted sales (in units).......................	360,000 units	270,000 units
Direct materials (total)	$270,000	$450,000
Direct labour...	$135,000	$210,000
Cost of external failures	$ 15,000	$ 30,000
Machine hours.......................................	18,000 mhrs	90,000 mhrs
Number of purchase orders	6,000 orders	12,000 orders
Number of production batches............	750 batches	7,500 batches

Budgeted manufacturing overhead costs for the period consisted of:

Processing of purchase orders	$ 60,000
Direct materials handling and storage	$ 210,000
Maintenance and amortization of equipment..............	$ 162,000
Cost of setting up machinery for new batches..............	$ 371,250
Quality inspection of each batch produced	$ 264,000
Cost of external failures...	$ 31,500
Fringe benefit costs for direct labour	$ 101,250
Total budgeted manufacturing overhead	$1,200,000

Required

1. What would be the total cost of one unit of "Loaves" if the company measured the direct materials and direct labour but:
   a. Allocated all manufacturing overhead costs based on direct labour costs?
   b. Allocated all manufacturing overhead costs based on the most logical driver of the activity?

2. Which costing system would management prefer? Why?

3. Tremblant Baking Company Ltd. is considering changing the layout of the factory and renting additional equipment at $425,000 per month. The new layout and equipment would allow the company to have separate production lines for each product line and therefore avoid changeovers from one line to another by using just-in-time production. This is expected to reduce the number of batches by 60 percent for each product line. It would also increase direct labour efficiency by 10 percent and decrease external failures by 50 percent. What would be the overall monthly savings to the company if the change is made?

Problem 25-9A   *Analyzing costs of quality*   *(Obj. 7)*

London Company Inc. is using the cost-of-quality approach to evaluate the source of direct materials. The company presently purchases the materials from an overseas supplier due to a much lower cost of purchase, but a local supplier has offered to supply the materials for 20 percent more, and provide materials of a higher quality and guarantee the quality of the materials.

The company is presently working at full capacity, but is still unable to meet demand. Information on its current annual operations includes:

Factory capacity	600,000 units
Average contribution margin per unit...........................	$8.00 per unit
Cost of materials..	$1,800,000
Cost of inspecting materials..	$ 40,000
Cost of inspecting production	$210,000
Cost of reworking faulty units prior to shipping.........	$ 60,000
Cost of warranty work...	$375,000
Cost of product liability claims.......................................	$450,000

10 percent of all production fails to pass the inspection and is destroyed.
40 percent of all product failures are due to faulty materials.

Required

1. Determine the total costs of quality in each of the following categories:
   - Prevention costs
   - Appraisal costs
   - Internal failure costs
   - External failure costs

2. What would be the annual gain or loss to the company if it improved the quality of direct materials?

Problems (Group B)

Problem 25-1B   *Product costing in an activity-based costing system*   *(Obj. 1)*

An IBM Canada factory assembles and tests printed circuit (PC) boards. Consider the following data regarding PC Board XR1, which is used in various computers:

Direct materials cost	$45.00
Activity costs applied	?
Manufacturing product cost...	?

The activities required to build the PC boards follow:

Manufacturing Activity	Cost Driver	Activity Costs Applied to Each Unit
1. Start station	Number of raw PC boards	1 × $ 1.80 = $1.80
2. Dip insertion	Number of dip insertions	20 × 0.25 = ?
3. Manual insertion	Number of manual insertions	12 × ? = 8.40
4. Wave solder	Number of boards soldered	1 × 3.50 = 3.50
5. Backload	Number of backload insertions	? × 0.80 = 5.60
6. Test	Standard time each board is in test activity	0.25 × 80.00 = ?
7. Defect analysis	Standard time for defect analysis and repair	0.16 × ? = 8.00
Total		$?

Required

1. Fill in the blanks in both the opening schedule and the list of activities.

2. How is labour cost identified with products under this product costing system?

3. Why might managers favour this activity-based accounting system instead of the older system, which applied all conversion costs on the basis of direct labour?

Problem 25-2B   *Product costing in an activity-based costing system*   *(Obj. 1, 2)*

Letourneau Furniture Company Inc. manufactures rocking chairs in its two factories in Quebec. The company uses activity-based costing. Its activities and related data follow.

Manufacturing Activity	Budgeted Cost of Activity	Cost Driver Used as Application Base	Activity Cost per Unit of Application Base
Materials handling	$ 600,000	Number of parts	$ 1.00
Assembling	3,000,000	Direct labour hours	15.00
Painting	170,000	Number of painted units	4.00

Two styles of chairs were produced in March—the standard chair and an unpainted chair, which has fewer parts and requires no painting. Their quantities, direct materials costs, and other data follow:

Product	Units Produced	Direct Materials Costs	Number of Parts	Assembling Direct Labour Hours
Standard chair	5,000	$100,000	100,000	7,500
Unpainted chair	1,000	20,000	15,000	1,200

Required

1. Compute the manufacturing product cost of the standard chairs and the unpainted chairs.

2. Suppose that "upstream" activities, such as product design, were analyzed and applied to the standard chairs at $5.00 each and to the unpainted chairs at $2.00 each. Similar analyses were conducted of "downstream" activities such as distribution, marketing, and customer service. The downstream costs applied were $21.00 per standard chair and $18.00 per unpainted chair. Compute the full product costs per unit.

3. Which product costs are reported in the external financial statements? Which costs are used for management decision making? Explain the difference.

4. What price should Letourneau's managers set for standard chairs in order to earn a unit profit of $21.50?

Problem 25-3B *Costing products with ABC rates and comparing to costs from single-rate system; clues that ABC passes cost-benefit test* **(Obj. 1, 4)**

The Software Department of NewNet Inc. develops software for Internet applications. The software market is very competitive, and NewNet Inc.'s competitors continue to introduce new products at low prices. NewNet Inc. offers a wide variety of different software—from simple programs that enable new users to create personal Web pages, to complex commercial search engines. Like most software companies, NewNet Inc.'s raw material costs are insignificant.

NewNet Inc. has just hired Jamie Lopez, a recent graduate of the University of Alberta's masters of business administration. Lopez asks department manager Sue Wong to join him in a pilot activity-based costing study. Lopez and Wong identify the following activities, related costs, and cost allocation bases.

Activity	Estimated Indirect Activity Costs	Allocation Base	Estimated Quantity of Allocation Base
Applications development	$3,000,000	# New applications	6 new applications
Content production	4,800,000	# Lines of code	15,000,000 lines
Testing	315,000	# Testing hours	2,100 testing hours
Total indirect costs	$8,115,000		

NewNet Inc. has recently developed two new applications:

- NewPage—for developing personal Web pages
- Eureka!—a commercial search engine

NewPage required 500,000 lines of code and 100 hours of testing, while Eureka! required 7,500,000 lines of code and 600 hours of testing. NewNet Inc. expects to produce and sell 30,000 units of NewPage and 10 units of Eureka!

Required

1. Compute the cost allocation rate for each activity.

2. Use the activity-based costing rates to compute the indirect costs of NewPage and Eureka! (Hint: First compute the total indirect costs allocated to each product line, and then compute the cost per unit.)

3. NewNet Inc.'s original single-allocation-base cost system allocated indirect costs to products at $100 per programmer hour. NewPage required 10,000 programmer hours, while Eureka! required 20,000 programmer hours. Compute the indirect costs allocated to NewPage and Eureka! under the original system. Then compute the indirect cost per unit for each product.

4. Compare the activity-based costs to the costs from the original system. How have the costs changed? Explain why the costs changed as they did.

5. What are the clues that NewNet Inc.'s ABC system is likely to pass the cost-benefit test?

Problem 25-4B *Activity-based management, target cost, and value engineering* **(Obj. 3)**

Even though Problem 25-3B shows that NewPage's ABC costs are lower than under the simpler original cost system, NewNet Inc.'s CEO Tony Millano is still concerned that the software's profitability may be less than expected. Millano asks Jamie Lopez to recommend a sale price that will yield a profit of $12 per unit, after direct production costs of $3 per unit, marketing and distributing costs of $5 per unit, and the indirect production costs of $22.50 per unit (from Problem 25-3B). Millano believes that the sale price must be $39 or less to reach estimated sales of 30,000 units. If Lopez's "cost-plus-based" recommended sale price exceeds $39, Millano authorizes him to establish a cross-functional value engineering team to squeeze out cost savings.

Required

1. Determine the sale price that yields a profit of $12 per unit. Will this meet Millano's target price?

2. Lopez establishes a value engineering team that finds new software writing routines can cut application development costs for the six new applications from $3,000,000 to $2,700,000. This would also save $600,000 in content production and require 14,000,000 instead of 15,000,000 lines of code. Testing would be unaffected. The value engineering team also finds that improved supply-chain management can cut NewPage's direct production costs from $3 per unit to $2 per unit. However, marketing and distribution costs for NewPage are unchanged.

   Given these cost savings, what are the indirect activity cost allocation rates for application development, content production, and testing?

3. If the value engineering team's suggestions are implemented, NewPage would require 480,000 lines of code and the same 100 hours of testing. What is the new indirect activity (production) cost per unit (including all three activities) for NewPage?

4. With these changes, can NewNet Inc. set a sale price of $39 and still earn a profit of $12 per unit?

Problem 25-5B *Recording manufacturing costs for a JIT costing system* **(Obj. 5, 6)**

Advanced Tech Products Ltd. produces pagers. The company has a JIT production system and uses JIT costing. Its production system has two trigger points: the purchase of raw materials and parts and the completion of pagers.

Advanced Tech Products Ltd. has two inventory accounts, Raw and In Process Inventory and Finished Goods Inventory. On August 1, 2002, the account balances were Raw and In Process Inventory, $2,000; Finished Goods Inventory, $5,000.

Advanced Tech Product Ltd.'s standard cost per pager is direct materials, $30; conversion costs, $20. The following data pertain to August manufacturing and sales activity:

Raw materials and parts purchased	$602,000
Conversion costs incurred	$388,000
Number of units completed	20,000
Number of units sold	19,800

Required

1. What are the major features of a just-in-time production system such as that of Advanced Tech Products Ltd.?
2. Prepare summary journal entries for August. Assume that there are no direct materials variances and that underapplied or overapplied conversion costs are closed to Cost of Goods Sold at the end of the month.
3. What is the August 31, 2002, balance of Raw and In Process Inventory?

Problem 25-6B *Recording JIT costs, second trigger point is sale* (Obj. 5)

Advanced Tech Products Ltd. of Problem 25-5B has a two-trigger-point JIT costing system, but now suppose that the second trigger point is the sale, not the completion, of pagers. The company has only one inventory account, labeled simply "Inventory." Only direct materials costs are assigned to Inventory; the account balance is the sum of the costs of materials in the storeroom (if any), in process, and in finished units that have not been sold.

Conversion costs are not inventoried. They are applied, at standard, to units sold. Continue to assume that overapplied or underapplied conversion costs are closed to Cost of Goods Sold at the end of the month.

Required

1. Prepare summary journal entries that correspond to the entries you prepared in Problem 25-5B, requirement 2.
2. Why might a company use the point of sale as the second trigger point instead of the point of completion?

Problem 25-7B *Analyzing costs of quality* (Obj. 7)

Shave Close Inc. is using a costs-of-quality approach to evaluate design-engineering efforts for a new electric shaver. The company's senior managers expect the engineering work to yield sizable savings in the costs of appraisal, internal failure, and external failure activities. The predicted reductions in activities over the two-year life of the shaver are shown below. Also shown are the budgeted unit activity costs.

Activity	Predicted Reduction in Activity Units	Unit Activity Cost
Inspection of incoming materials	200	$30.00
Inspection of work in process	200	37.50
Number of defective units discovered in-house	3,000	22.50
Number of defective units discovered by customers	800	45.00
Lost sales to dissatisfied customers	200	82.50

Required

1. Calculate the predicted quality-cost savings from the design-engineering work.
2. Suppose that Shave Close Inc. spent $100,000 on design engineering for the new shaver. What is the net benefit of this "preventive" quality activity?

3. What major difficulty would Shave Close Inc. managers have in implementing this costs-of-quality approach? What alternative approach to quality improvement could they use?

4. How will what you learned from this problem help you manage a business?

Problem 25-8B *Using an activity-based costing system, evaluating whether to change to just-in-time production* **(Obj. 2, 4)**

Commercial Baking Company Ltd. produces and sells two product lines with the following budgeted results for October, 2003:

	Loaves	**Rolls**
Number of sales orders...............	6,000 orders	14,000 orders
Budgeted production and sales (in units)	600,000 units	320,000 units
Direct materials (total)...............	$460,000	$640,000
Direct labour...............	$160,000	$240,000
Cost of external failures...............	$ 40,000	$ 80,000
Machine hours...............	30,000 mhrs	130,000 mhrs
Number of purchase orders...............	4,000 orders	8,000 orders
Number of production batches...............	2,000 batches	18,000 batches

Budgeted manufacturing overhead costs for the period consisted of:

Processing of purchase orders...............	$ 108,000
Direct materials handling and storage...............	$ 220,000
Maintenance and amortization of equipment...............	$ 176,000
Cost of setting up machinery for new batches...............	$ 528,000
Quality inspection of each batch produced...............	$ 308,000
Cost of external failures...............	$ 120,000
Fringe benefit costs for direct labour...............	$ 140,000
Total budgeted manufacturing overhead...............	$1,600,000

Required

1. What would be the total cost of one unit of "Loaves" if the company measured the direct materials and direct labour but:
   a. Allocated all manufacturing overhead costs based on direct labour costs?
   b. Allocated all manufacturing overhead costs based on the most logical driver of the activity?

2. Which costing system would management prefer? Why?

3. Commercial Baking Company Ltd. is considering changing the layout of the factory and renting additional equipment at $450,000 per month. The new layout and equipment would allow the company to have separate production lines for each product line and therefore avoid changeovers from one line to another by using just-in-time production. This is expected to reduce the number of batches by 50 percent for each product line. It would also increase direct labour efficiency by 15 percent and decrease external failures by 40 percent. What would be the overall monthly savings to the company if it made the change?

Problem 25-9B *Analyzing costs of quality* **(Obj. 7)**

The Great Lakes Software Company Inc. is using the cost-of-quality approach to evaluate the source of direct materials. The company presently purchases the direct materials from an out-of-town supplier. A local supplier has offered to supply the materials for 15 percent more, but provides materials of a higher quality and guarantees the quality of the materials.

The company is presently working at full capacity, but is still unable to meet demand. Information on its current annual operations includes:

Factory capacity..	2,000,000 units
Average contribution margin per unit..........................	$10 per unit
Cost of materials...	$3,600,000
Cost of inspecting materials...	$120,000
Cost of inspecting production	$400,000
Cost of reworking faulty units prior to shipping.........	$200,000
Cost of warranty work..	$720,000
Cost of product liability claims.....................................	$880,000

5 percent of all production fails to pass the inspection and is destroyed.
30 percent of all product failures are due to faulty materials.

Required

1. Determine the total costs of quality in each of the following categories:
   - Prevention costs
   - Appraisal costs
   - Internal failure costs
   - External failure costs
2. What would be the annual gain or loss to the company if it improved the quality of direct materials?

Challenge Problems

Problem 25-1C   *Explaining activity-based costing*   **(Obj. 1)**

Much is said today about activity-based costing and the fact that it is being adapted by a wide range of companies.

You are a new accounting graduate who has just joined Three Hills Mfg. Co. Ltd., a small family-owned company that manufactures a range of products for the cottage and camping trade. Three Hills had sales of $3,000,000 in 2002.

The company's cost-accounting system is fairly straightforward—add raw materials; add direct materials and overhead; divide costs by number of units produced to calculate manufactured cost.

Required

Marie Whittaker, the president of Three Hills Mfg. Co. Ltd., has asked you to explain activity-based costing to her and her executive committee, and specifically to explain how it would help the company. Make assumptions you think are necessary in providing advice to her.

Problem 25-2C   *Understanding the management of quality*   **(Obj. 7)**

"The quality of goods and services is a major feature of global competition. Businesses that deliver the best-quality products [and services] gain market share." Four types of quality costs (prevention costs, appraisal cost, internal failure costs, external failure costs) are discussed on page 1402.

Required

Your educational institution is interested in the management of quality in the educational process. Apply the four types of quality-related costs to your educational institution; indicate how they might be used to improve the quality of your educational experience.

Extending Your Knowledge

Decision Problems

1. Costing jobs with a single overhead rate and then with ABC rates; making a decision on the basis of resulting product costs   (Obj. 1, 2)

National Electronics Systems Ltd. is a government contractor that specializes in electronics systems for traffic control. The company's current job order cost accounting system has two direct cost categories—direct materials and direct labour. Indirect manufacturing cost (overhead) is applied to jobs at the single rate of $23 per direct labour hour.

A task force headed by National's senior management accountant recently designed an ABC system with five activities. The ABC system retains the current system's two direct cost categories. Thus, it budgets only overhead costs for each activity. Pertinent data follow.

Activity	Cost Driver Used as Application Base	Cost per Unit of Application Base
Materials handling	Number of parts	$ 0.75
Machine setup	Number of setups	500.00
Machining	Machining hours	32.00
Assembling	Assembling direct labour hours	18.00
Shipping	Number of shipments	1,500.00

All data necessary for both budgeting and job costing with this ABC system are collected automatically.

National Electronics Systems Ltd. has been awarded two new contracts, which will be produced as Job A and Job B. Budget data relating to the contracts follow.

	Job A	Job B
Direct materials cost	$262,500	$45,000
Direct labour cost	240,000	18,000
Number of parts	15,000	2,000
Number of setups	6	4
Number of machining hours	3,000	700
Assembling direct labour hours	1,500	200
Number of shipments	1	1
Total direct labour hours	8,000	600
Number of output units	100	10

Required

1. Compute the manufacturing product cost per unit for each job using the current costing system (with two direct cost categories and a single overhead application rate).

2. Suppose that National Electronics Systems Ltd. adopts the ABC system for product costing. Compute the manufacturing product cost of each job with this system, which has five activity-based overhead application rates instead of a single rate.

3. Which costing system more accurately assigns to jobs the costs of the resources consumed to produce them? Explain.

4. A dependable company has offered to produce both jobs for National Electronics Systems Ltd. for $8,000 per output unit. National may subcontract (buy from the outside company) either Job A only, Job B only, or both jobs. Which course of

action will National managers take if they base their decision on (a) current system costs? (b) ABC system costs? Which course of action will yield more income? Explain.

2. Activity-based management, target cost, and value engineering (Obj. 1, 2, 3)

To remain competitive, National Electronics Systems Ltd.'s management believes the company must produce Job B-type traffic controllers (from Decision Probem 1) at a target cost of $8,900. National just joined a business-to-business e-market site that management believes will enable the firm to cut direct material costs by 10 percent. National's management also believes that a value engineering team can reduce assembly time.

Compute the assembly cost saving per Job B-type traffic controller required to meet the target cost. (*Hint:* Begin by calculating the direct material, direct labour, and allocated activity cost per traffic controller.

Special Business Decisions and Capital Budgeting

CHAPTER OBJECTIVES

After studying this chapter, you should be able to

1 Identify the relevant information for a special business decision

2 Make five types of short-term special business decisions

3 Explain the difference between correct analysis and incorrect analysis of a particular business decision

4 Use opportunity costs in decision making

5 Use four capital-budgeting models to make longer-term investment decisions

6 Compare and contrast popular capital-budgeting models

Intrawest Corporation, headquartered in Vancouver, is a world leader in leisure services. Originally a real estate company, Intrawest ventured into the leisure services area in 1986 when it acquired Blackcomb Mountain, a destination ski resort in Whistler, British Columbia. Throughout the 1990s the company continued to acquire resort properties in British Columbia, Quebec, Alberta, Ontario, and the United States. These ski destinations provided Intrawest with over 5.5 million skier visits in 1998.

In 1998, the company made its first move into the warm-weather resort segment by acquiring a resort on the Gulf Coast of Florida and two golf courses in Arizona. Mr. Joe Houssian, Chairman, President, and Chief Executive Officer, stated in the 2000 Intrawest annual report that in 2000, Intrawest bought an equity stake in Compagnie des Alpes based in France and started its first village development in Europe at Les Arcs.

Also in the 2000 annual report, Mr. Dan Jarvis, Executive Vice President and Chief Financial Officer, stated:

> Over the next three years [Intrawest] will add 4,500 units of new accommodation and 400,000 square feet of shops, restaurants, and other commercial space in our villages.

How does Intrawest determine if an investment for a new property acquisition is warranted? The answer is capital budgeting. Intrawest's long-term strategy is growth through resort property acquisition. But how does Intrawest management determine the long-term viability of the acquisition?

Acquisitions must meet certain requirements—they must be profitable and they must provide an adequate return on investment. The company's acquisition team would want to compare the amount of investment needed to acquire a destination resort with the additional cash flow the company will generate from the acquisition.

These comparisons are done using management accounting techniques. One of the most common and widely used techniques is net present value, which attempts to determine the present value of the future cash flows of an investment and compare them with its cost.

We'll see how companies like Intrawest use management accounting techniques to decide which long-term investments to make.

Source: Intrawest Corporation, 2000 Annual Report.

THIS chapter will deal with *long-term* special decisions such as those Intrawest has made with respect to investments in Europe and expansion of its facilities. We'll tackle those long-term special decisions in the second half of the chapter. But first we need to consider *short-term* special decisions.

Intrawest Corporation
www.intrawest.com

Using Relevant Information

OBJECTIVE 1
Identify the relevant information for a special business decision

Business managers develop and implement strategies. A **strategy** is a set of business goals and the tactics to achieve them. The main financial goals in business are to earn profits and to build a strong financial position. Decisions centre on how to achieve those goals.

Decision making means choosing among alternative courses of action. To choose, managers

- Identify the alternative courses of action
- Gather information relevant (useful) for making the decision
- Analyze the information to compare alternatives
- Choose the best alternative to achieve the strategic goal

Exhibit 26-1 illustrates the decision-making process. Computers are ideally suited for decision analysis.

Managers often select the course of action that maximizes expected operating income. To do this, they analyze relevant information. **Relevant information** has two distinguishing characteristics. It is

- expected *future data* that also
- *differs among alternatives*

.... **THINKING IT OVER**

You are considering replacing your Pentium III computer with the latest model. Is the $1,900 you spent (in 2000) on the Pentium relevant to your decision about buying the new model?

A: The $1,900 cost of your Pentium model is irrelevant. The $1,900 is a *past* (sunk) cost that has already been incurred, so it is the same whether or not you buy the new computer.

Suppose you are buying your first car. You are deciding whether to buy a Toyota or a Ford. The cost of the car you want to buy, the insurance premium on this car, and the cost to maintain the car are all relevant because these costs

- will be incurred in the *future* (after you decide to buy the car), and
- will *differ between alternatives* (Each car has a different cost, and the maintenance and insurance costs will also differ.)

The cost of the car, the insurance, and the maintenance are called relevant because they can affect your decision of which car to purchase. Costs that were incurred in the past and costs that do not differ between alternatives are *irrelevant* because they do not affect your decision. For example, a campus parking sticker will cost the same whether you buy the Toyota or the Ford, so that cost is irrelevant to your decision.

The same distinction applies to all situations—*only relevant data affect decisions.* Let's consider another application of this general principle.

Suppose that Ingo Knitting Ltd. is deciding whether to use pure wool or a wool blend in a line of sweaters. Assume Ingo predicts the following costs under the two alternatives:

| | Expected Materials and Labour Cost per Sweater | | |
	Wool	Wool Blend	Cost Difference
Direct materials	$10	$6	$4
Direct labour	2	2	0
Total cost of direct materials and direct labour	$12	$8	$4

The cost of direct materials is relevant because this cost differs between alternatives (the wool costs more than the wool blend). The labour cost is irrelevant because that cost is the same for both alternatives.

The point is worth emphasizing

> **Relevant information is expected future data that differ among alternative courses of action.**

Managers should base their decisions on expected future data rather than on historical data. Historical data often are supplied by the accounting system and are useful guides to predictions. However, historical data by themselves are irrelevant for making decisions about the future.

EXHIBIT 26-1

How Businesses Make Special Decisions

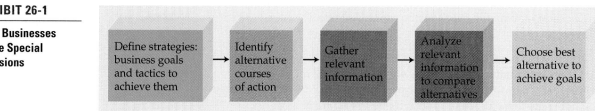

Short-Term Special Decisions

OBJECTIVE 2
Make five types of short-term special business decisions

Our approach to making decisions is called the *relevant information approach*, or the *incremental analysis approach*. This approach applies to a wide variety of special decisions. We now consider five short-term special decisions:

- Special sales orders
- Dropping products, departments, and territories
- Product mix
- Outsourcing (make or buy)
- Selling as is or processing further

As you study these decisions, keep in mind that two keys in analyzing short-term special business decisions are

- Focus on *relevant* revenues, costs, and profits
- Use a *contribution margin approach* that separates variable costs from fixed costs.

Special Sales Order

Suppose that Magna International, a manufacturer of automobile parts, ordinarily sells oil filters for $3.20 each. An e-commerce company has offered Magna $35,000 for 20,000 oil filters, or $1.75 per filter ($35,000/20,000 = $1.75). This sale will not affect regular business in any way. Furthermore, the special sales order

- Will not change fixed costs
- Will not require any additional variable non-manufacturing expenses
- Will use manufacturing capacity that would otherwise be idle

Magna International
www.magnaint.com

To set the stage for the analysis, examine the hypothetical income statement for the oil filter division of Magna in Exhibit 26-2. Suppose Magna made and sold 250,000 oil filters before considering the special order. Using the conventional (absorption costing) income statement on the left-hand side of Exhibit 26-2, the manufacturing cost per unit is $2.00 ($500,000 ÷ 250,000). This suggests that Magna should *not* accept the special order at a sale price of $1.75, because each oil filter costs $2.00 to manufacture. But appearances can be deceiving!

The right-hand-side of Exhibit 26-2 shows the more helpful contribution margin income statement. Recall from Chapter 22 that contribution margin income statements separate variable expenses from fixed expenses. Chapter 22 compares

EXHIBIT 26-2

Conventional Absorption Costing Format and Contribution Margin Format Income Statements for Magna International

HYPOTHETICAL MAGNA INTERNATIONAL—OIL FILTER DIVISION
Income Statement
For the Year Ended December 31, 2002

Conventional (Absorption Costing) Format		Contribution Margin Format		
Sales revenue	$800,000	Sales revenue		$800,000
Less manufacturing cost of goods sold	500,000	Less variable expenses: Manufacturing................	$300,000	
Gross margin..........	300,000	Marketing and administrative	75,000	375,000
Less marketing and administrative		Contribution margin		425,000
expenses..............	200,000	Less fixed expenses: Manufacturing................	$200,000	
		Marketing and administrative	125,000	325,000
Operating income..	$100,000	Operating income		$100,000

conventional and contribution margin income statements. Managers find this contribution margin format more useful for decision making because it shows how sales volume affects costs and income. The contribution margin income statement shows that the *variable* manufacturing cost per unit is only $1.20 ($300,000 ÷ 250,000). Now let's reconsider the key question facing Magna: How would the special sale affect the company's operating income?

Correct Analysis: Contribution Margin Approach

The correct analysis shown in Exhibit 26-3 is an incremental approach that follows the two key guidelines for special business decisions:

1. Focus on relevant revenues, costs, and profits, and
2. Use a contribution margin approach.

Exhibit 26-3 shows that this special sale increases revenues by $35,000 (20,000 × $1.75). The only cost that will differ between the alternatives is the variable manufacturing cost, which is expected to increase by $24,000 (20,000 × $1.20). The other costs do not enter the analysis because they are irrelevant. Variable marketing and administrative expenses will be the same whether Magna accepts the special order or not, because no special efforts were made to get this sale. Fixed expenses are unchanged because Magna has enough idle capacity to produce 20,000 extra oil filters without requiring additional facilities.

To decide whether to accept the special order, Magna compares the additional (incremental) revenues with the additional (incremental) expenses of producing the goods. As long as the increase in revenues exceeds the increase in expenses, the sale contributes to profits. Management predicts that the order will increase operating income by $11,000, as shown in Exhibit 26-3, so they should accept the special order.

Thus, the guiding principle in special order decisions is:

> **Special orders increase income if the revenue from the order exceeds the *extra* variable and fixed costs incurred to fill the orders.**

Exhibit 26-4 gives the contribution margin income statements both without the special sales order (column 1) and with it (column 2). Column 3 shows the differences from accepting the special order, an $11,000 increase in operating income.

We have shown two correct ways of deciding whether to accept or reject a special sales order at a sales price less than total cost per unit:

- An incremental analysis that quickly summarizes the differences (Exhibit 26-3)
- An analyis of total revenues, expenses, and operating income under both courses of action (Exhibit 26-4)

Which should you use? The answer depends on your question. The *incremental* analysis answers the question: What will be the *difference* in revenues, expenses, and operating income if the business accepts the special order? The *total* analysis shows the summary of differences and answers an additional question: What will be the *total* revenues, expenses, and operating income under each course of action? Managers can use either analysis to decide whether to accept or reject a special sales order.

EXHIBIT 26-3

Incremental Analysis of Special Sales Order

Expected increase in revenues—sale of 20,000 oil filters × $1.75 each.	$35,000
Expected increase in expenses—variable manufacturing costs:	
20,000 oil filters × $1.20 each..	24,000
Expected increase in operating income	$11,000

HYPOTHETICAL MAGNA INTERNATIONAL—OIL FILTER DIVISION
Income Statement
For the Year Ended December 31, 2002

	(1) Without Special Order, (250,000 Units)	(2) With Special Order, (270,000 Units)	(3) Difference, 20,000 Units Total	Per Unit
Sales.................................	$800,000	$835,000	$35,000	$1.75
Variable expenses:				
Manufacturing..................	300,000	324,000	24,000	1.20
Marketing and administrative...............	75,000	75,000	—	—
Total variable expenses........................	375,000	399,000	24,000	1.20
Contribution margin.............	425,000	436,000	11,000	0.55
Fixed expenses:				
Manufacturing..................	200,000	200,000	—	—
Marketing and administrative...............	125,000	125,000	—	—
Total fixed expenses..........	325,000	325,000	—	—
Operating income	$100,000	$111,000	$11,000	$0.55

EXHIBIT 26-4

Total Analysis of Special Sales Order—Income Statement without and with the Special Order

WORKING IT OUT

What if, by accepting the special order, Magna will have to buy a piece of stamping equipment that costs $12,000 in order to mark the oil filters with the e-commerce company's logo? The equipment will then be discarded. How does this affect your decision?

A:

Expected increase in operating income................	$11,000
Less cost of equipment	(12,000)
Loss from the special order.......	$(1,000)

Incorrect Analysis: Ignoring the Nature of Fixed Costs

Now consider an incorrect analysis of the special sales order decision. The conventional approach, using only the left-hand side of Exhibit 26-2, leads to an incorrect measure of the change in expenses resulting from the sale.

OBJECTIVE 3
Explain the difference between correct analysis and incorrect analysis of a particular business decision

Total manufacturing costs..	$ 500,000
Units produced	÷ 250,000
Manufacturing product cost per unit ($500,000/250,000)...........	$ 2.00

A manager who follows this incorrect approach reasons that it costs $2.00 to make an oil filter, so it is unprofitable to sell the product for less than $2.00. *The flaw in this analysis arises from treating a fixed cost as though it changes in total like a variable cost does.* Manufacturing one additional oil filter will only cost $1.20—the variable manufacturing cost. *Fixed expenses are irrelevant to the decision because Magna will incur the fixed expenses whether or not the company accepts the special sales order.* Producing 20,000 more oil filters will not increase *total* fixed expenses. As volume changes, manufacturing costs increase at the rate of $1.20 per unit, not $2.00 per unit. In the correct (contribution margin) approach, the variable expenses are relevant, and the fixed expenses are irrelevant.

Short-Term versus Long-Term: Other Factors to Consider

Our special sales order analysis focused on short-term expected effect on operating income. We also must consider long-term factors. How will the special order affect Magna's regular customers? Will acceptance of the order at $1.75 per unit hurt Magna's ability to sell the product at the regular price of $3.20? Will regular customers find out about the special price and balk at paying more? And how will competitors react? Will this sale start a price war?

Accepting the order yields an $11,000 advantage in operating income. Will potential disadvantages offset this income? The sales manager may think so and

LEARNING TIP

A company cannot survive in the long run by producing products that consistently sell for less than full cost. Management must also consider how to survive if there is chronic excess capacity in the factory: rather than accept a series of special orders that do not cover full costs, the business might consider downsizing.

reject the order. In turning away the business, the manager would say that the company is better off passing up $11,000 now to protect its long-term position and customer relations. Rejecting the special sales order may be an $11,000 "investment" in the company's long-term future.

To make special sales order decisions, we analyzed changes in revenues and costs among the different alternatives. We will use this same approach of analyzing differences in revenues and costs for the remaining short-term special decisions.

Dropping Products, Departments, Territories

To decide whether a company should drop a product line, a department, or a territory, let's modify our Magna example. We will assume that Magna already is operating at the 270,000-unit level, as shown in column 2 of Exhibit 26-4. Suppose that the company is now considering dropping the air cleaner product line with $35,000 (20,000 units) in sales and total variable costs per unit of $1.15. A contribution margin income statement that is divided by product line follows:

	Total	Product Line Oil Filters	Air Cleaners
Units	270,000	250,000	20,000
Sales revenue	$835,000	$800,000	$ 35,000
Variable expenses	405,000	375,000	30,000
Contribution margin	430,000	425,000	5,000
Fixed expenses:			
Manufacturing	200,000	185,185*	14,815*
Marketing and administrative	125,000	115,741†	9,259†
Total fixed expenses	325,000	300,926	24,074
Operating income (loss)	$105,000	$124,074	$(19,074)

*$200,000/270,000 units = $0.74074 per unit; 250,000 units × $0.74074 = $185,185; 20,000 units × $0.74074 = $14,815

†$125,000/270,000 units = $0.46296 per unit; 250,000 units × $0.46296 = $115,741; 20,000 units × $0.46296 = $9,259

Suppose that to measure product-line operating income, Magna allocates fixed expenses in proportion to the number of units sold. Dividing the fixed manufacturing expense of $200,000 by 270,000 units yields a fixed manufacturing cost of $0.74074 per unit. Allocating this unit cost to the 250,000 units of the oil filter product line results in a fixed manufacturing cost of $185,185 for this product. The same procedure allocates $14,815 to air cleaners. Fixed marketing and administrative expenses are allocated in the same manner. This allocation method results in an operating loss of $19,074 for air cleaners. Should Magna drop the air cleaner product line?

The analysis depends on whether fixed costs change.

Fixed Costs Remain Unchanged As in the special sales order example, follow the two key guidelines for special business decisions: (1) focus on relevant data items, and (2) use a contribution margin approach. The relevant items are still the changes in revenues and expenses, but now we are considering a decrease in volume rather than an increase. If fixed costs will in fact remain the same whether or not the air cleaner product line is dropped, the fixed costs are not relevant to the decision. Only the revenues and variable expenses are relevant.

The preceding table shows that the air cleaner product line has a positive contribution margin of $5,000. If this product line is dropped, the company will forego this $5,000 contribution. Exhibit 26-5 verifies this amount—expected revenue

EXHIBIT 26-5

Dropping a Product—Fixed Costs Unchanged

Expected decrease in revenues:	
Sale of air cleaners (20,000 × $1.75)	$35,000
Expected decrease in expenses:	
Variable manufacturing expenses—(20,000 × $1.50)	30,000
Expected decrease in operating income	$ 5,000

decreases by $35,000, and expected variable expenses decrease by $30,000, a net $5,000 decrease in operating income (since fixed costs are unaffected). This analysis suggests that management should *not* drop air cleaners.

As Exhibit 26-5 and 26-6 show, the key to deciding whether to drop products, departments, or territories is to compare the lost revenue against the costs that can be saved from dropping. The decision rule is:

> **If the lost revenues from dropping a product, deparment, or territory exceed the cost savings from dropping → Do not drop.**
>
> **If the cost savings exceed the lost revenues from dropping a product, department, or territory → Drop.**

Fixed Costs Change Don't jump to the conclusion that fixed costs never change and are always irrelevant. Suppose that Magna had employed a supervisor to oversee the air cleaner product line. The supervisor's $28,000 salary can be avoided if the company stops producing air cleaners. Exhibit 26-6 shows how this additional savings affects the analysis.

In this situation, operating income will increase by $23,000 if Magna drops air cleaners. Here a "fixed cost" *is* relevant, so managers must consider the change in the cost. Special decisions should take into account all costs affected by the choice of action. Managers must ask: What costs—variable *and* fixed—will change?

WORKING IT OUT

Refer to the previous Working It Out. By how much would Spiff's operating income change if $7,500 of the fixed costs could be eliminated?

A: It would increase by $800 because the decrease in fixed costs is greater than the decrease in contribution margin ($7,500 − $6,700).

STOP & THINK

The Magna example considers the $28,000 paid to the supervisor a fixed cost. But how can this be a "fixed" cost if it is eliminated by dropping the air cleaner product line?

Answer: Some fixed costs are directly traceable to a particular product line. The supervisor is employed specifically to oversee the air cleaner product line. Dropping air cleaners eliminates the need for the supervisor, so Magna can save the $28,000 it would otherwise pay that employee.

Recall that fixed costs are fixed *only* within the relevant range of production. Magna usually produces 20,000 air cleaners. Elimination of the air cleaner line is outside Magna's normal (relevant) range of production, so "fixed" costs can change.

EXHIBIT 26-6

Dropping a Product—Fixed Costs Change

Expected decrease in revenues:		
Sale of air cleaners (20,000 × $1.75)		$35,000
Expected decrease in expenses:		
Variable manufacturing expenses (20,000 × $1.50)	$30,000	
Fixed expenses—supervisor salary	28,000	
Expected decrease in total expenses		58,000
Expected increase in operating income..		$ 23,000

Product Mix—Which Product to Emphasize

Companies do not have unlimited resources. They must decide which products to emphasize and which to deemphasize. This decision affects profits. If salespersons push products with low profit margins at the expense of products with higher profit margins, the company's operating income may decrease.

Consider Esprit, a clothing manufacturer that produces shirts and pants. The following data suggest that shirts are more profitable than pants:

WORKING IT OUT

A firm makes two products, a hand mixer and a can opener. It takes 1/2 hour to make a hand mixer and 2 hours to make a can opener.

	Hand Mixer	Can Opener
Sale price	$8	$10
Variable cost	6	5
Contribution margin	$2	$ 5

If only 200,000 labour hours are available, which product should be produced?

A: Produce the mixer.

	Hand Mixer	Can Opener
Contribution margin	$ 2	$ 5
Hours required	1/2	2
Contribution margin per hr.	$ 4	$2.50

Producing the mixer will yield a profit of $800,000 (200,000 × $4); producing the can opener will yield a profit of only $500,000 (200,000 × $2.50).

	Product	
	Shirts	**Pants**
Per unit:		
Sale price	$30	$60
Variable expenses	12	48
Contribution margin	$18	$12
Contribution margin ratio:		
Shirts—$18/$30	60%	
Pants—$12/$60		20%

However, an important piece of information is missing—the time it takes to manufacture each product. This factor, called the **constraint**, restricts production or sale of a product. In some companies, the constraint is production capacity. The factory or labour force may be unable to produce more than a certain number of units. Constraints vary from company to company. The constraint that limits how much the company can produce may be labour hours, machine hours, materials, or square metres of shelf space. For example, storage may be limited to 5,500 square metres of space in a warehouse. Some companies are constrained by sales. Competition may be stiff, and the business may be able to sell only so many units.

Esprit can produce either 20 pairs of pants *or* 10 shirts per machine hour. The company can sell all the shirts and pants it produces. The company has 2,000 hours of capacity. Which product should it emphasize?

To answer this question, follow the guiding principle:

> **To maximize profits, produce the product with the highest contribution margin *per unit of the constraint.***

In our example, Esprit can sell all the pants and shirts it makes, so production (machine hours) is the constraint. Thus, Esprit should produce the product with the highest contribution margin per machine hour.

Exhibit 26-7 first determines the contribution margin per machine hour for each product. Pants have a higher contribution margin per machine hour ($240 = 20 pairs of pants x $12 per pair) than shirts ($180 = 10 shirts x $18 per shirt). Esprit will earn more profit by producing pants. Exhibit 26-7 proves this by multiplying the contribution margin per machine hour by the available number of machine hours. Esprit can earn $480,000 of contribution margin by producing pants, but only $360,000 by producing shirts.

Exhibit 26-7 shows that Esprit should *not* produce the product with the highest contribution margin *per unit* (shirts). The key point is that Esprit will earn more profit if it produces the product with the higher contribution margin per unit of the (machine hours) constraint—pants.

Notice that the analysis in Exhibit 26-7 has once again followed the two guidelines for special business decisions: (1) focus on relevant data (contribution margin in this example, because only sales revenue and variable costs are relevant), and (2) use a contribution margin approach.

EXHIBIT 26-7

Product Mix—Which
Product to Emphasize?

	Product	
	Shirts	Pants
(1) Units that can be produced each hour	10	20
(2) Contribution margin per unit	× $18	× $12
Contribution margin per hour (1) × (2)	$180	$240
Capacity—number of machine hours	× 2,000	× 2,000
Total contribution margin at full capacity	$360,000	$480,000

STOP & THINK

Why are Esprit's fixed expenses irrelevent in the decision to produce pants or shirts?

Answer: Esprit will use the same capital assets to make either pants or shirts. The fixed expenses will be the same whether the company makes pants or shirts, so the fixed expenses are irrelevant.

Outsourcing

Manufactured goods often include specialized parts. Overhead garage doors, for example, are activated by electronic controls. Overhead Door Company Ltd., a garage-door manufacturer, must decide whether to manufacture the control device itself or buy from a supplier. City Furniture Company Ltd. may ask, Should we stain and lacquer the furniture we manufacture or hire another company to do the finish work? These make-or-buy decisions are often called **outsourcing** decisions, because managers must decide whether to buy a component product or service, or to produce it in-house. Assuming that quality is unaffected, at the heart of the make-or-buy decision is *how best to use available facilities.*

Let's see how managers make outsourcing decisions. DefTone, a manufacturer of music CDs, is deciding whether to make the paper liners for the CD jewel boxes in-house, or whether to outsource them to Mūz-Art Inc., a company that specializes in producing the paper liners. DefTone's cost to produce 250,000 liners is:

	Total Cost (250,000 liners)
Direct materials	$ 40,000
Direct labour	20,000
Variable overhead	15,000
Fixed overhead	50,000
Total manufacturing cost	$125,000
Cost per liner ($125,000/250,000)	$0.50

Mūz-Art offers to sell DefTone the liners for $0.37 each. Should DefTone make the liners or buy them from Mūz-Art? DefTone's $0.50 unit cost of manufacturing the liner is $0.13 higher than the cost of buying it from Mūz-Art. At first glance, it appears that DefTone should outsource the liners. But the correct answer is not so simple. To make the best decision, you must compare the difference in expected future costs between the two alternatives. Which costs will differ depending on whether DefTone makes or buys the liners?

By purchasing the part, DefTone can avoid all variable manufacturing costs and reduce its fixed overhead cost by $10,000. (Fixed overhead will decrease to $40,000.) Exhibit 26-8 shows the differences in costs between the make and buy alternatives.

WORKING IT OUT

Z Inc. has been purchasing a part for $3.00. Z Inc. believes that it can make the part by utilizing excess capacity. Z Inc. predicts that it will need 50,000 of the parts. The unit costs have been estimated as follows:

Direct materials	$1.25
Direct labour	0.80
Variable overhead	0.50
Var. cost per unit	$2.55

Fixed costs will not change if the part is produced. Should Z Inc. make or buy the part?

A: Make the part.

Var. cost to make ($2.55 × 50,000)	$127,500
Var. cost to buy ($3.00 × 50,000)	150,000
Advantage to making	$ 22,500

EXHIBIT 26-8

Outsourcing Decision

Liner costs:	Make Liners	Buy Liners	Difference
Direct materials	$ 40,000	$ —	$40,000
Direct labour	20,000	—	20,000
Variable overhead	15,000	—	15,000
Fixed overhead	50,000	40,000	10,000
Purchase cost from Mūz-Art Inc. (250,000 × $0.37)	—	92,500	(92,500)
Total cost of liners	$125,000	$132,500	$(7,500)
Cost per unit—250,000 liners	$0.50	$0.53	$(0.03)

The decision: It would cost less to make the liners than to buy them from Mūz-Art. The net savings from making 250,000 liners is $7,500, which works out to $0.03 each. This savings exists despite the "make" alternative's $10,000 of incremental fixed overhead cost.

This example shows that *fixed costs are relevant to a special decision when those fixed costs differ between alternatives*. Exhibit 26-8 also shows that outsourcing decisions follow our two guidelines for special business decisions: (1) focus on relevant data (variable and fixed manufacturing costs in this case), and (2) use a contribution margin approach that separates variable costs from fixed costs. These guidelines help managers answer the fundamental question: What difference does the proposed change make?

Best Use of Facilities   Suppose that buying the liners from Mūz-Art Inc. will release factory facilities that DefTone can use to manufacture more CDs at an annual profit of $18,000. DefTone's managers must decide among three alternatives:

1. Use the facilities to make CDs.
2. Buy the liners and leave facilities idle.
3. Buy the liners and use facilities to make more CDs.

The alternative with the lowest *net* cost is the best use of DefTone's facilities. Exhibit 26-9 compares net cost under the three alternatives.

This analysis of net cost indicates that DefTone should buy the liners from Mūz-Art and use the vacated facilities to make more CDs. If the facilities remain idle, DefTone will forgo the opportunity to earn $18,000.

Special decisions often include qualitative factors—that is, factors that are difficult to quantify. For example, DefTone managers may believe they can better control quality by manufacturing liners themselves. This argues for DefTone making the liners. But Mūz-Art may be located very close to DefTone's assembly plant. Mūz-Art may be able to achieve a higher on-time delivery rate than DefTone's own plant. This

WORKING IT OUT

Refer to the previous Working It Out. Suppose that making the part increases fixed costs by $5,000 and that Z Inc. has an opportunity to rent idle facilities to Y Inc. for $20,000. How do these changes affect the decision?

A: There is a $2,500 advantage to buying the part.

	Make	Buy
Variable costs to make	$127,500	
Fixed costs to make	5,000	
Cost to buy		$150,000
Rent of space		(20,000)
Net cost	$132,500	$130,000

Fixed costs are relevant to this decision because they are different under the two alternatives. The fixed costs are $5,000 more if the part is made rather than purchased.

EXHIBIT 26-9

Best Use of Facilities

	Make Liners	Buy Liners and Leave Facilities Idle	Buy Liners and Make Additional CDs
Expected cost of obtaining 250,000 liners (from Exhibit 26-8)	$125,000	$132,500	$132,500
Expected profit contribution from additional CDs	—	—	(18,000)
Expected net cost of obtaining 250,000 liners	$125,000	$132,500	$114,500

would favour buying from Mūz-Art. DefTone's managers should consider these qualitative factors as well as revenue and cost differences in making their decision.

Outsourcing decisions are increasingly important in today's globally wired economy. In the past, make-or-buy decisions often ended up as "make," because coordination, information exchange, and paperwork problems made buying from suppliers too inconvenient. The Internet has largely eliminated these problems. Business-to-business applications allow companies to tap into suppliers' and customers' information systems and business processes, even if those suppliers and customers are located halfway around the world. Paperwork vanishes, and information required to satisfy the most stringent just-in-time delivery schedule is available in real time. As a result, companies are focusing on their core competencies, and outsourcing more and more other functions.

Like Nortel Networks, Cisco Systems, Dell, and Nike, world-class competitors have discovered that their core competency lies not in manufacturing, but in research

Nortel Networks Limited
www.nortelnetworks.com

Cisco Systems, Inc.
www.cisco.com

Dell Computer Corp.
www.dell.ca

Nike, Inc.
www.nike.com/Canada Limited

Accounting and the *e*-World

We Brand it, You Make it: The Outsourcing Trend

Your cell phone may sport the Motorola, Inc. logo, but there's a good chance it was actually make by a little-known company based in Singapore, Flextronics International Ltd. In May 2000, Motorola announced that it expects to outsource over $30 billion of consumer-electronics production. It was the largest outsourcing agreement to date between a name-brand electronics company and a contract manufacturer. In 1998, contract manufacturing was a $60 billion industry. By 2003 it will grow to nearly $150 billion.

According to a *Purchasing* magazine survey, 81 percent of electronics buyers cited cost as their reason for outsourcing everything from motherboards and set-top boxes to entire products. How do contract manufacturers like Flextronics and Solectron do the job more cheaply than original equipment manufacturers (OEMs)? "We leverage our overhead," says Solectron's CFO Susan Wang. In other words, orders from multiple clients keep contract manufacturers' factories busy around the clock and cover overhead costs.

OEMs are also rushing to outsource manufacturing so they can concentrate on the activities that add value. Product development, marketing, and customer support are all areas in which OEMs can gain a competitive edge. The manufacturing process is increasingly viewed as a commodity. "OEM is an oddity as an acronym," says Pamela Gordon of Technology Forecasters, a consulting firm. "What it really means is a company whose brand name goes on the product."

Because of the importance of distinguishing their brand name, OEMs must ensure that far-flung contract manufacturers in Brazil, Mexico, or Hungary deliver quality products. Most OEMs with multi-million-dollar or multi-billion-dollar manufacturer contracts maintain a team of their own people to oversee quality control. For Motorola, the Internet will play a major role in overseeing contract manufacturers around the globe. After announcing the Flextronics deal, both companies said they plan to use Internet technology to tie themselves more closely together and streamline Motorola's supply chain.

Based on: Scott Thurm, "Motorola Plans to Outsource Production To Flextronics in $30 Billion Agreement," *Wall Street Journal*, May 31, 2000, p. A3. Paul Gibson, "The Asset Paradox," *Electronic Business*, April 2000, pp. 120–126. James Carbone, "What Buyers Look For in Contract Manufacturers," *Purchasing*, March 23, 2000, pp. 32–38. John Teresko, "E-collaboration," *Industry Week*, June 12, 2000, p. 31–36.

and development, and in brand marketing. Such companies outsource much of their manufacturing to contract manufacturers like Flextronics and Yue Yuen Industrial Holdings, which operate huge manufacturing factories in countries where labour is less expensive, such as Mexico and Taiwan.

Cisco currently operates three factories that make its most sophisticated components, but outside suppliers directly fill 55 percent of Cisco's customers' order. Hewlett Packard is a leader in laser printers, but it outsources production of the laser mechanisms to Canon. Outsourcing doesn't stop at production. Eastman Kodak decided to outsource its cafeteria and security operations, and BP Amoco is considering outsourcing its accounting function.

Many outsourcing decisions are short-term in nature, but Cisco's decision to subcontract most of its manufacturing is a long-term one. When making decisions with long-term consequences, managers identify and analyze the relevant costs and benefits of different alternatives, as DefTone did in Exhibits 26-8 and 26-9. The only difference is that these cost and benefit calculations may extend many years into the future. In this case, managers discount these costs and benefits to their present values, as we explain in the second half of the chapter.

Sell As Is or Process Further?

Petro-Canada
www.petro-canada.ca

Should a product be sold as it is, or should the product be processed further into another item? For example, suppose that Petro-Canada spent $20,000 to produce 50,000 litres of regular gasoline. Assume Petro-Canada can sell this regular gasoline for $0.48 per litre, for a total of $24,000 (50,000 × $0.48) (Note: Gasoline taxes are not included in these prices.) Alternatively, Petro-Canada could further process this regular gasoline into premium-grade gas. Suppose the additional cost to process the gas further is $0.025 per litre, for an additional cost of $1,250 (for 50,000 litres). Assume the sale price of premium gasoline is $0.53 per litre, for a total of $26,500.

As in other special business decisions, managers need to know which items are relevant. The $20,000 cost of producing the 50,000 litres of regular gasoline is *not* relevant to Petro-Canada's sell or process further decision. Why? Because the $20,000 is a **sunk cost**—a past cost that cannot be changed regardless of which future action is taken. Exhibit 26-10 shows that the $20,000 has been incurred whether Petro-Canada sells the regular gasoline as is or processes it further into premium gasoline.

EXHIBIT 26-10

Diagram of Petro-Canada's Sell As Is or Process Further Decisions

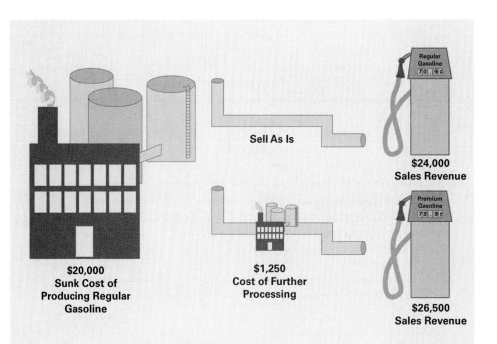

EXHIBIT 26-11

Sell As Is or Process Further
Decision

	Sell As Is	Process Further
Expected revenue from selling 50,000 litres of regular gasoline at $0.48 per litre...............................	$24,000	
Expected revenue from selling 50,000 litres of premium gasoline at $0.53 per litre...........................		$26,500
Additional costs of $0.025 per litre required to convert 50,000 litres of regular gasoline into premium gasoline....................		(1,250)
Total net revenue	$24,000	$25,250
Difference in net revenue		$1,250

Exhibits 26-10 and 26-11 show that the relevant items that differ between Petro-Canada's (1) sell as is and (2) process further alternatives are

- Expected revenues
- Expected costs of processing further

The analysis indicates that Petro-Canada should process the gasoline into the premium grade, because the $2,500 extra revenue ($26,500 − $24,000) outweighs the $1,250 cost of the extra processing.

Thus, the key guideline for sell as is or process further decisions is:

Process further only if the extra sales revenue (from processing further) exceeds the extra costs of additional processing.

STOP & THINK

Some companies have obsolete inventories that cannot be sold at regular prices. How should managers decide whether to sell the units as is or to incur additional manufacturing costs to rework them?

Answer: This is a sell or process further decision. Managers should predict the additional costs of reworking the inventory. Then they should forecast the additional revenues. If reworking will lead to additional revenues that exceed the additional costs, they should process further. If not, they should sell the units as is.

Opportunity Cost

OBJECTIVE 4
Use opportunity costs in decision making

We have illustrated five types of special business decisions. For each of these special decisions, managers decided on one course of action—and thereby rejected the opportunity to take other actions. When the managers rejected alternatives, their companies incurred an opportunity cost. An **opportunity cost** is the benefit that can be obtained from the next-best course of action in a decision. Opportunity cost is *not* an outlay cost that is recorded in accounting. An outlay cost requires a cash payment sooner or later, but an opportunity cost does not.

An example of an opportunity cost is the salary forgone by an engineer who may quit her job with Telesat Canada to start her own business. Suppose that this engineer analyzes her two job opportunities as follows:

	Open an Independent Business	Remain a Telesat Employee
Expected salary income from Telesat Canada		$ 60,000
Expected revenues	$200,000	
Expected expenses	120,000	
Expected net income	$ 80,000	$60,000

Telesat Canada
www.telesat.ca

The opportunity cost of staying with Telesat is the forgone $80,000 of net income from the independent business. The opportunity cost of starting a new business is the $60,000 salary from Telesat.

How do managers use opportunity costs in decision making? Consider two examples.

1. *Suppose the Telesat engineer has a third job opportunity—employment by Newbridge Networks (NN).* To determine the best alternative, the engineer can compare NN's offer with the $80,000 opportunity cost of not opening an independent business. If the engineer's goal is to maximize her personal income, she will accept NN's offer only if it exceeds her $80,000 opportunity cost. (The Telesat salary is irrelevant because opportunity cost is the benefit from the next-best course of action.)
2. *Refer to Exhibit 26-11.* Suppose Petro-Canada is approached by a customer who needs 50,000 litres of regular gasoline. The customer is willing to pay more than $0.48 per litre. Petro-Canada's managers can use the $25,250 ($26,500 − $1,250) opportunity cost of not further processing the gas to determine the sale price that will provide an equivalent income ($25,500/$50,000 = $0.51). If the customer offers more than Petro-Canada's opportunity cost of $0.51 per litre, Petro-Canada will be better off selling the regular gasoline. If the customer offers less than $0.51, Petro-Canada will be better off further processing the gas.

The special decisions we reviewed here pertain to relatively short periods of time, such as a year. In this time-frame:

- Many costs are fixed and do not vary with the volume of goods or services produced. This is why short-term special business decisions use the contribution margin approach that distinguishes variable from fixed costs.
- There is no need to worry about the time value of money. Managers do not bother computing present values of revenues and expenses for short-term decisions.

In the next half of the chapter, we turn to longer-term special decisions, like Intrawest's decision to add 4,500 units of new accommodation. For long-term decisions:

- Few, if any, costs are fixed.
- Managers often take into account the time value of money.

The approach to long-term decisions will reflect these differences.

But before moving on to long-term special decisions, stop for a moment to review the Decision Guidelines that summarize key points from our discussion. Then work through the mid-chapter summary problems.

Decision	Guidelines
What information is relevant to a short-term special business decision?	Relevant data: 1. are expected *future* data that 2. *differ* among alternatives.
What are two key guidelines in making short-term special business decisions?	Key guidelines: • Focus on *relevant* data • Use a *contribution margin* approach that separates variable costs from fixed costs.
When will accepting a special sales order increase income?	If the revenue from the order exceeds the extra variable and fixed costs incurred to fill the order, then operating income will increase.
When will dropping a product, department, or territory increase income?	If the cost savings exceed the lost revenues from dropping a product, department, or territory, then dropping will increase operating income.
To maximize profit, which product should be emphasized when there is a constraining factor?	Emphasize the product with the highest contribution margin per unit of the constraint.
How to decide whether to sell a product as is or process further?	Process further only if the extra sales revenue (from processing further) exceeds the extra costs of additional processing.
How to determine the opportunity cost of a decision?	The opportunity cost of a decision is the benefit forgone by not choosing the next-best course of action.

Mid-Chapter Summary Problems
for Your Review

Problem 1. Aziz Inc. produces two styles of sunglasses, a standard model and a deluxe model, with the following per-unit data:

	Per Pair	
	Standard	**Deluxe**
Sale price	$20	$30
Variable expenses	16	21

The company has 15,000 machine hours of capacity available. Seventy pairs of the standard model can be produced in an hour, compared with thirty pairs of the deluxe model. Which style should the company emphasize?

Problem 2. Just Do It! Ltd. has the following manufacturing costs for 40,000 pairs of its high-tech hiking socks:

Direct materials	$ 20,000
Direct labour	80,000
Variable overhead	40,000
Fixed overhead	80,000
Total manufacturing cost	$220,000
Cost per pair of socks ($220,000/40,000) .	$5.50

Another manufacturer has offered to sell Just Do It! similar socks for $5.00, a total purchase cost of $200,000. By purchasing the socks outside, Just Do It! can save $50,000 of fixed overhead cost. The released facilities can be devoted to the manufacture of other products that will contribute $60,000 to profits. Identify and analyze the alternatives. What is the best course of action?

Solutions to Review Problems

Problem 1.

	Style of Sunglasses	
	Standard	Deluxe
Sale price per pair	$20	$30
Variable expense per pair	(16)	(21)
Contribution margin per pair	$4	$9
Units that can be produced each machine hour	× 70	× 30
Contribution margin per machine hour	$280	$270
Capacity—number of hours	× 15,000	× 15,000
Total contribution margin at full capacity	$4,200,000	$4,050,000

Decision: The company should emphasize the standard model because it has the higher contribution margin per unit of the constraint—machine hours.

Problem 2.

		Buy Socks	
	Make Socks	Keep Facilities Idle	Make Other Products
Relevant costs:			
Direct materials	$ 20,000	—	
Direct labour	80,000	—	
Variable overhead	40,000	—	
Fixed overhead	80,000	$ 30,000	$ 30,000
Purchase cost from outsider			
(20,000 × $10)	—	200,000	200,000
Total cost of obtaining socks	220,000	230,000	230,000
Profit from other products			(60,000)
Net cost of obtaining 20,000 pairs of socks	$220,000	$230,000	$170,000

Decision: Just Do It! should buy the socks from the outside supplier and use the released facilities to make other products.

Capital Budgeting: Payback and Accounting Rate of Return

We have seen how managers make special business decisions of a short-term nature. Now let's turn to decisions that have long-term effects on business operations.

Think back to Intrawest Corp. in the chapter-opening story. Management's decision to expand the number of accommodation units by 4,500 will tie up resources for years to come. How did Intrawest decide that the expansion would be a good investment? The accommodation expansion met two conditions:

- First, the investment was part of the company's long-term plan. The expansion was a planned part of Intrawest's long-term strategy.
- Second, Intrawest's managers used capital budgeting techniques to analyze the expected financial effects of the investment.

Capital budgeting is a formal means of analyzing long-term investment decisions. The term describes budgeting for the acquisition of *capital assets*—assets used for a long period of time. Examples of capital budgeting decisions include expanding ski resorts, building new accommodations, or acquiring new ski lifts.

Before proceeding, you need to understand this: Capital budgeting is not an exact science. No matter how precise your calculations, they are based on predictions about an uncertain future. To become a successful decision maker, you must recognize and cope with uncertainty.

Because capital budgeting decisions have effects far into the future, your predictions must consider many unknown factors, such as changing consumer preferences, competition, and government regulations. The farther into the future the decision extends, the more likely that actual results will differ from predictions. Long-term decisions are thus riskier than short-term decisions.

We now discuss four popular capital budgeting decision models: payback, accounting rate of return, net present value, and internal rate of return. Three of these models compare the *net cash inflows from operations* each alternative generates. Generally accepted accounting principles are based on accrual accounting, but capital budgeting focuses on cash flows. The desirability of a capital asset depends on its ability to generate net cash inflows—that is, inflows in excess of outflows—over the asset's useful life.

Payback Period

Payback is the length of time it will take to recover, in net cash inflows from operations, the dollars of a capital outlay. The payback model measures how quickly managers expect to recover their investment dollars. The shorter the payback period, the more attractive the asset, all else being equal. Computing the payback period depends on whether cash flows are equal each year, or whether they differ over time. We consider each in turn.

Payback with Equal Cash Flows   Tierra Firma Inc., a manufacturer of high-quality camping gear, is considering investing $240,000 in information technology (hardware and software) to develop a portal, or interface, with a business-to-business (B2B) electronic market. The portal will enable employees throughout the company to enter the electronic market of certified suppliers to purchase goods and services appropriate to their jobs. Accountants will be able to buy office supplies, and maintenance workers will be able to buy parts. The portal will incorporate controls on the kinds of goods and services each employee can buy, as well as preset spending limits. Tierra Firma expects the portal to save $60,000 a year for the six years of its useful life. The savings will arise from reducing the number of purchasing personnel the company employs, and from lower prices on the goods and services purchased.

When net cash inflows are equal each year, managers compute the payback period as follows:

$$\frac{\text{Payback}}{\text{Period}} = \frac{\text{Amount invested}}{\text{Expected annual net cash inflow}}$$

In general, net cash inflows can arise from an increase in revenues, a decrease in expenses, or both. In Tierra Firma's case, the net cash inflows result from lower expenses. Tierra Firma computes the investment's payback as follows:

$$\frac{\text{Payback period for}}{\text{B2B portal}} = \frac{\$240,000}{\$60,000} = \text{4 years}$$

> **OBJECTIVE 5**
> Use four capital-budgeting models to make longer-term investment decisions

>  **WORKING IT OUT**
>
> A company is considering a new production method that will save $130,000 a year in manufacturing costs. New equipment will cost $800,000 and will be amortized on a straight-line basis over a 10-year life with a $40,000 salvage value. Compute the payback period.
>
> **A:**
> $$\frac{\$800,000}{\$130,000} = 6.2 \text{ years}$$

Exhibit 26-12 verifies that Tierra Firma expects to recoup the $240,000 investment in the B2B portal by the end of year 4, when the accumulated cash inflows (savings) total $240,000.

Tierra Firma is also considering investing $240,000 to develop a Web site to sell its camping gear. The company expects the Web site to generate $80,000 in cash inflows each year of its three-year life. The investment payback period is computed as follows:

$$\text{Payback period for Web site development} = \frac{\$240,000}{\$80,000} = 3 \text{ years}$$

Exhibit 26-12 verifies that for Web site development, the $240,000 investment is recouped by the end of year 3 when the accumulated net cash inflows total $240,000. Thus, the payback criterion favours Web site development because it recovers the investment more quickly.

A major criticism of the payback model is that it does not consider profitability. The payback technique can lead managers to make unwise decisions.

For example, consider the projects' useful lives. The Web site's useful life is the same as its payback period—three years. Exhibit 26-12 shows that the Web site will merely cover its cost and provide no profits. But the B2B portal has a useful life of six years. It will continue to generate net cash inflows for two years beyond its payback period. This will give the company an additional net cash inflow of $120,000 ($60,000 × 2 years). Unlike the Web site, the B2B portal will be profitable. After considering the assets' useful lives, the B2B portal appears to be the better investment.

Payback with Unequal Annual Cash Flows   The payback equation only works when net cash inflows are the same for each period. When periodic cash flows are unequal, you must accumulate net cash inflows until the amount invested is recovered. Suppose Tierra Firma's B2B portal will generate net cash inflows of $100,000 in Year 1, $80,000 in Year 2, and $50,000 in Years 3 through 5, and $30,000 in Year 6. Exhibit 26-13 shows the payback schedule for these unequal annual cash flows.

By the end of Year 3, we have recovered $230,000. Recovery of the amount invested ($240,000) occurs during Year 4. Payback occurs in 3.2 years:

$$\text{Payback} = 3 \text{ years} + \frac{\$10,000 \text{ needed to complete recovery in Year 4}}{\$50,000 \text{ net cash inflow in Year 4}} \times 1 \text{ year}$$

$$= 3 \text{ years} + 0.2 \text{ years} = 3.2 \text{ years}$$

Managers often compare the payback period with the asset's useful life. The asset's payback period must be shorter than its useful life. If an asset like information

EXHIBIT 26-12

Payback—Equal Annual Net Cash Inflows

| | | Net Cash Inflows | | | |
| | | B2B Portal | | Web site Development | |
Year	Amount Invested	Annual	Accumulated	Annual	Accumulated
0	$240,000	—	—	—	
1	—	$60,000	$ 60,000	$80,000	$ 80,000
2	—	60,000	120,000	80,000	160,000
3	—	60,000	180,000	80,000	240,000
4	—	60,000	240,000		
5	—	60,000	300,000		
6	—	60,000	360,000		

EXHIBIT 26-13

Payback—Unequal Annual
Net Cash Inflows

| | Amount | Net Cash Inflow | |
Year	Invested	Each Year	Accumulated
0	$240,000	—	—
1	—	$100,000	$100,000
2	—	80,000	180,000
3	—	50,000	230,000
3.2	—	10,000	**240,000**
4	—	40,000	280,000
5	—	50,000	330,000
6	—	30,000	360,000

technology has a payback period of five years and a useful life of three years, the company will never earn a profit from the technology asset. How much shorter than the useful life the payback period must be is a business decision that varies by industry and business conditions. When the business is deciding between two or more assets, the asset with the shortest payback period is the most profitable *only if all other factors are the same*. This leads to the following decision rule:

> **Make investments only if payback is *shorter* than the asset's useful life. Investments with shorter payback periods are more desirable, *all else being equal*.**

The payback method highlights cash flows, a key factor in business decisions. And, payback is easily understood. Advocates view it as a way to eliminate proposals that are unusually risky (projects with lengthy payback periods). However, a major weakness of payback is that it ignores profitability.

Accounting Rate of Return

Companies are in business to earn profits. One measure of profitability is the rate of return on investment. The **accounting rate of return** on an asset is computed by dividing the operating income that an asset generates by the amount of the investment in the asset:

$$\text{Accounting rate of return} = \frac{\text{Average annual operating income from asset}}{\text{Average amount invested in asset}}$$

The accounting rate of return focuses on the operating income an asset generates. Operating income from an asset can be computed as net cash inflow from the asset minus amortization on the asset. Exhibit 26-14 computes accounting rate of return for Tierra Firma's B2B portal in the original payback example. Recall that Tierra Firma expects the portal to generate annual net cash inflows of $60,000. The portal's development costs $240,000 and it has a useful life of six years with no residual value. Annual straight-line amortization is $40,000 ($240,000/6 years). Exhibit 26-14 shows that Tierra Firma expects the portal to generate average annual operating income of $20,000 ($60,000 − $40,000).

The accounting rate of return is an *average*. It measures the average rate of return from using the asset over its entire life. First, consider the average annual operating income. If operating income varies by year (as in the second payback example), compute the *total* operating income over the asset's life. Then divide the total by the number of years of life to find the *average* annual operating income from the asset.

Second, consider the average amount invested. The book value of the asset

WORKING IT OUT

Using the data from the previous Working It Out, compute the accounting rate of return.

A:

$$\frac{\$130,000 - \$76,000}{(\$800,000 - \$40,000)/2}$$

$$= 14.2\%$$

EXHIBIT 26-14

Accounting Rate of Return

$$\text{Accounting rate of return} = \frac{\text{Average annual operating income from asset*}}{\text{Average amount invested in asset}} = \frac{\text{Average annual net cash inflow from asset} - \text{Annual amortization on asset}}{[\text{Amount invested in asset} + \text{Residual value}]/2}$$

$$= \frac{\$60,000 - \$40,000^{\dagger}}{(\$240,000 + \$0)/2} = \frac{\$20,000}{\$120,000} = 0.167 = 16.7\%$$

*Operating income also can be computed as revenues minus operating expenses.
†$40,000 = $240,000/6 years

decreases as it is used and amortized. Thus, the company's investment in the asset declines over time. If the asset's residual value is zero, the average investment is half the asset's cost. Exhibit 26-14 shows that the average amount invested in Tierra Firma's B2B portal from the original payback example is $120,000 ($240,000/2).

If the asset's residual value is not zero, the average amount invested is greater than half the asset's cost. For example, assume that residual value of the portal's technology is $30,000. The annual amortization declines to $35,000 [($240,000 – $30,000)/6]. The accounting rate of return is:

$$\text{Accounting rate of return} = \frac{\$60,000 - \$35,000}{(\$240,000 + \$30,000)/2} = \frac{\$25,000}{\$135,000} = 0.185 = 18.5\%$$

Companies that use the accounting rate of return model set a minimum acceptable rate of return on investment projects. They invest only in assets with accounting rates of return equal to or greater than the minimum required rate. Suppose that Tierra Firma requires a rate of return of at least 20 percent. Would its managers approve an investment in the B2B portal technology in Exhibit 26-14? No, because the average annual return (16.7%) is less than the company's minimum acceptable rate (20%). Thus the decision rule is:

> **Invest in assets whose expected accounting rate of return exceeds the company's required accounting rate of return.**

Capital Budgeting: Discounted Cash-Flow Models

Chapter 15 introduced the concept of present value. A dollar received today is worth more than a dollar to be received in the future. Why? Because you can invest today's dollar and earn income on that dollar. Suppose you can choose between receiving a dollar today and a dollar one year from today. If you receive $1.00 today and deposit it in a bank that pays 6 percent interest, a year from today you will have $1.06 (the original $1.00 plus $0.06 interest). Presumably, you would rather receive the $1.00 now, which will grow to $1.06 a year from today, rather than simply receive $1.00 a year from today. The fact that money can be invested to earn income over time is called the **time value of money**, and this explains why businesses as well as individuals would rather receive cash sooner than later.

The time value of money means that the timing of capital investments' net cash flows is important. Consider two $10,000 investments that both promise future cash receipts of $11,000. Investment 1 will bring in cash of $5,500 at the end of each of the next two years. Investment 2 will return the full $11,000 at the end of the second year. Which investment is better? Investment 1, because it brings in cash sooner. Its $5,500 net cash inflow at the end of the first year can be reinvested right away to earn additional returns.

Neither the payback period nor the accounting rate of return recognize the time value of money. That is, these models fail to consider the *timing* of the net cash flows an asset generates. *Discounted cash-flow models*—the net present value and the internal rate of return—overcome this weakness. Many large industrial firms in Canada use discounted cash flow methods to make capital budgeting decisions. These models are also used by companies that provide services, like Intrawest.

Net Present Value

JVC is considering the manufacture of two products, CD players and VCRs. The products require different specialized equipment that each cost $1,000,000. Each machine has a five-year life and zero residual value. The two products have different patterns of predicted net cash inflows:

JVC Canada
www.jvc.ca

	Annual Net Cash Inflows	
Year	CD Players	VCRs
1	$ 305,450	$ 500,000
2	305,450	350,000
3	305,450	300,000
4	305,450	250,000
5	305,450	40,000
Total	$1,527,250	$1,440,000

KEY POINT
The alternative that produces the highest net present value of all cash flows is the most desirable.

Total net cash inflows are greater if JVC invests in the CD player project. However, the VCR project brings in cash sooner. To decide which investment is better, we use **net present value (NPV)** to bring cash inflows and outflows back to a common time period. We *discount* these expected future cash flows to their present value, using JVC's minimum desired rate of return. We then compare the discounted cash inflows with the discounted cash outflows to decide which, if any, projects to undertake.

Management's minimum desired rate of return on an investment is called the **discount rate**. Synonyms are **hurdle rate, required rate,** and **cost of capital**. The discount rate depends on the riskiness of investments. The higher the risk, the higher the discount rate. JVC's discount rate for these investments is 14 percent.

Net Present Value with Equal Periodic Cash Flows (Annuity) JVC expects the CD players to generate $305,450 of new cash inflow each year. This kind of stream of equal periodic cash flows is an **annuity**. The present value of an annuity is computed by multiplying the periodic cash flow ($305,450 in this case) by the present value of an annuity of $1, obtained from the present value of an annuity table in Exhibit 26-15. The table indicates that the present value of an annuity of $1 received each year for five years, discounted at 14% per year, is $3.433. That is, the value today of receiving $1 at the end of each year for the next five years, discounted at 14%, is $3.433. Another way to think about this is that if JVC invested $3.433 today at a 14% annual interest rate, there would be just enough money to pay out $1 at the end of each year for the next five years.

Panel A of Exhibit 26-16 uses this present value of an annuity factor (3.433) to compute the present value of the CD-player project's net cash flows. JVC's managers multiply the $305,450 to be received each year by the present value factor for a five-year annuity of $1 discounted at 14% (3.433), to obtain the present value of the net cash inflows, $1,048,610. After subtracting the $1,000,000 investment, the net present value of the CD-player project is $48,610.

WORKING IT OUT

Using the data from the Working It Out on page 1445, compute the net present value with a 12% minimum desired rate of return.

A:
PV of manufacturing
  cost savings
  ($130,000 × 5.650)..... $ 734,500
PV of residual value
  ($40,000 × 0.322)....... 12,880
Initial investment .... (800,000)
NPV............................... $ (52,620)

The proposal should be rejected.

EXHIBIT 26-15

Present Value of Annuity of $1

				Present Value of Annuity of $1					
Period	4%	5%	6%	7%	8%	10%	12%	14%	16%
1	0.962	0.952	0.943	0.935	0.926	0.909	0.893	0.877	0.862
2	1.886	1.859	1.833	1.808	1.783	1.736	1.690	1.647	1.605
3	2.775	2.723	2.673	2.624	2.577	2.487	2.402	2.322	2.246
4	3.630	3.546	3.465	3.387	3.312	3.170	3.037	2.914	2.798
5	4.452	4.329	4.212	4.100	3.993	3.791	3.605	3.433	3.274
6	5.242	5.076	4.917	4.767	4.623	4.355	4.111	3.889	3.685
7	6.002	5.786	5.582	5.389	5.206	4.868	4.564	4.288	4.039
8	6.733	6.463	6.210	5.971	5.747	5.335	4.968	4.639	4.344
9	7.435	7.108	6.802	6.515	6.247	5.759	5.328	4.946	4.607
10	8.111	7.722	7.360	7.024	6.710	6.145	5.650	5.216	4.833
11	8.760	8.306	7.887	7.499	7.139	6.495	5.938	5.453	5.029
12	9.385	8.863	8.384	7.943	7.536	6.814	6.194	5.660	5.197
13	9.986	9.394	8.853	8.358	7.904	7.103	6.424	5.842	5.342
14	10.563	9.899	9.295	8.745	8.244	7.367	6.628	6.002	5.468
15	11.118	10.380	9.712	9.108	8.559	7.606	6.811	6.142	5.575
16	11.652	10.838	10.106	9.447	8.851	7.824	6.974	6.265	5.669
17	12.166	11.274	10.477	9.763	9.122	8.022	7.120	6.373	5.749
18	12.659	11.690	10.828	10.059	9.372	8.201	7.250	6.467	5.818
19	13.134	12.085	11.158	10.336	9.604	8.365	7.366	6.550	5.877
20	13.590	12.462	11.470	10.594	9.818	8.514	7.469	6.623	5.929

Appendix A provides a fuller table for the present value of an annuity of $1.

A positive net present value means that the project earns more than the target rate of return. A negative net present value means that the project fails to earn the target rate of return. This leads to the following decision rule:

Invest in projects with a positive net present value.

In JVC's case, the CD-player project is an attractive investment. The $48,610 positive net present value means that the CD-player project earns more than JVC's 14% target rate of return.

Another way managers can use present value analysis is to *start* the capital budgeting process by computing the total present value of the net cash inflows from the project, to determine the maximum the company can invest in the project and still earn the target rate of return. For JVC, the present value of the net cash inflows is $1,048,610. This means that JVC can invest a maximum of $1,048,610 in the CD-player project and still earn the 14% target rate of return. Since JVC's managers believe they can undertake the project for $1,000,000, the project is an attractive investment.

Net Present Value with Unequal Periodic Cash Flows In contrast to the CD-player project, the net cash inflows of the VCR project are unequal—$500,000 in Year 1, $350,000 in Year 2, and so on. Because these amounts vary by year, JVC's managers must compute the present value of each amount separately:

Year	Present Value of $1 from Exhibit 26-17, 14% Column	Net Cash Inflow	Present Value of Net Cash Inflow
1	0.877	× $500,000 =	$438,500
2	0.769	× 350,000 =	269,150

	Present Value at 14%	Net Cash Inflow	Total Present Value
Panel A: Net Present Value with Equal Cash Flows			
CD player Project:			
Present value of equal annual net cash inflows for 5 years at 14%	3.433*	× $305,450 per year =	$ 1,048,610
Investment			(1,000,000)
Net present value of the CD player project			$ 48,610
Panel B: Net Present Value with Unequal Cash Flows			
VCR Project:			
Present value of each year's net cash inflows discounted at 14%:	**Year**		
	1	0.877† × $500,000 =	$ 438,500
	2	0.769 × 350,000 =	269,150
	3	0.675 × 300,000 =	202,500
	4	0.592 × 250,000 =	148,000
	5	0.519 × 40,000 =	20,760
Total present value of net cash inflows			1,078,910
Investment			(1,000,000)
Net present value of the VCR project			$ 78,910

*Present value of annuity of $1 for 5 years at 14%, Exhibit 26-15.
†Present value of $1 for 1 year, 2 years, 3 years, and so on, at 14%, Exhibit 26-17.

EXHIBIT 26-16

Net Present Value

Panel B Exhibit 26-16 includes these present-value computations, along with similar computations for years 3 to 5. The exhibit indicates that the total present value of the VCR project's net cash inflows is $1,078,910. After subtracting the $1,000,000 investment, Panel B shows that the VCR project has a total net present value of $78,910. This positive net present value means that JVC expects the VCR project to earn more than the 14% target rate of return. Thus, the VCR project is an attractive investment.

STOP & THINK

Use the present value of $1 table in Exhibit 26-17 to find the present value of an *annuity* of $1 for five years, discounted at 14%. Compare the result to the present value of an annuity of $1 factor from the table in Exhibit 26-15.

Answer: Exhibit 26-17 shows that at a 14% discount rate, the present value of $1 received:

In one year is	$0.877
In two years is	0.769
In three years is	0.675
In four years is	0.592
In five years is	0.519
Total present value of $1 received at the end of each year for five years, discounted at 14% is	$3.432

Except for a slight rounding error, this sum ($3.432) equals the present value of an annuity of $1 for five years discounted at 14%, shown in Exhibit 26-15 ($3.433). This shows how entries in the present value of an annuity table (Exhibit 26-15) are the sums of the present value of $1 factors from the present value of $1 table (Exhibit 26-17).

EXHIBIT 26-17

Present Value of $1

Present Value of $1

Period	4%	5%	6%	7%	8%	10%	12%	14%	16%
1	0.962	0.952	0.943	0.935	0.926	0.909	0.893	0.877	0.862
2	0.925	0.907	0.890	0.873	0.857	0.826	0.797	0.769	0.743
3	0.889	0.864	0.840	0.816	0.794	0.751	0.712	0.675	0.641
4	0.855	0.823	0.792	0.763	0.735	0.683	0.636	0.592	0.552
5	0.822	0.784	0.747	0.713	0.681	0.621	0.567	0.519	0.476
6	0.790	0.746	0.705	0.666	0.630	0.564	0.507	0.456	0.410
7	0.760	0.711	0.665	0.623	0.583	0.513	0.452	0.400	0.354
8	0.731	0.677	0.627	0.582	0.540	0.467	0.404	0.351	0.305
9	0.703	0.645	0.592	0.544	0.500	0.424	0.361	0.308	0.263
10	0.676	0.614	0.558	0.508	0.463	0.386	0.322	0.270	0.227
11	0.650	0.585	0.527	0.475	0.429	0.350	0.287	0.237	0.195
12	0.625	0.557	0.497	0.444	0.397	0.319	0.257	0.208	0.168
13	0.601	0.530	0.469	0.415	0.368	0.290	0.229	0.182	0.145
14	0.577	0.505	0.442	0.388	0.340	0.263	0.205	0.160	0.125
15	0.555	0.481	0.417	0.362	0.315	0.239	0.183	0.140	0.108
16	0.534	0.458	0.394	0.339	0.292	0.218	0.163	0.123	0.093
17	0.513	0.436	0.371	0.317	0.270	0.198	0.146	0.108	0.080
18	0.494	0.416	0.350	0.296	0.250	0.180	0.130	0.095	0.069
19	0.475	0.396	0.331	0.277	0.232	0.164	0.116	0.083	0.060
20	0.456	0.377	0.312	0.258	0.215	0.149	0.104	0.073	0.051

Appendix A provides a fuller table for the present value of $1.

Exhibit 26-16 shows that both the CD-player and the VCR projects have positive net present values. Therefore, both are attractive investments. If JVC wants to pursue only one of the two projects, the net present value analysis in Exhibit 26-16 favours the VCR project. The VCR project should earn an additional $78,910 beyond the 14% required rate of return, while the CD-player project returns only an additional $48,610 beyond the required rate of return.

This example illustrates an important point about present-value analysis. The CD-player project promises the greater *total* amount of net cash inflows, but the *timing* of the VCR cash flows—higher near the beginning of the project—gives the VCR investment a higher net present value. The VCR project is more attractive because of the time value of money. Its dollars, which are closer to the present, are worth more now than the more-distant dollars of the CD-player project.

Net Present Value of a Project with Residual Value Many assets yield cash inflows at the end of their useful lives. The present value analysis must consider this residual value, discounting it to its present value to determine the total present value of the project's net cash inflows. The residual value is discounted as a single amount—not as an annuity—because it will be received only once, when the asset is sold.

Suppose JVC expects the equipment to manufacture CD players to be worth $100,000 at the end of its five-year life. To determine the CD-player project's net present value, we discount $100,000 for five years at 14 percent—using the present value of $1 factor from Exhibit 26-17—and add its present value ($51,900), as shown in Exhibit 26-18.

Compare Exhibits 26-16 and 26-18. The discounted residual value in Exhibit 26-18 raises the CD-player project's net present value to $100,510, which is higher than the VCR project. If JVC expects VCR equipment to have zero disposal value, then the CD-player project is more attractive.

CD-Player Project	Present Value at 14%		Net Cash Inflow		Total Present Value
Present value of annuity of equal annual net cash inflows for 5 years at 14%..........................	3.433*	×	$305,450 per year	=	$ 1,048,610
Present value of residual value..........................	0.519**	×	$100,000	=	51,900
Total present value of net cash inflows					1,100,510
Investment..					(1,000,000)
Net present value of the CD-player project.......					$ 100,510

*Present value of an annuity of $1 for 5 years at 14%, Exhibit 25-15.
**Present value of $1 for 5 years at 14%, Exhibit 26-17.

EXHIBIT 26-18

Net Present Value of a Project with Residual Value

Sensitivity Analysis   There is great uncertainty surrounding capital budgeting decisions that affect cash flows far into the future. JVC's managers might want to know whether their decision would be affected by:

- Changing the discount rate from 14% to 12% or to 16%
- Changing the net cash flows by 10%
- Changing the residual value of the equipment

Managers use spreadsheets to perform these kinds of sensitivity analyses quickly and easily. After entering the basic information for net present value analysis, managers perform sensitivity analyses with just a few keystrokes. The computer quickly displays the results.

STOP & THINK

Suppose JVC uses a 6% discount rate rather than the 14% discount rate from Exhibit 26-16. Would the net present value of the CD-player project (assuming zero residual value) be higher or lower using the 6% rate than the original 14% rate? Why?

Answer: The higher the discount rate, the lower the present value (today) of dollars to be received in the future. Similarly, the lower the discount rate, the higher the present value of dollars to be received in the future. Because lower discount rates lead to higher present values, discounting the cash flows at 6% rather than 14% *increases* the net present value of the CD-player project, as follows:

CD-Player Project	Present Value at 6%	Net Cash Inflow		Total Present Value
Present value of annuity of equal annual net cash inflows for 5 years.........	4.212* ×	$305,450	=	$1,286,555
Investment..				(1,000,000)
Net present value at 6%..............................				286,555
Net present value at 14% (from Exhibit 26-16)..................................				(48,610)
Difference..				$ 237,945

*Present value of an annuity of $1 for 5 years at 6%, Exhibit 26-15.

Internal Rate of Return

Another discounted-cash-flow model for capital budgeting is the internal rate of return (IRR). The **internal rate of return (IRR)** is the rate of return (based on discounted cash flows) a company can expect to earn by investing in the project. The higher the IRR, the more desirable the project. The lower the IRR, the less desirable. The internal rate of return is the discount rate that makes the present value of the project's cash flows equal to zero.

Exhibit 26-19 shows that JVC's CD-player project's IRR is 16 percent. The 16-percent rate produces a net present value of zero. To see why, we follow three steps:

1. Identify the expected net cash inflows ($305,450 for five years) exactly as in calculating the net present value.

2. Find the discount rate that makes the total present value of the cash inflows equal to the present value of the cash outflows. This is easy when the investment in the project consists of a single immediate cash outflow followed by a series of equal cash inflows (an annuity). You can work backwards to find the discount rate that makes the present value of the annuity of cash inflows equal to the amount of the investment by solving the following equation for the annuity present value (PV) factor:

WORKING IT OUT

The Lethbridge School District is considering the purchase of a lawn tractor. The tractor will cost $10,000 and have a 10-year life. It will save approximately $1,627 a year in operating labour costs. Compute the internal rate of return.

A:

$$\frac{\$10,000}{\$1,627} = 6.146$$

Look in the present value of annuity table at the 10-year row; 6.145 (which is very close to the calculated 6.146) is in the 10% column. Therefore, the IRR is 10%.

Investment = Expected annual net cash inflows × Annuity PV factor		
$1,000,000 =	$305,450	× Annuity PV factor
Annuity PV factor =	$\dfrac{\$1,000,000}{\$305,450}$	= 3.274

3. Turn to the table presenting the present value of an annuity of $1 (Exhibit 26-15). Scan the row corresponding to the project's expected life—period 5, in our example. Choose the column with the number closest to the annuity PV factor that was calculated. The 3.274 annuity factor is in the 16% column. Therefore, the IRR of the CD player project is 16 percent. JVC expects the project to earn an annual rate of return of 16% over its life.

To decide whether the project is acceptable, compare the IRR with the minimum desired rate of return. If the IRR is equal to or greater than the minimum rate, the project is acceptable. Otherwise, it is not. That is, the decision rule is:

> **Invest in projects whose internal rate of return
> exceeds the required rate of return.**

If CD players were the only investment under consideration, JVC would invest in CD players because their 16% IRR exceeds the 14% discount rate. But recall that

EXHIBIT 26-19

**Internal Rate of Return,
CD-Player Project**

	Present Value at 16%		Net Cash Inflow		Total Present Value
Present value of annuity of equal annual net cash inflows for 5 years at 16%..............................	3.274*	×	$305,450	=	$ 1,000,000 †
Investment..					(1,000,000)
Net present value of the CD-player project.......					$ 0††

*Present value of annuity of $1 for 5 years at 16%, Exhibit 26-15.
†Slight rounding error.
††The zero difference proves that the IRR is 16%.

the VCR project has a higher net present value than the CD-player project. The VCR investment also has a higher IRR. Because the VCR project has unequal cash inflows, however, computation of the VCR's IRR requires a trial-and-error procedure that is covered in more advanced courses. (Spreadsheet software and even calculators can perform these necessary computations.)

Comparing Capital Budgeting Models

OBJECTIVE 6
Compare and contrast popular capital-budgeting models

Payback period, net present value, and internal rate of return are all based on cash inflows and outflows. Only the accounting rate of return is based on accrual accounting revenues and expenses. Payback is the simplest to compute, but it ignores profitability and the time value of money. The accounting rate of return considers profitability, but it also ignores the time value of money. Only net present value and internal rate of return consider the time value of money.

How do the net-present-value and IRR approaches compare? Net present value indicates the amount of the excess (or deficiency) of a project's present value of net cash inflows over (or under) its cost—at a specified discount rate. But net present value does not show the project's unique rate of return. The internal rate of return shows the project's rate but fails to indicate the dollar difference between the project's present value and its investment cost. In many cases the two methods lead to the same investment decision.

The discounted cash-flow models are superior because they consider both the time value of money and profitability. The time value of money enters the analysis through the discounting of future dollars to present value. Profitability is built into the discounted cash-flow methods because they consider all cash inflows and outflows—the determinants of profit—over the life of a project. The payback model considers only the cash flows necessary to recover the initial cash invested.

Exhibit 26-20 summarizes the strengths and weaknesses of the payback, accounting rate of return, and discounted cash-flow methods. Managers often use more than one model simultaneously to gain different perspectives on risks and returns. For example, Intrawest's managers could decide to pursue capital projects with positive net present values, provided that those projects have a payback of four years or less.

Intrawest's use of both payback and discounted cash-flow methods is typical of Canadian and U.S. companies. The payback method is most popular in Japan. Discounted cash-flow methods are more popular in Ireland and South Korea.

LEARNING TIP

Remember that payback, net present value, and internal rate of return are all based on *cash inflows and outflows*. Only the accounting rate of return is based on accrual accounting *revenues and expenses*. Also, only net present value and internal rate of return take into account the time value of money.

EXHIBIT 26-20

Capital-Budgeting Decision Models

Model	Strengths	Weaknesses
Payback	Easy to understand Based on cash flows Highlights risks	Ignores profitability and the time value of money
Accounting rate of return	Based on profitability	Ignores the time value of money
Discounted cash-flow models: Net present value Internal rate of return	Based on cash flows, profitability, and the time value of money	Difficult to determine discount rate

Suppose that BioChem Pharma Inc., a pharmaceutical company, is considering two drug-research projects. Project A has a net present value of $232,000 and a 3-year payback period. Project B has a net present value of $237,000 and a payback period of 4.5 years. Which project do you think the managers will accept?

Answer: Many managers would accept Project A. Net present value is a better guide to decision making than is the payback period. But managers would consider the 2.2-percent [($237,000 − $232,000)/$232,000] difference between the NPVs to be insignificant. In contrast, the 50-percent [(4.5 years − 3.0 years)/3.0 years] difference between payback periods is significant. The uncertainty of receiving operating cash flows increases with each passing year. Managers often forgo small differences in expected cash inflows to decrease the risk of investments.

Take a moment to review the different capital budgeting methods by studying the Decision Guidelines. This will help solidify your understanding of capital budgeting before you work on the summary review problem.

DECISION GUIDELINES   *Major Business Decisions*

Decision	Guidelines

How to decide whether a long-term investment is worthwhile?	Capital budgeting analysis suggests that investments may be worthwhile if:
	• Payback period is shorter than asset's useful life
	• Accounting rate of return on asset exceeds required rate of return
	• Discounted cash flow methods:
	  Net present value (NPV) is positive
	  Internal rate of return (IRR) exceeds required rate of return

How to compute the payback period with • Equal annual cash flows?	$\text{Payback period} = \dfrac{\text{Amount invested}}{\text{Expected annual net cash inflow}}$
• Unequal annual cash flows?	Accumulate cash flows until amount of investment is recovered.
How to compute the accounting rate of return?	$\text{Accounting rate of return} = \dfrac{\text{Average annual operating income from asset}}{\text{Average amount invested in asset}}$ $= \dfrac{\text{Average annual net cash inflow from asset} - \text{Annual amortization on asset}}{(\text{Amount invested in asset} + \text{Residual value})/2}$
How to compute net present value with • Equal annual cash flows?	$\begin{array}{c}\text{Present value of}\\ \text{annuity of \$1} \\ \text{(Exhibit 26-15)}\end{array} \times \begin{array}{c}\text{Annual net cash}\\ \text{inflow or outflow}\end{array}$
• Unequal annual cash flows?	Compute the present value of each year's net cash inflow or outflow (present value of $1 from Exhibit 26-17 × net cash inflow or outflow) and add up yearly present value
How to compute internal rate of return with • Equal annual cash flows?	$\begin{array}{c}\text{Annuity PV factor}\\ \text{(Use Exhibit 26-15)}\end{array} = \dfrac{\text{Investment}}{\text{Expected annual net cash inflow}}$
• Unequal annual cash flows?	Trial and error, spreadsheet software, or calculator.
Which capital budgeting models are best?	Discounted cash-flow models (net present value and IRR) are best because they incorporate both profitability and the time value of money.

Summary Problem
for Your Review

ZetaMax Ltd. is considering buying a new bar coding machine for its Calgary factory. The data for the machine follow:

Cost of machine...	$48,000
Estimated residual value	6,000
Estimated annual net cash inflow	13,000
Estimated useful life	5 years
Required rate of return...................................	16%

Required

1. Compute the bar coding machine's payback period.
2. Compute the bar coding machine's accounting rate of return.
3. Compute the bar coding machine's net present value (NPV).
4. Would you decide to buy the bar coding machine? Give your reason.

Solution to Review Problem

Requirement 1

$$\text{Payback period} = \frac{\text{Amount invested}}{\text{Expected annual net cash inflow}} = \frac{\$48,000}{\$13,000} = 3.7 \text{ years}$$

Requirement 2

$$\text{Accounting rate of return} = \frac{\text{Average annual operating income from asset}}{\text{Average amount invested}}$$

$$= \frac{\text{Average annual net cash inflow from asset} - \text{Annual amortization on asset}}{(\text{Amount invested in asset} + \text{Residual value})/2}$$

$$= \frac{\$13,000 - \$8,400*}{(\$48,000 + \$6,000)/2}$$

$$= \frac{\$4,600}{\$27,000}$$

$$= 0.170$$

$$= 17\%$$

$$*A = \frac{\$48,000 - \$6,000}{5 \text{ years}} = \$8,400$$

Requirement 3

Present value of annuity of equal annual net cash inflows at 16% ($13,000 × 3.274**)...	$ 42,562
Present value of residual value ($6,000 × 0.476†)	2,856
Total present value of net cash inflows	45,418
Investment	(48,000)
Net present value	$ (2,582)

**Present value of annuity of $1 for 5 years at 16%, Exhibit 26-15.
†Present value of $1 for 5 years at 16%, Exhibit 26-17.

Summary

1. **Identify the relevant information for a special business decision.** *Relevant information* is expected future data that differ among alternative courses of action. Historical data are irrelevant per se, but often they help managers make predictions about the future.

2. **Make five types of short-term special business decisions.** Two keys to making short-term special business decisions are (1) focusing on relevant items (relevant revenues and relevant costs), and (2) using a contribution margin approach that separates variable costs from fixed costs. Managers use these techniques when deciding whether to accept or reject a special sales order; whether to drop a product, department, or territory; which product to emphasize when a constraint is present; outsourcing; and whether to sell a product as is or to process it further. Managers often select the course of action that is expected to produce the most operating income.

3. **Explain the difference between correct analysis and incorrect analysis of a particular business decision.** Correct analysis of a business decision focuses on differences in revenues and expenses. The conventional absorption costing approach to decision making may mislead managers into treating a fixed cost as a variable cost. The contribution margin approach is more useful because it highlights how sales volume affects expenses and income.

4. **Use opportunity costs in decision making.** *Opportunity cost* is the benefit that can be obtained from the next-best course of action in a decision. Opportunity cost is not an outlay cost, so it is not recorded in the accounting records.

5. **Use four capital-budgeting models to make longer-term investment decisions.** *Capital budgeting* is a formal means of analyzing long-term investment decisions. Four popular capital-budgeting methods are payback, accounting rate of return, net present value, and internal rate of return. *Payback* is the length of time it will take to recover the dollars invested. The *accounting rate of return* is the average annual operating income from an asset divided by the average amount invested in that asset. *Net present value (NPV)* discounts the project's expected future cash flows by the minimum desired rate of return. The project's *internal rate of return (IRR)* is the discount rate that makes the net present value of the project's cash flows equal to zero.

6. **Compare and contrast popular capital-budgeting models.** The discounted cash-flow methods—net present value and internal rate of return—are conceptually superior to the payback and accounting rate of return. Payback ignores profitability and the time value of money. Accounting rate of return ignores the time value of money. Net present value and IRR consider both profitability and the time value of money.

Self-Study Questions

Test your understanding of the chapter by marking the best answer for each of the following questions.

1. Relevant information for decision analysis *(pp. 1429–1430)*
   a. Remains constant regardless of the alternative courses of action
   b. Is used in some but not all business decisions
   c. Varies with the alternative courses of action
   d. Excludes direct materials and direct labour because they are fixed

2. Suppose that fixed costs remain unchanged. To decide whether to make a sale at a special price, compare *(p. 1431)*
   a. Expected change in gross margin (sales minus cost of goods sold) with and without the sale

   b. Expected change in revenues with expected change in fixed expenses
   c. Expected change in revenues with expected change in selling expenses
   d. Expected change in revenues with expected change in variable expenses

3. To decide whether to drop a product, a manager should *(pp. 1434–1435)*
   a. Consider all costs that change
   b. Consider only variable costs
   c. Consider all costs that remain unchanged
   d. Consider only fixed costs

4. Pontchartrain Ltd.'s $0.47 manufacturing cost per unit includes fixed cost of $0.19. Acme, Inc. offers to sell the product to Pontchartrain for $0.35 per

unit. The make-or-buy decision hinges on the comparison between Pontchartrain's $0.47 manufacturing cost and the total cost if the products are purchased from Acme. That total cost is (pp. 1437–1440)

a. $0.28   c. $0.54
b. $0.35   d. $0.66

5. Sunk costs are (p. 1440)
   a. Relevant to most business decisions
   b. The costs of the next-best alternative
   c. Equal to the residual value of a capital asset
   d. Irrelevant in business decisions

6. Capital budgeting is a (an) (p. 1445)
   a. Amortization method
   b. Short-run decision
   c. Alternative to the payback method
   d. Way to analyze long-range investment decisions

7. A machine costs $45,000. It is expected to earn operating income of $6,000 and to generate a $7,500 net cash inflow annually. Expected residual value is $5,000 at the end of five years. What is the asset's payback period? (pp. 1445–1447)
   a. 5 years   c. 7½ years
   b. 6 years   d. 9 years

8. The accounting rate of return of the machine in Self-Study Question 7 is (p. 1447)
   a. 15 percent   c. 26.7 percent
   b. 24 percent   d. 37.5 percent

9. The time value of money is an important part of (p. 1448)
   a. Payback analysis
   b. Accounting rate of return analysis
   c. Net-present-value analysis
   d. All capital-budgeting methods

10. Payback analysis and net-present-value analysis indicate that a particular investment should be rejected, but the accounting rate of return is favourable. What is the wisest investment decision? Give your reason. (pp. 1449–1451)
   a. Reject because of net-present-value analysis
   b. Reject because of payback analysis
   c. Accept because of favourable accounting rate of return
   d. Cannot decide because of differences among the methods' results

Answers to the Self-Study Questions follow the Similar Accounting Terms.

Accounting Vocabulary

Accounting rate of return (p. 1447)
Annuity (p. 1449)
Capital budgeting (p. 1445)
Constraint (p. 1436)
Cost of capital (p. 1449)
Discount rate (p. 1449)
Hurdle rate (p. 1449)
Internal rate of return (IRR) (p. 1454)
Net present value (NPV) (p. 1449)

Opportunity cost (p. 1441)
Outsourcing (p. 1437)
Payback (p. 1445)
Relevant information (p. 1430)
Required rate of return (p. 1449)
Strategy (p. 1429)
Sunk cost (p. 1440)
Time value of money (p. 1448)

Similar Accounting Terms

Constraint	Limiting Factor
Discount rate	Rate of return; Hurdle rate; Cut-off rate; Cost of Capital; Target rate
Incremental analysis	Relevant cost analysis
Strategy	Business goals

Answers to Self-Study Questions

1. c   2. d   3. a

4. c   Fixed cost ($0.19) + Cost of outside units ($0.35) = $0.54

5. d   6. d   7. b $45,000/$7,500 = 6 years

8. b $$\frac{\$6,000}{(\$45,000 + \$5,000)/2} = \frac{\$6,000}{\$25,000} = 24\%$$

9. c   10. a

Assignment Material

Questions

1. How do special decisions differ from ordinary day-to-day business decisions? Give examples of special decisions.

2. Briefly describe how managers use relevant information in making special decisions.

3. Discuss the roles of expected future data and historical data in decision analysis. On which data are special decisions based?

4. Name two key guidelines for making short-term special decisions.

5. Identify two income statement formats. Which is more useful for deciding whether to accept a special sales order? Why?

6. Identify two long-run factors managers should consider in deciding whether to accept a special sales order.

7. What is the similarity between a special sales order decision and a decision to drop a product? The difference?

8. Which cost is more likely to change in a short-term decision situation, a fixed or a variable cost? Can both costs change?

9. Outline how to decide which product to emphasize when there is a limiting factor. Give four examples of limiting factors.

10. Which is relevant to decision analysis, an asset's sunk cost or its residual value? Give your reason, including an explanation of each.

11. What is an opportunity cost? How does it differ from an ordinary accounting cost?

12. Give an example of a decision that is based on opportunity cost. Discuss the role of opportunity cost in making the decision.

13. What are decision models? Why are they helpful in capital budgeting?

14. Name three capital-budgeting decision methods. State the strengths and the weaknesses of each method. Which method is best? Why?

15. Which capital-budgeting method is: (a) based on operating income; (b) based on cash flows without regard for their timing or profitability; (c) based on the time value of money.

16. How is the payback period computed for assets that generate equal annual cash flows? How does the estimated useful life of a capital asset affect the payback computation?

17. How can managers use the accounting rate of return in capital-budgeting decisions?

18. How can the accounting rate of return be computed when the annual amounts of operating income vary?

19. Explain why a positive net present value indicates an attractive investment project and a negative net present value indicates an unattractive project.

20. Which capital-budgeting strategy is better? (a) Pick the best capital budgeting method and use it exclusively. (b) Use more than one capital budgeting method. Explain your answer.

Exercises

Exercise 26-1   *Accept or reject a special sales order*   *(Obj. 1, 2)*

The Hockey Hall of Fame in Toronto has approached All-Sports Manufacturing Company Ltd. with a special order. The Hall wishes to purchase 100,000 monogrammed hockey pucks for a special promotional campaign and offers $0.80 per puck—a total of $80,000. All-Sports' total manufacturing cost per puck is $1.13, broken down as follows:

Variable costs:	
Direct materials..........	$0.18
Direct labour..............	0.12
Variable overhead......	0.33
Total variable cost......	0.63
Fixed overhead cost.......	0.50
Total cost	$1.13

Prepare a quick summary to help determine whether All-Sports should accept the special sales order. Assume that All-Sports has excess capacity.

Exercise 26-2   *Retain or drop a product line (fixed costs unchanged)*   *(Obj. 1, 2, 3)*

Top managers of Lethbridge Builders' Supply Co. Ltd. are alarmed that operating income is so low. They are considering dropping the building materials product line. Company accountants have prepared the following analysis to help make this decision:

	Total	Hardware	Building Materials
Sales	$500,000	$290,000	$210,000
Variable expenses	270,000	140,000	130,000
Contribution margin	230,000	150,000	80,000
Fixed expenses:			
Manufacturing	145,000	70,000	75,000
Selling and administrative	90,000	55,000	35,000
Total fixed expenses	235,000	125,000	110,000
Operating income (loss)	$ (5,000)	$ 25,000	$ (30,000)

Fixed costs will not change if the company stops selling building materials.

Prepare a quick summary to show whether Lethbridge Builders' Supply Co. Ltd. should drop the building materials product line. Explain the error of concluding that dropping building materials will add $30,000 to operating income.

Exercise 26-3   *Retain or drop a product line (fixed costs change)*   *(Obj. 1, 2)*

Refer to the data of Exercise 26-2. Assume that Lethbridge Builders' Supply Co. Ltd. can avoid $85,000 of fixed expenses by dropping the building materials product line. Prepare a quick summary to show whether Lethbridge Builders' Supply Co. Ltd. should stop selling building materials.

Exercise 26-4   *Which product to emphasize?*   *(Obj. 1, 2)*

Avant-Garde Fashions Ltd. sells both designer and moderately priced women's wear. Profits have fluctuated recently, and top management is deciding which product line to emphasize. Accountants have provided the following data:

	Designer	Moderately Priced
Per item:		
Average sale price	$200	$90
Average variable expenses	70	32
Average contribution margin	$130	$58
Average fixed expenses	20	9
Average operating income	$110	$49

The Avant-Garde store in Moncton, New Brunswick, has 1,200 square metres of floor space. If it emphasizes moderately priced goods, 600 items can be displayed in the store. Only 300 designer items can be displayed for sale. These numbers are also the average monthly sales in units.

Prepare an analysis to show which product to emphasize.

Exercise 26-5   *Deciding whether to make or buy*   *(Obj. 1, 2, 3)*

MicroTech Systems Ltd. manufactures an electronic control that it uses in its final product. The electronic control has the following manufacturing costs per unit:

Direct materials..	$ 7.00
Direct labour	1.00
Variable overhead.....................................	1.50
Fixed overhead	5.50
Manufacturing product cost..................	$15.00

Another company has offered to sell MicroTech the electronic control for $11 per unit. If MicroTech buys the control from the outside supplier, the manufacturing facilities that will be idled cannot be used for any other purpose. Should MicroTech make or buy the electronic controls? Explain the difference between correct analysis and incorrect analysis of this decision.

Exercise 26-6   *Determining best use of facilities*   *(Obj. 1, 2)*

Refer to Exercise 26-5. Assume that MicroTech Systems Ltd. needs 80,000 of the electronic controls. By purchasing them from the outside supplier, MicroTech can use its idle facilities to manufacture another product that will contribute $175,000 to operating income. Identify the incremental costs that MicroTech will incur to acquire 80,000 electronic controls under three alternative plans. Which plan makes the best use of MicroTech's facilities? Support your answer.

Exercise 26-7   *Deciding whether to sell or process further*   *(Obj. 1, 3, 4)*

Rizik Custom Cabinets Inc. has damaged some custom cabinets, which cost the company $8,000 to manufacture. Owner Jan Rizik is considering two options for disposing of this inventory. One plan is to sell the cabinets as damaged inventory for $1,500. The alternative is to spend an additional $700 to repair the damage and expect to sell the cabinets for $2,250. What should Rizik do? Support your answer with an analysis that shows expected net revenue under each alternative. Identify the opportunity cost of each alternative.

Exercise 26-8   *Computing payback with equal cash flows*   *(Obj. 5)*

Adkins Inc. is considering acquiring a processing factory. The purchase price is $1,457,000. The owners believe that the factory will generate net cash inflows of $485,700 annually. It will have to be replaced in seven years. Use the payback model to determine whether Adkins Inc. should purchase this factory.

Exercise 26-9   *Computing payback with unequal cash flows*   *(Obj. 5)*

Kumar Manufacturing Inc. is adding a new product line that will require an investment of $1,454,000. Managers estimate that this investment will generate net cash inflows of $310,000 the first year, $280,000 the second year, and $250,000 each year thereafter. Compute the payback period of this investment.

Exercise 26-10   *Determining accounting rate of return*   *(Obj. 4, 5)*

Barker Mills Inc. is shopping for new equipment. Managers are considering two investments. Equipment manufactured by Li Inc. costs $400,000 and will last for five years, with no residual value. The Li equipment is expected to generate annual operating income of $48,000. Equipment manufactured by Veras Products Ltd. is priced at $550,000 and will remain useful for six years. It promises annual operating income of $92,750, and its expected residual value is $30,000.

Which equipment offers the higher accounting rate of return? What is the opportunity cost of purchasing from each manufacturer? How would Barker Mills Inc. managers use the notion of opportunity cost in making their decision?

Exercise 26-11 *Computing net present value* *(Obj. 5)*

Use net present value to determine whether Prestige Products Ltd. should invest in the following projects:

Project A: Costs $295,000 and offers 8 annual net cash inflows of $65,000. Prestige Products Ltd. demands an annual return of 14 percent on projects like A.

Project B: Costs $435,000 and offers 9 annual net cash inflows of $80,000. Prestige Products Ltd. requires an annual return of 12 percent on investments of this nature.

What is the net present value of each project? What is the maximum acceptable price to pay for each project?

Exercise 26-12 *Computing internal rate of return* *(Obj. 5)*

Refer to Exercise 26-11. Compute the internal rate of return of each project, and use this information to identify the better investment.

Challenge Exercise

Exercise 26-13 *Determining product mix* *(Obj. 1, 2)*

Each morning in the summer, Ken Gaver stocks the drink case at Ken's Beach Hut in Wasaga Beach, Ontario. Ken has 35 linear metres of refrigerated display space for cold drinks. Each linear metre can hold either 18 375-ml cans or 12 625-ml plastic or glass bottles. Ken's sells three types of cold drinks:

- Coca-Cola in 375-ml cans, for $1.25 per can
- Coca-Cola in 625-ml plastic bottles, for $1.50 per bottle
- Evian in 625-ml glass bottles, for $2.00 per bottle

Ken's pays its suppliers:

- $0.25 per 375-ml can of Coca-Cola
- $0.30 per 625-ml bottle of Coca-Cola
- $0.70 per 625-ml bottle of Evian

Ken's monthly fixed expenses include

Hut rental..	$ 250
Refrigerator rental.........................	50
Ken's salary....................................	1,000
Total fixed expenses......................	$1,300

Ken's can sell all the drinks stocked in the display case each morning.

Required

1. What is Ken's constraining factor? What should Ken's Beach Hut stock in order to maximize profits?
2. Suppose Ken's refuses to devote more than 20 linear metres to any individual product. Under this condition, how many linear metres of each drink should Ken's Beach Hut stock? How many units of each product will be available for sale each day?

Beyond the Numbers

Beyond the Numbers 26-1 *Dropping a product line* *(Obj. 2)*

Suppose a national drugstore chain decided to stop selling cigarettes. Cigarettes have gross margins as high as 20 to 30 percent. A decision to eliminate the cigarette product line would have a significant effect on the company's gross margin.

Why might the drugstore chain decide to drop the cigarette product line and give up such a large profit?

Beyond the Numbers 26-2 *Required rate of return* *(Obj. 5)*

Answer the following questions.

1. In discounted cash flow analysis, does a higher discount rate (a higher required rate of return) increase or decrease the present value of the cash flow?

2. When performing discounted cash flow analysis, managers typically use different discount rates for riskier projects than for less risky projects. Would managers use higher or lower discount rates for riskier projects? Why?

3. Husky Oil Ltd. is one of the larger oil refiners in Canada and is also aggressive in oil explanation. Would managers use a higher or lower discount rate for oil refining projects than for oil exploration projects? Give your reason.

Ethical Issue

Roberta Chin is the chief financial officer (CFO) of Ultima Inc., a diversified company with a broad range of products in the food-service and household-products industries. Chin recently convinced Ultima's top management to sell the company's old mainframe computer and replace it with a system of desk-top computers located at the company's 20 factories and offices.

The CFO and her task force asked two vendors to propose systems that meet Ultima's operating needs. The first vendor's proposal would require a $1,040,000 upfront investment for hardware, software, and training. Its relevant net cash savings are predicted to be $400,000 per year for the four-year decision period. The second vendor's proposal would require a $2,000,000 initial outlay. Its relevant annual net cash savings are $740,000. Both systems would have no residual value at the end of four years.

Ultima uses the net-present-value model to evaluate investment proposals. The company's minimum desired rate of return on investments of this nature is 16 percent. However, Chin is sure that if she were to use a 14-percent discount rate for this decision, no one would challenge her. Chin would like to accept the proposal of the second vendor, a company owned by a close friend of hers.

Required

1. Compute the net present value of the two proposals. Use Ultima Inc.'s 16-percent discount rate. Which proposal should the company accept?

2. Compute the net present value of each proposal using 14 percent as the discount rate. Is this rate acceptable in this case? Would it be unethical for Chin to make her selection on the basis of the 14-percent computations?

Problems (Group A)

Problem 26-1A *Accepting or rejecting a special sales order* *(Obj. 1, 2)*

Acme Printing Ltd.'s contribution margin income statement for July, 2003, reports the following:

Sales in units	760,000
Sales	$190,000
Variable expenses:	
Manufacturing	$ 58,000
Marketing and administrative	34,000
Total variable expenses	92,000
Contribution margin	98,000
Fixed expenses:	
Manufacturing	58,000
Marketing and administrative	16,000
Total fixed expenses	74,000
Operating income	$ 24,000

Coast Vineyards Inc. wants to buy 100,000 labels from Acme. Acceptance of the order will not increase Acme's marketing and administrative expenses. Acme's factory has unused capacity to manufacture the additional labels. Coast Vineyards has offered $0.18 per label, which is considerably below the normal selling price of $0.25 per label.

Required

1. Prepare an incremental analysis to help determine whether Acme Printing Ltd. should accept this special sales order.

2. Prepare a total analysis to show Acme's operating income with and without the special sales order.

3. Identify long-run factors that Acme should consider in deciding whether to accept the special sales order.

Problem 26-2A *Keeping or dropping a product line* **(Obj. 1, 2, 3)**

The income statement of Sea Products Ltd. highlights the losses of the frozen seafood division:

	Product Line		
	Fresh Seafood	**Frozen Seafood**	**Total**
Sales	$630,000	$227,500	$857,500
Cost of goods sold:			
Variable	$100,000	$ 64,000	$164,000
Fixed	90,000	41,000	131,000
Total cost of goods sold	190,000	105,000	295,000
Gross margin	440,000	122,500	562,500
Marketing and administrative expenses:			
Variable	270,000	108,000	378,000
Fixed	80,000	49,500	129,500
Total marketing and administrative expenses	350,000	157,500	507,500
Operating income (loss)	$ 90,000	$ (35,000)	$ 55,000

Sea Products is considering discontinuing the frozen seafood product line. The company's accountants estimate that dropping frozen seafood will decrease fixed cost of goods sold by $32,000 and decrease fixed marketing and administrative expenses by $15,000.

Required

1. Prepare an incremental analysis to show whether Sea Products Ltd. should drop the frozen seafood product line.

2. Prepare a total analysis to show Sea Products Ltd. operating income with and without the frozen seafood division. Prepare the income statement in contribution margin format.

3. Explain the difference between correct analysis and incorrect analysis of the decision to retain or drop the frozen seafood product line.

Problem 26-3A *Determining product mix* *(Obj. 1, 2)*

Green's Outdoor Store Ltd. of Canmore, Alberta, specializes in outdoor furniture and barbeques. Red Green and Dorothy Seton, the owners, are expanding the store. They are deciding which product line to emphasize. To make this decision, they assemble the following data, which suggest that the line of patio sets, with the higher contribution margin, is more profitable:

	Per Unit	
	Patio sets	**Barbeques**
Per unit:		
Sale price.....................................	$500	$200
Variable expenses	260	110
Contribution margin	$240	$ 90
Contribution margin ratio........	48%	45%

After the renovation, the store will have 710 square metres of floor space. By devoting the new floor space to barbeques, Green's Outdoor Store can display 30 units of merchandise. If patio sets are emphasized, 20 units can be displayed. Green and Seton expect their company's merchandise to turn over once a month. That is, they expect monthly sales to equal the maximum number of units displayed.

Required

1. Identify the limiting factor for Green's Outdoor Store Ltd.

2. Prepare an analysis to show which product line to emphasize.

Problem 26-4A *Outsourcing; best use of facilities* *(Obj. 1, 2)*

WaterTime Products Ltd. manufactures swim fins. Cost data for producing 2,000 pairs of fins each year are as follows:

Direct materials............................	$21,000
Direct labour.................................	15,000
Variable overhead.........................	5,600
Fixed overhead.............................	38,400
Total manufacturing costs	$80,000

Zenith Diving Products Inc. will sell WaterTime the fins for $35 per pair. WaterTime would pay $1.80 per pair to transport the fins to its warehouse.

Required

1. WaterTime Products Ltd.'s accountants predict that purchasing the fins from Zenith Diving Products Inc. will enable the company to avoid $12,000 of fixed overhead. Prepare an analysis to show whether WaterTime should make or buy the fins.

2. Assume that the WaterTime facilities freed up by the purchase of the fins from Zenith Diving can be used to manufacture swim masks. The masks will contribute $35,000 to profit. Total fixed costs will be the same as if WaterTime used the factory to make fins. Prepare an analysis to show which alternative makes the best use of WaterTime's facilities: (a) make fins, (b) buy fins and leave facilities idle, or (c) buy fins and make masks.

Problem 26-5A *Deciding whether to sell as is or process further; identifying opportunity costs (Obj. 1, 2, 4)*

Vixon Petroleum Inc. produces a variety of petroleum products. Assume that Vixon has spent $300,000 to refine 60,000 litres of petroleum distillate. Suppose Vixon can sell the distillate for $5.50 a litre. Alternatively, Vixon can process the distillate further and produce cleaner for tape heads. Assume that the additional processing will cost another $1.25 a litre, and that the cleaner can be sold for $7.60 a litre. To make this sale, Vixon must pay a sales commission of $0.10 a litre and a transportation charge of $0.15 a litre.

Required

1. Prepare a diagram of Vixon Petroleum Inc.'s alternatives, using Exhibit 26-10, page 1440, as a guide.
2. Identify the sunk cost in this situation. Is the sunk cost relevant to Vixon's decision?
3. Prepare an analysis to indicate whether Vixon Petroleum Inc. should sell the distillate or process it into tape-head cleaner. Show the expected net revenue difference between the two alternatives.
4. Identify the opportunity cost of each option. Explain how managers can use opportunity cost to make this decision.

Problem 26-6A *Capital budgeting (Obj. 5, 6)*

Cinnalicious Ltd., maker of the original gourmet cinnamon bun, is considering two possible expansion plans. Plan A is to open eight stores at a cost of $3,220,000. Expected annual net cash inflows are $690,000 with residual value of $350,000 at the end of the seven years. Under Plan B, Cinnalicious would open 12 stores at a cost of $4,200,000. This investment is expected to generate net cash inflows of $1,050,000 each year for seven years, which is the estimated useful life of the properties. Estimated residual value of Plan B is zero. Cinnalicious uses straight-line amortization and its top managers require an annual return of 14 percent.

Required

1. Compute the payback period, the accounting rate of return, and the net present value of each plan. What are the strengths and weaknesses of these capital-budgeting models?
2. Which expansion plan should Cinnalicious Ltd.'s management choose? Why?
3. Estimate the internal rate of return (IRR) of Plan B. How does Plan B's IRR compare with the discount rate?

Problem 26-7A *Capital budgeting (Obj. 5, 6)*

Auburn Investments Inc. operates a resort on Lake Memphremagog in the Eastern Townships region of Quebec. The company is considering an expansion. The architectural plan calls for a construction cost of $5,200,000. Top managers of Auburn believe the expansion will generate annual net cash inflows of $700,000 for ten years. Architects and engineers estimate that the new facilities will remain useful for ten years and have a residual value of $2,400,000. The company uses straight-line amortization, and its shareholders demand an annual return of 12% on investments of this nature.

1. Compute the payback period, the accounting rate of return, and the net present value of this investment.
2. Make a recommendation to Auburn management as to whether the company should invest in this project.

Problem 26-8A *Accepting or rejecting a special order; use opportunity cost in decision making* **(Obj. 1, 2, 5)**

Gupta Manufacturing Ltd. produces cell phones with the following budgeted revenues and costs per unit based on the production and sale of 50,000 units:

Selling price..		$115.00
Cost of goods sold:		
Direct materials...	$7.00	
Direct labour	16.00	
Variable overhead.....................................	12.00	
Fixed overhead	10.00	
Total cost of goods sold		45.00
Gross margin...		70.00
Marketing and administrative costs:		
Variable marketing costs	11.00	
Fixed marketing costs..............................	12.00	
Fixed administrative costs	20.00	
Total marketing and administrative		43.00
Operating income.....................................		$ 27.00

Note:

The factory has a maximum capacity of 60,000 cell phones.

The variable marketing costs consist of $5.00 per cell phone for packaging and delivery, and a sales commission equal to 5 percent of sales.

Required

1. A salesperson has brought an offer from Future Shop to purchase 12,000 units at a price of $65.00 per unit delivered. This is a one-time-only order.
   (a) What costs would be irrelevant to the decision of whether or not to accept this special order?
   (b) Are there any opportunity costs relevant to the decision?
   (c) What would be the gain or loss to the company if it accepted the order?
2. What other qualitative factors should the company consider in accepting or rejecting the order?

Problem 26-9A *Outsourcing; opportunity costs and decision making; capital budgeting* **(Obj. 1, 2, 5, 6)**

WaTec Ltd. is presently manufacturing a component for its main product, a high-speed external modem. The component has the following costs based on the expected annual production of 20,000 units:

Direct materials...	$20,000
Direct labour..	40,000
Variable manufacturing overhead	14,000
Factory rent	50,000
Factory supervision...	42,000
Total cost of production....................................	$166,000

Other information:

- Demand for the component is expected to increase to 30,000 units per year (present capacity is 40,000 units per year).
- A supplier has offered to sell up to 40,000 units per year to WaTec at a price of $7.00 per unit.
- If the company were to buy the component from an outside supplier, any idle space in the factory could be used to:
  a. Produce and sell a new product that would have a contribution margin of $3.00 per unit. This product would use 40 percent of the factory space, employ the same supervisors as the original component, and require fixed marketing costs of $25,000 to obtain a demand for 30,000 units.
  b. The balance of the factory space would be occupied by marketing staff who are currently using outside facilities rented at a cost of $20,000 per year.

Required

1. What would be the overall benefit or loss to WaTec if it were to purchase the component from the supplier?
2. What qualitative factors should WaTec consider in outsourcing decisions?
3. Assume WaTec's managers decide to continue producing the component, and a machine is available that will automate the process. The machine would cost $80,000 and would last for five years with an expected residual value of $10,000. It would reduce direct material costs by 10 percent and direct labour costs by 60 percent, but would increase variable overhead by 20 percent and would require a part-time machine operator at a cost of $15,000 per year.

   Use the net-present-value approach (discount rate of 10 percent) to determine whether or not WaTec should purchase the machine, assuming demand is expected to be 30,000 units per year for the next two years and 40,000 units per year for the following three years.

Problems (Group B)

Problem 26-1B   *Accepting or rejecting a special sales order*   **(Obj. 1, 2)**

Play Day Corporation manufactures toys in Sydney, Nova Scotia. Play Day Corporation's contribution margin income statement for May, 2002 contains the following:

Sales in units	42,000
Sales	$420,000
Variable expenses:	
Manufacturing	$ 84,000
Marketing and administrative	100,000
Total variable expenses	184,000
Contribution margin	236,000
Fixed expenses:	
Manufacturing	116,000
Marketing and administrative	85,000
Total fixed expenses	201,000
Operating income	$ 35,000

eToy Ltd. wishes to buy 4,000 toys from Play Day Corporation. Acceptance of the order will not increase Play Day's marketing and administrative expenses. Play Day Corporation's factory has unused capacity to manufacture the additional toys. eToy Ltd. has offered $8.00 per toy, which is considerably below the normal selling price of $12.00.

Required

1. Prepare an incremental analysis to help determine whether Play Day Corporation should accept this special sales order.

2. Prepare a total analysis to show Play Day's operating income with and without the special sales order.

3. Identify long-run factors that Play Day Corporation should consider in deciding whether to accept the special sales order.

Problem 26-2B *Keeping or dropping a product line* *(Obj. 1, 2, 3)*

Members of the board of directors of Environmental Electric Inc. have received the following income statement for the year ended December 31, 2002.

| | Product Line | | |
	Industrial Products	Household Products	Total
Sales...	$405,000	$421,000	$826,000
Cost of goods sold:			
Variable...	$ 50,000	$ 55,000	$105,000
Fixed..	241,000	86,000	327,000
Total cost of goods sold....................	291,000	141,000	432,000
Gross margin	114,000	280,000	394,000
Marketing and administrative expenses:			
Variable...	86,000	92,000	178,000
Fixed	58,000	31,000	89,000
Total selling and administrative			
expenses...	144,000	123,000	267,000
Operating income (loss)........................	$ (30,000)	$157,000	$127,000

Members of the board are surprised that the industrial products division is losing money. They commission a study to determine whether the company should delete the industrial products line. Company accountants estimate that dropping industrial products will decrease fixed cost of goods sold by $95,000 and decrease fixed marketing and administrative expenses by $15,000.

Required

1. Prepare an incremental analysis to show whether Environmental Electric Inc. should drop the industrial products line.

2. Prepare a total analysis to show Environmental Electric Inc.'s operating income with and without industrial products. Prepare the income statement in contribution margin format.

3. Explain the difference between correct analysis and incorrect analysis of the decision to retain or drop the industrial products line.

Problem 26-3B *Determining product mix* *(Obj. 1, 2)*

Bouchard Compu Products Inc., located in Hull, Quebec, produces two lines of computer mouse; cordless and standard models. The owners are expanding the factory, and they are deciding which product line to emphasize. To make this decision, they assemble the following data, which suggest that the cordless product line is more profitable:

	Per Unit	
	Cordless mouse	Standard mouse
Sale price	$45	$30
Variable expenses	15	12
Contribution margin	$30	$18
Contribution margin ratio	67%	60%

After the factory expansion, the factory will have a production capacity of 2,200 machine hours per month. The factory can either manufacture 20 units of the cordless mouse each machine hour or 50 units of the standard mouse each machine hour.

Required

1. Identify the limiting factor for Bouchard Compu Products Inc.
2. Prepare an analysis to show which product line to emphasize.

Problem 26-4B   *Outsourcing; best use of facilities*   *(Obj. 1, 2)*

Pinafore Sailing Ltd. manufactures sailboats. Currently the company makes the boats' seat cushions. The cost of producing 1,200 seat cushions is:

Direct materials	$7,260
Direct labour	1,440
Variable overhead	960
Fixed overhead	2,400
Total manufacturing costs for 1,200 units	$12,060

Tarantino Inc. will sell seat cushions to Pinafore for $8 each. Pinafore would pay $0.90 per unit to transport the seat cushions to its manufacturing facility, where it would add its own Pinafore label at a cost of $0.12 per seat cushion.

Required

1. Pinafore's accountants predict that purchasing the seat cushions from Tarantino Inc. will enable the company to avoid $900 of fixed overhead. Prepare an analysis to show whether Pinafore should make or buy the seat cushions.
2. Assume that the Pinafore facilities freed up by the purchase of seat cushions from Tarantino can be used to manufacture another product that will contribute $2,300 to profit. Total fixed costs will be the same as if Pinafore had produced the seat cushions. Prepare an analysis to show which alternative makes the best use of Pinafore's facilities: (a) make seat cushions, (b) buy seat cushions and leave facilities idle, or (c) buy seat cushions and make another product.

Problem 26-5B   *Deciding whether to sell as is or process further; identifying opportunity costs*   *(Obj. 1, 2, 4)*

Bank Chemicals Inc. has spent $320,000 to refine 84,000 litres of acetone, which can be sold for $3.40 a litre. Alternatively, Bank Chemicals can process the acetone further and produce 77,000 litres of lacquer thinner that can be sold for $4.91 a litre. The additional processing will cost $0.89 per litre of lacquer thinner. To sell the lacquer thinner, Bank Chemicals must pay a transportation charge of $0.30 per litre and administrative expenses of $0.16 a litre.

Required

1. Prepare a diagram of Bank Chemicals Inc.'s decision, using Exhibit 26-10 (page 1440) as a guide.
2. Identify the sunk cost. Is the sunk cost relevant to Bank Chemicals' decision?
3. Prepare an analysis to indicate whether Bank Chemicals should sell the acetone or process it into lacquer thinner. Show the expected net revenue difference between the two alternatives.
4. Identify the opportunity cost of each alternative. Explain how managers use the notion of opportunity cost in making their decision.

Problem 26-6B   *Capital budgeting   (Obj. 5, 6)*

Organic Foods Ltd. operates a chain of grocery stores that specialize in health foods. The company is considering two possible expansion plans. Plan A is to open three stores at a cost of $6,420,000. This plan is expected to generate net cash inflows of $625,000 each year for 20 years, the estimated life of the store properties. Estimated residual value is $3,000,000. Under Plan B, Organic Foods would open eight smaller stores at a cost of $7,396,000. Expected annual net cash inflows are $875,000, with zero residual value at the end of 19 years. Organic Foods' top managers require an annual return of 8 percent.

Required

1. Compute the payback period, the accounting rate of return, and the net present value of these two plans. What are the strengths and weaknesses of these capital-budgeting models?
2. Which expansion plan should Organic Foods Ltd.'s owners choose? Why?
3. Estimate Plan B's internal rate of return (IRR). How does the IRR compare with the company's discount rate?

Problem 26-7B   *Capital budgeting   (Obj. 5, 6)*

 Pacific Developers Inc., in Surrey, B.C., is considering purchasing a water park for $1,850,000. Top managers of Pacific Developers believe the new facility will generate annual net cash inflows of $385,000 for eight years. Architects and engineers estimate that the facility will remain useful for eight years and have a residual value of $600,000. The company uses straight-line amortization, and its shareholders demand an annual return of 16% on investments of this nature.

Required

1. Compute the payback period, the accounting rate of return, and the net present value of this investment.
2. Make a recommendation to Pacific Developers management as to whether the company should invest in this project.

Problem 26-8B   *Accepting or rejecting a special order; using opportunity cost in decision making   (Obj. 1, 2, 5)*

Florian Ltd. produces patio chairs with the budgeted revenues and costs per unit based on the production and sale of 40,000 chairs shown on the next page.

Note:
   The factory has a maximum capacity of 45,000 chairs.

   The variable marketing costs consist of $1.50 per unit for delivery and a sales commission equal to 5 percent of sales.

Selling price		$64.00
Cost of goods sold:		
Direct materials	$ 7.50	
Direct labour	13.50	
Variable overhead	9.00	
Fixed overhead	5.00	
Total cost of goods sold		35.00
Gross margin		29.00
Marketing and administrative costs:		
Variable marketing costs	4.50	
Fixed marketing costs	6.00	
Fixed administrative costs	14.00	
Total marketing and administrative		24.50
Operating income		$ 4.50

Required

1. A salesperson has brought an offer from Zellers to purchase 7,000 units at a price of $46.00 per unit delivered. This is a one-time-only order.

   (a) What costs would be irrelevant to the decision of whether or not to accept this special order?

   (b) Are there any opportunity costs relevant to the decision?

   (c) What would be the gain or loss to the company if it accepted the order?

2. What other qualitative factors should the company consider in accepting or rejecting the order?

Problem 26-9B   *Outsourcing; opportunity costs and decision making; capital budgeting (Obj. 1, 2, 5, 6)*

Fundy Manufacturing Ltd. is presently manufacturing a component of its main product, battery chargers. The component has the following costs based on the expected annual production of 10,000 units:

Direct materials	$ 50,000
Direct labour	45,000
Variable manufacturing overhead	15,000
Factory rent	40,000
Factory supervision	37,500
Total cost of production	$187,500

Other information:
- Demand for the component is expected to increase to 25,000 units per year (present capacity is 30,000 units per year).
- A supplier has offered to sell up to 30,000 units per year to Fundy Manufacturing Ltd. at a price of $13.75 per unit.
- If Fundy were to buy the component from an outside supplier, any idle space in the factory could be used to:
  a. Produce and sell a new product that would have a contribution margin of $8.00 per unit. This product would use 40 percent of the factory space, employ the same supervisors as the original component, and require fixed marketing costs of $45,000 to obtain a demand for 10,000 units.
  b. The balance of the factory space would be occupied by salespeople who are currently using outside facilities rented at a cost of $30,000 per year.

Required

1. What would be the overall benefit or loss to Fundy Manufacturing Ltd. if it were to purchase the component from the supplier?
2. What qualitative factors should Fundy consider in outsourcing decisions?
3. Assume Fundy managers decide to continue producing the component, and a machine is available that will automate the process. The machine would cost $400,000 and would last for 5 years with an expected residual value of $50,000. It would reduce direct material costs by 20 percent and direct labour costs by 25 percent, but would increase variable overhead by 10 percent and would require a machine operator at a cost of $30,000 per year.

   Use the net-present-value approach (discount rate of 16 percent) to determine whether or not Fundy should purchase the machine, assuming demand is expected to be 25,000 units per year for the next two years and 30,000 units per year for the following three years.

Challenge Problems

Problem 26-1C *Understanding the difference between correct analysis and incorrect analysis of a particular business decision* *(Obj. 3)*

A number of years ago, I spent my sabbatical at KPMG in its Toronto office. I would ride Via Rail to and from Toronto every day. One day several other passengers and I got into a debate with the conductor about the costs of carrying the 80 or so people who commuted to Toronto from Kitchener-Waterloo and Guelph every weekday. Our fare was about $20 per round-trip. The train originated in London, Ontario, and went to Toronto; at night it made the return trip.

The conductor told us that it cost Via Rail $50 per passenger round-trip and so the railroad was losing $30 each time it carried one of us to Toronto and back.

Required

Explain the fault in the conductor's reasoning. Or did Via Rail really lose $30 every time it carried me to Toronto and back?

Problem 26-2C *Understanding capital budgeting models* *(Obj. 7)*

The text lists a number of decision models that can be used for capital budgeting decisions. The models are very useful because they help organizations make capital budgeting decisions in an unbiased way.

Required

Do you believe that organizations make their capital budgeting decisions totally on the basis of the decision models discussed in Chapter 26?

Extending Your Knowledge

Decision Problems

1. Deciding whether to purchase a new machine (Obj. 1, 5, 6)

Suppose that Intel is considering a new computer-controlled etching machine for etching trenches in the surfaces of silicon wafers. The company processes these wafers into semi-conductor chips. The etching machine costs $900,000, and an additional $250,000 would be required for installation. Thus $1,150,000 is the required cash outlay for the investment.

Assume the new etching machine would replace an existing machine that was purchased five years ago for $715,000. That machine has five years of useful life remaining. Intel must either keep the old machine or replace it with the new machine. The expected useful life of the new machine is five years. Suppose Intel managers believe that the machine would save $355,000 per year in cash operating costs. However, annual maintenance cost would be $40,000 higher with the new machine than with the old.

Disposal values of the machines are as follows:

	Old Machine	New Machine
Now.............	–0–	—
In 5 years.......	–0–	$150,000

Assume Intel has a minimum desired rate of return of 14 percent on assets of this type.

Required

1. Is the $715,000 cost of the old machine relevant to the decision of whether to keep or replace the old machine? Why or why not? (*Hint:* What are the requirements for a cost to be relevant?)

2. Which of the four capital budgeting methods is best for making this decision? Use that model to decide which course of action is better for Intel. (*Hint:* Identify the relevant items—*future* costs and benefits that *differ* between the alternatives.)

2. Outsourcing e-mail (Obj. 1, 2)

BKFin.com Inc. provides banks access to sophisticated financial information and analysis systems over the Web. The company combines these tools with benchmarking data access including e-mail and wireless communications so that banks can instantly evaluate individual loan applications and entire loan portfolios.

BKFin.com's CEO Aamer Sheikh is very happy with the company's strong growth. To better focus on client service, Sheikh is considering outsourcing some functions. CFO Isabelle Wang suggests that the company's e-mail may be the place to start. She recently attended a conference and learned that companies like Placer Dome, Continental Airlines, and DellNet were outsourcing their e-mail function. Sheikh asks Wang to identify costs related to BKFin.com's inhouse Microsoft Exchange mail application, which has 2,300 mailboxes. This information follows:

Variable costs:	
E-mail license	$6 per mailbox per month
Virus protection license..................	$1 per mailbox per month
Other variable cost.......................	$7 per mailbox per month
Fixed Costs:	
Computer hardware costs	$85,100 per month
$6,900 monthly salary for two information technology staff members who work only on e-mail	$13,800 per month

Required

1. Compute the total cost per mailbox per month of BKFin.com's current e-mail function.
2. Suppose Mail.com, a leading provider of Internet messaging outsourcing services, offers to host BKFin.com's e-mail function for $8 per mailbox per month.

If BKFin.com outsources its e-mail to Mail.com, BKFin.com will still need the virus protection software, its computer hardware, and one information technology staff member who would be responsible for maintaining virus protection, quarantining suspicious e-mail, and managing content (e.g., screening e-mail for objectional content). Should CEO Sheikh accept Mail.com's offer?

3. Suppose for an additional $5 per mailbox per month, Mail.com will also provide virus protection, quarantine, and content management services. Outsourcing these additional functions would mean that BKFin.com would not need either an e-mail information technology staff member or the separate virus protection license. Should CEO Sheikh outsource these extra services to Mail.com?

Comprehensive Problem
for Part Seven

Budgeting Operating Costs and Evaluating a Proposed Product Line

Brunk Extrusion Ltd. is evaluating a proposal to add a new product line of containers for sulphuric acid. The container line requires an investment of $4,760,000 for equipment. The equipment is expected to have a three-year life and zero disposal value.

Brunk Extrusion's managers predict that 52,000 containers can be sold in each of the next three years, at $102 per container. The company's *initial* budget includes total cash operating costs of $9,360,000 ($3,120,000 per year) and total amortization of $4,760,000. Brunk Extrusion's top managers desire an operating contribution of 15 percent of sales for investments of this type.

Required

1. Brunk Extrusion's managers believe that improved employee efficiencies will reduce average operating cost by $2 per container. For the containers, compute (a) desired average operating cost, (b) original budgeted cost, (c) improved efficiency cost, and (d) required value-engineering cost reduction.

2. Compute the net present value of the container project, assuming that Brunk Extrusion's discount rate is 16 percent. Use the containers' desired average operating cost as the starting point in computing annual operating cash inflows. Should the company accept or reject the project? Why?

Appendix A

Present-Value Tables and Future-Value Tables

This appendix provides present-value tables (more complete than those appearing in Chapter 26) and future-value tables.

Table A-1   *Present Value of $1*

Periods	1%	2%	3%	4%	5%	6%	7%	8%	9%	10%	12%
1	0.990	0.980	0.971	0.962	0.952	0.943	0.935	0.926	0.917	0.909	0.893
2	0.980	0.961	0.943	0.925	0.907	0.890	0.873	0.857	0.842	0.826	0.797
3	0.971	0.942	0.915	0.889	0.864	0.840	0.816	0.794	0.772	0.751	0.712
4	0.961	0.924	0.888	0.855	0.823	0.792	0.763	0.735	0.708	0.683	0.636
5	0.951	0.906	0.883	0.822	0.784	0.747	0.713	0.681	0.650	0.621	0.567
6	0.942	0.888	0.837	0.790	0.746	0.705	0.666	0.630	0.596	0.564	0.507
7	0.933	0.871	0.813	0.760	0.711	0.665	0.623	0.583	0.547	0.513	0.452
8	0.923	0.853	0.789	0.731	0.677	0.627	0.582	0.540	0.502	0.467	0.404
9	0.914	0.837	0.766	0.703	0.645	0.592	0.544	0.500	0.460	0.424	0.361
10	0.905	0.820	0.744	0.676	0.614	0.558	0.508	0.463	0.422	0.386	0.322
11	0.896	0.804	0.722	0.650	0.585	0.527	0.475	0.429	0.388	0.350	0.287
12	0.887	0.788	0.701	0.625	0.557	0.497	0.444	0.397	0.356	0.319	0.257
13	0.879	0.773	0.681	0.601	0.530	0.469	0.415	0.368	0.326	0.290	0.229
14	0.870	0.758	0.661	0.577	0.505	0.442	0.388	0.340	0.299	0.263	0.205
15	0.861	0.743	0.642	0.555	0.481	0.417	0.362	0.315	0.275	0.239	0.183
16	0.853	0.728	0.623	0.534	0.458	0.394	0.339	0.292	0.252	0.218	0.163
17	0.844	0.714	0.605	0.513	0.436	0.371	0.317	0.270	0.231	0.198	0.146
18	0.836	0.700	0.587	0.494	0.416	0.350	0.296	0.250	0.212	0.180	0.130
19	0.828	0.686	0.570	0.475	0.396	0.331	0.277	0.232	0.194	0.164	0.116
20	0.820	0.673	0.554	0.456	0.377	0.312	0.258	0.215	0.178	0.149	0.104
21	0.811	0.660	0.538	0.439	0.359	0.294	0.242	0.199	0.164	0.135	0.093
22	0.803	0.647	0.522	0.422	0.342	0.278	0.226	0.184	0.150	0.123	0.083
23	0.795	0.634	0.507	0.406	0.326	0.262	0.211	0.170	0.138	0.112	0.074
24	0.788	0.622	0.492	0.390	0.310	0.247	0.197	0.158	0.126	0.102	0.066
25	0.780	0.610	0.478	0.375	0.295	0.233	0.184	0.146	0.116	0.092	0.059
26	0.772	0.598	0.464	0.361	0.281	0.220	0.172	0.135	0.106	0.084	0.053
27	0.764	0.586	0.450	0.347	0.268	0.207	0.161	0.125	0.098	0.076	0.047
28	0.757	0.574	0.437	0.333	0.255	0.196	0.150	0.116	0.090	0.069	0.042
29	0.749	0.563	0.424	0.321	0.243	0.185	0.141	0.107	0.082	0.063	0.037
30	0.742	0.552	0.412	0.308	0.231	0.174	0.131	0.099	0.075	0.057	0.033
40	0.672	0.453	0.307	0.208	0.142	0.097	0.067	0.046	0.032	0.022	0.011
50	0.608	0.372	0.228	0.141	0.087	0.054	0.034	0.021	0.013	0.009	0.003

Table A-1 (cont'd)

14%	15%	16%	18%	20%	25%	30%	35%	40%	45%	50%	Periods
0.877	0.870	0.862	0.847	0.833	0.800	0.769	0.741	0.714	0.690	0.667	1
0.769	0.756	0.743	0.718	0.694	0.640	0.592	0.549	0.510	0.476	0.444	2
0.675	0.658	0.641	0.609	0.579	0.512	0.455	0.406	0.364	0.328	0.296	3
0.592	0.572	0.552	0.516	0.482	0.410	0.350	0.301	0.260	0.226	0.198	4
0.519	0.497	0.476	0.437	0.402	0.328	0.269	0.223	0.186	0.156	0.132	5
0.456	0.432	0.410	0.370	0.335	0.262	0.207	0.165	0.133	0.108	0.088	6
0.400	0.376	0.354	0.314	0.279	0.210	0.159	0.122	0.095	0.074	0.059	7
0.351	0.327	0.305	0.266	0.233	0.168	0.123	0.091	0.068	0.051	0.039	8
0.308	0.284	0.263	0.225	0.194	0.134	0.094	0.067	0.048	0.035	0.026	9
0.270	0.247	0.227	0.191	0.162	0.107	0.073	0.050	0.035	0.024	0.017	10
0.237	0.215	0.195	0.162	0.135	0.086	0.056	0.037	0.025	0.017	0.012	11
0.208	0.187	0.168	0.137	0.112	0.069	0.043	0.027	0.018	0.012	0.008	12
0.182	0.163	0.145	0.116	0.093	0.055	0.033	0.020	0.013	0.008	0.005	13
0.160	0.141	0.125	0.099	0.078	0.044	0.025	0.015	0.009	0.006	0.003	14
0.140	0.123	0.108	0.084	0.065	0.035	0.020	0.011	0.006	0.004	0.002	15
0.123	0.107	0.093	0.071	0.054	0.028	0.015	0.008	0.005	0.003	0.002	16
0.108	0.093	0.080	0.060	0.045	0.023	0.012	0.006	0.003	0.002	0.001	17
0.095	0.081	0.069	0.051	0.038	0.018	0.009	0.005	0.002	0.001	0.001	18
0.083	0.070	0.060	0.043	0.031	0.014	0.007	0.003	0.002	0.001		19
0.073	0.061	0.051	0.037	0.026	0.012	0.005	0.002	0.001	0.001		20
0.064	0.053	0.044	0.031	0.022	0.009	0.004	0.002	0.001			21
0.056	0.046	0.038	0.026	0.018	0.007	0.003	0.001	0.001			22
0.049	0.040	0.033	0.022	0.015	0.006	0.002	0.001				23
0.043	0.035	0.028	0.019	0.013	0.005	0.002	0.001				24
0.038	0.030	0.024	0.016	0.010	0.004	0.001	0.001				25
0.033	0.026	0.021	0.014	0.009	0.003	0.001					26
0.029	0.023	0.018	0.011	0.007	0.002	0.001					27
0.026	0.020	0.016	0.010	0.006	0.002	0.001					28
0.022	0.017	0.014	0.008	0.005	0.002						29
0.020	0.015	0.012	0.007	0.004	0.001						30
0.005	0.004	0.003	0.001	0.001							40
0.001	0.001	0.001									50

The column headers are grouped under **Present Value**.

Table A-2 *Present Value of Annuity $1*

Periods						Present Value					
	1%	2%	3%	4%	5%	6%	7%	8%	9%	10%	12%
1	0.990	0.980	0.971	0.962	0.952	0.943	0.935	0.926	0.917	0.909	0.893
2	1.970	1.942	1.913	1.886	1.859	1.833	1.808	1.783	1.759	1.736	1.690
3	2.941	2.884	2.829	2.775	2.723	2.673	2.624	2.577	2.531	2.487	2.402
4	3.902	3.808	3.717	3.630	3.546	3.465	3.387	3.312	3.240	3.170	3.037
5	4.853	4.713	4.580	4.452	4.329	4.212	4.100	3.993	3.890	3.791	3.605
6	5.795	5.601	5.417	5.242	5.076	4.917	4.767	4.623	4.486	4.355	4.111
7	6.728	6.472	6.230	6.002	5.786	5.582	5.389	5.206	5.033	4.868	4.564
8	7.652	7.325	7.020	6.733	6.463	6.210	5.971	5.747	5.535	5.335	4.968
9	8.566	8.162	7.786	7.435	7.108	6.802	6.515	6.247	5.995	5.759	5.328
10	9.471	8.983	8.530	8.111	7.722	7.360	7.024	6.710	6.418	6.145	5.650
11	10.368	9.787	9.253	8.760	8.306	7.887	7.499	7.139	6.805	6.495	5.938
12	11.255	10.575	9.954	9.385	8.863	8.384	7.943	7.536	7.161	6.814	6.194
13	12.134	11.348	10.635	9.986	9.394	8.853	8.358	7.904	7.487	7.103	6.424
14	13.004	12.106	11.296	10.563	9.899	9.295	8.745	8.244	7.786	7.367	6.628
15	13.865	12.849	11.938	11.118	10.380	9.712	9.108	8.559	8.061	7.606	6.811
16	14.718	13.578	12.561	11.652	10.838	10.106	9.447	8.851	8.313	7.824	6.974
17	15.562	14.292	13.166	12.166	11.274	10.477	9.763	9.122	8.544	8.022	7.120
18	16.398	14.992	13.754	12.659	11.690	10.828	10.059	9.372	8.756	8.201	7.250
19	17.226	15.678	14.324	13.134	12.085	11.158	10.336	9.604	8.950	8.365	7.366
20	18.046	16.351	14.878	13.590	12.462	11.470	10.594	9.818	9.129	8.514	7.469
21	18.857	17.011	15.415	14.029	12.821	11.764	10.836	10.017	9.292	8.649	7.562
22	19.660	17.658	15.937	14.451	13.163	12.042	11.061	10.201	9.442	8.772	7.645
23	20.456	18.292	16.444	14.857	13.489	12.303	11.272	10.371	9.580	8.883	7.718
24	21.243	18.914	16.936	15.247	13.799	12.550	11.469	10.529	9.707	8.985	7.784
25	22.023	19.523	17.413	15.622	14.094	12.783	11.654	10.675	9.823	9.077	7.843
26	22.795	20.121	17.877	15.983	14.375	13.003	11.826	10.810	9.929	9.161	7.896
27	23.560	20.707	18.327	16.330	14.643	13.211	11.987	10.935	10.027	9.237	7.943
28	24.316	21.281	18.764	16.663	14.898	13.406	12.137	11.051	10.116	9.307	7.984
29	25.066	21.844	19.189	16.984	15.141	13.591	12.278	11.158	10.198	9.370	8.022
30	25.808	22.396	19.600	17.292	15.373	13.765	12.409	11.258	10.274	9.427	8.055
40	32.835	27.355	23.115	19.793	17.159	15.046	13.332	11.925	10.757	9.779	8.244
50	39.196	31.424	25.730	21.482	18.256	15.762	13.801	12.234	10.962	9.915	8.305

Table A-2 *(cont'd)*

					Present Value						
14%	**15%**	**16%**	**18%**	**20%**	**25%**	**30%**	**35%**	**40%**	**45%**	**50%**	**Periods**
0.877	0.870	0.862	0.847	0.833	0.800	0.769	0.741	0.714	0.690	0.667	1
1.647	1.626	1.605	1.566	1.528	1.440	1.361	1.289	1.224	1.165	1.111	2
2.322	2.283	2.246	2.174	2.106	1.952	1.816	1.696	1.589	1.493	1.407	3
2.914	2.855	2.798	2.690	2.589	2.362	2.166	1.997	1.849	1.720	1.605	4
3.433	3.352	3.274	3.127	2.991	2.689	2.436	2.220	2.035	1.876	1.737	5
3.889	3.784	3.685	3.498	3.326	2.951	2.643	2.385	2.168	1.983	1.824	6
4.288	4.160	4.039	3.812	3.605	3.161	2.802	2.508	2.263	2.057	1.883	7
4.639	4.487	4.344	4.078	3.837	3.329	2.925	2.598	2.331	2.109	1.922	8
4.946	4.772	4.607	4.303	4.031	3.463	3.019	2.665	2.379	2.144	1.948	9
5.216	5.019	4.833	4.494	4.192	3.571	3.092	2.715	2.414	2.168	1.965	10
5.453	5.234	5.029	4.656	4.327	3.656	3.147	2.752	2.438	2.185	1.977	11
5.660	5.421	5.197	4.793	4.439	3.725	3.190	2.779	2.456	2.197	1.985	12
5.842	5.583	5.342	4.910	4.533	3.780	3.223	2.799	2.469	2.204	1.990	13
6.002	5.724	5.468	5.008	4.611	3.824	3.249	2.814	2.478	2.210	1.993	14
6.142	5.847	5.575	5.092	4.675	3.859	3.268	2.825	2.484	2.214	1.995	15
6.265	5.954	5.669	5.162	4.730	3.887	3.283	2.834	2.489	2.216	1.997	16
6.373	6.047	5.749	5.222	4.775	3.910	3.295	2.840	2.492	2.218	1.998	17
6.467	6.128	5.818	5.273	4.812	3.928	3.304	2.844	2.494	2.219	1.999	18
6.550	6.198	5.877	5.316	4.844	3.942	3.311	2.848	2.496	2.220	1.999	19
6.623	6.259	5.929	5.353	4.870	3.954	3.316	2.850	2.497	2.221	1.999	20
6.687	6.312	5.973	5.384	4.891	3.963	3.320	2.852	2.498	2.221	2.000	21
6.743	6.359	6.011	5.410	4.909	3.970	3.323	2.853	2.498	2.222	2.000	22
6.792	6.399	6.044	5.432	4.925	3.976	3.325	2.854	2.499	2.222	2.000	23
6.835	6.434	6.073	5.451	4.937	3.981	3.327	2.855	2.499	2.222	2.000	24
6.873	6.464	6.097	5.467	4.948	3.985	3.329	2.856	2.499	2.222	2.000	25
6.906	6.491	6.118	5.480	4.956	3.988	3.330	2.856	2.500	2.222	2.000	26
6.935	6.514	6.136	5.492	4.964	3.990	3.331	2.856	2.500	2.222	2.000	27
6.961	6.534	6.152	5.502	4.970	3.992	3.331	2.857	2.500	2.222	2.000	28
6.983	6.551	6.166	5.510	4.975	3.994	3.332	2.857	2.500	2.222	2.000	29
7.003	6.566	6.177	5.517	4.979	3.995	3.332	2.857	2.500	2.222	2.000	30
7.105	6.642	6.234	5.548	4.997	3.999	3.333	2.857	2.500	2.222	2.000	40
7.133	6.661	6.246	5.554	4.999	4.000	3.333	2.857	2.500	2.222	2.000	50

Table A-3 *Future Value of $1*

| | | | | | | | **Future Value** | | | | | | | |
Periods	1%	2%	3%	4%	5%	6%	7%	8%	9%	10%	12%	14%	15%
1	1.010	1.020	1.030	1.040	1.050	1.060	1.070	1.080	1.090	1.100	1.120	1.140	1.150
2	1.020	1.040	1.061	1.082	1.103	1.124	1.145	1.166	1.188	1.210	1.254	1.300	1.323
3	1.030	1.061	1.093	1.125	1.158	1.191	1.225	1.260	1.295	1.331	1.405	1.482	1.521
4	1.041	1.082	1.126	1.170	1.216	1.262	1.311	1.360	1.412	1.464	1.574	1.689	1.749
5	1.051	1.104	1.159	1.217	1.276	1.338	1.403	1.469	1.539	1.611	1.762	1.925	2.011
6	1.062	1.126	1.194	1.265	1.340	1.419	1.501	1.587	1.677	1.772	1.974	2.195	2.313
7	1.072	1.149	1.230	1.316	1.407	1.504	1.606	1.714	1.828	1.949	2.211	2.502	2.660
8	1.083	1.172	1.267	1.369	1.477	1.594	1.718	1.851	1.993	2.144	2.476	2.853	3.059
9	1.094	1.195	1.305	1.423	1.551	1.689	1.838	1.999	2.172	2.358	2.773	3.252	3.518
10	1.105	1.219	1.344	1.480	1.629	1.791	1.967	2.159	2.367	2.594	3.106	3.707	4.046
11	1.116	1.243	1.384	1.539	1.710	1.898	2.105	2.332	2.580	2.853	3.479	4.226	4.652
12	1.127	1.268	1.426	1.601	1.796	2.012	2.252	2.518	2.813	3.138	3.896	4.818	5.350
13	1.138	1.294	1.469	1.665	1.886	2.133	2.410	2.720	3.066	3.452	4.363	5.492	6.153
14	1.149	1.319	1.513	1.732	1.980	2.261	2.579	2.937	3.342	3.798	4.887	6.261	7.076
15	1.161	1.346	1.558	1.801	2.079	2.397	2.759	3.172	3.642	4.177	5.474	7.138	8.137
16	1.173	1.373	1.605	1.873	2.183	2.540	2.952	3.426	3.970	4.595	6.130	8.137	9.358
17	1.184	1.400	1.653	1.948	2.292	2.693	3.159	3.700	4.328	5.054	6.866	9.276	10.76
18	1.196	1.428	1.702	2.026	2.407	2.854	3.380	3.996	4.717	5.560	7.690	10.58	12.38
19	1.208	1.457	1.754	2.107	2.527	3.026	3.617	4.316	5.142	6.116	8.613	12.06	14.23
20	1.220	1.486	1.806	2.191	2.653	3.207	3.870	4.661	5.604	6.728	9.646	13.74	16.37
21	1.232	1.516	1.860	2.279	2.786	3.400	4.141	5.034	6.109	7.400	10.80	15.67	18.82
22	1.245	1.546	1.916	2.370	2.925	3.604	4.430	5.437	6.659	8.140	12.10	17.86	21.64
23	1.257	1.577	1.974	2.465	3.072	3.820	4.741	5.871	7.258	8.954	13.55	20.36	24.89
24	1.270	1.608	2.033	2.563	3.225	4.049	5.072	6.341	7.911	9.850	15.18	23.21	28.63
25	1.282	1.641	2.094	2.666	3.386	4.292	5.427	6.848	8.623	10.83	17.00	26.46	32.92
26	1.295	1.673	2.157	2.772	3.556	4.549	5.807	7.396	9.399	11.92	19.04	30.17	37.86
27	1.308	1.707	2.221	2.883	3.733	4.822	6.214	7.988	10.25	13.11	21.32	34.39	43.54
28	1.321	1.741	2.288	2.999	3.920	5.112	6.649	8.627	11.17	14.42	23.88	39.20	50.07
29	1.335	1.776	2.357	3.119	4.116	5.418	7.114	9.317	12.17	15.86	26.75	44.69	57.58
30	1.348	1.811	2.427	3.243	4.322	5.743	7.612	10.06	13.27	17.45	29.96	50.95	66.21
40	1.489	2.208	3.262	4.801	7.040	10.29	14.97	21.72	31.41	45.26	93.05	188.9	267.9
50	1.645	2.692	4.384	7.107	11.47	18.42	29.46	46.90	74.36	117.4	289.0	700.2	1,084

Table A-4 *Future Value of Annuity of $1*

Periods	1%	2%	3%	4%	5%	6%	7%	8%	9%	10%	12%	14%	15%
						Future Value							
1	1.000	1.000	1.000	1.000	1.000	1.000	1.000	1.000	1.000	1.000	1.000	1.000	1.000
2	2.010	2.020	2.030	2.040	2.050	2.060	2.070	2.080	2.090	2.100	2.120	2.140	2.150
3	3.030	3.060	3.091	3.122	3.153	3.184	3.215	3.246	3.278	3.310	3.374	3.440	3.473
4	4.060	4.122	4.184	4.246	4.310	4.375	4.440	4.506	4.573	4.641	4.779	4.921	4.993
5	5.101	5.204	5.309	5.416	5.526	5.637	5.751	5.867	5.985	6.105	6.353	6.610	6.742
6	6.152	6.308	6.468	6.633	6.802	6.975	7.153	7.336	7.523	7.716	8.115	8.536	8.754
7	7.214	7.434	7.662	7.898	8.142	8.394	8.654	8.923	9.200	9.487	10.09	10.73	11.07
8	8.286	8.583	8.892	9.214	9.549	9.897	10.26	10.64	11.03	11.44	12.30	13.23	13.73
9	9.369	9.755	10.16	10.58	11.03	11.49	11.98	12.49	13.02	13.58	14.78	16.09	16.79
10	10.46	10.95	11.46	12.01	12.58	13.18	13.82	14.49	15.19	15.94	17.55	19.34	20.30
11	11.57	12.17	12.81	13.49	14.21	14.97	15.78	16.65	17.56	18.53	20.65	23.04	24.35
12	12.68	13.41	14.19	15.03	15.92	16.87	17.89	18.98	20.14	21.38	24.13	27.27	29.00
13	13.81	14.68	15.62	16.63	17.71	18.88	20.14	21.50	22.95	24.52	28.03	32.09	34.35
14	14.95	15.97	17.09	18.29	19.60	21.02	22.55	24.21	26.02	27.98	32.39	37.58	40.50
15	16.10	17.29	18.60	20.02	21.58	23.28	25.13	27.15	29.36	31.77	37.28	43.84	47.58
16	17.26	18.64	20.16	21.82	23.66	25.67	27.89	30.32	33.00	35.95	42.75	50.98	55.72
17	18.43	20.01	21.76	23.70	25.84	28.21	30.84	33.75	36.97	40.54	48.88	59.12	65.08
18	19.61	21.41	23.41	25.65	28.13	30.91	34.00	37.45	41.30	45.60	55.75	68.39	75.84
19	20.81	22.84	25.12	27.67	30.54	33.76	37.38	41.45	46.02	51.16	63.44	78.97	88.21
20	22.02	24.30	26.87	29.78	33.07	36.79	41.00	45.76	51.16	57.28	72.05	91.02	102.4
21	23.24	25.78	28.68	31.97	35.72	39.99	44.87	50.42	56.76	64.00	81.70	104.8	118.8
22	24.47	27.30	30.54	34.25	38.51	43.39	49.01	55.46	62.87	71.40	92.50	120.4	137.6
23	25.72	28.85	32.45	36.62	41.43	47.00	53.44	60.89	69.53	79.54	104.6	138.3	159.3
24	26.97	30.42	34.43	39.08	44.50	50.82	58.18	66.76	76.79	88.50	118.2	158.7	184.2
25	28.24	32.03	36.46	41.65	47.73	54.86	63.25	73.11	84.70	98.35	133.3	181.9	212.8
26	29.53	33.67	38.55	44.31	51.11	59.16	68.68	79.95	93.32	109.2	150.3	208.3	245.7
27	30.82	35.34	40.71	47.08	54.67	63.71	74.48	87.35	102.7	121.1	169.4	238.5	283.6
28	32.13	37.05	42.93	49.97	58.40	68.53	80.70	95.34	113.0	134.2	190.7	272.9	327.1
29	33.45	38.79	45.22	52.97	62.32	73.64	87.35	104.0	124.1	148.6	214.6	312.1	377.2
30	34.78	40.57	47.58	56.08	66.44	79.06	94.46	113.3	136.3	164.5	241.3	356.8	434.7
40	48.89	60.40	75.40	95.03	120.8	154.8	199.6	259.1	337.9	442.6	767.1	1,342	1,779
50	64.46	84.58	112.8	152.7	209.3	290.3	406.5	573.8	815.1	1,164	2,400	4,995	7,218

Glossary

Absorption costing The costing method that assigns all manufacturing costs to products (p. 1242).

Accounting rate of return A measure of profitability computed by dividing the operating income that an asset generates by the amount of the investment in the asset (p. 1447).

Activity-based costing (ABC) A system that focuses on activities as the fundamental cost objects and uses the costs of those activities as building blocks for compiling costs (p. 1380).

Activity-based management (ABM) Using activity-based cost information to make decisions that increase profits while satisfying customer needs (p. 1387).

Allocation base A common denominator for systematically linking indirect costs to products. Ideally, the best measure of the cause-and-effect relationship between manufacturing overhead costs and production volume (p. 1146).

Annuity A stream of equal periodic amounts (p. 1449).

Appraisal costs Costs incurred in detecting poor-quality goods or services (p. 1402).

Backflush costing A standard costing system that starts with output completed and works backward to apply manufacturing costs to units sold and to inventories (p. 1398).

Benchmarking Comparison of current performance with some standard. The standard often is the performance level of a leading outside organization (p. 1336).

Breakeven point The sales level at which operating income is zero: Total revenues equal total expenses (p. 1231).

Budget Quantitative expression of a plan of action that helps managers to coordinate and implement the plan (p. 1089).

Budgeted manufacturing overhead rate Another name for predetermined manufacturing overhead rate (p. 1147).

Capital budgeting A formal means

of analyzing long-range investment decisions (p. 1445).

Capital expenditures budget A company's plan for purchase of property, plant, equipment, and other long-term assets (p. 1274).

Cash budget Details how the business expects to go from the beginning cash balance to the desired ending balance. Also called the statement of budgeted cash receipts and payments (p. 1280).

Constraint The factor that restricts production or sale of a product; also called the limiting factor (p. 1436).

Continuous improvement A philosophy requiring employees to continually look for ways to improve performance (p. 1108).

Contribution margin The excess of sales revenues over variable expenses (p. 1227).

Contribution margin income statement Groups variable and fixed expenses separately and features the contribution margin (p. 1227).

Contribution margin per unit The excess of the sales revenue per unit (sale price) over the variable expense per unit (p. 1232).

Contribution margin ratio The ratio of the unit contribution margin to the sale price (p. 1232).

Controlling Acting to implement planning decisions and then evaluating the performance of operations and employees (p. 1089).

Conversion costs All manufacturing costs other than direct materials costs (p. 1180).

Cost allocation The process of distributing manufacturing overhead and other indirect costs among cost objects (p. 1146).

Cost assignment The process of tracing direct costs and allocating indirect costs to cost objects (p. 1146).

Cost behaviour Description of how costs change in response to a change in a cost driver (p. 1223).

Cost-benefit analysis The weighing of costs against benefits to aid decision making (p. 1090).

Cost driver Any factor that affects costs (p. 1136).

Cost object Anything to which costs are assigned (p. 1092).

Cost of capital Another name for the discount rate (p. 1449).

Cost of goods manufactured Manufacturer's counterpart to the merchandiser's purchases; the cost that is added to finished goods inventory during a period (p. 1099).

Cost tracing The process of assigning direct costs, such as direct materials and direct labour, to cost objects (p. 1146).

Cost-volume-profit (CVP) analysis Expresses the relationships among costs, volume, and profit or loss. An important part of the budgeting system that helps managers predict the outcome of their decisions (p. 1223).

Customer service The support provided to customers after the sale (p. 1092).

Design Detailed engineering of products and services, or processes for producing them (p. 1092).

Direct cost Cost that is conveniently identified with and traceable to a particular department (p. 1092).

Direct labour The compensation of employees who physically convert materials into the company's products; labour costs that are conveniently traceable to finished goods (p. 1094).

Direct materials Materials that become a physical part of a finished product and whose costs are separately and conveniently traceable through the manufacturing process to finished goods (p. 1094).

Discount rate Management's minimum desired rate of return on an investment; also called the hurdle rate, cutoff rate, required rate, cost of capital, and target rate (p. 1449).

Distribution Delivery of products or services to customers (p. 1092).

Efficiency variance The difference between the actual quantity of an input and the standard quantity of the input, multiplied by the standard unit price (p. 1338).

Equivalent units A measure of the amount of work done during a production period, expressed in terms of fully complete units of output (p. 1181).

Expected values A computation of expected outcome in an uncertain situation, calculated as the sum of each possible outcome multiplied by the probability of that outcome (p. 1108).

External failure costs Costs incurred when poor-quality goods or services are detected after delivery to customers (p. 1402).

Factory overhead Another name for manufacturing overhead (p. 1094).

Financial budget Projects cash inflows and outflows and the period-ending balance sheet (p. 1274).

Finished goods inventory Completed goods that have not been sold (p. 1091).

First-in, first-out (FIFO) process costing method A process costing method that assigns to each period's equivalent units of production that period's costs per equivalent unit (p. 1189).

Fixed cost Cost that does not change in total despite wide changes in volume (p. 1227).

Flexible budget A set of budgets covering a range of volume rather than a single volume level (p. 1325).

Flexible budget variance A difference between an actual result and a flexible budget amount (p. 1330).

Full product costs The costs of all resources that are used throughout the value chain for a product (p. 1093).

Hurdle rate Another name for the discount rate (p. 1449).

Indirect cost Cost that cannot be traced to a single department; costs other than direct costs (p. 1093).

Indirect labour Manufacturing labour costs other than direct labour; labour costs that are difficult to trace to specific products (p. 1095).

Indirect manufacturing cost Another name for manufacturing overhead (p. 1094).

Indirect materials Materials whose costs cannot conveniently be traced directly to particular finished products (p. 1095).

Internal failure costs Costs incurred when poor-quality goods or services are detected before delivery to customers (p. 1402).

Internal rate of return (IRR) The rate of return that makes the net present value of a project equal to zero (p. 1454).

Inventoriable product costs All costs of a product that are regarded as an asset for financial reporting under GAAP (p. 1093).

Job cost record Document used to accumulate the costs of a job (p. 1137).

Job costing Costing system used by companies that manufacture products as individual units or in small batches that vary considerably in terms of resources consumed, time required, or complexity (p. 1135).

Just-in-time (JIT) Production system designed to eliminate waste by such means as sequentially arranged production activities, low setup times, demand-pull production scheduling, and a high level of employee training and commitment (pp. 1106, 1396).

Just-in-time (JIT) costing A standard costing system that starts with output completed and then assigns manufacturing costs to units sold and to inventories. Also called backflush costing (p. 1398).

Labour time record In a job costing system, the document that identifies the employee, the time spent on a particular job, and the labour cost charged to the job (p. 1140).

Management by exception The practice of directing management attention to important deviations from budgeted amounts (p. 1295).

Manufacturing company A company that uses labour, factory, and equipment to convert raw materials into new finished products (p. 1091).

Manufacturing overhead All manufacturing costs besides direct materials and direct labour (p. 1094).

Margin of safety Excess of expected sales over breakeven sales (p. 1238).

Marketing Promotion of products or services (p. 1092).

Master budget The comprehensive budget that includes the operating budget, the capital expenditures budget, and the financial budget (pp. 1274, 1324).

Materials inventory Materials on hand that are intended for use in the manufacturing process (p. 1091).

Materials ledger The subsidiary ledger of the Materials Inventory general-ledger account that includes a separate record for each type of raw material (p. 1138).

Materials requisition Request for materials, prepared by manufacturing personnel (p. 1138).

Merchandising company A company that buys ready-made inventory for resale to customers (p. 1091).

Mixed (semivariable) cost Cost that is part variable and part fixed (p. 1225).

Net present value (NPV) The decision model that computes the expected net monetary gain or loss from a project by discounting all expected future cash inflows and outflows to their present value, using a minimum desired rate of return (p. 1449).

Operating budget Sets the expected revenues and expenses—and thus operating income—for the period (p. 1274).

Opportunity cost The benefit that can be obtained from the next-best course of action in a decision (p. 1441).

Outsourcing A make-or-buy decision, where managers must decide whether to buy a component product or service, or to produce it in-house (p. 1437).

Overallocated (manufacturing) overhead The balance that results when actual overhead costs are lower than allocated overhead costs, due to the overhead allocation being too high (p. 1150).

Overhead flexible budget variance The difference between the actual overhead cost and the flexible budget amount for actual production; also called overhead controllable variance (p. 1348).

Payback The length of time it will take to recover, in net cash inflows from operations, the dollars of a capital outlay (p. 1445).

Period costs Operating costs that are expensed in the period in which they are incurred (p. 1095).

Planning Choosing goals and deciding how to achieve them (p. 1088).

Predetermined manufacturing overhead rate The rate used to allocate to each job its share of manufacturing overhead cost, calculated at the beginning of the period before actual costs are known. The calculation is total estimated manufacturing overhead costs divided by total estimated quantity of the manufacturing overhead allocation base (p. 1147).

Prevention costs Costs incurred to avoid poor-quality goods or services (p. 1402).

Price variance The difference between the actual unit price of an input and the standard unit price of the input, multiplied by the actual input quantity (p. 1338).

Prime costs Direct materials plus direct labour (p. 1122).

Process costing System for assigning costs to goods that are mass produced in a continuous sequence of steps (p. 1135).

Production cost report Summary of the activity in a processing department for a period (p. 1194).

Production or purchases Resources used to produce a product or service, or the purchase of finished merchandise (p. 1092).

Production volume variance The difference between the overhead cost in the flexible budget for actual production and the standard overhead applied to production (p. 1349).

Relevant information The expected future data that differ among alternative courses of action (p. 1430).

Relevant range A band of volume in which a specific relationship exists between cost and volume (p. 1225).

Required rate of return Another name for discount rate (p. 1449).

Research and development (R&D) The process of researching and developing new or improved products

or services, or the process of producing them (p. 1092).

Responsibility accounting A system for evaluating the performance of each responsibility centre and its manager (p. 1292).

Responsibility centre A part, segment, or subunit of an organization whose manager is accountable for specified activities (p. 1292).

Sales mix Combination of products that make up total sales (p. 1230).

Sales volume variance The difference between an amount in the flexible budget and a corresponding amount in the static (master) budget (p. 1330).

Sensitivity analysis A what-if technique that asks what a result will be if a predicted amount is not achieved or if an underlying assumption changes (pp. 1234, 1285).

Service company A company that provides intangible services, rather than tangible products (p. 1091).

Standard cost A carefully predetermined cost that usually is expressed on a per-unit basis (p. 1335).

Statement of budgeted cash receipts and payments Another name for the cash budget (p. 1280).

Static budget A budget prepared for only one level of volume (p. 1324).

Strategy A set of business goals and the tactics to achieve them (p. 1438).

Sunk cost A past cost that is unavoidable because it cannot be changed no matter what action is taken (p. 1440).

Supply chain management Companies exchange information with their suppliers and their customers to reduce costs, improve quality, and speed delivery of goods and services from suppliers, through the company itself, and on to the end customers (p. 1106).

Target cost The allowable cost to develop, produce, and deliver a product or service (p. 1389).

Target price What customers are willing to pay for a quality or service (p. 1389).

Throughput time The time between receipt of purchased materials and

completion of finished products (p. 1106).

Time record In a service company, the document that identifies the employee and the time spent on each job (such as a client or project) (p. 1152).

Time value of money The fact that income can be earned by investing money for a period of time (p. 1448).

Total quality management (TQM) A formal effort to improve quality throughout an organization's value chain (p. 1107).

Transferred-in costs Costs incurred in a previous process that are carried forward as part of the product's cost when it moves to the next process (p. 1190).

Trigger points Points in operations that prompt entries in the accounting records (p. 1399).

Underallocated (manufacturing) overhead The balance that results when actual overhead costs are higher than allocated overhead costs, due to the overhead allocation rate being too low (p. 1150).

Value chain Sequence of all business functions in which value is added to a firm's products or services (p. 1092).

Value engineering (VE) Systematically evaluating activities in an effort to reduce costs while satisfying customer needs (p. 1387).

Variable cost Cost that changes in total in direct proportion to changes in volume of activity (p. 1223).

Variable costing The costing method that assigns only variable manufacturing costs to products (p. 1242).

Variance The difference between an actual amount and the corresponding budgeted amount (p. 1324).

Weighted-average process costing method A process costing method that costs all equivalent units of work to account for each period with a weighted average of that period's and the previous period's costs per equivalent unit (p. 1194).

Work in process inventory Goods that are in the manufacturing process but are not yet complete (p. 1091).

Index

Check Figures

P23-5B	No check figure	**P25-1B**	Req. 1. Manufacturing product cost, $97.30
P23-6B	Saskatchewan operating income variance, $4,500 F	**P25-2B**	Req. 4. Sale price per unit, $114.00
P23-7B	Custom Travel operating income, $12,750	**P25-3B**	Req. 2. NewPage indirect cost per unit, $22.50
P23-8B	Req. 2. Financing required, $95,998	**P25-4B**	Req. 3. Indirect product cost per unit, $20.30
P23-1C	No check figure	**P25-5B**	Req. 3. Balance, August 31, 2002, $3,000
P23-2C	No check figure	**P25-6B**	Req. 1. Conversion costs overallocated by $8,000
DP 1	Req. 1. Cotton: Cash excess, $554; Linen: Cash deficiency, $574	**P25-7B**	Req. 2. Net benefit of design engineering, $33,500
DP 2	Req. 3. Cost assigned to ending inventory, $101,285.71	**P25-8B**	Req. 3. Overall benefit to the company of the change, $97,000
		P25-9B	Req. 2. Annual gain from increased material quality, $420,000
P24-1A	7,500-unit operating income, $32,625	**P25-1C**	No check figure
P24-2A	Total operating expenses sales volume variance, $41,925 U	**P25-2C**	No check figure
P24-3A	Req. 2. Overhead production volume variance, $700 U	**DP 1**	Req. 1. Manufacturing product cost: Job A, $6,865; Job B, $7,680
P24-4A	Req. 1. Actual direct labour hours, 3,432 hours	**DP 2**	Revised total manufacturing cost, $89,000
P24-5A	Direct materials price variance, $2,376 F		
P24-6A	Req. 3. Gross margin, $44,390	**P26-1A**	Req. 1. Expected increase in income, $10,400
P24-7A	Req. 3. Gross margin, $936,225	**P26-2A**	Req. 1. Expected decrease in operating income, $8,500
P24-8A	Req.2. Overhead flexible budget variance, $165,000 U	**P26-3A**	Req. 2. Total contribution margin at capacity, Patio Sets, $4,800.17
P24-1B	50,000-unit operating income, $66,450	**P26-4A**	Req. 1. Advantage to making, $20,000
P24-2B	Total operating expenses sales volume variance, $4,000 U	**P26-5A**	Req. 3. Advantage to processing further, $36,000
P24-3B	Req. 2. Overhead production volume variance, $65,000 F	**P26-6A**	Req. 1. Net present value of: Plan A, ($121,280; Plan B, $302,400
P24-4B	Req. 1. Actual direct labour hours, 2,895 hours	**P26-7A**	Req. 1. Net present value, ($472,200)
P24-5B	Direct materials price variance, $1,512 F	**P26-8A**	Req. 1. Incremental profit from special order, $121,000
P24-6B	Req. 3. Gross margin, $140,960	**P26-9A**	Req. 1. Benefit of purchasing the component, $14,000
P24-7B	Req. 3. Gross margin, $353,900		
P24-8B	Req.2. Overhead flexible budget variance, $8,000 U	**P26-1B**	Req. 1. Expected increase in operating income, $24,000
P24-1C	No check figure	**P26-2B**	Req. 1. Expected decrease in operating income, $159,000
P24-2C	No check figure	**P26-3B**	Req. 2. Total contribution margin at capacity, Cordless Mouse, $1,320,000
DP 1	Flexible budget operating income, $153,250		
DP 2	Flexible budget receipts from donations, $243,750	**P26-4B**	Req. 1. Advantage to making, $264
CP 1	Req. 2. Breakeven sales in units, 7,330 chairs	**P26-5B**	Req. 3. Advantage to selling as is, $11,480
		P26-6B	Req. 1. Net present value of: Plan A, $361,250; Plan B, $1,007,500
P25-1A	Req. 1. Manufacturing product cost, $131.60	**P26-7B**	Req. 1. Net present value, ($5,440)
P25-2A	Req. 4. Sale price per unit, $68.80	**P26-8B**	Req. 1. Incremental profit from special order, $26,400
P25-3A	Req. 2. Commercial container indirect cost per unit, $88.00	**P26-9B**	Req. 1. Cost of purchasing the component, $3,750
P25-4A	Req. 3. Indirect product cost per unit, $1.42		
P25-5A	Req. 3. Balance, December 31, 2003, $7,000	**P26-1C**	No check figure
P25-6A	Req. 1. Conversion costs underallocated by $46,000	**P26-2C**	No check figure
		DP 1	Req. 2. Net present value, ($9,245)
P25-7A	Req. 2. Net benefit of design engineering, $3,500	**DP 2**	Req. 1. Total costs per mailbox, $57
P25-8A	Req. 3. Overall benefit to the company of the change, $23,275	**CP 1**	Req. 1a. Desired average operating cost, $86.70
P25-9A	Req. 2. Annual gain from increased material quality, $226,000		